Heidegger and Classical Thought

SUNY series in Contemporary Continental Philosophy

Dennis J. Schmidt, editor

Heidegger and Classical Thought

Edited by
AARON TURNER

Published by State University of New York Press, Albany

© 2024 State University of New York

All rights reserved

Printed in the United States of America

No part of this book may be used or reproduced in any manner whatsoever without written permission. No part of this book may be stored in a retrieval system or transmitted in any form or by any means including electronic, electrostatic, magnetic tape, mechanical, photocopying, recording, or otherwise without the prior permission in writing of the publisher.

Links to third-party websites are provided as a convenience and for informational purposes only. They do not constitute an endorsement or an approval of any of the products, services, or opinions of the organization, companies, or individuals. SUNY Press bears no responsibility for the accuracy, legality, or content of a URL, the external website, or for that of subsequent websites.

For information, contact State University of New York Press, Albany, NY
www.sunypress.edu

Library of Congress Cataloging-in-Publication Data

Name: Turner, Aaron, 1984– editor.
Title: Heidegger and classical thought / edited by Aaron Turner.
Description: Albany : State University of New York Press, [2024] | Series: SUNY series in contemporary continental philosophy | Includes bibliographical references and index.
Identifiers: LCCN 2024000341 | ISBN 9781438499062 (hardcover : alk. paper) | ISBN 9781438499079 (ebook) | ISBN 978438499055 (pbk. : alk. paper)
Subjects: LCSH: Heidegger, Martin, 1889–1976—Knowledge and learning. | Classical philology.
Classification: LCC B3279.H49 H3413 2024 | DDC 480—dc23/eng/20240305
LC record available at https://lccn.loc.gov/2024000341

Contents

Introduction   1
    Aaron Turner

Part 1: Heidegger and Early Greek Thought

1. Heidegger, Tragedy, and the Ethics of the Uncanny: Reading Sophocles's *Antigone*   13
   Charles Bambach

2. Heidegger's "Pre-Aristotelians": Nietzsche and Heidegger on Anaximander   39
   Babette Babich

3. Alien Historicity: Ancestral Fictions in Heidegger, Derrida, and H. P. Lovecraft   97
   Mark Payne

4. Disciples of Empedocles: Hölderlin, Nietzsche, and . . . Heidegger?   113
   David Farrell Krell

Part 2: Heidegger and Plato

5. From Parmenides to Plato via Thucydides: On the Way to Metaphysics   137
   Aaron Turner

6. Another Chorology: Reading Heidegger's Plato Books   163
   Bret W. Davis

7. The Philosopher and the City: Heidegger Reading Plato's
   Republic   217
   Dennis J. Schmidt

Part 3: Heidegger and Aristotle

8. Heidegger's Perversion of Virtue Ethics, 1924   239
   Sacha Golob

9. The Temporality of Life: Reading Aristotle with and
   Against Heidegger in Two Unpublished Seminars from
   1923–1925   257
   Francisco J. Gonzalez

10. The Sky, from Below: Heidegger, Aristotle, and the
    Orientation of the Gaze   293
    Claudia Baracchi

11. Pity, Fear and *Catharsis* from a Heideggerian Perspective 321
    Robert Eaglestone

12. Rationalizing the Animal in Humanity: On Speaking with
    Neither Cause nor Purpose   337
    Laurence Hemming

13. Hiding in Plain Sight: Κίνησις at the Core of Heidegger's
    Work   361
    Thomas Sheehan

14. Animal and World in Heidegger and Aristotle   383
    Sara Brill

Abbreviations   417

Contributors   425

Index   429

Introduction

Heidegger and Classical Thought

Aaron Turner

The present volume emerged out of a small colloquium I organized in London in November 2018 entitled "Heidegger and the Classics." The aim of the colloquium was to bring together a group of classicists and a group of Heideggerians for the purpose of establishing a dialogue concerning Martin Heidegger's apparent estrangement from classical scholarship and the case for his rehabilitation. The verdict was inconclusive. While the workshop was extremely rich in discourse, it became clear that the question of Heidegger's relationship with classical thought, constitutive of both the discipline of classical philology and ancient modes of thought, requires a far more extensive interrogation than a one-day workshop can provide. The aim of the present volume takes up the task that the workshop was only able to suggest, namely it sets out how laying the foundations for addressing the question of Heidegger's engagement with classical thought can begin. The volume asks: What does Heidegger still offer to the discourse of classical thought? In what way can Heidegger contribute to the work being carried out by classicists in the twenty-first century, and how might classical readings of what we find in the vast range of materials in Heidegger's *Collected Works* (or *Gesamtausgabe*) allow fresh perspectives on classical texts to emerge? Finally, it asks how Heidegger's engagement with classical thought informs his own philosophical inquiries?

While Heidegger's affiliation and involvement with the Nazi regime has been used as a justification for marginalizing his work within the discourse of classical thought, his unconventional interpretations of Greek thought and his radical translations of Greek words have also been harshly criticized. One such critic was Marcel Detienne, who challenged Heidegger's etymological interpretation of ἀλήθεια, attempting instead to produce philological, philosophical, and historical arguments to undermine Heidegger's interpretation. Regarding Heidegger himself, Detienne wrote, "Few scholars of Antiquity or educated readers are aware of how carefully Heideggerians and "deconstructionists" have built a veritable wall to separate themselves from the explorations of Greek scholars."[1] The critique of Heidegger's interpretation of ἀλήθεια was taken up more recently by Thomas Cole[2] and Gregory Nagy,[3] while Heideggerians are undoubtedly well aware of Paul Friedländer's critique of Heidegger's etymological account of the α-privative in the word ἀλήθεια.[4]

Broader criticisms of Heidegger's contributions to the study of classical texts have been frequent. As Glenn Most observes, "For the professional classicist, there is almost nothing at all of interest in Heidegger's work on Greek philosophy and poetry, which no doubt says as much about professional classicists as it does about Heidegger. Heidegger's work remains entirely marginal to the classics profession, except for a very few classicists who are themselves largely marginal . . . what is interesting about Heidegger's Greeks is not that they are Greeks, but that they are Germans and they are Heidegger's."[5] The testament of Most's remarks is confirmed by the noticeable paucity of Heidegger or Heideggerian thought in modern classical scholarship. Still, the conspicuously absent figure of Heidegger in classical scholarship is somewhat surprising given that his shadow has loomed large over the development of classical studies and its methods over the past sixty years. Heidegger, to some degree, has influenced some of the most significant intellectual advancements of the twentieth century, including postmodernism, hermeneutics, experientialism, intertextuality, spatial theory, and the so-called linguistic turn, all of which had a tremendous impact on the ways that modern classicists engage with antiquity. In a field that has indirectly reaped the rewards of Heidegger's expansive influence, the philosopher himself remains a forgotten and obscure figure.

This is perhaps even more surprising considering just how ingrained within classical philology Heidegger became following the publication of *Being and Time* in 1927. While Heidegger was predominantly concerned with Plato and Aristotle in the preceding years, after 1927 he became more and more entrenched in early Greek thinking, particularly the fragments of Anaximander, Heraclitus, and Parmenides, especially between 1932 and

1944.⁶ According to Otto Pöggeler, following a seminar in Davos in 1929, Heidegger made his "departure from every merely academic philosophy."⁷ In a letter to Elisabeth Blochmann written shortly after the seminar in April 1929, Heidegger himself suggested that while he "gained nothing" philosophically from the seminar, he made truly valuable connections with Ernst Cassirer and two classical philologists, Kurt Riezler and Karl Reinhardt.⁸ Contrary to Detienne's claim, Heidegger then became increasingly engaged with classical philology, which was being taken in new directions. In his lectures on *Die Grundbegriffe der Metaphysik* from 1929–1930, Heidegger remarks that the failings of a purely grammatical approach to classical texts was, after centuries, beginning to falter, and so like philosophy, "here too we see a process of transformation, the transfer of philology to new foundations" (GA 29/30: 438). Throughout the 1930s, Heidegger frequently corresponded with a number of prominent philologists, including Werner Jaeger, Walter Otto, Wolfgang Schadewaldt, Bruno Snell, and Julius Stenzel, and it is surely no coincidence that his fascination with the early Greek thinkers peaked at this time.⁹ As he writes in a letter to Karl Jaspers in 1932 shortly after the conclusion of his lecture series on Anaximander and Parmenides (GA 35), "I devoted the last year entirely to the Greeks and, even in this sabbatical semester, they aren't letting me go."¹⁰ The extent to which Heidegger's engagement with the classical philologists of his day was fruitful both for the development of his own interpretation of early Greek thinking and, likewise, for the progress of classical philology in Germany, remains an important question.¹¹

The importance of this question lies at the heart of the *Heidegger and Classical Thought* research project that emerged out of the 2018 workshop, which began the following year and that Laurence Hemming and I have been running ever since. Contrary to Most's claims that "there is almost nothing at all of interest in Heidegger's work on Greek philosophy and poetry," our research project has illuminated a relationship between Heidegger and classical thought that hitherto has not only been ignored by classicists but has even been overlooked by Heidegger scholars themselves. The present volume is a foundational component of this research project, bringing together scholars in both classics and philosophy and aiming at determining what Heidegger still offers to classical discourse in terms of both his own interpretations of ancient thought and his own original contributions to modern philosophical thought that might allow classicists to cultivate fresh perspectives and incorporate new modes of thought into their research.

The book is divided into three sections.

Heidegger and Early Greek Thought

The first section of this volume considers the relation of Heidegger's thought and the development of Greek thought in the sixth and fifth centuries. While Heidegger's engagement with Greek philosophy cannot so easily be systematized, there is a noticeable reverse chronological trend in his treatment of ancient philosophers. In the 1920s, prior to the publication of *Sein und Zeit* (1927), Heidegger's emerging philosophy of fundamental ontology was deeply grounded in Aristotelian metaphysics. Following the completion of *Sein und Zeit*, Heidegger's so-called turn (*die Kehre*) redirected his inquisition of truth. Where prior to and throughout *Sein und Zeit* Heidegger's philosophy considered "man in relation to Being," in the decades that followed his focus shifted to consider "Being and its truth in relation in man." While Heidegger had occasionally engaged with Plato prior to the *Kehre*, it was in the 1930s that a more direct and prolonged confrontation with Platonic metaphysics took place. Heidegger's engagement with the early Greek thinkers, particularly Anaximander, Heraclitus, and Parmenides, has been evident since at least 1922: these three figures had a profound influence on the direction of Heidegger's *Kehre*. The subject of this opening section, then, is Heidegger's treatment of Greek thought prior to Plato.

The chapters that constitute this section concern precisely Heidegger's engagement with early Greek thought. Given Heidegger's vast oeuvre spanning seven decades and the integral place of the early development of Greek thinking within this body of work, it is extremely surprising that Heidegger's treatment of such thought, especially that pertaining to Heraclitus, Parmenides, and Anaximander, has received such minimal attention in the scholarship. For Charles Bambach, the grounding of Heidegger's later philosophy can be attributed to his engagement with pre-Platonic thought: in this instance, Sophocles. Bambach considers two readings of Sophocles's *Antigone* by Heidegger in 1935 and in 1942. He suggests that the strikingly different interpretations that Heidegger offers of the same play between these readings elucidates the shift in Heidegger's thought as he prepares the way for his refutation of modern technological modes of thought. In this way, Bambach sheds light on Heidegger's reliance on Greek tragedy as a way of understanding some of the most pressing philosophical problems of his corpus.

The subject of Babette Babich's chapter is Heidegger's diminution of both Nietzsche's status as a "classical philologist" and his readings of the

Presocratics. Babich argues that, for Heidegger, Nietzsche's own interpretations of ancient philosophy, and particularly his readings of Heraclitus, Parmenides, and Anaximander, serve only to articulate a contest of power relations that Nietzsche himself deploys as a clichéd interpretation of the will to power. In Mark Payne's chapter, the temporal structures of past, present, and future that comprise the first-person experience of historicity that Heidegger questions in *Being and Time* (but ultimately gives no definitive answer) can be exemplified through the kairotic logic of historical fiction. For Payne, the relationship between historicity and temporality is proposed according to the logic of the graft: an intervention in the organismic processes of a living being that is viable insofar as the graft either does or does not "take," by succeeding in attaching itself to its host. The metaphor of the graft is pursued through an analysis of H. P. Lovecraft's *At the Mountains of Madness*, where Payne identifies the conditions that would determine the success of Western modernity's efforts to graft itself onto a Greek stock. David Farrell Krell considers Heidegger's indirect relationship with Empedocles. While Heidegger engaged himself deeply with Parmenides, Heraclitus, and Anaximander, it is something of a mystery that Empedocles remained elusive across Heidegger's vast oeuvre. For Krell, this is particularly surprising given the prominence of Empedocles in the works of arguably later Heidegger's two greatest influences: Hölderlin and Nietzsche. This chapter serves to locate the implicit presence of Empedocles within the development of Heidegger's later thought.

Heidegger and Plato

The second section of this volume examines Heidegger's encounter with Plato. Heidegger's relationship with Plato was simultaneously deeply polemical and profoundly reverential. While Heidegger frequently praised the bravery and ingenuity of Plato's philosophy for its radical stance against the tide of empty rhetoric that had pervaded Greek philosophy since the arrival of Sophism in the late fifth century, he was fundamentally critical of the course that Western philosophy took following Plato's development of early metaphysics. For Heidegger, Plato's transformation of λόγος into διαλέγεσθαι and reconceptualization of ἀλήθεια as a mode of propositional truth laid the foundations for metaphysical thought and, ultimately, the rise of technological modes of human understanding. Through Plato, Aristotle, Descartes, Kant, Hegel, and Nietzsche, philosophy enacted the abandonment of Being. According to Heidegger, Nietzsche's attempt to save estern philosophy from the nihilism of Platonism produced in fact the culmination of metaphysical thought. For Nietzsche, nihilism signifies the "devaluation of the highest values" that is brought about by the death of God. By God, Nietzsche means the Christian God, and by the death of God, he means the whole suprasensory realm pertaining to God and along with it the deterioration and nullity of those transcendental values derived through the Christian interpretation of Platonic metaphysics. According to Heidegger, Nietzsche succeeds not in bringing about the end of metaphysics but, in fact, fulfilling its destiny by elevating valuative thought to the highest mode of human comportment toward the world and thus abandoning Being as the fundamental question of philosophy.[12]

Despite his critique of Platonic metaphysics and the negative effect it had on the development of Western thought, Heidegger was profoundly influenced by the revolutionary nature of Plato's philosophy. The chapters that comprise this section are concerned precisely with both Heidegger's confrontation with the origins of metaphysical thought in Plato and the intimately close readings of Platonic philosophy that resonated so much with Heidegger's own concerns. My own chapter considers the nature of the gradual transition of truth-as-unconcealment to truth-as-correctness in the context of Thucydides's *History of the Peloponnesian War*. Thucydides began composing the historical narrative during the outbreak of the war in 431 BC and continued to write it until at least 404 BC, when the war concluded. Thucydides himself was a product of the "intellectual revolution" of the late fifth century and he is acknowledged generally as the "father of scientific historiography." His *History*, then, is fertile ground for excavating the seeds of metaphysical truth that were sown by Parmenides and that germinate in Plato a century later.

For Bret W. Davis, Heidegger's engagement with Platonic metaphysics extended beyond the more direct confrontations of the 1930s and continue in more indirect terms within his 1944–1945 *Country Path Conversations*, which Heidegger dubbed his "Plato book." In this work, which rarely mentions Plato by name, Heidegger employs Platonic forms of dialogue to further undermine Platonic metaphysics. Davis's chapter thus enables not only a more nuanced understanding of Plato dialogues in relation to the beginning of Platonic metaphysics but also for an understanding of *Country Path Conversations* and other later writings of Heidegger. Dennis J. Schmidt looks at three lecture courses and one speech in which Heidegger judges the task and place of philosophy in the world either by simply citing or by actually reading and interpreting Plato. In all these texts, Heidegger turns to Plato's *Republic* as offering something productive to be understood. For Schmidt, by looking closely at what Heidegger sees—and perhaps more importantly does not see—in Plato is illuminating for the larger question of how we are to understand the task philosophy and its relation to life itself.

Heidegger and Aristotle

The third section of this volume is devoted to Heidegger's fundamental relationship with Aristotle. Heidegger was so heavily influenced by Aristotle that he recommended his students "study Aristotle for ten to fifteen years" before reading Nietzsche and his own work.[13] While he featured less in Heidegger's later work, Aristotle was a constant presence in *Being and Time* and Heidegger's various lecture courses throughout the 1920s. For Heidegger, Aristotle was the last great Greek philosopher who radicalized and revolutionized Platonic metaphysics by recognizing the highest existential possibility of man not in φρόνησις (practical wisdom), like Plato, but in σοφία (theoretical knowledge). For Heidegger, Aristotle's overturning of Plato's thought occurs primarily because Aristotle discovers a higher level of ἀληθεύειν than Plato is able to see. Unlike Plato, who recognized ἀγαθόν (the Good) as fundamentally related to πρᾶξις (doing), Aristotle separates ἀγαθόν from πρᾶξις so that it becomes an object of pure θεωρία.

Throughout the 1920s until the publication of *Being and Time* in 1927, Heidegger's principal interest was phenomenology. While Edmund Husserl, Heidegger's teacher, introduced his young student to the *problematic* of phenomenology, it was through his engagement with Aristotle that Heidegger defined his own philosophy as the reformulation of phenomenology toward the task of fundamental ontology. Of this development, Heidegger later wrote: "The clearer it became to me that the increasing familiarity with phenomenological seeing fruitful for the interpretation of Aristotle's writing, the less I could separate myself from Aristotle and other Greek thinkers. Of course, I could not immediately see what decisive consequences my renewed preoccupation with Aristotle was to have."[14] But while Heidegger was deeply indebted to Aristotle for his own philosophical development, Aristotelian metaphysics launched Western philosophy on to a disastrous course through which *sophia* became the highest mode of human comportment toward the world. Heidegger's aim in the development of fundamental ontology is not to reprioritize *phronesis* above *sophia* but to transcend the distinction entirely. In this way, Heidegger's ultimate reverence of Aristotelianism is simultaneously a fundamental denunciation of metaphysics that results directly from Aristotle. The purpose of this section is to engage with and elucidate the nuanced and complicated relationship between Heidegger and Aristotle.

For Heidegger, one of the central aspects of both his early engagements with Aristotle and the scope of *Being and Time* was the problem of human authenticity, which commentators have often framed in line with a broadly Aristotelian ethics. For Sacha Golob, the apparent relation of Heideggerian authenticity and Aristotelian *eudaimonia* is problematic because human authenticity is too ontological to be identifiable with *eudaimonia*. Golob examines the relationship between *phronesis* and Heidegger's Pauline appeal to moments of crisis and suggests that by comparing the mundane everydayness of Heideggerian authenticity against recent expositions of Aristotelian (and, to some extent, Kantian) norms of ethical automatism with *eudaimonia*, a distinction is revealed between the two.

In Francisco J. Gonzalez's chapter, the complicated relationship between Heidegger and Aristotle is brought to light in a new way by considering the temporality of life in two unpublished seminars the former gave between 1923 and 1925. Gonzalez challenges Heidegger's interpretation of some of the most important Aristotelian texts dealing with *kinesis* (motion), *energeia* (activity), and time by demonstrating that, for Aristotle, these notions are guided by the phenomenon of life, not that of world. However, Gonzalez argues that even this challenge shows how Heidegger can draw our attention to the continuing philosophical significance of Aristotle's physics and metaphysics that is usually missed by contemporary classical scholars. In Claudia Baracchi's chapter, the originality of Heidegger's reading of Aristotle's *Ethics*—particularly regarding the continuity of *phronesis* and *sophia*, both considered in terms of "gazing"—is emphasized. Baracchi argues that despite both orientations remaining essentially of/in the order of the phenomenal, the inveterate and conventional polarity of practical wisdom and theoretical knowledge is reasserted. She suggests that, however construed in unusual terms (in relation to *techne*, etc.), *sophia* ends up being opposed to and detached from what concerns action. Robert Eaglestone's chapter offers a provisional

Heideggerian reading of fear, pity, and catharsis in Aristotle's *Poetics*. For Eaglestone, fear and pity are not simply contingent feelings but also have a profounder ontological significance. This is why ancient tragedy is existentially significant because it has disclosive power not only for our lives but also, in care and concern, for what Heidegger identifies as part of the fundamental structure of our being-in-the-world.

For Laurence Hemming, the phrase ζῷον λόγον ἔχον—"living being that is possessed of language and speaking"—is a central aspect of Heidegger's interpretations of Aristotle. His chapter seeks to explore this phrase, by following the contours of Heidegger's inquiry, into the phrase itself, into the history of metaphysics, and into the history of being. Hemming demonstrates the breadth of the discussion and how it relates to both classical and contemporary sources, concluding by asking where (or rather in whom) might Heidegger locate the origin—or perhaps the ἀρχή—of language? Thomas Sheehan reveals that in a personal conversation between himself and Heidegger it was stressed that an understanding of Heidegger's work could not be accomplished without a fundamental understanding of (1) Aristotle's doctrine of *kinesis*, and (2) Heidegger's use of it in the development of his concept of *Dasein*. Sheehan's chapter shows how the implicit ("secret") foundation of human *Dasein* in Heidegger is rooted in how Heidegger "retrieves" the existential possibilities he discovers in *Physics* III, 1–3.

Finally in this section, Sara Brill considers the relation of animal and world in both Heidegger and Aristotle. Brill argues that Heidegger's misreading of ancient Greek approaches to living being and human animality, particularly in Aristotle, provides a false foundation to the conceptual framework of "being-in-the-world" that is integral to Heidegger's project. She argues that Heidegger's model of animality stands at far remove from the alignment of vitality and vividness evident in a variety of strands of Greek literature, and the association between embodiment, signification, and sociality that accompanies them; a sensibility that proves decisive for Aristotle's zoological investigations.

Ultimately, the fourteen chapters that constitute this volume serve neither to condemn nor condone Heidegger's ostracism from classical discourse but rather to prepare the way for a possible reconciliation between classical scholarship and one of the greatest philosophers of the twentieth century, whose engagement with ancient thought is both vast and instructive.

Notes

1. Marcel Detienne, *The Masters of Truth in Archaic Greece* (New York: Zone Books, 1996 [1967]), 26.

2. Thomas Cole, "Archaic Truth," *Quaderni Urbinati di Cultura Classica* 13 (1983): 7–28.

3. Gregory Nagy, *Homeric Questions* (Austin: University of Texas Press, 1996), 122–29.

4. Though many are prone to forget that Friedländer scaled back this critique of Heidegger in the third edition of his *Plato* book (Paul Friedländer, *Plato: An Introduction*, 3rd ed., translated by Hans Meyerhoff (Princeton, NJ: Princeton University Press, 1969), vii.

5. Glenn W. Most, "Heidegger's Greeks," *Arion* 10, no. 1 (2002): 96.

6. Cf. David C. Jacobs, ed., *The Presocratics after Heidegger* (New York: State University of New York Press, 1999), which provides an excellent analysis of the condition of Presocratic studies after Heidegger's explosive interpretations.

7. Otto Pöggeler, "Heidegger's Political Self-Understanding" in *The Heidegger Controversy. A Critical Reader* (Cambridge, MA: MIT Press, 1993), 211.

8. Joachim W. Storch, ed., *Martin Heidegger-Elisabeth Blochmann Briefwechsel 1918–1969* (Marbach am Neckar: Marbacher Schriften, 1989), 29.

9. Many of these letters are due to published as part of Heidegger's *Briefausgabe*, which has been edited by Alfred Denker and Holger Zaborowski since 2010. While the specific content of these letters will remain a mystery until publication, I'm convinced they'll shed some light on Heidegger's transformative and hugely important engagement with Anaximander, Heraclitus, and Parmenides between 1932 and 1944.

10. Walter Biemel and Hans Saner, eds. *The Heidegger-Jaspers Correspondence 1920–1963*, tr. Gary E. Aylesworth (Amherst, NY: Humanity Books, 2003).

11. For a broader analysis of Heidegger's relationship with classical philology, see my chapter, "Der Abbruch und Anfang des Philosophierens: Heidegger, Parmenides, and Altertumswissenschaft" in *Heidegger and Parmenides*, ed. Laurence Hemming and Aaron Turner (Lanham: Rowman & Littlefield, forthcoming).

12. Cf. GA 6.1; 6.2.

13. GA 8: 78.

14. OTB: 78.

Part 1
Heidegger and Early Greek Thought

1

Heidegger, Tragedy, and the Ethics of the Uncanny

Reading Sophocles's *Antigone*

CHARLES BAMBACH

Tragedy and the German Mission:
Reading the Ister Lectures

Greek tragedy begins with reversal. Even at the beginning of the tragic scene there is no secure site from which the action proceeds. Everything always already appears in terms of oppositions and contrarieties. The stranger is unmasked as the native; the *tyrannos* shown to be the *basileus*; the icon of purity is exposed as the miasma; the figure most rooted in the home suffers the fate of the exile. Such tragic reversal is, moreover, always marked by profound ambiguity and enigma. We find such double-dealing language expressed paradigmatically in the riddling discourses of the prophet Tiresias. In *Oedipus Tyrannus*, frustrated by the dense and impenetrable augury of the prophet—"This day will show your birth and bring your ruin"—Oedipus replies: "How riddling and obscure in excess are all your words."[1] Sophocles proves himself a master of this doubling discourse and deploys it to pose questions that offer no easy answers. Instead, the questions remain open, providing a portal through which the viewer must pass if s/he is to enter into the heart of the tragic paradox that defines the action onstage. Tragedy—as a genre and as a philosophical problem—emerges out of the paradoxical, inconsistent, and indefinite elements that come together to shape the interpretive possibilities of both the tragic characters and their audience. Through the masterful language of the poet-dramatist, we are confronted by words and phrases whose meaning becomes contentious, even as the tragic characters keep insisting on their own univocal, exclusive renderings of what constitutes the truth for them. Single meanings are upended through dialogic interplay, not merely of the characters who speak but of language itself. Here language in all its poetic density opens up its meanings to the force of strife, contradiction, ambiguity, and reversal. Again, it is Tiresias who, in *Antigone*, speaks of a doubled confusion and reversal of the two main characters, Creon and Antigone. Near the end of *Antigone*, as the entire world of the *polis* is spinning out of control, he utters these words to Creon:

> You've confused the upper and lower worlds.
> You settled the living person without honor
> in a tomb; you keep up here that which belongs
> below, a corpse unburied and unholy.[2]

In this world of reversals and confusion, Tiresias utters what the German poet Friedrich Hölderlin called "the pure word"—the utterance that ushers in "a counter-rhythmic interruption" within tragic speech that splits it in two.[3] In this caesura initiated by Tiresias's pure word, Hölderlin finds the power of a tragic language that "transports (*entrückt*) the human being from its orbit of life, the very mid-point of its inner life, and tears (*reisst*) it into the *excentric* orbit of the dead." In this, the German poet asks us to bear witness to the uncanny monstrousness that characterizes human existence. Moreover, in doing so, he uncovers a concealed path that leads from Sophoclean tragedy to a renewed form of German identity and self-reflection. For Hölderlin, the very enigmas, reversals, ambiguities, and inversions presented by Sophoclean tragedy harbor within themselves the hidden cipher for understanding ethical dilemmas. In his translations of both *Oedipus Tyrannus* and *Antigone*, Hölderlin finds a way to pose ethical questions that point toward the most essential questions about who we are. Through his presentation of language's most extreme oppositions/contradictions, Hölderlin locates a concealed grammar for helping us to grasp the contradictions at the heart of our own existence.

In what follows I want to take up Hölderlin's insights into the *ethical* character of Greek tragic language by looking at how it shapes the insights of Martin Heidegger.[4] Heidegger turns to a reading of Sophocles in two of his lecture courses: *Introduction to Metaphysics* (1935) and *Hölderlin's Hymn 'The Ister'* (1942). The two lecture courses share the same focus: a detailed analysis of the first choral ode from *Antigone* and its classic definition of the human being as *deinos*. There, in the doubled, enigmatic, and inverted language of the chorus's song, Heidegger finds "the fundamental word of this tragedy, indeed of Greek tragedy as a whole, and with that the fundamental word of Greek antiquity."[5] But what for Heidegger proves absolutely essential to Greek antiquity comes to him not solely through the tragic word of Sophocles. It comes, rather, through the poetic translation of such a word in the work of Hölderlin. Sophocles's tragic insights offer a singular interpretation of the Greek world and its historicity, but modern Germans need the mediating force of the poet "of" the Germans (Hölderlin) "the poet—that is, founder—of German beyng," in order to properly approach "the poetic work of Sophocles named *Antigone* that, as a poetic work, is a founding of the entire Greek Dasein."[6]

There are many different questions and problems that emerge out of Heidegger's two readings of the first choral ode in *Antigone* in 1935 and 1942.[7] Here, however, I wish to look at the later reading from SS 1942 that can hardly be read apart from its political and historical context. What begins as a lecture course on Hölderlin's late hymn "The Ister," focused on the meaning of the river as the locality for the sojourn or abode (*Aufenthalt*) of human beings upon the earth, suddenly veers off into a lengthy discussion of Sophocles's first choral ode from *Antigone*: this discussion eventually constitutes almost half of the volume. But why? Why does Heidegger decide to focus on the question of uncanniness in *Antigone*? And why does he decide to forgo analysis of the play itself (except for a brief account of the introductory dialogue between Antigone and Ismene) in order to focus on the choral ode above all else? Moreover, why does the language of the ode appear to Heidegger as more "essential" than the dramatic action? And why does Heidegger's discussion of the ode concentrate so intensely on the Sophoclean notion of the *polis*? To address these questions we will need to understand that for Heidegger what is ultimately at stake in his analysis of the *polis* is less an interest in "the political" than one on the question of poetic dwelling, grasped as the "*Aufenthalt* or sojourn of human beings as historical in the midst of beings."[8] This emphasis on *Aufenthalt* will be conceived within the human being's *ethos* that abjures any interpretation of "the ethical" as it is commonly understood. For Heidegger, the essence of Sophoclean tragedy lies in exposing the enigmatic status of human dwelling in terms of its ethicality. What becomes most essential for Heidegger is that human dwelling takes place for the Greeks only within the historical structure of the *polis*. But the authentic meaning of the *polis* remained concealed to the Greeks themselves, Heidegger maintains. The philosophical reflections on the *polis* offered by Plato in *The Republic* and Aristotle in *The Politics* were "thought at the end of the great Greek era" and were not "adequate even to question the *polis* at all, and to do so in the Greek sense."[9] In order to think the essence of the Greek *polis*, then, "we must think more Greek than the Greeks themselves." But to do so, Heidegger reminds his German listeners, the Germans themselves must "think more German than all Germans hitherto." And for this, what is needed is the hymnal poetizing of Hölderlin. Hölderlin alone was able to grasp how Greek tragic language, with its ironic reversals and chiasms, was able to express the hidden meaning behind the action that transpired on stage. In this, he found authentic kinship with the works of Sophocles. In this bond Heidegger will situate not merely the tragic action of the plays themselves but the need of contemporary Germans for these tragic insights. Moreover, what will distinguish Heidegger's 1942 reading of *Antigone* from his 1935 interpretation is this essential meaning of Germany's need for homecoming. If earlier Heidegger had emphasized the role of *techne* in the Greek experience of the *polis*, now he stresses the essential meaning of the *Aufenthalt* of human beings within the *polis* as sojourn and as abode. As he understands it, "The *polis* conceals within itself the possibility of a counterturning abode (*gegenwendigen Aufenthalt*)" that is marked by an oppositional unity whose structural dynamic he sees at work in Hölderlin and that for him holds the key to Germany's own historical mission and search for its identity.

As a way of defining Germany's proper mission, Heidegger will turn to Hölderlin's hymnal poetizing to reconfigure Sophocles's understanding of the human being as uncanny. In Hölderlin's hymns, Heidegger traces the outlines of a confrontation between the native and foreign as a way to open the path for a philosophical homecoming of the Germans through an encounter with the ancient Greeks. In this way, the German *Volk* stands in an uncanny relation to the Greeks as the foreign "other." In doing so, however, they also become foreign to themselves as a *Volk* and thereby enter into an essential relation to what they can be. This futural vocation of the Germans as the *Volk* that is "auserwählt" as "the chosen one" to "save the West" will mark Heidegger's lectures with a doubled legacy. On the one hand, they stand as a powerful indictment of traditional ethics and its tendency to run roughshod over the ethical enigmas of Greek tragic presentation. On the other hand, they also come to us as a grotesque form of German national self-congratulation at a critical moment in the history of the West where the fate of modern Europe hangs in the balance. In this doubled way, the Ister lectures themselves come to embody the very uncanniness whose essence they seek to explore and confront.

Here I want to examine these enigmatic lines of inquiry within Heidegger's work precisely as they relate to his encounter/confrontation (*Auseinandersetzung*) with Sophocles. Within Heidegger's history of being, Sophocles does not stand merely as a singular Greek dramatist, nor does *Antigone* come to us as a specific historical drama. Rather, both playwright and play come to us as intimations of the first Greek beginning, a beginning whose inaugural power is so great that it "determines and prevails in advance out beyond everything proceeding from it."[10] It is this originary Greek *arche* that comes to shape Heidegger's narrative of Western history as a history of being, one whose concealed power has long been occluded by the metaphysical projections of philosophers since Plato and Aristotle. But this reading of Sophocles has its own context, defined by the patriotic revival of Hölderlin after Germany's defeat in 1918 and the way it rekindled a certain nationalistic approach to Greek antiquity. Against this reception, Heidegger's engagement with "the" Greeks—(which ones? from which historical era? under which contemporary optic?)—emerges out of the embers of the First World War.[11] Within a cultural landscape pervaded by the nihilistic prophecies of Oswald Spengler's *Decline of the West*, German academics turned to the ancient Greeks as a way to reconstitute the role of "the" Germans within the long narrative history of the West.[12] In asserting their singular destiny as the true inheritors of the Greek tradition, many German academics turned to the work of Hölderlin and Nietzsche to reposition themselves as the only ones capable of "saving the West," as Heidegger put it.[13] In an epoch where Spengler's talk of decline or *Untergang* became a generational anthem, Heidegger, cribbing from Nietzsche's *Thus Spoke Zarathustra*, spoke of an *Übergang* or "crossing-over" to another beginning for the West. Here the German "reflection on the first beginning" in the Greeks would come to serve as "a thrust into the crossing-over," one marked by "all of the ambiguity that is proper to a historical crossing-over."[14]

During the 1930s Heidegger began to construct his own narrative of the West's decline, framed around the forgetting of the concealed essence of early Greek *aletheia*. On this reading, in Western metaphysics' establishment of truth as correctness, *adaequatio*, certitude, and objectivity, what came to be forgotten—and, more essentially, was never properly acknowledged—was that "the question of truth is ambiguous."[15] If the metaphysical thinking of Plato and Aristotle had established new standards of truth as "presence" and "correctness," for Heidegger it was the earlier Greek thinkers and poets—especially Anaximander, Heraclitus, Parmenides, Pindar, and Sophocles—who had grasped the essence of truth as un-concealment, marked by what Heidegger called *Zwiefalt* and *Zweideutigkeit*—doubledness and ambiguity.[16]

Doubledness, Ambiguity, and the Question of Truth

For these early Greeks the question concerning truth was first and foremost a question about "the enigma of the essential two-foldedness of *physis*."[17] This question becomes for Heidegger one whereby the originary power of *physis* gets covered over and concealed by the subjectivity of a metaphysical thinking that questions being from beings alone, leaving the question of being itself all the more enigmatic. In his Heraclitus lectures from SS 1944, Heidegger characterizes the human relation to being as ambivalent (*zwiespältig*) since it involves both a turning toward being that, at the same time, remains a turning away from being.[18] For Heidegger, it was above all in Greek tragedy that this doubledness, ambivalence, and ambiguity would play itself out in the riddling enigmas of ethical life. Such ethical enigmas were not solved in the unfolding of Greek tragedy's plot, action, or characters. On the contrary, these questions remained ever more questionable as indications of a necessity to take up such questions once again in a more originary way. As Heidegger put it in his first set of Hölderlin lectures, "the historical being of humans is shot through with ambiguity and essentially so."[19] It is as the poetic manifestation of such ambiguity that Heidegger turns to tragedy as a way of refocusing the ethical imagination of contemporary Germans. For Heidegger, this confrontation with tragedy appears as a way of rethinking the very *Fragestellung* of ethical discourse in the philosophical tradition.

As Heidegger argues, our usual modes of understanding tragedy conceive it in terms of our "lived experience" *(Erlebnis)*, a concept rooted in the values of German humanism. But such an approach only seals us off from the Greek tragic tradition "and has made the Greek world completely inaccessible."[20] What is required, Heidegger insists, is a renewed focus on the ambiguities of tragic *language*, not psychology, character development, motive, political aims, or questions of gender. What stands before us as our proper task is to reengage the tragic language of Sophocles, midwifed through Hölderlin's poetry and his translations, as a way of reclaiming tragedy's ethical power to move us toward a historical decision about who we are. As Heidegger put it in one of his Black Notebook entries from the late 1930s: "Meditation *(Besinnung)* must have the power to leap back while yet remaining in the leap ahead and to incorporate expressly into the forward leap that which is overleapt." Such a meditation has the potential to prepare a "transformation of beyng" that will allow us to "press toward a decision concerning the essence and vocation *(Bestimmung)* of the Germans and thus press toward the destiny of the West."[21] The hope for fulfilling this vocation, in Heidegger's estimation, lies with the Germans' own ability to heed the word of Hölderlin—especially with regard to his understanding of Sophoclean tragedy.

Greek-German Kinship

Hölderlin's poetic river hymns offer Heidegger an opening for him to stage his own remarkable reading of Western history as a history of beyng that depends on an essential and "special" relationship between the ancient Greeks and modern Germans. Here Heidegger thinks of "the special inner kinship of the German language with the language of the Greeks and their thinking."[22] As both Rainer Marten and Glenn Most have argued, however, Heidegger's "Greeks" are hardly the models of standard classical philology. Instead, they are selectively chosen exemplars that comport with Heidegger's own narrative of the history of beyng.[23] Sophocles is no exception, nor is Heidegger's choice of the first choral song of *Antigone* (vv. 332–370). Heidegger considers this chorus to be the site that poetizes the essence of Greek Dasein and comes to express the historical commencement of

Western humanity. What comes to language in this choral song is the insight of all Greek tragedy for Heidegger—namely, that the essence of truth is marked by conflictual intimacy (*Innigkeit*), a unifying opposition between hiddenness and unhiddenness, concealment and revelation that reigns throughout all being.[24] It is the tragic poet who stands at the crisscross of this conflict and is able to let the *Innigkeit* of authentic dwelling come to presence. From out of this tragic conflict, we learn how human essence is not a given but is, rather, concealed in the strife-ridden history of humanity's own attempts to define its essence. As Heidegger put it in one of his lectures from WS 1942/43: "For the possibility and necessity of 'tragedy' itself has its single source in the conflictual essence of *aletheia*."[25] Hölderlin understood this conflictual essence of truth and let it guide his own understanding of the human being. Perhaps nowhere in his corpus is this conflictual understanding of the human being as carefully drawn as in his own tragedy, *The Death of Empedocles*. There we find the core of this insight in Empedocles' chiastic utterance: "Ich bin nicht, der ich bin/ I am not who I am."[26] For both Hölderlin and Heidegger, the human being is at odds with itself, caught in the doubling discourse of a language that it seeks to master and control and yet which, despite all the human being's best efforts, eludes its grasp. In this sense, tragedy is less about flawed character, poor decisions, or the appointment of fate than about grappling with paradoxes that exceed human grasp. As Jean-Pierre Vernant writes, "Actions take place within a temporal order over which the human being has no control . . . his actions elude him; they are beyond his understanding."[27] Tragedy opens its viewers to a world of antinomies without offering "a solution that could eliminate the conflicts either by reconciling them or by stepping beyond the oppositions. And this tension, that is never totally accepted nor entirely obliterated, makes tragedy into a questioning to which there can be no answers." Heidegger seizes upon this ambiguity within the language of tragedy and by reading these tensions as aporiae that offer not *Aufhebung* but reversal, not *Überwindung* but *Übergang*, he finds a way to grasp the homelessness of modern humanity, not as socioeconomic anomie or political discontent but as a call for a transition within the history of being.

To arrive at this daring interpretation of *Antigone*, Heidegger will have to overdetermine or ignore much of the action in the play. For example, Heidegger will not focus on the overweening self-assertion of Creon or on Antigone's dismissal of her own filial obligations within the *polis*, except for the female custom of burial for the dead. Sophocles tells us in the play that Antigone goes to her death unwept (*aklautos*), unmarried (*agamos*), lamented by no friend (*aphilos*), and without the wedding song (*anhymenaion*, vv.876, 917).[28] In both his and the chorus's eyes, she fails to share in the common language of her community, remaining outside the boundaries that define communal life. She dares to abandon not only the laws and precepts that Creon has set down in the *polis*, but in decisive ways she also abandons her own family. Her insistence on burying her dead brother takes precedence over all living beings, including her sole surviving family member (Ismene) and her future consort (Haemon) with whom she might form a new family. In a very concrete sense she is *deinos* (uncanny [*unheimlich*], un-homely [*unheimisch*]) since her decisions transport her far beyond what the choral song names "the hearth" (*parestia* or para-Hestia, v. 372). And here Heidegger designates Antigone as "the supreme uncanny."[29] In doing so, he raises her above everyone else within the *polis*, "not quantitatively, but in an essential way." Moreover, he clearly designates Antigone as the *sole* figure of the uncanny to whom the chorus refers at the end of the first choral song when they refer to that one who "shall not be entrusted to my hearth" (vv. 372–73).

The Ethical Question of Tragedy: Heidegger and Sophocles

Before proceeding to a closer reading of Heidegger's interpretation of Antigone understood in and through this ode, however, we need first to consider some crucial issues. Several critics have censured Heidegger for "not paying attention to the plot of the tragedy and arguing as though it had nothing to do with human interaction, but everything with the disclosure of being."[30] Jacques Taminiaux rightly observes that Heidegger's focus on the word *deinon* "deliberately overlooks the use of the word elsewhere in the drama," especially regarding those uses that describe the actions of Creon. Jean Greisch likewise notes that with his intense—and exclusive—focus on the first choral song, Heidegger's "resolutely ontological interpretation of the chorus obscures the fact that violence and aporicity manifest themselves nowhere better than in the tragic action."[31] Yet these criticisms, well aimed and unassailable as they are, miss the most essential insights within Heidegger's analysis. Perhaps it is best to remember that Heidegger's aim in the Ister lectures is not to offer an interpretation of Sophocles's play *Antigone*. Rather, he turns to a reading of the first choral song so as to confront the riddles and paradoxes of ethical life within the *polis*: riddles that express the conflicts and ambiguities within ethics as such. Dismissing the discourse of "ethics" as a failed metaphysical program bent on finding rules and directives, one forged with the same machinational reckoning as modern technological calculation, Heidegger looks to Sophocles for an originary language of poetic dwelling that holds open the path for ethical thinking. Here perhaps we ought to pause and reflect on Heidegger's larger hermeneutic aims in his reading of ancient sources. In his own approach to tragic, poetic, and philosophical sources, Heidegger did not seek to offer "interpretations" of texts. On the contrary, his philosophical energy was devoted to opening paths within texts that set the reader upon a way of thinking. In this sense, his focus in the Ister lectures is to draw upon Sophocles's poetic language as a "founding of truth" that grasps language as the proper abode for human beings, their proper *ethos*.[32] Insofar as the first choral ode of *Antigone* comes to us as "a poetic work that poetizes the essence of human beings," it opens just such a path of thinking.[33] Heidegger leaves the dramatic (and philological) details of *Antigone* aside to reclaim the play's tragic expression of how Sophocles's insight into the essential homelessness of the human being stands before us as a way of grasping the very ethicality of human existence as an open question that demands our attention.

Drawing on this sense of *Antigone* as a poetic text that opens a path of thinking about the riddles and enigmas of ethical life within the *polis*, Heidegger's focus is less on the motivations and actions of Antigone the character. That is, Heidegger sets aside an analysis of her family history, the political situation in Thebes, the conflict with her uncle Creon, to concentrate on how Antigone comes to embody Sophocles's chiastic language about the doubled nature of the human being as that being whose own essence is turned against itself. In this way, Antigone functions not as a character among characters in a plot that unfolds both the logic and contradictions of tragic action. On the contrary, she is that singular figure whose essence is expressed in the first choral song's designation of the human being as *deinon*—the uncanny one, the one whose essence is to undertake actions against its own essence. At this juncture, Sophocles's language becomes essential in that the chorus's designation of Antigone as the one who is both *hypsipolis/apolis* and *pantoporos/aporos*—at the same time—comes to express the doubled nature of human being as tragic. Here the language of the chorus becomes "the essential middle of the tragedy (*Wesensmitte*) . . . that poetically gathers around it the whole of the poetic work."[34] What this essential middle mediates is the essence of tragedy as the tragedy of language; and because Antigone is this essential middle, for Heidegger "she is the purest poem itself." In other words, what comes to language in this case is neither the word of Sophocles nor that of Antigone: it is "the essence of poetizing" that poetizes not beings, but being. Hence, for Heidegger, "what essentially prevails as being (*was west als das Sein*) and is never a being (*ein Seiendes*) . . . can be said only in poetizing or thought in thinking." As Heidegger grasps the tragic unfolding of the drama, it is Creon who directs himself toward becoming the master of beings; Antigone is left to confront the uncanniness of being. What is at stake, then, for Heidegger is less the struggle between family/state, male/female, politics/religion, individual will/communal need, than it is a fundamental confrontation at the very heart of human dwelling: namely, that the human being is not at home in being, precisely there where it attempts to dwell in the home. Here the human being's mode and manner of habitation, settlement, and abiding in its abode—in other words, its *ethos*—is marked by a profoundly tragic contradiction. For it is precisely there where it is settled in the habitudes of its habitat that the human being becomes unsettled and at odds with its own form and manner of habitation. It is this ethical paradox that constitutes for Heidegger the poetic essence of tragedy.

An Ethics for a World at War? (The Question of the Homeland)

Any understanding of Heidegger's Ister lectures that approaches them from the perspective of Greek tragedy confronts a fundamental danger—not only to Heidegger but to tragedy itself. Heidegger turns to tragedy not to offer insights into the workings of Sophoclean drama. On the contrary, tragedy becomes for him a way of understanding the dynamic between two intersecting themes that shape the hymnal poetizing of Hölderlin. If we remember to situate the discussion of *Antigone* within this lecture on "The Ister," then two intersecting themes come to appearance. Firstly, that Heidegger's engagement with this river hymn—in the middle of a world war—concerns the question of poetic dwelling. Secondly, that the question of poetic dwelling shaped by the relation of the native and the foreign constitutes one of the classic issues within Sophoclean tragedy. For Heidegger, dwelling is not something that humans can achieve of their own volition; it is never secured through planning, arrangement, design, or calculative thinking. At the same time, it is not something attained by reading or writing poetry, as if by deploying poetic language in the service of poetic dwelling we might somehow achieve it. Rather, poetic dwelling concerns our *ethos*, our way of responding to the claim that being makes upon us. As Heidegger tells us, "The word *ethos* originally means dwelling, sojourn (*Aufenthalt*). So understood, it means the sojourn of the human being, its sojourning/abiding (*Sichaufhalten*), dwelling in the middle of beings as a whole. The essential feature of *ethos*, of this sojourning, is the way in which the human being holds fast to beings (*hält sich*) and in this way maintains and holds itself *(sich selbst behält und hält)*, and lets itself be held *(sich hälten lässt)*. This being at home in *ethos*, the knowing thereof, is 'ethics.'"[35] Understood in this way, as a reflection on the meaning of the human sojourn upon the earth and in it, Heidegger's reading of *Antigone* within his lecture course on Hölderlin's "The Ister" unfolds some of the most powerful ethical insights in his entire corpus. Within Greek tragedy we see how the human being is exposed to a world that exceeds it, in a way that manifests its attunement to being—or lack thereof. For Heidegger, Antigone shows her attunement to being by coming to dwell at the very center of chiastic crossings and contradictions that marks being's appearance. Part of what makes *Antigone* so relevant to Heidegger is the way it addresses the question of the native and the foreign and how this speaks to the situation of the Germans in the middle of the Second World War.

Against this background, there are several strands of Heidegger's pro-German, antiforeign bias that make themselves known in SS 1942 when he delivers the Ister lectures. We can see this in his remarks about the resettlement of German nationals on the eastern reaches of the Danube, his embrace of a politics of German expansion in Eastern Europe for *Lebensraum* and his claim that "the Anglo-Saxon world of Americanism has resolved to annihilate Europe, that is, the homeland (*Heimat*), and that means the commencement of the Western world."[36] For him, the Second World War stands as a struggle between America's lack of any sense of "history" and the German attempt to retrieve the power of the Greek commencement against "the ultimate American act of American historylessness and self-devastation."[37] At the same time as he is delivering these lectures on the Ister, he writes to his friend Kurt Bauch:

> We stand in an epoch that lacks a total sense of history. That is to say: the essence of history has still not come to be settled at all. . . . As a consequence of this still barely thought histor-

ylessness, the "concept" of the West has faded away. "Europe" means something wholly other. But I can only see this fading away of the West as a kind of sparing and safeguarding and thereby as a concealed transformation of its essence. We will be the land of evening (*Land des Abends*) for a night of the morning (*Nacht des Morgens*). And *only* the Germans can do this because in them is preserved the inceptual vocation of the Greeks."[38]

A few months later he writes to Bauch that "slowly the world-historical trial of the Germans is coming closer," the one in which "the founding vocation of the Germans lies concealed."[39] What emerges from this preoccupation with the German vocation is a narrative of Western history as a history of being that depends on the German retrieval of the first Greek beginning. Such a retrieval is to serve as a way of preparing the path of an other beginning.

Because the history of the West since the fifth century BCE has been shaped and dominated by metaphysical thinking, Heidegger turns to the hymnal poetizing of Hölderlin that, he insists, "falls outside of all metaphysics, insofar as its poetizing of the rivers necessarily poetizes the historicity of human beings."[40] It is in Hölderlin's poetic work—and in his translations of Sophocles and Pindar—that a nonmetaphysical relation to the ancient Greeks comes into view, one whose task becomes "to thoughtfully reflect on the essence of history." Before we can begin such thoughtful reflection, however, Heidegger emphasizes that we must break with the notion of Greece as an ideal model for the perfection of humankind put forward by Winckelmann and German Classicism. Hölderlin's Greece, Heidegger argues, is "never 'classical antiquity,'" nor is it the product of a romantic yearning to return to Arcadia. Moreover, Hölderlin's relationship to the Greek world is even "more conflictually intimate" (*inniger*) than Nietzsche's since it acknowledges the need to confront the Greeks as other and foreign.

> For only where the foreign is known and acknowledged in its essential oppositional character does there exist the possibility of a genuine relationship, that is, of a uniting that is not a confused mixing but a conjoining in distinction. By contrast, where it remains only a matter of refuting, or even of annihilating the foreign, what necessarily gets lost is the possibility

of a passage through the foreign, and thereby the possibility of a return home into one's own, and thereby that which is one's own itself. . . . The essence of one's own is so mysterious that it unfolds its ownmost essential wealth only from out of the supremely thoughtful acknowledgment of the foreign. This mystery of the coming to be at home of human beings as historical is the poetic care of the poet of the river hymns. This poet . . . must therefore enter into a historical dialogue with the poets of the foreign land, and indeed with those poets in whose poetizing there spoke to him a telling of human beings in their becoming homely. That is why we hear everywhere in Hölderlin's hymnal poetizing the countering resonance of a poetic work that poetizes the essence of human beings. We mean the first stationary song of the chorus in Sophocles's *Antigone* tragedy.[41]

In his reading of the *Antigone* ode, via Hölderlin, Heidegger unearths a great truth having to do with ethics, *ethos*, and the prospect of dwelling authentically in the homeland. There we find a Heidegger who (despite all his German exceptionalism and his apprehension about other nations, cultures, languages, and lines of descent) takes up a fundamentally ethical reflection on the meaning of the native, the national, and the homeland as our proper place of dwelling upon the earth. Moreover, in these same reflections we find crucial hints, beckonings, and intimations of an ethics that, breaking with the metaphysical "ethics" of right and wrong, offers penetrating insights into a fitting relation between the proper and the strange, the native and the foreign, oneself and/as the other. If the question of ethics has to do with the authentic possibility of dwelling—and if dwelling is understood as bound up with the question of our sojourn/ *ethos*/*Aufenthalt* that comes to define our habitual haunts, habitat, and settlement—then the question shaping the Ister lectures can be understood as fundamentally ethical since it is this question of poetic dwelling that defines our way of "being properly homely" (*das eigentliche Heimischsein*).[42]

Tragedy As the Counterturning Relation between the Homely: Unhomely

As the basis for his new sense of ethics, Heidegger turns to a text from antiquity: the first choral song from *Antigone*. Drawing upon Antigone's status as the most uncanny of all human beings, Heidegger writes that "there must presumably be an intrinsic relation between the becoming homely, that is, being unhomely of human beings as poetized by Hölderlin, and *that* human being who is poetized by Sophocles as *to deinotaton*, which we translate: *das Unheimlichste*, the most uncanny."[43] What would it mean to speak of an ethics "of" the uncanny? As if in dwelling in nearness to its prevailing power, we would become intimate with the conflictual forces that dwell at its center? How would an ethics of the uncanny appear from out of the language of tragedy? Moreover, how might we think of an ethics that would move away from the orbit of rules and proscriptions to open up a new sense of the ethical that understood the tragic essence of the human being? It is through his engagement with Hölderlin's Sophocles that Heidegger attempts such a reading of *Antigone*.

Hölderlin's Ister hymn beautifully traces the course of human dwelling and does so by configuring it in terms of the tragic figure of reversal that reigns in Sophoclean tragedy. We find this figure of chiastic inversion in the hymn's first verse where a river hymn commences with fire. We see other figures of reversal in terms that juxtapose heat and coolness, night and day, verticality (trees, rocks) and horizontality (the even flow of the river), moon and sun, East and West, Greek and German. Just after the midpoint of the poem, Hölderlin jars the flow of the poem's own riverine unfolding by imagining it as undergoing a reversal:

> Yet almost this river seems
> To travel backwards and
> I think it must come from
> The East.
> Much could
> Be said about this.[44]

We can find the tragic source for this image of a river's reversal in a text Hölderlin was translating at the time of his Ister hymn, a choral song from Euripides's *Medea* (vv. 410–11): "Flow backward to your sources, sacred rivers,/And let the world's great order (*dike*) be reversed."[45] What Heidegger will draw from this sense of reversal is an understanding of human being as *to deinon*—the uncanny (*unheimlich*), unhomely one (*unheimisch*). What makes the human being uncanny is its way of being essentially unhomely—that is, that it is not "at home" within its own essence. As Andrew Benjamin has put it, "Heidegger's translation of *ta deina* as *das Unheimliche* . . . does not oppose the 'homely' (*heimliche*) to the 'unhomely' or uncanny (*Unheimliche*). The point is more significant. Both are already present together."[46] One is tempted to extend Benjamin's insight to say here that the uncanny and the unhomely are always already present together with the native and the homely, but in a way that exposes each to the monstrous possibilities of reversal. And yet, in another sense, there is no reversal of the homely in the unhomely since homeliness always already harbors within itself the unhomely and, in turn, the unhomely remains ever open to the possibility of the homely. This constitutes the tragic situation of the human being. For Heidegger, no human being better expresses this tragic condition than Antigone.

Antigone exceeds all other human beings by becoming homely in being unhomely.[47] That is, she takes up into her own essence the strange, alien, unsettling, and monstrous elements of the human situation. She exposes herself to them in all their utter uncanniness and knowingly makes them her own. It is not by happenstance or through a turn of misfortune that she does so. On the contrary, she becomes at home in this unhomeliness in a way that exceeds her father/brother Oedipus, whose own passage into the world of the *deinos* occurs without his own decision. As Heidegger puts it, "In fittingly accommodating herself (*pathein*) (v. 96) . . . to that against which nothing can prevail . . . Antigone comes to be removed from all human possibilities and placed into direct conflict over the site of all beings."[48] Creon too suffers the loss of the homely in the deaths of his wife and son, but he does not choose this for himself. Antigone chooses her own death, which for Heidegger is "her becoming homely, but a becoming homely within and from out of her being unhomely." Hence, Antigone "is not just any *deinon* . . . Antigone is the supreme *deinon*." Heidegger pays special attention to three aspects of Antigone's uncanniness, all of which are sung in the first choral ode. These have to do, first, with her relation to the *polis* (*hypsipolis/apolis*); second, with the irruption of Antigone's own power that "ventures forth in all directions" (*pantoporos*) even as it winds up being a nihilistic venturing forth into nothing (*aporos* v.360). Thirdly, it has to do with the sense of being at home in the hearth (Hestia) and being expelled from the hearth (*parestios* v.372).

Hypsipolis/Apolis

The chorus's first song in *Antigone* characterizes the human being as *deinon*; Heidegger reads this to mean that human existence first arises and comes to be in the *deinon*. Because Antigone understands this uncanny origin of human existence and knowingly embraces it as the very measure of her ethical dwelling upon the earth, not recoiling from the demand such an insight places upon her, she is in Heidegger's terms "the supreme uncanny."[49] As this "most unhomely human being, and thus the most uncanny of all that is uncanny," Antigone expresses the doubling essence of the human being as that being turned against itself in and as a reversal. In tragic terms, she is nothing but a *katastrophe*, understood in its Greek sense as a turn (*strophe*) that overturns all in its path even as it turns downward (*kata*), against, and away from, what it is. As Heidegger puts it, "Human beings themselves in their essence are a *katastrophe*—a reversal that turns them away from their own essence. Among beings, the human being is the sole catastrophe."[50] What fissures human being is a cut, a rending that emerges from out of human being itself and not from the social-political conditions within which the human being confronts its contradictions. Hence, all interpretive focus on the conflict between religion and the state, the family and the city, Creon's male-patriarchal authority versus Antigone's status as a female member of the household, misses the essential point of the tragedy in Heidegger's estimation. What the chorus sings of is the fundamental doubling and opposition that underlie all human options within the *polis*, not merely those facing Creon or Antigone. Yet Antigone presses these options to their limits—and then beyond such limits to a realm that exceeds all limits, the realm of *Übermass* (excess, exceeding the measure).[51] Nowhere is the poetic truth of such *Übermass* more properly expressed than in the first choral song with its designation of the human being as *pantoporos/aporos* and *hypsipolis/apolis*.

It is within this context that Heidegger characterizes the human being as "the unhomely one." We most properly come into the homely through deprivation, Heidegger claims. That is, we are exposed to the most proper sense of unhomeliness/uncanniness as a form of absence. It is in lacking an essential bond to the home that we come to an awareness of the home. Moreover, it is in this interwoven and mutually implicating relation of presence and/as absence that the un/homely manifests itself. For Sophocles, this takes the form of the human being as that being who is *pantoporos*, that is, the one who finds passage everywhere, who overcomes all hindrances to forge a way forward, the being who always uncovers a means of escape and can ferry its way across any impasse. As Heidegger puts it, this is the being that "ventures forth in all directions" yet is without direction; the one who "everywhere find its way through," who unfailingly finds the porous rift in the fold and presses through this porosity to gain access to its own design—and yet finds there no designation or purpose at the end of its enterprising explorations. This being who is "*pantoporos* is a being that experiences everything and yet remains without experience."⁵² Even as it presses ahead everywhere, however, this being is at the same time *aporos,* incapable of circumventing human fate, marked by mortality. As the chorus sings: "It is from death alone that he can find no means of escape" (v. 361–62). And while most human beings shuttle back and forth on their mortal journey between shaping circumstances to match their will and falling victim to circumstances due to lack of foresight or the frailty of their own designs, Antigone stands out as that being who knowingly exceeds all these precarious dangers to embrace her own fate as "being-towards-death."⁵³ Antigone, on Heidegger's reading, "takes as her all-determinative point of departure that against which nothing can prevail." That is, she not only negotiates the perilous relation between the *pantoporos/aporos*; much more than this, she goes beyond the measure of the city, exceeding the city, looming over all its incursions into the truth of a shared life with others, surpassing the city's own excursions from out of its center.

Whereas most translators have rendered Sophocles's terms *hypsipolis:apolis* as "high in the city""":cityless," Heidegger offers a different path. For him, the *polis* is essentially neither the state (*Staat*) nor the city (*Stadt*) since "the *polis* does not let itself be determined 'politically.' "⁵⁴ Rather, the *polis* is " 'the stead' (*die Statt*): the site (*die Stätte*) of the abode (*Aufenthalt*) of human history that belongs to humans in the midst of beings."⁵⁵ It is "this site of the abode, that is, the site of being homely in the midst of beings as a whole" that expresses the authentic meaning of the *polis* to the Greeks. This sense of the *polis* undergoes a counterturn in *Antigone,* one that shows that the essence of the home lies in the unhomely and the essence of the *polis* lies in that which undermines, exceeds, or proves destructive of the *polis*. It is in this sense that Heidegger understands the *hypsipolis/apolis* relation. What Antigone exposes is this counterturning/ *Gegenwendigkeit* that manifests the doubled essence of human being—its ability to surpass all others even if, in so doing, it loses the very center of its own existence. This constitutes tragedy's core, its way of showing/ manifesting the reversals that undermine all the incursions and excursions that the self attempts, turning them against it. Antigone becomes the exemplar of such reversals in that she embodies this *deinon* character of human being as the terrible wonder, the unhomely homely one, the one who is both most proper and, beyond all others, has lost the sense of the proper. In being banished from the *polis*, she comes to be at home in the exilic, simultaneously preserving "the most intrinsically unhomely" in its "most intimate belonging to the homely."[56] Yet Heidegger does not see all this primarily as a way to read *Antigone* or Greek tragedy or Hölderlin's relation thereto. For him, what manifests itself here above all else is a decision about the direction of Western humanity, one that is shaped by a "historical-poetic necessity" about how to contend with the counterturning essence of the human being as both "being at home and being unhomely" at the same time.[57]

In her homecoming to the unhomely, Antigone not only fulfills her own "destiny" (*Geschick*), a destiny that is fitting (*schicklich*), but through this very accomplishment, she fulfills the "proper history of the humankind she belongs to."[58] Only through her intimacy with the hearth, Hestia, the homely, does she attune herself to that which is *deinon*, that which threatens the hearth. Here Antigone fulfills what Heidegger calls "the law of history"—that any hope of historical homecoming must confront the looming threat of the unhomely that lies concealed at the hearth of the home. In this way, Antigone stands as the essence of poetic dwelling as that which "demands a going away" from the home (native) into what is not of the home (foreign) in order to authentically dwell within the home as the proper.[59] "Antigone *is* the poem of being unhomely in the proper and supreme sense," Heidegger claims. But is this so? Does Sophocles understand her, as Heidegger does, as "the purest poem"? In his ambition to read *Antigone* as the source for a futural Hölderlinian homecoming for the Germans, Heidegger all too readily dismisses a good deal of the play that takes place outside the context of the first choral ode. As part of this neglect, Heidegger seems to miss how destructive of both the family and the *polis* Antigone truly is. Yes, Antigone's daring refusal to bend under the yoke of the new king elicits the chorus's respect and makes her *hypsipolis*, the highest in the estimation of the *polis*. But her actions also render her cityless, banished to a grave beneath the earth. The tragic consequences here do not simply apply to Antigone as a singular character. They extend to the whole *polis* as well, making her the agent of a strategy that proves destructive for the *polis*'s own existence. Antigone is *hypsipolis* in that through her willful designs, she exceeds the limits and boundaries of life within the *polis*. In exceeding these limits, and surpassing the needs and measures of the city, she becomes *apolis*, an exile from its very center.

For Heidegger, Sophocles's portrayal of the *hypsipolis/apolis* double bind is, then, not simply a way to characterize Antigone but belongs more powerfully to "the essential abode" of the human being. As Heidegger conceives it, "What is worthy of poetizing in this poetic work is nothing other than becoming homely in being unhomely."[60] For him it is precisely Antigone's not-being-at-home that opens a pathway for her becoming-at-home. That is, it is in being unsettled and without a home that Antigone truly finds her home within being. It is in achieving a state of being unsettled and without a place in the *polis* (i.e., being *apolis*) that Antigone towers over the polis as the *hypsipolis*. In this belonging to the site of her homelessness Heidegger uncovers the proper *ethos* of poetic dwelling. And this reading is crucial for Heidegger's own sense of an *ethos* of dwelling poetically on the earth. But it seems as if in pursuing such a reading, one that focuses on the conflictual tension between the *hypsipolis* and the *apolis*, Heidegger loses sight of the importance of the *oikos* in Sophocles's tragedy. This is not merely a minor difference in interpreting the play in its dramatic detail, I would argue, but has pressing consequences for how Heidegger formulates an *ethos* of poetic dwelling. For here Heidegger either forgets or wholly overlooks Antigone's inward-directed posture and self-willed temper that abandons any genuine sense of the Other. In one of her very last speeches, Antigone confesses: "I'm a strange new kind of inbetween thing aren't I/not at home with the dead nor the living" (v.852)[61] The Greek term here—*metoikos*—traditionally designates a "resident alien" or metic who is *meta-oikos*: "between" (dative) "besides" (in a doubled and ambiguous sense), even "beyond" the *oikos*, "the abode, house, settlement, community."[62] And Antigone embodies all of these ambiguous and contradictory aspects of that being who is "beyond" the *oikos* in several distinctive ways. The consequences here for Heidegger's reading are telling.

In his characterization of Antigone as "the purest poem," Heidegger too easily forgets how Antigone embodies the failure of human existence, at least within a Sophoclean measure. In embracing her being-toward-death, Heidegger sees Antigone as taking responsibility for the nullity at the heart of the human project to master all beings. In this way, he contends, Antigone expresses an authentic relationship to being. But we can also notice here Heidegger's errant misprision of Sophocles's own sense of the *deinon*. In her embrace of death Antigone does step out of the site of all beings; moreover, this gesture is doubly uncanny in that it both banishes her from the hearth, even as it brings her to loom over the site of all beings. Such a reading forgets, or even perhaps refuses, to see how such action violates the highest measure of the hearth as the site of human flourishing. In Antigone's reckless disregard for the *nomoi* of the family within the ancient Greek world, she fails in several crucial ways. Never quite able to extricate herself from the thread and ties of family relations, her determined attempt to bury her brother Polyneices manifests only one side of familial obligation. Her arrogant, intractable comportment toward her sister, her uncle, and to the usual demands placed upon young Greek maidens—yes, to bury the dead, but also to wed, bear children, and set the family's needs above her own—mark her as *dysmoron* ("without a fate," vv. 865, 919, 1018, 1234). To be *dys-moron* means to have a *moros* (fate, destiny) that has gone awry, erred, or missed the mark (*dys*) [etymologically tied to *moira* (part, share, lot)]. For Hölderlin, being *dysmoron* signifies a "lack of measure" and of being without a fate *(schicksallos)*. If *moros* means lot, part, or share, then being *dysmoros* signifies having no allotment, no share, no parceling out of a fate. Here Antigone shows that she has only partially fulfilled her obligations to the *oikos*. She is, yes, a sister and a daughter (and to her father, both at once); but she is not a wife or mother and so remains in deadly, crucial ways *aphilos* (v. 876). As she laments in her last exchange with the chorus: "Accursed, unwed, alien, foreign, and strange, I am nowhere at home on this earth" (vv. 876–78). We hear this in her plaintive cry: "unwept, unwed, unloved, I go . . . no one will lament me" (vv. 821–22).[63]

Antigone against the Measure of Poetic Dwelling

Given this reading of Antigone within Sophocles's tragedy, we can well understand how her isolation within her own native sphere renders her, paradoxically, as foreign. Here Antigone's own sense of herself—within the *oikos* and the *polis*—casts her against any traditional sense of *ethos* as well as simply "proper." In a very real sense, given her contorted family history, her proper is im-proper. When, in her last speech, she refers to her "tomb" and "bridal chamber" in the earth below as her "dwelling-place" (*oikesis*) (v. 892), those who have been following the pathway of her chosen death are not surprised. This final utterance reinforces her yearning to be homeward bound. It is in this "caverned prison" (vv. 891–92) that she finds union with the dead where, she announces "I go to meet my own" (*emautes*) (v.893).

It is precisely in this situation of homelessness that Heidegger finds the authentic expression of tragic discourse. For him, Antigone achieves the highest of human possibilities in "fittingly accommodating herself (*pathein*)" to the uncanny as the *to deinon*. But there are several problems here. Firstly, in terms of the tragedy itself, at the end of her life Antigone seems not "to take upon herself the uncanny" which then manifests "her belonging to being."[64] On the contrary, in her last speeches (vv. 838-52; 876-82; 891-928) she expresses the pain of her isolation, lamenting that she must die "before the term of my life is spent" (v. 896) and that "my descent will be the saddest of all." As Charles Segal argues, what the text expresses is "Antigone's growing horror of being entombed alive."[65] At the end she comes to the realization that even below in Hades she faces the prospect of being a resident alien (*metoikos*). Rather than embracing her "being-towards-death," as Heidegger imagines it, Antigone wallows in self-pity at her plight. As Karl Reinhardt puts it, the closer she comes to death "the more bitter and accusing becomes her final backward glance at the realm and government of the living which is expelling her (916 ff.)."[66]

In his reading of Antigone as the supreme uncanny, Heidegger seems inattentive to his own insight into "the double and counterturning relation" that governs "every poros."[67] Heidegger is right that "the polis . . . is not some isolated realm" but, rather, operates "within a manifold of other realms of human ventures and pervadings (*poros*)." But at a critical juncture in his reading, he forgets the looming presence of countervailing reversal. By raising Antigone to the status of "the supreme uncanny," he misses her own "self-willed . . . temper" (*autognotos . . . orga*) that leads to her destruction. In her "reckless daring" (*tolmas, but* v. 371) she is banished from the hearth—and it is this tragic turn away from the *oikos* that consigns her to be cityless (*apolis*). All of her incursions to secure a bond between herself and her family "lead nowhere" (*aporos*). It is in this sense that, on my reading, she fails to fulfill the most essential element of a Heideggerian form of poetic dwelling, one that marks our sojourn or *Aufenthalt* upon the earth as one that is attuned to the other and able to recognize the other in her otherness. In her self-willed embrace of that which is her own at the expense of that which is foreign, strange, and other, Antigone reverses "the law of homecoming" so crucial to Heidegger in the Ister lectures. Her actions reflect the nihilism of a Nietzschean will to power turned against itself, rather than a Hölderlinian sense of homecoming. This reading does not wholly subvert Heidegger's notion of poetic dwelling; it simply questions whether the Antigone of Sophocles's play genuinely carries out such an *ethos*. Part of an authentic form of a poetic *ethos* lies in the power of commemoration (*Andenken*), on whose basis alone we make ready the inauguration of what is to come. In her persistent attachment to the past, however, Antigone forecloses any such opening to the future. In her relentless cleaving to the proper, she achieves a reversal into the improper. At the end of his lectures on Hölderlin's "Andenken" from WS 1941–42, as he reflects on the proper *ethos* of homecoming, Heidegger writes: "The sojourn (*Aufenthalt*) in the foreign and the learning of the foreign, not for the sake of the foreign, but for the sake of one's own, demands that enduring waiting that no longer thinks of one's own."[68] It is in failing to carry out this law of homecoming that Antigone founders on the shore of her own abode.

In this failure to grasp the essentially other-directedness of authentic dwelling, Antigone remains caught in the selfsame iron cage of language that Sophocles so deftly constructs. Moreover, in her denial of the ethical force of the other—as what is strange, foreign, and improper—Antigone loses the thread of the Sophoclean bond to community, family, hearth, and, perhaps above all, language. Antigone never succeeds in going beyond her own circumscribed fate. Such an approach to language and human dwelling could scarcely serve as the proper measure for either a Hölderlinian or Heideggerian measure of a proper poetic dwelling. That Heidegger himself was unable to grasp this offers us a powerful sense of his own difficulty in thinking the relation of the native and the foreign.

Notes

1. *Sophocles, I* ed. Hugh Lloyd-Jones (Cambridge, MA: Harvard University Press, 1994), 368–69.

2. Elizabeth Wyckhof, trans. *Sophocles I* (Chicago: University of Chicago Press, 2013), 60. Cf. Loeb edition, 102–3.

3. Friedrich Hölderlin, *Essays and Letters*, ed. Jeremy Adler and Charlie Louth (London: Penguin, 2009), 318/ Hölderlin, *Sämtliche Werke und Briefe*, II, ed. Jochen Schmidt (Frankfurt: Deutscher Klassiker Verlag, 1994), 850–51. Hereafter abbreviated as DKV.

4. Here I want to acknowledge the helpful work of several others, including Dennis Schmidt, *On Germans and Other Greeks* (Bloomington: Indiana University Press, 2001) and "The Monstrous, Catastrophe, and Ethical Life: Hegel, Heidegger, and Antigone," *Philosophy Today* 59, no. 1 (2015): 61–72, as well as Andrew Benjamin, *Place, Commonality, and Judgment: Continental Philosophy in the Ancient Greeks* (London: Bloomsbury, 2012); Jean Greisch, "Who Stands Fast?

Do Philosophers Make Good Resistants?" In *Bonhoeffer and Continental Thought*, ed. B. Gregor and J. Zimmermann (Bloomington: Indiana University Press, 2006); and Norman Swazo, " 'Preserving the *Ethos*': Heidegger and Sophocles' *Antigone*," *Symposium* 10 (2006): 441–71.

    5. HHI: 67/GA 53: 82.

    6. GA 39: 214, 216/HGR: 195, 197.

    7. Some of the works that deal with these differences include Claire Geiman, "Heidegger's *Antigones*," in *A Companion to Heidegger's Introduction to Metaphysics*," eds. R. Polt and G. Fried (New Haven, CT: Yale University Press, 2000), 161–82; Jacques Taminiaux, "Plato's Legacy in Heidegger's Two Readings of *Antigone*," in *Heidegger and Plato*, ed. C. Partenie and T. Rockmore (Evanston: Northwestern University Press, 2005), 22–41; and Scott M. Campbell, "The Tragic Sense of Life in Heidegger's Readings of *Antigone*," in *The Science, Politics and Ontology of Life Philosophy* (London: Bloomsbury, 2013), 185–96.

    8. HHI: 87/GA 53: 108.

    9. HHI: 81/GA 53: 99.

    10. HHI: 100/GA 53: 125.

    11. Cf. my book, *Heidegger's Roots: Nietzsche, National Socialism and the Greeks* (Ithaca, NY: Cornell University Press, 2003).

    12. Cf. For example, the rise of the interest in pre-Socratic philosophy: Glenn Most, "Polemos Panton Pater: Die Vorsokratiker in der Forschung der Zwanziger Jahre" in *Altertumswissenschaft in den 20er Jahre*, ed. Hellmut Flashar (Stuttgart: Steiner, 1995), 87–114.

    13. GA 13: 16; GA 55: 69, 108; GA 80: 693, as well as the Black Notebooks GA 98: 285–86.

    14. GA 45: 186–97.

    15. GA 45: 37.

    16. GA 53: 107; GA 55: 340, 343–45.

    17. GA 55: 159–60.

    18. GA 55: 343–44.

    19. HGR: 34/GA 39: 36.

    20. PA: 73/GA 54: 108.

    21. BN II: 14/GA 95: 18.

    22. GA 16: 679.

    23. Rainer Marten "Heidegger und die Griechen," *Internationale Zeitschrift für Philosophie* 23 (1993): 34–50 and Glenn Most "Heidegger's Greeks," *Arion* 10 (2002): 83–98.

    24. For Hölderlin's notion of *Innigkeit* cf. "Über das Tragische" DKV II: 425–439; One of the other crucial sources for Heidegger's *Innigkeit* is Heraclitus. Cf. GA 39: 116–18; 133–35; 249–50, and 256–2260.

    25. PA: 90/GA 54: 134.

    26. Hölderlin, DKV II: 406.

27. Jean-Pierre Vernant, *Myth and Tragedy* (New York: Zone Books, 1990), 82, 38.

28. See Paul Hammond, *The Strangeness of Tragedy* (Oxford: Oxford University Press, 2009), 100–105 for more on Antigone's lack of filial ties.

29. HHI: 104/GA 53: 129.

30. Jacques Taminiaux, "Plato's Legacy in Heidegger's Two Readings of *Antigone*," 36–38.

31. Jean Greisch, "Who Stands Fast? Do Philosophers Make Good Resistants?," in *Bonhoeffer and Continental Thought*, ed. B. Gregor and J. Zimmermann (Bloomington: Indiana University Press, 2006), 86.

32. BW: 199/GA 5: 62.

33. HHI: 55/GA 53: 69.

34. HHI: 119–120/GA 53: 148–50.

35. GA 55: 205–6.

36. HHI: 54/GA 53: 58.

37. Cf. A letter from Heidegger to his brother Fritz on June 7, 1942 where he speaks of the measurelessness of Americanism HAS: 83 and in GA 54: 249 his eschatological vision of Germany's mission to save the West in World War II is on full display.

38. HKB: 78. The land of evening translates *Abendland*, which designates the West or Occident; *Morgenland* designates the land of the rising sun, Asia. Moreover, in passages written during the battle of Stalingrad, Heidegger writes: "the highest form of suffering is dying one's death as a sacrifice for the preservation of the truth of being. This sacrifice is the purest experience of the voice of being" (GA 54: 249–50).

39. HKB: 85.

40. HHI: 53–54/ GA 53: 66–67.

41. HHI: 54–55/GA 53: 67–69.

42. HHI: 137/GA 53: 171.

43. HHI: 69/GA 53: 84.

44. Friedrich Hölderlin, *Selected Poems and Fragments*, translated by Michael Hamburger (London: Penguin, 1998), 256–57.

45. *Euripides, I* ed. Richmond Lattimore (Chicago: University of Chicago Press, 1955), 73; *Euripides IV*, trans. A.S. Way (Cambridge: Harvard University Press, 1980), 316–17.

46. Andrew Benjamin, *Place, Commonality, and Judgment: Continental Philosophy in the Ancient Greeks* (London: Bloomsbury, 2012), 101.

47. GA 53: 69.

48. HHI: 103–4/GA 53: 128–29.

49. HHI: 104/GA 53: 129.

50. HHI: 77/GA 53: 94.

51. GA 53: 169.

52. HHI: 75/GA 53: 92.
53. GA 53: 128–29. This point is extended in William McNeill, "A Scarcely Pondered Word" in *Philosophy and Tragedy*, ed. Miguel de Beistegui and S. Sparks (London: Routledge, 2000), 169–89.
54. GA 53: 99.
55. HHI: 82–84/ GA 53: 101–4.
56. HHI: 104/GA 53: 129.
57. HHI: 56/GA 53: 69.
58. HHI: 109/GA 53: 136.
59. HHI: 142/GA 53: 178.
60. HHI: 121/GA 53: 151.
61. Sophocles, *Antigone*, Anne Carson, trans. (London: Oberon, 2015), 39.
62. *A Greek-English Lexicon* ed. Liddell, Scott, and Jones (Oxford: Clarendon Press, n.d.) 1121.
63. Cf. Anne Carson's translation of *Antigone*, 39–40.
64. GA 53: 129.
65. Sophocles, *Antigone* trans. Charles Segal (Oxford: Oxford University Press, 2007), 149.
66. Karl Reinhardt, *Sophocles* (London: Blackwell, 1979), 83.
67. HHI: 89/GA 53: 111.
68. HHR: 162/GA 52: 190.

2

Heidegger's "Pre-Aristotelians"
Nietzsche and Heidegger on Anaximander

BABETTE BABICH

There is no philological concept of philology, because philology as such is not something philological.

—Martin Heidegger[1]

There is a science which specifically considers beings as beings and that which in these beings is already there in advance and indeed in themselves.

—Aristotle[2]

Beginnings and Successions

Heidegger's Pre-Aristotelians[3] is a rubric for what Heidegger named "first philosophy," including not only his concern with beginnings but following Husserl's (differently minded) characterization of the methodology of phenomenology as first science[4] as Heidegger amplifies the method of phenomenology as hermeneutic. In this lineage, Heidegger's student, Hans-Georg Gadamer wrote a "prehistory" of metaphysics in addition to a 1996 study on the inception or beginning of philosophy.[5] There is an echo of this in the American Anaximander scholar Charles Kahn who was himself continuing Francis Macdonald Cornford's investigations into the "origins" of Greek theory of knowledge and cosmology.[6] Here there are several themes to weave together in part necessitated by the elusive question of 'style' (this Jacques Derrida exemplifies in characteristically striking fashion as he writes, "The title of this discussion will be the question of style. But my subject shall be woman.")[7] By speaking of Heidegger's Pre-Aristotelians, I underline issues of style beyond Nietzsche's Pre-Platonics and Hermann Diels's Pre-Socratics, as Heidegger advances a doxographic characterization of antiquity after Aristotle. Today Aristotelianism is mainstream,[8] and I will argue that only Nietzsche offers an alternative.

On Students and Teachers

Gadamer, a student of classical philology foregrounding Plato,[9] was inclined to tell his students that the only way to differentiate philosopher and philologist was when one or the other "fell short." The quip is quintessential Gadamer. As I relate it here, as Gadamer's student, it is a piece of successional apocrypha. There is a tradition of "Successions" literature[10] and Nietzsche, who was, like Gadamer, a student of classical philology, writes on succession throughout his ten years of Basel lecture courses on Plato's dialogues along with some 260 pages of courses on "The Pre-Platonic Philosophers," with a separate course on *Die Διαδοχαί der vorplatonischen Philosophen*.[11] Dovetailing with Heidegger's claim that the "essence" of philology is "nothing philological," Gadamer's remark slips neatly into the "concinnity" about which the Canadian philosopher, Graeme Nicholson writes.[12]

In lectures given at the University of Marburg in 1926, Heidegger contrasts philosophy with the "positive" sciences (each of which have, in the Comtean sense, a positive object), defining philosophy as "the *critical* science" [die *kritische* Wissenschaft]."[13] Differentiating beings and Being as such, Heidegger undertakes to articulate what he regards as a comprehensive philosophy of science[14] in his reflections on foundational ontology, that is, what he calls, following Husserl, "scientific philosophy."[15] And, after *Being and Time*, in his 1929 inaugural lecture at the University of Freiburg, Heidegger elaborates the notion of *Wissenschaft*, which he will also unpack in his lecture courses on Nietzsche (and knowledge and science) in connection with passion [*Leidenschaft*]: "What happens to us, essentially, in the grounds of our existence, when science becomes our passion?"[16] As Heidegger goes on to say, recollecting Husserl's programmatic return to the 'things themselves': "in all the sciences we relate to beings themselves . . . No particular way of treating objects of inquiry dominates the others. Mathematical knowledge is no more rigorous than philological historical knowledge. It merely has the character of exactness which does not coincide with rigor."[17]

Heidegger echoes Aristotle. Thus his lectures has been connected with his debates with Rudolf Carnap and Ernst Cassirer that some argue to have instigated the "continental divide," as Michael Friedman in particular has contended, arguing influentially, that this conflict has been foundational for twentieth-century philosophy.[18] A review of Heidegger's reading of logic[19] along with his attention to mathematics and, via Husserl,[20] to the concerns of Frege and Russell is necessary to understand both Heidegger's original (and complex) claim as well as Carnap's critique.[21] Not limited to Carnap alone, this criticism was a long-standing charge contra Heidegger and concerning talk of the "nothing"—itself a fundamental philosophical problem ever since Parmenides, the so-called father of logic, who notably proscribes any talk of nothing/ non-being. The publication of Heidegger's "black notebooks" can give us a sense of Heidegger's concern with Carnap's criticism along with the archness of his assessment of the rigor of the critique: "The nothing is conceded. With a studied indifference science abandons it as what 'there is not.'"[22] Heidegger invokes Parmenides in addition to citing Hegel's reply to Parmenides in his *Science of Logic*—"Pure Being and pure Nothing are therefore the same"[23]—which via a tour through the themes of *Being and Time*, on anxiety and Dasein, brings Heidegger to ask, "Why are there beings at all, and why not rather nothing?"[24]

This is the Leibnizian question Heidegger reprises at the outset of his 1935 course, *An Introduction to Metaphysics*. Gadamer's conjoint reflection on philology/philosophy recalls Nietzsche's conclusion to his 1869 inaugural lecture at the University of Basel, to the extent that Nietzsche inverts Seneca's caution: *Itaque quae philosophia fuit, facta philologia est* [Thereby what was philosophy has been made into philology].[25] Nietzsche's "*philosophia facta est quae philologia fuit*" [what was philology has now been made philosophy][26] consequently inverts this classical relation.

I raise the question of Heidegger's "return" to the ancients "as a question" in Nietzsche's spirit as Nietzsche contends in his late preface to *The Birth of Tragedy* that he was the first to recognize "*the problem of science*" as such, "as problematic, as questionable [*als problematisch*, *als fragwürdig*]."[27] The notion of "return" for Heidegger[28] features further metonymic resonances with Nietzsche with respect to the "Preplatonics." If Pierre Hadot emphasizes that the idea of "return" is at the heart of Platonic and Stoic cosmology[29] we should also recall Cornford, once again, given his familiarity (this is rare among classicists) with Nietzsche's inaugural lecture at Basel.[30] Thirty years younger than Nietzsche, Cornford, a superb translator of Plato and the author of an important study of the *Timaeus* that remains insightful with respect to ancient cosmology, Cornford reminds us in a fashion that almost seems to converge with Nietzsche's or Hölderlin's voice, that Empedocles does not *invent* his doctrine of the "exile of the soul and its wanderings round the wheel of rebirth"[31] invoking further scholarship to argue that this account is already "found in Pindar's second Olympian, written for Theron of Acragas where Empedocles was born at a date when Empedocles was a boy," including a reference beyond Pindar to Erwin Rohde's *Psyche*.[32] Other arguments would bring in Walter Burkert as well as recent scholarship on the Derveni Papyrus, along with Denis O'Brien who makes a similar case for Empedocles.[33]

Complicating traditional accounts of the importance of Aristotle via Brentano for the early Heidegger,[34] Heidegger's epigraph for *Being and Time* is drawn from Plato's *Sophist* (244a). A number of scholars have highlighted the importance of Plato in Heidegger's thinking and, as evidenced by his 1926 *Basic Concepts of Ancient Philosophy*,[35] both Plato *and* Aristotle constitute the tradition of Heidegger's Being question as a concern with the very, as I began by noting, "*beginning* of philosophy."[36] According to convention, the first philosopher is Thales. Heidegger begins doxographically by reminding us that Aristotle (indebted as he is for his knowledge of "the history of this great era [*großen Zeit*] to the Platonic Academy") is our sole source for Thales. Emphasizing the Preplatonic character of early Greek philosophy, Nietzsche underlines in his own lectures on early Greek philosophy that "multiple" sources attest that "[Thales] did not write," further emphasizing Aristotle (along with Eudemus) as originally setting Thales into "ancient *written* traditions."[37] In this context Heidegger also claims that Aristotle sets the terms for "Theophrastus, Simplicius and the Doxography."[38] The issue of firstness is crucial for Heidegger: invoking Anaximander as "first philosopher,"[39] Heidegger proposes "another beginning."[40]

Heidegger limits his discussion of Anaximander in *Die Grundbegriffe der antiken Philosophie* to scarcely more than a page.[41] Similarly spare,

Nietzsche dedicates four pages to Anaximander, describing Anaximander's "lapidary" saying as "the boundary stone of philosophy."[42] By contrast, Nietzsche will dedicate a full third of his *Philosophy in the Tragic Age of the Greeks* to Anaxagoras, invoking Kant in a cosmological focus that continues into Nietzsche's reflections on the *Timaeus* in *The Gay Science*, cautioning against the conceptual solecism of conceiving "the world as a living being."[43] For his part, Heidegger begins his lecture on Anaximander's "Saying" [*Spruch*] citing Nietzsche's translation followed by Diels translation, a tactic setting the two together in source dependency. I argue that this constellation must be read historically beyond its expression in Heidegger's title: "The Saying of Anaximander and its Translations: Nietzsche and Diels [*Der Spruch des Anaximander und seine Übersetzungen: Nietzsche und Diels*].[44] Conventionally enough, Heidegger cites Simplicius's version in Greek before quoting Diels's 1882 edition.[45] Here, I do not claim that Heidegger's reading of Anaximander is Nietzschean, a point Heidegger reduces to Wagner's influence (perhaps given that Nietzsche's lectures on the tragic age of the Greeks were conceived for public presentation at Bayreuth).[46] At the same time, I have argued that Heidegger's debts to Nietzsche are profound and complicated. Thus still speaking on the *inception* of philosophy (given in English as "commencement") in his Nietzsche lectures, Heidegger maintains that such an origin "does not leap outside the history of the first [beginning], does not renounce what has been, but goes back into the grounds of the first beginning."[47] Instead, for Heidegger, "Beginning is the handing-over that is tradition. Preparation of such a beginning takes over that questioning by which the questioner is handed over to that which answers. Primordial questioning itself never replies. For primordial questioning, the sole kind of thinking is one that attunes the human to hear the voice of Being."[48] The human being attuned to "the voice of Being" highlights an esoteric source. The reference is to Parmenides, already mentioned above, and to Heraclitus, qua "obscure," and, in this same succession, to Plato.

The esoteric attunement takes us to Plato's "unwritten teaching" beyond Plato and beyond Heidegger's own references to readings of Plato to the so-called Tübingen school, via Hans Joachim Krämer and Konrad Gaiser and Giovanni Reale,[49] but also including others. And it should be noted that Krämer gives us a bibliographic list in chronological order in which Boeckh, Hermann, Becker, and, latterly, Cornford make an appearance but—and this omission is consistently observed by scholars of ancient philosophy—Nietzsche's name does not.[50] I note here that the reference to the so-called 'esoteric' Plato must be conceived in addition to other "esoteric" traditions, including geometry as such (and Pythagoras) quite as, in addition to David Lachterman,[51] Walter J. Ong traces this at the outset of his book, *Ramus: Method and the Decay of Dialogue*.[52] Ong may be compared with Heidegger's reflection on science and calculative thinking as he features an epigraph from Hugh of St. Victor's *Didascalicon*, which asks *and* answers, rather like Angelus Silesius: "Why do you follow the windings of the river? Lay hold of the source, and you have all."[53] Notably, the section of Ong's chapter on Peter of Spain may be read as useful background to Ivan Illich's commentary on Hugh of St Victor, *In the Vineyard of the Text*, as an exploration of loci as such: "Peter's Places."[54] With this range of references, the "esoteric," as Nietzsche who uses this express term tells us, has to do with *what* is said/unsaid and not less with the one *to whom* it is said/unsaid.[55] We need this differential context to ask the Heideggerian "who" question. Here we may also note that the esoteric is (at least) part of the reason Heidegger's language tends to inspire some, who hang on his every word, spoken *and* unspoken, while others dismiss him outright.

SPEAKING WISDOM: ON FRAGMENTS AND THEIR DISCONTENTS

We have a problem with the words we read in English even before we begin to read Heidegger on Anaximander. In translation, the titular phrasing of "The Anaximander Fragment" includes an ambiguity that permits the reader to assume that a "fragment" of Anaximander's writings is somehow extant in some fashion. This is a common error, beyond Anaximander, that Catherine Rowett early in her career (writing as Catherine Osborne) sought to correct albeit without reading Nietzsche, who emphasized this very lack of historical record in his lectures on pre-Platonic philosophers.[56] By invoking Anaximander's "fragment," Krell's translation suggests that Heidegger echoes Diels's *Die Fragmente der Vorsokratiker*. If some scholars continue to regard Diels's "fragments" as canonic, classical philology has a long tradition of challenging the conception of literal "fragments" that could be regarded, in Heidegger's language as cited above, as constituting the static, "positive" subject matter of classical philology. Thus Heidegger's "*Der Spruch des Anaximander*" might be better rendered as "The Saying of Anaximander." For his part, Nietzsche foregrounds what he describes as the "*sporadisch-spruchmäßige Vorstufe der Philosophie*,"[57] highlighting the apothegms themselves as the "sporadic-aphoristic preliminary-stage of philosophy," observing that what we call philosophy begins with such "aphorisms" or "sentences" [*Sentenzen*], qua summary bits of wisdom not unlike sayings already to be found in Homer and Hesiod (and Pindar as already noted by citing Cornford above).

In his lecture, "*Die Vorstufen des σοφὸς ἀνήρ*," Nietzsche reviews the sayings attributed to "Demetrius Phalereus . . . Cleobulus, Solon, Chilon, Pittacus, Thales, Bias Periander. Each had 20 or more sayings."[58] And in his Basel lectures beginning in 1869 on the topic of *The Preplatonic Philosophers*, Nietzsche emphasizes that both Homer and Hesiod are to be read with attention to what is absent from these classical sources, that is, failing any attribution to this sage or that. Thus—and this observation is particularly relevant for Nietzsche's interpretation of Anaximander—the concept of ownership or "property" [*Eigenthum*] (i.e., that an idea might be the coin of a given sage) does not seem to feature in Hesiod, underlining the "extraordinary abundance" of "popular wisdom," as Nietzsche specifically lists different attributions and notes that Hesiod himself draws upon this popular tradition with "both hands" [*er greift mit vollem Händen zu*].[59] As such broad sources to be mined, Nietzsche recounts the sayings of the so-called seven sages [*Weisesprechung der 7*][60] including the Delphic Oracle itself—a source for Plato, as we will return to this point—in a longer tradition of cryptic, "gnomic" sayings, echoed throughout ancient and medieval texts and already for Nietzsche of long-standing provenance in the *Iliad* itself: "*die Gnomologie*."[61]

Specialist as Nietzsche was on what we today name source scholarship—specifically and comprehensively, Diogenes Laërtius—Nietzsche parses such "archaic formulae" as "ethical sentences" characterized in terms of "physiognomy" whereby the pronouncements associated with the Delphic Oracle would offer less revelation/futural "predictions" than ethical teachings or admonitions to "human conscience," thereby explaining their archaeological prominence as inscribed "on columns and other visible loci."[62] To this extent, as Nietzsche explains, given the antique tendency to associate a given saying with not just one but several different sages, the philological challenge will be to justify one attribution over another as *Spruchtafeln* [tablets of sayings] are compiled. This is critical philology, as Nietzsche will later use the term, to the extent that what is at issue is not a fixed list of sages as such but to emphasize that these remain unspecified owing to this profusion such that, formally, "it suffices to *seek* the 7."[63]

How is the contemporary scholar to check claims about the sayings themselves or the sages? Are there not authorities? To ask this may miss the historiographical point for Nietzsche, given that the sourcebooks to be consulted for such a check—the presumptively "attested" canonic authorities, the concordances, the handbooks and histories of early Greek philosophy—are all of them compiled by philologists. This Nietzsche underlines throughout his university lectures, as he writes them as if speaking to such future (and this is a common word for Nietzsche) philologists. Thus like Heidegger's lecture courses—and like Hegel's—Nietzsche's courses were written for his students in contrast with his expressly popular lectures on *Philosophy in the Tragic Age of the Greeks*, composed for Wagner's public in Bayreuth. Mindful of the distinction between destined audiences, Nietzsche also wrote about teaching and gave public lectures in Basel on what he named the "future of our educational institutions"[64] specifically on the topic of teaching philology to future teachers of philology (just as Kant famously wrote the *Prolegomena* for "future teachers of metaphysics"). Thus Heidegger's option in his lecture on Anaximander's "Saying" to cite not Nietzsche's university lectures, but Nietzsche's popular *Philosophy in the Tragic Age*[65] is striking.

More significant than Nietzsche's lectures for a study of Anaximander are the sources themselves and, as sources, stand in relation to one another. Nietzsche's three studies on the sources of Diogenes Laërtius, published seriatim from 1867 to 1970 in *Rheinisches Museum für Philologie*, then the leading journal of classical philology,[66] were key for Diels. As Diogenes Laërtius tells us of Anaximander in his brief articulation of his "life," here citing the Loeb edition:

> [Anaximander] laid down as his principle and element that which is unlimited without defining it as air or water or anything else. He held that the parts undergo change, but the whole is unchangeable; that the earth, which is of spherical shape, lies in the midst, occupying the place of a centre; that the moon, shining with borrowed light, derives its illumination from the sun; further, that the sun is as large as the earth and consists of the purest fire.[67]

We will return below to the complicated notion of "principle" and to the ἄπειρον, Anaximander's "unlimited" or "boundless" as Nietzsche says.

Elsewhere, writing on hermeneutics, I emphasize Nietzsche's indebtedness to his teachers, that is to both Friedrich Ritschl (1806–1876),[68] for the sake of textual philology, as well as to the archaeologist, philologist, and Mozart expert, Otto Jahn (1813–1869) for the sake of a specifically *phenomenological* hermeneutic dimension, the latter evident in Nietzsche's gnomic reference to the "boundary stone" as such and thus to archaeological or what Nietzsche named "monumental" inscription.[69]

Above I highlighted the interpretive consequences of translating Heidegger's "*Der Spruch des Anaximander*" as "fragment" as opposed to "saying." In a related fashion, beyond the intimation that scholars possess a material fragment, Nietzsche's remonstration to his students emphasizes that already to attribute the saying to Anaximander presupposes that one has a hermeneutic method of exegesis, reading between sources assumed extant and distinct.[70] In the case of Heidegger, and Nietzsche concisely indicates the point of phrasing, a further complication is the loss of Heidegger's own focus on *saying* as this amplifies his invocation of Nietzsche's *Zarathustra* as advocate, that is: as speaker. At the same time, we take over, often uncritically, what received sources claim as the legacy of Theophrastus and Simplicius.[71]

Heidegger's lecture reflects on the tradition of translating Anaximander's saying: "Beings are spoken of in such a way that their Being is expressed. Being comes to language as the Being of beings."[72] Thereby Heidegger transposes this tradition throughout his text on his own terms. Hence, although beginning with Nietzsche's translation of Anaximander, Heidegger offers no gloss (this does come later, paratactically, in the strategy we recognize from his *Introduction to Metaphysics*, or from his readings of Hölderlin or Trakl, or even in his "What Are Poets For?," writing about Rilke on the "Open," with his own "tacking" translation of Anaximander's saying), but moves in his 1941–1942 lecture to reflect on power, which he links not to Nietzsche's notorious (unpublished manuscript) *The Will to Power* but Nietzsche's partly published—Nietzsche would only publish three books—*Thus Spoke Zarathustra*:

> At the summit of the completion of Western philosophy these words are pronounced: "To stamp Becoming with the character of Being—that is the highest will to power." Thus writes Nietzsche in a note entitled, "Recapitulation." According to the character of the manuscript's handwriting we must locate

it in the year 1885, about the time when Nietzsche, having completed Zarathustra, was planning his systematic metaphysical magnum opus. The "Being" Nietzsche thinks here is "the eternal recurrence of the same." It is the way of continuance through which will to power wills itself and guarantees its own presencing as the Being of Becoming. At the outermost point of the completion of metaphysics the Being of beings is addressed in these words.[73]

Where is Anaximander? Ensconced in the Platonic as in the Aristotelian doxographic tradition (as this differs from Nietzsche's reading backward from Plato, as we here bracket the question of Aristotle for Nietzsche), Anaximander is not at stake for Heidegger any more than Anaximander himself would seem to be especially key to either Aristotle or to Plato. Thus in a lecture dedicated to Anaximander, Heidegger reads Parmenides and Heraclitus as "the names of the two thinkers, contemporaries in the decades between 540 and 460, who at the outset of Western thought uniquely belong together in thinking the true."[74]

Reading Parmenides is at the heart of Heidegger's *Introduction to Metaphysics*, a "fully reworked" (much has been much written on this reworking in a specifically Nazi context) lecture course that Heidegger began in 1935 at the University of Freiburg, eight years after *Being and Time*: "It is customary in describing the beginning of Western philosophy to oppose the doctrine of Heraclitus to this doctrine of Parmenides. A much-quoted saying is attributed to Heraclitus: *panta rhei*, everything is in flux. Accordingly, there is no being. Everything 'is' becoming."[75] Heidegger opposes Parmenides to Heraclitus, that is, Plato, on becoming. Writing in his unpublished "Black Notebooks," Heidegger seems to reflect on the question of whether Nietzsche might yet serve as "transition, i.e., a preparation for another' beginning of the history of beyng?"[76] Here Heidegger retrains the Being question: "Nietzsche is a transition only in the sense that he metaphysically anticipates the consummation of modernity and thereby posits the end appropriate to the history of being, and with this end (which he himself was not able to recognize and know as such, because he still thinks metaphysically, as the ultimate and definitive proponent of metaphysics) the possibility of a preparation of the decision in favor of the other beginning is made ready."[77] There has been a great deal of commentary on the opposition/difference/distinction/contrast between *Nietzsche/Heidegger*, commonly asking, in effect: Is Heidegger's Nietzsche *right*? Is Heidegger's Nietzsche *wrong*? Expectedly, and with the signal distinction of Jacques Derrida and Reiner Schürmann, as well as the present author, such readings privilege the commentator's reading of Nietzsche as opposed to engagement with Heidegger's reading in order, absent such a reading, to assess Heidegger one way or another. And readers rarely, as this is even more complicated, engage Nietzsche's reading of his Pre-Platonic philosophers.[78]

With respect to the inception of philosophy, Heidegger argues that in "Nietzsche's thinking, there is nothing referring to this beginning in its neediness and its essence."[79] Taking pains to underscore the danger of influence, for Heidegger a mimetic danger, Nietzsche can be "synonymous with a certain imitation of his thought,"[80] yielding "a new 'form' [»*Gattung*«] of 'literature,'[81] a literary trend in which Heidegger himself may (obviously) be counted and several scholars highlight a certain agonistic tension. Various political elements dominate in this just to the extent that Nietzsche, on Heidegger's reading (and not only Heidegger's reading), articulates war-inflected modernity as the "unconditional empowerment of power for unrestricted violence [*unbedingte Ermächtigung der Macht zur schrankenlosen Gewalt*]. We may also suspect we are entering the first phase of the onset of this consummation. What possesses the decisive character, however, is only the knowledge of this basic content of the final Western metaphysics, which in turn depends on knowledge of how the essence of metaphysics as a whole is to be understood in terms of the history of being."[82] Readings of Heidegger's interpretation of Nietzsche and readings of antiquity (these tend to be separate) remain "steeped" in a range of the same problems to the present day as it is supposed that Heidegger's Nazism inspires his interest in "his" own Presocratics.[83] The dates in question seem rarely to be an issue for such readings, typically claiming a Nazism *avant la lettre*, as this would apply to his early lecture courses.

Thinking through chronology and history as "the historical, the genuinely historical," Heidegger undertakes to raise a question that is the question of the ἀρχή,[84] a question Schürmann expressly seeks to articulate and that we will return to below. The question of the ἀρχή, for Heidegger, "precedes and determines all history."[85]

Adding complexity to these reflections, Nietzsche offers a sustained engagement with chronology as a historical problem.[86] To this same extent, the doctrine of "succession" is at issue. This for Nietzsche is the hermeneutic matter of determining the dates for the "Pre-Platonic" thinkers themselves as the problem of history and philology. And when we read Diels's 1879 *Doxographi Graeci*,[87] Diels, himself a Theophrastus expert, tells us we must have recourse to Theophrastus.[88]

Built into the reflection on succession is a reference to Aristotle as ultimate authority: here the problem is that of beginnings, and that is, as Nietzsche argues, a matter of source research. Thus J. A. Philip reminds us that "it is only when we can see the development of an idea in its context that we can hazard any conjecture as to gaps in our tradition or as to its beginnings when those beginnings are unclear. We can no longer juggle the doxography against Aristotle, or Aristotle against himself, to justify any hypothesis as to earlier thought. We can no longer build on the Successions to fill gaps in the thought structure of earlier thinkers."[89] Philip's comment seems to echo Nietzsche's arguments regarding the Successions, Nietzsche's Διαδοχαί.

Yet, for Heidegger, Nietzsche hardly counts as a scholarly authority any more than he counts as such for Philip or, indeed, for most readers interested in classical philology/ancient philosophy today. For Heidegger, "Nietzsche's fulfilment of metaphysics is the foundation of the final period of the modern age . . . the age of consummate meaninglessness."[90] Identifying a "Roman" Nietzsche as Heidegger speaks of him (by contrast with a supposedly "Greek" Nietzsche), Heidegger institutes a contrast with Nazi absorption. As Heidegger goes on to note, then-contemporary Nietzsche interpretations foregrounded "the Nietzsche of the Wagner period and without yet penetrating to the point whereby Nietzsche rejects the Greeks in favour of the Romans and the Will to Power, i.e., 'technology.' . . . one continues to see 'technology' . . . as mere 'deviltry' and romanticism."[91]

By informing us that Nietzsche thinks "in a purely Roman fashion," Heidegger can conclude that Nietzsche never could "comprehend the Greek beginning of Western thought,"[92] and just this will be asserted as Heidegger's own new beginning. Here and elsewhere there is no lack of Nietzsche-*ressentiment*—we may, after Max Scheler's *Ressentiment*, call it that—in engaging Nietzsche either positively or negatively. Thus Heidegger tells us that he is the *only* thinker to fulfill "Nietzsche's thought" as opposed to those engaged in what he here dismisses as "historiological trifling" or theft [*historische Spielerei oder Dieberei*].[93] Only Heidegger has the capacity to bring Nietzsche beyond himself into the promised land of the history of being.

How to Invent Fragments:
On History and Hermeneutic Dogma

> Wo hält sich doch der liebe Mann auf? Warum blieb er so lange incognito? *A propos* wissen Sie mir nicht eine Silhouette von ihm zu bekommen?
>
> —Nietzsche, *Homer und die klassische Philologie*

Everything historically transmitted from the past depends on texts, sayings, aphorisms, quotations, "fragments."[94] There is the tradition of received *doxa*—thank you Theophrastus/Aristotle (or Simplicius or Aetius)[95]—and there is the separate question of the "person" as in Nietzsche's inaugural lecture at Basel, asking, Who is Homer? Or else, in the philosophical tradition, as Nietzsche teaches his students to ask: Who is Pythagoras? As Nietzsche frames the question in his lectures: Was there a historical Pythagoras? This is parallel to the question of the historical Homer or the historical Jesus as this classic question, via "David Strauss, the Confessor and Writer" was the first of Nietzsche's *Untimely Meditations*.[96] To this extent, Nietzsche's "meditations" concern the question of history, including "Richard Wagner in Bayreuth" as inquiries into "the history of the evolution of culture since the Greeks."[97] In this fashion we may begin to trace Plato's Socrates, Arrian's Epictetus, and who knows who, certainly *someone's* "Nicomachean" Aristotle just as Nietzsche has his own Aristotle and Heidegger likewise. What is quoted, that is, what is said to be said, embraces the very first philosophical text: the Anaximander "saying." The saying as Heidegger begins with Simplicius is transmitted as a quote, complete with a famously judgmental gloss, as "rather poetic."

Above we noted that Osborne (Rowett), writing on Hippolytus, reminds us that we have the texts we have filtered through citations, quotations, other texts.[98] Christian Benne, author of an above-referenced study of Nietzsche and historical-critical philology, traces the genesis of the manuscript to the book.[99] And throughout his life, Pierre Hadot sought to explain exegesis and commentary and primary sources, as we sometimes suppose these to be original, emerging fully formed, without prior influence, and thereby "first": thus reminding us that not everything is written down and emphasizing, as Nietzsche emphasizes, that Goethe observes that only certain bits of what is written are subsequently transmitted. "Literature," in consequence, as Friedrich Kittler cites Goethe's

Wilhelm Meisters Lehrjahre: "is the fragment of fragments; the least of what had happened and of what had been spoken was written down; of what had been written down only the smallest fraction was preserved."[100] Speaking of this same Goethean reflection on the fragment, for Nietzsche "the most wretched accidents, sudden eclipses of men's minds, superstitious paroxysms and antipathies, cramped or lazy writing fingers, down to book worms and rainfall, all determine whether or not a book will live on another century or turn into ashes and mould."[101]

Here, to begin again, we recall Heidegger's citation of Nietzsche's translation in *Der Spruch des Anaximander*: "Whence things have their origin, there they must also pass away according to necessity; for they must pay penalty and be judged for their injustice, according to the ordinance of time."[102]

Heidegger's next sentence takes us to Zarathustra: "Thus translates the young Nietzsche in a treatise completed in 1873 entitled *Philosophy in the Tragic Age of the Greeks*. The treatise was published posthumously in 1903, thirty years after its composition."[103] These days, German-speaking scholars tend to use the little orange Reclam edition of *Die Vorsokratiker* in Jaap Mansfeld's translation, which like all such renderings, including Nietzsche's and Diels's to be sure, cites Simplicius/Theophrastus.[104]

Elsewhere, I call attention to Heidegger's thematization of Nietzsche's style as this also inspires Derrida, where Heidegger names Nietzsche's Zarathustra as one who speaks on behalf of others, a *Fürsprecher*.[105] So regarded, *Thus Spoke Zarathustra* is a register of different speeches and interlocutors, beginning with Zarathustra addressing the sun itself, invoking an overflowing cup (micturition, think Joyce), a forest saint, and so on. Zarathustra speaks differently depending on those he is speaking to: the crowd in the marketplace, the fallen tightrope walker, the despisers of the body, the night, life herself, eternity, his followers, his animals.

Nietzsche taught Plato's dialogues (under the title page: *Plato amicus sed* [Plato, a friend but]), in a course on Plato thematizing Plato's antecedents,[106] recollecting the so-called unwritten teaching, key to the esoteric tradition no matter whether one reads the esoteric as conventional Straussian or more rigorously, more saliently, by way of the Tübingen school (including disputes) already referenced with the respect to the esoteric as such.[107] The origin of this "unwritten teaching," qua teaching about the unwritten, is no secret doctrine but scholarly 'esoterica,' as Plato underlines apocrypha in the *Phaedrus*.

Limited to the texts we have, we have noted the circular authority of Aristotle but also, as Nietzsche puts this, following Goethe, on what Heidegger characterizes as the "rare and the seldom."[108] In the case of Nietzsche's philological reflections, the "rare" is the accident that is the "text" metonymically characterized as a "fragment." But not only is little preserved, text-wise and materially (apart from literal fragments such as we have them, like the Derveni Papyrus), but we lack context for most of what has been preserved, failing what Nietzsche calls "personality" (cue Diogenes Laertius), as such references to the person apart from any written text can be all we have, as in the case of Thales or Pythagoras or Socrates.[109]

Thus Nietzsche emphasizes that philologists effectively find themselves in a "field of shards" [*Trümmerfeld*].[110] Using recognizably Heideggerian language, Gadamer reminds us that our prejudices are determinative: "Anyone who quotes, already interprets by means of the form in which he or she presents the text of the quotation."[111]

What can this mean? Once again, do we not "have" a range of fragments, specifically as collected in Diels? Is there not a tradition of Presocratic/Preplatonic thinkers? Have these thinkers not already been, as we cited Diels's *Doxographi Graeci* above, already *canonized* and so set in basic scholarly order? Here, keeping to the first such "fragment" as Heidegger begins with this, we can go back not only to Kathleen Freeman, who translated Diels's translations or else to Kirk and Raven (and Schofield) but also to Charles Kahn's *Anaximander and the Origins of Cosmology*.[112] For Kahn, drawing on the same Burnet Heidegger cites, we have considerable work to do just to figure out what words in the fragment transmitted to us may properly be said to belong to Anaximander and which must be ascribed to the commentator or tradition. It is to Osborne/Rowett's credit that she reminds us that much that was perhaps too hastily discarded may need to be reinstalled as authentic bits—this is also the strategy Gadamer uses in his own discovery, of which he was rightly proud, and which, methodically, he has explained, of a heretofore unrecognized and thus unknown and thus new Heraclitus fragment[113]—while different formerly received terms may have to be reclassified to make the text make sense on the terms of our own generation or (as historically such judgments tend to be more perspicuous) another.

But surely the original fragments—did I not just quote Nietzsche's formula of a "field of shards"—can be selected out? What else is hermeneutics for? Certainly scholarly practice proceeds in this fashion—I call this the "raisin theory" of philosophy/philology: whereby one reads certain texts less for the author's words than for the bits (i.e., the raisins) featured as quotations. This is the fate of Diogenes Laërtius in particular or Kirk and Raven's *Presocratics* where readers can bracket the editor(s)'s or compiler's interpretive commentary (matters are not advanced with the new Kirk, Raven, and Schofield) or Diels (which we know as Diels-Kranz). Thus in an Anglophone context, students of early Greek philosophy read the "Presocratics" set off, in the case of Kirk, Raven, and Schofield, by boldface type, offset. These offset bits are regarded as "the texts," that is: as the "fragments," themselves. The same is the case with Kahn's less well-known collection/reordering of the fragments of Heraclitus.[114] Same thing with more recent collections and including the more broadly parsed, multivolume, bilingual Laks/Most Loeb edition.

Typically scholars, even students of scientific philology, so Nietzsche argues, exclude context.[115] But it is for this reason of exclusion, leading to a project of excavation and discarding, that Nietzsche uses his own Platonic metaphor for science, not unlike Heidegger's usage, invoking the goddess of truth, Aletheia, to describe the field of classical philology in the latter sections of his *On the Birth of Tragedy*, speaking of archaeology and its discontents/motivations using the models as he variously does of a search for precious stones or a fetishist disrobing a woman.[116]

At stake is the word, Heidegger reminds us, at the close of his essay on "Heraclitus B 50"—"The word of thinkers knows no authors, in the sense of writers."[117] For Heidegger, more concisely, the "word of thinkers has no authority."[118] By contrast, Nietzsche begins *The Preplatonic Philosophers* lectures by raising the question of the so-called sages as a philological query together with the range and kind of traditions surrounding those named sages and thus called "wise" and including the title, the name, the word "philosopher"[119] per se. Interestingly, making a recognizably "Socratic" point, the typical tack in such ascription is refusal or denial. For anyone who accepts a description as philosopher or claims such a description for their own part—as Plato underlines the point, echoing Heraclitus and Parmenides—can be no philosopher, as the second-century Menippean satirist Lucian later parodizes the point in his *Philosophies for Sale*.[120] Nietzsche details the gesture of deflection. And the same deflection is arguably at work—note the *topoi* at hand in Plato's *Apology*—apostrophizing the person of Socrates and thereby setting Socrates into the thus preferred "succession." Nietzsche writes numerically and thus structurally with respect to the earlier attribution of the term "wise":

Beautiful but varying legends concerning the selection of the 7. Fishermen fish out a tripod from the sea and the Milesian community leadership designates it for the wisest. . . . 1) to whom is the tripod first sent (Thales Pittakus Bias) 2) who gets it finally 3) in what order 4) from whence the tripod 5) where is it set up (Miletus Delphi Thebes). The seven number seems to be already stamped in the form of these legends (not yet).[121]

Heidegger squares off contra Nietzsche with a technique borrowed from him, using what he calls fruitful contestation, or *Auseinandersetzung*. In this fashion, Heidegger contends that "Nietzsche thinks purely Roman style and in his own metaphysics can never conceive the Greek beginning of Western thinking."[122]

The problem with this contestation is that Nietzsche is no accepted authority in classics, as this is a matter of received convention. Nietzsche had no authority in Heidegger's day, and this did not change. So the question remains: What did Heidegger mean by claiming that Nietzsche, Graecist as he was, theorist of Greek lyric and who discovered the basis for what is now conventional Greek prosody via his rhythmic research on the ancient Greek ictus, "thinks purely Roman style"? Might Heidegger have been claiming that Nietzsche taught in Latin? Teaching in Latin, in Nietzsche's day—and in Heidegger's day—was common practice in university, most especially in philological instruction. What is more, Nietzsche published studies of Diogenes Laërtius in Latin.[123] No part of that was exceptional or noteworthy given that Latin was the *lingua franca* of scholarship. Arguably Heidegger's judgment about Nietzsche's "Roman style" concerned Nietzsche's qualifications, much as Heidegger also judged the qualifications of his contemporaries with reference to their teachers. If so, Heidegger would not have been wrong as Nietzsche's teacher, Friedrich Ritschl, was a Latinist (thus Nietzsche's lifelong pride in his own stylistic prowess with reference to Sallust).

Heidegger's rhetoric assimilates Nietzsche to Heidegger's own oppositional tensions: defining the "authentic" Nietzsche as a thinker who thinks the Roman rather than the Greek converges with his assessment of leading Nazi interpretations of the day about which he makes parallel claims. Indeed, we can trace this in Heidegger's 1939 lecture course on "The Will to Power as Knowledge." Thus a focus on "power" and "will" continues to dominate accounts of both Nietzsche and politics as well as commentaries on Nietzsche and antiquity.

By adding hermeneutics to his rhetorical account, Heidegger's efforts to read Anaximander's saying contra Nietzsche's account of Anaximander's first *ethical* philosophy (to use Nietzsche's characterization of Anaximander), permits Heidegger to assert that it will not be Nietzsche but Heidegger himself who *rediscovers* Presocratic philosophy by retrieving the beginning of Western thought even before its inception with Anaximander and Heraclitus and Parmenides. In this way, as Heidegger explains at the outset of his *Introduction to Metaphysics*, what is at stake is the "inception" or beginning [*Anfang*] of philosophy. Heidegger likewise parses this by way of the Latin, reminding us here that in doing so we designate the texts (proto-scientific and proto-philosophical as we also periodize tradition) as "primitive."[124]

Thus Spake Anaximander, Thus Spake Heidegger

> jemand, der so etwas geschrieben habe, sei wissenschaftlich todt
>
> —Hermann Usener

By dismissing Nietzsche's readings by assessing them as more "Roman" than Greek and characterizing Nietzsche as (popularly) allied to the Wagnerianism of his era, Heidegger echoes the judgment of mainstream classicists. This is all well-known. Privately, in his *Nachlaß*, Heidegger insists/predicts that the "fable that Nietzsche rediscovered 'pre-Platonic philosophy' will one day come to light in its fabulosity [*Fabelhaftigkeit*]; for Nietzsche has indeed bequeathed the most superficial interpretation of these thinkers, i.e., of what they thought, due to his very great obliviousness regarding what is reserved for essential thinking as that which is to be thought."[125] There is a certain dissonance here given that any scholars who might have claimed otherwise would seem to have been either a decided minority or utterly nonexistent. Thus above I underlined that despite his contributions regarding the sources of Diogenes Laërtius, and despite his contributions to Greek prosody, Nietzsche is not conventionally assumed crucial for ancient philology or ancient philosophy. So just what author would have inspired Heidegger's objections? Given historical context, Heidegger may have been alluding to Karl Joël, who in 1906 wrote *Der Ursprung der Naturphilosophie aus dem Geiste der Mystik*.[126] If Joël is today mostly obscure, at the time he was Nietzsche's successor as professor at Basel as of 1902.

Joël refers to Nietzsche's Basel lecture courses, *Preplatonic Philosophers*, in his 1921 study of ancient philosophy. Indeed, accustomed as we are to one (re)discovery of the wheel after another, typically with no mention of antecedent thinkers, it can be striking to note that Joël's preface cites a paragraph of predecessors, listing distinguished alternatives. This included the miraculous year (as Heidegger himself cites the year) 1903, when Joël's own book (so he informs his reader) originally appeared.[127] Indeed, if we had not largely forgotten Joël, we would not need to rediscover, thanks to Alberto Bernabé Pajares and others, a certain Orphic tradition that is no less relevant for Nietzsche.[128]

Nevertheless, in Heidegger's public lecture on Anaximander, we find no reference to Nietzsche's Basel lectures on *Die vorplatonischen Philosophen* (although we know that Heidegger was familiar with these lectures inasmuch as he cites them in the *Nachlaß* version of his own lecture course, GA: 78).[129]

Thus it can seem that there is a certain anxiety of influence such that Heidegger begins his reading of the Anaximander fragment by quoting Nietzsche only to "dead-silence" him. Similarly, we may read Heidegger's *Nachlaß* note in his Black Notebooks, denouncing the "fabulosity" of any claims for Nietzsche's own "rediscovery" of "pre-Platonic philosophy."[130] If Heidegger uses Nietzsche's terminology of the *Preplatonics* in place of Diels's *Presocratics*, while offering the parallel rubric of *Pre-Aristotelians*, it is not to call attention to Nietzsche but and much rather because Heidegger's referent is Hegel.

The claim that a scholar has been subjected to dead silencing (*Todschweigerei*) would not be to say that that scholar is *never* cited or his work irrelevant. Ordinary scholarly norms (paradigms, received views) function by bracketing, that is to say silencing, whole ranges of individual scholars and collective traditions. Thus if Nietzsche's pathbreaking studies on Diogenes Laërtius and source scholarship was as foundational as it was, and few would dispute this, the fact of it has never managed to ensure either acknowledgment or influence. This is not least because Diogenes Laërtius is regarded, in the words of the Anglophone editorial authorities behind *The Presocratic Philosophers* (Kirk, Raven, and Schofield), as "trivial," if immediately qualified as "important."[131] When Jonathan Barnes dubs Diogenes Laërtius "night-porter to the history of Greek philosophy," he adopts Nietzsche's metaphor, clarifying that "no-one can enter unless Diogenes has given him the key."[132] For today's specialists, Nietzsche remains as "dead" to ancient philosophical/philological scholarship as he was for

Usener, who warned his own students that anyone who wrote as Nietzsche did had to be regarded as "scientifically dead"—"*wissenschaftlich todt.*"[133]

Reading this, we suppose this quality of being dead to scholarship would have been a matter of Nietzsche's "bombast" or unclear style. But recalling Nietzsche's contribution to "source scholarship" established with his publications on Diogenes Laërtius in the *Rheinisches Museum für Philologie*,[134] we can observe that these contributions were quite conventional, and Diels would have been able to draw on Nietzsche's research as a matter of course for both his 1879 *Doxographi Graeci* and 1903 *Fragmente der Vorsokratiker*[135] quite as it is Diels himself who informs us that, had things gone as originally designed, he would have collaborated with Nietzsche on the latter.[136]

There is a parallel to be drawn with Heidegger, if classicists do not typically read Heidegger and matters are hardly helped as Heidegger is both influenced by and refuses Nietzsche. Here one may wonder at the energy Heidegger dedicates to sidelining an influence on classics, namely Nietzsche's, that does not exist, as mainstream classicists tend to refuse both Heidegger *and* Nietzsche.

With Heidegger's *An Introduction to Metaphysics* and its focus on Parmenides, along with his lectures of the 1940s on Anaximander as on Heraclitus, Heidegger claimed for his own part to have "rediscovered" Presocratic philosophy. The focus on the "beginning" captivated Gadamer, as Heidegger claims that the ancients displayed an "inability to retain the beginning."[137] More than simple reproach, this claim leads to the necessity of nothing other than *repetition*: "to draw once again more deeply than ever from its source."[138]

To be sure, both Heidegger and Nietzsche may be read in terms of their rediscovery of the Greeks. For Heidegger, Anaximander is concerned with the Being question; for Nietzsche, Anaximander is the first "ethical" philosopher, a firstling that also makes sense of Anaximander's cosmogenesis/cosmodicy.

Once again: Heidegger's "The Saying of Anaximander" foregrounds the numerological coincidence of the 1903 publication of Diels's *Die Fragmente der Vorsokratiker* and Nietzsche's (posthumous) *Philosophie im tragischen Zeitalter der Griechen*, included in the *Nachlass* volumes appearing in 1903 (although Heidegger references the 1913 Kroner edition).[139] In addition, Heidegger knew that this same popular volume grew out of Nietzsche's active decade as professor of classics teaching lecture courses such as "Introduction to Plato's Dialogues,"[140] "The Pre-Platonic

Philosophers," "Aristotle's Rhetoric,"[141] and ancient rhetoric in general, as well courses on ancient Greek lyric poetry,[142] and the "succession question" at the University of Basel.[143]

In his public lecture, Heidegger focuses on the popular Nietzsche, presented as one "from whose philosophy (all too coarsely understood) Spengler predicted the decline of the West—in the sense of the Western historical world."[144] Thus when Heidegger begins by citing Nietzsche's translation from his *Philosophy in the Tragic Age of the Greeks*,' *before* he cites Diels, it is because Nietzsche's commentary, published nine years earlier, would have been known to Diels precisely on account of his engagement with and rendering of Anaximander: "But where things have their origin, there too their passing away occurs according to necessity; for they pay recompense and penalty to one another for their recklessness, according to firmly established time."[145] Heidegger will spend the rest of his essay unpacking the fragment.

On this point, Françoise Dastur has reminded us that we need to find access to the saying of Anaximander "outside the saying itself, in the experience from which it is the expression."[146] Dastur develops the Derridean gift/donation along with Heidegger's *Brauch*, setting her reading in opposition to the language of compensation as Nietzsche uses this language (the concepts mine and thine are key to Nietzsche). This also has the benefit of taking the discussion back to Heidegger's "gift of Being." For Dastur: "This more originary gift is therefore letting the beings belong to Being, a *Gehörenlassen*."[147] On the topic of further debts and Anaximander, Gary Shapiro takes this reflection a little further with reference to Nietzsche.[148]

Whose Nietzsche? Whose Greeks?

I argued above that haunting Heidegger's reflections on Nietzsche and his claimed "invention" of the "Preplatonic Philosophers" is a hidden community, namely the philologists of the received tradition who remain for their part disinclined to note Nietzsche's contributions. One leading (recognized) name displaces another. As evidenced by the most recent Loeb publication of the texts associated with Presocratic/Platonic thought, now generically retitled as *Early Greek Philosophy*, the assumptions Heidegger makes in his reflection on Anaximander insist upon an audience of importantly opposed personages in classics scholarship, representing "irrational" contra "rational" scholarship. These authors are hardly invoking Peter Ramus (as cited by Ong noted above) but specifically Aristotelian schematism. The ghost of Karl Popper, who also sought to go "back" to the Presocratics, namely to Parmenides (albeit in a limitedly Whiggish modality),[149] may lurk in this distinction.

In the case of Heidegger, one might name Wolfgang Schadewaldt (who, in addition to classics also wrote on the significance of translation in Hölderlin) or Karl Reinhardt, who was significant in connection with Nietzsche as well as Alfred Bauemler,[150] who edited a then-influential collection of Nietzsche's unpublished writings,[151] along with Ernst Bertram.[152] Here, Pierre Hadot's introduction to Bertram's *Versuch einer Mythologie* can help to clarify some of Heidegger's references to myth and to Wagner, along with—and quite influentially given his discussion of Hölderlin—Stefan Zweig,[153] in the ambit of Wilamowitz, Nietzsche's antagonistic contemporary.[154] And there is Werner Jaeger. Perhaps more significantly still (I owe this clue to Gadamer in a personal remark), there would be Paul Natorp who in 1890 wrote on Aristotle and the Eleatics.[155]

Complicating the discussion, the sharpness of Heidegger's claims with respect to Nietzsche undergoes a certain evolution. He is a bit more generous in his *Introduction to Metaphysics*: "Nietzsche was a victim of the current (and false) opposition between Parmenides and Heraclitus. This is one of the main reasons why in his metaphysics he did not find his way to the decisive question, even though he understood the great age of Greek beginnings with a depth that was surpassed only by Hölderlin."[156] Here Heidegger argues that "Nietzsche is the last thinker to have sacrificed himself in favor of 'Platonism'; for through the inversion of Platonism he completely enveloped himself in it and allowed the overturned and the inverting to run out ultimately into the indifferentiation of the sheer powering of power."[157] Whenever one invokes Nietzsche, especially for Heidegger, "power" takes on metonymic overtones. Prophet of nihilism, Nietzsche is also prophet of the *Übermensch*, as this concept remains the deathless (in so many ways) signifier of Nazi thinking, posterchild for today's sellers of transhumanism and posthumanism along with AI robotics and DNA hacking protocols.[158] To "overcome"—note the Nietzschean and Heideggerian language of overcoming—humanity is "our" destiny, which means that we must invoke Crispr genes[159] or more saliently and to the current moment, mRNA on offer in today's vaccine mandates/marketing strategies, so as to hack ourselves into whatever futurist upgrades might be forthcoming. We will return to this point below, as transhumanists, like any cargo cult, are metaphysical beasts, inspired by the hope of technological messianism and a new Second Coming: out with the old human, in with the new transhuman, the *Übermensch*.

Thus Heidegger, including a reference to Spengler's 1931 *Der Mensch und die Technik*, clarifies the *Übermensch*:

> The terms, in the sense of Nietzsche's metaphysics does not mean, contrary to popular opinion, a human being who has outgrown the normal size, with a gigantic bone structure, as muscular as possible, with a low forehead, etc. Instead "super-human" is an essentially metaphysical-historical concept and signifies the human hitherto, always already determined as *animal rationale*, who has passed into the essential domain of the will to power as the reality of all that is real. Therefore Nietzsche can say that the human who has not yet become the super-human is the "animal that has not yet been determined [*festgestellt*]," i.e., the animal about whose essence a final metaphysical decision has not yet been made.[160]

We are not better off when we attempt to compare these translations, reading Heidegger in English, reading Diels's renderings as we know them in the case of Anaximander, through Kahn together with Kirk and Raven and latterly Schofield, alongside Nietzsche. What seems true is that we are presented with a formidable catena of reception and authority, tacking through German and Greek and English. Heidegger makes things no easier when he reflects that "when a translation is only literal it is not necessarily faithful. It is faithful only when its terms are words which speak from the language of the matter itself."[161]

In their translation of Heidegger's 1942 *Parmenides* lecture, André Schuwer and Richard Rojcewicz (rightly) opt to leave Heidegger's Greek not only in Greek but without transliteration into Roman letters and without additional translation, translating only Heidegger's own glosses or translations.[162] For his part, Heidegger insists that "the more difficult task is always the translation of one's own language into its ownmost word."[163] I argue that this sensibility informs Heidegger's readings of Hölderlin's poetry, but here in connection with rendering Greek into German, Heidegger reflects on the most dangerous hermeneutic "forehaving" patent in the unthought and thus tenacious prejudice to the effect that we moderns who speak German would understand the German word without a problem since it belongs, after all, to our (the echo is to Hölderlin) language; whereas, on the contrary, to translate a Greek word we must first learn that foreign tongue.[164]

The issue here is the challenge of translating Greek to German to English. Thus Heidegger, having thought through, over many pages, the Greek ψεῦδος and the Latin *falsum*, with respect to his most famous rendering of ἀληθές/ἀλήθεια as "unconcealing" or "disclosing," reminds us that "the erroneous becomes *falsum*," and that what is at stake is not Nietzsche's doing any more than it is Descartes's: it is larger than both. Thus (and the thought of the Reich as such cannot be bracketed): "The political, which as πολιτιχόν arose formerly out of the essence of the Greek word πόλις, has come to be understood in the Roman way. Since the time of the *Imperium*, the Greek word 'political' has meant something Roman. What is Greek about it now is only sound."[165] In addition to vacuity, there is violence. As Heidegger reflects on Anaximander's saying:

> We are bound to the language of the saying. We are bound to our mother tongue. In both cases we are essentially bound to language and to the experience of its essence. This bond is broader and stronger, but far less apparent, than the standards of all philological and historical facts—which can only borrow their factuality from it. So long as we do not experience this binding, every translation of the fragment must seem wholly arbitrary. Yet even when we are bound to what is said in the saying, not only the translation but also the binding retain the appearance of violence, as though what is to be heard and said here necessarily suffers violence.[166]

Tacking between translations and assumptions, Heidegger tells us that Anaximander's "saying speaks of that which, as it approaches, arrives in unconcealment, and which, having arrived here, departs by withdrawing into the distance."[167]

By contrast, Nietzsche flags Anaximander as *first* philosopher because with Anaximander, as opposed to Thales and other "precursors" who merely "say" but *write* nothing, there is, as Nietzsche emphasizes, and quite precisely *philologically*, a text, a quote, in this sense a saying, to be deciphered as such, even if in "rather poetic terms." To this "oracular legend," this "boundary stone of Greek philosophy," Nietzsche asks: "How shall we interpret you?"[168]

In both his popular lectures—that is, those offered at Bayreuth, as well as those presented over the years at his university at Basel—Nietzsche indicts the injustice of those beings who remain or tarry in being, corresponding to Heidegger's aletheic reading of lingering, the inherent errancy of everything that presences by lingering including "gods and men, temples and cities, sea and land, eagle and snake, tree and shrub, wind and light, slope and sand, day and night."[169] And Heidegger speaks because Anaximander speaks of ἀδικία, of injustice, as Nietzsche says: "It is your guilt that causes you to tarry in existence,"[170] whereby Heidegger's reading of Anaximander's saying returns to Nietzsche's account: "As they linger awhile, they tarry. They hang on. For they advance hesitantly through their while, in transition from arrival to departure. They hang on; they cling to themselves. When what lingers awhile delays, it stubbornly follows the inclination to persist in hanging on, and indeed to insist on persisting; it aims at everlasting continuance and no longer bothers about *dike*, the order of the while."[171] The dependency of Heidegger's reading of Anaximander on Nietzsche's account is tacit, reducing Nietzsche to a temporal coincidence alongside Diels. Declaring, once again and as we have seen, "that the genuine Nietzsche thinks purely in the *Roman* way and in his own metaphysics could never grasp the Greek beginning of Western thinking,"[172] Heidegger thereby assimilates Nietzsche to the (at the time Nazi) opposition, which same assimilation makes Nietzsche a "mix't figure," to use Nietzsche's characterization of Plato's style, but not less as we saw above, a Roman-German:[173] a judgment Heidegger shared with leading Nazi interpretations of his day as with readings of Nietzsche and power today.

It can be noted that Heidegger, along with Hegel (whom he cites as authoritative source), and thereby Aristotle[174] is ensconced quite as we are in the doctrine we began by noting, that is the doctrine of "succession" as Nietzsche would term it.[175] For his part, Gadamer turns to Plato, more careful than Heidegger. Thus I began by referring first to Gadamer and only then to Nietzsche, as we continue to need what Nietzsche named an "introduction" to Plato's dialogues given that we continue to lack nearly everything antecedent to Plato. Thus for Nietzsche, *faute de mieux*, "Plato must serve for us as a substitute [*Ersatz*] for the great writings of the pre-platon[ic] philosophers that have been lost."[176] Nietzsche's point is that if we imagine, contrafactually, that there was no Plato, we would be constrained or condemned to begin our philosophy with Aristotle but would thus be, by the same token, all the more impoverished when it comes to reading those thinkers who are, thus Nietzsche's language of the "preplatonics," as not only artists but philosophers.

Heidegger's Pre-Aristotelians

> Nietzsche hat mich kaputtgemacht.
>
> —Heidegger, on Gadamer's telling[177]

Nietzsche introduces the designation "preplatonic" in order to count Socrates among these thinkers in the tradition of those sages who, like Thales, did not write and thereby count among proto-philosophers. The same distinction permits Nietzsche to characterize Plato himself as "mix't" or mongrel. Heidegger counters this with the charge of Nietzsche's "Platonism," introducing Aristotle via Hegel on the history of philosophy. As Heidegger explains, this is how what we take to be the authoritative text comes to be established: "The Φυσικῶν δόξαι of Theophrastus became the chief source for manuals of the history of philosophy in Hellenistic times. These manuals prescribed the interpretation of the original writings of the early thinkers which may have survived to that time and founded the subsequent doxographical tradition in philosophy. Not only the content but also the style of this tradition made its mark on the relation of later thinkers—even beyond Hegel—to the history of thought."[178] In this fashion, Heidegger sets Aristotle as a stumbling block for his own courses on Nietzsche, in place of Lotze as prelude: "It is advisable, therefore, that you postpone reading Nietzsche for the time being, and first study Aristotle for ten to fifteen years."[179] The problem when it comes to taking Aristotle as prelude to the study of Nietzsche is Nietzsche's rarely addressed opposition to Aristotle.

There is no lack of Aristotle in the tradition because Aristotle (plus Theophrastus) *is* the tradition, the scholarly air we breathe. This makes Aristotle invisible, but it also makes him, as Heidegger says, the "scientific apex of ancient philosophy." For Heidegger, Aristotle "advanced to the limits which Greek philosophy could reach, given its general approach and its problematics. He unified in a positive way the fundamental motifs of the previous philosophy."[180]

In his early lecture course, "Basic Concepts of Ancient Philosophy," Heidegger explains philosophical wonder in terms of questioning and the capacity for holding to questioning as such, noting that what we call "common sense," by contrast with philosophy and this since antiquity, dispenses with the need to question inasmuch as it "believes it understands everything because it is unaware of any higher possibilities of questioning."[181] For Heidegger, "the scientific problem is not an arbitrary question, one randomly spluttered out [*Spatzen*], but is a deliberately posed question, the predelineation and discussion of possible ways, means, and factual motifs, i.e., motifs offered by the interrogated object itself for its own determination. The most multifarious knowledge of everything possible is not yet science. What is essential (the problem) is a capacity to question, drawn from, and developed in conformity with, the matter at issue itself."[182] Again, Heidegger sets his own reading of Anaximander in the order of succession:

> About 530 A.D. the Neoplatonist Simplicius wrote an extensive commentary on Aristotle's *Physics*. In it he reproduced the Anaximander fragment, thus preserving it for the Western world. He copied the fragment from Theophrastus' φυσικῶν δόξαι. From the time Anaximander pronounced his saying—we do not know where or when or to whom—to the moment Simplicius jotted it down in his commentary more than a millennium elapsed. Between the time of Simplicius' jotting and the present moment lies another millennium-and-a-half.

The intervals are those of scholastic commentary, the scope of philology, and of history. Importantly, in English, we are inevitably followers of Theophrastus as we read Anaximander, as Theophrastus is cited in Simplicius, as we are told in Kirk, Raven, and Schofield. We thus know that the prelude that highlights coming into being is the commentator's own explication or gloss: ". . . some other apeiron nature, from which come into being all the heavens and the world in them. And the source of coming-to-be for existing things is that into which destruction, too, happens 'according to necessity' [translating κατὰ τὸ χρεών]; for they pay penalty [translating διδόναι δίκην] and retribution to each other for their injustice according to the assessment of Time [personified as Chronos]."[183]

I have already noted that Heidegger begins by citing the Greek, then Diels's edition of Simplicius before citing Nietzsche's translation and then going on to Diels's translation. I also noted that in received or mainstream classics Nietzsche's voice is hardly present. If he is mentioned, it is only as a cow-catcher, with classicists publishing tracts and books telling their readers what all the fuss concerning Nietzsche was about, a fuss that in classics has, for some time, beginning in Nietzsche's day, ceased to be "a thing." Thus, we noted that Nietzsche was designated "dead to the profession" by the same Hermann Usener who, so Diels relates to us, had tasked Nietzsche to work together with Diels on a collective edition of ancient Greek philosophers.[184]

Death

Jede Übersetzung ist eine Auslegung

—Heidegger, GA: 78

To that which is real [*Dem, was wahrhaft ist*] we cannot ascribe the predicates of perishable things:

—Nietzsche, KGW II$_4$, 242

"Aus der Fuge—Out of Joint"

Dasein, anxiety, death, Heidegger's inaugural lecture at Freiburg, reprises the themes of *Being and Time*. Here I note that Nietzsche's reading of Anaximander emphasizes a traditional gnomology [*Gnomologie*] inscribed or incised as effectively, affectively *ethical* remonstration. Thus Nietzsche tells us that Anaximander is the first ethical philosopher, here to cite his reference to a singular "lapidary sentence":

> That which truly is, concludes Anaximander, cannot possess definite characteristics, or it would come-to-be and pass away like all the other things. In order that coming to be shall not cease, primal being must be indefinite. The immortality and everlastingness of primal being does not lie in its infinitude or its inexhaustibility, as the commentators of Anaximander generally assume, but in fact that it is devoid of definite qualities that would lead to its passing. Hence its name, "the indefinite."[185]

For Nietzsche what is at stake in the ethical beyond the cosmological is the address to the self as it is, and as Heidegger would say, as it dwells—or as Nietzsche says, "tarries"—on the earth. As Heidegger writes in *Being and Time* of speaking and of silence but above all listening "as in hearing the voice of the 'friend' whom every Dasein carries with it,"[186] as we quoted Nietzsche above saying that the Oracle at Delphi addresses the "conscience" of those who seek counsel: γνῶθι σεαυτόν, know thyself, the reflex, σεαυτόν being key.

To this day, scholars in both philology and philosophy dispute the meaning/translation of Anaximander's terms, most all of them especially including τὸ ἄπειρον. Heidegger, who unpacks in his essay nearly every word of the saying, does not address this concept, key as it is for Nietzsche, other than peripherally.

At issue for Heidegger is the question of ownership: *Eigenthum*, as Nietzsche warns his students, is something of a solecism,[187] crucial for us as we seek to know *who* wrote a text, although this was a concern that was less crucial for the Greeks. Modern scholarship wishes to know the author, ascertained according to its satisfaction (or "taste" or "aesthetic judgment" as Nietzsche puts it in his 1869 lecture on Homer). Thus we ask: Is this Anaximander's saying? Where does the proper saying begin? Are these words Anaximander's own, a precipitate of the doxographic tradition, or an artifact of subsequent commentary? Interestingly, and to the point of Nietzsche's gnomic emphasis or in the constellation of archaeological and phenomenological hermeneutics, the most "scientific" achievements of recent provenance for classics, as for ancient philosophy, accrue less to exegetical clarifications of this or that text, or scholarly claims for or against "authenticity," but perfectly ontic fragments. These would be "real world" findings—beyond those collated as "fragments," we have archaeological finds: in papyrus (preserved or even, most significantly for philosophy in the case of the Derveni Papyrus, burnt remnants) or in gold, in bronze, stone, clay, etc.[188] Here speaking of the use/detriment of classics, that is the utility or damages of "history" for life, in contrast with the historical "antiquarian," there is the archaeological or "monumental," as Nietzsche describes it. To this same extent, the Derveni Papyrus and the debates (and disputes) concerning its interpretation can be salutary. But note that it is key, if rare, that one must read not merely the Derveni Papyrus discovered in 1962, along with the complicated material history of its reconstitution and the history of conflicted interpretations (ongoing and bitter) but also, so I argue, the Derveni Krater itself, the latter a dithyramb in bronze that offers as much to be "read," if this is more challenging, as the text itself and its disputed deciphering.[189] To this extent, hermeneutics is, as Nietzsche would say, *both* antiquarian *and* monumental, meaning that it is concerned with both texts as well as archaeological finds and their decipherment in addition, as Nietzsche emphasizes this material's consequentiality, to the fairly literal destruction of both at the hands of classicists.

As a parallel, I will cite a colleague, Val Dusek, citing an article I wrote in order to explain Patrick Aidan Heelan's ideas in the context of "reading" scientific instruments: "[T]he scientific experimentalist is not 'reading' his instruments as one reads a text but rather as one might "read"—metaphorically speaking—a painting, a landscape, a face, a gesture."[190] In the same hermeneutic fashion, Nietzsche tells us that one "reads" ancient monuments, including the Oracle at Delphi, specifically as we quoted him above, including inscriptions inscribed on monuments, or etched in stone—think of Epicurus, specifically the perfectly *monumental* discovery ("uncovered" would hardly be the word), transmitted to the philological world at the end of the nineteenth century in Nietzsche's own lifetime (more than 2.37 meters high and 80 meters wide), legacy of the second-century CE Epicurean, Diogenes of Oinoanda, found in Turkey in 1884.[191] In just this way one must begin to "read" Greek statues and other artifacts including sarcophagi.[192]

Relevant in this context is the parallel between philosophy as practice—what Heidegger calls τέχνη read via Aristotle and not Plato[193]—and the concern with life after death. Together with a Dionysian element that may be seen to have Empedoclean overtones, this may be connected not with the popular notion of will to power but with Nietzsche's reprise of the esoterica doctrine of eternal recurrence.

Here referring to descent, thus to perishing rather than to tarrying, as Nietzsche says (or lingering or hanging on), we are also speaking of an end. It is this Heidegger glosses, and everyone who has read Xenophon can follow (above I note that Lucian might be more useful): "The word κατὰ precedes τὸ χρεών. It means 'from up there,' or 'from over there.' The κατὰ refers back to something from which something lower comes to presence, as from something higher and as its consequent. That in reference to which the κατὰ is pronounced has in itself an incline along which other things have fallen out in this or that way."[194] Here it is important to underline that what analytic philosophy distinguishes as "history of philosophy" is a distinction specific to its own disciplinary divisions. To this extent, and no more than Nietzsche himself, Heidegger does not articulate "history of philosophy." By contrast, qua classicist, Nietzsche reflected on the doing of history, as it were, in terms of its scientific or scholarly constitution in addition to his reflections on its uses (and disadvantages), down to determining, this is hermeneutics, what is only rarely given from data beyond the text (eclipses being in short supply in recorded time) for the sake of determining chronology.

If Heidegger is less concerned with what we philosophers today in the aforementioned analytic modality regard as "history of philosophy" than with Anaximander's saying as he reads it, there are hermeneutic challenges. Thus Heidegger—and every other commentator—tells us: we do not know where "the fragment" (note here the determinate force of naming the saying a "fragment") begins.[195] Thus, with all due scientific rigor, Heidegger begins by citing:

Ἀναξίμανδρος [. . .] ἀρχὴν. . . . τῶν. . . . ὄντων . . . λέγει . .
. μήτε ὕδωρ μήτε ἄλλο τι τῶν καλουμένων εἶναι στοιχείων, ἀλλ' ἑτέραν τινὰ φύσιν ἄπειρον, ἐξ ἧς ἅπαντας γίνεσθαι τοὺς οὐρανοὺς καὶ τοὺς ἐν αὐτοῖς κόσμους· ἐξ ὧν δὲ ἡ γένεσίς ἐστι τοῖς οὖσι, καὶ τὴν φθορὰν εἰς ταῦτα γίνεσθαι κατὰ τὸ χρεών· διδόναι γὰρ αὐτὰ δίκην καὶ τίσιν ἀλλήλοις τῆς ἀδικίας κατὰ τὴν τοῦ χρόνου τάξιν, ποιητικωτέροις οὕτως ὀνόμασιν αὐτὰ λέγων.[196]

As Heidegger repeats: "These are precisely the words in reference to which Theophrastus complains that Anaximander speaks in a rather poetic manner."[197] In addition to a range of further questions, there are questions of "exact definition" as Diogenes Laërtius notes (and, once again, on Nietzsche's reading) regarding τὸ ἄπειρον.[198] Here, starting from the outset of the fragment as we are told: "ἐξ ὧν δὲ ἡ γένεσις," is the question of origination or genesis [ἡ γένεσίς][199] of what is (ἐστι τοῖς οὖσι "existing things").

As Heidegger writes: "γένεσίς does not at all mean the genetic in the sense of the 'developmental' as conceived in modern times; nor does φθορὰν mean the counterphenomenon to development—some sort of regression, shrinkage, or wasting away. Rather, γένεσίς and φθορὰν are to be thought from φύσις, and within it, as ways of luminous rising and decline."[200] Heidegger proceeds to transpose the terms into his conception of coming into appearance/concealment/withdrawal: "γένεσίς is coming forward and arriving in unconcealment. Φθορὰ means the departure and descent into concealment of what has arrived there out of unconcealment.

The coming forward into and the departure to become present within unconcealment between what is concealed and what is unconcealed. They initiate the arrival and departure of whatever has arrived."²⁰¹

To this extent, Heidegger focuses on Beings coming into being. Hence in his 1926 Marburg lecture course he notes that the saying refers to "beings [*Seienden*]." Twenty years later, as he dates it, Heidegger apostrophizes that part of the saying he takes to be Anaximander's own: "In the dawn of Being's destiny, beings, τὰ ἐόντα, come to language. From the restrained abundance of what in this way comes, what does the Anaximander saying bring to utterance? According to the presumably genuine text, the saying reads: 'κατὰ τὸ χρεών· διδόναι γὰρ αὐτὰ δίκην καὶ τίσιν ἀλλήλοις τῆς ἀδικίας.' "²⁰² And what follows adds the standard translation: "According to necessity; for they pay one another recompense and penalty for their injustice."²⁰³

After thinking through Homer on the meaning of those currently "present," via Homer's recourse to Calchas, a soothsayer, a seer—one who, as one having seen—sees the future [*Er sieht das Futurum aus dem Perfektum.*]²⁰⁴ that is present [*Anwesende*] Heidegger glosses *injustice*, that is, '*aus der Fuge*,' which Krell and Capuzzi render, thanks to Shakespeare, as the "*out of joint*":

> The saying clearly says that what is present is in ἀδικία, i.e., is out of joint. However, that cannot mean that things no longer come to presence. But neither does it say that what is present is only occasionally, or perhaps only with respect to some one of its properties, out of joint. The saying says [*Der Spruch sagt*]: what is present as such, being what it is, is out of joint. To presencing as such jointure must belong, thus creating the possibility of its being out of joint. What is present is that which lingers awhile [*Das Anwesdende ist das je Weilige*].²⁰⁵

The focus for Heidegger is beings qua present precisely as they linger or remain. This is the key to "justice"/"injustice" and what Heidegger extracts from the equation is Platonism to be replaced, via Hegel, by Aristotelian doxography.²⁰⁶ As Heidegger writes, it is Hegel himself, palimpsest for so much, who "provides the basis for the classification of the early thinkers as Preplatonic and Presocratic precisely by grasping them as Pre-Aristotelians."²⁰⁷

As Heidegger emphasizes, both Nietzsche and Diels suggest another reading (as Heidegger notes their translations, despite the differences in their orientation and assumptions, telling us that nevertheless they are "in essence" the same, often coinciding, as he tells us, down to the very word).[208] By contrast, Heidegger undertakes a philological, hermeneutic corrective reading, citing the Greek (and eliding as he does so), before Nietzsche's and Diels's versions:

· διδόναι γὰρ αὐτὰ δίκην (Nietzsche)
τῆς ἀδικίας (Diels)

Here Heidegger continues: " 'They must pay [a] penalty,' Nietzsche translates; 'They pay recompense,' Diels translates, "for their injustice" But the saying says nothing about payment, recompense, and penalty; nor does it say that something is punishable, or even must be avenged, according to the opinion of those who equate justice with vengeance."[209]

The most creative readings of Heidegger's essay—I have already cited Dastur and Shapiro along with Derrida and others—will echo this elimination of the language of payment, recompense, penalty. Heidegger is explicit: *Bezahlung*. Thus Heidegger writes, "The more strictly we think in ἀλλήλοις the manifold of beings lingering awhile, the clearer becomes the necessary relation of ἀλλήλοις to τίσις."[210]

To this end, Heidegger repeats one of the stock criticisms of Nietzsche, noting that Nietzsche passes over ἀλλήλοις, which is key to his own reading as we shall see, as Diels for his part does not.[211]

But the focus is on usage, regard, reck [*Ruch*]. Some commentators have recourse to the poet, Gerard Manley Hopkins's usage of "reck," but it should be noted that Hopkins himself was only heeding John Milton's dismissal of the standard run of heedless shepherds, new breed of younger scholars and poets in his *Lycidas*:

What recks it them? What need they?
They are sped,

That, given the context of regret and mourning, Milton had something of Anaximandrian justice in mind can be argued, as Milton tells his reader that *Lycidas* was composed for "a learned friend, unfortunately drowned in his passage from Chester on the Irish Seas, 1637; and by occasion," and here the parallel seems overdetermined, "foretells the ruin of our corrupted Clergy, then in their height." Thus mindful of Anaximander, we note the reckoning that presages the reck to follow:

> How well could I have spared for thee, young swain,
> Enow of such as, for their bellies' sake,
> Creep, and intrude, and climb into the fold!
> Of other care they little reckoning make
> Than how to scramble at the shearers' feast,
> And shove away the worthy bidden guest. . . .

Arguably, Anaximander might help us unlock the knottiest Miltonian formula: "But that two-handed engine at the door / Stands ready to smite once, and smite no more." Thus justice is restored, just as earlier the poet had underlined, repeating

> But, oh! the heavy change, now thou art gone,
> Now thou art gone and never must return! . . .

In Heidegger's explication of "reck" [*Ruch*], we read: "The more unequivocally this relation emerges, the more clearly we recognize that the διδόναι τίσιν ἀλλήλοις, each one giving reck to the other, is the sole manner in which what lingers awhile in presence lingers at all, i.e., διδόναι δίκην, granting order."[212] The paratactic Heidegger elsewhere emphasizes serves him here, substantively, as he explains: "The καὶ between δίκη and τίσιν is not simply the vacuous conjunction "and." It signifies the essential process. If what is present grants order, it happens in this manner: as beings linger awhile, they give reck to one another."[213]

One might argue that the greatest service Heidegger offers contemporary readers of Anaximander gets them off the hook in life, thrown as they are into existence as having to be. Nietzsche's Anaximander underlines that coming to be, ex-isting is always already transgression: always already and before one is born, before coming into being until one goes out of being, a transgression, rectified by dissolution. This sits badly with the ethos and promise of Judeao-Christian humanism.

Here we may cite Heidegger's hermeneutic addressed to the tradition, including both Nietzsche and Diels: "We usually translate τίσις by 'penalty.' This leads us to translate διδόναι as 'to pay.' Whatever lingers awhile in presence pays penalty; it expends this as its punishment (δίκη). The court of justice is complete. It lacks nothing, not even injustice—though of course no one rightly knows what might constitute injustice."²¹⁴ As Heidegger goes on to clarify: "Surely, τίσις can mean penalty, but it must not, because the original and essential significance of the word is not thereby named. For τίσις, is "esteem" [*Schätzen*]. To esteem something means to heed it, and so to take satisfactory care of what is estimable in it. The essential process of esteem, which is to satisfy, can, in what is good, be a magnanimous action; but with respect to wickedness giving satisfaction may mean paying a penalty."²¹⁵ Only this is essential to Heidegger's readers. And even scholars who may not seem to be following Heidegger benefit from the exemplary illustration of hermeneutic reading.

What makes this reading as rich as it has proven to be for commentators like Derrida—and others, like Dastur as cited above—is Heidegger's focus is not on τὸ ἄπειρον but τὸ χρεών: "Anaximander says, τὸ χρεών. We will dare a translation which sounds strange and which can be easily misinterpreted: τὸ χρεών, usage [*der Brauch*]."²¹⁶ Tacking between the question of τὸ ἄπειρον as that from which presencing, and to which withdrawal may be understood with respect to beings coming into and going out of being qua existents, Heidegger refers to things that *are* much rather than *are not*. Just this account of ἄπειρον is explicitly side-lined, mentioned at the start without featuring in a reading which, as noted can seem to look at each and every word.

The claim only holds for the text we read in *Holzwege*, or in translation in *Early Greek Thinking* because the collected works, *letzter Hand*, show us that Heidegger goes on to detail the "relationship" [*Verhältnis*] between the two parts of the saying, including a section dedicated to Anaximander's "other word" Ἀρχή τῶν ὄντων ἄπειρος.²¹⁷

As promised above, I here return to this 'other word,' τὸ ἄπειρον, which Diogenes Laërtius glosses as the "unbounded." Dirk Couprie and Radim Kočandrle have reminded us in their reading of Anaximander, to be sure without naming Heidegger and without naming Nietzsche (although they approvingly cite Detlev Fehling's study of Presocratic material cosmology,²¹⁸ and thus following Aetius). Couprie and Kočandrle summarize the received view on the Aristotelian ἀρχή:

> It is well known that the question about the origin of everything has its roots in Aristotle's explication of ἀρχή as "source," "origin," "principle," and "cause." Aristotle interpreted the explications of the origin of all things and the continuing nature

of the present world given by his predecessors as the search for the ἀρχή. Consequently, in the doxography Anaximander's supposed concept of ἀρχή is generally understood through the Aristotelian paradigm of the principles and causes, and particularly in terms of the material cause.[219]

Here Couprie's translation should be cited owing to his material focus, also emphasized in an older multiauthored collection, *Anaximander in Context*, and reprised more recently in a dedicated coauthored monograph:

Whence things have their origin,
Thence also their destruction happens,
As is the order of things;
For they execute the sentence upon one another
The condemnation for the crime -In conformity with the ordinance of Time.[220]

Today's scholarship on the ἄπειρον is indebted not only to Theophrastus—as Heidegger tells us citing Diels's edition of Simplicius[221]—but Aetius, who duly echoes Aristotle.[222] The literature is vast although there is, as noted above, a clear recent shift to the material as such, going back to Kahn and others on the tradition of nature philosophers. Thus qua physical origination of this heterogeneity, ἀλλ' ἑτέραν τινὰ φύσιν ἄπειρον, what may be translated as the unbounded, infinite, or as Nietzsche clarifies in contrast with what he refers to as Aristotle's "misreading" of this same infinite, as the *in-definite*, is the *undefined*. To this extent, Diogenes Laërtius specifies τὸ ἄπειρον, as this has been variously translated as the "unbounded," "unlimited," but also perhaps helpfully as "incompassable" as Gottschalk writes,[223] rendering the same ἄπειρον (as noted: this is disputed) as that out of which[224] same unbounded everything that is is adjudged as rightfully (this rightfulness is not in dispute) returning or perishing (this perishing as such *is* disputed).[225]

Above I cited Couprie, around whose name a fruitful coterie of engagements has been gathering for decades, although there are other voices. Here it is important to note, as this is Nietzsche's own reflection in his inaugural lecture on the even more extensively discussed Homer question, that those who claim to have resolved such issues only do so on their own terms an insistence that inevitably ensures the durability of the problem. It helps, for the sake of scholarship, to read one's colleagues, perhaps, as Nietzsche argues, with a certain generosity.

"They Hang On"

Above I have offered a slow reading, if not as slow as Heidegger's own, and broader as I also include Nietzsche, tacking through Heidegger's analyses of Anaximander's saying. To cite Kirk/Raven/Schofield's *The Presocratic Philosophers*, a translation that follows Diels's *Die Fragmente der Vorsokratiker*: [Fr.] 111. . . . "some other apeiron nature, from which come into being all the heavens and the worlds in them. And the source of coming-to-be for existing things is that into which destruction, too, happens 'according to necessity; for they pay penalty and retribution to each other for their injustice according to the assessment of Time,' as he describes it in these rather poetical terms."[226] Recall Nietzsche's Anaximander: "Whence things have their origin, there they must also pass away according to necessity; for they must pay penalty and be judged for their injustice, according to the ordinance of time."[227] As the attention to Anaximander's cosmology makes clear, Anaximander's concern is nature, however much we have a tendency to read this religiously, thus Couprie and Kočandrle cite Giovanni Semerano's innovative etymology (from the Semitic, the Hebrew, and the Akkadian), all "meaning 'earth' " and thus yielding "something like 'dust thou art, and unto dust shalt thou return.' "[228]

As cosmodicy, one may also note τὸ ἄπειρον, the unbounded, unlimited, or as Nietzsche insists, the nondifferentiated, is violated, transgressed by every coming to be. To this extent ἄπειρος is the "whence" from which "things have their origin," and ἄπειρος is the "thence" to which "they must also pass away according to necessity." Here to conclude, what is at issue is Heidegger's emphasis on whiling, tarrying, hanging on. Once again, recall Nietzsche who tells us that the gnomic utterances of the Oracle at Delphi offer an ethical reflection, "an appeal to the human conscience [*ein Appel an das menschliche Gewissen*]"[229] demanding of those who seek the oracle: Who are you to ask this? What does it mean that you seek such and such an answer?"[230]

For Nietzsche, Anaximander counts in this gnomic fashion, as first "ethical" philosopher, a tradition of gnomic utterances: "For they must pay [a] penalty and be judged for their injustice, according to the ordinance of time." This Heidegger challenges: no penalty, no payment but only reck and regard and to this now we add Heidegger's whiling, tarrying, hanging on.

Existence so understood as expressly, as specifically delimited existence, under one form or set of limits or borders or bounds as opposed to another, is the existence that is always, as Heidegger reminds us, *in each case mine*, whether taken up as a project (authentically so) or not (the garden variety and standardly 'inauthentic' way of living that is most immediately and throughout most of our lives, the way we live). Here the archaic point is that this being, this existence, much rather than not being (in existence), is opposed to other aspects or forms or determinations or boundedness of so being. It is this that opposition that borrows against or infringes on or transgresses every *other* possibility.[231] Of necessity.

Thus, one may characterize the ἄπειρον as without properties and without proprietary distinction: no mine, no thine. This goes some distance toward the insistence that we hear in Heidegger (Parmenides on Being contra Heraclitus on becoming), but it is for Nietzsche a matter of ethical comportment: "All that becomes and passes away atones [*büßt*], must give τίσις and δίκη τῆς ἀδικίας! How can something pass away that has a right to be [*ein Recht hat zu sein*]? Given that we see all things passing away, consequently all things are in the wrong. To that which is real [*Dem, was wahrhaft ist*] we cannot ascribe the predicates of perishable things: it is something other [*es ist etwas anderes*], for us however to be indicated only negatively."[232] The relevance is clear for Heidegger as he is also aware of the lecture course,[233] even if his lectures draw exclusively on the popular *Philosophy in the Tragic Age of the Greeks* to distinguish his own reading from what he identifies (contra Nietzsche to be sure) as the Platonism of Nietzsche's thinking along with that of the so-called long nineteenth century and onward. For Heidegger both the Preplatonic and Presocratic belong to this same tradition and if Diels may appear to be more sober, Heidegger opts for still greater sobriety via Aristotle and that is to say: Theophrastus. We noted this earlier and, once again, Heidegger clarifies that he has his terminology from Hegel's exposition " 'of the first philosophers as 'Nature Philosophers' and indeed as Pre-Aristotelians."[234]

For Nietzsche, "The individual who breaks off from the unlimited must nonetheless return once again to the same, in accordance with the order of time (κατὰ τὴν τοῦ χρόνου τάξιν)"[235] Thus Anaximander speaks specifically of injustice, indicating thereby that to perish is anything but an injustice, which can remind us of the Stoic philosophers, especially Epictetus who, likewise inviting the language of expiation, emphasize the notion of return. Thus, for example, should a cup break (or be stolen or otherwise lost) or should a favorite servant, spouse, or child die, Epictetus invites us to reflect: "If you kiss your child, or your wife, say that you only kiss things which are mortal, and thus you will not be disturbed if either of them dies" (Epictetus, *Enchir.* §3). With this, Epictetus offers what may strike modern readers as an overly harsh remonstration, urging them not to be disturbed and explaining that by nature such things are not only finite and fragile but not one's own. This is key for Epictetus to begin, as he writes in the first section of the *Enchiridion* transmitted to us via Arrian: "Things not in our control are body, property, reputation, command, and, in one word, whatever are not our own actions" (*Enchir.* §1)[236] with this the remonstration to respond to all such losses: "It is returned."

Thus to quote Epictetus:

> Never say of anything, "I have lost it"; but, "I have returned it." Is your child dead? It is returned. Is your wife dead? She is returned. Is your estate taken away? Well, and is not that likewise returned? "But he who took it away is a bad man." What difference is it to you who the giver assigns to take it back? While he gives it to you to possess, take care of it; but don't view it as your own, just as travelers view a hotel. (*Ench.* §11)

The thought of cyclical time likewise, Epictetus' analogy, "just as travellers view a hotel" refers to possessions as to one's offspring, one's spouse, and indeed one's body, one's life.

If we are thus invited to set aside traditional assumptions of privilege, in a Schopenhauerian mood, Nietzsche points his question by asking, again to recall this question: "What is your existence worth? And if it is worthless, why are you here? Your guilt, I see, causes you to tarry in your existence."[237]

William J. Richardson reminds us that Heidegger wrote "The Anaximander Saying" in a time of widespread need after WWII, specifically and crucially for Heidegger, "during the enforced retirement of the de-Nazification period."[238] Here one may suppose that this would color Heidegger's reflection on our tendency to seek to outstay our time. Currently in today's pandemic era—as this can seem a sustained epoch of fear, that would be the politics of crisis thinking—it can seem that a certain drive toward immortality is characteristic of the nineteenth-century in the Promethean dream of Mary Shelley's *Frankenstein*, which Prometheanism many post-Heideggerian theorists of technology prefer to emphasize quite by contrast with Heidegger's emphasis on questioning.[239] In this we recall our aspiration to the transhuman ideal: a desire to escape mortal definition, or determination by which we mean nothing grander than to eclipse mortality, undo death, become cyborg, a machine, a thing, DNA hacked, and computer coded, name it whatever you like, as long as we do not die.

Günther Anders (1902–1993), one of Heidegger's students and near contemporary of Gadamer's, articulated a different Prometheanism as he replied to Heidegger on technology. For Anders, the Aeschylean connection is crucial to his reading. Our mortality constitutes our Promethean "shame" as Anders invokes Goethe's Prometheus—with Schiller bleeding through (and perhaps also with Beethoven). In today's post-Covidian mentality, as fear infuses contemporary articulations of transhumanism, we see the thought of death as unwarranted and corrigible (provided only enough people die to meet the requisites of population reduction and zero-carbon ideals). In our technological era, we do not regard death as Epictetus tells us that are to regard death as part of our essence (mortals) as we are part of the *Nous* of the universe or as Anaximander also underlines as necessary.

Today, posthuman, transhuman, we ambition another vision of ourselves beyond the nineteenth-century second law of thermodynamics and its closed economy. We do not see ourselves as did Heraclitus, Empedocles, and the Pythagoreans and Plato himself, as returning, that is, as cyclical wanderers on the earth through circles of thousands of years. To this extent, we hardly hold discourse with our own shade like Nietzsche's 'wanderer' and his Lucianic shadow, nor do we anticipate that a demon might come (here to be contrasted with Socrates's account of his *daimon*) to tell us the doctrine of eternal recurrence contra an afterlife of heaven (or of hell): it was a thought Nietzsche found so edifying he claimed that thinking the thought of eternal recurrence could break humanity in two.

For us, in a Judeo-Christian schema, qua *ens creatum*, we are made *imago dei*: being *beyond* estimation, *beyond* price. And even as we no longer believe in a deity we continue to believe in the unmeasured value of being human as of life eternal. To this same extent we do not suppose it to be our "guilt" that induces us to "whiling," to use Heidegger's language: to tarry as we wish to tarry in existence. Rather our guilt occasions our dying, "created" as we take ourselves to be in the likeness of the deathless, the divine. From a religious perspective, from the perspective of Heideggerian everyday inauthenticity, here to use Tracy Strong's language, "Death always comes from outside the frame."[240]

Apart from deity, within the frame, Epictetus exemplifies Hadot's constant *prosoché* or "vigilance," the value of meditation on death as on other execrable, terrible things: "Let death and exile and every other thing which appears dreadful be daily before your eyes; but most of all death: and you will never think of any thing mean nor will you desire anything extravagantly" (*Ench.* §27).

Notes

1. BCAP: 5.
2. BCAP: 8.
3. There are many who write on Heidegger and Aristotle; useful in the specific context of Heidegger's thought, may be Alfredo Guzzoni's doctoral dissertation, *Die Einheit des on πολλαχος λεγομενον bei Aristoteles* (Freiburg im Briesgau, 1957) and Rudolf Boehm, *Das Grundlegende und das Wesentliche. Zu Aristoteles' Abhandlung "Über das Sein und das Seiende" (Metaphysik Z)* (The Hague: Nijhoff, 1965). See, too, Franco Volpi, *Heidegger e Aristotle* (Rome: Editore Laterza, 2010) in addition to Jussi Backman, "Being Itself and the Being of Beings: Reading Aristotle's Critique of Parmenides (*Physics* 1.3) after Metaphysics," *Epoché: A Journal for the History of Philosophy*, 22: 2 (2018): 271–91. And see too, albeit with no reference to Heidegger, the multivolume Loeb edition: *Early Greek Philosophy*, André Laks and Glenn W. Most (eds.) (Cambridge, MA: Harvard University Press, 2016).
4. Edmund Husserl, *First Philosophy: Lectures 1923/24 and Related Texts from the Manuscripts (1920–1925)*, trans. Sebastian Luft and Thane M. Naberhaus (Dordrecht: Springer, 2019). I discuss this, as Heidegger also reads this via Kant, in Babich, On the 'Very Idea of a Philosophy of Science': On Chemistry and Cosmology in Nietzsche and Kant," *Axiomathes* 31 (2021): 703–26.
5. Hans-Georg Gadamer, "Zur Vorgeschichte der Metaphysik," *Gesammelte Werke, 6 Griechische Philosophie II* (Tübingen: Mohr Siebeck, 1983), 9–29 and Gadamer, *Der Anfang der Philosophie* (Stuttgart: Reclam, 1996).
6. I cite both authors below.
7. Jacques Derrida, "The Question of Style" in *The New Nietzsche: Contemporary Styles of Interpretation*, ed. David Blair Allison, trans. Ruben Berezdivin (New York: Delta, 1979), 176–89.
8. This is, of course, an old concept. See Joachim Ritter's helpful 1954 essay, "Aristoteles und die Vorsokratiker" in *Metaphysik und Politik: Studien zu Aristoteles und Hegel* (Frankfurt am Main: Suhrkamp, 1969), 17; and, in English, one may, in English, recall the translation of Book Alpha from Aristotle's *Metaphysics*, A. E. Taylor's *Aristotle and his Predecessors. Being a Translation of the First Book of the Metaphysics* (Chicago: Open Court, 1927 [1906]) in addition to Harold F. Cherniss's *Aristotle's Criticism of Pre-Socratic Philosophy* (Baltimore: Johns Hopkins University Press, 1935). Today, see André Laks, *The Concept of Presocratic Philosophy: Its Origin, Development, and Significance*, Glenn W. Most, trans. (Princeton, NJ: Princeton University Press, 2018) or, for an expressly analytically minded discussion—note the titular use of "history of philosophy": Catherine Collobert, "Aristotle's Review of the Presocratics: Is Aristotle Finally a Historian of Philosophy?" *Journal of the History of Philosophy* 40, no. 3 (July 2002): 281–95.
9. Thus André Laks rightly, I think, cites Gadamer's note that Plato formed the center of his scholarship as epigraph to "Gadamer, Parmenides und die

Vorsokratiker. Eine kritische Würdigung," in *Wissen und Bildung in der antiken Philosophie*, ed. Christoph Rapp and Tim Wagner (Stuttgart: Metzler, 2006), 61–72. Cf. Gadamer, "Heideggers Rückgang auf die Griechen," in *Theorie der Subjektivität*, ed. Konrad Cramer et al. (Frankfurt am Main, Suhrkamp, 1987), 397–424. To be sure, although attention to Plato is significant, this does not always mean familiarity with Nietzsche's lecture courses on Plato, see note below, such that Nietzsche's view of Plato is supposed to be limited to his remarks in his published writings. See for example, Monique Dixaut, *L'autre manière de philosopher* (Paris: Fayard, 2015).

10. See for a useful discussion, Jaap Mansfeld on Hippolytus and Aetius in Mansfeld, *Heresiography in Context: Hippolytus'* Elenchos *as a Source for Greek Philosophy* (Amsterdam: Brill, 1992), 20f.

11. Friedrich Nietzsche, *Vorlesungsaufzeichnungen 1871/72–1874–75. Kritische Gesamtausgabe II_4*, 613–32. Hereafter cited as KGW II_4.

12. See Graeme Nicholson's arch Aristotelian (and accordingly Ur-Heideggerian) parsing of "*Concinnitas*" in Nicholson, *Illustrations of Being* (Atlantic Highlands, NJ: Humanities Press, 1992), 272–273. More broadly one should note, in addition to others who thematize Heidegger and Aristotle, Walter Brogan's *Heidegger and Aristotle: The Twofoldness of Being* (Albany: State University of New York Press, 2006) as well as the contributions to Alfred Denker et al., eds., *Heidegger und Aristoteles* (Alber: Freiburg im Breisgau, 2007); and Alasdair MacIntyre's *After Virtue* (Notre Dame: University of Notre Dame. 1984), chs. 9 and 18.

13. Heidegger, *Die Grundbegriffe der antiken Philosophie*, GA 22 (Frankfurt: Klostermann, 1993 [1926]), 6. See too for a discussion of Husserl and Nietzsche and crisis, Babich, "Crisis and Twilight in Heidegger's "Nietzsche's Word 'God is Dead'" Zaborowski, ed., *Martin Heidegger: Holzwege—Klassiker auslegen* (Berlin: de Gruyter, 2024), 135–154.

14. Thus philosophy is necessary and by definition: "If the mathematician wished to say what mathematics is, not by presenting mathematical problems and proofs, but by talking about mathematics, its objects and method, then he could no longer employ mathematical concepts and proofs, just as little as the physicist could employ experiments to show and prove the essence of physics." GA 22, 6.

15. BCAP: 6.

16. BW: 96. Originally published as 'Was ist Metaphysik?' the text can be found in *Wegmarken* (Frankfurt am Main: Klostermann, 1978), 103–21.

17. BW: 96.

18. See Michael Friedman, "Carnap, Cassirer, and Heidegger: The Davos Disputation and Twentieth Century Philosophy," *European Journal of Philosophy*, 10, 3 (2002: 263–274 along with Friedman's *A Parting of the Ways: Carnap, Cassirer, and Heidegger* (Chicago: Open Court, 2000). Jean Grondin argues that such appellations are always articulated from an explicitly Anglophone (and thus analytic) perspective. See Grondin's chapter, "Continental or Hermeneutical

Philosophy: The Tragedies of Understanding in the Analytic and Continental Perspectives" in John Sallis and Charles Scott (eds.) *Interrogating the Tradition: Hermeneutics and the History of Philosophy* (Albany: State University of New York Press, 2000), 75–83. And see, too, Peter Gordon, *Continental Divide: Heidegger, Cassirer, Davos* (Cambridge: Harvard University Press, 2010) as well as for a summary assessment and further references, Babich, "The Analytic-Continental Divide: 'An Idea No Longer of Any Use . . . Superfluous . . . Let Us Abolish It!,'" *Borderless Philosophy*, 5 (2022): 1–47.

19. See Daniel O. Dahlstrom, *Heidegger's Concept of Truth* (Cambridge: Cambridge University Press, 2001 and cf., too, the earlier version of this text in German: 1996) as well as Dahlstrom's "Heidegger's Method: Philosophical Concepts as Formal Indications," *The Review of Metaphysics* 47, no. 4 (June 1994): 775–95 as well as, conventionally and usefully, Jitendranath Mohanty, "Heidegger on Logic," *Journal of the History of Philosophy* 26, no. 1 (1988): 107–35 along with Holger Zaborowski, "Wahrheit, Sein und Zeit: Zu Heideggers Vorlesung aus dem Winter Semester 1925/26 *Logik. Die Frage nach der Wahrheit* (GA 21)" in *Heidegger und die Logik* (Amsterdam: Rodopi, 2006), 161–83.

20. See Richard Tieszen, *Phenomenology, Logic and the Philosophy of Mathematics* (Cambridge: Cambridge University Press, 2005) as well as with a clear but subtle reference to Heidegger, the Gadamer student, John J. Cleary, "Abstracting Aristotle's Philosophy of Mathematics" in Babich, ed., *Hermeneutic Philosophy of Science, Van Gogh's Eyes, and God: Essays in Honor of Patrick A. Heelan, S.J* (Dordrecht: Kluwer, 2002), 163–176 including a footnote explicating without mentioning the Heideggerian 'as' via Allan Bäck's account of "Aristotle's theory of reduplication whereby "a qua proposition is actually a condensed demonstrative syllogism in which the qua term functions as a middle term and as a cause." 176. Cleary proceeds here to offer his own take.

21. See, for one discussion, Jürgen Ludwig Scherb, „Nichtet das Nichts wirklich nicht? Analyse und Explikation oder: eine deutsche Vorkriegsdebatte europäisch belichtet," *Phil. Jahrbuch* 115. Jahrgang / I (2008): 79–98 as well as, more recently, Peter Bernhard's provocative, "'Sie diskutieren sehr gern, aber sehr dilletantisch': Carnaps Vorträge am Dessauer Bauhaus" in *Logischer Empirismus, Lebensreform und Die Deutsche Jugendbewegung*, ed. Christian Damböck, Günther Sandner, and Meike G. Werner (Frankfurt: Springer, 2022), 227–46.

22. BW: 96. Cf. Rudolf Carnap, "Überwindung der Metaphysik durch logische Analyse der Sprache," *Erkenntnis* 2 (1931): 219–41. See further my essay "Heidegger's Philosophy of Science: Calculation, Thought, and *Gelassenheit*" in Babich, ed., *From Phenomenology to Thought, Errancy, and Desire* (Dordrecht: Kluwer, 1995), 589–99.

23. BW: 110.

24. BW: 112.

25. Seneca, *Epistulae morales*, 108.

26. Friedrich Nietzsche, "Homer und die klassische Philologie," in *Frühe Schriften*, ed. Carl Koch and Karl Schlechta (Munich: C. H. Beck, 1994), 5:305. See for a discussion Babich, "Friedrich Nietzsche" in Niall Keane, ed. *Blackwell Companion to Hermeneutics* (Oxford: Wiley, 2015), 366–77.

27. To cite Nietzsche's late preface to his first book, *The Birth of Tragedy*, Nietzsche, *Kritische Studienausgabe* (Berlin: de Gruyter, 1980), 1:13.

28. See the contributions to Michael Steinmann, ed., *Heidegger und die Griechen* (Frankfurt am Main: Klostermann, 2007) as well as, somewhat more idiosyncratically, Werner Beierwaltes, "Heideggers Rückgang zu den Griechen," *Bayerische Akademie der Wissenschaften Philosophisch-Historische Klasse Sitzungsberichte* 1 (1995), 5–30. Useful in this essay is its mythognomic references to Schulz and to Carl Schmitt.

29. Pierre Hadot, *The Inner Citadel*, trans. Michael Chase (Cambridge, MA: Harvard University Press, 1998 [1992]). That Hadot means the point in a fair Nietzschean sense is clear (Nietzsche cites the same reference): "Nature's will, however, is always the same; and the only thing its continuous action can accomplish is the repetition of this world, with precisely this beginning, precisely this end, and the entire course of events situated between these two moments. Thus, this world returns eternally: 'There will be another Socrates, a Plato, and every man with the same friends and the same fellow-citizens . . . And this renewal will not happen once, but several times; rather, all things will be repeated eternally.' This is why the sage, like universal Reason, must intensely wish for each instant: he must wish intensely for things to happen eternally exactly as they do happen." Ibid., 75–76.

30. See Cornford, *From Religion to Philosophy: A Study in the Origins of Western Speculation* (New York: Harper and Row, 1957 [1912]) and Walter Burkert's habilitation, *Weisheit und Wissenschaft: Studien zu Pythagoras, Philolaos und Platon* (Nürnberg: Hans Carl, 1962) as well as, magisterially, Denis O'Brien, *Empedocles' Cosmic Cycle: A Reconstruction from the Fragments and Secondary Sources* (Cambridge: Cambridge University Press, 1969). Instructively O'Brien, like Heidegger, follows Aristotle to read his Empedocles. Cf., further O'Brien's "Life Beyond the Stars: Aristotle, Plato and Empedocles (*De Caelo* I.9 279a11–22),"in R. A. H. King, ed., *Common to Body and Soul* (Berlin: De Gruyter, 2006), 49–102.

31. Cornford, *From Religion to Philosophy*, 228.

32. "Rhode, *Psyche*, ii, 216." Cited in Cornford, *From Religion to Philosophy*, 228.

33. See to begin with, again, Burkert's *Weisheit und Wissenschaft* in English as *Lore and Science in Ancient Pythagoreanism*, E. L. Minar Jr., trans. (Cambridge: Harvard University Press, 1972) as well as, for a preliminary introduction to his own work on the Derveni Papyrus, Alberto Bernabé, "What is a Katábasis? The Descent into the Netherworld in Greece and the Ancient Near East," *Les Études classiques* 83 (2015): 15–34.

34. There are many who have written on this relationship over decades and decades but see for a start, Franco Volpi, "*Being and Time*: A 'Translation' of the *Nicomachean Ethics*?," trans. John Protevi in *Reading Heidegger from the Start* (Albany: State University of New York Press, 1994).

35. BCAP: 44.

36. My emphasis. Thus Gadamer publishes, via a transcription of his oral lectures in Italy, translated back into German by Joachim Schulte, *Der Anfang der Philosophie* (Stuttgart: Reclam, 1988). The lectures themselves reprise Gadamer's final lecture course given in Heidelberg and he was to be sure giving classes on the Greeks—when I was a student at Boston College in the early 1980s (I took all of these courses and confess that what I wanted to hear was his more specific reflections on method and hermeneutics), in English as *The Beginning of Philosophy* (London: Bloomsbury, 2016).

37. Nietzsche, „Die vorplatonische Philosophen (Vorlesung Sommer 1872, 1873, 1876)," in: Nietzsche, *Gesammelte Werke. Vierte Band* (Munich: Musarion, 1921), 270. My emphasis.

38. GA 52: 52.

39. Martin Heidegger, "The Anaximander Fragment," in EGT: 13–58; also published in *Arion: A Journal of Humanities and the Classics*, New Series 1, no. 4 (1973–1974): 576–626. Originally "Der Spruch des Anaximander" in *Holzwege* (Frankfurt am Main: Klostermann, 1957 [1946]), 296–343; "Das anfängliche Sagen des Seins im Spruch des Anaximander" (1941), *Vorlesungen 1923–1944, Grundbegriffe*, ed. Petra Jaeger (Frankfurt am Main: Klostermann, 1981), GA 51, Abt. 2, 94–123. See too: GA 78. Cf, in addition to others, to be sure, Jacques de Ville, "Rethinking the Notion of a 'Higher Law': Heidegger and Derrida on the Anaximander Fragment," *Law and Critique* 20 (2009): 59–78.

40. See, generally, Joseph Fell, "Heidegger's Notion of Two Beginnings," *The Review of Metaphysics* 25, no. 2 (December 1971): 213–37 and helpfully, if focused on Heraclitus not Anaximander, Daniel Dahlstrom's contribution "Being at the Beginning: Heidegger's Interpretation of Heraclitus" in Dahlstrom's edited collection, *Interpreting Heidegger: Critical Essays* (Cambridge: Cambridge University Press, 2011), 135–55.

41. BCAP: 44.

42. Nietzsche, *Philosophy in the Tragic Age of the Greeks*, trans. Marianne Cowan (Washington, DC: Regnery, 1962), 45, 46. Cf., *Die fröhliche Wissenschaft*, KSA 3, 467.

43. See for a discussion of Nietzsche and Anaxagoras, the closing section of Babich, "Enstehungsgeschichte" in *Nietzsches Antike. Beiträge zur Altphilologie und Musik* (Berlin: Academia, 2020), 15–48. For Nietzsche and ancient cosmology, see Babich, "On the Very Idea of a Philosophy of Science."

44. GA 78: 1.

45. Heidegger cites "*Simplicii in Aristotelis Physicorum libros quttuor priores commentaria*. Ed. Hermannus Diels. Reimer, Berlin 1882." Ibid.

46. Nietzsche composed his *Philosophy in the Tragic Age of the Greeks* for popular, public presentation at Bayreuth but the point of contrast with his university lecture courses is made more complex as the posthumous publication of Nietzsche's university lectures elided his Anaximander lecture to a single paragraph on half a page in the 1921 Musarion edition (p. 275), where an editorial footnote simply refers the reader back to the popular lecture series: "[1] [Further pp. 168ff.)," in place of Nietzsche's stylistically and substantively different discussion in his university lectures: KGW II$_4$, 239–251.

47. N3: 182.

48. N3: 182–83.

49. Hans Joachim Krämer, *Der Ursprung der Geistmetaphysik: Untersuchungen zur Geschichte des Platonismus zwischen Platon und Plotin* (Amsterdam: B. R. Grüner, 1964) as well as Konradin Gaiser, *Platons ungeschriebene Lehre Studien zur systematischen und geschichtlichen Begründung der Wissenschaften in der Platonischen Schule* (Stuttgart: Klett-Cotta, 1968). See for contemporary reception, limited as this is, in addition to the contributions to Dmitri Nikulin, ed., *The Other Plato: The Tübingen Interpretation of Plato's Inner-Academic Teachings* (Albany: State University of New York Press, 2013) as well as, significantly emphasizing both the breadth of research and context, the late Thomas Szlezák's scholarly criticism of Tanja Staehler's assessment of the so-called 'esoteric' Plato,' in Szlezák/Staehler's "Plato's Unwritten Doctrines: A Discussion," *J. anc. philos. (Engl. ed.), São Paulo* 8, no. 2. (2014): 160–166 and for a recent, if elliptic reference to some of the complexities of tracing this tradition, Holger Schmid, "The Greatest Music: New Footnotes" in François Renaud und Anne Sheppard, eds., "*Platon mousikos*" (Amsterdam: Brill, in press).

50. Krämer, *The Foundations of Metaphysics: A Work on the Theory of the Principles and the Unwritten Doctrines of Plato with a Collection of the Fundamental Documents*, trans. John R. Catan (Albany: State University of New York Press, 1990).

51. See David Lachterman, *The Ethics of Geometry: A Genealogy of Modernity* (London: Routledge, 1989).

52. Walter J. Ong, *Ramus: Method and the Decay of Dialogue* (Cambridge: Harvard University Press, 1958).

53. Ong, *Ramus*, 53.

54. Ong, *Ramus*, 63ff. Cf. Ivan Illich, *In the Vineyard of the Text* (Chicago: University of Chicago Press, 1996).

55. Thus this may not be reduced to today's Straussians if there are many readings of the Straussian unwritten. Thus Tracy B. Strong (1943–2022) reminds me that he took care as editor of *Political Theory* to bring out, contra certain hindrances, Geoff Waite's "On Esotericism: Heidegger and/or Cassirer at Davos," *Political Theory* 26, no. 5 (October 1998): 603–51.

56. Catherine Osborne [Rowett], *Rethinking Early Greek Philosophy: Hippolytus of Rome and the Presocratics* (Ithaca, NY: Cornell University Press, 1987). See too, in addition to his 1968 *Greek Papyri*, Eric G. Turner, *Greek Manuscripts of the Ancient World* (Princeton: Princeton University Press, 1971).

57. Nietzsche, KGW II$_4$. This text appears in the Musarion edition that would have been available to Heidegger, 260ff.

58. See here the Musarion edition of Nietzsche's lectures, 267.

59. Nietzsche, KGW II$_4$, 224.

60. Nietzsche, KGW II$_4$, 225.

61. Nietzsche, KGW II$_4$, 225.

62. Nietzsche, KGW II$_4$, 226.

63. Nietzsche, KGW II$_4$, 226. Note that by the time we get to Hugh of St Victor, the '7' Nietzsche emphasizes among the Greeks as the '7 sages' will have become the 7 liberal arts.

64. See for discussion, editorially modified as published: Babich, "From Nietzsche's 'Educational Institutions' to Jaspers and MacIntyre and Newman on 'The Idea of the University,'" *Existenz* 15, no. 2 (Fall 2020): 17–31 as well as Babich, "Hermeneutics, Love, and Education: Reading Gadamer, Nietzsche, and Illich" in Andrzej Wierciński, ed., *A Hermeneutic Teacher* (Amsterdam: Brill/Fink, 2024).

65. Here it should be underlined that this latter, in addition to Nietzsche's *Birth of Tragedy Out of the Spirit of Music* was, as most criticisms fail to note, oriented to the same broad readership as Erwin Rohde's two volume *Psyche: Seelencult und Unsterblichkeitsglaube der Griechen* (Tübingen: Mohr, 1903).

66. Nietzsche, "De Laertii Diogenis fontibus. I," *Rheinisches Museum für Philologie* (1868), 632–53 and "De Laertii Diogenes fontibus (II), *Rheinisches Museum für Philologie* (1869), 188–88 as well as "Fridericus Nietzsche. Analecta Laertiana. Scripsit," *Rheinisches Museum NF XXV* (1870), 217–31.

67. Diogenes Laërtius, *Lives of the Eminent Philosophers*, R.D. Hicks, trans. (Cambridge: Loeb Classical Library, 1925), chap. 1.

68. See further, Babich, "Friedrich Nietzsche" in *The Blackwell Companion to Hermeneutics*, ed. Niall Keane and Chris Lawn (Oxford: Blackwell, 2016), 366–67.

69. See for context, Christian Benne, *Nietzsche und die historisch-kritische Philologie* (Berlin: Walter de Gruyter, 2012).

70. It is helpful to read Hadot on exegesis between disparate received sources (and not less prejudices inherited from a given textual tradition), as Hadot discusses this with respect to readings of Greek influences on St Augustine in the work of Pierre Courcelle. See Hadot, *Philosophy as a Way of Life* (Oxford: Blackwell, 1981).

71. See Heidegger, "The Anaximander Fragment." For a discussion including a footnote detailing the instaurations of Heidegger's Anaximander lecture, see Jan Kerkmann, "Die Subordination der δίκη unter das Sein in Heideggers Aufsatz Der Spruch des Anaximander (1946)" in *Dike und Physis*, 71–166. For a reflective

discussion specifically distinguishing between *Beginn* and *Anfang*, distinctions lost in translation, see Jussi Backman, *Complicated Presence: Heidegger and the Postmetaphysical Unity of Being* (Albany: State University of New York Press, 2015), especially the first chapter. Note here that others who write on Nietzsche and Anaximander include the thoughtful Gary Shapiro, "Debts Due and Overdue: Beginnings of Philosophy in Nietzsche, Heidegger, and. Anaximander" in *Nietzsche, Genealogy, Morality: Essays on Nietzsche's Genealogy of Morals*, ed. Richard Schacht (Los Angeles: University of California Press, 1994), 358–75.

72. EGT: 22.
73. EGT: 22.
74. PA: 1.
75. IM: 97.
76. GA 96: 11.
77. GA 96: 11.
78. See for example, the contributions to the collective volume edited by the present author along with Alfred Denker and Holger Zaborowski, eds., *Heidegger & Nietzsche* (Amsterdam: Brill, 2012) among a range of monographs in addition to the serried remarks offered in editorial and translator's appendices to Heidegger's Nietzsche lectures.
79. GA 96: 12.
80. GA 96: 12.
81. GA 96: 176.
82. GA 96: 176.
83. See on this point: Sabrina P. Ramet, "The Relationship between Martin Heidegger's Nazism and his Interest in the Pre-Socratics," *Religion Compass* 6, no. 9 (September 2012): 426–40. See, too, on an ethical and political level together with a reading of Jünger, Michael Allen Gillespie, "Martin Heidegger's Aristotelian National Socialism," *Political Theory* 28, no. 2 (April 2000): 140–66. More generally, see Charles Bambach, *Heidegger's Roots: Nietzsche, National Socialism, and the Greeks* (Ithaca, NY: Cornell University Press, 2003) together with the contributions to David C. Jacobs, ed., *The Presocratics After Heidegger* (Albany: State University of New York Press, 1999). Gillespie himself draws on Walter Brogan's contribution to the latter.
84. Reiner Schürmann, *From Principles to Anarchy: Heidegger on Being and Acting* (Bloomington: Indiana University Press, 1982).
85. PA: 1.
86. See the first chapter, already cited above, of Babich, *Nietzsches Antike*.
87. Diels, *Doxographi Graeci. collegit recensuit Prolegomenis Indicibusque instruxit* (Berlin: G. Reimer/Weidmann 1879).
88. See for discussion Mansfeld as well as, earlier, J. A. Philip, "Fragments of the Presocratics," *Phoenix* 10, no. 3 (Autumn, 1956): 116–23, including a helpful

diagram, 119. Significant for Philip's discussion is Hermann Koller's *Die Mimesis in der Antike. Nachahmung, Darstellung, Ausdruck* (Bern: Francke 1954). Cf. with reference to Plato and doxography, Han N. Baltussen, *The Presocratics and Plato: Peripatetic Dialectic in the* De Sensibus (Leiden: Brill, 2000) although of course making no reference to Nietzsche or Heidegger for that matter as the text is directed to contemporary authors who write on the Presocratics and only these.

89. Philip, "Fragments of the Presocratics," 123.

90. "Die Vollendung der Metaphysik durch Nietzsche ist die Begründung des letzten Zeitalters der Neuzeit: wir nennen es das Zeitalter der vollendeten Sinnlosigkeit." GA 96, 93.

91. The focus here for Heidegger is on the young Nietzsche "der Wagnerzeit und ist noch nicht dahin vorgedrungen, daß der eigentliche Nietzsche das Griechentum zurückweist zugunsten des Römertunis und des Willens zur Macht und d. h. der »Technik.« Man ist noch so »geistig«, daß man die »Technik« immer noch »romantisch« als bloße »Teufelei« und Romantik sieht. Wohin man historisch den Beginn Neuzeit legt, ist nicht wesentlich—vollends dann nicht, wenn man in diesen Beginn Gedanken und Fragen hineinfälscht, die schon aus einer wesenhaften Überwindung der Neuzeit durch die Überwindung der abendländischen Metaphysik überhaupt entsprungen sind." GA 96: 198.

92. "Dabei vergißt man leicht, daß der eigentliche Nietzsche rein römisch denkt und in seiner eigentlichen Metaphysik nie den griechischen Anfang des abendländischen Denkens begreifen kann." GA 96: 199.

93. GA 96: 12.

94. I borrow the title of this section and its spirit, from Tracy Burr Strong's "How to Write Scripture: Hobbes on Words and Authority," *Critical Inquiry* 20, no. 1 (1993): 128–59.

95. On Aetius, see Jaap Mansfeld and David Runia, *Aetiana: The Method and the Intellectual Context of a Doxographer: The Sources* (Leiden: Brill, 1997) but also Lebedev, "Did the Doxographer Aetius Ever Exist?" *Philosophie et Culture: Actes du XVIIe congrès mondial de philosophie* 3 (1988): 813–17 and Jan Bremmer, "Aëtius. Arius Didymus and the Transmission of Doxography," *Mnemosyne, Fourth Series* 51, Fasc. 2 (April 1988): 154–60.

96. Note that the Pythagoreans as a school or a sect are not in doubt. Thus a later lecture on these follows the lecture on Leucippus and Democritus, cf. KGW II$_4$, 340–350. As Nietzsche notes: "What one calls Pythagorean philosophy is something much later, hardly earlier than the 2nd half of the 5th Century." KGW II$_4$, 252. But Nietzsche's lecture continues systematically, "What now do we actually know of Pythagoras' life according, respectively, to three sources, legends, rational history, newer superstitions? As good as nothing." KGW II$_4$, 259.

97. Nietzsche, Richard Wagner in Bayreuth," §4, *Kritische Studien Ausgabe*, 1: 446.

98. Osborne, *Rethinking Early Greek Philosophy*.

99. Benne, *Die Erfindung des Manuskripts: Zur Theorie und Geschichte literarischer Gegenständlichkeit* (Frankfurt am Main: Suhrkamp, 2015).

100. Friedrich Kittler, "Gramophone, Film, Typewriter," Dorothea von Mücke and Phillippe L. Similon, trans. *October* 41 (Summer 1987): 101–18, here: 105.

101. Nietzsche, *Philosophie im tragischen Zeitalter der Griechen*, in English as: *Philosophy in the Tragic Age of the Greeks*, 36–37.

102. Cited following EGT: 13. Heidegger's lecture, dating from the end of Heidegger's time in Marburg, was first presented in Freiburg in 1932 and again ten years later and appeared in print in 1946. See GA: 78, citation above.

103. Ibid.

104. Elsewhere I have argued that it is significant that Heidegger was for a time involved with an authoritative philological and philosophical edition of Nietzsche's complete works. See Babich, "Heidegger's Black Night: The Nachlass and Its Wirkungsgeschichte" in Ingo Farin and Jeff Malpas, eds., *Reading Heidegger's Black Notebooks: 1931-1941* (Cambridge: MIT Press, 2016), 59–86. Thus we may be puzzled to note, just given that a scholarly edition of Nietzsche's complete works had been available since 1922, why Heidegger, of all scholars, would begin by citing a popular chapbook, composed—and thus the first sentence mentions both Goethe *and* Wagner—for the sake of a lecture presentation at Bayreuth.

105. Heidegger, "Who Is Nietzsche's Zarathustra?" in *The New Nietzsche: Contemporary Styles of Interpretation*, David B. Allison, ed. (New York: Dell, 1977), 64–79: I cite this here although Heidegger's essay also appears elsewhere because it is here disseminated most widely in the literature.

106. Nietzsche, KGW II$_4$, 1.

107. See on this, again, Krämer, *Plato and the Foundations of Metaphysics*.

108. Heidegger, *Beiträge zur Philosophie (Vom Ereignis)*, GA 65, Friedrich Wilhelm von Hermann, ed. (Frankfurt am Main: Klostermann, 2017 [1989]), 417.

109. See again, Babich, "Enstehungsgeschichte."

110. Hadot, *Philosophy as a Way of Life*.

111. Gadamer, *The Beginning of Philosophy*.

112. Kahn, *Anaximander and the Origins of Cosmology* (New York: Columbia University Press, 1960).

113. See for references and discussion, Babich, "Understanding Gadamer, Understanding Otherwise." *Agora Hermeneutica*. International Institute for Hermeneutics. Online: https://www.academia.edu/66050431/Understanding_Gadamer_Understanding_Otherwise.

114. Kahn, *The Art and Thought of Heraclitus* (Cambridge: Cambridge University Press, 1979).

115. There are a range of discussions of this ancient distinction and correspondence, quite beyond my apocryphal reference to a teacher's word and beyond Nietzsche's famous conclusion to his inaugural lecture in Basel. See for

one such, focused on the question of rank order: Andreas Arndt, *Philologie und Philosophie. Philologia ancilla philosophiae? Zur Philosophie der Philologie* (Tübingen: Max Niemeyer Verlag, 1998) as well as, once again, Benne's *Nietzsche und die historisch-kritische Philologie.*

116. Nietzsche, *The Birth of Tragedy*, §15.

117. EGT: 78.

118. EGT: 78.

119. See for a discussion the first part of Babich, "Entstehungsgeschichte."

120. See further Babich, "Nietzsche's Zarathustra and Parodic Style: On Lucian's *Hyperanthropos* and Nietzsche's *Übermensch*," *Diogenes* 232, no. 4, 2010): 81–104.

121. Nietzsche, KGW II$_4$, 229.

122. GA 96: 159.

123. Cited above and see too: Nietzsche, *Beiträge zur Quellenkunde und Kritik des Laertius Diogenes* (Basel: Carl Schultze's Universitætsbuchdruckerei, 1870).

124. GA 40: 12.

125. GA 96: 178. See, more broadly: Ingeborg Schüßler, "Heidegger und Diels: Editorische Notiz zu Heideggers Vorlesungsmanuskript ,Der Spruch des Anaximander.' GA 78," *Heidegger Studies 27, Enowning-Thinking, the Onefold of Hermeneutic Phenomenology, Interpreting Gestalt and History* (2011): 237–42. As Schüßler points out, Heidegger sets Nietzsche's rendering alongside Diels but repeatedly cites, as she notes, Nietzsche's rendering.

126. Joël, *Der Ursprung der Naturphilosophie aus dem Geiste der Mystik. Mit Anhang Archaische Romantik* (Jena: Eugen Diederichs Verlag, 1906).

127. Joël refers to its publication three years earlier in 1903 as part of the "Programm zur Rektoratsfeier der Universität Basel," v.

128. See for discussion and some references, Babich, "Blood for the Ghosts: Reading Ruin's *Being With The Dead* With Nietzsche," *History and Theory* 59 (2020): 255–69.

129. See, however, for an early general discussion of Nietzsche and classics, Hugh Lloyd-Jones, "Nietzsche" in his *Blood for the Ghosts: Classical the 19th and 20th Centuries* (London, 1982), 165–81 in addition to the more specific notes below. At the time of Heidegger's Anaximander lecture, Nietzsche's lecture courses had been available for more than two decades in various published versions of Nietzsche's (unauthorized) *Nachlaß*.

130. Thereby, but this is a task for future research, Heidegger tells us this was a then-current claim. Cf. for a discussion (thus not directly illuminating on point), Jan Kerkmann, *Dike und Physis. Philosophische Studien zu einer Schlüsselkonstellation bei Heidegger, Nietzsche und Heraklit* (Berlin: Tectum, 2019) as well as Philipp Christian Kastropp who raises the more general question concerning the very idea of rediscovery in Heidegger. See Kastropp, *Seinsentdeckungen, Seinsverdeckungen* (Bielefeld: transcript Verlag, 211–74).

See for a discussion, with specific reference to history, Babich, "*Machenschaft* and *Seynsgeschichte* in the Black Notebooks," *Journal of the British Society for Phenomenology* (2020). Online: November 21, 2019. https://www.tandfonline.com/doi/full/10.1080/00071773.2019.1690167.

131. Geoffrey S. Kirk, John E. Raven, and Malcolm Schofield, eds., *The Presocratic Philosophers* (Cambridge: Cambridge University Press, 1983), 2.

132. Nietzsche, "Er ist der Nachtwächter der griechisch. Philosophiegeschichte, man kann nicht in sie hinein, ohne daß einem nicht von ihm der Schlüssel gegeben wird." Here citing Jonathan Barnes translation in "Nietzsche and Diogenes Laertius," *Nietzsche-Studien* 15 (1986): 16–40, here 18, citing Nietzsche, *Historisch-kritische Gesammtausgabe: Werke*, ed. Joachim Mette (Munich: Beck, 1933–1943), 5:126.

133. The quote goes back to Nietzsche himself who reports this secondhand and James Porter reviews Nietzsche's contributions to the discipline of classics to conclude that "any influence Nietzsche may have had in the field of Presocratic philosophy will have consisted in a misprision and a reduction of the views variously on offer in his published and unpublished writings." Porter, *Nietzsche and the Philology of the Future* (Stanford: Stanford University Press, 2000), 391.

134. See too, Nietzsche, "Beiträge zur Kritik der griechischen Lyriker," *Rheinisches Museum für Philologie. Neue Folge* 23 (Frankfurt a/M: Sauerländer, 1868): 480–89 as well as Nietzsche, "Der Florentinische Tractat über Homer und Hesiod, ihr Geschlecht und ihren Wettkampf," *Rheinisches Museum für Philologie. Neue Folge* 25 and 28 (Frankfurt am Main: Verlag von Johann David Sauerländer, 1870–1873), 528–40; 211–49.

135. Hermann Diels, *Die Fragmente der Vorsokratiker* (Berlin: Weidmann, 1903). That there are elements of a certain *Wirkungsgeschichte* to be reflected (more is needed than can be offered here) may be evidenced by the publication of Diels, *Doxographi Graeci* (Berlin: Wiedemann, 1879). See Heidegger on this constellation—it is not the subject of his discussion but a prelude to his reading of Anaximander first published in 1950. Vgl. Heidegger, *Der Spruch des Anaximander*, Hg. Ingeborg Schüssler (Frankfurt: Klostermann, 2010).

136. Mansfeld and Runia, *Aetiana*. See for discussion, again, the authors "Entstehungsgeschichte," specifically, 21–25.

137. IM: 155.

138. IM: 191.

139. *Nietzsches Werke. Nachgelassene Werke. Von Friedrich Nietzsche. Aus den Jahren 1872–1875*, Vol. 10 (Leipzig: C. G. Naumann, 1903). The text also appears in the first Kröner volume of Nietzsche's posthumous writings. Nietzsche, *Aus dem Nachlaß 1869–1873. Nietzsches Werke. Taschen-Ausgabe. Band I* (Leipzig: Alfred Kröner Verlag, 1921). However the text had already appeared in 1894.

140. Nietzsche includes a title epigraph: „*Plato amicus sed—/ Plato und sein Vorgänger. / Ein Versuch/denen zu nützen welche [sich dazu vorbereiten wollen,

Plato zu lesen.] Plato lesen wollen und für nöthig halten, sich dazu vorzubereiten,' KGW II₄, 3. Included here are several courses: ‚Einführung in das Studium der platonischen Dialoge' [WS1871–1872]; ‚Ueber Platons Leben und Schriften' [WS 1873–1874]; ‚Ueber Platons Leben und Lehre [SS 1876] as well as one of the last classes he taught before taking early retirement, ‚Einleitung in das Studium Platons' [WS 1878/1879].

141. Taught at least three times from 1874 to 1878.

142. See for references and discussion in German, including preliminary references to further reading, Babich, "Nietzsches Lyrik. Archilochos, Musik, Metrik" in: Christian Benne and Claus Zittel (eds.) *Nietzsche und die Lyrik. Ein Kompendium* (Frankfurt am Main: Metzler, October 2017), 405–29 and, in English, "Who is Nietzsche's Archilochus? Rhythm and the Problem of the Subject" in Charles Bambach and Theodore George (eds.) *Philosophers and their Poets: Reflections on the Poetic Turn in Philosophy Since Kant* (Albany: SUNY, 2019), 85–114.

143. See again, Nietzsche, *Die Διαδοχαί der vorplatonische Philosophen* [1868–1869] (Philologische Niederschriften und Notizen aus der Leipziger Zeit)—WV: 162; the editors date this lecture course as offered both in 1874 and 1876.

144. EGT: 17.

145. Nietzsche, already cited above, in translation: *Whence things have their origin, there they must also pass away according to necessity; for they must pay penalty and be judged for their injustice, according to the ordinance of time.*

146. Dastur, "Heidegger on Anaximander," here 183.

147. Ibid., 186.

148. See again: Shapiro, "Debts Due and Overdue."

149. Karl Popper, *The World of Parmenides: Essays on the Presocratic Enlightenment* (Avon: Routledge, 1998) and see too Feyerabend's response to Popper's reading in his posthumous *Conquest of Abundance: A Tale of Abstraction versus the Richness of Being* (Chicago: University of Chicago Press, 1999), 60–82. Informative and complicated in this respect, relevant to both Nietzsche and Heidegger, and as I have already referenced John Cleary's reading of Aristotle and mathematics, is Feyerabend's signal reference to Sabetai Unguru, "On the Need to Rewrite the History of Greek Mathematics," *Archive for History of Exact Sciences* 15, no. 1 (1975): 67–114.

150. Bauemler, *Nietzsche, der Philosoph und Politiker* (Leipzig: Reclam, 1931).

151. Bauemler, *Die Unschuld des Werdens. Der Nachlass, ausgewählt und geordnet von Alfred Baeumler* (Leipzig: Kröner, 1931).

152. Bertram, *Nietzsche: Versuch einer Mythologie* (Berlin: Bondi, 1918).

153. Zweig, *Der Kampf mit dem Dämon: Hölderlin Kleist Nietzsche* (Leipzig: Insel-Verlag, 1925).

154. For a discussion from the side of the more influential Wilamowitz for classics as a discipline, see William M. Calder III, "The Wilamowitz-Nietzsche Struggle: New Documents and a Reappraisal," *Nietzsche-Studien* 12 (1983):

214–54. But cf., instructively from the perspective of the history of ideas, James Q. Whitman, "Nietzsche in the Magisterial Tradition," *Journal of the History of Ideas* 47, No. 3 (1986): 453–468.

155. Paul Natorp, "Aristotle und die Eleaten," *Philosophische Monatshefte* 26 (1890): 1–16; 147–69. And see, too, Otto Gilbert, "Aristoteles' Urteile über die pythagoreische Lehre," *Archiv für Geschichte der Philosophie*, 22 (1909): 28–48, 145–65. See more peripherally on this theme, Mirko Wischke, "Ist es Notwendig, Die Vergangenheit zu Verstehen?: Friedrich Nietzsche und Hans-Georg Gadamer über das „Rätsel der Wertsetzung," *Perspektiven der Philosophie*, 28 (2002): 301–25.

156. IM: 126.

157. GA 96: 179.

158. There is no shortage of such discussions but for a range of these, see the contributions to Yunus Tuncel, ed., *Nietzsche and Transhumanism: Precursor or Enemy?* (Cambridge: Cambridge Scholars, 2017).

159. This has been hyped for a while: see the online news article by Daniel Fraga, "Genome Editing—Bringing the Übermensch to a Shelf Near You," *Next Nature*, 28 September 2015. https://www.nextnature.net/2015/09/genome-editing-bringing-ubermensch-shelf-near/.

160. PA: 68. Translation altered.

161. EGT: 14.

162. PA: Translators' Foreword, xv. This is an option that needs mention as Heidegger translations often transliterate/Romanize the Greek entirely, where the original text includes it, indeed even, most notoriously perhaps, in the case of Heidegger's *Einführung in die Metaphysik* where Heidegger cites Sophocles's Greek chorus where English translations exclude the Greek altogether. See for a discussion of Heidegger on translation, including further references, Tom Greaves, "Heidegger" in: Piers Rawling and Philip Wilson, eds., *The Routledge Handbook of Translation and Philosophy* (London: Routledge, 2018), 49–62.

163. PA: 13.

164. Ibid.

165. PA: 45.

166. EGT: 19.

167. EGT: 31. Translation slightly modified.

168. Nietzsche, *Philosophy in the Tragic Age of the Greeks*, 46.

169. EGT: 40.

170. EGT: 43.

171. EGT: 45.

172. BN III: 157.

173. This is the force of Most's dismissal of Heidegger along with a culture of Graecist scholarship: "since all idealizations of the Greeks are ultimately Roman in inspiration, Heidegger's Greeks may be described as being Germans in togas." Most, "Heidegger's Greeks," *Arion*, 3rd series, 10, no. 1 (2002): 83–98, 95.

174. See, again, Cherniss, *Aristotle's Criticism of Presocratic Philosophy*.
175. J. B. McDiarmid, "Theophrastus on the Pre-socratic Causes," *Harvard Classical Studies*, Vol. LXI (1953): 85–56.
176. Nietzsche, *Einleitung in das Studium der platonischen Dialoge*, KGW 11_4, 8.
177. Gadamer, "Heidegger und Nietzsche. Zu: 'Nietzsche hat mich kaputtgemacht," *Aletheia* 9, no. 10 (1996): 19. I talk about this fairly disquieting notion—at least for certain Heideggerians, most notably Bill Richardson—at the outset of my *Words in Blood, Like Flowers* (Albany: State University of New York Press, 2006).
178. EGT: 15.
179. WCT: 73.
180. BCAP: 18.
181. BCAP: 23. See further on questioning, Babich "Heidegger's Questioning After Technology," *Gatherings: The Heidegger Circle Annual* 13 (2023): 1–45.
182. BCAP: 23. Translation slightly altered.
183. Kirk and Raven, *The Presocratic Philosophers*, 118.
184. See again for their discussion, Mansfeld and Runia, *Aëtiana*.
185. Nietzsche, *Philosophy in the Tragic Age of the Greeks*, 47.
186. BT: 163.
187. Nietzsche, KGW II_4, 224.
188. Cf. here Alberto Bernabé, "La théogonie orphique due papyrus de Derveni," *Kernos*, 15, no. 5 (2002): 91–129. For more references and discussion see, especially the footnotes to, my review essay, again, Babich, "Blood for the Ghosts."
189. See Babich, *Nietzsches Plastik. Ästhetische Phänomenologie im Spiegel des Lebens* (Oxford/Berlin: Peter Lang, 2021), 135. Richard Janko, "Review of The Derveni Papyrus, edited by Theokritos Kouremenos, George M. Parássoglou, and Kyriakos Tsantsanoglou," *Bryn Mawr Classical Review* 29 Oktober 2006. Online. https://bmcr.brynmawr.edu/2006/2006.10.29/.
190. Cited in Val Dusek, "Patrick Heelan's Phenomenology and Hermeneutics of Observation in Quantum Mechanics," *AI & Society* (2021).
191. See for a discussion and references, the author's "Epicurean Gardens and Nietzsche's White Seas" in Vinod Acharya and Ryan J. Johnson, eds., *Nietzsche and Epicurus: Nature, Health and Ethics* (London: Bloomsbury, 2020), 52–67.
192. See for a hermeneutic illustration, Babich, "Dionysian Redemption, Ariadne's Death, Asses' Ears—and Nietzsche's Debts," *New Nietzsche Studies*, Vol. 11, No 34 (Fall 2021/Spring 2022), 99–130, here: 106–107.
193. See for John van Buren's somewhat giddy reading between Heidegger and Plato, to the benefit of Aristotle, and citing index-card-style stacking references, Heidegger's definition of philosophy " 'as the greatest *mousike*,' 'Plato would never define philosophy as a *techne*!,' " and so on in van Buren, *The Young Heidegger* (Bloomington: Indiana University Press, 1994), 234.
194. EGT: 49.

195. As Heidegger writes, "The text from Simplicius's commentary on the Physics is traditionally accepted as the Anaximander fragment. However, the commentary does not cite the fragment so clearly that we can ascertain with certainty where Anaximander's saying begins and where it ends." Heidegger, "The Anaximander Fragment," 30.

196. GA 78: 1.

197. Heidegger, "The Anaximander Fragment," 30, cf. *Der Spruch des Anaximander*, GA 78, 1.

198. Thus Dirk Couprie and Radim Kočandrle summarize: "Ἄπειρος has two meanings: (1) 'infinite,' 'without end,' and (2) 'inexperienced,' 'not acquainted with.' The second meaning has hardly ever been taken seriously in connection with Anaximander. In the first meaning, the words ἄπειρος and ἀπείρων were also associated with the description of nets, fetters or rings. Usually, the meaning 'infinite' is brought into relation with πέρας, 'end,' 'limit.' Kahn suggests a connection with the verbal root per, as in πείρω, περάω, περαίνω. Then the meaning of ἄπειρος is not nominal, but verbal: 'what cannot be passed over or traversed from end to end.'" Couprie and Kočandrle, "Anaximander's 'Boundless Nature,'" *Peitho / Examina Antiqua* 1, no. 4 (2013): 63–91, here p. 66.

199. Not, to be sure, for Heidegger, see his reflections, EGT: 30–45 and so on.

200. EGT: 30, cf. GA 78: 1.

201. EGT: 30, cf. GA 78: 1.

202. EGT: 40; translation slightly altered. GA 5: 353.

203. Ibid.

204. GA 5: 546.

205. EGT: 41; GA 5: 354.

206. Thus Heidegger clarifies what he means by speaking of Nietzsche's "inverted Platonism" by way of "Hegels philosophische Auslegung der »älteren Philosophen« im Ausgang von Aristoteles." GA 78: 15.

207. EGT: 15.

208. Heidegger's point of departure for his own "slow" rendering is thus that both Diels and Nietzsche despite all their differences, "stimmen sie in allem Wesentlichen und beinahe bis aufs Wort miteinander überein." GA 78: 15.

209. EGT: 42. Translation slightly modified.

210. EGT: 47.

211. This is to be sure a very frequently made criticism of Nietzsche, most well known perhaps with Nietzsche's rendering of Pindar's Second Pythian Ode. See for a discussion and partial overview of this debate in the literature, Babich, "Between Hölderlin and Heidegger: Nietzsche's Transfiguration of Philosophy," *Nietzsche-Studien*, 29 (2000): 267–301.

212. EGT: 47.

213. EGT: 47.

214. EGT: 45.

215. EGT: 45.

216. EGT: 52. As Heidegger continues here: "Usage now designates the manner in which Being itself presences as the relation to what is present, approaching and becoming involved with what is present as present: τὸ χρεών." Ibid., 53.

217. GA 78: 217.

218. Detlev Fehling, *Materie und Weltbau in der Zeit der frühen Vorsokratiker* (Innsbruck: Verlag des Instituts für Sprachwissenschaft der Universität Innsbruck, 1994).

219. Dirk Couprie and Radim Kočandrle, "Anaximander's 'Boundless Nature,'" 65.

220. Couprie with Robert Hahn and Gerrard Naddaf, *Anaximander in Context*. And see, Couprie and Kočandrle, "Anaximander's 'Boundless Nature.'"

221. Heidegger's first footnote to GA 78 thus cites Hermann Diels, *Simplicii in Aristotelis Physicorurm libros quattuor priores commentaria* (Berlin: Reimer, 1882), here: GA 78, 1.

222. For a related study see Kočandrle, "Infinite Worlds in the Thought of Anaximander," *The Classical Quarterly* 69, no. 2 (March 9, 2020).

223. See H. B. Gottschalk, "Anaximander's Apeiron," *Phronesis* 10, no. 1 (1065): 37–53.

224. Elizabeth Asmis summarizes some of the different definitions in her essay, "What is Anaximander's Apeiron?," *Journal of the History of Philosophy* 19, no. 3 (July 1981): 279–97. As Asmis begins by noting, Burnet uses the language of the "boundless" to characterize a reserve or "stock from which the waste of existence is continually made good," in John Burnet, *Early Greek Philosophy* (London: Adam & Charles Black, 1930), 53. Frances M. Cornford locates this "outside the world as the 'eternal' background of the cycle of change and becoming" in Cornford, *Principiura Sapientiae* (Cambridge: Cambridge University Press, 1955), 171. Kahn describes the *apeiron* as "primarily a huge, inexhaustible mass, stretching away endlessly in every direction" in Kahn, *Anaximander and the Origins of Greek Cosmology*, 233.

225. Whence things have their origin, / Thence also their destruction happens, / According to necessity; For they give to each other justice and recompense / For their injustice / In conformity with the ordinance of Time. Anaximander. But as R. J Hankinson, reminds us in his *Cause and Explanation in Ancient Greek Thought* (Oxford: Clarendon, 1998), quoting Simplicius to do so, what comes into being is not owing to "alteration of the element but by the separating off (*apokrinesthai*) of the opposites by the eternal motion. (Simplicius, On the 'Physics' 1. 2. 24. 17–25 = 12 A 9 DK = 101 a KRS)," 8. And likewise, there seems to be a balance and a return built into the same cyclic generation and destruction: to quote Hankinson quoting Anaximander: "And the things from which existing things are generated are also those into which they are destroyed."

226. Kirk, Raven, Schofield, *The Presocratic Philosophers*, 118. Cf. Hermann Diels, *Die Fragmente der Vorsokratiker*, ed. Walther Kranz (Berlin: Weidmannsche Buchhandlung, 1931 [1903]), 89. Note that Diels who stresses "*Indirekter Rede*"

does not include the comment on poetic terminology and see too Charles Kahn's *Anaximander and the Origins of Cosmology* (New York: Columbia University Press). Cf. "The things that are perish into the things out of which they come to be, according to necessity, for they pay penalty and retribution to each other for their injustice [*adikias*] in accordance with the ordering of time [*chronou*], as [Anaximander] says in rather poetical language."

227. In German: „Woher die Dinge ihre Entstehung haben, dorthin müssen sie auch zu Grunde gehen, nach der Nothwendigkeit; denn sie müssen Buße zahlen und für ihre Ungerechtigkeiten gerichtet werden, gemäß der Ordnung der Zeit." Nietzsche, *Die Philosophie im tragischen Zeitalter der Griechen*, in Nietzsche, *Kritische Studienausgabe* (Berlin: de Gruyter, 1980), Vol. 1, 818.

228. Couprie and Kočandrle, "Anaximander's 'Boundless Nature,'" 66.

229. KGW II$_4$, 226.

230. Tracy Strong makes this the signature of his reading of Nietzsche and rhetoric: "In Defense of Rhetoric: Or How Hard It Is to Take a Writer Seriously," *Political Theory* 41, no. 4 (2013): 507–32.

231. There are many readings of this and here I mention Peg Birmingham, "Ever Respectfully Mine: Heidegger on Agency and Responsibility" in *Ethics and Danger*, ed. Arleen Dallery and Charles Scott (Albany: State University of New York, 1992) as well as Leslie MacAvoy, "The Heideggerian Bias Toward Death: A Critique of The Role of Being-Towards-Death in the Disclosure of Human Finitude," *Metaphilosophy* 27, no. 1/2 (January/April 1996): 63–77.

232. KGW II$_4$, 242.

233. Citing it in GA 82: 2, and via the 1913 Kroner edition, GA 78: 17.

234. GA 78: 20.

235. Ibid.

236. Cited here following the George Long translation that may also be found online. https://www.gutenberg.org/files/10661/10661-h/10661-h.htm.

237. Nietzsche, *Philosophy in the Tragic Age of the Greeks*, 49.

238. William J. Richardson, *Heidegger: Through Phenomenology to Thought* (The Hague: Martinus Nijhoff, 1974 [1963]), 514.

239. Theorists include Donna Haraway and Bruno Latour as well as Bernard Stiegler and Mark Coeckelbergh among others.

240. I owe this phrase—with all its truth—to Tracy Burr Strong (1943–2022).

3

Alien Historicity

Ancestral Fictions in Heidegger, Derrida, and H. P. Lovecraft

MARK PAYNE

In *Being and Time,* Martin Heidegger conducts a provisional inquiry into the nature of historicity as the subjective condition of being historical. Jacques Derrida, reflecting on the provisional nature of this inquiry in *Heidegger: The Question of Being and History,* suggests that it stalls because of the unresolved vegetal metaphorics that govern it. Whereas Heidegger proposes historicity as a form of belonging, according to the logic of natural growth, Derrida suggests that it should instead be considered according to the logic of the graft: not outside the metaphorics of vegetal life but not as the natural ownness of trunk and branch.

Heidegger's inquiry into the first-personal character of historicity in *Being and Time* precedes the sustained effort in his later work to affirm the priority of the Greeks for the affordances of our access to Being in the era of Western technology's ubiquity. And yet this inquiry into historicity as belonging still takes as its example of the claim of the past upon the present "the remains of a Greek temple." Even here, a common-sense appeal to local conditions of historical belonging stemming from family or ethnos is not constitutive of the claim. As articulated, therefore, the first personal character of historicity can only have the form of an expropriation, the claim of an alien origin that is retroactively metabolized as one's own.

The ownness of historicity as a first-personal condition is always a retroactive outcome. The self that recognizes its expropriation by the past enacts a responsive appropriation toward what claims it, negating the alieneity of expropriation. I will not consider here how the appropriation of an alien historicity might be conceived as first personal experience in the sustained engagement with the Greeks in Heidegger's later work, and not just because such a framing of relationality as first personal is itself alien to the project of that work. Instead, I will look at the staging of this appropriation in H. P. Lovecraft's speculative fiction *At the Mountains of Madness*, written a few years after the publication of *Being and Time*, which takes as its theme the subjective appropriation of the Greeks as an alien origin.

Lovecraft is best known for the linked tales of cosmic horror known as the Cthulhu mythos, whose foundational role in the emergence of speculative fiction as a transnational genre has been monumentalized in the Library of America edition of his work and rejected by contemporary writers in this genre who abhor his white supremacist racism.[1] Of these tales, *At the Mountains of Madness* is the perfect tool with which to pursue the inquiry into the nature of historicity as a subjective condition of historical belonging because it explicitly stages this condition in the form of a graft. The university team that discovers the remains of an alien civilization in the ice-bound canyons of Antarctica in Lovecraft's story acknowledge their continuity with a historical form of life with which they have no natural relation of descendance. Historicity is produced in them as they metabolize the realization that what they thought of as their ownmost endeavor, precisely because it was a natural outgrowth of their local circumstances and history, has a historical precedent of which they had no conception. They appropriate the expropriation of their local self-understanding, grafting themselves to an alien stock.

In *Being and Time* II.5.73, Heidegger brackets the analogy between historicity and the lived temporality of Dasein as a naïve and unexamined presupposition. With regard to the latter, neither the proposition that as first-personal experience the future emerges for us a clarification of the claims of the past, nor that we enact our future as the resolution of these claims, demands strenuous assent. Likewise, we can readily assent to the proposition that attending to this emergence belongs to Dasein's care for its own being. But even if we typically say that history is structured as past, present, and future in the same way as our first-personal temporal experience, it has not yet been properly asked whether our apprehension of our being in history is structured in the same way as that of our being in time: "The 'past' is manifestly different from *one's having been*, with which we have become acquainted as something constitutive for the ecstatical unity of Dasein's temporality. This, however, only makes the enigma ultimately more acute; why is it that the historical is determined *predominantly* by the 'past,' or, to speak more appropriately, by the character of having-been, when that character is one that temporalizes itself equiprimordially with the present and future?"[2] In the constitution of the historical, *having-been* outranks present and future, whereas in temporality, one's having-been ranks equally with present and future as the opening for their emergence. Having-been is determinative for the experience of historicity, as one's having-been is not for temporality. As an experience of belonging in time, historicity is the claim of the past above all others. Even if the temporal being of Dasein and the being of history are structured alike in their directionality, as is clearer in the derivation of the German *Herkunft* and *Zukunft* from *kommen*, Dasein's engagement by historicity is an expropriation—a brake on its self-resolution in the orientation toward futurity that interrupts and punctuates its forward movement.

It is at this incongruence between historicity and temporality that Derrida's intervention takes aim; it points to an incomplete thought—a vector, or feeler of thinking—that has not been afforded adequate support: "The problem of historicity is *grafted* onto that of temporality—that signifies, of course, that historicity is not temporality, and that the confused concept of *becoming* should not obscure their specificity, but this graft signifies above all that historicity can be thought in its root only on the basis of the movement of temporality, of an ontological interrogation into what the temporality of *Da-Sein* signifies."[3] And when Derrida returns to the question in a subsequent seminar, it is to underscore that the metaphorical logic of vegetality according to which the inquiry into the relationship between historicity and temporality was opened, and a preliminary access to its experiential conditions afforded, has at the same time made it impossible to discover the congruence of the structures it was intended to reveal:

> Historicity must be rooted in temporality as its condition of possibility. Having recognized this, one is then threatened by another danger, the very one that Heidegger must confront here. Namely, that if one considers solely or primarily the rootedness of historicity in temporality, one runs the risk—and this is what

happens here—of no longer finding anything original about what is rooted, about the rooted with regard to the root. The originality of historicity with respect to temporality suddenly becomes impossible to find; it is now only a modification of temporality.[4]

According to the vegetal logic of the root, a trunk produces branches of the same kind as itself through the automatic processes of natural life, whereas the graft points to difference, artificiality, and the supplement, which, if it "takes," grows together with the stock onto which it is grafted, without being or becoming of the same kind. What is grafted, whether skin or branch, lives through the care of an outside agent who takes its "taking" in hand and fosters its survival. Someone has to do the grafting, whereas a branch grows by itself.

With the logic of the graft in mind as the condition for the successful production and integration of historicity into temporality, let us now turn to Lovecraft's story in which this process is staged as first-personal historical self-understanding. Lovecraft was a fanatical admirer of the Greeks. In his autobiographical reminiscence, "A Confession of Unfaith," he attributed the invention of his own distinctive kind of horror fiction, which he called "cosmic horror," to his childhood reading of classical authors: "The most poignant sensations of my existence are those of 1896, when I discovered the Hellenic world, and of 1902, when I discovered the myriad suns and worlds of infinite space." These sensations were inextricably linked in his response to Greek culture. What he discovered in both Greek materialist philosophy and Greek mythological literature was an unflinching response to the universal insignificance of human life. After these twin discoveries, he proclaimed himself "for evermore a Graeco-Roman," and dedicated himself to restaging for the readers of his own fiction the sensations that classical literature and philosophy had produced in him.[5]

What's not to like? you might think: another triumph for ancient atheism and another monument to the convergence of Greek literature and historical materialism. Unfortunately, Lovecraft was also a fanatical white supremacist who saw the Greeks as a "super-race" precisely because of the cosmic materialism that freed them from the mental servitude common to all other races alike, which shrank from the materiality of life and took refuge in its supposed divine origin, as a defensive response to the horror of participating in the substrate of bare life with living beings as a whole. Pondering organized religion's survival into the age of Darwinism and Einsteinian physics, Lovecraft looks back to the Greeks and reflects: "There is nothing to wonder at in the long survival and hard death of such a system. Its overthrow comes only as a result of the most conclusive and gigantic array of contrary evidence. The wonderful thing is that it should have been extensively challenged by an important section of Greek philosophers as far back as Democritus. However—perhaps one should not wonder at anything Greek; the race was a super-race."[6]

The Greeks were a "super-race" because of their tolerance for contemplating what other races can't bear to behold. The term is not Lovecraft's invention. It is a typical marker of American exceptionalism as the survival and extension of the Greek miracle.[7] The two postures are inextricable from one another. Lovecraft the admirer of the Greeks cannot be disentangled from Lovecraft the white supremacist, precisely because his understanding of the Greeks as unique among races is the very thing that sustains his understanding of himself as a white supremacist safeguarding their racial legacy for the future: decentering ourselves from the universe and deanthropomorphizing our understanding of the planet we inhabit. Whereas all other cultures before and since have shielded themselves from this knowledge with the invention of gods, and other ways of construing the earth as human beings' natural home, the Greeks were the first and only people to face the absolute materiality of life, and the arbitrary and meaningless nature of our own participation in that life, a legacy that the America of his day is struggling to preserve as a racial heritage. As he puts it in his reply to his critics, "In Defense of Dagon": "Greece, whose culture was the greatest of all, antedated Christianity and originated materialism. Modern civilisation is the direct heir of Hellenic culture—all that we have is Greek."[8]

For Lovecraft, there is no conflict between *logos* and *mythos* in his understanding of the Greeks. On the contrary, the convergence between the two is one of the features of Greek culture that sets them apart as a super-race. Whereas mythological story telling in every other culture conceals the truth about the cosmos from its audience, Greek mythological literature tells the same story as Greek materialism. It is only the form of disclosure that is veiled, a procedure Lovecraft came to prefer for his own writing, as a mode of revelation intended only for the intellectual and spiritual elite who could bear the burden of knowledge and its sensations.

It is a long way from the Mediterranean to McMurdo Sound, where *At the Mountains of Madness* begins, but readers of the great tales of cosmic horror should bear in mind that Lovecraft cut his teeth on neo-Hellenic fabulations like the short story "The Tree" that he is defending in "In Defence of Dagon." What is wrong with these early stories from the perspective of the mature work is that they are too obvious in their advocacy of Greek culture and its values. In "The Tree," the trees of a Greek sacred grove whisper in Greek against the illusions of humankind. They "reveal the truth to the midnight searcher as they chaunt knowingly over and over again "οἶδα!" "οἶδα!"⁹ The later work will reject such overtness, and conceal an injunction to become undeceived that remains essentially Greek in the less obvious forms of penguins, protoplasm, and white mist.

At the Mountains of Madness narrates the discovery of the ruins of a lost civilization in the mountain valleys of Antarctica by a scientific expedition from Lovecraft's fictional Ivy League institution, Miskatonic University. The narrator, Dr. William Dyer, is a professor of geology, and the other members of the expedition are an array of Lovecraft's favorite academic types: a biologist, a geologist, and an anthropologist, and the graduate students who support their research. As always with the tales of cosmic horror, there are all manner of allusions and cross-references to other works of Lovecraft and his circle that ground the work in a fictional world that extends beyond the story itself, and that in this case retrospectively incorporates Edgar Allan Poe's polar novella, *The Narrative of Arthur Gordon Pym*.

Little remains above ground of the civilization that the expedition discovers, and what does remain has long since been covered by the polar ice cap. In any case, the majority of the building work is inside the mountains, and to explore it, Dyer and a companion must proceed through subterranean passages that access the gigantic labyrinthine structures excavated out of the rock. The walls of these passages are lined with reliefs from which Dyer pieces together the history of the lost civilization. He determines two things about the beings that created the reliefs. First, they were originally aliens, but these off-world colonists at some point lost the technology that would have allowed them to escape the earth when its climate became inhospitable and glaciation overwhelmed what had been a lush, tropical zone when they first settled it. Second, in the construction of their polar civilization, these beings, known as the Old Ones, made use of a form of servile labor called Shoggoths. To be more specific, the Old Ones did not simply make use of the Shoggoths, they created them out of nothing as "formless protoplasm," a fungible substratum of bare life that was infinitely adaptable to their purposes. At some point in their history, however, this servile class rebelled, and a number of slave wars ensued, hastening the Old Ones' demise. The Shoggoths themselves then fashioned a series of reliefs that mock and debase the artistic achievements of the Old Ones, in which the latter had delighted to reflect upon the achievements of their culture.

The Old Ones were once an industrial civilization. Before they came to Earth "they had passed through a stage of mechanized life on other planets but had receded upon finding its effects emotionally unsatisfying." Having found that they were able to do without "the more specialized fruits of artificial manufacture," they chose, when they came to this planet, to create life—not machines—for their own use, "at first for food and later for other purposes," initiating the sequence of bioengineering achievements that will eventually produce the Shoggoths. Lovecraft reiterates this point; the Old Ones prefer living slaves to machines: "They had done the same thing on other planets, having manufactured not only necessary foods, but certain multi-cellular protoplasmic masses capable of moulding their tissues into all sorts of temporary organs under hypnotic influence and thereby forming ideal slaves to perform the heavy work of the community."[10]

It is this achievement that is celebrated in the endless sequence of sculptured friezes that constitute the high point of the Old Ones' civilization, the contemplation of which is their favorite form of cultivated leisure: "Historical interest and pride obviously formed their chief psychological element." The friezes, that is to say, are intended both to communicate their achievements to posterity, and also to induce a kind of commemorative rapture in the Old Ones themselves. They are the expression of racial pride in a form of self-realization that has not held back from allowing its own telos as the domination of life to manifest itself in just this way. The Shoggoths are not merely of instrumental value to the Old Ones. They are not just "living tools," as Aristotle calls slaves. They are what allowed the Old Ones to become who they were, and to contemplate themselves as the ones who dared to become what they were,[11] audacity being the Promethean reflection that W. E. B. Du Bois, in *The Souls of White Folk*, singled out as white supremacism's distinctive form of self-congratulation in the early twentieth century: "The using of men for the benefit of masters is no new invention of modern Europe. It is quite as old as the world. But Europe proposed to apply it on a scale and with an elaborateness of detail of which no former world ever dreamed. The imperial width of the thing,—the heaven-defying audacity—makes its modern newness."[12]

At the Mountains of Madness dates from a time toward the end of Lovecraft's life in which his political commitments had turned from the whimsical Anglophile loyalism of his youth to a more serious engagement with some form of American national socialism that could preserve the achievements of white civilization from its imminent deluge by a racialized underclass. The Old Ones' will to become and own what they became looks like a reflection of Lovecraft's reading of Nietzsche as this informed his political sympathies at this time.[13] Likewise, the "hypnotic suggestion" by which the Old Ones control the Shoggoths for as long as they can reflects his grasp of the work of ideology in the political world of the 1920s.

Crucially, however, Lovecraft also understands that the power of ideology doesn't last forever unless it continues to work its magic upon its creators; unless they too continue to immerse themselves in its rapturous self-intoxication. The Old Ones' civilization begins to decline when they come to simply depend on the Shoggoths, rather than actively enjoying the spectacle of how they have created life for their own use. The idea is more Rousseauian than Hegelian. While it is true that the slave class comes to an understanding of itself through its servile labor, it is not the case that the Old Ones are denied self-understanding through their outsourcing of such labor. Rather, as an unintended consequence of this outsourcing, the Old Ones gradually lose sight of what their own powers had once been, as well as what they were capable of in the past and so assiduously recorded in their historical friezes. To put it simply, they forgot who they once were, rather than not knowing in the first place.

Lovecraft offers his readers an extended overview of the decline and fall of the Old Ones' civilization as it is instantiated in their monuments, in which his classical models are evident:

> At last a mighty metropolis rose on the bottom of that Stygian sea, its architecture much like that of the city above, and its workmanship displaying relatively little decadence because of the precise mathematical element inherent in building operations.
>
> The newly bred Shoggoths grew to enormous size and singular intelligence, and were represented as taking and executing orders with marvellous quickness. They seemed to converse with the Old Ones by mimicking their voices—a sort of musical piping over a wide range, if poor Lake's dissection had indicated aright—and to work more from spoken commands than from hypnotic suggestions as in earlier times.
>
> They were, however, kept in admirable control. The phosphorescent organisms supplied light with vast effectiveness, and doubtless atoned for the loss of the familiar polar auroras of the outer-world night.

Art and decoration were pursued, though of course with a certain decadence. The Old Ones seemed to realise this falling off themselves; and in many cases anticipated the policy of Constantine the Great by transplanting especially fine blocks of ancient carving from their land city, just as the emperor, in a similar age of decline, stripped Greece and Asia of their finest art to give his new Byzantine capital greater splendours than its own people could create. That the transfer of sculptured blocks had not been more extensive, was doubtless owing to the fact that the land city was not at first wholly abandoned.

By the time total abandonment did occur—and it surely must have occurred before the polar Pleistocene was far advanced—the Old Ones had perhaps become satisfied with their decadent art—or had ceased to recognise the superior merit of the older carvings. At any rate, the aeon-silent ruins around us had certainly undergone no wholesale sculptural denudation, though all the best separate statues, like other moveables, had been taken away.[14]

The artwork that the Shoggoths themselves produce in the aftermath of the failed "war of resubjugation" against them is a détournement of the Old Ones' ideology as it is expressed in the high culture of their sculptured friezes. It turns the forms and motifs of this culture against its creators in a way that produces considerable unease in its human discoverers. The Miskatonic University team find it "more like a parody than a permutation of that tradition," the "degenerate murals aping and mocking the things they had superseded." And it is this story of a civilization's decline and fall, its displacement by the triumph of its own servile class, that inspires recognition and sympathy in the story's narrator. Dyer's initial aversion to the Old Ones is metabolized into transhistorical and trans-species affinity by the sensation of cultural kinship, his appropriation of the Old Ones as ancestors in a scientific civilization whose values he himself instantiates in the world of the present: "Poor Old Ones! Scientists to the last—what had they done that we would not have done in their place? God, what intelligence and persistence! What a facing of the incredible, just as those carven kinsmen and forbears had faced things only a little less incredible! Radiates, vegetables, monstrosities, star spawn—whatever they had been, they were men."[15]

If the appropriation is difficult for Dyer, who must metabolize these alien ancestors after witnessing some members of his team gruesomely dismembered by their last survivors, it is almost as difficult for the reader who is asked to consider the claim of these alien ancestors upon himself. But the pain of expropriation is the very thing Lovecraft wants his readers to experience. There is a moment of urgency, a window of opportunity, when a superior civilization can recognize that its powers are ebbing away from it, before its very eyes. The common threat that grounds the sensation of kinship with the unique past the scientists discover—unique in the sense that its culture is just like their own, the unique culture of a super-race—is never made explicit in the story as a present danger to the Western civilization from which their expedition originates. The reader has to make this connection for himself. But if he fails to recognize and act on this kairotic moment, his culture is doomed too; there can be no going back. He must not refuse the acknowledgment that Dyer's ancestors are his ancestors too; alien ancestry is the very thing that makes the stakes of historicity in the story clear.

In his introduction to the Modern Library edition of *At the Mountains of Madness*, China Miéville, following S. T. Joshi, notes the legibility of a racialized proletariat in the Shoggoths, allegorizing the story as a Spengler-inspired vision of the downfall of the West.[16] But *At the Mountains of Madness* is as much a call to arms as it is a tragedy or an elegy. The turn to alien ancestry allows the reader to recognize his culture's inextricable dependence upon a history of racialized labor but also to recognize that this culture's persistence rests on a willingness to acknowledge and embrace the will to create such a culture as a form of self-realization in the first place. Lovecraft wants his readers to understand that they do not have to go the way of the Old Ones unless they choose to.

For all the acuteness of their analysis, even Joshi and Miéville miss the extent to which dominion over life itself is the ground of the Old Ones' self-regard. The Old Ones lived through a period of industrial civilization and rejected it because they found its effects upon themselves to be emotionally unsatisfying in comparison to biological slavery, in which their self-realization was visible to them as mastery over life itself. The perpetuation of superiority through an intervention in the processes of life, and the enactment of your own will by other living beings, affords a kind of pleasure in contemplation that mechanical civilization never can. A robot cannot provide the same enjoyment as a living being enslaved for your own use.

The Old Ones' commitment to the enslaved labor of living beings organismically different from themselves tells us something about the

Greeks too. The link that Lovecraft forges between slavery and contemplation is his answer to a question that his own industrial civilization had asked about the value of studying ancient culture: if the Greeks were so smart, how come they didn't invent industrial technology? And if they didn't, what's the point of knowing about them? Lovecraft's answer to this question is that the Greeks did not invent technology because they chose not to. They preferred the spectacle of slavery, the coercion of life to one's own ends, because of the emotional and intellectual satisfaction it affords. The "super-race" that he calls the Greeks knew themselves, for the first time in human history, as living beings whose life was entirely material; they enacted this realization as willing mastery over other living beings.

One way of distinguishing between a mechanical system and a living being is that the latter is autotelic. An organism has goals that it pursues for its self-realization even when it is composed of subsets of organs and systems that have their own routines. (Contemporary biology may think otherwise on this point, but it holds for the purposes of the story.) The Old Ones' creation of the Shoggoths is a détournement of such autotelic processes for the sake of a good outside the organism itself, and this détournement is itself a constituent of the pleasure they take in contemplating their achievement. Violating the natural ends of an organism may itself be an inducement and source of pleasure. There is no such thing as the "living tool" of Aristotle's definition of the slave. There are the living and there are tools, and the harms that can be inflicted on each of them are different in kind. Aristotle's definition conceals the nature of the delight that the Old Ones take in the Shoggoths, the recognition that they enjoy using the living for their own ends, precisely because they are living, when they could have used machines instead.

As it reaches its climax, *At the Mountains of Madness* turns into a fantasy of all-consuming whiteness. Its setting is "the white, aeon-dead world of the ultimate south," or more simply, "the great white south." To the Old Ones, Lovecraft's scientist heroes look like "frantic white simians." The only other animal on the scene is a "huge, unknown species larger than the greatest of the known king penguins, and monstrous in its combined albinism and virtual eyelessness." Even the Shoggoths "belch pallidly" with "sinister curling . . . white mist" as they try to hunt the explorers down.

At one level, there is nothing remotely surprising that the story should end with an incoherent whiteout. As Toni Morrison observed of Lovecraft's model, Poe's *Arthur Gordon Pym*, images of incomprehensible, impenetrable, inarticulate whiteness are typically generated in early American fiction "whenever an Africanist presence is engaged," and their function is to substitute "paralysis and incoherence" for the sense of an ending: "These images of blinding whiteness seem to function as both antidote for and meditation on the shadow that is companion to this whiteness."[17]

Morrison urges her readers to examine the self-reflexive character of this generative chaos, rather than allowing it to shut down reflection. So let us try to heed her injunction. Lovecraft's scientists are still closer to the Shoggoths than they are to the Old Ones, even in the Old Ones' present degraded state. The Old Ones' ruins are a challenge and an aspiration. The expedition cannot communicate their sensations of kinship to the Old Ones themselves, but they must bring the story of their decline back home, where it can function as a warning to their own kind. From this perspective, even the penguins are functional: sightless witnesses to the Old Ones' achievements, they have long since lived on friendly terms with what remains of them, despite themselves being an inferior form of life, unable to capitalize on the manifest superiority that surrounds them.

The ancestral aliens of *At the Mountains of Madness* are the necessary supplement to the whiteness of the expeditionary team. The Old Ones stand outside their local human time and figure the historical super-race of antiquity to which Western civilization must graft itself to produce its own singularity from out of the circumambient mass of ordinary world cultures. Lovecraft knew a lot about the ancient Mediterranean and Near East, and was something of an expert on Babylonian astronomy. This contextual knowledge did nothing to change his understanding of Greek exceptionalism because what he valued about the Greeks was not what they knew, but the existential posture that they made of their knowledge—the heroic, unconsoled materialism he called "cosmic horror." This is the essence of their alienness, the alienation from the livingness of the life world, that sets them apart. This allows them to be recombined with later historical forms of life to produce the second-order historical singularity of the graft.

Willing domination of the matter of life is the essence of the sensation of kinship that makes this graft possible. Old Ones, Shoggoths, and humans are all made of the same stuff, but solidarity in the substrate of shared life brings with it no feelings of kinship with living beings as a whole. As the expedition dissects, so the Old Ones dismember, and this, as Dyer recognizes, instantiates the commonality of their stance toward life. The degrees of affinity between the living can, and therefore will, be manipulated for the self-realization and self-understanding of those who have the will to enact their own ends. The materiality of shared life entails no obligations other than the obligation to experiment: to venture to become makers of the living, mind-manipulated tools of which the Greeks could only dream in the automata of Hephaestus.

From this perspective, *At the Mountains of Madness* allows for a particular conjuncture of the ancestral and the unspeakable. The graft that Lovecraft wants to take is white America onto classical antiquity, and this can only be accomplished through the figure of the alien. What the alien allows is the possibility that slavery can be imagined and expressed not as an accident of historical existence—an unfortunate lack of available labor power that had to be circumvented somehow, and so is a historically contingent fact of the human past precisely because it was unavoidable in its time—but can instead emerge from this condition of deplorable obscenity as an occasion for contemplative pleasure. For those eager for the graft to succeed, the horrors don't have to be bracketed with faux historical piety as horrors at all but can instead become a motive for self-recognition, self-realization, and self-congratulation. There is great explanatory value in the story for a kind of thinking we are reluctant to engage with, and if there is a reason to read Lovecraft after all, this is probably it.

In *Being and Time*, Heidegger ponders how the historical artifact in a museum context gives access to the world of the past from which it has come down to us. In the case of such an object, considered as an occasion for contemplation, the loss of the world it once belonged to is spatially enacted in its setting, yet somehow accompanies it all the same. As Da-sein is "being there," so Da-gewesen ("having been there"), clings to its remainders—"for instance, the remains of a Greek temple"—advancing with them into the unknown future where they wait to make their claim as someone's past.[18] What we have seen, in fact, is that this dislocation is the very condition of expropriation and appropriation for future Dasein, on which these remains make their claim as an alien historicity. And from this perspective, the problem with Dasein's historicity is that it is not vegetal enough. The "for instance" of the Greek temple is hardly unmotivated; it constructs lineation according to a logic of the graft whose outcomes have always been eyed in advance for the affordances they offer as myth-historical backstops to the open-endedness of continuous historical human being.

In conclusion, therefore, I suggest that we consider instead the nature of relation as it operates in the presence of historical artifacts that point to Da-gewesen without its having been characterized in advance for the sake of expropriation and appropriation; for instance, the remains of Stonehenge. In *Pagan Britain*, Ronald Hutton suggests that the lack of evidence for continuous historical activity around the Neolithic monuments that their builders erected with such zest might lead us to reconsider "the nature of monumentality in a prehistoric society." If "the act of making a Neolithic monument may have been the vital activity in itself, a prolonged ritual of tremendous importance for religious and social life rather than simply a process aimed at an end result: a structure which would stand as witness to its makers and their beliefs,"[19] then these monuments cannot (and were not intended to) produce the kind of grafting that Heidegger and Lovecraft have in mind.

Instead, we can cognize in them a more basic affordance of the historical artifact as a "life-adjacent producer of memory or as a mode of preserving life."[20] The absence of messaging is what makes the stones so compelling as a site of historicity that is not keyed to particular historical achievements, but to historical human life in its most abstract and generic form. They afford us a way of imagining those who came before as merely bearers of life, in a relation of vegetal continuity with our own. This affordance is a very particular kind of ecological perspective. We do not access our continuity with shared life as a whole, which is what an ecological perspective typically wants our self-understanding to open up onto. Instead, it offers a perspective that is more narrowly human, yet without the usual valorized markers of humanness: culture, and history in the sense of ethnically specific records, of the kind that produce the sensations of historical continuity in *At the Mountains of Madness*. We are severed from the other branches of the tree of life as we experience the singularity of what it is to be human, while at the same time we feel a stronger solidarity along an axis of humanness that has been evacuated of any content beyond the mere fact of ancestral presence.

For all the museum-like contextualization at the visitor center, Stonehenge will always be a different kind of heritage site than a medieval castle, and not simply because it is so much older. Its antiquity is unparseable in the face it presents to us. What it reflects back to our inquiry is the simple fact of ancient human presence, rather than ancient human presence in any culturally specific form that we can recognize. It is not even legible as an intention to communicate, as a rock painting or petroglyphs are legible, where even if we do not understand the content of the message, we do at least understand that they are intended as communication.[21] Sites like Stonehenge connect us to Earth in a more basic and indeterminate way. We aren't grafted onto a history by recognizing human agents in the past with goals and mentalities like our own. Instead we are interpellated as the latest human carriers in the transmission of life, as subjects of life that is itself unchosen, the human iteration of the living substance through which life passes and is gone.

Notes

1. Some notable dissenters to Lovecraft as founding father include N. K. Jemisin, Nnedi Okorafor, and Jeff VanderMeer. The World Fantasy Award used to come with a bust of Lovecraft's head, and Okorafor's reflections on being presented with it on the occasion of her winning the award in 2011 fostered a larger discussion about the history of race and exclusion in speculative fiction as a whole.

2. BT: 433.

3. Jacques Derrida, *Heidegger: The Question of Being and Time* (Chicago: University of Chicago Press, 2016), 92. See also Hans Ruin, *Enigmatic Origins: Tracing the Theme of Historicity through Heidegger's Works* (Stockholm: Almqvist and Wiksell, 1994), especially 165–75, where he argues that "the unresolved tension between a 'temporal' and a 'historical' analysis of Dasein" in *Being and Time* reflects the inconclusive determination of the temporal structure of being itself that the book leaves unanswered as it breaks off, to be taken up again in the interrogation of the priority between the historical and the temporal in the works that follow directly upon it.

4. Derrida, *Heidegger: The Question of Being and Time*, 156.

5. H. P. Lovecraft, *Collected Essays. Volume 5: Philosophy; Autobiography and Miscellany* (New York: Hippocampus Press, 2006), 145–49.

6. Lovecraft, *Collected Essays. Volume 5: Philosophy; Autobiography and Miscellany*, 60.

7. Francis Jennings in Roxanne Dunbar-Ortiz, *An Indigenous Peoples' History of the United States* (Boston: Beacon Press, 2015), "American culture is seen as not only unique but better than all other cultures, precisely because of its differences from them." Cf. Dunbar-Ortiz, *Collected Essays. Volume 5: Philosophy; Autobiography and Miscellany*, 117.

8. Lovecraft, *Collected Essays. Volume 5: Philosophy; Autobiography and Miscellany*, 61.

9. Lovecraft, *Collected Essays. Volume 5: Philosophy; Autobiography and Miscellany*, 54.

10. H. P. Lovecraft, *At the Mountain of Madness* (New York: Modern Library Classics, 2013), 240–47.

11. Lovecraft, *At the Mountain of Madness*, 247.

12. W. E. B Du Bois, *Writings* (New York: Library of America, 1987), 932.

13. Sunand Tryambak Joshi, *The Weird Tale: Arthur Machen, Lord Dunsany, Algernon Blackwood, M. R. James, Ambrose Bierce, H. P. Lovecraft* (Austin: University of Texas Press, 1990), 170–77, 214–28.

14. H. P. Lovecraft, *The Classic Horror Stories* (Oxford: Oxford World's Classics, 2013), 253–54.

15. Lovecraft, *The Classic Horror Stories*, 272–75.

16. Joshi, *The Weird Tale: Arthur Machen, Lord Dunsany, Algernon Blackwood, M. R. James, Ambrose Bierce, H. P. Lovecraft*, 171, 218; China Miéville, "H. P. Lovecraft," in H. P. Lovecraft, *At the Mountain of Madness*), xix–xxii.

17. Toni Morrison, *Playing in the Dark: Whiteness and the Literary Imagination* (Cambridge, MA: Harvard University Press, 1992), 32–33.

18. BT: 430–32.

19. Ronald Hutton, *Pagan Britain* (New Haven, CT: Yale University Press, 2015), 39–40.

20. Dorian Z. Bell; post for class discussion. I would like to take this opportunity to thank Dorian, and the other students in my 2020 seminar on ancestral fiction, as well as the students in my 2019 seminar on Lovecraft, for significantly advancing my understanding of what is at stake in the historicity of *At the Mountains of Madness*.

21. See Edgar Garcia, *Signs of the Americas: A Poetics of Pictography, Hieroglyphs, and Khipu* (Chicago: University of Chicago Press, 2020) for a compelling account of the continuing vitality of such deep transhistorical messaging in the cultures of the Americas.

4

Disciples of Empedocles
Hölderlin, Nietzsche, and . . . Heidegger?

DAVID FARRELL KRELL

for Will McNeill

German philosophy as a whole . . . is the most fundamental kind of romanticism and homesickness that has ever been seen: this longing for the best that ever was. One no longer feels at home anywhere. In the end, one longs to be back somewhere where one can feel at home; only there does one want to *be* at home. And that is the world of Greece! . . . above all, the world of the Presocratics—of all Greek temples the one most reduced to rubble!

—Friedrich Nietzsche

Are not those philosophers foolish who complain about what another philosopher has *failed* to read and discuss? Why harp on what a thinker has *not* thought about, as though life could be anything other than a series of more or less haphazard choices and inevitable, regrettable exclusions, lapses, near misses, and gaps?

Does Heidegger ever discuss the fragments of Empedocles? Does he refer at all to Empedocles in the hundred-plus volumes of his collected writings? The answer to the second question, my friend Will McNeill assures me, is *yes*. The answer to the first question, as to whether Heidegger discusses the extant *fragments* of Empedocles, is, I believe, *no*. Will McNeill has generously sent me all the references to "Empedocles" that he could find in the *Gesamtausgabe*, almost all of them references to Hölderlin's *The Death of Empedocles*. In what follows I will discuss these references, although I first want to speculate on the question, however foolish it may appear to be, as to why the extant fragments of Empedocles's thinking play no role in Heidegger's thought. They play no role, I say, but they *should* do so. And that *should* is so strong that one might argue that indeed they *do* play a role, if only offstage, concealed in the wings like Hamlet's ghost—or like Kypris Aphrodite concealed at the heart of being.

My paper has three parts: (1) a rumination on possible reasons for the absence of Empedocles's fragments from Heidegger's responses to early Greek thinking; (2) Heidegger's mentions of Empedocles, principally as *Hölderlin's* Empedocles, but sometimes also as *Nietzsche's* Empedocles; and (3) some suggestions about several Empedoclean fragments that may be essential to Heidegger's task of thinking.

What might the reasons be for Empedocles's absence from Heidegger's preoccupation with the Greeks? A first reason, the *hermeneutical*, may be that there is simply too much material from Empedocles that survives. Although one might assert the same of Parmenides and Heraclitus, Heidegger's two principal inspirations, it is clear that Heidegger works by reduction, not by expansion. Only a very small handful of fragments from Parmenides and Heraclitus serve his hermeneutic. Even when there is only one fragment to be interpreted, as in the case of Anaximander, Heidegger cuts much of it away, considering certain phrases Stoic or Aristotelian or otherwise "inauthentic." With Empedocles, both his fragments on "nature" or "birth" and those strange asseverations that tradition calls his *Purifications*, require an entire narrative. One can cite a pithy line or two from *The Four Quartets*, but what does one cite from *Light in August*? Empedocles is closer to Faulkner than to Eliot, even if his poetry is glorious.

A second reason may be that Empedocles comes too late. As a pupil of Parmenides, he might be held to be epigonal. Heidegger is keen on "the oldest," the most archaic, so old that it can be called *anfänglich*, and Empedocles is arguably none of those things. His originality stems from something other than antiquity. Indeed, Matthew Arnold was not entirely wrong to see in Empedocles a paragon of "the modern," the "psychological." Even though Empedocles is a contemporary of Sophocles, many would associate him with Euripides.

A third reason, related to his supposed "modernity," might be that Empedocles's cosmological speculations on love and hate in the sphere of being smack of psychology and prosopopoeia. It is no accident that Freud felt Empedocles to be his greatest ally and precursor in the antique world, perhaps even more significant to him than Plato and Aristophanes.

A fourth reason may be that Empedocles's *Purifications*, presuming there was such a "book," with its emphasis on blood crimes and guilt, infanticide and patricide, is simply too close to "moral" and "dramatic" themes that Heidegger would find objectionable—*ontic* themes quite remote from the ontological realm. Recall his eschewal of the "legal" and "moral" interpretations of Anaximander, that is, his treatment of ἀδικία not as "injustice" but as *Un-Fug*, the being "out of joint" of beings as a whole. In the same vein, Empedocles appears to emphasize the seamless quality of nature, in which plants, animals, humans, and gods are intimately related. If Empedocles declares that at one time he was both boy and girl, bush and bird, and flying fish leaping o'er the sea, that seems to make him an ancient avatar of Rilke, not a thinker like Heidegger, who insists on "an abyss of essence" that separates human from animal.

A fifth reason may be that Empedocles is simply too "political" a figure for him, indeed, a political figure of the "left." It is no accident that Camus's *L'Homme révolté* takes Empedocles as its ancient hero. Aristotle himself declares Empedocles to be a democrat. Likewise, both Hölderlin and Nietzsche take Empedocles to be an eminently political figure, one whose struggles with the citizens of Acragas form the basis of the *dramas* they are attempting to write about him. Related to this "political" tendency is the association of Empedocles with things female. Strangely, Heidegger himself will cite more than once the figures of Rhea and Panthea in Hölderlin's *Der Tod des Empedokles*, even though the story of Panthe(i)a might suffice to induce Heidegger to wash his hands of the ancient physician and magus altogether.

And yet, after all these proffered reasons, one still has the sense that Empedocles is often close to some of Heidegger's dearest themes and questions, perhaps too close, *zu innig, zu einzig*, as Hölderlin would say. Such closeness was certainly something that troubled Freud when it came to Nietzsche, if not Empedocles. Among the themes that would have, or at least ought to have, attracted Heidegger to Empedocles—and this list is merely a beginning—would be:

- Like Heidegger, Empedocles invokes a fourfold or quaternity: parallel to, though not identical with, Heidegger's earth and sky, mortals and deities, are the "four roots" or "rhizomes," ῥιζώματα, of Empedocles, to wit, fire and air, earth and water. These "roots" are forever intertwined, so that, as Heidegger says of *his* quaternity, if one names any one of them, one must think the other three along with it.

- Like Heidegger, who elaborates the "strife" between world and earth in *The Origin of the Work of Art*, Empedocles thinks of the Strife (Νεῖκος) that shares with Love (Φιλία) the sphere of being, which is the sphere that *gathers* differences into one.

- Like Heidegger, who his life long thinks about the inherence of *Verborgenheit* in all *Entbergung*, that is, the intrinsic belonging of concealment to all revealing, Empedocles is a thinker of ἀπάτη, that is, a kind of "deception" that is neither willful nor accidental, but, if one may attach such a word to Empedocles, *ontological*.

- Like Heidegger, who takes thinking to be intimately related to poetry, indeed, to be *devoted to* poetry, Empedocles the sage, physician, theurgist, and magician writes glorious poetry. Neither Hölderlin nor Nietzsche would have had anything to do with Empedocles had it not been for the magnificent dramatic poetry. Can Heidegger afford to be deaf and blind to it?

It may be, however, that among the fragments of Empedocles that have survived, Heidegger has whether wittingly or unwittingly taken some of them up into his own thinking. There are at least two such borrowings: first, Heidegger's Parmenidean (but also Empedoclean) preoccupation with thinking and being as *presencing*; second, Heidegger's fascination with the "trembling" or "shivering" of the "last god" in his *Beiträge zur Philosophie*. Both "borrowings" will be discussed in what follows.

This brief list of issues, to repeat, is a mere beginning. Let me turn now to Heidegger's rare mentions of Empedocles, once again with thanks to Will McNeill, first in the context of Nietzsche's thought, and then, even more fruitfully, in the context of Hölderlin's mourning-play, *The Death of Empedocles*.

During his Heraclitus seminar of 1943, Heidegger makes a reference to Nietzsche's "heroes" of thought, namely, Heraclitus, Empedocles, Spinoza, and Goethe.[1] He does not elaborate, not even on the proximity of Heraclitus to Empedocles in this list. Nor does he elaborate on the strange absence, or presence-in-absence, of Empedocles in Nietzsche's 1873 *Philosophy in the Tragic Age of the Greeks*. In that text, which Nietzsche hoped would be a publication to follow his *Birth of Tragedy from the Spirit of Music*, it becomes clear that Heraclitus is Nietzsche's incomparable hero of thought. Empedocles, by contrast, receives only a handful of mentions—not because he is insignificant, however, but because Nietzsche is simultaneously working on a tragic drama that will have Empedocles as its hero. Not only that, but some twelve years later, when Nietzsche is composing *Thus Spoke Zarathustra*, many of his notes on a possible Empedocles drama return to haunt him. Particularly important for Nietzsche is Empedocles's intended death by suicide, as an *affirmative* suicide, that is, as testimony to the thought of eternal return. However, Nietzsche is never able to write that part of *Zarathustra*; the death of his hero will be *postponed* indefinitely.[2]

Let me present only two of the many plans for Nietzsche's tragic drama, the first from the period 1870-72, when Empedocles is uppermost in his mind, the second from 1883, as he is sketching out what appears to be a Zarathustran drama for the proposed fourth part of the work. Here is one of the many Empedocles plans:

> Greek memorial festival. Signs of collapse. Outbreak of plague. The Homeric rhapsode. Empedocles appears as a god in order to heal.
> Infection with fear and pity. Antidote: tragedy. When one of the minor characters dies, the heroine tries to go to him. Empedocles, enflamed, holds her back; she grows ardent for him. Empedocles shudders before the face of nature.
> The plague spreads.
> Final day of the festival—sacrifice of Pan on Etna. Empedocles puts him to the test and reduces him to ruins. The people flee. The heroine remains. In an excess of pity, Empedocles wants to die. He leaps into the breach, only managing to shout, "Flee!"—She: Empedocles! and then she follows him. An animal rescues itself near them. Lava surrounds them. (8[30] 1870-72; KSA 7: 233-34; cf. 233-37)

One could say a great deal about the reminiscences of, and differences from, the Empedocles plans of *Hölderlin* that we see in Nietzsche's

Empedocles sketches. But I will restrain myself. Let me merely present the first of those plans from a dozen years later in Nietzsche's life, as he is writing *Zarathustra*:

Plan for *Zarathustra* 4.

1. The victory procession, the plague-ridden city, the symbolic heap of ruins. 30[3]

2. Proclamations concerning the future: his pupils recount *their deeds*. 30

3. His final speeches, with auguries, interruptions, rainfall, death. 30

4. The group at his grave—the oath-takers—magnificent midday—full of *premonitions*, serene and *spine-tingling*. 30 (16[55] 1883; KSA 10: 518)

There can be no doubt that Heidegger knew (of) these materials. He served with Walter Otto and Hans Joachim Mette on the editorial committee that was preparing a new edition of Nietzsche's works in the mid-1930s, and Heidegger himself specialized in the *Nachlass*, the unpublished notes—among them these plans for an Empedoclean-Zarathustran drama. The upshot of these notes is that Empedocles is the figure that connects Nietzsche's fascination with the Greek beginnings with the hero of his magnum opus and its communication of the eternal recurrence of the same, so that this Empedoclean connection ought to have been crucial for Heidegger's reading of Nietzsche. There is some slight evidence in the lecture courses on Nietzsche that it was a theme, at least to the extent that Heidegger is aware of the continuity of Nietzsche's thought from his early focus on the Greeks to Zarathustra's thought of recurrence. Yet Heidegger merely touches here and there on such continuity, and never, as far as I know, with an explicit mention of Empedocles.

As for the connection between Nietzsche and Hölderlin's Empedocles, there is also no doubt that Heidegger knew of Nietzsche's extraordinary essay, written while still a pupil at Schulpforta, "A Letter to My Friend, in Which I Recommend That He Read My Favorite Poet," dated October 19, 1861. Nietzsche, who had just turned seventeen, seems to be chiding proleptically none other than Heidegger, whose readings of Hölderlin stress the late hymns and say very little about either *Hyperion* or *Der Tod des Empedokles*:

> And, by the bye, you seem to believe that he wrote no more than poems. Thus it is clear that you do not know his *Empedocles*, this extremely significant dramatic fragment, in whose melancholy tones resounds the future of the hapless poet, the living grave of years spent insane—yet not, as you believe, in turgid blather, but in the purest Sophoclean language and in an infinite plenitude of profound thoughts. . . .
>
> In the never-completed mourning-play *Empedocles*, the poet unfolds for us his own nature. Empedocles' death is a death resulting from divine pride and contempt for humankind, from a surfeit of the earth and a hunger for the gods. Whenever I read it in its entirety, this work in particular always shatters me; a divine height is achieved in this *Empedocles*. . . .
>
> You will surely forgive me if in my enthusiasm I have at times had recourse to hard words against you; I only wish—and this you must take as the purpose of my letter—that you be moved to acknowledge and to evaluate without prejudice this poet whose name the majority of his nation scarcely knows.
>
> Your friend,
>
> F. W. Nietzsche[4]

As we know, Nietzsche's German teacher at Schulpforta, Herr Koberstein, gave him a B– for the "Letter," and encouraged the boy to devote his energies to a "healthier" and "more German" poet. Heidegger would have given a much better grade, we may suppose, and he would have noted that there is in fact no more German poet than Hölderlin. Yet let us try to leave Nietzsche behind and ask what it is that Heidegger himself says about *Hölderlin's* Empedocles.

Let me begin with the best known of Heidegger's references to Hölderlin's mourning play, *The Death of Empedocles*: there are three of them, and they appear very close to one another in the fifth and final section of Heidegger's 1936 Rome lecture, "Hölderlin and the Essence of Poetry," now the second chapter of *Erläuterungen zu Hölderlins Dichtung*.[5] These three references occur as Heidegger is interpreting the lines from

Hölderlin's late poem *In lieblicher Bläue* that declare, "Full of merit, yet poetically dwells / The human being on this earth." The first reference is to lines 1716–17 of the first version: "The one / Through whom the spirit speaks must part betimes."[6] Heidegger follows young Nietzsche's intuition when he takes this departure of the ancient Greek magus to prefigure Hölderlin's own early "departure." The second reference is to Empedocles's being *hinausgeworfen*, "cast out" from the comforts of everyday life and exposed to that most dangerous of gifts, language. The third reference, perhaps the most enduring in its impact, shows Heidegger identifying himself with the leading female character of Hölderlin's play, Panthea, about whom we will have to inquire. For the moment, Heidegger affirms her words, "To be him, that is life, and / We others are the dream of life" (ll. 102-03 of the first version; DE 41). For Heidegger, of course, that dream is "the actual," "the efficacious," or "the real," *das Wirkliche*, namely, the act of thinking the essence of poetry.

These are the three most famous references to Hölderlin's Empedocles. Yet they do not tell us much about either Heidegger's reading of the play or the significance of its hero for him.

In 1944 Heidegger says something that hints at the importance of Empedocles for both Nietzsche's entire career of thought and Hölderlin's late hymns, and what he says seems to me to be decisive: "Is it an accident that the two great solitaries whose work is shaping our own future, Hölderlin and Nietzsche, encountered in their solitude the figure of Empedocles, holding converse with him and trying to define themselves in their tasks by means of that dialogue" (75: 337). Apart from that rhetorical question, however, Heidegger's notes that appear under the rubric "On Hölderlin's *Empedocles*-Fragments" (75: 331–37) treat the theme of Hölderlin's "gods" without many references to the specifics of the mourning play itself. In general, Heidegger finds the *hymns* to be decisive, whereas the drama merely "intimates" and "searches for" the "grounding of the time-space of the truth of beyng."[7] An exception to this rule is the following brief sketch:

Empedocles

With the first words spoken by Panthea: the place where Empedocles is standing [*der Standort des Empedokles*]. Garden." . . . in the veiled / Penumbra, near the bubbling spring." Near the concealed origin. *Safeguarded.*—

Thus he is *seen*—his *image*—the first essential profile in which he shows himself.⁸

Empedocles is near the origin, at the beginning, safeguarding the earth. He is *seen*, even if in shadow, at the very *place* where essential poetry and essential thought meet.

I will return in a moment to the final pages of these notes from 1944, the most significant we have from Heidegger on Hölderlin's Empedocles. But I want to pause in order to observe something strange, namely, the fact that this is not the first time Heidegger focuses on the *female* personages of Hölderlin's play. Here it is Panthea who defines the *Ort* or "place" of the philosopher-poet. Arguably, Heidegger is always in search of this "place" of poetry, all the way to his *Er-ört-erung* or "placement" of Georg Trakl's singular unsung poem a decade later. Here, with Panthea, it is the woman whom Empedocles is said to have cured—Diogenes Laertius tells us the story—in a remarkable way. Given up for dead, the young woman had ceased breathing, her body already growing chill. Empedocles, discovering the last traces of warmth at the center of her torso, manages to spread that warmth over her entire body, restoring the woman to life. She recovers consciousness and from that moment on is an acolyte of her physician. There is even a suggestion—and Nietzsche makes this the center of *his* planned Empedocles drama—that she leaps into the crater of Etna with Empedocles. Hölderlin does not make this *Liebestod* a part of his mourning-play, but he does give Panthea an important role in the first version. And, if I am right, the roles of Panthea and Delia (or Rhea) are taken over by the figure of Manes in the third and final version of the play.

If we go back ten years from the 1944 notes, back to the very first Heidegger course on Hölderlin, "Hölderlin's Hymns, *Germanien* and *Der Rhein*,"⁹ we find three telling references to *Der Tod des Empedokles*, the second one a reference likewise to Panthea and Rhea (renamed Delia). In the first reference,¹⁰ Heidegger expatiates on one of Hölderlin's most important words, to wit, *Innigkeit*. Heidegger explicitly rejects the common understanding of *Innigkeit* as "*Innerlichkeit*," namely, some sort of "interiority." Rather, *Innigkeit* is somewhere between our words "intimacy" and "intensity." (It is perhaps telling that "an intimate intensity" and "an intense intimacy" are the most common meanings of the word in the popular phrase, *Ich liebe Dich heiss und innig*, "I love you ardently and *innig*." Only a Cartesian would take the word to mean interiority.) And this is where the magus of Acragas comes in, for the figure of Empedocles is marked by excessive *Innigkeit*, a surplus of intimacy and intensity, in Hölderlin's plans for his play. In the poem "Archipelagus," Hölderlin calls the Greeks *das innige Volk*, and Heidegger, going in search of *Innigkeit*, turns to the theoretical essays that Hölderlin wrote between the second and third versions of *Der Tod des Empedokles*. Heidegger cites the essay "The Basis of Empedocles," which contrasts tragic drama with the tragic ode: "What the tragic dramatic poem expresses is the most profound intensity" (DE 142). Heidegger does not announce his departure from Hölderlin here: he insists that the late hymns reflect the greatest intensity, whereas Hölderlin, by contrast, stresses here that *drama*, not the tragic ode, achieves the greatest intensity. For Heidegger, intensity has to do with "the relationship of an historical people to their gods."[11] Yet the *Innigkeit* stressed by Hölderlin is the *excessive intensity and singularity* of the tragic hero, Empedocles, caught up in struggles with the leaders of the city, with the gods of his youth, and even with his most fervent followers, Panthea and Pausanias. Empedocles hopes to resolve these struggles by making his suicide an affirmative act. The "strife" in question is that between "art" and "nature," or between the "organizational" and what Hölderlin calls "the aorgic," that which cannot be tamed or subdued, the excessive, the ecstatic. Allow me simply to say, if only by way of capitulation, that Hölderlin's theory of tragic dramatic art is one of the most difficult themes in all of Hölderlin studies. Heidegger does not enter into it, as far as I can see, and so I will reluctantly move on.[12]

The second reference to *The Death of Empedocles* comes much later in Heidegger's early lecture course.[13] Here too Heidegger chooses a scene with the women to indicate what it means for a poet to institute or found (*stiften*) beyng for a historical people. "The two priestesses of the Vesta," writes Heidegger, "Panthea and Rhea, enter the garden of Empedocles in Agrigent, on the island of Sicily, his homeland, and they enter into a dialogue concerning Empedocles the thinker and poet." Heidegger then presents the following extract, which contains the "dream of life" reference we heard earlier on:

Panthea

I follow traces that he leaves—what, beyond him,
Is there for me to follow? ah! and if I've grasped him,
What's that? To be him, that is life, and
We others are the dream of life.—

His friend Pausanias has also told me much
About him—the young man sees him
Day in, day out, and Jove's eagle is
Not prouder than Pausanias—this I do believe!

Rhea

I find no fault, dear love, in what you say,
And yet my soul mourns wondrously
About all this; I want to be like you,
And then again I don't. Do all of you on
The island act like this? We too take
Our pleasure in great men, and one of them
Is now the very sun to every Athenian woman,
Sophocles! to him among all mortals first of all
The most resplendent nature of young womanhood
Appeared and granted him a pure memorial of itself
Within his soul—
every woman wishes she could be a thought of this
Amazing man, and every one of us would gladly save
The ever lovely beauty of her youth before it wilts
Depositing that beauty in the poet's soul
And each inquires and riddles as to which of the city's
Young women that tender earnest heroine may be
Who hovered there before his soul, the one he calls
Antigone; and all grows bright
About our brows when this friend of gods
On cheerful festive days enters the theater;
Yet our delight is free from trouble
And never does our loving heart lose itself
As yours does, captive to a painful worship—
(DE 41).

Heidegger says no more about this scene, which is full of tension between the Athenian Rhea (or Delia) and the Agrigentian Panthea, but he immediately takes up the reference to Sophocles, who is so important for his reading of Hölderlin's hymns, especially because of the second choral ode of *Antigone*. Yet in bypassing Empedocles, who is on the verge of Etna, Heidegger bypasses the theme of being unto death—in which one would have expected him to show considerable interest.

The third and last reference to *The Death of Empedocles* in the 1934–35 lecture course is perhaps the least telling of the three, since Hölderlin's mourning-play, according to Heidegger, is still in search of (but not yet in the full presence of) *Innigkeit*. Hölderlin's own struggle, according to Heidegger, has as its goal "to establish a new beginning for the poetry of our people," *um der Dichtung unseres Volkes einen neuen Anfang zu setzen*.[14] I once heard it said, by someone who knew quite well Hölderlin's hymns after his "return to the fatherland," that the word *Volk* in Hölderlin's mouth means the folks in the immediate neighborhood of Stuttgart. *Germanien* is a kind of suburb of Tübingen, or perhaps the countryside along the Neckar flowing south to Horb. I myself have argued that if Hölderlin's poetry is a decisive "test" for the German people, that test consists in their becoming more French—in the sense of the Revolutionary Girondists Hölderlin encountered in Bordeaux.[15]

It is noteworthy that Heidegger nowhere cites the *third* version of Hölderlin's play, where, arguably, the extraordinary diction of Hölderlin's late hymns is already heard—yet not as an institution of beyng and not as the decisive new beginning of poetry for a historical *Volk* that is ripe for *decision*. Rather, the third version, with the conflict between Manes and Empedocles at center stage, ends with the raveling and dissolution of Empedocles's resolve to end his life. Arguably, the language of this extraordinary version achieves the greatest and most intimate intensity through the *failure* of national identity and the *impossibility* of the affirmative decision to perform the tragic deed.

Since a reference to Bordeaux has only now fallen, one has to concede that Heidegger's commentary on Hölderlin's *Andenken*, "Remembrance," heads precisely in that same direction. And Empedocles is met along the way. Heidegger reverts to a theme he had raised in his very first Hölderlin course, namely, that passage in "The Basis of Empedocles" in which Hölderlin writes about the need for the tragic poet to deny or renounce (*verleugnen*) his or her own person and situation, projecting all of that into "the foreign" in order to see what the drama is essentially about, namely, the struggle between the individual and destiny. Oddly, the context in Heidegger's *Andenken* course is Hölderlin's reference to *die braunen Frauen*, "the brown women." Heidegger takes these to be the women of ancient Greece, whereas they may well be the African women who are in Bordeaux because of the notorious slave trade: slavers arriving from the coasts of Africa often stopped for supplies at Bordeaux before continuing on to the West Indies and the southern states of the United States. Over many decades, a large African population developed in and around the port city. Much could be said about that, and about the impression the "brown women" made on Hölderlin, but this is not the place for such a discussion.[16]

In any case, a more specific reference to Empedocles comes later in the course, when Heidegger cites some lines by Hölderlin's hero, who in this first version of the play is on the very verge of his leap:

Am Scheidetag weissagt unser Geist,
Und wahres reden, die nicht wiederkehren.
(CHV 1: 823) [17]

The day on which we part, our spirit augurs all,
And they tell true who never will recur.
(DE 93)

Heidegger interprets these lines, not in terms of Empedocles's impending suicide but as a positively thought withdrawal from beings (*das Seiende*) and the preservation of a thought of being (*das Sein*): withdrawal and sheltering (*Verbergung*) allow beings to be "more in being" (*seiender*) than every metaphysics of "causation."[18]

In the 1942 *Ister* course, we find a shortened form of the speech by Rhea (or Delia) that invokes Sophocles, who becomes very important for this course, as he did for Heidegger's *Introduction to Metaphysics* in 1935. And thus the circle closes on Heidegger's references to Hölderlin's *Death of Empedocles*.[19]

However, I promised several pages back to return to Heidegger's remarks in 1944 on Hölderlin's *Death of Empedocles*. Allow me to do so in all brevity, simply by citing what I take to be Heidegger's principal theses. In at least two of these sketches,[20] Heidegger explicitly refers to *both* the mourning-play *and* the late hymns as sources for his "incipient thinking" of *Ereignis*, or the "appropriative event." His language, in what follows, is that convoluted and even contorted and stilted language that is familiar to readers of the *Black Notebooks* from the late 1930s and the 1940s:

Hölderlin's position in the history of beyng is thus experienced in the particularity of his poetic realm, which is founding in a proleptic way [*vorausstiftenden Dichtertums*], poetically grounding as it does the other beginning of our history.

But *Empedocles* is the thinker from the midpoint of the first beginning, in whose figure Hölderlin proleptically poetizes the thinker of the other beginning, and in the hymns he grounds the space for this thinker. The figure of this thinker must be made visible by a disclosive return to Da-sein, in which the thinker—grounding Da-sein—is himself grounded and which he—not only as a "thinker" in the narrower sense—insistently examines. Only from the opening of such Dasein must a view into the beyng of beings as a whole be possible, a beyng whose truth is grounded in that Dasein.

Working on the notes to the versions of the *Empedocles* should get us underway in this direction. Such work does not wish to be *the* interpretation of this poetry; it belongs entirely and solely to preparing the other beginning and it claims no "literary-critical" correctness and validity. It stands and falls with the question of beyng that is developed in "the appropriative event."

•

Hölderlin's Empedocles

If one were able actually to place Hölderlin's Empedocles in the space Hölderlin demands and articulates for it, and to ground it—historically—then one would succeed, moving farther into the future, in achieving what it was that Nietzsche wildly, compulsively, and in a discordant way sought in his *Zarathustra*—the figure of the poet and thinker who finds and inheres in the place where it can be decided whether the gods and God—inconceivably distant and remote—are moving toward us or away from us. We need these figures that inhere in such a place, as the locality of supreme decision. And therefore we must once again—as remote as we are from all this—bring before our inner eye the essence of these beings who are in-between [*das Wesen dieser Zwischenwesen*].

•

The tragic character of the one who knows . . .

Heidegger's interrogation ("Is it an accident that the two great solitaries. . ."), with which we began, follows this reference to the tragic knower. And, finally, we have another two book-pages[21] that are devoted to quotations from or references to Nietzsche's *Zarathustra* and Hölderlin's poems, among them "Nature and Art or Saturn and Jupiter."

However, I can sense my readers' impatience. In this volume on Heidegger and the *Greek* classics, why all this fuss about Hölderlin and Nietzsche, "classics" themselves, but even so? Does Heidegger not take up the fragments of Empedocles directly? Is there nothing in those fragments for a thinker of beyng and Da-sein? It seems certain that both Nietzsche and Hölderlin had access to at least some of the fragments of Empedocles, and that their plans for and versions of a tragic drama on Empedocles were informed at least to some degree by the fragments themselves. Because Heidegger, as far as I can see, never cites the fragments of Empedocles, it is impossible to tell what he may have known of them or thought about them. Yet in a recent book I speculate that a number of the fragments certainly should have gripped him.[22]

In what follows I cite a number of fragments from the Diels-Kranz collection of Presocratic fragments that I believe ought to have fascinated and inspired Heidegger.[23] Let me begin with a fragment that is reminiscent of Parmenides's ἐὸν ἔμμεναι, which occupies Heidegger during the entire second half of his 1951–52 lecture course, *Was heisst Denken?* This fragment from Empedocles (DK B106), in the Kirk, Raven, and Schofield rendering, reads: πρὸς παρεὸν γὰρ μῆτις ἀέξεται ἀνθρώποισιν, "Men's wit grows according as they encounter what is present" (KRS 311).[24] Yet it takes only a bit of "tweaking" to understand the fragment in such a way that it means precisely what Heidegger takes Parmenides to be saying: μῆτις is not "wit" or "cleverness" but fateful and skillful *thinking* itself, which responds to the goddess; παρεόν becomes not merely what is present, *das Seiende-im-Ganzen*, but the *presencing* and accompanying *absencing* by which beings come into the open and withdraw into concealment. If that translation of παρεόν is admissible, the fragment summarizes quite capably the effort of Heidegger's later thinking of being.

Immediately prior to this fragment is DK B105, one of the most discussed and admired of Empedocles's fragments. According to this fragment, thinking transpires not in the head but in and around the heart, "which dwells in the sea of blood surging forth and back, / Where is especially what human beings call thought. / For the blood that flows about the human heart—this is thought [αἷμα γὰρ ἀνθρώποις περικάρδιόν ἐστι νόημα]." Heidegger's own way of saying this, or of *trying* to say this, is *in die Acht nehmen*, "taking heed." J. Glenn Gray and Fred D. Wieck, in their translation of *Was heisst Denken?*, render Heidegger's words as "taking to heart." The reference to "heart" may be merely an accident of translation on their part, yet the phrase is also reminiscent of Boris Pasternak's portrait of Doctor Zhivago, who, as a thoughtful human being, "took everything to heart." True, that may be a mere association or literary allusion, from out of the blue, as it were. However, if one recalls Aristotle's account of the soul, "which is in a way all things," one may say that the psyche—especially the blood-psyche of the ancient Greeks—is that saline solution that goes to meet all its blood relatives in the world of beings. And if this last is more than a "mere" metaphor, then the hematic mix of pericardial thinking has to do with Φιλία, and Love with the goddess Kypris Aphrodite, who lies concealed at the center of being—even if, as we will soon hear, mortal males most often fail to discern her, perhaps because of Νεῖκος, the Strife in which they are so often entangled.

Now, Heidegger calls this goddess Aletheia, and he finds her at the center of Parmenides's *Proem*. Yet for Parmenides too (DK B12–13), the goddess in question is none other than Kypris, so that Empedocles, in his most famous fragments, is indeed a faithful disciple of Parmenides. For example, in fragment 17:

> A twofold tale I shall tell: at one time they grew to be one
> Out of many, at another time they became many out of one.
> Double is the birth of mortal things and double their collapse.
> For the one is brought to birth and destroyed by the coming
>   together
> Of all things, the other is nurtured and disperses as they separate
> Again. And these things never cease their endless interchange,
> Now through Love all coming together into one,
> Now again each scattering by the hatred that is Strife.
> Insofar as they have learned to become one from many,
> And again, as the one falls apart and become many,
> Thus far do they come into being and have no steadfast life.
> Yet insofar as they never cease their continual ring dance
> They exist forever changeless in the cycle.
> (DK B17, ll. 1–13)

The ultimate paradox of Empedocles's "twofold tale," which may be duplicitous as well as duplex, is that everything changes, such that change endures forever. Empedocles signs his own name to this paradox: beings "have no *steadfast* life," οὔ σφισιν ἔμπεδος αἰών. Nothing is ἔμπεδος, and that pronouncement is signed, or countersigned, by "Empedocles." Everything is moved in the cycle of lovehate, which itself is forever unmoved, "changeless in the cycle," ἀκίνητοι. The fragment continues, elaborating on the twofold:

> I tell a twofold tale: at one time they became one out of many,
> At another they separated and became many out of one,
> Fire and water and earth and air up above;
> Off to the side, Strife; the whole well-harmonized,
> And in the center, Love, equal in breadth and in height;
> Look at her, think with your eyes, do not be abashed.
> You know her, she surges in the limbs of mortals;
> Thanks to her they think of love and do unifying deeds,
> Crying out her name: O Delight! O Aphrodite!
> As she spins there among the other elements, no
> Mortal male can recognize her. But you must follow
> The course of my words: they will not deceive you.

The duplicity of the twofold lies perhaps in Empedocles's reference to Ἀπάτη, the goddess or titaness Deceit, who is always associated with Kypris Aphrodite as her companion. Would it not be possible to think the possibility of deceit or deception as *Verborgenheit*, "concealment" in Heidegger's sense? And if one reverts to the "early" Heidegger, who thinks revealing and concealing in terms of "the nothing," "benumbment," and "anxiety," is not Empedocles the most anxious of the pre-Platonic philosophers? Is he not "under way" in the most drastic sense? Fragment DK B115:

> There is an oracle of Necessity, ancient decree of the gods,
> Eternal and sealed with broad oaths:
> When anyone sins and pollutes his own limbs with bloodshed,
> One who by his deep flaw makes false the oath he swore
> By the daimons whose portion is long life,
> For thrice ten thousand years he wanders apart from the blessed,
> Being born throughout that time in all manner of mortal forms,

> Exchanging one harsh path of life for another.
> The force of aither chases him into the sea,
> The sea spews him onto the floor of the earth,
> The earth casts him into the rays of the blazing sun,
> And the sun chases him back to the aither.
> Each receives him from the other, but all abhor him.
> Of these I too am now one, exiled from the gods, a fugitive,
> Having put my trust in raving Strife.

In the epoch that embraces the stretch of Heidegger's and our own lives, there can be no doubt that "raving Strife" is on the upsurge. For ours is the epoch of "the last god." Empedocles describes the rule of Love in the sphere—and the upsurgence of Strife—in the following way: when Love prevails and orders the sphere, all seems well, and harmony permeates the "rounded sphere celebrating its joyous solitude" (DK B27, ll. 22–23). Yet as Strife begins to attain supremacy in the sphere, Simplicius tells us, citing Empedocles's own words, a more erratic motion arises, "For one by one all the limbs of the god began to quiver [πελεμίζετο]" (DK B31, l. 15; KRS 295).

"The limbs of the god began to quiver." A strange notion. Hesiod uses the word πελεμίζω at least twice in his *Theogony* (ll. 458, 842), referring to the earth's trembling beneath Zeus's thunderbolts and his footfall. However, with Empedocles, according to Simplicius, it is the god himself who quivers or trembles—as Hölderlin imagines it centuries later in the third version of his *Death of Empedocles*. At first it is the philosopher of Acragas who trembles:

> When brother fled from brother, when lovers passed
> Each other by in ignorance, when fathers failed
> To recognize their sons, when human words no more
> Were understood, nor human laws, that was when
> The meaning of it all assailed me and I trembled:
> It was my nation's parting god!
> (DE 185; ll. 421–26)

Yet the philosopher's trembling, reminiscent of Zarathustra's "shudder" before the enormity of the thought of eternal return, is a response to the quaking and shivering of an apprehensive deity itself, as the ancient Egyptian priest Manes has already declared in that third and final version:

> The lord of time, grown apprehensive of his rule,
> Looms with glowering gaze above the consternation.
> His day extinguished, lightning bolts still flash, yet
> What flames on high is inflammation, nothing more;
> What strives from down below is savage discord.
> (DE 184; ll. 367–71)

When we hear Manes's cry, "What flames on high is inflammation, nothing more," how can we not be reminded of Heidegger's remarkable commentary on Georg Trakl's *Geist* as "flame," the flame of both good and evil, in "Die Sprache im Gedicht," along with Jacques Derrida's treatment of that flame in *De l'esprit*? When we think of Empedocles's four roots, and of the mortals being tossed from one element to the other as they fail to see Aphrodite at the center, tossed from sea to earth to sun to aither, how can we not be astonished by a fourfold that has purged itself of all false piety? When we perceive the shivering god of Empedocles, how can we not be reminded of Heidegger's *Beiträge zur Philosophie*, which cites the quivering, trembling, or shivering of the "last god"?[25]

This *Zittern des letzten Gottes* is one of the most insistent themes of the *Beiträge*, written in 1936–38, and it is surely one of the most bizarre themes of that text. It appears to be a relapse in Heidegger's thinking, the return to an onto-mytho-theo-logy he elsewhere—both in *Being and Time* and in "The Onto-Theo-Logical Constitution of Metaphysics"—resists and wishes to leave behind. Indeed, most interpreters of Heidegger, in my experience, are happy to ignore this quivering and trembling "last god." Among the most striking phrases in this work of 1936–38, which is nothing short of apocalyptic, is *die Erzitterung des Seyns*, "the trembling of beyng" itself, a phrase that appears over and over throughout the work. The phrase first appears in the *Beiträge* at GA 65: 4, 8, and 21, but it continues to reverberate—or to tremble—throughout the text, achieving its most significant force in what were meant to be the final sections of the work, namely, "The Futural Ones" and "The Last God."[26] Such quivering, shivering, or trembling of the last god is highly reminiscent of remarks by both Schelling and Nietzsche, and it has to do with both the "birthing" or "generating" (*Göttern*, surely connected with *gattern*) and the passage or passing-by (*Vorbeigang*) of the last god, who is caught in the net of spacetime, which is the network of the mortals.[27]

In conclusion, I cannot conceal the fact that as I was working through Nietzsche's and Hölderlin's Empedocles plans, once again confronting the political and erotic struggles that characterize both these tragic dramas, I could not suppress the thought that these struggles were recapitulated in Heidegger's very public political debacle of the 1930s, his having put his trust in raving Strife, and in his many merely private engagements with Kypris. I will not say that these entanglements are what caused him to take some distance on Empedocles himself and his remarkable fragments, but I can affirm, on the nod from Hölderlin and Nietzsche, that a reflection on Empedocles's thought and his fate would have nurtured Heidegger in an essential way. It would have encouraged him to set aside for a long moment his militant decisionism, his demand for a "grounding" and a "founding" of a "new beginning" for his "historical people." A pericardial thinking might have aided his lifelong effort to allow concealment to play a role in every revelation, every presencing.

Such a thinking would doubtless nurture us as well. For are we not ourselves fugitives and exiles in our troubled times? Do we not, with every passing day, sense that we are wandering "across the plains of Doom [Ἄτης ἂν λειμῶνα (DK B118)]"?

Notes

1. GA 55: 30.

2. In what follows I rely on my very first book, no longer in print, but available electronically. See Krell, *Postponements: Woman, Sensuality, and Death in Nietzsche* (Bloomington: Indiana University Press, 1986). The materials I present below appear in Friedrich Nietzsche, *Kritische Studienausgabe der Werke*, ed. Giorgio Colli and Mazzino Montinari, 15 vols. (Berlin and New York: Walter de Gruyter, 1980), cited as KSA with volume and page number.

3. The *Nachlass* editors have not speculated on the number 30, which appears after each of the four points. Surely not thirty pages, but surely more than thirty lines—a mystery.

4. Friedrich Nietzsche, *Jugendschriften 1861–1864*, 4 vols., ed. Hans Joachim Mette (Munich: Deutscher Taschenbuch Verlag, 1994, first published by C. H. Beck Verlag, 1933–40), 1:1–5.

5. Fourth, expanded edition (Frankfurt am Main: V. Klostermann, 1971), 44–45.

6. See Friedrich Hölderlin, *The Death of Empedocles: A Mourning-Play* (Albany: State University of New York Press, 2008), 96. I will refer to this translation as DE with page number in the body of my text.

7. GA 75: 335.

8. GA 75: 335.
9. GA 39.
10. GA 39: 116–18.
11. GA 39: 118.
12. Interested readers should examine DE 139–57 for these extremely dense essays by Hölderlin. I hope that my detailed commentary on them (DE 254–62), along with my "Analysis" of the entire Empedocles complex (DE 275–306), may provide some help.
13. GA 39: 215–16.
14. GA 39: 258.
15. Allow me to refer to Krell, *Struck by Apollo: Hölderlin's Journey to Bordeaux and Back and Beyond* (Albany: State University of New York [SUNY] Press, 2023). The book follows the trail of Hölderlin's journeys in 1801–2 from Nürtingen to Bordeaux and then back to Stuttgart, well over a thousand kilometers each way, some of it by foot, some by post-coach. *Struck by Apollo* stresses the importance of France for Hölderlin's late poetry and for his personal life.
16. See *Struck by Apollo*, 112 and 115–16.
17. That is, *Friedrich Hölderlin Sämtliche Werke und Briefe*, 3 vols., ed. Michael Knaupp (Munich: Carl Hanser Verlag, 1992). I will cite this work as CHV by volume and page.
18. GA 52: 100–101.
19. GA 53: 70; cf. GA 39: 215–16.
20. GA 75: 336–37.
21. GA 75: 338–39.
22. See Krell, *The Sea: A Philosophical Encounter* (London: Bloomsbury Academic, 2019), ch. 4, "Full of Gods," esp. 143–60, on which the following remarks are based.
23. Hermann Diels and Walther Kranz, *Die Fragmente der Vorsokratiker*, 6th ed., 3 vols. (Zürich: Weidmann, 1951); I cite this work as DK with fragment number.
24. That is, G. S. Kirk, J. E. Raven, and M. Schofield, *The Presocratic Philosophers: A Critical History with a Selection of Texts*, 2nd ed. (Cambridge, UK: Cambridge University Press, 1983).
25. GA 65. For Heidegger's reading of Trakl's "Grodek" and other poems, see his *Unterwegs zur Sprache* (Pfullingen: G. Neske Verlag, 1959), esp. 59–60. And for Derrida's remarkable response to spirit as flame, see *De l'esprit: Heidegger et la question* (Paris: Galilée, 1987) throughout but especially its final chapters.
26. The transcript prepared by Heidegger's brother Fritz ends with these two brief but powerful sections. Unfortunately, the editor of MHG 65 decided to place an earlier section, with whose "placement" Heidegger himself was admittedly dissatisfied, at the very end of the book, thus destroying the dynamics of the entire text.

27. See GA 65: 4, 8, 21, 59, 120, 158, and elsewhere. For the references to Schelling and Nietzsche, see Krell, *The Tragic Absolute: German Idealism and the Languishing of God* (Bloomington: Indiana University Press, 2005), 131n21.

Part 2
Heidegger and Plato

5

From Parmenides to Plato via Thucydides

On the Way to Metaphysics

Aaron Turner

Introduction

The development of Greek philosophy from Parmenides to Plato can be characterized to some extent as the gradual emergence of ancient metaphysics that laid the groundwork for Western thought. For Martin Heidegger, the fundamental consequence of this process is the essential transition of ἀλήθεια from truth-as-unconcealment to truth-as-correctness, which he lays out most explicitly in his 1931–32 lecture series, *Vom Wesen der Wahrheit: Zu Platons Höhlengleichnis und Theätet* (GA 34) and his 1942 essay, *Platons Lehre von der Wahrheit*.[1] It has frequently been claimed that Heidegger retracted the basic thesis of this lecture series in 1964, when he wrote, "Der natürliche Begriff von Wahrheit meint nicht Unverborgenheit, auch nicht in der Philosophie der Griechen."[2] Heidegger's apparent "retraction" of his *truth*-thesis was supposedly a response to both Paul Friedländer's opposition to Heidegger's interpretation of ἀλήθεια as "unconcealment" in his 1954 book, *Platon: Seinswahrheit und Lebenswirklichkeit*,[3] and Heribert Boeder's 1959 essay "Der frühgriechische Wortgebrauch von Logos und Aletheia," which argues that ἀλήθεια in epic poetry remained firmly grounded in human *Miteinandersein* (being-with-one-another) and its development emerged out of that context.[4] Indeed, in Joan Stambaugh's English translation of GA 64, she observes in a footnote that "this statement has profound implications for Heidegger's book *Platons Lehre von der Wahrheit*."[5] But was this really a retraction?

Taken on its own, it would certainly seem so. However, in the same chapter there are numerous remarks that suggest Heidegger remained convinced of his *truth*-thesis. Only a few paragraphs later, he asks: "Was heißt ratio, νοῦς, νοεῖν, Vernehmen? Was heißt Grund and Prinzip und gar Prinzip aller Prinzipien? Läßt sich dies jemals zureichend bestimmen, ohne daß wir die Ἀλήθεια griechisch als Unverborgenheit erfahren und sie dann, über das Griechische hinaus, als Lichtung des Sichverbergens denken?"[6] Likewise, a few pages earlier Heidegger entertains the notion of interrogating Aristotelian ἐνέργεια or Platonic ἰδέα in the context of a binding character of presence but then says, "Wir können diese seltsamerweise in der Philosophie stets unterlassenen Fragen nicht einmal fragen, solange wir nicht erfahren haben, was Parmenides erfahren mußte: die Ἀλήθεια, die Unverborgenheit."[7] Evidently, Heidegger had not entirely abandoned his *truth*-thesis. Remarkably, in the preface to the second edition of his *Plato* book published in 1969, Friedländer scales back his earlier definitive position on ἀλήθεια:

> This second edition of the introductory volume of my work on Plato does not differ basically from the first edition. Only chapter XI, "*Aletheia*, A Discussion with Martin Heidegger," has undergone substantial revision. My opposition to Heidegger's interpretation of the Platonic concept of truth remains unchanged. Yet, recent extensive analysis of the meaning of *alētheia* in the older literature has more clearly brought out the various early meanings of the concept. It has become clear that the aspect of unhiddenness most stressed by Heidegger was present very early, but so were the elements that later combined in Plato's lofty concept of *alētheia*.[8]

Despite both Friedländer's partial concession and the broader context of Heidegger's thesis in GA 14, the problem of Heidegger's interpretation of the transformation of ἀλήθεια in Greek thought that gave rise to metaphysical thought remains controversial.

One often overlooked element of this debate is the historical conditions that make possible the transformation of truth in Plato—if one does indeed take place. The space between Parmenides and Plato is more than a century. Over the course of this time, which constitutes most of the fifth century and the early fourth century, the Greek world underwent a significant intellectual shift. Heidegger rarely, if ever, remarks on the nature of this intellectual shift and yet the ground of this shift is key to understanding the relationship between Parmenides and Plato. Of course, it is not only Parmenides that Heidegger engages with in his attempt to determine the originary Greek notion of truth. From 1932 onward, Heidegger begins to identify an essential relationship between Parmenides, Heraclitus, and Anaximander, which ultimately allows Heidegger to understand the ontological character of early Greek thinking as a unity. But still, the historical conditions of the fifth century BC that instigated the radical reassessment of truth that Heidegger suggests Plato undertook in the fourth century is seldom explored in the *Gesamtausagabe*. This chapter seeks to illuminate the fundamental character of this intellectual shift through consideration of two texts, Thucydides's *History of the Peloponnesian War* and Hippocrates's *On the Sacred Disease*. It will be shown that, for Parmenides, Thucydides, and Plato, the emergence of metaphysics in ancient thought was a necessary countermeasure to the emerging systematization of δόξα (seeming).

The Emergence of the Ontological Difference

The possibility of the emergence of the ontological difference is a consequence of the earliest thinking about being in Western thought. Heidegger identifies the earliest explicit engagement with the question of being in the fragment of Anaximander, which reads: "Ἐξ ὧν δὲ ἡ γένεσίς ἐστι τοῖς οὖσι καὶ τὴν φθορὰν εἰς ταῦτα γίνεται κατὰ τὸ χρεών· διδόναι γὰρ αὐτὰ δίκην καὶ τίσιν ἀλλήλοις τῆς ἀδικίας κατὰ τὴν τοῦ χρόνου τάξιν." Heidegger's initial engagement with the Anaximander fragment in 1932 (GA 35) is illuminating but lacks the precision of his prolonged interpretation in 1942 (GA 78). Here, Heidegger translates the fragment: "Aus welchem her aber das Entstehen sich bringt den jeweiligen Anwesenden auch sogar das Entgehen zu diesem hin (als dem Selben) entsteht füglich dem Brauch; gehören lassen nämlich sie (die Jeweiligen) Fug (dem Brauch) darum auch Ruch einander (aus der Verwindung) des Un-Fugs füglich der als der Erweilnis fügenden Zu- und Einweisung."[9] According to Heidegger, Anaximander is the first to grasp being—that which is (*das Seiende*)—as presencing.

The notion of the ontological difference, though never acknowledged or addressed explicitly, emerges through Parmenides. Against the emerging threat of Sophistry, Parmenides attempts to elevate ἀλήθεια beyond the reach of δόξα. While the problem of δόξα as a mode of ἀληθεύειν goes back at least as far as Thales (DL: 1.1.35), it was not until Parmenides that the philosophical distinction between ἀλήθεια and δόξα was explicated. In Parmenides's poem, the goddess Ἀλήθεια initially alludes to two ways of questioning (ὁδοὶ διζήσιος). On the First Way, the δίζησις concerns ὅπως ἔστιν, the "how it is" of "what-is" (Being—ἐόντα) (DK 28 B2 1–2). The Second Way, the goddess warns, is impassable to humans. This δίζησις concerns that which could not possibly be—ὡς χρεών ἐστι μὴ εἶναι—non-Being, in relation to what-is, whereby all Being remains necessarily absent. In non-Being, there is no persuasion toward nothingness and nothing is disclosed or produced (οὐ γὰρ ἀνυστόν) from inquiries into what-is-not (DK 28 B2, 5–8). In the poem, the goddess proceeds to guide Parmenides toward a mode of disclosive questioning that allows the truth of what-is to manifest itself.

Later in the poem, the goddess Ἀλήθεια reveals to Parmenides the perils of a Third Way, the way of δόξα. The way of δόξα is the way that unknowledgeable humans (εἰδότες οὐδέν) generally proceed, which they forge for themselves (πλάττουαι), their heads at once here and at once there (δίκρανοι) (DK 28 B6, 4–6). Humans do not lack νόος, the capacity to apprehend, but along this Third Way a waylessness (ἀμηχανίη) sets in that disorientates their alignment (ἰθύνειν) and, led by an ignorance of the way, produces errancy.

The poem does not produce a means to traverse the First Way—this way is untraversable for humans—but provides an orientation for humans already underway on the Third Way to look out for the signs, the σήματα, of the First Way in order to interrogate and disclose the ground of δόξα (DK 28 B8, 55). As the goddess concludes,

> τόν σοι ἐγὼ διάκοσμον ἐοικότα πάντα φατίζω,
> ὡς οὐ μή ποτέ τίς σε βροτῶν γνώμη παρελάσσῃ (DK 28 B8, 60–61).[10]

Parmenides represents a significant rupture in the development of Greek thought. Where the Milesians (Thales, Anaximander, Anaximenes) enquired into the γένεσις and φθορά, the emerging and passing away, of τὰ ὄντα (what-is), Parmenides elevated τὸ ὄν (Being) beyond the temporal and existential parameters of his predecessors. Why? Charles Kahn asks: "What problems did Parmenides inherit from his predecessors to which his own doctrine of "Being" might be a response?"[11] Rather, it should be argued that Parmenides is not responding to the problems beset by his predecessors but rather those introduced by his successors: the Sophists. Classical scholarship has long characterized Parmenides as an exponent of the so-called Pre-socratic tradition of natural philosophy. By casting Parmenides in this light, the significance of the fundamental relation of ἀλήθεια and δόξα within the Poem is obscured.

Anaxagoras's immediate concern was dispelling the Milesian notion of emergence and withdrawal: "τὸ δὲ γίνεσθαι καὶ ἀπόλλυσθαι οὐκ ὀρθῶς νομίζουσιν οἱ Ἕλληνες· οὐδὲν γὰρ χρῆμα γίνεται οὐδέ ἀπόλλυται, ἀλλ' ἀπὸ ἐόντων χρημάτων συμμίσγεταί τε καὶ διακρίνεται. Καὶ οὕτως ἂν ὀρθῶς καλοῖεν τό τε γίνεσθαι συμμίσγεσθαι καὶ τὸ ἀπόλλυσθαι διακρίνεσθαι" (DK 59 B17).[12] Likewise, Empedocles:

οἱ δ' ὅ τι κεν κατὰ φῶτα μιγὲν φῶς αἰθέρος ἵκῃ
ἢ κατὰ θηρῶν ἀγροτέρων γένος ἢ κατὰ θάμνων
ἠὲ κατ' οἰωνῶν, τότε μὲν τὸν . . . γενέσθαι·
εὖτε δ' ἀποκρινθῶσι, τὸ δ' αὖ δυσδαίμονα πότμον
εἰκαίως καλέουσι νόμῳ δ' ἐπίφημι καὶ αὐτός. (DK 31 B9)[13]

In positing the μῖξις and διάλλαξις/ἀποκρίνω of being, both Anaxagoras and Empedocles sought to overcome the Milesian duality of γένεσις and φθορά/ὄλεθρος. It is often suggested that in developing this thesis of μῖξις and διάλλαξις/ἀποκρίνω that Anaxagoras and Empedocles are presenting a solution to the problem of Parmenidean τὸ ἐόν, which denied the possibility of γένεσις and φθορά/ὄλεθρος. As Furley writes: "Both philosophers accept this conclusion but argue that physical change can nevertheless be described without writing contradictions or nonsense, so long as it is interpreted as the 'mingling together' and 'coming apart' of 'things that are' before, during and after the change."[14] Anaxagoras, though, initiates a fundamental shift in Greek thought by introducing a principle of reason into his cosmology.

For Anaxagoras, lying at the foundation of κόσμος exists νοῦς, which replaces Parmenides's τὸ ἐόν and brings κόσμος into τάξις, good arrangement. Anaxagoras is seemingly drawing on Heraclitus's notion of Λόγος, which, as τὸ Ἕν, is the gathering-together of τὰ ἐόντα, which reveals ἀλήθεια, if only humans could attune themselves to what Λόγος says: "(τοῦ δὲ) λόγου τοῦδ' ἐόντος ἀεὶ ἀξύνετοι γίνονται ἄνθρωποι καὶ πρόσθεν ἢ ἀκοῦσαι καὶ ἀκούσαντες τὸ πρῶτον· γινομένων γὰρ (πάντων) κατὰ τὸν λόγον τόνδε ἀπείροισιν ἐοίκασι, πειρώμενοι καὶ ἐπέων καὶ ἔργων τοιούτων, ὁκοίων ἐγὼ διηγεῦμαι κατὰ φύσιν διαιρέων ἕκαστον καὶ φράζων ὅκως ἔχει. τοὺς δὲ ἄλλους ἀνθρώπους λανθάνει ὁκόσα ἐγερθέντες ποιοῦσιν, ὅκωσπερ ὁκόσα εὕδοντες ἐπιλανθάνονται" (DK 22 B1).[15] See as well: "τοῦ λόγου δ' ἐόντος ξυνοῦ ζώουσιν οἱ πολλοὶ ὡς ἰδίαν ἔχοντες φρόνησιν" (DK 22 B2).[16] As the gathering-together of what-is, Heraclitus does not conceive of Λόγος in any causal sense. Like Parmenides's τὸ ἐόν, Λόγος is the letting-appear of τὰ ἐόντα, toward which humans must orient themselves.

Anaxagoras's fundamental contribution to the development of Greek thought is the disjunction of νοῦς from τὰ ἐόντα. "πάντα χρήματα ἦν ὁμοῦ· εἶτα νοῦς ἐλθὼν αὐτὰ διεκόσμησε" (DL. 2.3.6).[17] For Anaxagoras, νοῦς is a distinct property that perdures outside of τὰ ἐόντα and initiates the process of μῖξις and διάλλαξις. It is precisely in this regard that Anaxagoras misunderstands Parmenides, specifically the notion that γὰρ αὐτὸ νοεῖν ἐστίν τε καὶ εἶναι (For thinking and Being are the same).[18] For Anaxagoras, the limit of human νοεῖν is αἴσθησις (perception).

If Anaxagoras is the first to misappropriate Parmenides's distinction of the ontological difference, then Leucippus is the second. According to Diogenes Laertius, Leucippus was a student of Zeno (DL. 9.30), who was himself educated under Parmenides. Along with his student, Democritus, Leucippus initiated the philosophy of "atomism," which would later ground Epicureanism. Leucippus, preceding Leibniz, established the earliest notion of the principle of sufficient reason: "οὐδέν χρῆμα μάτην γίνεται, ἀλλὰ πάντα ἐκ Λόγου τε καὶ ὑπ' ἀνάγκης" (DK 67 B2).[19] Likewise, Democritus was singularly interested in establishing cause: "βούλεσθαι μᾶλλον μίαν εὑρεῖν αἰτιολογίαν ἢ τὴν Περσῶν οἱ βασιλείαν γενέσθαι."[20] For Democritus, who wrote more prolifically than Leucippus, the ground of cause is the nexus of το πλῆρες and τό κενόν, the full and the void, assigned respectively, ὄν and μὴ ον, being and nonbeing (so, for Democritus, even nonbeing *is*). Τό πλῆρες and τό κενόν order the relation of change in terms of ρυσμός (relation), διαθιγή (contact), and τροπή (turning). Thereby, το πλῆρες and τό κενόν are apprehended through three basic categories: σχῆμα, (configuration), τάξις, (order) and θέσις (position).

Like Anaxagoras and Empedocles, the Atomist position put forward by Leucippus and Democritus put severe limits on the capacity of human experience to infer the underlying nature of what-is. "νόμῳ ψυχρόν, νόμῳ θερμόν, ἐτεῇ δὲ ἄτομα καὶ κενόν": καὶ πάλιν, "ἐτεῇ δὲ οὐδὲν ἴδμεν· ἐν βυθῷ γὰρ ἡ ἀλήθεια" (DL. 9.11.72).[21] Democritus, then, differentiates between appearance and what-is, denying the possibility of human knowledge of the latter.

The Emergence of Sophistry

The emergence of the Sophists across Greece in the early fifth century coincided with the gradual rise of democracy within the Greek states. The possibilities that democratic institutions opened up for participation in community affairs necessitated the introduction of new modes of education, namely rhetoric. The educators were the Sophists. Public effectiveness was demonstrated most succinctly through rhetoric, but the Sophists also taught practical, political, and historical knowledge, as well as theoretical cognitions. Through imparting a mastery of λόγος, the art of διαλέγεσθαι (dialectic) materialized. The object of Sophistic διαλέγεσθαι was to view any state of affairs from various sides, not to absolutize one side, but to form δόξαι for oneself. Through the Sophists, the fundamental divisions of λόγος and ἔργον, φύσις and νόμος, and ἀλήθεια and δόξα were established and had a profound effect on the development of Greek thought throughout the fifth century.

The philosophy of Sophistry itself developed, much like the later philosophers of nature, Anaxagoras and Empedocles, in response to Parmenides and the aftermath of the establishment of the ontological difference. The earliest Sophist, Protagoras, developed a doctrine of truth that was considered by Plato and Aristotle to be directly opposed to Parmenidean "monism." For Protagoras: "πάντων χρημάτων μέτρον ἄνθρωπον εἶναι, τῶν μὲν ὄντων ὡς ἔστι, τῶν δὲ μὴ ὄντων, ὡς οὐκ ἔστιν" (*Theat.* 151e8–152a8).[22] Truth, then is not the unconcealment of τὸ ἐόν but is relative to the individual's own comportment to the world. Protagoras's concern for his pupils was a practical affair. He criticized both Prodicus and Hippias for teaching their students λογισμούς τε καὶ ἀστρονομίαν καὶ γεωμετρίαν καὶ μουσικήν (arithmetic, astronomy, geometry, and music) when εὐβουλία (good judgment) in one's own affairs and the affairs of the city was a much worthier lesson (*Prot.* 318e–319a).

Likewise Gorgias, who held likelihood (εἰκός) as a more useful resource than pure truth: "Τεισίαν δὲ Γοργίαν τε ἐάσομεν εὕδειν, οἳ πρὸ τῶν ἀληθῶν τὰ εἰκότα εἶδον ὡς τιμητέα μᾶλλον, τά τε αὖ σμικρὰ μεγάλα καὶ τὰ μεγάλα σμικρὰ φαίνεσθαι ποιοῦσιν διὰ ῥώμην λόγου" (Plato, *Phaedrus* 267A).[23] Gorgias was a pupil of Empedocles. While Empedocles "established" (κεκινηκέναι) rhetoric as a τέχνη of philosophical significance, Gorgias popularized it across the Greek world. Gorgias himself developed a philosophical doctrine that directly opposed Parmenidean τὸ ἐόν, entitled Περί τοῦ μὴ ὄντος ἢ Περίφύσεως (On non-Being, or, On Nature).[24] The fundamental principle of Gorgias's work is the notion that humans have recourse only to δόξα, rendering ἐπιστήμη redundant. For Gorgias, directly contradicting Parmenides, δόξα is the highest mode of ἀληθεύειν.

Greek thought in the fifth century, therefore, can be characterized as establishing the priority of δόξα over ἀλήθεια. Like Parmenides, whose ontological difference between Being and beings both confronted Sophistic δόξα and simultaneously set into relief the task of Sophistry, Plato, in the fourth century, confronts the challenge of δόξα as a mode ἀληθεύειν. Plato's establishment of metaphysics through the Theory of the Forms as an overcoming of Sophistic δόξα was the ground of Heidegger's work beginning in the 1930s. That being said, Heidegger seldom comments on the development of metaphysics during the fifth century. The remainder of this chapter will consider the role of Thucydides as a precursor to Plato's confrontation with Sophistry.

Thucydides and the ἀληθεστάτη πρόφασις

Thucydides began composing his historical narrative during the outbreak of the war in 431 and continued to write it until at least 404, when the war concluded. Thucydides himself was a product of the "intellectual revolution" of the late fifth century and is generally acknowledged as the "father of scientific historiography." His *History*, then, is fertile ground for excavating the seeds of metaphysical truth that germinate in Plato half a century later.

Like Parmenides, Thucydides is concerned above all with safekeeping truth, which can be discerned only through the ἐπιφανεστάτων σημείων (the clearest signs). He writes: "οὔτε ὡς ποιηταὶ ὑμνήκασι περὶ αὐτῶν ἐπὶ τὸ μεῖζον κοσμοῦντες μᾶλλον πιστεύων, οὔτε ὡς λογογράφοι ξυνέθεσαν ἐπὶ τὸ προσαγωγότερον τῇ ἀκροάσει ἢ ἀληθέστερον, ὄντα ἀνεξέλεγκτα καὶ τὰ πολλὰ ὑπὸ χρόνου αὐτῶν ἀπίστως ἐπὶ τὸ μυθῶδες ἐκνενικηκότα, ηὑρῆσθαι δὲ ἡγησάμενος ἐκ τῶν ἐπιφανεστάτων σημείων ὡς παλαιὰ εἶναι ἀποχρώντως" (Thuc. 1.22.1).[25] On account of Thucydides's rigorous historical methodology, his *History* is conceived of in modernity as the earliest example of scientific historiography. This primordial characterization of

Thucydides's work has served only to obscure the genuinely groundbreaking strides that Thucydides takes toward historical consciousness. Identified as merely a precursor to the scientific historiography that developed in the nineteenth century, and despite some tension in the twentieth century, Thucydides continues to predominate the philosophy of history in the twenty-first century. His status as the "father of scientific historiography" is little more than a nominal title that serves only to illustrate the immense "progress" that has been made since antiquity.

Of the origins and cause of the Peloponnesian War, Thucydides writes: "τὴν μὲν γὰρ ἀληθεστάτην πρόφασιν, ἀφανεστάτην δὲ λόγῳ, τοὺς Ἀθηναίους ἡγοῦμαι μεγάλους γιγνομένους καὶ φόβον παρέχοντας τοῖς Λακεδαιμονίοις ἀναγκάσαι ἐς τὸ πολεμεῖν: αἱ δ' ἐς τὸ φανερὸν λεγόμεναι αἰτίαι αἵδ' ἦσαν ἑκατέρων, ἀφ' ὧν λύσαντες τὰς σπονδὰς ἐς τὸν πόλεμον κατέστησαν" (Thuc. 1.23.6).[26] In this passage, Thucydides differentiates between two degrees of truth. He distinguishes the "truest cause" (ἀληθεστάτη πρόφασις), which emerges out of Athenian power and Spartan fear, from the "publicly alleged reasons" (αἱ δ' ἐς τὸ φανερὸν λεγόμεναι αἰτίαι), which he proceeds to explain in terms of the breakdown of political alliances. The aim of this chapter is to consider the essential relation of πρόφασις and αἰτία in this passage in order to understand Thucydides's historical notion of ἀλήθεία.

While the subject of Thucydides's rendering of ἀληθεστάτη πρόφασις in relation to the φανερὸν λεγόμεναι αἰτίαι has been widely discussed in modern scholarship, the general consensus is split between two prevailing interpretations. One is signified in the most common translation of ἀληθεστάτη πρόφασις as "true cause" or "real cause." In the original Greek ἀληθεστάτη means something like "truest" or, to be truer to its root etymology, "most unhidden." In English this is usually translated as "real" or "true." The "real" cause represents the "deeper" cause while the αἰτίαι belong to "surface" causes. Pelling distinguishes between the war's "underlying causes" and "the immediate occasion which precipitated the war." The former, he suggests, "makes it clear that there was a war waiting to happen" while the "'grounds and rifts' explain why it happened in 431 rather than 435 or 427."[27] Hornblower, likewise, stresses that ἀληθεστάτη πρόφασις must be understood as "'underlying cause,' as opposed to the 'reasons openly given out at the time.'" The distinction is one between "profound and superficial causes."[28]

The second interpretation of ἀληθεστάτη πρόφασις pertains to its status as a "precondition" of the war that enables the war to occur on account of the αἰτίαι. Rawlings, the progenitor of this alternative interpretation, argues that the use of πρόφασις at Thuc. 1.23.6 lacks any causal force at all, at least according to our own "modern scientific conception" of causation. He identifies its usage here according to its προ-φαίνω heritage together with its medical connotation which he translates as 'precondition.' ". . . πρόφασις was not a primary, sufficient, or necessary cause . . . Thucydides is simply doing a diagnosis of the illness that was the war: Corcyra and Potidaea were a precipitant of the conflict. They were not necessary causes or even sufficient causes they were altogether accidental; they were obvious to anyone; the war could have occurred without them; they precipitated the war, just as in 2.48.3 a prior illness precipitated the plague."[29] Rawlings' thesis finds support from Lebow, who concurs that "Thucydides was not suggesting that the rise to power of Athens was the truest cause of war, only that it was the most important precondition."[30] For Shanske, who produced a lengthy refutation of Rawlings' study, the translation of πρόφασις as 'precondition' is problematic because it omits "the core meaning of πρόφασις (namely, something specious)." Shanske is here invoking the original pre-technical meaning of πρόφασις and thus translates ἀληθεστάτη πρόφασις as the 'most revealing pretext.'[31] Likewise, Orwin suggests that "a more plausible rendition [of πρόφασις] is casus belli, that is, that issue or issues alleged as sufficient justification for resorting to war."[32]

Interpreting πρόφασις as 'pretext,' though, falters on three fronts. Firstly, as we suggested above, its clear contrast with αἰτία implies Thucydides is using it in a medical sense. Secondly, Thucydides states that the ἀληθεστάτη πρόφασις was ἀφανεστάτη δὲ λόγῳ (least apparent in speech). Presumably, though, for a pretext to be a pretext it needs to be spoken as a justification. And thirdly, the pretext is qualified by ἀληθεστάτη, and 'truest pretext' is an oxymoron.

While Rawlings' thesis that πρόφασις at 1.23.6 should be understood as 'precondition' has amassed support in subsequent scholarship, the significance of its grounding in contemporary medical terminology has not been so adequately developed. Thucydides's familiarity with medical science is generally recognized in his account of the plague in Book Two where he employs technical terminology to describe the symptoms.[33] Even the rigorous nature of Thucydides's historical methodology has often been attributed to the medical writers.[34] Concerning the problem of πρόφασις, though, and the nature of its relation to the αἰτία, surprisingly little attention has been directed toward its resolution since Rawlings.

Part of the issue lies in the various meanings that both terms represent across the Hippocratic corpus. That such inconsistencies exist between the medical writers is compounded by the fact that we are unable to accurately date medical documents, which means we are also unable to accurately determine the particular texts that Thucydides was drawing on. In general, owing to these pitfalls, modern scholarship is less inclined to attribute the ideas and particular word usages of specific texts to Thucydides. Instead, he is typically characterized as a "literary historian who has used Hippocratic ideas as they suit him and who has departed from them when they do not."[35]

Ἀληθεστάτη: The Truest Truth

In order to understand the distinction between the ἀληθεστάτη πρόφασις and the φανερὸν λεγόμεναι αἰτίαι, the significance of the latter will be made clear first. Immediately after his remarks on the causes of the war, Thucydides proceeds to recount the various events and disputes that, according to popular opinion, instigate the outbreak of the conflict between the Athenians and the Spartans. The term αἱ δ᾽ ἐς τὸ φανερὸν λεγόμεναι αἰτίαι is often translated as 'complaints made by either side' and, true to form, complaints comprise the majority of this account. The dispute over Epidamnus between the Corinthians and Corcyraeans is arbitrated by the Athenians, who must ally themselves with those who express the most persuasive appeal. The Corinthian appeal is founded on principles of justice and convention: "ὡς μὲν οὖν αὐτοί τε μετὰ προσηκόντων ἐγκλημάτων ἐρχόμεθα καὶ οἵδε βίαιοι καὶ πλεονέκται εἰσὶ δεδήλωται· ὡς δὲ οὐκ ἂν δικαίως αὐτοὺς δέχοισθε μαθεῖν χρή" (Thuc. 1.40.1).[36] Advantage, on the other hand, largely constitutes the appeal of the Corcyraeans. They suggest that, owing to the strength of their navy in light of the imminent conflict with the Spartans, the Athenians would benefit more from an alliance with Corcyra (Thuc. 1.33.2-2). Consequently, the Corinthians fought naval battles against the combined forces of the Corcyraeans and the Athenians and were soundly beaten. Thucydides writes: "αἰτία δὲ αὕτη πρώτη ἐγένετο τοῦ πολέμου τοῖς Κορινθίοις ἐς τοὺς Ἀθηναίους, ὅτι σφίσιν ἐν σπονδαῖς μετὰ Κερκυραίων ἐναυμάχουν" (Thuc. 1.55.2).[37] The principal complaint of the Corinthians, in terms of both the Athenian alliance with Corcyra and their conduct in breaking the treaty, is that the Athenians have acted unjustly.

The affair of Potidaea, which further still made the Corinthians hostile to Athens, resulted in a Corinthian appeal to Sparta designed to excite the Peloponnese states to declare war against Athens. Once again, the main thrust of the Corinthian speech is geared towards demonstrating the unjust activities of the Athenians. "ἵνα μὴ ἄνδρας τε φίλους καὶ ξυγγενεῖς τοῖς ἐχθίστοις προῆσθε καὶ ἡμᾶς τοὺς ἄλλους ἀθυμίᾳ πρὸς ἑτέραν τινὰ ξυμμαχίαν τρέψητε" (Thuc. 1.71.4).[38] Finally, the Spartan decision is made. Following speeches by Archidamus and Sthenelaidas, the Spartans commit to war. This series of events, broadly speaking, constitutes the αἰτίαι. Thucydides's exposition of the αἰτίαι immediately succeeds his decisive statement that the ἀληθεστάτη πρόφασις was Spartan fear of the growth of Athenian power and concludes with the same statement. He writes that "the Spartans were not so much swayed by the speech of their allies (οὐ τοσοῦτον τῶν ξυμμάχων πεισθέντες τοῖς λόγοις) but according to their own fear of the growth of Athenian power (ὅσον φοβούμενοι τοὺς Ἀθηναίους μὴ ἐπὶ μεῖζον δυνηθῶσιν)" (Thuc. 1.88.1).

The complaints that constitute the αἰτίαι pertain exclusively to νόμος. That is, they are grounded in argumentation that draws solely from those adventitious conventions and agreements that serve to organize and direct ἀνθρωπεία φύσις. Thucydides's criticism of the everyman's common-sense appeal to obviousness is the foundation of his characterization of the τὸ φανερὸν λεγόμεναι αἰτίαι. He is not saying that the αἰτίαι had no bearing on the outbreak of war, but that such attributions to νόμος lack the essential truth that his ἀληθεστάτη πρόφασις conveys. What, then, is the essential truth of ἀληθεστάτη πρόφασις?

If ἀληθεστάτη corresponds to ἀνθρωπεία φύσις in its opposition with νόμος then in what sense does it qualify πρόφασις? The controversy surrounding Thucydides's use of the term here is based on the question of whether he is using the term in its technical, medical context or in its traditional, pretechnical usage. What is more perplexing is that, given the further ambiguity surrounding the use of πρόφασις following its adoption by the medical writers in the fifth century, it is difficult to determine precisely what meaning Thucydides attaches to its employment in this crucial passage, meaning that even if we could ascribe to it with certainty its technical sense, the task of determining its precise function in this specific context represents a major problem. Across the Hippocratic corpus, πρόφασις encompasses a number of different meanings and, furthermore, without sufficient means of dating the production of these medical essays we have no clear way of knowing when the various meanings were established. As a result, attributing a specific meaning of πρόφασις to its employment at 1.23.6 is in danger of being both speculative and anachronistic.

The etymology of πρόφασις is itself ambiguous. Its construction could either stem from προ-φῆμι, meaning "spoken-forth," and so typical translations would include "pretext" or "reason given" or "justification." Alternatively, it could stem from προ-φαίνω, signifying a "showing-forth" of something. Whatever its etymology, since Homer πρόφασις has been employed to signify something deceptive, and so is often translated as 'pretext.' The assimilation of ordinary Greek words into the technical lexicon of the Presocratic, Sophistic, and Hippocratic writers, however, endowed words with new meanings and πρόφασις is one such candidate. According to Hankinson, "a πρόφασις is simply the ostensible reason or surface cause for [a disease], as contrasted with its full cause or complete reason (generally denoted in the Hippocratic corpus by the term αἴτιον)."[39] The use of πρόφασις, then, retains its specious quality, while αἴτιον serves to demonstrate the true cause. According to Galen, though, "Hippocrates uses the term πρόφασις of those things that are falsely called causes, as is the general custom, but he often applied it to evident causes, and sometimes to any kind of cause in general" (*On Hippocrates' 'Epidemics,'* 17 A 52). Across the Hippocratic corpus, πρόφασις could signify an ostensible or surface cause, a precipitating factor, or the full cause of a disease. The direct contrast between αἰτία and πρόφασις is a development attributable to the medical writers.

The distinction between αἰτία and πρόφασις in Hippocratic treatises and the distinction between ἀληθεστάτη πρόφασις and αἱ δ' ἐς τὸ φανερὸν λεγόμεναι αἰτίαι in Thucydides should give us just cause to assert that Thucydides *intends* the distinction to echo the medical division. If it is accepted, then, that Thucydides employs πρόφασις in its medical capacity, how then should it be delineated in light of the various meanings of the term across the Hippocratic corpus in order to identify its meaning in relation to the cause of the war? We find in one specific Hippocratic text, *On the Sacred Disease*, some considerable correlations between its content and Thucydides' narrative. Like Thucydides, the author of *On the Sacred Disease* is deeply critical of the everyman's 'common sense' predilection to obviousness. He writes: "ἴσως δὲ οὐχ οὕτως ἔχει ταῦτα, ἀλλ' ἄνθρωποι βίου δεόμενοι πολλὰ καὶ παντοῖα τεχνέονται καὶ ποικίλλουσιν ἔς τε τἆλλα πάντα καὶ ἐς τὴν νοῦσον ταύτην, ἑκάστῳ εἴδει τοῦ πάθεος θεῷ τὴν αἰτίην προστιθέντες."⁴⁰ This statement echoes Thucydides's observation at 1.20 that the everyman accepts as truth the evidence closest to hand (οὕτως ἀταλαίπωρος τοῖς πολλοῖς ἡ ζήτησις τῆς ἀληθείας, καὶ ἐπὶ τὰ ἑτοῖμα μᾶλλον τρέπονται). Both Thucydides and the Hippocratic author impress upon their readers the need for a more considered, diligent approach to ascertaining cause. Furthermore, Thucydides's description of the plague contains an expression that is remarkably close to an expression used in *On the Sacred Disease*. Where Thucydides speaks of the plague's indiscriminancy, he writes that it struck "without cause" (ἀπ' οὐδεμιᾶς προφάσεως) (Thuc. 2.49.2). Similarly, in *On the Sacred Disease*, when the author speaks of the cause of madness, he writes that it struck "without any apparent cause" (ἀπὸ μηδεμιῆς προφάσιος ἐμφανέος). Such similarities, of course, do not provide sufficient evidence that Thucydides was familiar with and influenced by a reading of *On the Sacred Disease*, but a path has opened up nonetheless that we are wont to tread.

How does the author of *On the Sacred Disease* conceive of αἰτία and πρόφασις and their relation? There are thirteen uses of αἴτια and its cognates in *On the Sacred Disease*. In most instances, it is employed in connection to certain misconceptions regarding causation. Responsibility in this way is usually attached to a deity (ὁ θεός, ὁ Ποσειδῶν, ὁ Ἄρης) or to those conjurors and charlatans (μάγοι καὶ ἀλαζόνες) that attributed the disease to the gods in the first place. What this attribution of αἰτία lacks is a *process*. The author of the treatise himself writes that "the brain is responsible for this affliction" (ἀλλὰ γὰρ αἴτιος ὁ ἐγκέφαλος τούτου τοῦ πάθεος). But the brain, as being responsible, does not act autonomously like the deity. Rather, the brain is receptive to a process that causes the onset of the disease. In the case of the present text: epilepsy.

The process is the πρόφασις. In this text, φύσις and πρόφασις are essentially related. As Hippocrates suggests, "φύσιν δὲ αὐτῇ καὶ πρόφασιν οἱ ἄνθρωποι ἐνόμισαν θεῖόν τι πρῆγμα εἶναι ὑπὸ ἀπειρίης καὶ θαυμασιότητος, ὅτι οὐδὲν ἔοικεν ἑτέρῃσι νούσοισιν."⁴¹ What does φύσις signify in the context of a disease? Across the Hippocratic corpus, φύσις means the natural constitution of human beings. The body is in a constant state of becoming. That φύσις is often associated with ἀρχή in reference to primal nature. The Hippocratic author of *Epidemics* (6.5.1) renders it: Νούσων φύσιες ἰητροί (The body's nature is the physician in disease).

If, in *On the Sacred Disease*, φύσις is the coming into being of the disease and the brain is responsible, what role does πρόφασις play? It was said that πρόφασις is process, so what underlies the process? It is asserted in the text that the sacred disease "attacks only those of a phlegmatic constitution, and does not attack the bilious" (SD: 3). For van der Eijk, πρόφασις means in this context only those external factors, such as the wind, rain, or sun, that triggers the disease: "The question remains why it is only these προφάσεις which are mentioned here in chapter 18, for it seems very improbable that they are more important as constitutive elements of the nature of the disease than the cause of the disease itself, the brain."[42] But πρόφασις is not solely indicative of these external elements. The πρόφασις of the disease as cause in bringing its φύσις into a state of becoming, is *the mingling of these external elements with the receptive factors already present in the body*, in this case, the phlegmatic constitution. In the case of epilepsy, according to our author, the disease triggers when the south wind changes the consistency of the brain and effects a build-up of phlegm which then brings about an epileptic seizure. The brain is identified as being responsible (αἴτιος) for the disease only in the sense that it is where the disease originates once the πρόφασις itself has taken place.

How does this interpretation of the relation between πρόφασις and αἰτία facilitate an interpretation of Thucydides's ἀληθεστάτη πρόφασις? The πρόφασις of the disease consists of two elements: the external factor and the inner constitution of the body. When the two elements are engaged, the disease comes into being. That is πρόφασις. For Thucydides, the ἀληθεστάτη πρόφασις of the war is the fundamental Spartan fear of the growth of Athenian power. But how does Thucydides demonstrate the truth of this statement?

The philosophical milieu out of which Thucydides emerges is a critical juncture in the development of Greek thought. It was illustrated earlier in this chapter that the rise of the Sophists during the fifth century occurred in part to the emergence of democracy across the Greek world and was fundamentally opposed to the alleged "monism" of Parmenides. Thucydides is a product of this crisis.

Thucydides is critical of sense perception in the determination of truth. For example, in anticipating future judgments of the present power of Athens and Sparta based on the physical remains of their respective cities, Thucydides predicts that, owing to its grandiose appearance, Athens would be conceived of as possessing twice its true power (διπλασίαν . . . τὴν δύναμιν), while the relative simplicity of Spartan architecture would produce the opposite effect (*Thuc.* 1.10.2). In his explication of his historical methodology, Thucydides again criticizes the gravitation to the "obviousness" of common sense when he suggests that "Men attach themselves to the evidence of their senses (τὰς ἀκοὰς τῶν προγεγενημένων) and accept uncritically (ἀβασανίστως) traditions of their own and other countries" (*Thuc.* 1.20.1). Such criticism immediately precedes the decisive statement at 1.23.6 concerning the ἀληθεστάτη πρόφασις and the αἱ δ' ἐς τὸ φανερὸν λεγόμεναι αἰτίαι.

Thucydides speaks of ἀνθρωπεία φύσις (Thuc. 3.84.2), which is typically translated as human nature, and also variably expressed in the narrative as τὸ ἀνθρώπινον (Thuc. 1.22.4) or φύσις ἀνθρώπων (Thuc. 3.82.2). The distinction between φύσις and νόμος is recognized by Heraclitus but becomes the foundation of the development of Sophistic thought. Like the Presocratics, Antiphon—a Sophist and contemporary of Thucydides—closely associates φύσις with ἀλήθεια.[43] In his tract, *On Truth*, φύσις, represented by ἀλήθεια, is prior to and superior over νόμος. Gagarin suggests that, for Antiphon, "φύσις is more real or truer than νόμος, or in other words, statements are true if and only if they correspond to φύσις, but not to νόμος." Justice (δίκη)—the core principle of νόμος—is, according to Antiphon, defined as "not transgressing the laws (νόμιμα) of the city in which one may happen to live." For Antiphon, the central aspect of φύσις is expediency or advantage.

For the dictates of the laws (τὰ τῶν νόμων) are adventitious, whereas the dictates of nature (τὰ τῆς φύσεως) are inescapable; dictates of the laws, based on agreement as they are, are not natural growths, whereas the dictates of nature, being natural growths, are not based on agreement . . . the whole reason for the examination of these things is the following: the majority of just causes, measured according to law, are inimical to nature (πολέμια τῆι φύσει) (DK 87 B44).[44]

Where the Sophists, though, conceive of φύσις and νόμος as absolute opposites, Heraclitus identifies a more reciprocal relation. In Fragment 114, he writes: τρέφονται γὰρ πάντες οἱ ἀνθρώπειοι νόμοι ὑπὸ ἑνὸς τοῦ θείου (For all human laws being cultivated according to the Divine one). While Thucydides was inevitably influenced by the Sophists, his understanding of the relation between φύσις and νόμος appears to be more in line with Heraclitus. What, then, is the nature of this relation?

For the Presocratics, φύσις could mean something like "the order of nature" in the same way that we conceive of the natural world. The English "nature," derived from the Latin *natura*, also denotes a thing's character, aspect, or kind. But φύσις also carries connotations of origin and growth. Cast into opposition with νόμος and transitioned into the realm of the human condition, φύσις undertakes a semantic shift. For the Sophists and for Thucydides, φύσις means the origin and growth of man as man *and* the character of man *distinct* from those man-made institutions. Thucydides demonstrates this distinction in his analysis of the revolution at Corcyra. "ξυνταραχθέντος τε τοῦ βίου ἐς τὸν καιρὸν τοῦτον τῇ πόλει καὶ τῶν νόμων κρατήσασα ἡ ἀνθρωπεία φύσις, εἰωθυῖα καὶ παρὰ τοὺς νόμους ἀδικεῖν, ἀσμένη ἐδήλωσεν ἀκρατὴς μὲν ὀργῆς οὖσα, κρείσσων δὲ τοῦ δικαίου, πολεμία δὲ τοῦ προύχοντος· οὐ γὰρ ἂν τοῦ τε ὁσίου τὸ τιμωρεῖσθαι προυτίθεσαν τοῦ τε μὴ ἀδικεῖν τὸ κερδαίνειν, ἐν ᾧ μὴ βλάπτουσαν ἰσχὺν εἶχε τὸ φθονεῖν" (*Thuc.* 3.84.2).[45] Like Antiphon, Thucydides characterizes man's φύσις as the enemy (πολέμος) of νόμος. Human nature lies beneath νόμος—it hides, in the Heraclitean sense— but political revolution (στάσις) lays bare the truth, the essential and primordial character, of man.

For Thucydides, νόμος develops from φύσις in order to restrain it but νόμος is at the same time a temporary configuration of ἀνθρωπεία φύσις that pertains to its essential character. Ἀνθρωπεία φύσις is the basic character of all human beings. If Thucydides's project is to comport his reader's understanding of the cause of the war from αἱ δ' ἐς τὸ φανερὸν λεγόμεναι αἰτίαι, grounded in νόμος, to his own ἀληθεστάτη πρόφασις, grounded in ἀνθρωπεία φύσις, then how does Thucydides delineate ἀνθρωπεία φύσις from νόμος? Thucydides recognizes that such an essence cannot be demonstrated by appealing to something immediately observable. Only through historical reflection can the enduring essence of man (τὸ ἀνθρώπινον) be revealed.

At the beginning of the *Archaeology*, Thucydides demonstrates the essential character of ἀνθρωπεία φύσις: "τῆς γὰρ ἐμπορίας οὐκ οὔσης, οὐδ' ἐπιμειγνύντες ἀδεῶς ἀλλήλοις οὔτε κατὰ γῆν οὔτε διὰ θαλάσσης, νεμόμενοί τε τὰ αὑτῶν ἕκαστοι ὅσον ἀποζῆν καὶ περιουσίαν χρημάτων οὐκ ἔχοντες οὐδὲ γῆν φυτεύοντες, ἄδηλον ὂν ὁπότε τις ἐπελθὼν καὶ ἀτειχίστων ἅμα ὄντων ἄλλος ἀφαιρήσεται, τῆς τε καθ' ἡμέραν ἀναγκαίου τροφῆς πανταχοῦ ἂν ἡγούμενοι ἐπικρατεῖν, οὐ χαλεπῶς ἀπανίσταντο, καὶ δι' αὐτὸ οὔτε μεγέθει πόλεων ἴσχυον οὔτε τῇ ἄλλῃ παρασκευῇ" (Thuc. 1.2.2).[46] Thucydides's ἀνθρωπεία φύσις is demonstrated in the mingling of its three core principles: acquiring power, maintaining power, and enhancing power. But in this environment the acquisition of power stagnates because the lack of security prohibits power's maintenance and enhancement. This pre-νόμος state is characterized by the absence of those institutions that are fundamental to human society: security from invaders, commerce, and agriculture.

The development of the *Archaeology* is the development of νόμος. Νόμος opposes and restrains ἀνθρωπεία φύσις in the constructing of social institutions and the establishing of agreements and conventions but such institutions and agreements are in themselves directed *toward* the goal of ἀνθρωπεία φύσις, toward the acquiring, maintaining, and enhancing of power. Through νόμος, power, in all its manifest forms—from the planting of the ground to the rise of naval empires—is given license to grow. Where νόμος displaces ἀνθρωπεία φύσις, it acts in its stead. While νόμος opposes and restrains ἀνθρωπεία φύσις it also *enables* it in its collective capacity to acquire, maintain, and enhance its own power (δύναμις) through the establishing of settlements and the building of walls. The object of νόμος is δύναμις and the substance of δύναμις is χρήματα. Through the accumulation of χρήματα, δύναμις increases. The *Archaeology*, then, charts the progress of the growth of δύναμις as it arises from both the restraint *and* the enabling of ἀνθρωπεία φύσις.

Farrar defines human nature in Thucydides as "the constant interaction of reason and desire."[47] Desire in the context of ἀνθρωπεία φύσις is always desire toward the acquiring, maintaining, and enhancing of δύναμις. What constitutes reason? In the above passage, Thucydides writes: τῆς γὰρ ἐμπορίας οὐκ οὔσης, οὐδ' ἐπιμειγνύντες ἀδεῶς ἀλλήλοις. The crucial term here, ἀδεῶς, meaning "without fear" is the primary factor prohibiting ἐμπορία and ἐπιμίγνυμι. Human beings *desire* resources but their fear of invasion *reasons* against the possibility of a sedentary, secure mode of living. Fundamental, then, to the development of νόμος is the negation of δέος (fear). Fear is one of the core foundations of reason in Thucydides. It is according to fear that walled settlements are established. Minos, likewise, recognizing the potential threat posed by piracy to his own revenues (τοῦ τὰς προσόδους μᾶλλον ἰέναι αὐτῷ), determined that it was necessary to eradicate the threat (Thuc. 1.4.1).

Fear is driven by the possibility of detriment and is therefore directed toward the maintenance of δύναμις, which in turn provides the platform for the enhancement of δύναμις. The suppression of fear in the *Archaeology* leads to the progression of society. Unconstrained by fear, the Athenians were among the first who laid aside their weapons and "adopted an easier and more luxurious way of life" (ἀνειμένῃ τῇ διαίτῃ ἐς τὸ τρυφερώτερον μετέστησαν—Thuc. 1.6.3). The emergence of tyranny occurred when rulers, having accrued significant wealth, employed caution (ἀσφάλεια) in their endeavors and neglected their obligations (ῥητὰ γέρα) to the community

(Thuc. 1.13.1; 1.17.1). The formation of the Delian and Peloponnesian Leagues following the Persian War occurs when smaller states, recognizing the potential threat of future Persian invasions, ally themselves with either Athens or Sparta (Thuc. 1.18.2–3). The fear, then, that necessitates the inception of νόμος is the same fear that necessitates συμμαχία. In the historical process of the essential character of ἀνθρωπεία φύσις, fear is the mediating factor that conjoins reason and desire.

Necessity (ἀνάγκη) is an intrinsic element of Thucydides's conception of ἀνθρωπεία φύσις. In fifth-century Greek thought, ἀνάγκη and φύσις are closely connected. For Parmenides, ἀνάγκη is the clasping-together of what-is (ἐόντα) in the constraint of its own limit (DK 28 B8.30). According to Schürmann, ἀνάγκη determines not things themselves but "their conjunction, their mutually belonging to one another, their interchange . . . necessity is a law governing not things or beings, but constellations of things and beings."[48] Transposed to the sphere of human reason, ἀνάγκη becomes embroiled in the νόμος-φύσις conflict. The Ἄδικος Λόγος in Aristophanes's *Clouds* equates ἀνάγκη and φύσις in order to justify one's adulterous and shameful conduct (1075). As Guthrie observes, "This association of necessity with nature is used as an argument by the opponents of νόμος, which they represent as an attempt to thwart natural forces that is rightly doomed to failure."[49] Antiphon, as we have seen, is one such critic of νόμος. His encouragement to act συμφερόντως in accordance with the precepts of φύσις is based on his conception of customs and laws as adventitious and products of agreement, while the laws of nature are ἀναγκαία (col. 1,23.2–3).

For Thucydides, ἀνάγκη retains its originary function of "clasping-together." As the force of necessity and constraint in human affairs, ἀνάγκη is the clasping together of reason and desire that constitutes ἀνθρωπεία φύσις. In turn, ἀνάγκη is regulated by fear, which grounds reason in its pursuit of desire. If ἀνθρωπεία φύσις, as the acquiring, maintaining, and enhancing of δύναμις, is the object of desire, then ἀνάγκη determines the measure of the interaction between the distinct elements of the threefold. It is according to ἀνάγκη, then, that in order to *acquire* δύναμις individuals form collectives and establish νόμος to govern its *maintenance*. The consequent *enhancing* of δύναμις is the accumulation of χρήματα that such an enterprise allows. In this way, ἀνάγκη is the ground of reason that compels the ἀνθρωπεία φύσις.

So, then, the truth of Thucydides's ἀληθεστάτη πρόφασις, which he identified as: "τοὺς Ἀθηναίους ἡγοῦμαι μεγάλους γιγνομένους καὶ φόβον παρέχοντας τοῖς Λακεδαιμονίοις ἀναγκάσαι ἐς τὸ πολεμεῖν." In identifying the truth of ἀληθεστάτη, Thucydides identifies in the Spartan decision to go to war (τὸ πολεμεῖν) the same concurrence of fear (φόβος) and necessity (ἀνάγκη) that directs the course of the *Archaeology*. In invoking fear and necessity, Thucydides elucidates the essential character of ἀνθρωπεία φύσις as *the acquiring, maintaining, and enhancing* of power. In their perception of τοὺς Ἀθηναίους μεγάλους γιγνομένους, the Spartans are necessitated to war (ἀναγκάσαι ἐς τὸ πολεμεῖν) because ἀνάγκη, acting under the directive of ἀνθρωπεία φύσις in the interest of maintaining its own δύναμις, demands it.

The πρόφασις of the war is the process of Athenian power, the external factor, exciting Spartan fear, the inner constitution. Spartan fear is grounded in Thucydides's idea of ἀνθρωπεία φύσις, in the maintenance of their own δύναμις that the Athenian growth of power (μεγάλους γιγνομένους) threatens. Ἀνθρωπεία φύσις, therefore, functions in the same way as the Hippocratic author of *On the Sacred Disease* conceives of the φύσις of a disease. The ἀληθεστάτη πρόφασις in its essential relation to ἀνθρωπεία φύσις is the process of the coming to presence of *the acquiring, maintaining, and enhancing* of power.

Conclusion

What I've shown in this chapter is the manner in which Heidegger's *truth*-thesis can be understood according to the historical conditions of the Greek "intellectual revolution" at the end of the fifth century BC. In the context of Plato's decisive confrontation with the Sophists, which fundamentally grounded his Theory of Forms that laid the foundations for Western metaphysics, Parmenides plays a crucial role. That Heidegger acknowledges this role is evident in the growing significance of Parmenides in the development of Heidegger's thought since at least 1922. What this chapter demonstrates is that Thucydides, drawing on the Hippocratic tradition, confronts Sophism in a much similar way. Thucydides himself emerges out of the Sophistic tradition and is clearly well-versed in the key debates of his day, particularly the division between φύσις and νόμος. Thucydides, though, transcends the division by grounding ἀλήθεια as fundamental ἀνθρωπεία φύσις while νόμος functions as the historical establishment of society through which ἀνθρωπεία φύσις as *the acquiring, maintaining, and enhancing* of power is directed toward the πόλις. In doing so, Thucydides structures his understanding of the Peloponnesian War on the foundation of the ἀλήθεια of ἀνθρωπεία φύσις which permits an explanation of the cause of the war in terms of fundamental human nature.

Notes

1. This essay was originally published in *Geistige Überlieferung, das zweite Jahrbuch* (Berlin: Helmut Küpper, 1942), 96–124. It was a revised version of an essay written in 1930/31, presumably a preamble to his lectures on Plato given in the Winter Semester of 1931/32 (GA 34).
2. "The natural concept of truth does not mean unconcealment, nor did it in the philosophy of the Greeks" (GA 14: 87).
3. Paul Friedländer, *Platon: Seinswahrheit und Lebenswirklichkeit* (Berlin: De Gruyter, 1954).
4. Heribert Boeder, "Der frühgriechische Wortgebrauch von Logos und Aletheia," *Archiv für Begriffsgeschichte: Bausteine zu einem Historischen Wörterbuch der Philosophie*, 4 (1959): 82–112.
5. OTB: 70.
6. "What does *ratio* mean, νοῦς, νοεῖν, perceiving? What does ground and principle and even the principle of all principles mean? Can this ever be adequately determined without us experiencing the Greek Ἀλήθεια as unconcealment and then thinking it, beyond the Greek, as openness of self-concealment?" (GA 14: 88).
7. GA 14: 85. "We cannot even ask these questions, strangely enough omitted in philosophy, until we have learned what Parmenides had to experience: Ἀλήθεια, unconcealment."
8. Paul Friedländer, *Plato: An Introduction*, 2nd ed. translated by Hans Meyerhoff (Princeton, NJ: Princeton University Press, 1969), p. vii.
9. GA 78: 203.
10. "I want to say completely how semblance is configured in the separate appearances. Thus (if you understand this) never will human opinion surpass you" (BWP: 142).
11. Charles Kahn, "The Thesis of Parmenides," *The Review of Metaphysics* 22, no. 4 (1969): 702.
12. "The Greeks do not think correctly about coming-to-be and passing-away; for no thing comes to be or passes away but is mixed together and dissociated from the things that are. And thus they would be correct to call coming-to-be mixing-together and passing-away dissociating."
13. "When they [sc. the four roots—earth, water, air, fire] are mingled together to form a man and so come to aether, or to form the race of wild beasts, or of plants, or of birds, then men speak of 'coming-to-be'; and when they come apart, then they speak of 'ill-fated death.' They are not right to call them so, but I myself comply with the customary belief."

14. David J. Furley, "Anaxagoras' Theory of Change: A Response to Parmenides," *The Society for Ancient Greek Philosophy Newsletter* (1975), 1. Cf. John Palmer: "By positing a plurality of such entities, Empedocles thought he could account for the phenomenal multiplicity and change Parmenides had allegedly felt compelled to deny. Thus on conventional views of Empedocles' response to Parmenides, Empedocles accepts his stricture against absolute genesis and destruction but accounts for the cosmos of change and plurality by transferring the attributes of Parmenidean Being to his own four elements or roots. Since these elements preserve the attributes of Parmenidean Being, there is no absolute coming to be or perishing"; See *Parmenides and Presocratic Philosophy* (Oxford: Oxford University Press, 2009), 272.

15. "Of the Λόγος being-forever do men prove to be uncomprehending, both before they hear and once they have heard it. For although all things happen according to this Λόγος, they are like the unexperienced experiencing words and deeds such as I explain when I distinguish each thing according to its nature and show how it is. Other men are unaware of what they do when they are awake just as they are forgetful of what they do when they are asleep."

16. "Although this Λόγος is common [to all], the many live as if they had a private understanding."

17. "All things were together; then came νοῦς and set them in order."

18. It has been argued that, in doing so, Anaxagoras fulfills the Parmenidean directive of establishing a "rational cosmology"; see Patricia Curd, *Anaxagoras of Clazomenae: Fragments and Testimonia* (Toronto: University of Toronto Press, 2007), 229. But there is no indication in the Poem of Parmenides that Being should be conceived of as a rational, causative entity.

19. "Nothing arises by chance; on the contrary, everything comes from definite foundations and by force of necessity."

20. "I would rather discover a single principle of reason than obtain the whole Persian Empire"; see Eusebius, *Preparation for the Gospel* 14.7.4 (68Bu8).

21. "Opinion/convention says hot or cold, but the reality is atoms and empty space," and again, "Of a truth we know nothing, for truth is in a well."

22. "The human being is the measure of all things: of beings, as they are, and of non-beings, as they are not.

23. "And shall we leave Gorgias and Tisias undisturbed, who saw that probabilities are more to be esteemed than truths, who make small things seem great and great things small."

24. It has been suggested that a "philosophical approach to Gorgias's On Not-Being exaggerates his intellectual sophistication and credits him with an uncharacteristic power of conceptualization." Gorgias "imitated" the philosophers, but what was really important to him was "rhetoric"; see George A. Kennedy, *Classical Rhetoric and Its Christian and Secular Tradition from Ancient to Modern Times* (Chapel Hill: University of North Carolina Press, 1980), 31. However,

Aristotle himself composed a work entitled Πρὸς τα Γοργίου (Against Gorgias), and it seems unlikely that Aristotle would engage with a simple babbler.

25. "[The reader] must not be misled by the exaggerated fancies of the poets, or by the tales of chroniclers who seek to please the ear rather than to speak the truth. Their accounts cannot be tested by him; and most of the facts in the lapse of ages have passed into the region of romance. At such a distance of time he must make up his mind to be satisfied with conclusions resting upon the clearest evidence which can be had."

26. "The truest cause, though the least apparent in speech, was the growing power of the Athenians and the fear that excited in the Spartans, necessitating them to war. The publicly alleged reasons set down by each side that contributed to the breaking of the treaty and the outbreak of war are as follows...."

27. Christopher Pelling, *Literary Texts and the Greek Historian* (London: Routledge, 1999), 87. Cf. Lionel Pearson "Prophasis and Aitia," *Transactions and Proceedings of the American Philological Association* 83 (1952): 217.

28. Simon Hornblower, *A Commentary on Thucydides Vol. 1* (Oxford: Oxford University Press, 1991), 65.

29. Hunter R. Rawlings III, *A Semantic Study of Prophasis to 400BC* (Hermes Einzelschriften, 1975), 78–97. Hornblower (1991, 65), on the other hand, suggests that "πρόφασις here, whatever its etymology . . . must mean 'underlying cause' as opposed to the 'reasons openly given out at the time.'" John Moles, "Narrative and Speech Problems in Thucydides Book I" in *Ancient Historiography and its Contexts: Studies in Honour of A. J. Woodman*, ed. Christina Kraus, John Marincola, and Christopher Pelling (Oxford: Oxford University Press, 2010), 15–39 argues that such a distinction between levels of causality is indicative of the Hippocratic contrast between αἴτια and πρόφασις. That being said, he observes that "the Hippocratics characteristically use the terms πρόφασις and αἴτια the other way round, and πρόφασις commonly means 'excuse.'" Thus, Thucydides is challenging the linguistic expectations both of medical language and of ordinary usage." Moles, though, is seemingly ignoring the multifaceted Hippocratic meaning of πρόφασις.

30. Richard Ned Lebow, *The Tragic Vision of Politics: Ethics, Interests and Orders* (Cambridge: Cambridge University Press, 2003), 108.

31. Darien Shanske, *Thucydides and the Philosophical Origins of History* (Cambridge: Cambridge University Press, 2006) 159.

32. Clifford Orwin, *The Humanity of Thucydides* (Princeton, NJ: Princeton University Press, 1994), 32–35.

33. Cf. D.L. Page, "Thucydides' Description of the Great Plague at Athens," *Classical Quarterly* 3, no. 3–4 (1953): 97–119.

34. Cf. Klaus Weidauer, *Thukydides und die hippokratischen Schriften* (Heidelberg: Heidelberger Forschungen, 1954). As Rosalind Thomas ("Thucydides' Intellectual Milieu and the Plague," in *Brill's Companion to Thucydides*, ed. Antonios Rengakos and Antonis Tsakmakis (Leiden: Brill, 2006), 87–108) writes, "It is

tempting, then, to think that Thucydides is aware of certain types of discourse, of style—not just vocabulary—that were associated with medical discussions" (102).

35. Simon Swain, "Man and Medicine in Thucydides," *Arethusa* 27, no. 3 (1994), 303–27, here 307.

36. "We have proved that our complaints are justified and that our adversaries are tyrannical and dishonest; we will now show you that you have no right to receive them."

37. "This was the first among the causes of the war, the Corinthians alleging that the Athenian fleet had taken part with the Corcyraeans and had fought against them in a time of truce."

38. "Do not betray friends and kindred into the hands of their worst enemies; or drive us in despair to seek the alliance of others."

39. R. J. Hankinson, *Cause and Explanation in Ancient Greek Thought*. Oxford: Oxford University Press, 1998), 58.

40. Hippocrates, *On the Sacred Disease*, 1: "But perhaps it will be said, these things are not so, but, not withstanding, men being in want of the means of life, invent many and various things, and devise many contrivances for all other things, and for this disease, in every phase of the disease, assigning the cause to a god."

41. Hippocrates, *On the Sacred Disease*, 3: "Men regard its nature and cause as divine from ignorance and wonder, because it is not at all like other diseases.

42. Philip van der Eijk, *Medicine and Philosophy in Classical Antiquity*. Cambridge: Cambridge University Press, 2009), 52.

43. As Morrison (1963, 45) observes, the word ἀλήθεια in Antiphon's title is likely to have had the same overtones as Democritus's ἐτεή. Behind a wide variety of names, he seeks those kinds of things which are based on nature, not convention. See James S. Morrison, "The "Truth" of Antiphon," *Phronesis* 8, no. 1 (1963): 35–49.

44. The extent to which Antiphon's tract was intended to genuinely instruct its readers has received considerable attention. Ostwald (1990, 304) suggests that Antiphon was attempting to "delineate the advantages that accrue to a human being from following, respectively, the dictates of society and those of nature," and so observes in the treatise an account of partial truth occupying both φύσις and νόμος through which his readers would "find a way to attaining the good life." Cf. Saunders 1978, 227: "It is a priori unlikely that Antiphon wished to decry all laws or rules or customs or conventions of all kinds whatsoever: both in theory and practice, such extreme anarchism is difficult to maintain, and there is no evidence that Antiphon was attracted to it."

45. "At such a time the life of the city was all in disorder, and human nature, which is always ready to transgress the laws, having now trampled them under foot, delighted to show that her passions were ungovernable, that she was stronger than justice, and the enemy of everything above her."

46. "There was no commerce, and they could not safely hold intercourse with one another either by land or sea. The several tribes cultivated their own soil just enough to obtain a maintenance from it. But they had no accumulations of wealth and did not plant the ground; for, being without walls, they were never sure that an invader might not come and despoil them. Living in this manner and knowing that they could anywhere obtain a bare subsistence, they were always ready to migrate; so that they had neither great cities nor any considerable resources."

47. Cynthia Farrar, *The Origins of Democratic Thinking: The Invention of Politics in Classical Athens* (Cambridge: Cambridge University Press, 1988), 135.

48. Reiner Schürmann, *Broken Hegemonies* (Bloomington: Indiana University Press, 2003), 88.

49. WKC Guthrie, *A History of Greek Philosophy: Volume 3, The Fifth Century Enlightenment, Part 1, The Sophists* (Cambridge: Cambridge University Press, 1971), 100.

6

Another Chorology
Reading Heidegger's Plato Books

BRET W. DAVIS

In a letter written to his wife at the time, Heidegger characterized his 1944–45 *Country Path Conversations* (*Feldweg-Gespräche*, GA 77/CPC) as his "Plato book."[1] It is, indeed, the first and one of the only texts Heidegger composed in the Platonic form of dialogue.[2] More significantly, Heidegger's postmetaphysical confrontation with Platonic metaphysics is at issue throughout the three imaginary conversations that make up the book, even though Plato is rarely mentioned by name. This essay attempts to explicate the dialogical confrontation with Plato that takes place there and in many of Heidegger's other writings—writings from which we must glean intimations of the content of another planned-yet-never-written "Plato book."[3] That unwritten book presumably would have been Heidegger's final attempt to address the content of Plato's dialogues directly, rather than (or perhaps in addition to) appropriating their form.

Much has been written about Heidegger's readings of Plato, and references will be made to some of this important scholarship. The reading of both Heidegger's written and unwritten "Plato books" undertaken in this essay will engage especially with John Sallis's post-Heideggerian rereading of the Platonic dialogues, especially his reading of the "chorology" in the *Timaeus*, which shows how what Plato writes about the *chōra* (χώρα) preemptively deconstructs the dyadic structure of what became Platonist metaphysics. This engagement with Sallis's *Chorology*[4] and other of his works on Plato enables not only a more nuanced understanding of the Platonic dialogues themselves in relation to what became the traditional conception of Platonic metaphysics but also a reading of *Country Path Conversations* and other writings of the later Heidegger as attempts to begin again with another—postmetaphysical—chorology.

Heidegger's Written and Unwritten Plato Books

On January 9, 1945, Heidegger wrote to his wife Elfride of feeling "increasingly clearly the need for simple saying; but this is difficult; for our language only applies to what has been up until now."[5] A month earlier, soon after having returned from a brief conscription into the *Volkssturm* to dig trenches in Alsace, Heidegger had left Freiburg on bicycle bound for his hometown Messkirch. Freiburg had been heavily bombed the night of November 27, 1944, with the old city almost completely destroyed. Once in Messkirch, Heidegger was preoccupied with safeguarding his manuscripts, which he eventually hid in a cave together with some manuscripts by Hölderlin, who a century before had lived out his remaining years—after his decent into madness—in a tower in Tübingen. Heidegger reportedly "had the idea of having one of the towers of Messkirch Castle restored with a view to working there."[6] Work on restoring the Messkirch tower, however, was delayed and in the end never completed.[7] In the early spring of 1945, Heidegger busied himself with attending to his manuscripts, teaching seminars to students who had retreated from besieged Freiburg to Wildenstein Castle in the vicinity of Messkirch, carrying on an affair with Princess Margot von Sachsen-Meiningen, and worrying about his two sons Jörg and Hermann, who were missing in action on the Russian front. It was no doubt difficult for him to find the rest and repose needed for thinking beyond the pressing needs of the day, and it seems that he fell into a bout of depression.

Yet on March 11, 1945, a reinvigorated Heidegger wrote Elfride to say: "I've got over the depression; I feel that my strength isn't at an end yet; perhaps the efforts of the last 7 years can resolve themselves into a quite simple saying."[8] One thinks of the often tortuous prose of the many solitary manuscripts—starting with *Beiträge zur Philosophie* (1936–38) and ending with *Die Stege des Anfangs* (1944)—on which Heidegger had been hard at work for what was in fact the previous eight or nine years, not to mention the many lecture courses, including his prolonged dialogical confrontation (*Auseinandersetzung*) with Nietzsche and his close readings of Hölderlin and the Presocratics. Then, on March 23, 1945, Heidegger wrote again to Elfride:

> Even though my condition is still physically delicate, in the last few days I've gained such remarkable momentum that I'm almost completely oblivious to food & sleep. I suddenly found a form of saying I would never have dared use, if only because of the danger of outwardly imitating the Platonic dialogues. I'm working on a 'conversation'; in fact I have the 'inspiration'—I really have to call it this—for several at once. In this way, poetizing & thinking saying [*das dichtende und denkende Sagen*] have attained a primordial unity, & everything flows along easily & freely. Only from my own experience have I now understood Plato's mode of presentation, & in some form or other the Plato book intended for you must one day become reality after all.[9]

The "Plato book" book that Heidegger was writing at the time did become a reality. The manuscript was completed within a couple of months—the third dialogue dated May 8, 1945—and according to his wishes the three dialogues were posthumously published together in 1995 as *Feldweg-Gespräche* (GA 77), translated in 2010 as *Country Path Conversations* (CPC).

However, in a letter to Elfride in 1950, Heidegger wrote that "the work in which I deal specifically with Plato's thought is to be yours . . . this work will one day be written."[10] Again in 1954 he makes a promise to her: "I shall eventually produce the Plato book after all."[11] And so, Heidegger evidently planned to write not just a book in the Platonic style of dialogue but also one explicitly about Plato's thought. It was never written. It seems that, despite all he did write about Plato, and in spite of his dialogical confrontation with Plato's thought that must be read between the lines of his own attempt to write dialogues or—as he would prefer to call them—conversations (*Gespräche*), Heidegger was never done with Plato.

The present essay, of course, cannot pretend to complete Heidegger's *Auseinandersetzung* with Plato for him, even if such completion were desirable. Rather, by examining the ambiguities and ambivalences in Plato's dialogues themselves along with Heidegger's increasingly critical and yet also at times ambiguous and ambivalent interpretations of those dialogues, I attempt (1) to delineate the major issues at stake in Heidegger's dialogical confrontation with Plato and/or Platonism, and (2) to elucidate what can be called the "other chorology" that issues from this dialogical confrontation.

While my main textual focus will be *Country Path Conversations*, I will also take into consideration other texts in which Heidegger is explicitly or implicitly engaging with Plato and/or Platonism, especially texts written after what might be called his "Plato booklet," *Plato's Doctrine of Truth*. This relatively concise and critical interpretation of Plato's Allegory of the Cave was written in 1940, based on a lecture course delivered in 1931–32.[12] It was first published in 1942, and subsequently published independently as a booklet as well as included in *Wegmarken/Pathmarks*.[13] Yet the summation of his *Auseinandersetzung* in that booklet was hardly Heidegger's last word on Plato and Platonism. Insofar as he sees Plato as the inauguration of the history of metaphysics, and insofar as he sees his own thought as stepping back to the origins of metaphysics in order to think what comes both before the beginning and after the closure of that history, Heidegger is never done with reading Plato, and we have only begun to understand and respond to his readings. In this essay I will offer a reading of both Heidegger's written and unwritten Plato books—that is, of both the book he wrote in the form of Platonic dialogues (in which he rarely mentions Plato) and the book he planned to write, based on his decades of engaging with Plato and with Platonism, but never did.

Heidegger's Platonic Dialogues: *Country Path Conversations*

Country Path Conversations (*Feldweg-Gespräche*), a set of three imaginary dialogues composed in 1944–45 and preserved for posthumous publication (in 1995), stands out among Heidegger's texts and not only because it is one of the very few texts he composed in this form. It was written at a pivotal moment in the development of Heidegger's thought. It marks the dramatic completion of a crucial turn in the fundamental attunement (*Grundstimmung*) or comportment (*Sichverhalten*) of his thought, a turn from the will (*Wille*) to releasement (*Gelassenheit*).[14] Moreover, it provides a kind of bridge between, on the one hand, Heidegger's confrontation with the history of metaphysics and its technological present and, on the other, his own attempt to speak and think in a different manner by way of a "simple saying" or a saying of "the simple," by which he means "the enigmatic" and by no means the easy; indeed, "the abyss of the simple"—

along with other locutions such as "the open-region" and "the healing expanse"—is one of the names given to what Heidegger elsewhere, using the language of the tradition, calls "being."[15]

The Guide in the first *Conversation* does not simply leap into a simple saying of the abyss of the enigmatic; he does not simply monologically walk off into the sunset of occidental (*abendländische*) metaphysics and thus toward the oriental (*morgenländische*) dawn of what the Tower Warden in the second *Conversation* calls a "non-metaphysical thinking" (*das nichtmetaphysische Denken*).[16] Rather, the Guide himself endeavors to think toward this "other thinking" (*das andere Denken*) (187/122) by way of relating it to the (at first) staunchly modern-metaphysical manner of thinking of the Scientist and the more "loosened up metaphysical manner of thinking" (*aufgelockerte metaphysische Denkweise*) (175/114) of the Scholar.

The conversion of the Scientist over the course of the first *Conversation* is the most dramatic occurrence and in many ways the most helpful in showing us the pathway from the currently dominant "worldview" of scientism to this other thinking that would no longer, as Heidegger says elsewhere, represent the world as a picture.[17] The claim that there is a sense in which natural science is applied technology, much discussed in the first *Conversation*,[18] was already made in Heidegger's lectures on Heraclitus in 1943 in a discussion of the primordial sense of nature as φύσις. And yet, there Heidegger says that "it would be foolish to want to persuade an agricultural chemist and a modern physicist of this [primordial pretechnological sense of φύσις]," since they only know how to approach matters in the technological manner of "doing something" with them.[19] The Guide in *Country Path Conversations* ignores this advice, as it were, and attempts to lead a physicist to a thoughtful encounter with the modern metaphysical worldview that underlies his work. The Guide, with the assistance of the Scholar, shows that even though, in the Scientist's experience, "Nature and nature alone, in the manner that it shows itself to us, has the last word in physics,"[20] the *first word* is in fact had by "the mathematical projection of nature,"[21] which representationally sets nature toward us in a particular manner; and it is precisely this prior objectification—which allows nature to show itself only as quantifiable material ready for calculative manipulation—that Heidegger means when he uses the term "technology."[22]

The first *Conversation* is remarkable for the manner in which the Guide leads the Scientist down the path into Heidegger's critique of the modern scientific and technological worldview. But many of us, insofar as we often go about our research on the history of Western philosophy, may most readily identify ourselves with the figure of the Scholar, whose careful steps often meditate the stretch between the Scientist, who tends to drag his feet, and the Guide, who tends to leap ahead. Or, as philosophers who often find ourselves cautiously following the lead of Heidegger's thinking, perhaps we find most illuminating the semantic space that opens up between the Guide and the Scholar in the first *Conversation*, between the Tower Warden and the Teacher in the second *Conversation*, and between the Younger Man and the Older Man in the third *Conversation*.

Plato before Platonism, Heidegger after Anti-Platonism

Yet, in what sense or senses can *Country Path Conversations* be understood as Heidegger's "Plato book"? Did he call it that just because it is written in the Platonic form of dialogue? Or, is the content as well as the form conceived with Plato in mind? In fact, as the present essay seeks to demonstrate in detail, Heidegger's dialogical confrontation with Plato's thought is in the background of his appropriation of the form of Platonic dialogue—and this is the case despite the fact that Plato is mentioned by name only twice in *Country Path Conversations*.[23] Plato's thought is at issue throughout the three *Conversations*, not only on account of the form of these texts but also on account of their content—which, indeed, calls into question the very division of matters into form and content.

In "The End of Philosophy and the Task of Thinking," Heidegger claims that "throughout the history of philosophy, Plato's thinking remains decisive in its sundry forms. Metaphysics is Platonism."[24] Heidegger's dialogical confrontation (*Auseinandersetzung*) with Plato thus cannot but be in the background of *Country Path Conversations* insofar as all three *Conversations* attempt to think back before and out beyond metaphysics, that is, insofar as they attempt to articulate and engage in a "non-metaphysical thinking."[25] It is as if confronting and recovering from the metaphysics of Forms first set forth in the Platonic dialogues requires thinking once more in the form of dialogue. Indeed, Heidegger's refusal to use the Greek-derived term *Dialog*, preferring instead the German *Gespräch* (57/37), is perhaps indicative of his marking a certain distance and difference from Plato precisely as he is apparently appropriating his literary form; the proximity and distance between *Dialog* and *Gespräch* would, as it were, echo the proximity and distance between what in *Contributions to Philoso-*

phy[26] is called the "first inception" of Western philosophy, which devolved into Platonic metaphysics, and the "other inception" of non-metaphysical thinking. It is as if Heidegger wants to intimate that he does not want to be misunderstood as simply *mimicking* the *form* of Plato's thought; as if the content of his *Country Path Conversations* is meant to appropriate in a manner that at the same time breaks the mold of Plato's paradigm.

Yet, let us proceed carefully. To begin with, there is a momentous question to which, it is fair to say, Heidegger does not always sufficiently attend: the question of what gets lost when the Platonic dialogues get reduced to statements of Platonic metaphysics. What gets lost when Plato gets translated into Platonism? John Sallis has led the way in raising and pursuing this momentous question.[27] He has influenced a new generation of re-readers of Plato who have unearthed in the Platonic dialogues core motifs and moments of recoil from the very metaphysics that, when unleashed from these reins of recoil, set sail as Platonism in the Western tradition—or even *as* the Western tradition, if we include under its determinations the manners in which Platonism essentially informed various philosophies and theologies, and how it remains determinant even in its eventual overturning and thus, according to Heidegger, consummation in positivism and in what Nietzsche calls his "inverted Platonism."[28]

Rereading Plato under the tutelage of Sallis's careful and compelling hermeneutics, one discovers in the Platonic dialogues time and again, *on the one hand*, a conspicuous thrust toward metaphysics, a separation of "the sensible" (τὸ αἰσθητόν) from "the intelligible" (τὸ νοητόν)—a separation of the realm of changing particulars from the realm of eternal Ideas (ἰδέες) or Forms (εἴδη) and an ontological, epistemological, and axiological subordination of the former to the latter; *on the other hand*, one discovers time and again a recessive recoiling from this thrust, an undercutting or at least endless complication of this metaphysical division. We can perhaps best hear Plato's own essentially ambivalent voice, not in an unwritten doctrine concealed behind the scenes, but rather precisely in the tension and interplay between this thrust and this recoil.

In an essay on the *chōra* (χώρα), and with his at times remarkable combination of clarity and nuance, Derrida explains the distinction, and the connection, between the Platonic dialogues and Platonism thus:

> Should one henceforth forbid oneself to speak of the philosophy of Plato, of the ontology of Plato, or even of Platonism? Not at all, and there would undoubtedly be no error of principle in

> so speaking, merely an inevitable *abstraction*. *Platonism* would mean, in these conditions, the thesis or the theme which one has extracted by artifice, misprision, and abstraction from the text, torn out of the written fiction of "Plato." . . . This will be called Platonism or the philosophy of Plato, which is neither arbitrary nor illegitimate, since a certain force of thetic abstraction at work in the heterogeneous text of Plato can recommend one to do so.[29]

Given the distinction as well as connection between Plato and Platonism, it will be important to bear in mind that Heidegger's critique of Plato is, for the most part, a critique of Platonism. Heidegger himself is—at least at times—quite explicit about this. At the beginning of one of his clearest and most extensive treatments of Platonism, namely the last third of his first lecture course on Nietzsche (1936–37), he writes: "We say "Platonism," and not Plato, because here we are dealing with the conception of knowledge that corresponds to that term, not by way of an original and detailed examination of Plato's works, but only by setting in rough relief one particular aspect of his work."[30]

Moreover, it is also crucial to bear in mind that, even on his own terms, Heidegger's thought is not an *anti-*Platonism. In *Country Path Conversations* as elsewhere, Heidegger accuses Nietzsche of remaining stuck in the horizon of Platonism precisely by having merely overturned Platonism. While in his interpretation of art Nietzsche began to twist free of the paradigmatic metaphysical opposition of the sensible and the intelligible, "the idea of value led his thinking—at least in its form of expression—to fall back into metaphysics."[31] Heidegger finds especially problematic the positing of values by the "will to power," for "the realm of a pure will to power . . . would have to remain only the counter-world to the Platonically thought world" (209/135). For Heidegger, "Any countermovement against metaphysics, and any mere turn away from it, always remains still caught in metaphysical representation" (188/122). This theme—namely that "by positing the opposite we just entangle ourselves yet further in a dependence on that from which we want to free ourselves" (154/100), that "everything revolutionary remains caught up in opposition. Opposition, however, is servitude" (51/33)—is repeated throughout *Country Path Conversations*.

The problem with willing to overcome metaphysics or nihilism is not just that it repeats the problem it is trying to solve—namely the "willing" that defines the subjectivity implicated in modern metaphysics and nihilism—but also that what Heidegger is searching for is not simply the binary opposite of the terms privileged in the hierarchies of metaphysics. Thus, he does not want the sensible over the intelligible; or immanence over transcendence; or even the historical over the transhistorical. Heidegger's thought is just as critical of one-world empiricism and positivism and historicism as it is of two-world Platonism. And the "non-willing," "Gelassenheit," and "waiting" called for in *Country Path Conversations* is not a passivity as opposed to activity; it is beyond the domain of this opposition, which Heidegger calls "the domain of the will."[32] Heidegger does not think in terms of "anti-" but rather in terms of "non-"; his "non-metaphysical thinking" (187/122) is not antimetaphysics but rather a thinking otherwise.

And so, the nonmetaphysical thinking Heidegger is presaging would not simply be an anti-Platonism, much less an anti-Platonic thinking. Rather, this nonmetaphysical thinking would be a rethinking of what was thought as well as what was at issue yet remained unthought by Plato, what was said as well as what was at issue yet remained unsaid in the Platonic dialogues. We could even say that it would be a matter of rethinking and resaying what was said and thought about that which cannot be properly said or thought, about that which cannot be fully appropriated by our speaking and thinking because our speaking and thinking have always already been both appropriated and expropriated by it. In this sense—in the sense, that is, of that which allows us to make limited sense of everything precisely by disallowing us to make unlimited sense of anything, and especially of it—we could say that Heidegger is intimating *another chorology*.

The Premetaphysical Festival of the Platonic Chorology

Even though Plato is mentioned by name only twice in *Country Path Conversations*, he is perhaps the referent, or at least one of the referents, of a significant, if enigmatic (or perhaps in this case merely cryptic) allusion. In the second *Conversation*, the Tower Warden attributes the thought that "thinking is a feast or festival" (*das Denken sei ein Fest*) to " 'he who is far greater' than both of us combined."[33] The other likely referent—and the ambiguity may well be intentional—is Hölderlin, whose poetic word is often, or perhaps always, concerned with the festival. Perhaps Heidegger is intimating that, like John the Baptist in conversation with the author of the Gospel of John, the Tower Warden in conversation with the Teacher is looking toward what is coming by alluding to the most futural (*zu-künftige*) of poets; and at the same time he is looking back at what has been and continues to essentially determine our historical being (*das Gewesene*) by way of alluding to Plato.

It is beyond the scope of this essay to discuss Heidegger's relation to Hölderlin and his poetic word regarding "the *wedding festival of humans and gods*."[34] Although Hölderlin is mentioned by name only once in *Country Path Conversations*, after 1934 he remains Heidegger's most intimate conversation partner, especially when he endeavors to think by way of "simple saying" rather than by dialogical confrontation with the metaphysical tradition. Nevertheless, here I wish to follow the implications of taking the reference to he who thought that "thinking is a festival" to be a reference to Plato.

Allusions to feasts and festivals abound in the Platonic dialogues, as does the idea that philosophical discourses and dialogues are in their own manner feasts and festivals. For example, near the beginning of the *Republic*, as Socrates begins his ascent back to the city, he engages in a feast of *logos* (see 352b, 354a) in which he dismantles Thrasymachus's aggressively proclaimed thesis that justice is whatever is advantageous for the stronger; in other words, might makes right. Socrates does not attempt to convert by external force—by might—but rather to educate through the power of *logos*, a power he trusts inheres in his partner in dialogue. And so he tells Thrasymachus that this was a "feast furnished by you . . . now that you have become gentle with me and are no longer angry" (354a).[35] A similar attempt to provide the occasion for such a conversion is foreshadowed at the beginning of the *Gorgias*, when Socrates arrives just after the rhetorician had displayed his powers of persuasion. The dialogue opens with Callicles's remark: "This is how they say you should take part in warfare and battle, Socrates." Socrates responds by subtly shifting the metaphor for what should be taking place by means of *logos*: "What," he asks, "have we arrived at the latter end of a feast, as the saying goes" (447a). The feast of *logos* suggested here would be a dialogue in which participants would not be willfully coerced into believing something but rather would be guided toward the light of reason that compels them not from without but from within. The noncoercive nature of dialogue is echoed in Heidegger's suggestions that a conversation is not a conversation at all "if it wills something,"[36] and that it is the course of the conversation, or the country path itself, that moves us (118/76, 202/131).

The images of a feast of *logos* to be found in the Platonic dialogues also include, of course, the entire setting of the *Symposium*, in which participants engage in a sober discussion about the most maddening and ecstatic of topics, namely love (ἔρως). In the first of the *Country Path Conversations*, it is suggested that thinking is "the festival of sobriety [*Das Fest der Nüchternheit*],"[37] and Heidegger may be intimating his preference for Plato's dialogical thinking over Hegel's dialectic, which Hegel describes as "the Bacchanalian revel [*der bacchantische Taumel*] in which no member is not drunk."[38] In a true conversation, presumably, one is not to be coerced either by irrational intoxication or by the "cunning of reason" operated by a teleologically driven world-spirit.[39]

Two of the most remarkable references to the idea of a feast of *logos* to be found in the Platonic dialogues appear in the *Timaeus* (20c) and the *Phaedrus* (227b, 247a–b). And the fact that this expression occurs in these two dialogues in particular is worth pondering. Despite all the rigor and sobriety involved in the festival of thinking that is the *Timaeus*, or rather precisely on their account, it cannot evade a descent into "bastard reasoning [λογισμῷ τινι νόθῳ]" (*Timaeus* 52b) and dreamlike discourse when it comes time to speak of the *chōra* (χώρα). Whereas in the middle of the *Republic* we find an ascent out of the cave all the way up toward that which is "beyond being," in the middle of the *Timaeus* we find a descent down toward what is, as it were, beneath being: beneath even the privative form of being that characterizes the changing particulars.

The *Timaeus* is the only dialogue in which Plato discusses the *chōra* in the sense of the "third kind" (τρίτον γένος), which is meant to enable the interrelation between sensible particulars and intelligible Ideas (48e–52). To be sure, as a common word meaning, among other things, place, land, and country, the term *chōra* frequently occurs in other Platonic dialogues, such as throughout the *Laws*. It is noteworthy that *chōra* shares the ambiguity of our English word "country"—as well as the English and German words "land" and "*Land*"—in that it can mean both the countryside that lies outside the city walls and the entire political unit that surrounds and includes the city. In the *Timaeus*, the word *chōra* is often translated as "space," and it is used, along with "receptacle" (ὑποδοχή), "nurse" (τιθήνη), "mother" (μητέρα), and "matrix" (ἐκμαγεῖον), in Plato's attempts to speak of the "third kind" that enables the production or genesis of the sensible particulars as imperfect and changing images of the intelligible Ideas as perfect and eternal originals.

The thought of the *chōra*—or rather the necessity yet inability to think the *chōra*, to bestow meaning and form on that which receives meaning and form precisely because it has no meaning and form of its own—this unavoidable thought of the unthinkable, this name for the unnamable, problematizes the very opposition that establishes and maintains the metaphysics of Platonism. As Timaeus speaks and Socrates silently listens, Plato preemptively undermines Platonism by introducing, out of necessity, the thought of a non-intelligible matrix of reality that is neither sensible nor intelligible but is needed if sensible things are to be or become in some sense images of intelligible Ideas.

In a key passage in his remarkable book on this topic, *Chorology*, Sallis writes:

> Thus, it is the χώρα that makes possible the doubling of being in an image, the duplicity of being. . . . But then, the very move that displaces or limits the twofold, namely, the introduction of the third kind, is at the same time what establishes the very possibility of the twofold, of the doubling of being in an image. . . . If one were to take metaphysics to be constituted precisely by the governance of that twofold, then the chorology could be said to bring both the founding of metaphysics and its displacement, both at once. Originating metaphysics would have been exposing it to the abyss, to the abysmal χώρα, which is both origin and abyss, both at the same time. Then one could say—with the requisite reservations—that the beginning of metaphysics will have been already the end of metaphysics.[40]

From Heraclitus to Heidegger's Other Chorology

The aim of the present essay is to demonstrate how Heidegger's later thought can be understood as a radical postmetaphysical rethinking of Plato's pre- or proto-metaphysical *chōra*. Although Sallis has in many respects cleared the way for such an interpretation, he has not himself pursued it, at least not in such terms. In fact, he writes: "In Heidegger's own brief discussions of χώρα, which conflate χώρα with τόπος and link

Platonism to the transformation of the essence of place into space defined as extension, there is little to suggest any originary engagement with the Platonic discourse on the χώρα."[41] However, I think we can clearly trace Heidegger's thinking of being in terms of "the open-region" (*die Gegnet*) in *Country Path Conversations* back to the Greek, if not specifically Platonic, notion of *chōra*.

Although *chōra* is not mentioned in *Country Path Conversations*, it is in the background—indeed, one is tempted to say that it *is* the background that is at issue. The *chōra* is rethought as the "region of all regions"[42] or "open-region" that is spoken of as the "open and yet veiled expanse" (206/132). Reading *Country Path Conversations* as developing a postmetaphysical chorology is supported by Heidegger's references to *chōra* in at least two previous texts. The first occurs in a parenthetical remark in *Introduction to Metaphysics* (a remark not read but purportedly written in 1935 and first published in 1953). Before the parenthetical remark, Heidegger says that the "Greeks have no word for 'space.' This is no accident, for they do not experience the spatial according to *extensio* but instead according to place (τόπος) as χώρα, which means neither place nor space but what is taken up and occupied by what stands there. The place belongs to the thing itself."[43] In other words, the modern and specifically Newtonian idea of space as a homogeneous container is foreign to the Greek understanding of a mutual belonging of place and thing. Heidegger says that the transition from thing-specific places to neutral space is portended, however, in Plato's doctrine of the *chōra*—at least, we should interject, in the way in which this doctrine gets taken up by Aristotle and the ensuing tradition. Heidegger paraphrases and then quotes in Greek a key passage from the *Timaeus*, according to which the *chōra* must be "bare of all manners of outward appearance [*Aussehen*, Heidegger's translation of Plato's εἶδος or ἰδέα]" so that it may receive the imprint of any of these forms without interference or imposition of an outward look of its own. In the parenthetical remark, Heidegger then suggests that "Platonic philosophy—that is, the interpretation of being as ἰδέα—prepared the transfiguration of place (τόπος) and of χώρα, *the essence of which we have barely grasped*, into 'space' defined by extension."[44] Insofar as Plato's *chōra* lends itself to being interpreted as spatially extended matter, into which the Demiurge as Craftsman would stamp the unities of eternal and perfect Ideas into the pluralities of changing and imperfect particulars, it plays an inceptual role in the development of the metaphysics of production. It has been the modern destiny of the history of this metaphysics to understand space as extension in terms of a mathematical grid through which things are reduced to calculable points of mass-energy.

Yet, in the parenthetical remark, Heidegger also says that we have scarcely begun to grasp the essence of *chōra*, and he offers a brief yet significant indication of how we may begin to do this: "Could not χώρα mean: that which removes itself from every particular [*das Sichabsonderde von jedem Besonderen*], that which gets out of the way [*das Ausweichende*], that which in this manner admits [*zuläßt*] and 'makes place' [*Platz macht*] precisely for another?"[45] Heidegger develops this brief remark—this hint of another chorology—in his lectures on "Heraclitus' Doctrine of *Logos*" in the summer semester of 1944.[46] There he writes: "The χώρα is the self-opening expanse which comes to encounter [*Die χώρα ist die sich öffnende, entgegenkommende Weite*]."[47] He translates *chōra* as "the region" (*die Gegend*) and even makes reference to the Tirolian dialect form of this word, *Gegnet*, which features prominently in the first of the *Country Path Conversations* written soon thereafter.

The context in which Heidegger begins to develop what I am calling his "other chorology" in the 1944 lectures is his translation and interpretation of Heraclitus's fragment 108: ὁκόσων λόγους ἤκουσα οὐδεὶς ἀφικνεῖται ἐς τοῦτο ὥστε γινώσκειν ὅ τι σοφόν ἐστι, πάντων κεχωρισμένον. Richard McKirahan translates this fragment as follows: "Of all those whose accounts [λόγοι] I have heard, no one reaches the point of recognizing that that which is wise is set apart from all."[48] Heidegger takes issue with similar German translations and gives the following rendering: "Of the many λόγοι I have (already) heard, none reaches the point of familiarity with this: that what is properly to be known in relation to all beings essentially unfolds from out of its (own) region [*Sovieler λόγοι ich (schon) vernommen habe, keiner gelangt dorthin, von wo aus er vertraut is damit, daß das eigentlich Zuwissende im Bezug auf alles Seiende aus seiner (eigenen) Gegend west*]."[49] Crucial here is Heidegger's rendering of πάντων κεχωρισμένον as "im Bezug auf alles Seiende aus seiner (eigenen) Gegend west" rather than as "von alles abgesondert, abgetrennt, ab-gelöst, ab-solutum."[50] Such metaphysical and theological misunderstandings of what Heraclitus means by *logos* (λόγος)—misunderstandings Heidegger says can be found in attempts to link Heraclitus's *logos* to Christ as *logos* in the opening lines of the Gospel of John—founder precisely insofar as they fail to see the sense of *chōra* implied in *kechōrismenon*. It is true that "κεχωρισμένον etymologically belongs to χωρίζω, χωρίζειν, which one translates as to divide, remove, set aside" (334). But in our exclusive attention to the setting apart of one thing from another, we forget what lies at the basis of such setting apart (*was dem zugrunde liegt*). What gets lost in the translations of *kechōrismenon* as *abgesondert, abgetrennt*, and so forth is precisely the *chōra* that underlies any *chōrizein*, any separation or articulation of the differences between phenomena. That this *chōra* gets forgotten, overlooked, is presumably because it does not present itself as an object, as a *Gegenstand*; it is, says Heidegger, "*Das Gegenstandlose der Gegend*," "the objectlessness of the region" (336). This is why, as Heraclitus says, no one recognizes it. In our exclusive attention to beings, we overlook being as the *chōra* that lets them be.

Heidegger interprets the *chōra* in this context as "the surrounding region, the given environs, which gives place to a sojourn [*die Umgebung, die umgebende Umgegend, die einen Aufenthalt einräumt und gewährt*]."[51] He relates it back to the verb χάω (whence also χάος), which means to yawn, to gape, to open oneself up. Heidegger then says: "ἡ χώρα as the given surroundings is thus 'the region' [ἡ χώρα *als die umgebende Umgegend ist dann »die Gegend«*]" (335).

In his 1944 lectures on Heraclitus's doctrine of *logos* (λόγος), which we have been examining, Heidegger understands *chōra* as being and as *logos*. He understands *logos* here in the same manner he does in the third text of *Country Path Conversations*, namely as the all-gathering or "the gathering toward the originally all-unifying One,"[52] the One that can let things be in their differences precisely as it holds them together; for "διαίρεσις, the Greeks well knew, is still and is already σύνθεσις."[53] Heidegger takes *logos* to be the referent of "that which is to be known" in Heraclitus's fragment 108, and his interpretation of the fragment bears the following fruit. "The Λόγος is as λόγος πάντων κεχωρισμένον: the all-surrounding region which, in relation to the whole of beings, opens itself for everything and comes to encounter everything [*die alles umgebende, für alles sich öffnende und allem sich entgegnende Gegend*]: the present [*Gegenwart*] into which each and every thing is gathered and sheltered; from out of it—out of the region as such—each thing emerges and receives its arising and its perishing, its appearing and its disappearing."[54]

The following year, Heidegger develops this thought in *Country Path Conversations*, where of the open-region (*die Gegnet*) it is said: "The open-region is the abiding expanse which, gathering all, opens itself so that in it the open is held and halted, letting each thing arise in its resting."[55] And: "This open seems to me to be something like a region, by means of whose enchantment everything which belongs to it returns to that in which it rests" (112/73). Heidegger also adds that, precisely on account of its radical openness, "the open-region [as such] draws itself back, goes away from us [*uns entgeht*], rather than coming to encounter us [*uns entgegenkommt*]" (114/74). The "horizon" is said to be the side of the open-region that comes to encounter us, "the side turned toward us of [this] surrounding open" (112/72). The horizon is a delimitation of the open-region, a delimited openness. The delimitation of a horizon within the open-region of being is an event of truth as ἀλήθεια, as *Lichtung*.

Thus, Heidegger's development of the thought of the *chōra* as *Gegend* or *Gegnet* is a development of his understanding of the truth of being as an event of un-concealment, as the clearing (*die Lichtung*), or as *Da-sein*, as long as we no longer understand the latter primarily in terms of the projection of the meaning of being on the part of the human. In his comments in the 1969 Seminar in Le Thor, Heidegger says that in order to counter the Sartrean misconception of "project" (*Entwurf*) as a performance of human subjectivity, "the thinking after *Being and Time* replaced the expression "meaning of being" with "truth of being." And, in order to avoid any falsification of the sense of truth, in order to exclude its being understood as correctness, "truth of being" was explained by "locality of being [*Ortschaft des Seins*]"—truth as place-hood [*Örtlichkeit*] of being. This already presupposes, however, an understanding of the place-being [*Ortseins*] of place. Hence the expression topology of beyng [*Topologie des Seyns*] . . ."[56] In and after *Contributions to Philosophy*,[57] Heidegger often, though not always, uses the archaic spelling of *Sein* (being), *Seyn* (beyng), to indicate the appropriating event (*Ereignis*) that is more originary than the metaphysical distinction between being as beingness (*Seiendheit*, whatness, *quidditas*, ἰδέα) and beings (*Seiende*). Heidegger's "topology of beyng" is thus his attempt to think beyond the ontological difference that founds metaphysics by thinking back before it, by stepping back to that region—or *chōra*—that undergirds and undercuts it, enabling its construction, deconstruction, and, perhaps, transmutation.[58]

Yet, we might ask, is the open-region—the *chōra*—of beyng a *topos*, an *Ort*? In his 1944 lectures on Heraclitus, Heidegger in fact marks a clear and important distinction between *chōra* and *topos*, *Gegend* and *Ort*, region and place or location.

> The place or location [*Ort*] is always in a region [*Gegend*] and has a given environs [*Umgebung*] around it which comes out of the surrounding-region [*Umgegend*]. . . . This open expanse,

however, is not the emptiness of a container, but rather an open that holds back, holds much in reserve, and, in its peculiar manner, of itself delimits itself. These limits, moreover, are themselves region-like and that means expansive and revealing. Because the region that can be understood in this way in each case surrounds and grants locations [*Orte*], and so first allows the arrangement and allocation of location, it is in a certain regard that which is essential [*das Wesenhafte*] to a location, its locality [*Ortschaft*].[59]

In this sense, we can understand Heidegger's "topology of beyng" as an attempt to develop an understanding of the place-being of place, where place is not simply a spatial location but is the qualitative space of intelligibility and perceivability that opens up with an event of unconcealment. The topology of beyng is none other than Heidegger's understanding of *alētheia* as clearing.

Yet, insofar as the clearing is an opening in a forest, and if we were to name the cleared space the *Da* (there) in the sense of the delimited openness of a horizon, we need a name for the surrounding forest itself, that is, for the mystery of the open-region as the "concealed essence of truth" that withdraws in any event of unconcealment; we need a name for the *lēthē* that remains held back in the event of *alētheia*. If *topos* names a delimited place, we need a name for the open-region in which the openings of such places take place. We need a name for the open-region that surrounds all delimited and therefore disclosive *topoi* and withdraws from them precisely in the radicality of its unlimited openness. That name could be, in Greek, *chōra*. And so, Heidegger could have spoken not of a "topology of beyng," but rather, in a more expansive sense—in the sense of an expanse that both holds within itself and withholds itself from the topoi of sense in which we reside[60]—he could have spoken of a *chorology of beyng*.

From Plato's Inceptual to Heidegger's Other Chorology

Having gotten a sense of the other chorology entailed in Heidegger's conception of the other inception of postmetaphysical thinking, it remains for us to examine more closely how it relates to the Platonic pre- or proto-metaphysical chorology. The Platonic chorology haunts the ontology of Platonism as a necessary and yet necessarily "bastard reasoning" that its dualistic metaphysical structure requires and yet cannot accommodate; in addition to being (Ideas) and becoming (particulars), there must be a "third kind" of thing, namely the *chōra*: the material-spatial receptical of the Ideas that makes the individuation and generation of particulars possible (*Timaeus* 47e–53c). In the middle of Plato's *Timaeus*, the explication of the genesis and structure of the world thus finds it necessary to delve into a chorology in its attempt to return to the beginning and retell this cosmogenic tale from the ground up. Yet this ground turns out to be quicksand on which Platonism either founders or builds upon only by covering it up—for example, with the translation of the χώρα into the technical concept of ὕλη.[61] Moreover, even if Aristotle's hylomorphism subordinated matter to form, potentiality (δύναμις) to actuality (ενέργεια), it was only through medieval theology and modern metaphysics that matter gets stripped of its inherent dynamic potentiality and is treated as a merely passive recipient of forms imposed upon it by a transcendent or transcendental subject.

Although the *Timaeus* first introduces the *chōra* in passive terms as a "receptacle," as though it were a shapeless malleable material that is given form by being stamped with the mold of the Ideas, it immediately adds to this the more ambiguous metaphor of "nurse" and connects the *chōra* to the primal movement of the morphological exchange among the elements (*Timaeus* 49a–d). It later speaks of the *chōra* as a dynamic, if still disordered, "winnowing basket" whose shaking movement separates the elements into different regions of space in advance of their arrangement into an ordered cosmos by God (*Timaeus* 52d–53b). Sallis writes that "the χώρα is a receptacle filled in the beginning with indeterminate powers in flux; it is the mother from whom, then, the elements come to be born."[62] Yet the subsequent reduction of the *chōra* to merely passive matter lays the productionist metaphysical ground for the technological reduction of beings to "standing-reserve" (*Bestand*) for the extraction of material resources and limitlessly transferable energy.[63]

Heidegger's postmetaphysical and posttechnological chorology attempts to "step back" behind this "history of being"—as the history of the devolution of Platonist metaphysics into the technological worldview—to the always self-concealing at the same time as self-revealing event of unconcealment. In effect, Heidegger rethinks the *chōra* as the open-region (*Gegnet*) of beyng (*Seyn*), and the orientation of his thinking is an avowedly enigmatic "going into nearness to farness," that is to say, an ek-static opening to the mystery of the forest of concealment that surrounds the horizonally delimited clearings of the sensible and intelligible worlds in which we in-statically dwell.[64]

It is as if, as it were, Plato's Divided Line, the linearity of which sustains the metaphysical oppositions of Platonism, is bent back around such that the "beyond being" (ἐπέκεινα τῆς οὐσίας) (Republic 509b) of the Good can no longer be clearly distinguished from the "before being" of the *chōra*, thus closing the space of metaphysics and clearing the way for a nonmetaphysical thinking grounded, or rather ungrounded, in another chorology.[65]

Heidegger's nonmetaphysical thinking does not attempt to get beyond the *chōra* but rather to thoughtfully dwell within it. *Country Path Conversations* thematizes and enacts a thinking that understanding itself as a "going into nearness"[66] to "the unprethinkable" (*das Unvordenkliche*) (146/95, 231/150), to "the enigmatic" (30–32/19–20, 81/51, 138/89, 213/138, 218/141) that cannot be captured in the horizons of thought because it is the open-region in which those horizons are themselves formed. As the Guide says in the first *Conversation*: "Insofar as we are those who think, we come into the nearness of the world [later emended to "the open-region"], yet, due to such nearness, we at the same time remain far from it; although this remaining is also a return in the sense of a turning to enter into releasement."[67]

Heidegger's chorology develops out of his turn from a transcendental-horizonal projection of world toward an indwelling releasement to the open-region.[68] This turn involves a return to nature, in the sense that human horizons are formed in response to the wider expanse of nature—as long as we understand "nature" not in the sense of one region of beings (i.e., as the collection of natural versus artificial or supernatural beings), but, to begin with, in the sense of what for Heidegger was the original Greek word for being, φύσις. As we have seen, one of the meanings of the Greek word *chōra* is country or countryside, as in what lies beyond the city walls and as what surrounds and thus includes the city. This sense presumably informs Heidegger's retrieval of the term and his translation of it as *Gegend* and *Gegnet* in the context of his retrieval of Heraclitus's sense of the originary belonging together of *physis* and *logos*.

The *chōra* in both Platonism—which, following Aristotle, reduces the *chōra* to *hyle* (matter)—and in Heidegger is connected to "nature" (φύσις, *Natur*). Yet everything depends on how we understand "nature." To make a long story short: whereas the productionist metaphysics of Platonism rooted φύσις in τέχνη, Heidegger seeks to return *technē* to its original rootedness in *physis*.[69] This originary understanding of *physis* would precede the subordination of *physis* to the model of *technē*, beginning with the image of a divine craftsman who imprints the Forms on the *chōra*, analogous to the manner in which a human craftsman shapes amorphous matter according to his design or a design he receives through inspiration from a transcendent source—in any case, a design foreign to the matter being shaped. This productionist model ultimately leads to the technological reduction of nature to natural resources, to standing-reserves for human projects by way of passing through the modern metaphysics of transcendental subjectivity, according to which such subjectivity constitutes objects by imposing its forms of intuition and categories of understanding on things. *Physis* becomes the nature of natural science by way of being subjected to objectification; scientific objects are formed when phenomena are constrained to show themselves according to the grid of "mathematical projection." By going back to the Presocratics, Heidegger endeavors to recover an originary sense of *physis*, an experience of nature not as one region of beings, much less a region that is all but deprived of being, but rather as beyng itself.

The development of Heidegger's attempt to recover a more originary sense of *physis* goes hand in hand with the development of his critique of technology—developments that begin precisely around the time of his failed rectorship and his turn from a voluntaristic embrace of Hitler's politics to a thoughtful dialogue with the poetry of Hölderlin, for whom nature was "the holy"—is certainly relevant. Since the publication of *Contributions to Philosophy* (GA 65), with its critique of *Machenschaft*, and of GA 90, which collects Heidegger's previously unpublished notes on Ernst Jünger from 1934 to 1954, the development of Heidegger's critique of technology has become more transparent. Particularly striking in this context is the second note in GA 90, which reads: "The interpretation of beings as a whole from and according to the Old Testament's creation-plan [*Schöpfungsplan*] and the planetary domination of the unconditional work-plan [*Arbeitsplan*] of the worker are metaphysically the same—both are carried and supported by the correspondingly reinterpreted homogenizing of ancient Platonic-Aristotelian metaphysics and its modern transmutation [*Abwandlung*]."[70]

Hence, Heidegger's *Auseinandersetzung* with modern technology is a confrontation with the theological as well as metaphysical legacy of Platonism. Insofar as Plato's *chōra* gets translated into *hyle*, and *hyle* comes to be understood as a merely passive material receptacle for the imprint of the Ideas, the *Timaeus*' demiurge (δημιουργός) becomes the craftsman who stands at the inception of the metaphysics of production. Analogously, in the beginning of Genesis the Creator God of the biblical tradition fashions an ordered cosmos out of a primeval watery chaos. More than a millennium later, Christian theologians reinterpret this creationist cosmogony in terms of the doctrine of *creatio ex nihilo*, a doctrine that dispenses with the *chōra* or reduces it to a *nihil negativum*. In the modern metaphysics of "transcendental-horizonal representation," it is human subjectivity that projects the a priori categories of understanding through which things can show themselves only by way of being turned into objects of representation. This transcendental "thinking as willing" then devolves into the technological "human attack on nature"[71] that is problematized in Heidegger's *Country Path Conversations*.

For Heidegger, the *chōra*, rethought as the *Gegnet* or open-region, is not a chaotic material or passive receptacle of eternal Ideas but rather the "concealed essence of truth" that "requires the human" in order to reveal itself in always finite ways.[72] It is the "abiding expanse" in which humans and things belong, in which they are allowed to rest in themselves. It is the open-region in which finite horizons are formed, horizons through which things can come to be known by humans, and potentially known as they show themselves from themselves rather than as they are reduced to representational objects or technological standing-reserve.

An Ambiguous Transformation of the Nature of Nature

At the inception of Platonic metaphysics, there occurred, according to Heidegger, a transformation in the essence of truth. In "Plato's Doctrine of Truth" (1931–32, 1940), Heidegger claims that "what remains unsaid in Plato's thinking is "a change in the determination of the essence of truth," namely a change from an understanding of truth as ἀλήθεια, as the unconcealment or unhiddenness of beings, to truth as the correctness (ὀρθότης) of human apprehension and assertion about beings.[73] With the determination of the being of beings as the Ideas, the *locus* of truth changes; truth is no longer the self-showing of things in unconcealment, it is the correspondence or agreement (ὁμοίωσις) of human representations and linguistic propositions to the Idea, the "outward look" (εἶδος), which in turn determines the being of a being from above, as it were. Natural things are given form by resembling something supernatural. They cannot show themselves in an intelligible manner from themselves; to make sense they must receive the imprint of a look—an *eidos*—from something supersensible that transcends them.

This change in the transformation of the essence and locus of truth accompanies a transformation of the essence and locus of nature, of φύσις. In this case, the older conception of *physis* is not replaced but rather a new, metaphysical sense of *physis* comes to be used alongside it. *Physis* derives from the verb φύειν, "to grow, to appear." Heidegger defines the original meaning of *physis* as "what emerges from itself (for example, the emergence, the blossoming, of a rose), the unfolding that opens itself up, the coming-into-appearance in such unfolding, and holding itself and persisting in appearance—in short, the emerging-abiding-sway [*das aufgehend-verweilende Walten*]."[74] For Plato, however, for a thing to appear as this or that, it must participate in an eternal and immaterial Idea that transcends its temporal and material becoming, a metaphysical essence that shapes its physical existence.

The term "metaphysics," to be sure, is a later invention; it was first used to designate the untitled book that Aristotle wrote after his *Physics* on "first philosophy," and only later became used to refer to what lies "beyond physical things" (μετὰ τὰ φυσικά). Rather than inventing the word "metaphysics" to speak of the Ideas, Plato gave the word *physis* a second meaning. This ambiguity is still evident today in the fact that we use the word "nature" to refer *either* to the essences of things *or* to things that are untouched by human artifice. The English word "nature" derives from the Latin *nasci*, "to be born," which in turn stems from the Proto-Indo-European root *gene-*, from which also come "genesis" and "generation." Sometimes the two senses of "nature" are understood to be related insofar as the qualities something is born with are thought to be those that are essential to it. Yet, for example, when someone asks about the nature of language or the nature of God, they are generally not asking about their genesis, and may in fact be asking about their timeless essences.

We owe this second, metaphysical sense of "nature" as "essence" to the new sense of *physis* formulated in what Socrates calls—in his autobiographical account in the *Phaedo* of how he became, as it were, a Platonic rather than a natural philosopher—his "second sailing" (*Phaedo* 99c-d). A "second sailing" (δεύτερος πλοῦς) "is what sailors do when in the absence of wind they take to the oars."[75] In this case, when Socrates's youthful attempts to look for natural causes of things ended up raising aporetic questions—such as about the peculiar nonphysical nature of numbers—that called for a different kind of inquiry, he redirected his search toward another, supernatural kind of cause of what makes things the things that they are. In Book 10 of Plato's *Laws*, the Athenian criticizes naturalistic explanations of things, saying: "Why, by *nature* [φύσιν] they mean what was there to begin with, but if we can say that soul [ψυχή] came first . . . it will be perfectly true to say that it is the existence of soul which is most eminently natural [διαφερόντως φύσει]" (*Laws* 892c). What the Athenian calls *psychē* here is akin to Anaxagoras's idea of *nous*, the idea that set the course for Socrates's second sailing. Socrates says that he was inspired when he heard someone reading a book by Anaxagoras "which said that is it νοῦς that sets all in order and causes all things" (*Phaedo* 97b–c). Although he was disappointed to find that Anaxagoras did not actually employ *nous* to explain the causes of things but rather, like others, gave naturalistic explanations based on the elements, Socrates himself set about to employ the rational soul or intellect rather than the senses to understand why things are as they are.

In other words, or rather in the now ambiguous use of the same word, we could say that Socrates turned away from "nature" in order to understand the "nature" of things. In effect, his second sailing launches what might be called the project of Platonism. Sallis deftly explains this as

> a tendency (not foreign to Platonic texts [in a footnote Sallis sketches the polysemous uses of the term φύσις in the *Timaeus*]) to let the word *nature* undergo a decisive semantic shift: from designating the domain of natural things (as presented through the senses), it comes to signify what something or someone is. If one were simply to follow this tendency, then it could be said that by looking into nature (in the first sense) Socrates came to a certain insight into his own nature (in the second sense). Then the discourse could expand into an account of the *nature of* things and even of the nature of nature. And yet, with this shift, one would have posited a nature beyond nature, dividing nature against itself.[76]

It would not be an exaggeration to say that this ontological as well as semantic split of "nature" into two distinct and even opposing domains and meanings—a split which inscribed, in a single yet ambiguous word, the two-world metaphysics of Platonism—henceforth determined the history of Western philosophy as a history of metaphysics.

In commenting on Charles Scott's critique of the notion of "nature" as a metaphysical essence that would grant us knowledge of a thing's generic qualities at the expense of blinding us to its singularity, Sallis writes of the "doubling of nature" that gave rise to Platonism and the entire Western tradition of metaphysics as follows:

> The fact that the word "nature" commonly has this double sense in the modern European languages, that it can signify both the manifold of natural things and the essence of something, even of something not natural—as when one speaks of the nature of art, for instance—attests to the force and consistency with which philosophy has determined nature precisely by projecting it beyond itself, by positing a nature beyond nature. In interrupting and dismantling this project, philosophy thus turns critically, deconstructively, against itself.[77]

It was Plato who inaugurated the tradition of metaphysics, with its turn away from natural things (existents) and toward their natures (essences). And yet, we need to remind ourselves again that there is much more going on in the Platonic dialogues than the inauguration of Platonist metaphysics. To begin with, even before the beginning, Plato writes of the *chōra* as "the nature [φύσις] that receives all bodies" (*Timaeus* 50b).[78] In Plato's chorology, one could say, a third kind of nature is from the beginning shown to be a necessary supplement to the doubling of nature into particulars and Ideas. Plato's chorology deconstructs, at the same time as it inaugurates, metaphysics.

In his postmetaphysical rereading of the pre- as well as protometaphysical ambivalences in the Platonic dialogues, Sallis points out that Socrates's second sailing does not simply set a course toward the metaphysical Ideas but rather is a turn to *logoi*, to human speech as the mediator between the two sense of nature.[79] Language is the psychophysical medium through which the things we perceive with our bodily senses are allowed to make meaningful sense to our minds. And, at least as long as we remain embodied beings bound to the earth, language is the medium though which we (always imperfectly) attain some idea of the Ideas that determine the nature of natural as well as artificial things. Sallis reminds us of the irreducibly dialogical nature of Plato's texts, and he questions whether Plato's understanding of dialogue is not in fact much closer to Heidegger's understanding of the "gathering of language" that takes place in a genuine *Gespräch* (conversation)—in which language is allowed to speak (*die Sprache spricht*) and humans speak only insofar as they respond (*entspricht*) to this speaking of language—than Heidegger was willing or able to acknowledge.[80]

There is much more to be said about language. For example, one could examine the resonances, as well as the dissonances, between, on the one hand, the manner in which *logos* mediates the intelligible and sensible realms in Plato's dialogues and, on the other hand, Heidegger's placement of language as the "dimension" (*Dimension*) of "dif-ference" (*Unter-schied*) and intimacy (*Innigkeit*) that holds together while holding apart the "twofold" (*Zwiefalt*) of world and things.[81] One could further attend to the way in which Sallis explores the similarities and relation between language and imagination in attending to the images of art alongside, or sometimes interweaving with, the spoken and sung (as well as written) word—and both in relation to the presentations of the phenomena of nature, beginning with what Sallis calls "the elementals."[82] One might also attend to Julia Kristeva's explicit use of the term *chōra* to indicate the field of prelinguistic semiotic rhythms produced by the psychosomatic drives, which both generate and disrupt the symbolic systems of meaning in which we dwell as conscious subjects.[83]

But here let us keep our focus on Plato. In order to lay the groundwork, as it were, for *logos* as the mediator between the sensible particulars and intelligible Ideas, the chorology in the *Timaeus* is, as it were, Plato's original attempt both to distinguish between and to mediate the two senses of *physis*. The *chōra* is a "third kind," different in kind than either the physical generation (γένεσις) of the things of "nature" or the metaphysical Ideas that impart an essential "nature" to those things.

The Persistent Prevalence of Plato's Supernatural Orientation

We have seen how Plato's chorology is more of an abyssal quicksand than a solid ground for the construction of Platonist metaphysics, a quicksand that was covered over and dissimulated in the translation of *chōra* into matter and into space. Still, even if we restore the enigmatic chorology to its rightful place in the Platonic text, and even if we let this expose the tension between a thrust toward, and a recoil from, metaphysics in our rereading of the Platonic text, where does this leave *physis* in the "first sailing" sense of "nature"—*physis* in the physical sense of the realm of things we can perceive with our bodily senses? Even if we attend to the recoiling moments in the Platonic dialogues that remind us that the mortal coil of human life and thought is bound to nature, does this alter their axiomatic orientation toward the supernatural? To pursue this question, let us turn to the *Phaedrus*, a prominent Platonic dialogue that speaks of two senses of a feast of *logos*.[84]

The centerpiece of this dialogue, Socrates's second speech, famously inscribes the doctrines of Platonist metaphysics with its mythical account of the tripartite soul consisting of two horses and a driver. This soul occasionally manages to grow wings and ascend to where the driver can glimpse the realm of the intelligible Ideas in the "place beyond the heavens" (ὑπερουράνιος τόπος) (*Phaedrus* 247c). For the most part, however, the driver, as the "best part of the soul" is alienated from this true home since, on account of the bad horse, it falls back into embodiment in the physical world.

The dialogue takes place between Socrates and Phaedrus. The latter recites a speech on love (ἔρως) by Lysias, who is said to have been in Athens the day before. Socrates comments, ironically, "No doubt Lysias was giving the company a feast of *logos*" (*Phaedrus* 227b). In order to convert Phaedrus away from understanding love as oriented toward physical pleasure to Socrates's own understanding of love as the philosophical ascent toward the metaphysical Ideas, that is, toward the true "feast" (δαίτη) or "banquet" (θοίνη) of the procession of the gods outside the rim of the celestial sphere (247a–b), he follows Phaedrus on a "walk outside the city walls" into the countryside. They wade barefoot across a stream and then sit and talk at a beautiful shady spot under a plane tree.

The *Phaedrus* stands out among the Platonic dialogues in that it takes place on an excursion outside of the city walls. However, having been lured out into the country by Phaedrus, it is Socrates's aim to lead Phaedrus back across the stream and thus return him to the city. Sallis reminds us that "the *Republic* concludes with the task of making a 'good crossing of the river [Λήθη]' (621c)," signifying "the ascent by which the soul returns from Hades to another life on earth."[85] Of course, the underworld of Hades—into which a lover not of wisdom but of the body (φιλοσώματος, Phaedo 68c) would fall—must be distinguished from the "place beyond the heavens" toward which earthling philosophers aspire on their upward journey. The *Republic* begins with a downward excursion out of the city, or rather to the outer limits of the city, namely to Piraeus, the harbor of Athens, where the city meets the open sea and where citizens mingle with foreigners. After attending the festival of Bendis, a goddess of the underworld, Socrates begins his ascent back to the city by engaging in a different kind of festival, the feast of *logos* with Thrasymachus referred to earlier (*Republic* 352b, 354a). In both cases, leaving the city is analogous to descending toward a realm of nature that is less than being, whereas returning to the city is viewed as an ascent on the upward journey toward the true being of the Ideas and ultimately toward the divine Good beyond being.

To be sure, just as there are gods and goddesses of the underworld, divinities can be found in the countryside as well. In the *Phaedrus*, when they reach the spot in the countryside, Socrates enthusiastically praises the natural scenery, and surmises that the stream is "consecrated to Achelous and some of the nymphs." Achelous is the chief river god, signaling the importance of the stream and, presumably, of making a good crossing of it back to the city. At the end of the dialogue, Socrates suggests that, before making their way back to the city, they first "offer a prayer to the divinities here." He then gives this prayer: "Dear Pan, and all ye other gods that dwell in this place, grant that I may become fair within, and that such outward things as I have may not war against the spirit within me" (*Phaedrus* 279b). Pan is a musician and also, as Socrates says elsewhere, "either *logos* or the brother of *logos*,"[86] suggesting perhaps that he represents the capacity for a certain kind of divine inspiration to unfold into *logos*. Pan is a god of music who is part man and part animal, and so perhaps he can also help humans achieve the virtue of moderation needed so that the desires of the body do not impede the desires of the spirit: in particular, the spiritual love for beauty and hence for truth that will bring humans from the countryside back to the city and, ultimately, back to their true home in the realm above the heavens.

It should be pointed out that, here as elsewhere, Plato is rewriting traditional accounts of the gods so as to put these myths at the service of philosophy.[87] Pan is traditionally portrayed as driving humans into an irrational frenzy with his music, and the nymphs or local nature deities are associated with musical and sexual seduction and abduction. Plato's *Phaedrus* is taming and reorienting, as it were, these divine powers of madness and ecstasy, reinterpreting them as inspiring forces of that beneficial "divine madness" that leads humans toward that realm above the heavens where they may feast on the real nourishment of the soul: the vision of the Ideas.

When first reaching the spot in the countryside, Socrates also mentions "the shrill summery music of the cicada choir" (*Phaedrus* 230c), and he later retells the myth of the cicadas. In its original pre-Platonic version, this myth can be understood as a warning against seduction by the Muses. When the Muses came into existence there was a race of humans who were "so thrilled by pleasure that they went on singing, and quite forgot to eat and drink until they actually died without noticing it" (259c). The first element of the Platonic reinterpretation of the myth is that, if we orient our love only toward pleasure, we will fail to take any part in that divine banquet of *logos* that is the true aim and sustenance of a properly human life.

Yet Socrates, in his second speech, is not simply calling on us to choose the saneness of reason over the madness of love but rather to engage in a kind of divine madness, a philosophical love that leads through earthly beauty upward toward the intelligible realm above the heavens. The cicadas, who are said to report back to the Muses, are accordingly interpreted as divine messengers who inspire us (*Phaedrus* 262d), and whose incessant singing reminds us to stay on this philo-sophical—or erotico-sophical—path to meta-physical wisdom and not get sidetracked by pursuing only physical pleasure. Specifically, "to the eldest, Calliope, and to her next sister, Urania, they tell of those who live a life of philosophy and so do honor to the music of these two Muses whose theme is the heavens and all the story of gods and men, and whose song is the noblest of them all" (259d tm). In other words, *the cicadas are reinterpreted as divine messengers sent to the countryside to remind us that our true home is not in the countryside.* The key point of Socrates' speech is that beauty is the shining of the supersensible in the sensible; it thus bridges the gap and leads us on our erotic path upwards from the country to the city and ultimately back to the true home of the highest part of our souls in that "place beyond the heavens."

Of course, in this Platonic dialogue it is hardly the case either that Phaedrus himself is truly trying to return to the country, or that Socrates thinks humans should stay walled up in the city. Phaedrus, after all, wants to use the countryside for an invigorating walk to refresh himself and in order to practice reciting the speech that he is concealing under his cloak. As Sallis writes in *Being and Logos*, one meaning of Socrates's question that opens the dialogue ("Phaedrus, my friend, where do you come from and where are you going?") and Phaedrus's answer (that he has come from listening to a speech by Lysias and going for a walk in the country) is that "men are formed in the city—this is where they come from—and they are formed especially by the speeches they hear in the city." Even when we go out into the countryside, it remains questionable: "Do men really go outside the city? Do they really succeed in getting beyond the walls?"[88] Or do they always see and experience the countryside through city speeches? Do they always only see φύσις through the framework of τέχνη—for example, as the work of a divine craftsman, as creatures great and small, or as a scenic landscape enframed as a vacation destination?

Socrates, for his part, "is beyond the city precisely by virtue of his way of being in the city."[89] As recounted in the *Apology*, Socrates understands himself as a gift to the city from God, called Apollo or Zeus (*Apology* 23b, 28e, 29d, 33c, 35d). "Socrates' way of being in the city (as gadfly), his specific mode of comportment to the men in the city (questioning), is not determined by the city nor by Socrates' 'genetic' bond to the city; it is determined, rather, by something which transcends the walls of Athens and of every particular city."[90] Nevertheless, what transcends the city is, for Socrates, not the countryside; it is not something natural. It is not nature but rather something divinely supernatural. The city lies between the countryside and the "place beyond the heavens" (ὑπερουράνιος τόπος) (*Phaedrus* 247c), just as humans, as combinations of body and soul, dwell between the visible world and the "intelligible realm" (νοητόν τόπον) (*Republic* 6.508b), and between the beasts of nature and the gods.

In the *Phaedrus*, Socrates shows his lack of interest in nature—in *physis* understood as the physical in opposition to the metaphysical, as the realm of the body rather than the realm of the soul. In regard to the scientific accounts of those so-called wise people (οἱ σοφοί) who debunk mythical beliefs—including those Presocratic philosophers whom Aristotle called φυσιολόγοι or "those who discuss nature"—he says: "I myself certainly have no time for the business, and I'll tell you why, my friend. I can't as yet 'know myself,' as the inscription at Delphi enjoins and so long as that ignorance remains it seems to me ridiculous to inquire into extraneous matters. Consequently I don't bother about such things, but accept the current beliefs about them, and direct my inquiries . . . rather to myself" (*Phaedrus* 229e–230a). Especially in the *Phaedo*, Socrates distances himself from the inquirers into the workings of the physical world and explains that the philosophical quest to "know thyself" involves a "liberation of the soul from the body" (ψυχῆς ἀπὸ τοῦ σώματος ἀπαλλαγήν). The practice of freeing the rational soul from distractions and desires of the body is an approximation and a preparation for that unfettered vision of the intelligible realm that can only happen in a disembodied afterlife. Socrates thus strikingly explains the practice of philosophy to be a "practicing dying and preparing for death" (αὐτοί ἐπιτηδεύουσιν ἢ ἀποθνῄσκειν τε καὶ τεθνάναι) (*Phaedo* 64a–c). Not surprisingly, the *Phaedo* in particular became the *locus classicus* for what Nietzsche and others decry as the body-despising and life-denying spirit of Platonism.

The Mortal Recoil: Earthbound After All?

And yet, Sallis persistently reminds us that, in the Platonic dialogues, "the upward way belongs inextricably together with a downward way, which is the way of corruption, the way of death, the way of concealment," and the way of earthly embodiment.[91] In his commentary on the *Phaedo*, Sallis reminds us that Socrates is here gearing his speech to two Pythagoreans, Simmias and Cebes. The term "philosopher" was probably first used among the Pythagorians, who took over a great deal from the mystery religion of Orphism. It is from this Orphic-Pythagorean tradition that Plato gleans the doctrines of reincarnation and—through the process of purification—the desideratum of liberating the soul from the body. Sallis writes:

> In the *Phaedo* there is much that derives from Pythagoreanism. . . . Yet, there is nothing taken over that is not, in one way or another, brought under interrogation. This is preeminently the case with the theme of purification, especially insofar as it is conceived as a means by which the soul would free itself of embodiment and of the attachment to nature and the earth that embodiment entails. In this interrogation what is fundamentally put in question is the bond of the human to φύσις and to the earth and the receptacle of φύσις.[92]

According to Sallis's provocative—indeed revolutionary—rereading of the *Phaedo*, Plato is not advocating for an understanding of philosophy as a liberation of the soul from the body but rather demonstrating—with dramatic hints and ironic ventriloquy of "obtrusively Orphic-Pythagorean diction and gestures"[93]—the hubris of thinking that this is possible.[94] The "second sailing" that Socrates ventures after turning away from a direct sensory investigation of natural things, Sallis points out, does not lead to a simple and straightforward intellectual vision of intelligible Ideas as the metaphysical causes of physical things.

> Rather, it is a turn to λόγοι as they call forth the beings themselves, the looks, the original causes. Yet, through this turn there is accomplished a return to the things of nature, a return in which these things become manifest in their look, in the look that shines through them and determines them in their being. In the second sailing the soul does indeed draw itself away from nature, but only in order that there might be a return of nature in the manifestness of its being.[95]

The *Phaedo* ends with Socrates's last words, namely "We owe a cock to Asclepius" (*Phaedo* 188), the god of healing. This has traditionally been understood—and derided especially by Nietzsche—to imply that life is one long illness from which the philosopher is freed by death.[96] Yet Sallis offers a competing—and rather compelling—counter-interpretation:

> What, then, is the illness from which there has been a recovery? It could hardly be a recovery from human emplacement in a body within nature upon the earth. Rather, the recovery—for Socrates but also for his friends—will have been from the presumption of an ascent into the company of the gods themselves, and from the danger that in venturing direct access to being itself one risks blinding one's very soul. It is a recovery that would free humans for a celebration of all that belongs to nature, that would enable them to embrace the return of nature.[97]

The recovery spoken of would thus be from the hubris of thinking that one could separate the rational soul from its earthbound embodiment. Ironically, the entire tradition of Platonists would have then missed the irony and pursued the hubris Socrates was warning against. Sallis's reading is thus as radically overturning as it is hermeneutically patient and persuasive.

And yet, I wonder whether Sallis goes a little too far in suggesting that Plato is unequivocally calling for a "celebration of all that belongs to nature" and an "embrace of the return of nature." It does seem persuasive to say that Plato is warning against the hubris of thinking we can, as embodied as well as rational beings, ever free ourselves completely from all things earthly—at least so long as we are embodied, and perhaps that means as long as we are alive in any sense. Nevertheless, the primary orientation of Plato's thought does generally seem to be away from nature, and his acknowledgment of an inevitable return of nature—and of the bodily in particular—hardly always seem celebratory. As Sallis himself notes, and quotes, in the final mythical tale at the end of the *Phaedo*, Socrates says that, while those who have committed bad deeds will be cast down into the various subterranean regions, "all who seem to have distinguished themselves in leading a holy life—it is they who are liberated and set free from these regions here within the earth, as though from prisons, and who, arriving at their pure dwelling up top, dwell on the surface of the earth. And of these people, the ones who have been sufficiently purified by philosophy live without bodies for all time to come" (*Phaedo* 114b–c). Nevertheless, Sallis reads this final myth of the *Phaedo*—which he calls "Socrates' swan song"—as a celebration of "a return of nature with the earth as its receptacle."[98] He writes:

> Hardly anything could be more remarkable than that Socrates' final discourse is a song of the earth, considering how often in the previous discourses, especially in the third, the body, the senses, nature, and the earth as the very receptacle of nature were denigrated as the locus that the true—or true-born—philosopher would strive to die away from. As Socrates' death draws near, he speaks only about the earth, and even what he says about the destiny of the various sorts of souls is in every case described in terms of the region of the earth to which they are finally transported. . . . Yet what seems most remarkable of all is the depiction of the purest and holiest souls: even they—even if they become so purified that they can live (even though they are dead) without bodies—even they go to dwell up on the surface of the earth. Not even they, though purified by philosophy, would take flight of the earth.[99]

And yet, I wonder whether this is a too literal reading of what Plato intended as allegory, in the manner in which the physical Sun is an earthly "offspring" and analogy for the metaphysical Good (*Republic* 6.508b). In the final myth of the *Phaedo*, as in the Allegory of the Cave in the Republic (*Republic* 7.515c–516c), is not the surface of the earth—which lies outside the cave or the cavernous underworld—a metaphor for the "intelligible realm" (νοητόν τόπον) (*Republic* 7.517b), that is, for the super-terrestrial (and indeed super-atmospheric) realm that Plato speaks of in the *Phaedrus* as the "place beyond the heavens" (ὑπερουράνιος τόπος) (*Phaedrus* 247c), the metaphysical realm to which the purified rational soul can ascend only after it leaves the binds of the body and the earth behind (see *Phaedo* 64–68)? After all, it is not only in the *Phaedo* that we find Socrates affirmatively discussing the Orphic doctrine expressed in the wordplay *sōma-sēma*: the teaching that the body (σῶμα) is like a tomb (σῆμα) from which the purified soul would be liberated into a super-corporeal afterlife (see *Phaedo* 80a–84b, *Gorgias* 493a, *Cratylus* 400b–c, and *Phaedrus* 250c).

Can We Learn from Trees in the *Chōra* Outside the *Polis*?

Despite the repeated reminders of the mortal recoil that binds us to earthly embodiment in this life, the predominant orientation of Socrates's discourses in the Platonic dialogues thus seems to remain, after all, the upward journey that ultimately is said to lead to a supernatural and incorporeal afterlife. In order to track this complicated yet persistent supernatural orientation—which became the all-too unequivocal metaphysical doctrine of Platonism—let us return to where we left off in the *Phaedrus*.

Although Socrates says that he does not have time for reductionistic scientific explanations of customary mythical stories, and so he just accepts those stories and gets on with his business of seeking to know himself (*Phaedrus* 229e–230a), he does not in fact simply accept those mythical stories as they have traditionally been told. Rather, he reinterprets and reorients them in a way that puts them in service to philosophy. Having reached the shady spot Phaedrus had in mind, Socrates enthusiastically praises the enchanting natural environment; yet, ironically, as we have seen, he interprets the divine sights and sounds he perceives in the countryside as reminders that he does not belong in the countryside: it is by talking to people in the city, not by communing with nature in the countryside, that he can stay on course in his journey back to the supernatural home of the highest part of his soul. Thus, after reaching the beautiful spot in the countryside, Socrates says that Phaedrus has been "the stranger's perfect guide." To which Phaedrus responds:

> "Whereas you [Socrates], my excellent friend, strike me as the oddest of men. You really do seem like a stranger [ἀτοπώτατος, literally someone out of place] being guided about, rather than like a native [ἐπιχωρίῳ, literally a person of the country]. You never leave the city to cross the border nor even, I believe, so much as set foot outside the city walls." Socrates replies: "You must forgive me, dear friend; I'm a lover of learning, and country regions [χωρία] and the trees won't teach me anything, whereas the people in the city do. (*Phaedrus* 230c–d tm)

By sharp contrast, it would seem,[100] Heidegger does think we can learn from country regions and from trees. In his 1949 essay, "Der Feldweg" ("The Country Path"), Heidegger reminisces about growing up among oak trees and learning from them about the slowness and steadiness of growth. He writes: "The oak tree itself spoke, saying that what lasts and bears fruit is grounded solely in such growth; and that growth means: to open oneself to the expanse of the heavens and at the same time to be rooted in the dark earth, and that everything sturdy flourishes only if humans are equally both prepared for the claim of the highest heaven and taken into the protection of the supportive earth."[101] The oak tree teaches us, in other words, that we belong in the between; we are beings whose life and growth are nurtured by dwelling always between the earth and the heavens. We do not exist in this between as beings who erotically strive—through increasingly disembodied levels of ἔρως—to return to an intelligible home above the heavens; our desire is not ultimately directed to a disembodied beholding of "the beautiful" (τὸ καλὸν) as such, "pure, undefiled, unmixed, unadulterated by human flesh and skin complexion, or any other such mortal nonsense" (*Symposium* 211e). Rather, our true home is in the between, and beautiful and meaningful things can be experienced only *there*, in the fourfold gathering (*Geviert*) of earth and sky, mortals and divinities.[102]

For Heidegger, even the divine does not subsist in a realm above the heavens; the divinities are not supernatural beings. Even God, or the Godhood (*Gottheit*) of which the divinities are said to be "the hinting messengers,"[103] is not a supernatural being.[104] In "Der Feldweg," Heidegger writes: "The expanse of all grown things, which abide about the country path, bestows world. As Eckhart, the old master of reading and living, said, in the unspoken of the language of this expanse, God is first God" (GA

13: 89). Trees can teach us to listen to the divine, not as a supernatural voice breaking into nature from a realm above the heavens, but rather as the silence and wordless sounds of the natural expanse in which we dwell among all living things. And this expanse bestows world, not as a stationary site cut off from nature behind city walls, but first of all as a country path on which we walk between cultivated fields and dark forests.

And yet, trees can teach us such things only if we let them show themselves from themselves rather than through rhetorical lenses crafted behind city walls; only if, that is, we "for once let the tree stand where it stands," namely, in the "country region" that abides in the "open-region." This "healing expanse," which "provides us with freedom," is intimated to the Younger Man in the third of the *Country Path Conversations* by "the rustling of the expansive forest" on his walk outside the walls of the barracks, walls that he identifies with "what is objective" (*das Gegenständliche*).[105] The problem, Heidegger later writes in *Was heisst Denken?*, is that "to this day, thought has never let the tree stand where it stands."[106] The problem is that we make it stand over against us as an object (*Gegenstand*) of our representation; the problem is that we allow the tree to show itself only through the idea of treeness (*das Baumhafte*) that we have projected upon it having preemptively climbed up above the tree itself.[107]

Where Is Truth—in Presencing or in Representation?

Understanding ourselves as *animal rationale*—a medieval version of the Aristotlean determination of human being as ζῷον λόγον ἔχον—we have come to think that: "Thinking is really nothing other than the representational setting-before [*Vor-stellen*] and setting-toward [*Zu-stellen*] of the horizon, that is, of the circle-of-vision, in which the outward look and the essence of objects—Plato named it the Idea of things—becomes visible to us."[108] In this statement, the Scholar in the first *Conversation* draws a line connecting modern "transcendental-horizonal representation" back to Plato's thought of the Ideas. Of course, this line is a long one and we need to examine it carefully—even more carefully than did Heidegger.

We have seen how, in "Plato's Doctrine of Truth" (1931–32, 1940), Heidegger claimed that "what remains unsaid in Plato's thinking is a change in the determination of the essence of truth," namely a change from an understanding of truth as ἀλήθεια, as the unconcealment or unhiddenness of beings, to truth as the correctness (ὀρθότης) of human apprehension and assertion about beings.[109] In Plato, truth is said to have been displaced from the display of things themselves to the correspondence of our thoughts and words about things with the Ideas that form the essences of things. In 1975, however, Heidegger reportedly said in a conversation with John Sallis that his essay "Plato's Doctrine of Truth" was no longer tenable, meaning, presumably, that the Platonic dialogues were not after all the site of a transformation of truth from unconcealment to correctness.

Where, then, does this leave matters? As Sallis puts the question, "How is the relation between the two determinations of truth to be reconfigured in the Platonic text once Heidegger's thesis of a change from one to the other has been set aside?" Sallis himself provocatively offers one possibility by way of unfolding the implications of a key statement found in "Plato's Doctrine of Truth." After the purportedly fateful change in the determination of truth, according to that essay: "The ἰδέα is not a presenting foreground [*ein darstellender Vordergrund*] of ἀλήθεια but rather the ground that makes ἀλήθεια possible."[110] This implies, however, "that prior to the change the ἰδέα is a presenting foreground of ἀλήθεια." Sallis develops this implication as follows:

> The ἰδέα would be the look by which things come to be present, the look that, shining through them, presents them as the things they are, that is, *in their unconcealment*. Yet as such the ἰδέα would be only foreground, would be set against the background of concealment from which the look of things would have to be wrested and to which these looks, the things themselves, would always remain attached. Thus the ἰδέα would be nothing other than the moment of unconcealment belonging to ἀλήθεια. . . . The reconfiguration of the two determinations of truth can now be very simply sketched. Truth as ἀλήθεια would make possible truth as correctness by setting forth a look, a presenting foreground, to which apprehension could correspond and so be correct. Yet the look would be bound to concealment, and consequently the apprehension would be bound always to take account of the bond to concealment.[111]

Remarkably, Sallis reveals that this doubling of truth—this interplay between truth as unconcealment and truth as the relation of correctness that unconcealment enables in its withdrawal into the background—is at play in the Platonic dialogues themselves. Moreover, those dialogues, in their moments of recoil, are found to intimate a "turn back into concealment," that is, a returning of our attention to the nonsublatable interplay between concealment (λήθη) and unconcealment (ἀλήθεια). What is remarkable about this reading is not just that it finds Heidegger's central thought of *alētheia* anticipated in Plato. After all, Heidegger found his way to this thought by way of returning to the Presocratics, and so we might simply conclude that Plato, as a watershed figure, had more in common with the Presocratics than Heidegger acknowledged. Yet what is also remarkable is that, while Sallis moves the line forward into the Platonic dialogues, so to speak, Heidegger, in his late writings, pushes it back further into the Presocratic Greeks.

In "The End of Philosophy and the Task of Thinking" (1966, 1969), where Heidegger famously, in response to Paul Friedländer's critique,[112] retracts the central claim of "Plato's Doctrine of Truth," namely "the assertion about the essential transformation of truth, that is, from unconcealment to correctness," the reason he gives for this retraction is *not* that Plato in fact did, after all, maintain an understanding of truth as unconcealment but rather that, *even in the Presocratic Greeks*,

> 'Αλήθεια, unconcealment in the sense of the clearing of presence, was originally experienced only as ὀρθότης, as correctness of representations and statements. But then the assertion about the essential transformation of truth, that is, from unconcealment to correctness, is also untenable. Instead we must say: ἀλήθεια, as the clearing of presence and presentation in thinking and saying, immediately comes under the perspective of ὁμοίωσις and *adaequatio*, that is, the perspective of adequation in the sense of the correspondence of representing with what is present.[113]

"'Αλήθεια is indeed named at the beginning of philosophy" by Presocratics such as Parmenides; but, Heidegger says, "It is not explicitly thought by philosophy," not even in the very beginning, for it immediately came under the sway of truth as correctness (ZSD 76/BW 446). The early Greeks did indeed "experience" *alētheia* as unconcealment; but, in order to "think it as the clearing of self-concealing," we must go "above and beyond the Greek [*über das Griechische hinaus*]" (79/448).[114]

Freeing Beings from Platonic Ideas

The metaphysical understanding of truth as correctness, as the adequation of representations to reality, is said to have first taken root in the Platonic doctrine of Forms or Ideas, according to which a mental idea was true insofar as it corresponds to a metaphysical Idea. So let us briefly turn our attention now to Heidegger's *Auseinandersetzung* with the discourse on the Ideas initiated by the Platonic dialogues and developed by the tradition of Platonism.

Section §110 of *Contributions to Philosophy* gives a sketch of the history of metaphysics beginning with "the concept of ἰδέα (εἶδος)." This concept is said to have originally meant "the look of something, what something gives itself out to be and makes of itself, that in which something is set back and thus is the being itself." It means "the *shining forth* of the *look* itself, what offers up a view and does so for a gaze." Originally, therefore, an *idea* as an *eidos* is not a metaphysical Idea determining the essence of things from above, much less an idea in our heads. Rather, it is the look given forth by the thing itself; it is the way a tree, for example, shows itself from itself.

However, Heidegger goes on to say, insofar as the emphasis is on "the *presencing*, the shining forth, of the view in the look and specifically as that which in *coming to presence* provides *constancy at the same time*," there originates the bond of the ἰδέα to the notion of "constant presence." Moreover, insofar as it is the look of treeness that remains constantly present, even though the particular tree may change, "Here originates the distinction between the τί ἔστιν ['what it is'] (*essentia, quidditas*) and ὅτι ['that it is'] (*existentia*) in the temporality of the ἰδέα."[115] In "Sketches for a History of Being as Metaphysics," Heidegger writes of this fateful division between essence or "whatness" and existence or "thatness," a division that ensues when ἀλήθεια "comes under the yoke of the ἰδέα." "The precedence of the ἰδέα brings the τί ἔστιν along with the εἶδος to the position of authoritative measure-giving being [*des maßgebenden Seins*]. Being is primarily whatness. . . . As authoritative measure-giving being, whatness displaces being, namely being in the primordial determination lying *before* the distinction of what and that, the determination which preserves for being the fundamental characteristic of inceptuality and emergence and presencing."[116] In his 1943 lectures on φύσις in Heraclitus, Heidegger says that the Greek ὄν was originally ambiguous: it is a participle which, like our English gerund "being," can be understood both nominally as *das Seiende* (a being) and verbally as *Sein* (τὸ εἶναι, *be-ing*, *to be*).[117] It was precisely the turning away from the verbal sense to the nominal sense and, moreover, the identification of this nominal sense with ἰδέα, that inaugurated metaphysics. Heidegger's thought is an attempt to return to the verbal sense of being understood at once as *physis* and as *alētheia*. The return to the things themselves is a return to the way in which things naturally show themselves from themselves at the same time as they withdraw back into concealment and so preserve their inexhaustible richness.

Heidegger's other chorology is thus an attempt not just to let things show themselves from themselves but also to let them return to that open-region of nature, the field of *physis*, in which they originarily belong. The world, he says, "insofar as it worlds, gathers everything, each to the other, and lets everything return to itself in its own resting in the selfsame."[118] Insofar as Heidegger's chorology calls for a proper human participation in the *logos* that is "the gathering toward the originally all-unifying One" (223/145), it calls for letting things return to rest in themselves. This would be a matter of letting things be as they are—as they are, that is, neither merely locked up "in themselves" nor merely exposed "to us," but rather, in the circulating course proper to their self-showing, "as things for themselves [*als Dinge für sich selbst*]" (139/90).

(Un)conclusion: Interpreting Plato's *Polis* as Heidegger's *Lichtung*

It is tempting to conclude this essay by summarizing the contrasts between Platonist metaphysics and Heidegger's postmetaphysical thinking. In 1929–30 Heidegger quotes Novalis as saying, "Philosophy is really a homesickness, an urge to be at home everywhere" (GA 29/30: 7/FCM 5). Yet the "first inception" of philosophy articulated in the Platonic dialogues repeatedly suggests that the true home of the highest part of our souls is elsewhere, not of this earthly world. Heidegger, in 1929–30, speaks of becoming at home *in the world*. To be sure, at this point he still views the world as formed by Dasein's transcendental-horizonal projection, which, in a sense, surpasses nature.[119] By the time he writes *Country Path Conversations*, however, Heidegger thinks of the environing horizonal world as situated within a nonanthropocentric open-region, a "healing expanse" that is most nearly sensed when we venture out on country paths that take us through "the rustling of the expansive forest."[120]

The Platonic dialogues take place within city walls, or, in the unique case of the *Phaedrus*, on an excursion out to the countryside that in the end leads back to the city. Heidegger's *Conversations*, by contrast, take place on country paths, and they deepen as they wander forth into dark forests. The path of Platonic *eros* leads primarily upward toward a realm above the heavens, toward a transcendence of nature (even if, so long as we remain embodied, there is an inevitable return of nature). Heidegger's *Gelassenheit* entails a being engaged (*eingelassen sein*) in the earth and an openness to the mystery of nature. To be more precise, Heidegger's *Gelassenheit* involves a being at home in not being at home in nature; it is a matter of being at home in an intelligible clearing that is surrounded by an endlessly bountiful yet also eerily boundless forest. Heidegger's path of thought does not aim to take us somewhere else but rather to let us, for once, be where we are. It does not aim at metaphysical transcendence to the supernatural, but rather at an indwelling that does not forget that our human being-in-the-world is, in turn, situated within the wider field of nature.

Thus may we summarize the differences. And yet, while the contrast with Platonic metaphysics may be clear, the relation of Heidegger's thought to the richness of the Platonic dialogues evades such clear-cut opposition. And so, let me close—or rather open back up—this essay by explicating Heidegger's attempt to recover a more primordial sense of *physis* in another one of his readings of Plato. In his 1942 lecture course, *Parmenides*, Heidegger looks back to what he calls the "fresh leaves" of the tree of Plato's texts rather than to the "foliage fallen on the ground" that became Platonism.[121] "It is almost as if," Heidegger says, "what was always already nearby and experienced is explicitly put into words only in the age of the completion of Greek humanity, a completion that is not a high peak but instead a high pass of transition to the end" (131/88).

Here Heidegger gives a highly original interpretation of the concluding myth of the *Republic*, the Πολιτεῖα.[122] He writes: "The last word of the Greeks that names λήθη in its essence is the μῦθος concluding Plato's dialogue on the essence of the πόλις."[123] What is first of all remarkable—and no doubt controversial—is how Heidegger claims that the "essence of the πόλις, i.e., the πολιτεῖα, is not itself determined or determinable 'politically'" (142/96). Building on the interpretation of "the pre-political essence of the πόλις" he gave the previous semester in his course on Hölderlin's *Der Ister*,[124] Heidegger says that "Πόλις is the πόλος, the pole, the place around which everything appearing to the Greeks as a being turns in a peculiar way."[125] He also says that "πόλις is, in its root, identical with the ancient Greek word for 'to be,' πέλειν: 'to emerge, to rise up into the unconcealed'" (133/90). "Hence the πόλις is not the notorious 'city-state' but is, rather, the settling of the place of the history of Greek humanity... . ...The πόλις is the abode, gathered together into itself, of the unconcealedness of beings" (133/90). The *polis* is thus, in other words, the site of *alētheia*.

To the experience of *alētheia*, of life in the *polis*, belongs an experience of *lēthē*, an experience of what is named in Plato's myth "τό τῆς Λήθης πεδίον—the field of withdrawing concealment [*das Feld der entziehenden Verbergung*]."[126] If *alētheia* is the *polis*, the abode of unconcealment in which mortals dwell, this abode is situated within a field—perhaps we might say a *chōra*, a country region—an uncanny forest that surrounds, exceeds, and encompasses the clearing, the "city," in which we are at home and go about our ordinary lives. We, however, no longer see beyond the city walls; we no longer take excursions in the countryside, even when (or precisely when) the vacation industry provides us with outdoor adventures. And we no longer notice that our homely cities, in which our ordinary lives are conducted, are situated in this surrounding uncanny (*unheimliche*), unhomely (*unheimische*), and even monstrously extraordinary (*ungeheuerliche*) region.

When Heidegger says that "being ... is precisely *the* τόπος for all beings,"[127] this is not simply a space of intelligibility but includes at its heart—or is included in, surrounded by—what Plato's myth calls a "δαιμόνιος τόπος," which Heidegger translates as an "*ungeheure Ortschaft*," a "monstrously extraordinary locality."[128] "For us," he says, "it is difficult to attain the fundamental Greek experience, whereby the ordinary itself ... is the monstrously extraordinary."[129] We no longer attend to the uncanny mystery of the "earth" that enables the emergence of—and may at any moment, and will certainly in due time, reclaim—our fortified cities and our embodied lives.

In his interpretation of the choral ode in Sophocles's *Antigone*, Heidegger speaks of the uncanny as "*das Un-heimische*," as "that unhomely that is the fundamental trait of human abode in the midst of beings."[130] We need to distinguish between what we might call an inauthentic and an authentic homelessness or being unhomely. The former is our "fallenness" or lostness among predetermined beings, our everyday "running around amidst beings" (*Umtrieben an das Seiende*)[131] and consequent forgetfulness of our true home in being. For "being is not some thing that is actual";[132] it does not provide a home in the sense of a constant presence that supports us, but rather withdraws its extraordinary excess in order to enable the delimitations of the horizons of an ordinary abode—an artistically and linguistically delimited "house of being." Dwelling in such a domesticated *world* while at the same time maintaining a nearness to the *earth*—that is, to the extraordinary excess of the open-region of being that lies outside and encompasses our horizonal homes—would be an authentic homelessness. Heidegger's thought calls for a being at home in not being at home, an ek-static standing out of our homeliness among beings as an indwelling (*Inständigkeit*) in the open-region of being in a manner that is "open to the mystery." In his reading of the choral ode as the core of *Antigone*, Heidegger thus says: "The counterplay [of this tragedy] is played out between being unhomely in the sense of being driven about amid beings without any way out, and being unhomely as becoming homely from out of a belonging to being . . . such that what is poetized is a becoming homely in being unhomely."[133]

In the following year, in his *Parmenides* lecture course, Heidegger elaborates on this unhomely abode as he looks back beyond the purported transformation of *alētheia* to correctness, back to the primordial unity of *alētheia* and *physis* intimated in Plato's *mythos*.

> We may call the δαιμόνιον the monstrously extraordinary [*das Un-geheure*], because it surrounds, and insofar as it everywhere surrounds, the present ordinary state of things and presents itself in everything ordinary, though without being the ordinary [*das Geheure*]. The monstrously extraordinary, understood in this way with regard to what is ordinary, is not the exception but rather the "most natural [*das Natürlichste*]" in the sense of "nature" as thought by the Greeks, i.e., in the sense of φύσις. The uncanny, the extraordinary, is that out of which all that is ordinary emerges, that within which all that is ordinary is suspended, usually without surmising it in the least, and that into which everything ordinary falls back.[134]

Heidegger's postmetaphysical chorology invites us to find our home, not up in the supernatural heavens but rather in the midst of the uncanny extraordinariness of the open-region of nature that surrounds—and ordinarily shows itself only as delimited by—the homely horizons of our everyday being-in-the-world.[135]

Notes

1. LW: 187. I have marked "tm" in cases where I have modified translations. A draft of this essay was first presented as part of a lecture course given at the Collegium Phaenomenologicum in July of 2013. I thank Drew Highland for inviting me to teach that course. And I thank the attendees, John Sallis foremost among them, for an intense and fruitful discussion afterward.

2. Other than the three texts gathered in *Country Path Conversations*, the only other two texts Heidegger composed in the form of dialogues were "Das abendländische Gespräch: 1946/1948" (GA 75: 57–196), a long, less polished, and unfinished dialogue written in the wake of *Country Path Conversations*; and "From a Conversation on Language (1953–54): Between a Japanese and an Inquirer" (GA 12, 79–146/OWL 1–54, translation of the title modified). Although the three dialogues in *Country Path Conversations* appear polished and complete, the editor of GA 77 informs us that in Heidegger's *Nachlaß* can be found sketches for continuations of all three (GA 77: 246/CPC 161). Heidegger published a revised excerpt of the first *Conversation* was in 1959 (GA 13: 37—74/DT 59–90). For some insightful reflections on the dramatic elements of Heidegger's dialogues, together with some comparisons with Plato's dialogues, see Drew A. Hyland, "Heidegger's (Dramatic?) Dialogues," *Research in Phenomenology* 45 (2015): 341–57; and three articles by Katherine Davies: "The Resistant Interlocutor: Plato, Heidegger, and the End of Dialogue," *Epoché: A Journal for the History of Philosophy* 23/1 (2018): 165–90; "Heidegger's Reading(s) of the Phaedrus," *Studia Phaenomenologica* 20 (2020): 191–221; and "Heidegger's Conversational Pedagogy," *Research in Phenomenology* 53, no. 3 (2022): 399–424.

3. LW: 212, 241.

4. John Sallis, *Chorology: On Beginning in Plato's Timaeus* (Bloomington: Indiana University Press, 1999).

5. LW: 182.
6. LW: 179.
7. See LW: 181, 186.
8. LW: 187.
9. LW: 187.
10. LW: 212.
11. LW: 241.
12. GA 34/ETP.
13. GA 9: 203–38/PM 155–82.

14. For a treatment of the development of Heidegger's path of thought that focuses on his turn from the will to nonwilling, see Bret W. Davis, *Heidegger and the Will: On the Way to Gelassenheit* (Evanston, IL: Northwestern University Press, 2007). For a sketch of the content of *Country Path Conversations*, see my Translator's Foreword to CPC.

15. GA 77: 95/61; see also 92/59, 138/89, 199/129, 205/132, 230/149.

16. GA 77: 187/CPC 122.

17. GA 5: 75—113/QCT 115-54.

18. GA 77: 5-12/3-11.

19. GA 55: 89.

20. GA 77: 17/CPC 11.

21. GA 77: 41-42, 141/CPC 26-27, 92.

22. On the fate of "nature" in the turn of Heidegger's thought that can be witnessed most clearly in *Country Path Conversations*, see Bret W. Davis, "Returning the World to Nature: Heidegger's Turn from a Transcendental-Horizonal Projection of World to an Indwelling Releasement to the Open-Region," *Continental Philosophy Review* 47/3 (2014): 373–97.

23. GA 77: 91, 209/CPC 58, 135.

24. ZSD 63/BW 433.

25. GA 77: 187/CPC 122.

26. GA 65/CP.

27. In addition to his *Chorology* (1999), see especially the following works by John Sallis: *Being and Logos: Reading the Platonic Dialogues*, 3rd ed. (Bloomington: Indiana University Press, 1996 [first edition 1975]); *Platonic Legacies* (Albany: State University of New York Press, 2004); and *The Figure of Nature: On Greek Origins* (Bloomington: Indiana University Press, 2016).

28. According to Heidegger, Nietzsche's reversal of Platonic oppositions is an overturning that consummates the history of metaphysics; Nietzsche is said to sometimes anticipate but never quite manage to "twist free" into a nonmetaphysical thinking. See Ni 180, 231–42/N1 154, 200–10; Ni 473–81/N3 3–9; Nii 199–202/N4 147–49. See also Davis, *Heidegger and the Will*, 151–57.

29. Jacques Derrida, "Khōra," translated by Ian Mcleod, in Jacques Derrida, *On the Name*, edited by Thomas Dutoit (Stanford: Stanford University Press, 1995), 119–20.

30. N1 151.

31. GA 77: 187/CPC 122.

32. GA 77: 109/CPC 70.

33. GA 77: 198/CPC 128.

34. EHD 103/EHP 126 tm.

35. Translations of passages from Plato's dialogues are generally taken from *The Collected Dialogues of Plato*, edited by Edith Hamilton and Huntington Cairns (Princeton, NJ: Princeton University Press, 1961). I have sometimes modified

these translations and, when commenting on Sallis's interpretations, often used his translations.

36. GA 77: 56/CPC 36.

37. GA 77: 137/CPC 89.

38. G. W. F. Hegel, *Phänomenologie des Geistes* (Frankfurt: Suhrkamp,1986), 46; *Hegel's Phenomenology of Spirit*, translated by A. V. Miller (New York: Oxford University Press, 1977), 27.

39. Heidegger's only explicit reference to Hegel in *Country Path Conversations* serves to distance his attempt to think the sense in which "physics is applied technology" from the "tricky tactics of reversal" one finds in the assertions of philosophers such as Hegel, who claims that "in order to be able to follow the thinking of metaphysics, one must attempt to stand on one's head and walk like that" (GA 77: 7/CPC 4).

40. Sallis, *Chorology*, 123. It is beyond the scope of this essay to do justice to the manner in which Sallis's own phenomenological thinking has—in the wake of and, at times, in critique of Heidegger—developed in part out of his careful engagement with Plato's chorology. Sallis has coupled a pursuit of the topic of imagination, which Heidegger dramatically brought to the fore in his Kant book and then abandoned, with a pursuit of the question of the "sensible," which cannot be reduced to the question of the "meaning" of being. With this coupling of imagination and the sensible, and drawing on early Greek discourses of the elements including their centrality to Plato's chorology, Sallis develops a thinking of "the elementals" that adds a concrete sensibility to the Heideggerian chorology discussed in the present essay. In addition to *Chorology* and his other works on Plato, some key works of Sallis in this regard are *Echoes: After Heidegger* (Bloomington: Indiana University Press, 1990); *Force of Imagination: The Sense of the Elemental* (Bloomington: Indiana University Press, 2000); and *Logic of Imagination: The Expanse of the Elemental* (Bloomington: Indiana University Press, 2012).

41. Sallis, *Chorology*, 111.

42. GA 77: 113/73.

43. EM 50/IM 72 tm.

44. EM 51/IM 73, emphasis added.

45. EM 51/IM 73 tm.

46. Note that, given that there are indications that at least some of the parenthetical remarks in *Introduction to Metaphysics* were in fact added after 1935, it may be that the passage quoted earlier was written after the Heraclitus lecture course of 1944 and after *Country Path Conversations* (1944–45). One can also hear an echo of the *chōra* in Heidegger's 1959 "Hölderlin's Earth and Heaven" when he speaks of "the Greek χορός" as the festive "round dance" in which the fourfold are gathered (EHD 174/EHP 198). After the original draft of the present essay was written and presented at the Collegium Phaenomenologicum in July of 2013, a fine English translation of Heidegger's 1943 and 1944 lectures on Heraclitus was

published (HC). Although I have kept my own translations and references to GA 55, the English translation includes the German pagination and so the context of the passages I cite from GA 55 can easily be found in that volume.

47. GA 55: 337.

48. Richard D. McKirahan, *Philosophy Before Socrates: An Introduction with Texts and Commentary* (Indianapolis: Hackett, 1994), 117.

49. GA 55: 330.

50. GA 55: 333.

51. GA 55: 335.

52. GA 77: 223/CPC 145. These terms are gleaned from Heidegger's translation and interpretation of Heraclitus's Fragment 50. See GA 55: 243–47; and VA 218/EGT 75.

53. GA 55: 337.

54. GA 55: 338.

55. GA 77: 114/CPC 74.

56. GA 15: 335/FS 41 tm.

57. GA 65/CP, written 1936–38.

58. See Sallis, *Platonic Legacies*, 86–90.

59. GA 55: 335.

60. see GA 77: 182/CPC 118.

61. In critique of Aristotle's misinterpretation of Plato's *chōra* as *topos* and as *hyle* (see *Physics* 192a, 209b), Sallis avers that these equations have no basis in the *Timaeus*. See Sallis, *Chorology*, 152; and *Platonic Legacies*, 31–32.

62. Sallis, *Platonic Legacies*, 42.

63. See Heidegger's essays collected in QCT and Davis, *Heidegger and the Will*, 173–78.

64. See GA 9: 197—98/PM 151; GA 77: 151–57, 205–6/CPC 99–103, 132–33; GA 13: 24/DT 55.

65. On the curious similarities between the before-being of the *chōra* and the beyond-being of the Good, see Sallis, *Platonic Legacies*, 54, 78. Sallis goes so far as to suggest: "Is it not in the chorology that one finds, then, a Platonic counterpart to the movement back through the first beginning ventured in [Heidegger's] *Contributions to Philosophy*?" "To be sure," he adds, "the chorology did not become part of the Platonic legacy; its reduction and effective exclusion is already at work as early as Aristotle. The Platonic chorology is rather something held back from the legacy, something not passed along, except for the traces remaining in the text of the *Timaeus*. Yet those traces endure beyond that Platonism that chorology already exceeds" (*Platonic Legacies*, 93). Sallis has pioneered the recovery of those traces. The question remains, however, in what sense or senses Plato's pre- or proto-metaphysical chorology, which both undercuts and underlies the "first inception" of metaphysics, is the counterpart to the other chorology involved in Heidegger's "other inception" of postmetaphysical thinking.

It is beyond the scope of the present essay to pursue the manner in which later Platonists and Neoplatonists took up the legacy of Plato's dialogues and of his so-called unwritten doctrines. The latter include the idea that, for there to be intelligible and sensible beings, the first principle of the One must, from the beginning, be complicated by the second principle of The Infinite Dyad (see Aristotle's *Physics* 209b13–15, and *Metaphysics* 987b25–988a15, 1081a22, 1081b22, 32–33). The Indefinite Dyad (ἀόριστος δυάς) is akin to, and perhaps even synonymous with, the *chōra*. The One is the principle of unity and determinateness, whereas the Infinite Dyad is the principle of multiplicity and indeterminacy. Both these primordial principles are coprimordially necessary for the generation of sensible and intelligible beings, and yet they are both before or beyond being and thus insensible and unknowable in themselves. For rethinking the relation between Heidegger's postmetaphysical thought and Plotinus in particular, the work of Reiner Schürmann is especially noteworthy. See his "Neoplatonic Henology as an Overcoming of Metaphysics," *Research in Phenomenology* 13 (1983): 25–41; and his *Broken Hegemonies*, translated by Reginald Lilly (Bloomington: Indiana University Press, 2003), 137–88. See also Sallis's engagement with Schürmann's work in "Platonism at the Limit of Metaphysics," in *Platonic Legacies*, 61–78. For a nuanced critique of Heidegger's metaphysical interpretation of Plato's Idea of the Good as failing to attend to the strategies and ironies at play in Plato's text and to the similarities to his own postmetaphysical thought, see Adraiaan T. Peperzak, "Heidegger and Plato's Idea of the Good," in *Reading Heidegger: Commemorations*, edited by John Sallis (Bloomington: Indiana University Press, 1993), 258–85. For a compelling argument that Socrates's method of elenctic discussion in Plato's early dialogues presents us with one model of the nonmetaphysical thinking "in the between" that Heidegger calls for in texts such as *Contributions to Philosophy* (GA65/CP), see Sean D. Kirkland, "Thinking in the Between with Heidegger and Plato," *Research in Phenomenology* 37 (2007): 95–111. Kirkland argues that not only are these early dialogues of Plato compatible with Heidegger's nonmetaphysical thinking, but that, in so far as Socrates is primarily concerned with human virtue, they "open up the possibility of engaging political and ethical problems, without betraying Heidegger's insight as to the limits of the metaphysical concepts that traditionally ground those discussions" (111). However, Gregory Fried argues that, in order to revive ethical and political thought after their foundering in "Heideggerian postmodernism," we need to return to a nondogmatic Plato who does not deny our finitude and yet who inspires us to repeatedly aspire toward the transcendent Good. See Gregory Fried, "Back to the Cave: A Platonic Rejoinder to Heideggerian Postmodernism," in *Heidegger and the Greeks*, edited by Drew A. Hyland and John Panteleimon Manoussakis (Bloomington: Indiana University Press, 2006), 156–76; on Plato in this regard, see also Drew Hyland, *Finitude and Transcendence in the Platonic Dialogues* (Albany: State University of New York Press, 1995), esp. 108–9, 176–78, 191–95. It is true that Heidegger failed to do more than suggest in passing that his thinking implied an "originary ethics" (GA 9: 356/PM: 271), and even commentators who are sympathetic with his aversion to metaphysical moralizing have bemoaned what Drew Hyland calls "Heidegger's longstanding antipathy toward 'the political,' toward 'ethics,' towards that whole set of issues that could be said to be associated with 'the polis'" (Hyland, "Heidegger's [Dramatic?] Dialogues," 349). While it is beyond the scope of the present essay to address this important issue, it is no doubt a momentous question for a postmetaphysical chorology whether it can provide the grounds—or groundless source—for ethical and political critique. Whether it is thought with or against (the letter or the spirit of) Plato's texts, might not this other chorology imply a kind of transcendence—or, rather, "trans-descendance"—toward the source of ethical and political thought and action? (The term "trans-descendance" was apparently first used by Jean Wahl, yet I borrow it from Kyoto School philosopher of Zen, Nishitani Keiji; see Bret W. Davis, "The Step Back Through Nihilism: The Radical Orientation of Nishitani Keiji's Philosophy of Zen," *Synthesis Philosophica* 37 [2004]: 139–59.) Does not this other chorology and, indeed, Heidegger's entire path of thought indicate a third way beyond both metaphysical transcendence and positivistic immanence? The question could be put thus: Do ethical and political thought and action require transcendence toward the supernatural, or might they receive their impetus and orientation from a trans-descendance toward a deeper sense of the natural?

66. GA 77: 155/102.
67. GA 77: 149/ CPC 97; see G 65–66/DT 86.
68. See Davis, "Returning the World to Nature."
69. See GA 65: §97.
70. GA 90: 5.
71. GA 77: 17/11, 33/21.
72. GA 77: 146–47/CPC 95–96.
73. GA 9: 201, 231/PM 155, 177; see also GA 34: 17–18/ETP 12.
74. EM 11/IM 15–16.
75. Sallis, *Figure of Nature*, 235.
76. Sallis, *Figure of Nature*, 232–33.
77. Sallis, *Platonic Legacies*, 132–33.
78. See Sallis, *Platonic Legacies*, 137.
79. See Sallis, *Figure of Nature*, 238.
80. See John Sallis, "Gathering Language," in John Sallis, *Elemental Discourses* (Bloomington: Indiana University Press, 2018), 34.
81. GA 12: 9–30/PLT 187–208.
82. Among his many works on art, see John Sallis, *Transfigurements: On the True Sense of Art* (Chicago: University of Chicago Press, 2008); and John Sallis, *Songs of Nature: On Paintings by Cao Jun* (Bloomington: Indiana University Press, 2020).

83. See Julia Kristeva, "The Semiotic *Chora* Ordering the Drives," in Julia Kristeva, *Revolution in Poetic Language*, translated by Margaret Waller (New York: Columbia University Press, 1984), 25–30.

84. My treatment of the *Phaedrus* in relation to Heidegger's thought will not pursue a textual analysis of Heidegger's own various treatments of this dialogue over the course of his career. In her "Heidegger's Reading(s) of the Phaedrus," Katherine Davies examines Heidegger's three explicit readings of the *Phaedrus*—in the 1924/25 *Plato's Sophist* lectures (GA 19: 308–52/PS 214—44); in a seminar on the *Phaedrus* in 1932 (GA 83: 85–150); and in the first lecture course on Nietzsche in 1936 (Ni 218–31/N1 188–99)—as well as in what she interprets as an implicit engagement in "Das abendländische Gespräch: 1946/1948" (GA 75: 57–196). In 1936 Heidegger says of Plato's *Phaedrus* that is "this dialogue must be accounted the most accomplished one in all essential respects" (Ni 222/N1 191), and Davies argues that Heidegger "remains steadfast in praising this Platonic dialogue above all others," and that "these readings provide fertile ground for reconsidering Heidegger's engagement with Plato over and above Platonism" (195). With regard to Heidegger's evolving interpretation of Nietzsche gathered in his two Nietzsche volumes (N1 and N2), Hannah Arendt remarks that there is an important sense in which in the first volume Heidegger still largely "goes along with" Nietzsche, while the second is written in an "unmistakable polemical tone" (Hannah Arendt, *The Life of the Mind* [San Diego: Harcourt Brace, 1978], part 2, 173). This pattern can also be detected in Heidegger's evolving interpretations of Plato, which become more critical—indeed polemical—the further along he progresses in developing his interpretative schema of the history of Western metaphysics, a historical narrative in which the figures of Plato and Nietzsche mark the beginning and end. In the 1936 Nietzsche lecture course, Heidegger in fact announces this critical turn in his interpretive approach when he writes: "We say 'Platonism' and not Plato, because here we are dealing with the conception of knowledge that corresponds to that term, not by way of an original and detailed examination of Plato's works, but only by setting in rough relief one particular aspect of his work" (Ni 177/N1 151). Yet Heidegger subsequently blurs this crucial distinction between "Platonism" and "Plato," for example in his programmatic "Plato's Doctrine of Truth," written in 1940 (GA 9: 203–38/PM 155–82), which interprets the Allegory of the Cave in Plato's *Republic* as the locus classicus for the transformation of the concept of truth from unconcealment to correctness. Yet, as Francisco Gonzalez points out, Heidegger's reading of the Allegory of the Cave in his 1931 lecture course (GA 34/ETP) was far more nuanced. See Francisco Gonzalez, *Plato and Heidegger: A Question of Dialogue* (University Park: Pennsylvania State University Press, 2009), 107–36. Noting that Heidegger mentions in a 1954 letter that "I've now made a decisive discovery" about "the transformation of λόγος in Plato," Katherine Davies suggests a recovery of his first extensive engagement with Plato's dialogues in the 1924–25 lecture course

published as *Plato's Sophist*, in which Heidegger claims that the central theme of the Phaedrus is λόγος (GA19: 315-16/PS 219; Davies, "Heidegger's Reading[s] of the Phaedrus," 210). Yet in his close reading of Heidegger's 1932 seminar on the *Phaedrus* (" 'I have to Live in Eros': Heidegger's 1932 Seminar on Plato's *Phaedrus*," *Epoché* 19/2: 217-40), Francisco Gonzalez explains how, whereas Heidegger's 1924–25 treatment of the *Phaedrus* had focused just on *logos*, his 1932 treatment focuses especially on the intimate relation of *logos* and *eros*, concluding that "the essence of every λόγος is the 'λόγος ερωτικός' " (GA 83: 313). Yet Gonzalez also indicates: "This intensive engagement with the notion of eros in Plato is, however, short lived. When Heidegger delivers again in 1933-34 his course *On the Essence of Truth*, . . . the notion of *Seinserstrebnis* that plays such a central role in the course as delivered in 1931–32 drops out completely. . . . Eros is clearly associated here with the transformation of being into ιδέα and truth into ὁμοίωσις and thus with the beginning of metaphysics. If Heidegger speaks of the beginning of 'philosophy' here, he clearly means the beginning of 'the *eros* for wisdom.' Many years later in the lecture, "Was ist das—die Philosophy?" Heidegger will speak of this transformation as one from φιλεῖν τὸ σοφόν understood as being in harmony or concord with the wise (Einklang, ἁρμονία), the kind of 'philosophy' that characterized the Presocratics, into a *striving after* [Streben nach] the σοφόν and thus philosophy understood as ὄρεξις and eros" (Gonzalez, 230; WP 50–51). Gonzalez wonders: while in 1932 "Heidegger suggests that the catastrophe for philosophy is when it ceases to be erotic, when it loses . . . its ground in the striving for being. How could eros have come to be seen by Heidegger as itself the catastrophe?" (Gonzalez, 230). However, if we take into consideration Heidegger's turn through an embrace of the will (*Wille*) in the 1930s toward a fundamental attunement of *Gelassenheit* (see my *Heidegger and the Will*), a turn away from projecting toward waiting, away from transcendence toward indwelling (see my "Returning the World to Nature"), this turn away from *eros*—especially given that Heidegger links *eros* with *orexis* and thus with the ancient germ of the modern metaphysics of will—makes more sense. Of course, Plato's philosophy as "*eros* for wisdom" is a far cry from what Heidegger criticizes as the "technological will to will." Moreover, Gonzalez draws our attention to later letters to his wife in which Heidegger personally continued to both identify and struggle with *eros*, philosophically as well as romantically—and indeed in the context of talking about the "Plato book" he still hoped to one day be able to write (LW 213, 246). Perhaps that Plato book would have clarified the relation between *eros*, will, and *Gelassenheit*; or perhaps it was Heidegger's inability to clarify that relation that prevented him from writing the book. In any case, when thinking about Heidegger's desire and inability to write that book, when reading Heidegger's various interpretations of the Platonic dialogues, and when developing our own interpretations, we should bear in mind a perceptive—and presumably retrospective—remark Heidegger made in 1951: "A dialogue of Plato—the *Phaedrus*, for example, the conversation on Beauty—can be interpreted in totally different spheres and respects, according to totally different implications and problematics. This multiplicity of possible interpretations does not discredit the strictness of the thought content. For all true thought remains open to more than one interpretation—and this by reason of its nature" (ZSD 68/WCT 71).

85. Sallis, *Being and Logos*, 113.
86. Sallis, *Being and Logos*, 175, citing *Cratylus* 408d.
87. See Bruce Gottfried, "Pan, The Cicadas, and Plato's Use of Myth in the Phaedrus," in *Plato's Dialogues: New Studies and Interpretations*, ed. Gerald A. Press (Lanham, MA: Roman and Littlefield, 1993), 179–94.
88. Sallis, *Being and Logos*, 107.
89. Sallis, *Being and Logos*, 107.
90. Sallis, *Being and Logos*, 58.
91. Sallis, *Being and Logos*, 534.
92. Sallis, *Figure of Nature*, 177.
93. Sallis, *Figure of Nature*, 192.
94. See Sallis, *Figure of Nature*, 247.
95. Sallis, *Figure of Nature*, 240–41.
96. See Friedrich Nietzsche, "The Dying Socrates" in *The Gay Science*, §340; and "The Problem of Socrates" in *Twilight of the Idols*, especially §§1 and 12.
97. Sallis, *Figure of Nature*, 247.
98. Sallis, *Figure of Nature*, 245–46.
99. Sallis, *Figure of Nature*, 245.
100. The contrast is complicated, and even softened, yet not eliminated by the following: near the end of the *Phaedrus*, after telling a myth about an Egyptian god who invented writing and a king who pointed out the dangers of relying on it, Socrates defends his telling of such tales by saying that "the authorities of the temple of Zeus at Dodana, my friend, said that the first prophetic utterances came from an oak tree. In fact, the people of those days, lacking the wisdom of you young people, were content in their simplicity to listen to trees or rocks, provided these told the truth" (*Phaedrus* 274c–275c). Socrates had prefaced his recounting of the tale from Egypt by saying: "I can tell you the tradition that has come down from our forefathers, but they alone know the truth of it. However, if we could discover that for ourselves, should we still be concerned with the fancies of mankind?" (274c). He goes on to contrast the dead speech of the written word with living speech that relies on the true knowledge that is "written in the soul of the learner" (276a). Myths and written texts must be employed merely as means to reawaken the inner *logos* inscribed in the human soul. The implication is that, on the "long detour" (274a) that is necessary to do this—a journey that includes the journey outside the walls of the city to the countryside where myths originated

from listening to trees and other natural phenomena, such as cicadas—at the end of the day one is to return from *mythos* to *logos*, from nature to the city, on the upward journey toward true knowledge and being.

101. GA 13: 88.

102. See "The Thing" in the 1949 Bremen Lectures (GA 79: 5–21/BFL 5–20), where Heidegger develops a number of thoughts first articulated in *Country Path Conversations*.

103. GA 79: 17/BFL 16.

104. On the *Gottesfrage* that accompanies Heidegger's lifelong path of thinking the *Seinsfrage*, see Bret W. Davis, "God or Gods (*Gott, Götter*)," in *The Cambridge Heidegger Lexicon*, ed. Mark Wrathall (Cambridge: Cambridge University Press, 2021), 357–61.

105. GA 77: 206/CPC 132.

106. WHD 18/WCT 44.

107. See GA 77: 87/CPC 55.

108. GA 77: 91/CPC 58.

109. GA 9: 201, 231/PM 155, 177.

110. GA 9: 234/PM 179 tm.

111. John Sallis, "Plato's Other Beginning," in *Heidegger and the Greeks*, 186–87; see also John Sallis, *The Verge of Philosophy* (Chicago: University of Chicago Press, 2008), 24.

112. Paul Friedländer, *Plato 1: An Introduction*, translated by Hans Meyerhoff (Princeton, NJ: Princeton University Press, 1969), chapter 11. The second edition of the German text, which added this chapter, was published in 1954. In a preface to the third edition, published in 1964, Friedländer writes: "Only chapter XI, '*Aletheia*: A Discussion with Martin Heidegger,' has undergone substantial revision. My opposition to Heidegger's interpretation of the Platonic concept of truth remains unchanged. Yet, recent extensive analysis of the meaning of *aletheia* in the older literature has more clearly brought out the various early meanings of the concept. It has become clear that the aspect of unhiddenness most stressed by Heidegger was present very early, but so were the elements which later combined in Plato's lofty concept of *aletheia*" (vii). In the concluding paragraph to his revised chapter on Heidegger, Friedländer writes: "In my discussion with Martin Heidegger, I have learned that my earlier opposition to the interpretation of *aletheia* as unhiddenness was unjustified. What stands unchanged is my criticism of Heidegger's historical construction [of a transformation of truth from unhiddenness to correctness in Plato]. For the result has become ever more clear. It was not 'first in Plato' that truth became correctness of perception and assertion. This meaning was present much earlier, i.e., in the old epic. For Plato, there is in ἀληθής and ἀλήθεια an equilibrium between the revealing truth, the unhidden reality, and the truthfulness which measures the reality by this truth" (229). In the

end, Heidegger and Friedländer come close to an agreement about the ambiguities of *aletheia* both before and in Plato. However, whereas Friedländer concludes that "Plato sharpened the concept, systematized it, and heightened it" by bringing "the three facets of the Greek *aletheia*"—"the ontological, the epistemological, and the existential"—together (229), Heidegger sees in this ambiguity an occlusion of the primordial sense of *aletheia* as unhiddennness or unconcealment (*Unverborgenheit*), as the forgetting of being (or beyng) as the "clearing of self-concealing presence, clearing of self-concealing sheltering" (ZSD 79/BW 448 tm) that inaugurates the tradition of metaphysics.

113. ZSD 78/BW 447.

114. For Sallis's critical and insightful reading of Heidegger's "Plato's Doctrine of Truth" and his engagement with Friedländer, see "At the Threshold of Metaphysics," in John Sallis, *Delimitations: Phenomenology and the End of Metaphysics*, collected writings edition (Indiana University Press, 1995), 170–85.

115. GA 65: 208–9/CP 163.

116. N2 458–59/EP 55–56 tm.

117. GA 55: 55, 57–58, 77.

118. GA 77: 149/CPC 98.

119. See Davis, "Returning the World to Nature."

120. GA 77: 205–6/CPC 132–33.

121. GA 54: 139–40, 144/PA 94, 97.

122. Indeed, the originality of Heidegger's interpretation may incline one to replace "Kant" with "Plato" in a response Heidegger is said to have given to a critique of his interpretation of Kant: "It may not be good Kant, but it is awfully good Heidegger." While this quote comes from a hearsay report by Bernd Magnus, in a later preface to his Kant book, Heidegger does, in print, offer this justification for the hermeneutical "violence" of his admittedly contentious interpretation of Kant: "In contrast to the methods of historical philology, which has its own agenda, a thoughtful dialogue is bound to other laws—laws which are more easily violated" (KPM xviii).

123. GA 54: 140/PA 95.

124. GA 53: 97–119/HHI 79–95.

125. GA 54: 132/PA 89.

126. GA 54: 180/PA 121.

127. GA 54: 141/PA 95.

128. GA 54: 174/PA 117 tm.

129. GA 54: 151/PA 102 tm.

130. GA 53: 113/HHI 91.

131. GA 9: 116/PM 92.

132. GA 53: 150/HHI 120.

133. GA 53: 147–48/HHI 118.

134. GA 54: 150–51/PA 101–2 tm.

135. The Kyoto School philosopher of Zen, Ueda Shizuteru, speaks in a related manner of "being-in-the-twofold-world" (*nijū-sekai-nai-sonzai*). See Ueda Shizuteru, *Kokū / sekai* [Empty Expanse / World], *Ueda Shizuteru shū* [The Collected Writings of Ueda Shizuteru], vol. 9 (Tokyo: Iwanami, 2002); Ueda Shizuteru, "Horizon and the Other Side of the Horizon," in *Contemporary Japanese Philosophy: A Reader*, ed. John W. M. Krummel (New York: Roman & Littlefield), 93–106. An examination of the Kyoto School's philosophies of "place" (*basho*), including what Ueda calls "nature as place" (*basho toshite no shizen*), in relation to Heidegger's thought and especially the other chorology I have sought to articulate in this essay will have to wait for another occasion.

7

The Philosopher and the City
Heidegger Reading Plato's *Republic*

Dennis J. Schmidt

Plato's life is bookended by two great traumas that are ineluctably entangled in his life as a philosopher. In his late twenties, he witnessed how his own city, Athens, convicted and executed by poison his beloved teacher, Socrates. In his late sixties, Plato travels to Syracuse in the hope of teaching a king how to philosophize, and the result was that Plato barely escaped with his life.[1] Wars and the rule of tyrants were a constant during Plato's life. These events—and others to be sure—left deep marks upon Plato's work; above all they set the question of the relation of the philosopher to the city in the heart of most every dialogue and letter that Plato wrote. One cannot deny that Plato's reflections on the relation of philosophy to life are deeply felt and genuinely probing, nor can one deny the deep sense of responsibility that continues to animate Plato's relentless sense of the obligation of the philosopher to life. In the end, Plato's work exhibits a deep moral concern, and that concern shapes the most important decisions we find in his work.

Heidegger's life encompassed two world wars in which one witnessed extreme violence, monstrous horrors, brutality, and repression on a scale and with a force never before seen. In his late twenties, poison gases defined the First World War, and twenty years later poison would be key to the mechanization of death camps. Heidegger would witness book-burning as well as the burning of human beings. He would see destruction of an unimaginable scale and the blinding flash of nuclear annihilation. These events do not seem to have left any significant marks upon Heidegger's work; in fact, when Heidegger does speak to these events one is left uncomfortable at best—or repelled. Nonetheless, one cannot deny that the question of the relation of philosophy to life is very much at the heart of Heidegger's work. One sees this clearly at the end of *Being and Time* when Heidegger writes that all philosophical questioning "arises out of an analytic of existence. . . . and is *folded back* into it."[2] In the end, for Heidegger philosophy is riveted to life and a world, and yet one is hard pressed to find this commitment to life as he understands it to be concerned with moral life.

The situations out of which Plato and Heidegger each write are shaped by profoundly different worlds, languages, and histories. Heidegger was especially critical of his own times and frequently located the deepest roots of what was so unhealthy in his times in Plato's own work which Heidegger would, when convenient, take as the real source of the metaphysical tradition that has ultimately distorted the world. Indeed, until the publication of Heidegger's lecture courses and many of his letters over the past few decades, there was little evidence that Heidegger regarded Plato as anything more than a sort of opponent and his work as opening the way to the Western world's essentially calculative conception of truth.[3]

And yet: there is one question that Plato and Heidegger share, and that neither would fully resolve, namely, the question of the relation of philosophy to the city and—even more—to life itself. It is, I believe, no accident that during the strange years from 1931 to 1942—years that would leave haunting and disturbing questions for anyone trying to read Heidegger today—Heidegger turns frequently to Plato to ask and answer this question of the place of philosophy in the world.[4] Importantly, for Heidegger's reading of Plato, this question is invariably answered by discussing a sort of "return" to the cave, to political life, to those still in need of liberation.

In what follows, my intention is to look at three lecture courses and one speech in which Heidegger judges the task and place of philosophy in the world either by simply citing or by actually reading and interpreting Plato. In all these texts, Heidegger turns to Plato's *Republic* as offering something productive to be understood. My sense is that looking closely at what Heidegger sees—and perhaps more importantly does not see—in

Plato is illuminating for the larger question of how to understand the task of philosophy and its relation to life itself.[5]

⁓

In the Winter Semester of 1931-32, Heidegger gave a lecture course entitled *Vom Wesen der Wahrheit* (GA 34), the first half of which was devoted to reading Plato's *Republic*. That seminar ended on February 26, 1932. Eighteen months later, beginning on November 7, 1933, Heidegger would repeat the topic of that course and even a fair amount of its content (GA 35/36).[6] Sandwiched between those two lecture courses, which were devoted largely to Plato's *Republic*, Heidegger would give his *Rektorratsrede* on 27 May 1933, and that text would end with a citation from the *Republic*. During tumultuous and politically charged years Heidegger's letters would also indicate just how deeply he was engaging Greek, especially Platonic, texts.[7] Taken together it is clear that Heidegger saw in those Platonic texts a sort of measure and means of understanding his own historical present.

Heidegger's remarks about Plato in these years focus primarily upon the Platonic conception of truth and his readings of the *Republic* tend to be coupled with the *Theatetus*. Heidegger's effort is largely to present a Plato who is en route to the metaphysical conception of truth, as either the last Greek or the first metaphysician. However, one topic that Heidegger takes up in these texts that is quite out of the ordinary is the question of the relation of the philosopher to power. He does this in two ways: first, by speaking about Plato's description of the fate of the philosopher who returns to the cave (*Republic*, Bk. VII); and second, by giving the final word in Heidegger's own Rectoral Address to Plato (*Republic*, Bk. VI).

Heidegger's discussion of "the return of the liberated person" ["Der Rücksteig des Freien in die Höhle"][8] has a strange aura of violence and death framing it. He remarks that the liberated person is destined to a peculiar sort of death, while that person, who has returned to free others still in the cave, must be "violent" ["ein Gewalttäiger sein"] and "tear away" ["Herausreißen"] the cave dwellers and bring them to the light.[9] Heidegger clarifies that this violence is not "crude" ["Roheit"] but an example of "spiritual strength" ["geistigen Strenge"]. He is also clear that the liberated person who possesses this strength, exercises such violence, and risks such a death is the philosopher. Heidegger stresses, but does not entirely explain, that the philosopher is not someone who is engaged in "culture" ["Bildung"], but someone who has philosophy as the fundamental character of his being. Heidegger makes clear that it remains a question whether there are truly philosophers any longer, but the poisons that can kill any philosopher "are far more poisonous, because they are hidden and slow, but insidious."[10] This means that "the genuine philosopher is thus powerless inside the realm of prevailing common sense"[11] and so, "the philosopher must remain alone [einsam bleiben] because that is what he *is* in his essence. His solitude [Einsamkeit] is not to be *talked about* [zu bereden]. Isolation [Vereinzelung] is nothing to be wished for. But precisely for that reason he must always be there in decisive moments and not yield [nicht weichen]. He will not misunderstand solitude in an external manner as a retreat into himself and a letting go of things."[12]

Heidegger's discussion in these two lecture courses of the philosopher's return to the cave dwellers presents an image of the philosopher as a hero, as someone of strength, conviction, and courage, and as someone who is necessarily solitary. The task of philosophy is a dangerous one since the philosopher will be a voice at odds with prevailing wisdom. In the end, the philosopher is a liberator. Becoming a liberator is the transformation that takes place upon exiting the cave: to be a philosopher is to understand the necessity of entering back into the cave, into the place of history. The relation between the philosopher and those who need to be liberated is dangerous, risky, and violent—from both sides.

Despite this image of a conflict between the philosopher and the city, there is also a sense in which Heidegger speaks of the philosopher as the fulfillment of the possibilities of being human, as an intensification of being human. Thus, we read: "one *is not* a human being insofar as one is bound in the cave, feeling comfortable and chatting, *one is* also *not* human insofar as one is in the opposite condition outside of the cave. Rather, the human being *is the transition* out of the cave into the light and back into the cave."[13] This movement is very much the same as the movement that Heidegger described in *Being and Time* as the movement of philosophy that "arises out of an analytic of existence. . . . and is *folded back* into it."[14] The task of philosophy is the same as the task of the human being.

Heidegger's remarks about human beings as defined by a philosophical way of being do not mean that everyone is already a philosopher; rather, it means that everyone has philosophy as a possibility. Most importantly, it means that philosophy is not a matter of a profession, a position, or engaging any canonical body of knowledge. It is fundamentally not an academic discipline, but a way of life: "The transformation of the essence of the human being in one's Dasein is not a change in one's external situation, rather it is the most inward change in the Being of human being."[15] Saying this pushes Heidegger a bit beyond himself to be sure, and it seems clear that the path to philosophy is still a narrow, extremely rigorous, and rather restricted one. Nonetheless, what one can see clearly is that Heidegger is deeply critical of the present state of philosophy as an academic discipline, and yet it remains the basic task of philosophy in the authentic sense to liberate people to become what they fundamentally are.

∼

Heidegger's Rektorratsrede, "Die Selbstbehauptung der deutschen Universität," is concerned with the nature of the university, the place of the university in the life of a people and culture, and with the limits of theorical knowledge in the face of other powers. It is a lecture that makes one quite uncomfortable—at the very least—for many reasons that I will not discuss here. Significantly, it also gives Plato's *Republic* the final word.

Heidegger opens this address and almost immediately cites a line from Aeschylus' *Prometheus Bound*. Heidegger's way of introducing this line is odd for several reasons, not the least of which is Heidegger's decision to introduce it by saying that the Greeks considered Prometheus to be the "first philosopher."[16] Heidegger then suggests that the line he will cite "expresses the essence of knowing." The line, which is spoken by Prometheus while he—like the cave dwellers in Plato's "Allegory of the Cave"—is chained in place, is "τέχνη δ' ἀνάγκης ἀσθενεστέρα μακρῷ."[17] Heidegger translates it as "Wissen aber ist weit unkräftiger denn Notwendigkeit" ["Knowledge is far less powerful than necessity"] (R: 11).[18] The decision to translate τέχνη as "Wissen," as "knowing," is an odd one and not entirely keeping in the spirit of Aeschylus's play where the context seems to clearly refer to Prometheus's own skillfulness and what is needed for him to be freed from his chains. In *Prometheus Bound* this line indicates that there is a power, the power of fated necessity, that is greater even then Zeus's own power. Prometheus warns the Chorus that his knowledge of this truth must be kept secret [συγκαλυπτέος].

Heidegger does not make an effort to contextualize his citation from Aeschylus; rather, he explains it by saying "this means that all knowledge about things is from the outset handed over to the superior power of destiny and such knowledge fails in the face of that power." Then Heidegger immediately moves to show that it is precisely this failure of knowledge when confronted by the "unfathomable inalterability" of things that leads knowledge to its own truth and this truth is shown to be the "theoretical" attitude. In this claim, as well as the following claim that "theory is itself was to be understood as the highest realization of genuine praxis" (R: 11), Heidegger turns Prometheus into the Platonic philosopher par excellence and as one who signals what is involved in the struggle for knowledge.

This struggle is what Heidegger has in mind when he concludes his Rectoral Address with a quotation from Plato's *Republic*: τά . . . μεγάλα πάντα ἐπιφαλῆ . . . (497d9), which Heidegger translates—again in a rather forced way—as "Alles Große steht im Sturm . . ." ["All that is great stands in the storm . . ."] (R.19). First, a comment on the translation, then on its context in *Republic*. Heidegger's translation of "ἐπιφαλῆ" as "storm" is stretched. The more common translation would be "at risk," "unstable," "prone to fall," or "precarious."[19] This is the only appearance of the word, "ἐπιφαλῆ" in the Platonic corpus and the context of its appearance in *Republic* makes clear that it is to be understood as referring to a risk or danger. It appears in Book VI when Socrates and Glaucon are discussing what cities might be worthy of philosophy. Socrates says that the difficulty is to make clear "By what means a city will avoid being destroyed by taking philosophy in hand." Then Socrates speaks the line that Heidegger cites: "Anything big risks a fall."[20] With this Heidegger's gives Plato the final word but he does so in a way that seems to emphasize the steadfastness of standing, the self-assertion of philosophy—for that is what has been pointed to throughout—in the turbulence of the times. The danger of the moment in which philosophy enters a city—the risk to which Socrates refers—is something Heidegger never explains, rather Heidegger seems to be suggesting that the task of philosophy is more like the heroism of holding fast in a time of turbulence. In doing this, Heidegger largely repeats the way he interprets the return of the philosopher to the cave in his lecture courses of the time: the philosopher is a "liberator" ["Befreier"] and one whose return to the city is tasked with wrenching—even violently so—others free of their bonds.[21]

Heidegger's engagement with Plato in the 1930's is quite intensive. In addition to the lecture courses of 1931/32 and 1933/34, Heidegger held seminars on Plato's *Parmenides* (1930/31) and *Phaedrus* (1932).[22] Plato would also play a not insignificant role in several lecture courses of the time, especially those devoted to Nietzsche that began in 1936 and ran for four years. While there are several themes that emerge in these engagements, Heidegger's overwhelming conviction guiding all of his readings of Plato in this period is clear and well expressed by Heidegger when he bluntly remarks: "Each of [Plato's] dialogues, indeed almost every part of every dialogue, points the way—either directly or indirectly—to the question of ἀλήθεια."[23] While summing up these many readings is risky business, one does come away with a sense that Heidegger persistently reads Plato without any sense of the drama or pathos or larger context of the dialogues. The idea that characters play a role in the formation of viewpoints does not come into Heidegger's understanding of the dialogues. He remains riveted to the question of ἀλήθεια and to the transformation that idea is said to undergo in the Platonic dialogues, even to the point that this focus might obscure or overlook other significant insights in the dialogues.[24] In particular, Heidegger seems to strip Plato's texts of their real political force and of the question of shared life they address. One sees this above all in the way in which Heidegger so thoroughly removes the idea of the good from any moral sense.[25] In other words, even in the *Republic*, even in Plato's most political of texts, Heidegger relentlessly ontologizes that text in such a way that the political questions become strictly philosophical concerns.

There is, however, one theme that Heidegger does note in Plato during these years that opens Heidegger to a new set of issues; more precisely, Heidegger is well aware that the story told in the Allegory of the Cave pivots on understanding the *necessity of a return to the cave*. Thus, Heidegger notes: "The human being *is not*, insofar as one is bound into the cave, feels content and chats with others, one *is* also *not* [a human being] insofar as one is in the opposite position outside of the cave; rather a human being *is the transition* out of the cave into the light and then *back into the cave*."[26] This, according to Heidegger is the "destiny" ["Schicksal"] of human being and this return is explained by the need to liberate others and by the need to enter into the "battle" ["Kampf"], the struggle, of truth and untruth that is history: "the philosopher *must* climb down into the cave, however not in order to be drawn into debates with those who live in the cave, but in order to take hold of this or that person who he believes he recognizes and lead him up on the steep path, not through a one-time deed, but through the happening of history itself."[27] One's return to the cave is necessitated by our essential philosophical existence.[28] In other words, the return is a way of continuing one's life as a philosopher and this means it is a way of fulfilling the real nature of one's existence.

One could argue—rightly I believe—that this return, which Plato characterizes as a "descent" ["κατέβην"], is understood quite differently for Plato; indeed, the movement of "going down" is very much at issue throughout the *Republic*, which opens with that word.²⁹ In the case of the return to the cave, it is important to remember that the philosopher does not want to return to the cave since to do so means leaving the light and the beauty one has found. It is also extraordinarily risky. Nonetheless, Socrates argues that the philosopher is compelled to gone down to the cave as a way of repaying a debt to the city for the education one received: "Our task . . . is to not permit them to stay there ["καταμένειν"] and to not let them stay there rather than go down ["καταβαίνειν"] again among the prisoners" (519c–d). This return to the cave is, in the end, the just thing to do even though it will mean compromising the philosophical life by returning to the world of shadows.³⁰

∼

There is of course another "going down" and an "ascent" in the final book, indeed final words, of the *Republic*. It is a tale that describes the descent of souls that are "pure" ["καθαράς"] who come down from "heaven" ["οὐρανοῦ"]; it is a story that ends with ascent of souls being born into new bodies, an ascent that is accompanied by "thunder and earthquakes and shooting stars" (621b).³¹ Socrates recounts this going down and ascending as a story told by the soldier Er who died in a battle but ascended back up to life ["ἀνεβίω"] after ten days so that he could be the messenger ["ἄγγελον"] to human beings about what awaits the dead.³² Heidegger will take up this section of the *Republic* in a lecture course devoted to Parmenides that he gave in 1942–43, that is after his resignation from the Rectorate and during the Second World War.³³ But before turning to Heidegger's reading, a few remarks about the "Myth of Er" will help set the framework for Heidegger's reading.

Socrates never explains how he came to know this story ["μῦθος"] of what Er, a soldier from Pamphylia³⁴, witnessed in the time after his death during which his soul traveled to a place that is described as a "demonic place" ["τόπον τινὰ δαιμόνιον"] while his body remained on the battlefield still intact and healthy ["ὑγιὴς"]. Although his tale is of a realm the living cannot know, Er's journey to the realm of the dead is limited in two ways: first, he must stay on a threshold where other souls are judged, he is not able to travel the full course that the dead must travel; and second, Er is there only to observe everything in that place so that he could be a messenger to human beings about what awaits the dead, Er is there only as a witness who will testify later and so he is not engaged in the events that he describes.³⁵ So the story Er tells is one that he observes and overhears in that place beyond any appearance for the living. The heart of the story that Er tells and that Socrates recounts in indirect speech that Socrates occasionally interrupts with his own commentary concerns the way some of the souls chose the pattern of their next life ["βίων παραδείγματα"] (619e).³⁶ Er describes the scene as "pitiful" ["ἐλεινήν"], "laughable" ["γελοίαν"], and "wonderful" ["θαυμασίαν"] (620a). The choices are indeed strange: human beings chose the life of an animal, men choose the life of a woman, animals chose the life of a human being, women become men, some souls that were just become unjust, and all sorts of mixtures are found.³⁷ Despite the strangeness and ridiculousness of this scene, it is clear that the choice is a grave, serious, and hazardous ["κίνδυνος"] one (618b)—it is the choice of the character of one's life to come, the choice of one's destiny—and despite the warning given to the souls not to be "careless" ["ἀμελείτω"] (619b), many do not examine their choices well. For the most part, the choice of a life is guided by the trace that remains of that soul's previous life ["κατά συνήθειαν του προτέρου βίου"] (620a). Several choices that Er witnesses are mentioned, but two in particular—the first and the last choices described—are of special note.

The first choice was made by a soul that had previously lived a life of virtue in a well-ordered polis, but only out of habit and "without philosophy" ["ἄνευ φιλοσοφίας"] (619d). Although this soul had lived a life of virtue it was not lived knowingly, but out of the habits bred by living in a well-ordered city rather than by having learned how to "distinguished the worthy from the worthless life" ["χρηστὸν καὶ πονηρὸν διαγιγώσκοντα"] (618c). As a result of lacking what knowledge belongs to philosophy this soul chose thoughtlessly and without looking carefully enough, and as a consequence, this soul chose a destiny that was full of evils. The final choice fell to the soul that had been Odysseus who, from the memory of its previous "troubles" ["πόνων"] chose a life of a "private person who minds his own business" ["ἀνδὸς ἰδιώτου ἀπράγμονος"] (620c).³⁸ The reluctance of the soul that learned from the life of Odysseus to choose a life of involvement in the affairs of others echoes the reluctance of the philosopher to return to the cave and engage others in the city. It also echoes the description Socrates gives of the just person as one who, "in private as well as public life" ["ἰδία καὶ δημοσία"] will keep away from "political affairs" ["τά γε πολιτικὰ ἐθελήσει πράττειν"] (592a). In other words, these choices highlight both the importance and the reluctance of the philosopher to enter into public life.

The tale that Er tells ends with the rebirth of the souls who have chosen a new life. Unlike Er, who returns to his body and who is able to tell this tale, all of the other souls enter the world as babies, and they do this by "going up" and having forgotten all that had preceded their arrival in the world with such destinies that they had chosen for themselves. They cannot speak, are at the mercy of those who can care for them, and they are vulnerable. Their utter inability to care for themselves and to articulate what they need other than as an inarticulate cry is how they enter the cave from which they will be urged to escape and to which they will be urged to return. Er returns fully able to testify to these events and for that reason "the tale was saved" ["μῦθος ἐσώθη"] and it might "save us" if we are "persuaded by it" (621c). It will "save" us if we come to understand what the souls of the dead wish that they knew while they were alive and on the earth: how "to choose the life at the mean . . . and avoid extremes on either side, both in this life as far as possible, and in all that is the next life" (619a) and it is clear that the only life that prepares one for this is the philosophical life.

Heidegger returns a discussion of Plato's *Republic* in his 1942–43 lecture course on Parmenides and this time his primary concern is the Myth of Er. He introduces this concern by suggesting that the Myth of Er serves as something of a completion or counterpoint to the Allegory of the Cave: "Plato's dialogue on the πόλις that contains a μυθος about ἀλήθεια, concludes the entire project at the end of the 10th book with another μυθος, one that reaches its highpoint in the saying of λήθη" (GA 54: 136). In other words, he introduces his reading of the Myth of Er as a continuation of the discussion of the struggle defining truth. The Myth of Er becomes the Myth of Lethe, of forgetfulness, that is the companion to the Allegory of the Cave as the Myth of Aletheia.[39] It is, to say the least, a quite novel way to characterize and approach this concluding myth of the *Republic*. Heidegger immediately acknowledges that the Myth of Er is so "expansive and rich that it is not really able to be presented" especially because the essential point is missing the experience of the basic character of myth and its relation to the metaphysics of Plato (GA 54: 136).

When Heidegger turns to the Myth of Er he notes that Socrates initially describes this myth as an "ἀπόλογον," which Heidegger translates as an "Abrede," and he clarifies this by calling it more precisely a "Verteidigung" ["defense"] (GA 54: 146). Doing this is odd insofar as it ignores the puns that populate this opening sentence; and insofar as it translates "ἀπόλογον" in a rather unusual way by calling it an "Abrede" which Heidegger explains by saying that this word sets the story that follows apart from what has been said thus far and in this way "preserves its truth" (GA 54: 146).[40] After introducing the nature of the myth that he will recount, Heidegger speaks of the place where everything that Er narrates happens; namely, of the "τόπον τινὰ δαιμόνιον" which Heidegger translates as the place of "das Un-geheure," as the "extra-ordinary" which is what is nonetheless "most natural" and is that "out of which all that is ordinary emerges" (GA 54: 150–51). Even more pointedly, Heidegger claims that "the "δαιμόνιον" defines the basic relation of being to human being" (GA 54: 173) and that this place of which speaks is a place where the essence of being comes to presence [west] in an eminent [ausgezeichneten] sense" (GA 54: 174). Heidegger does not discuss the choices made, but rather focuses upon the "final place within this realm of the extra-ordinary, the one at which the wanderer must stop . . . [and it] is the τὸ Λήθης πεδίον, the field of withdrawing hiddenness in the sense of oblivion ["das Feld der entziehenden Verbergung im Sinne der Vergessung"]" (GA 54: 175).[41] This, even more than the choices of a life, will be what Heidegger takes to be the summit and real meaning of this final tale told in the *Republic*.

Heidegger notes that this field that all souls must, of necessity, pass through before birth is itself "empty" ["leer"] and has nothing ordinary about it. Plato describes it as "a place of terrible, scorching, stifling heat, barren of everything that grows" (621a). In this desolate, lifeless field the travelers encounter only a river, but Heidegger notes that "even the name of this river shows that it is appropriate for this place and that it too in in the service of the essence of λήθη . . . it is called Ἀμέλης, which means "without care" ["Ohnesorge"]."[42] This river cannot be contained in any vessel; it is by nature elusive. However, what is most important about these waters is that the travelers, those who have just chosen new souls in preparation for birth, are required to drink from this river and so forget all that they have come to learn in this place. Before any soul can be born, it must drink some measure ["μέτρον"] of this water and those who lack "good sense" ["φρονήσει"] drank more than the proper measure. Heidegger explains that in this case "φρονήσει," which he translates first as "insight" ["Einblick"] and then as "to have a view of the essential" ["den Blick haben für das Wesenhafte"], means the same as "philosophy."[43] Only Er was "prevented" ["κωλυθῆναι"] from drinking these waters, and this is the reason the tale was saved ["ἐσώθη"] from being forgotten. Only Er returns as himself. In fact, he seems to return as more than what he had been, as something of the philosopher par excellence; however, we know nothing of Er's own fate, only that did not know how he "suddenly" ["ἐξαίφνης"] returned to his body.[44] But in what sense might this tale that Er is able to tell save us?

Heidegger's emphasis in his telling of this tale is not about the choice of soul, but the drinking of the water. Those who drink the proper measure, those who possess "good sense" ["φρονήσει"], are the ones who are born with the chance of "doing well" ["εὖ πράττωμεν"] (621d). Those are the ones Heidegger calls philosophers. Those who lack this insight are those who are "lacking philosophy" ["die Philosophie-losen"].[45] Heidegger is clear that philosophy here does not refer to any cultural good, any discipline or body of knowledge that one "possesses." Philosophy is rather an "attentiveness" ["Achtsamkeit"]. The philosopher too has drunken something of the waters of forgetting, but only the proper measure and this thanks to a peculiar ["φρονήσει"]. The possibility that Er's story holds for us is the admonition to cultivate the good sense of philosophy. This good sense is a matter of how one lives, of the attentiveness characteristic of the "φρονήσει."[46] Heidegger, in this academic lecture course given in a university at the time of a brutal war, does not say more about what this philosophical life entails. Nonetheless, he does at least recognize that this myth that Er tells and that brings Plato's dialogue on political life to a close stands as testimony to the importance of a philosophical life that is dedicated to cultivating and caring for life here, in this world.

While Heidegger indicates the importance of the attentiveness and care that are at risk in the tale Er tells, that care is quickly translated in his reading into a care for truth. Heidegger will identify the δαιμόνιος τόπος that is the site for the Myth of Er as the real meaning of the name of goddess of truth in Parmenides poem.[47] When he does this Heidegger seems to shift the stakes that are at risk away from the life of a soul.

∽

The Myth of Er, a tale about what awaits the dead, ends with a story of birth, of beginnings that are shaped by choices made at another time, beginnings that are radically new and yet full of history: no one is born without some measure of destiny that is always already at work. These births are shrouded in mystery and are spectacular, like stars shooting up from out of the earth, they enter bodies and are birthed into the world of appearances. What is not said is that these new births are sent into the world, into the cave, completely helpless and vulnerable. They cannot care for themselves, they cannot speak and cannot survive without the help of others. They are utterly helpless without others, they need the care of others.[48] These new beings are, as the Heidegger of just a few years earlier would have called them, thrown into the world and set on a path to death.[49]

That much of the *Republic* concerns the education of children[50] should not be forgotten at this point. Both Plato and Heidegger are in agreement that the summit of this education, the goal that is most significant for the right order of the polis, is found when that education leads to the life of a philosopher. They are, however, not so clearly in agreement about just what such a life entails nor what special obligations that person has to the city, to others. Neither is foolish enough to believe that such special obligations that open up in the philosophical life imply a special talent or skill for leadership, for ruling.

Upon seeing Heidegger shortly after he resigned as Rector of the University of Freiburg, one of his friends famously said: "So, back from Syracuse?" The reference is clear as is the implication: Heidegger, like Plato who took a third trip to Syracuse in the hope of finding he could still have an influence upon the tyrant, had succumbed to the philosophical temptation to assume that philosophers do have a special talent for leading or at least advising those who lead.[51] The implication of course is that there is a sort of arrogance defining philosophy—or at least philosophers—in both cases and that Syracuse, or Berlin, is simply the name for the locus of this arrogance.

I began by noting that both Plato and Heidegger lived through times of real crisis, of tyranny, and of war. They are not at all unique in this, indeed it is difficult to find times in history when such crises are not at the forefront of the times.[52] The question then that *we*—not simply Plato or Heidegger, but everyone who wants to lay claim to living a philosophical life—*must ask* is just what philosophy can contribute to such times.[53] During the years 1931 to 1943, Heidegger repeatedly turned to Plato to think through this question. His readings, especially of the *Republic*, tend to strip Plato's thought of its deeply political character and of its almost concrete ethical force. For Heidegger, the question of truth, the basic philosophical question, takes over the question of the relation of the philosopher to the city. One sees this especially in Heidegger's discussion of the Myth of Er where Heidegger translates this presentation of birth into the world—an event that reminds us that human beings are profoundly vulnerable and in need of one another—into a question of truth. In many ways Heidegger's readings of Plato during these years are full of insight and have the merit of calling attention to much that is typically neglected in readings of Plato. However, these readings often, indeed most often, miss the strongest point that one finds in Plato. It is a point that Plato, whose teacher he loved was executed by his city *for leading the life of a philosopher*, thought about throughout his life. Sadly, especially for those of us who have learned much from Heidegger, this seems to be something that Heidegger never really brought himself to consider.

Notes

1. On this, see Debra Nails, "The Life of Plato in Athens," in *A Companion to Plato*, ed. H. Benson (London: Blackwell, 2006), 1–12. For a discussion of the third trip to Syracuse with special attention to the Seventh Letter, see *Plato at Syracuse* (New York: Parnassos, 2019). It is clear that Plato went to Syracuse on this third visit with a great deal of skepticism and an awareness of the risks that such a trip contained for him.

2. BT: 436. For a discussion of this "fold" in *Being and Time*, see my "Honoring One's Commitments," in *Commonplace Commitments*, ed. Peter S. Fosel, Michael J. McGandy, and Mark D. Moorman (Lewisburg, PA: Bucknell University Press, 2016), 106–12.

3. The only substantial and best-known text on Plato that he published during his lifetime was "Plato's Doctrine of Truth" (1941). There were extended remarks on Plato in Heidegger's *Nietzsche* volumes, but the texts that Heidegger wrote on Plato now available to us significantly expand our sense of how Heidegger engaged Plato. One of the most important consequences of these newly available texts is that we can now see just how deeply and carefully Heidegger did engage Plato. His interpretations of Plato are no less controversial, but they are clearly neither one-sided nor even consistent. So, we have Heidegger writing to his wife in the final months of WWII: "Only now, on the basis of my own experience, do I understand the Platonic form of presentation and, in some form or other, I must complete the Plato book that I've promised you" (*Mein liebes Seelchen*, 235) and then, a few years later, Heidegger comments to Georg Picht during a walk the two took outside of Hinterzarten in the Black Forest that "I must confess that the structure of Platonic thought is completely obscure to me" (Günter Neske, ed., *Erinnerungen an Martin Heidegger* [Pfullingen: Neske Verlag, 1977], 203).

Nietzsche's remark in *Jenseits von Gut und Böse* that Plato possessed a "Sphinix-nature" seems the most appropriate way to describe Heidegger's engagement with Plato; for Heidegger, Plato remained a riddle and a challenge. The reasons for this are, in some sense, easy to identify: Heidegger almost never takes the dialogue as an exchange between characters into account, he never provides a dramatic context for his readings of Plato, and the evolution of a thought in conversation seems ignored. Platonic dialogues have a "felt" dimension, they communicate something of the people engaging in discussion, the place of the discussion, and the larger context for remarks. It is this "felt" sense that seems lacking in most every one of Heidegger's discussions of Plato.

4. Adjectives like "strange," "haunting," and "disturbing" are quite inadequate to characterize what sort of questions and problems Heidegger's actions and decisions during this time pose for anyone who draws upon Heidegger. The purpose of this paper is not to take up the question of Heidegger's own political engagement. That is an important issue but, for the most part, it is one that lies outside of the scope of this essay. However, I have attempted to address this point several times; see, for instance, "Changing the Subject," in *Graduate Faculty Journal of the New School* 14, no. 2–15, no. 1 (1991), 441–64; "The Baby and the Bathwater," in *Heidegger and Practical Philosophy*, ed. Raffoul and Pettigrew (Albany: State University of New York Press, 2002), 159–72; "Philosophical Life and Moral Responsibility," in *International Yearbook for Hermeneutics*, Bd. 19 (2019), 113–28; and *On Germans and Other Greeks* (Bloomington: Indiana University Press, 2001).

5. Let me stress at the outset that my intention is quite narrow both in terms of the period I will consider, the texts that are at issue—for both Plato and Heidegger—and in terms of the leading question I want to address. I simply want to look at a selected set of Heidegger's lectures between 1931 and 1942, and only those that consider either the "Allegory of the Cave" or the "Myth of Er"—in other words, only those concerned with the *Republic* (this omits the *Theatetus* and *Phaedrus*, both dialogues that claimed Heidegger's attention in these years). Finally, I am interested primarily in addressing the question of the relation of the philosopher to the polis, and this as a matter of a peculiar sort of "return." There is a substantial literature on the larger question of the relation of Heidegger and Plato. Here I mention only a few of the books that are especially worth attention and directly on the questions surrounding this relation: Alain Boutot, *Heidegger et Platon* (Paris: PUF, 1987); Gregory Fried, *Towards a Polemical Ethics: Between Heidegger and Plato* (London: Rowman & Littlefield, 2021); Francisco Gonzales, *Plato and Heidegger: A Question of Dialogue* (University Park: Pennsylvania State University Press, 2009); Drew Hyland, *Questioning Platonism* (Albany: State University of New York Press, 2004); Catherine Zuckert, *Postmodern Plato's* (Chicago: University of Chicago Press, 1996).

6. Comparing these lecture courses, especially their respective treatments of the "return" to the cave of "one who is liberated," is an interesting project, but is outside of the scope of this essay.

7. See especially Heidegger's letters to Blochmann—April 10, 1932; October 5, 1932; December 19, 1932; March 30, 1933—all of which speak about his engagement with Plato and encourage Blochmann to continue with her reading of Platonic texts (he mentions in particular Plato's Seventh Letter).

8. GA 34: 79.

9. GA 34: 81.

10. GA 34: 84.

11. GA 34: 84. In GA 35/36: 182, Heidegger describes the powerlessness of the philosopher as having his language transferred into the language of the cave dwellers, and of his inner life becoming a nullity.

12. GA 34: 84.

13. GA 36/37: 187.

14. BT: 436.

15. GA 35/36: 205. See also p. 208 where Heidegger offers a list of what is not a matter of philosophy.

16. This is, of course, not a commonplace decision. There are references to Prometheus in Plato—*Protagoras* (320d-322e), *Philebus* (16c-d), *Gorgias* (523d-e), and *Statesman* (274 b-d)—but none refer to him as a "philosopher," let alone the first one. One way of understanding this claim is developed by Sarah Kofman, *Comment n' en sortir?* (Éditons Galilée, Paris, 1983): 71–94. See also, Claude Calame, "The Pragmatics of "Myth" in Plato's Dialogues: The Story of Prometheus in the *Protagoras*," in *Plato and Myth*, ed. C. Collobert, P. Destrée and F. Gonzalez (Leiden: Brill, 2012): 127–44.

Heidegger seldom refers to Aeschylus or Prometheus. One of the few other references however likely comes from these years; it is in GA 94: 95, one of the "Schwarzehefte" notes found in a notebook dated October 1931. That reference does link Aeschylus's *Prometheus* and the "beginning of philosophy." The reference to Aeschylus in *GA* 36/37 is quite on point: "The Dasein of the Geeks is . . . a great, monstrous [ungeheurer] *struggle* [*Kampf*] with the most monstrous and dark powers such as appears in the tragedy of Aeschylus," p. 144.

17. The text could also be translated as "Skill is far less significant than necessity." The word ἀσθενεστέρα refers to weakness, sickness, and insignificance. It is, for instance, the word that Plato uses in the Seventh Letter to describe the "weakness of language" that leads anyone of intelligence not to put into written symbols one's most serious thoughts (342e–43a).

18. The lines from Aeschylus are 514–23. See Jacques Taminiaux, "The Platonic Roots of Heidegger's Political Thought," *European Journal of Political Theory* 6, no. 1 (January 2007), 11–29 for an interesting reading of the Rectoral Address that recognizes the importance of this citation from Aeschylus. Taminiaux argues that Heidegger's speech "can be seen as a kind of repetition of . . . Plato's *Republic*" (p. 14). For a fine reading of the Rectoral Address that recognizes both the Platonic and Nietzschean roots of that text, see Charles Bambach, *Heidegger's*

Roots (Ithaca, NY: Cornell University Press, 2003), 69–111. The importance of Nietzsche, who Heidegger refers to as "the last German philosopher" (13) in the R, should not be undervalued for a fuller understanding of the Rectoral Address.

Also of importance is the seldom discussed, but quite revealing, text of the two lectures that Heidegger gave to foreign students enrolled in the University of Freiburg: "Die Deutsche Universität." Those lectures were given in August 15 and 16, 1934 (see GA 16: 285–307). That text speaks of the task of the university as the *"liberation"* [*"Befreiung"*] of human beings from what binds them: "Liberation, freedom . . . will be the enchanting words and slogans of the coming centuries" (290). The word "Befreiung" is the same word Heidegger used in his lecture course to describe what the philosopher returning to the cave must do.

19. This is the only appearance of the word, "ἐπιφαλη" in the Platonic corpus. One is tempted to hear a sort of quiet reference to the "Sturmabteilung" [Storm Division], which was the Nazi Party's paramilitary wing founded in 1921. The often-loaded vocabulary of the Rectoral Address frequently shapes the framework of that speech in quite complicated ways. On the vocabulary of Heidegger's political speeches see Karl Jaspers, *Notizen zu Martin Heidegger*, ed. H. Saner (München: Piper Verlag, 1989), 238–43. One of the most interesting treatments of Heidegger's vocabulary in the Rectoral Address is Derrida's discussion of the word "Geist" in *De l'esprit* (Paris: Éditons Galilée, 1987).

20. This translation is by Joe Sachs. Bloom translates the line as "For surely all great things carry with them the risk of a fall." The more common German translation would be: "Denn alles Große hat ja seine Schwierigkeit"—the word "ἐπιφαλη" is typically interpreted as "zum Fall geneigt," "wankend," or "unsicher."

21. For a careful and comprehensive treatment of Heidegger's "Rectoral Address" in relation to Plato, see Francisco Gonzalez, "Heidegger's 1933 Misappropriation of Plato's *Republic*," in *Ermeneutica e Filosofia Antica*, ed. Franco Trabbatoni and Mariapaola Bergomi (Milan: Quaderni Di Acme, 2012), 63–119.

22. These are published in GA 83.

23. GA 45: 222.

24. This is a point that Heidegger will concede in letters that he exchanged with Gadamer in the late 1960s and 1970s. He also pressed Gadamer to write his "Plato book" and to draw out what Heidegger himself had failed to accomplish in his readings of Plato. I have this from conversations with Gadamer and the still unpublished letters that Heidegger and Gadamer exchanged over fifty years. Of special interest here are Gadamer's *Gesammelte Werke*, Bd. 5–7, Mohr Siebeck Verlag, Tübingen, 1991.

25. One of the clearest examples of this is found in GA 36/37: 186–200. Heidegger tends to understand the possibility of moral sense as ineluctably wedded to a Christian notion of good and evil. For Heidegger, the idea of the good has the task "of making unconcealedness at all possible" ["die Unverborgenheit *überhaupt* zu ermöglichen"] p. 192. Plato is clear that the idea of the good has its

moral sense, so one reads a passage in the Allegory of the Cave that Heidegger ignores; namely, that one must look to the good in order "to act prudently in private or public" ["ἐμφρόνως πράξειν ἢ ἰδίᾳ ἢ δημοσίᾳ"] 517a.

26. GA 36/37: 187; emphasis added.

27. GA 36/37: 183.

28. Significantly, Heidegger does not say that this return is driven by the need for the philosopher to govern; indeed, in a lecture course of 1936–37 Heidegger will say "in Plato's *Republic* that the "philosophers" are destined to be rulers [βασιλεῖς] is already the essential debasement [Herabsetzung] of philosophy" (GA 45: 180). To be sure, this remark comes after the debacle of the Rectorat, nonetheless, even in the remarks at the time of the Rectorate, there is no clear sense of *governing* that defines the need for a return.

29. "κατέβην" is used seven times in the *Republic*, always as a decisive movement (372a, 328c, 359d, 511b, 516e, 519d, 614d). On this see the fine reading of Plato's *Republic* in John Sallis, *Being and Logos* (Bloomington: Indiana University Press, 1996) esp. chap. 5.

30. In the end, this return and way in which it is compelled remains unresolved. On this, see Baracchi, *Of Myth, Life, and War in Plato's* Republic Bloomington: Indiana University Press, 2002), 205–7.

31. Compare *Timaeus* 41d–e, where every soul is carried by a star.

32. The movements of κατέβην and ἀνεβην in the myth reenact a sort of reverse movement of that described in the Allegory of the Cave. My comments on the "Myth of Er" will be limited to those that are especially relevant to my general concern with Heidegger's reading of Plato and especially upon the discussion of the relation of the philosopher to the city. There is much more to be said than I will begin to address here and of course much has been written about this passage; I simply note here a few of readings of this part of the *Republic* that were especially helpful to me in this essay: Giorgio Agamben, *The Use of Bodies*, trans. A. Kotsko (Stanford: Stanford University Press, 2015), esp. 249–62; Claudia Baracchi, *Of Myth, Life, and War in Plato's*, esp. 177–226; Patrick J. Deneen, *The Odyssey of Political Theory* (Oxford: Rowman & Littlefield, 2000), esp. 81–130; Stephen Halliwell, "The Life-and-Death Journey of the Soul," in *The Cambridge Companion to Plato's* Republic (Cambridge: Cambridge University Press, 2007), 445–73; Gert-Jan van der Heiden, *The Voice of Misery* (Albany: State University of New York Press, 2019), esp. 111–22; Francisco Gonzales, *Plato and Heidegger*, esp. 225–55; Catherine Malabou, "Odysseus' Changed Soul," in *Contemporary Encounters with Ancient Metaphysics*, ed. Abraham Jacob Greenstein and Ryan J. Johnson (Edinburgh: Edinburgh University Press, 2017), 30–46. There are other myths in Platonic dialogues about what awaits the dead. Both *Gorgias* and *Phaedo* offer quite different stories in this regard. On this, see Julia Annas, "Plato's Myths of Judgment," *Phronesis* 27, no. 2 (1982): 119–43.

33. For my treatment of other sections of this lecture course, see my *Idiome der Wahrheit* (Frankfurt: Klostermann Verlag, 2013), 13–38, and "Putting Oneself in Words . . ." in Lewis Edwin Hahn ed., *Library of Living Philosophers: Gadamer* (Chicago: Open Court, 1995), 483–95.

34. "Pamphylia" means something like "every race/tribe."

35. Er thus occupies a position similar to the one Socrates describes of his own witnessing of the festival in Book I, like Er Socrates does not participate in the events. This is one among the many reasons one can say that "the myth of Er's journey to the 'other place' mirrors Socrates' descent to the Piraeus"; Baracchi, *Of Myth, Life, and War in Plato's* Republic, 222.

36. Catherine Malabou rightly notes that "a striking fact in the myth is that among the various models of lives the life of a philosopher was nowhere to be found" (Malabou, "Odysseus' Changed Soul," 40).

37. It is also strange and unexplained just how Er is able to recognize the souls of famous people. This is the same puzzle that one faces in Odysseus's descent into the underworld in *Odyssey* Bk. XI. The link between the word for the shades of the dead and image, εἴδολον, is worth considering on this point. On this, see my *Between Word and Image* (Bloomington: Indiana University Press, 2012), 28–35.

38. This remark is reminiscent of Socrates comment about the need to care above all for the "polity within oneself" ["τῆς ἐν αὐτῳ πολιτείας"] (608b).

39. Prior to turning to the Myth of Er, Heidegger had developed an extended treatment of the notion of ψευδος as incorrectness. The discussion of λήθη is an effort to show that it, not ψευδος, is the true counterpart that defines ἀλήθεια as a struggle. On this, see Francisco Gonzalez, *Plato and Heidegger*, 225–32.

40. On the meaning of "Abrede" see van der Heiden, *The Voice of Misery*, 116–18. "Ἀλκίνου ἀπόλογος" was a phrase used to describe a lengthy and tedious story, and the phrase that Heidegger translates as "eines wackeren Mannes" ["a brave man"] is "ἀλκίμου μὲν ἀνδρός" which is almost the same as Ἀλκίνου—with a mu instead of a nu (and Ἀλκίμου was the father of Mentor and friend of Achilles). In short, Heidegger takes this characterization of the tale as an "ἀπόλογον" only by taking the word out of a quite intricate context that is defined by multiple puns. There are other odd ways in which Heidegger introduces this discussion; for instance, here he translates the Greek word "πολέμῳ" as "Gefecht" ["skirmish"] whereas he has previously—and frequently—translated it as "Kampf" ["struggle"]. Given the timing of this lecture course—it was held during the period of the German defeat at Stalingrad where there were heavy casualties. Most of Heidegger's students during this time were women or wounded soldiers.

41. For an interesting discussion of these descriptions of hiddenness and oblivion, see Rudolf Bernet, "Le secret selon Heidegger et 'La letter volée de Poe," in *Archives de philosophie* 68, no. 3 (2005): 379–400.

42. GA 54: 176–77. Heidegger distinguishes the "τόπον τινὰ δαιμόνιον" from the river of carelessness by saying that it is "after" (p. 178) the trip through the "τόπον τινὰ δαιμόνιον" that the travelers encounter this river. This is somewhat surprising, and yet he does not defend this decision nor clarify what is at stake in this distinction.

43. GA 54: 178.

44. In a sense, Er, who is a warrior of "every race," is utterly unique in the world since he alone among everyone living has witnessed and testified to this life "over there."

45. GA 54: 179.

46. So, "one can be struck by the claim of being without knowing what that is, and without being able to respond to this claim of being with a thinking that is appropriate" (GA 54: 179).

47. GA 54: 188.

48. On this, see my "Birth, Death, and Unfinished Conversations," in *Gadamer's Hermeneutics and the Art of Conversation, International Studies in Hermeneutics and Phenomenology* 2, ed. Andrzej Wierciński (2010), 107–15; "Another Interrupted Conversation," in *Oxford Literary Review*, special ed. M. Naas 36, no. 2 (2014): 306–8; and "Where ethics begins. . . . ," in *Epochē* 22, no. 1 (2017): 159–75; see also, van der Heiden, 121–22.

49. The phrase used in GA 54 is "todesträchtigen Gang" ["death drawn passage"] (p. 192). The role of birth in *Sein und Zeit* is quite understated, but still central. One sees this in the notion of "thrownness," but also in remarks such as the one Heidegger makes in his discussion of history in Chapter Five that "das faktische Dasein existiert gebürtig und gebürtig stirbt es" (374).

50. This is especially the case for the Allegory of the Cave.

51. I am not going to try to litigate the question of what Plato's trip to Syracuse meant for Plato. Among the many books devoted to this question, one of the most interesting is a collection of essays—some of which do compare Plato and Heidegger on this question—Heather L. Reid and Mark Ralkowski, eds., *Plato at Syracuse* (Sioux City, IA: Parnassos, 2019). My concern is not simply about how to understand Plato—or even Heidegger—here, but whether this idea of going to Syracuse, where Syracuse is the name of an idea rather than a place, is a constitutive liability of philosophy in general.

52. This is likely why Hegel described history as the "slaughter bench of the happiness of peoples" and the times not defined by crises as the "blank pages" of history, see Hegel, *Vorlesungen über die Philosophie der Geschichte* Bd. 12 (Frankfurt: Suhrkamp Verlag, 1970), 35. On this see my "Blank Pages, Storms and Other Images of History," in *Research in Phenomenology* XXIX, no. 1 (1999), 13–30.

53. On this see my "Thinking in Times of Crisis: What to Do," *International Yearbook for Hermeneutics* Bd. 20 (2020): 55–65. The Scylla and Charybdis that one needs to navigate are the double risks of turning philosophy into politics or of ontologizing political life.

Part 3

Heidegger and Aristotle

8

Heidegger's Perversion of Virtue Ethics, 1924

Sacha Golob

Heidegger's debt to Aristotle is, of course, vast: Volpi went so far as to ask whether *Being and Time* was a translation of the *Nicomachean Ethics*.[1] In this chapter, I want to investigate a fundamental divergence between the two, a rejection by early Heidegger of one of the central tenets of Aristotelian ethics. This rejection begins in the years before *Being and Time* and the forces behind it extend into the postwar period. I will focus in particular on GA 18, 1924's *Basic Concepts of Aristotelian Philosophy*: what Heidegger's Aristotle rejects there, in effect, is the notion of character.

What makes this rejection so complex and revealing is that Heidegger's interpretative approach forces him to present disagreement as discovery: as an insight into a true Aristotle who has remained concealed. My claim here is not the familiar one that Heideggerian history of philosophy is exegetically "violent" or that it frequently tells us more about Heidegger than about its supposed target. Rather, it is more specific. Texts such as *Basic Concepts of Aristotelian Philosophy* present a unique exegetical situation. This is because Heidegger lacks several of the interpretative tools that will justify his radical reading of Kant just a few years later: I will examine in particular his changing conception of "philology." The result is that, while commentators routinely talk of Heidegger's "appropriation" of Kant, Heidegger's early use of Aristotle is simultaneously more complex and less refined.[2] "Perversion" is, one might think, scarcely a rigorous term, but it is, I will argue, the best description of what follows.

239

Before proceeding, a few words on scope. I cannot remotely do justice to the breadth of the Aristotle-Heidegger relationship in this chapter. Instead, I will keep the exegetical focus tight, concentrating on GA 18. I will not discuss GA 19, the *Sophist* lectures from the same year, in any detail, although I believe what I say here harmonizes with them. I will also not discuss wider issues such as Heidegger's appeal to phronesis-like judgments in *Being and Time*: that would require a far fuller analysis of authenticity [*Eigentlichkeit*] than I can offer here.[3]

I begin by highlighting some of the relevant aspects of Aristotle's story on virtue acquisition (§1). I will then provide a similar overview of the nearest parallel in Heidegger's own early philosophy, the transition to authenticity (§2). With this background in place, I turn directly to GA 18, focusing on Heidegger's treatment of "*hexis*" (§3). In particular, I examine his introduction of classically hermeneutic themes into Aristotle, themes that exert a radical and distorting influence on his reading of virtue (§4). I close with an assessment of some of the philosophical and exegetical consequences of these results (§5).

(§1) Aristotle on Virtue Acquisition

I want to start by highlighting a few aspects of Aristotle's account of what we now call "moral" virtue acquisition or the acquisition of virtues of character—for example, courage. All of what follows is, of course, open to vast debate, but we need an orthodox Aristotelian position on the table to see how Heidegger's reading differs.

There are five aspects of the standard Aristotelian story I want to highlight. For simplicity, I focus solely on the *Nicomachean Ethics*, ignoring complexities introduced by the *Eudemian*.

First, virtue acquisition occurs via habituation, with agents becoming temperate or courageous by performing temperate or courageous actions (NE: 1103a17-b1). As such, it mirrors the acquisition of other, more mundane, capacities such as lyre playing or building (NE: 1103a26-b2). Indeed, Russell goes as far as to say that Aristotle "does not offer any special theory of acquiring the virtues because he thinks that there is no special problem involved in understanding how virtues are acquired. On the contrary, Aristotle thinks of that process as a particular instance of something people do all the time: getting better at something through practice and training."[4] I will not assume this strength of reading, but the fact that it is possible will be useful to bear in mind. The end result of the process is a relatively robust set of motivational and epistemic capacities. Of particular importance will be the idea that virtue requires what Crisp renders as "a firm and unshakeable character," Sachs as "being in a stable condition and not able to be moved all the way out of it" and Irwin as "a firm and unchanging state" (NE: 1105a29–35).[5] I follow Irwin in using "state" for "hexis" and its cognates: as Annas notes, this has become the "established translation."[6]

Second, Aristotle's model faces familiar "internalization" problems. How can merely performing a given action, no matter how often, yield the kind of robust, multifaceted, internal state that Aristotle posits? This in turn threatens the analogy with ordinary skills: as Broadie observes, "The more he stresses the differences, the more one is entitled to wonder how merely performing the actions leads to moral character."[7] One consequence is that Aristotle's theory naturally lends itself to the idea of partial or imperfect or failed internalization: cases, such as the *Nicomachean Ethics*'s "civic courage," say, or the courage characteristic of Sparta discussed in the *Politics*.

Third, as a process of habituation, virtue acquisition is necessarily temporally extended: it cannot happen overnight. Many contemporary Aristotelians regard this as almost a conceptual truth given their attendant picture of moral psychology. Here, for example is Annas: "If we think of habits, we can see that there is no shortcut. I cannot become generous overnight, however genuine my conversion from meanness to generosity, just as I cannot stop worrying overnight. In each case my feelings change as a result of modifying my behavior."[8] She elaborates on this rejection of a "conversion model" elsewhere: "Scrooge may have been converted suddenly to compassion and kindliness on Christmas Eve, but the story is careful to tell us that he continued over time the process of becoming a compassionate person. Coming to see that being loyal or brave is a worthwhile way to live is just the first step. Becoming virtuous requires habituation and experience."[9]

Fourth, the stable state produced by habituation must have a particular structure: it is not sufficient that nonrational parts of the soul merely happen to desire what is rationally appropriate (NE: 1102b33–1103a1). Rather, our desires should so aim *on account of* their obedience to reason, accepting its authority, as a child accepts the authority of their father or a servant their master (NE: 1138b11).

Fifth, Aristotle's account has direct pedagogical consequences. Most obviously, the centrality of long-term habituation and the fact that one can still learn by copying actions even without a mature understanding of them, places the focus squarely on the education of the child under the guidance of a teacher. As Aristotle puts it: "It makes no small difference, then, to be habituated in this or that way straight from childhood, but an enormous difference or rather all the difference (NE: 1103b.24–25)."[10] This chimes, of course, with the rejection of a "conversion model": the primary aim is to develop the young rather than, as Annas puts it, to "jolt and shock" the mature out of existing habits.[11]

(§2) Heidegger on Anxiety and Authenticity

I now want to introduce the nearest parallel in Heidegger's own early philosophy, the transition from inauthenticity to authenticity. I am not, of course, claiming that this is equivalent to virtue acquisition. Nor is the account that follows intended as anything like a complete analysis: in particular, I deliberately gloss over Heideggerian technicalities, such as the relationship between human and Dasein, when they are not relevant here. But it will prove a useful foil.

In particular, I want to highlight a specific mood [*Stimmung*]. In GA 18, Heidegger equates such states with Aristotelian *pathe*: through both we become orientated toward the world, encountering specific objects or goals as "mattering" to us in various ways.[12] Withy has provided an extremely helpful overview of this alignment of the *pathe* and Heideggerian *Befindlichkeit*.[13] My concern, however, is not with the broad issue per se, but with one very specific case: anxiety.

Heidegger identifies anxiety as central to the process of becoming authentic: it "provides the phenomenal basis" for understanding our "originary wholeness of being" and thus for the self-understanding or "self-transparency" that he equates with authenticity.[14] Such anxiety consists in a sudden experience of a loss of meaning and import: our world "collapses," the goals to which we have been committed appear as "utterly insignificant."[15] As Dreyfus and Rubin put it, "All meaning and mattering slip away"; Withy summarizes it as "a crisis or rupture in our everyday lives"; Blattner as a "condition in which nothing matters."[16] Pippin aptly locates the state within a broad modern focus on "radical" and "complete" failures of meaning, comparing it to Melville's Bartleby.[17]

If we now juxtapose even this brief sketch with the Aristotelian account of virtue acquisition, several points are striking.

First, anxiety, at least in the episodic, global form to which Heidegger ascribes such philosophical significance, is presented as a sudden onset state: a "collapse" of meaning.[18] It is not the product of habituation: indeed, SZ's only mention of "habit" is to dismissively assert that authenticity "can hardly be confused with an empty 'habitus.'"[19]

Second, while Heidegger recognizes some complex sense in which we can be "ready" for anxiety, this is absolutely not "a particular instance of something people do all the time," raising "no special problem," as Russell maintained about Aristotelian training.[20] On the contrary, achieving this readiness in *Being and Time* requires appeal to complex existential notions such as "wanting-to-have-a-conscience."[21] Later lectures, such as GA 29/30 on the (for Heidegger) closely related state of profound boredom, admit that such readiness is a "strange or almost insane demand."[22] Notably, any idea of becoming authentic by copying the acts of the authentic is deeply problematic in a Heideggerian context. This is because Heidegger is profoundly worried by agents who, lacking direct, personal engagement with some phenomenon, repeat what they have seen others do or say with regard to it: in the absence of a "primary relationship" with the object, this amounts simply to "gossip" or "passing the word along."[23] Heidegger's sympathies here are with Luther rather than Aristotle: mimicry of the target behavior by agents without the relevant internal state is closer to hypocrisy than learning.

Third, the status Heidegger allocates to anxiety immediately problematizes the priority of anything like "rational" over "non-rational" parts of the soul. Of course, Heidegger himself is suspicious of the distinction and his own "moral psychology" has no corresponding divide. However, one can see the problem if we ask why should we take the experience of anxiety to be veridical or significant? Why is the sudden belief that all options lack significance, a significance to which every previous training and argument has attested, not simply a sign that the agent is akratic or worse? It is hard for an Aristotelian to see such bursts of anxiety as respectful of reason's paternal authority.

Fourth, the surrounding pedagogical landscape will clearly be very different. It is hard to think of an Aristotelian topic on which Heidegger has less to say than children: *Being and Time* never uses the term, and GA 18 excizes childhood from Aristotle's own text, mentioning them only in passing.[24] One obvious reason is the Christian influences that push Heidegger toward the "jolt and shock" side of Annas's distinction:

commentators have frequently stressed the influence of *phronesis* on Heidegger's account of resolute choice, but there is, of course, also the strong influence of Luther's *Augenblick*, the instant in which we are all changed.[25]

(§3) Heidegger on *Hexis*

With this background in place, I want now to turn directly to GA 18, 1924's *Basic Concepts of Aristotelian Philosophy*. Heidegger's avowed aim is to reconstruct the distinctive contours of the Greek experience of being through an analysis of Aristotle's fundamental concepts: "We are pursuing . . . the clarification of the being structure of the being-there of human beings, for Aristotle. In his explication, that which was already vital in the history of the Greek interpretation of being-there explicitly comes to fulfillment."[26] Aristotle is thus taken as a representative spokesperson for Greek thought: hence Heidegger talks casually of "infer[ing] the meaning, for Aristotle and the Greeks" of theoretical research (GA 18: 39) or grasping "their basic possibilities of speaking to their world" by analyzing "the basic Aristotelian concepts."[27]

Given this premise, Heidegger's task is to piece together, as accurately as possible, Aristotle's own position. The famous "violence" of Heideggerian history of philosophy is not trumpeted here, as it will be in 1927 when he moves to Kant. Instead, Heidegger presents his project as philological rather philosophical: "Here, we offer no philosophy, much less a history of philosophy. If philology means the passion for knowledge of what has been expressed, then what we are doing is philology . . . The lecture has no philosophical aim at all; it is concerned with understanding basic concepts in their conceptuality. The aim is philological in that it intends to bring the reading of philosophers somewhat more into practice."[28] Unsurprisingly, the situation is far more complex than this suggests.

The place to begin is with Heidegger's remarks on "*hexis*." What, Heidegger asks, "does it genuinely mean to come into a determinate *hexis*?" In particular, in what sense is "habituation" the path to it?[29]

What is striking is that Heidegger's answer rejects any appeal to training, practice, or the skill analogy. Here is one of the key passages. It is best understood as three claims, each following from the previous and separated by the ellipses: first a definition of training, then of action, then a conclusion regarding their consequent incompatibility. "Training has the precise sense of reducing deliberation . . . It is essential to action that it proceeds by deliberating . . . With training, the possibility of action [*Handlung*] is ruled out: deliberating and resolving, the how of action— precisely that on which it depends."[30] The claim is that "training," which he immediately equates with "practice" [*Übung*], is at odds with action insofar as the latter requires deliberation and resolution.

Heidegger now explains this claim: behavior based on training or "frequently undergoing" [*Öfter-Durchmachen*] or "skill" is insufficiently flexible, insufficiently adjusted to the demands of the given moment. He contrasts it to what he dubs "repetition" [*Wiederholung*], a repetition that does not imply the stability one associates with Aristotelian virtue states. "The manner and mode of habituation [*Gewöhnung*], in the case of action, is not practice but repetition. Repetition does not mean the bringing-into-play of a stable state or skill [*festsitzenden Fertigkeit*], but rather *acting anew in every moment on the basis of the corresponding decision* [*entsprechenden Entschluss*] . . . Every state as stable routine breaks down in the face of the moment [*Augenblick*]."[31] The idea of repetition will eventually be reworked in *Being and Time*'s theory of historicity, for example when authentic Dasein draws on past exemplars.[32] But here the only positive content it receives is acting "anew" in each situation, that is, in a way that meets the specific demands of that moment. I will say more on this in §4. Skill and practice, by contrast, are presented as rote or routine behaviors.

It is worth pausing to address the complex translation issues in play here. Metcalf and Tanzer render "*festsitzende Fertigkeit*" as "settled completeness." This obscures the link to the ordinary German use of *Fertigkeit* for "skill": one might easily render "*festsitzende Fertigkeit*" as "established skill." However, it has the great benefit of foregrounding the tie with "*hexis*," typically rendered in English as "stable disposition" or "state," and with the idea that such states emerge from habituation, captured via the links between "*fertig*" and "complete" or "finished." To do justice to this characteristically Heideggerian polyphony, I have left both "stable state" and "skill" in the translation.[33]

What is evident is that Heidegger is pushing against practice, the skill analogy and the resulting idea of stable states or dispositions. This immediately requires him to embark on an extensive reworking of Aristotle's claims. For example, Aristotle's talk of becoming virtuous by "acting-frequently" does not supposedly "mean 'often' in the sense of a duration," that is, a regularly performed behavior. Instead, again, it is really a reference to the "moment": what precisely that amounts to we will shortly see.[34]

Before proceeding, I want to set aside one possible, but I think mistaken and uninteresting, explanation for Heidegger's remarks. On that explanation Heidegger would have equated training, skill, or "stable states" with unthinking automaticity, what Sherman called the "mechanical view" on which Aristotelian virtue is devoid of rational engagement, a "mindless process" as Broadie puts it.[35] His point would then simply be that Aristotelian virtue is not like this—and hence should not be understood be understood in terms of training or the resultant stable states.

This reading is uninteresting because Heidegger would simply be echoing a standard observation made by almost all Aristotle commentators. Furthermore, he would be expressing that point in a mangled and misleading way: rather than arguing that training, skill, or stable states need not imply mindlessness, he would be assuming that they do and thus separating Aristotle from them. This would, furthermore, be an extremely odd assumption for him to make. This is because the only people who naturally do so are those, most famously Kant, who assume that the only alternative to mindlessness is reflection and who thus conflate anything below the level of reflection with mechanistic routine.[36] But Heidegger, whose entire philosophy of mind rests on a rejection of reflection's primacy, is an unlikely candidate for the error: indeed, in GA 18 itself he warns that "reflection is but a certain outré form in which being-there is conscious of itself."[37]

Yet if Heidegger is not making a bizarrely mangled version of a stock point, what is he doing?

(§4) Heidegger's Aristotle on Hermeneutics and the Good

To understand see the answer, we need to introduce two other pieces of the puzzle. The first is Heidegger's hermeneutic epistemology, the second his rejection of a substantive notion of the good. Crucially, as we will see, he projects both on to Aristotle. I will take them in turn. The basic of Heidegger's epistemology is well illustrated by the following remark:

It was an error of phenomenology to believe that phenomena could be correctly seen merely through unprejudiced looking. But it is just as great an error to believe that, since perspectives are always necessary, the phenomena themselves can *never* be seen and that everything amounts to contingent, subjective . . . standpoints. From these two impossibilities, we obtain the necessary insight that our central task and methodological problem is to arrive at the *right* perspective. We need to take a preliminary view of the phenomenon but precisely for this reason it is of decisive importance whether the guiding perspective is adequate to the phenomenon, i.e., whether it is derived from its substantial content or not (or only constructed). It is not because we must view it from some perspective or other that the phenomenon gets blocked off to us, but because the perspective adopted most often does not have a genuine origin in the phenomenon itself.[38]

In short, "our central task" is to engage in a continuous process of adjusting and recalibrating our standpoint in order "to arrive at the right perspective." The "mode of discovery" must be "as it were, regulated and prescribed by the entity to be discovered and by its mode of being."[39] Heidegger places particular emphasis on the fact that familiar principles or concepts or tools will often be unsuitable because they are not sufficiently attentive to the dynamics of the domains in question;[40] for example, one cannot simply appeal to modal logic without recognising that the notions of modality appropriate to different entities are not even coextensive.[41]

This same model is central to Heidegger's Aristotle. It is for example, how he understands "*paideia*," echoing *Being and Time*'s insistence on avoiding 'off the shelf' categories in favour of those tailored to the situation.

> The decision lies in the *paideia*, whether the access [to a phenomenon] is originary or whether the speaker has access only from hearsay . . . He who has the right instinct, the right *paideia*, will be able to decide whether it makes sense to treat logic mathematically or to set up the history of Christianity with categories from art history . . . Today, this *hexis* is entirely neglected; it is also difficult to appropriate, and even more difficult to obtain.[42]

Note *hexis* being aligned with the capacity for a situation-specific response: the "neglected" hexis is one that would allow the right approach to a phenomenon, avoiding the careless imposition of inappropriate categories. Indeed, for Heidegger's Aristotle the need to avoid "presupposed theories," that is, assumptions not drawn from the phenomenon itself, becomes *the* foundational metaphysical requirement: "Exposing nature in its being-there depends upon our way not being blocked by presupposed opinions and theories."[43] Likewise with aporias, the key is whether the speaker are has "a definite fundamental experience of the matter itself" or "lack[s] the right perspective on the matter about which he speaks."[44] Heidegger particularly stresses the role of affect in this process of calibration and orientation.[45]

As Heidegger develops this hermeneutic picture, he increasingly uses Aristotle's talk of "the mean" to make the same point. For example, he uses it to gloss the comment on affects just cited: "One understands what "coming into the genuine frame of mind" means: coming into the mean, coming from the aforementioned degrees into the mean. The mean is nothing other than the *kairos*, the entirety of circumstances, the how, when, whither, and about which."[46] This notion of the "entirety of circumstances" in turn is aligned with a full grasp of the situation or moment before us—and this ties back to *hexis*, now understood as the capacity for a situation-specific response. "This being-composed, this being-oriented toward the moment, is the sort of possibility that has seized being-there itself *on the basis of its particular situation*. . . . In the manner and mode that we, correspondingly, are present to our being in the full presence of the situation encountered, we grasp *hexis*."[47] Note how far we are now form the standard model of *hexis* as a stable, that is, *cross-situational*, state or disposition. Instead, it is precisely a *variable* openness to the distinctive nature of each *"particular situation"*—above all, an openness unhampered by any "presupposed opinions and theories."

In aligning the mean with a hermeneutic engagement with each situation, Heidegger inevitably also separates it from the idea of a cross-situational good grounded in teleological facts about human nature. Here is a clear example: "*For our being, characterized by particularity, no unique and absolute norm can be given. It depends on cultivating the being of human beings, so that it is transposed into the aptitude for maintaining the mean. But that means nothing other than seizing the moment.*"[48] Heidegger's point is not the trivial one that Aristotle rejects rigid moral rules. Instead, he is making a much stronger claim: the only substantive norm identifiable is "seizing the moment," that is reacting appropriately, in the hermeneutic sense, to the demands of the situation.

Once again, he fuses this back to his new reading of *hexis*: "Aristotle says of *hexis*—more precisely of the ability to have the moment at one's disposal in the proper mode—that it "preserves the mean"; it brings me into the genuine being that corresponds to the circumstances."[49] *Hexis* has now been fully hermeneuticized: it is the ability to respond to the specifics of each distinctive situation. "For in *hexis* lies the primary orientation toward the *kairos*: "I am there, come what may!" This being-there, being on- the-alert in one's situation, in relation to its matter, characterizes *hexis*."[50] We can understand see why Heidegger was so skeptical of habituation. The complaint was not the Kantian one that habituation is unreflective. Rather, it is the hermeneutic one that habituation, by establishing a set pattern of action, implies an inflexibility, a settled cross-situational state set prior to and independent of each of the phenomena we encounter. From a hermeneutic point of view, that cannot be acceptable. *This* is why: "Every completeness as stable routine breaks down in the face of the moment [*Augenblick*]."[51] We can also see how the instabilities characteristic of Heidegger's own work will emerge: for example, the tension between the hermeneutic and the existentialist. If this grip on "the moment" is authorized by an experience of anxiety that seems to elude verbal expression, to what extent is it compatible with an open giving and exchange of reasons? Exacerbated by Heidegger's suspicions about public discourse as mere "idle talk," his hermeneutics is, ironically, often on the point of collapsing into voluntarism, simultaneously eulogising attentive interpretation while privatising the resources for interpretation's justification.[52]

(§5) The Perversion of Virtue Ethics

We are now finally in a position to see how Heidegger has reconfigured the Aristotelian text—and his stance on *hexis* is the key. Heidegger's collapse of the mean into "the moment" implies that the only source of normativity is the "full presence of the situation encountered" and the need for a response that does it justice in the hermeneutic sense.[53] There is no other "no unique and absolute norm," no *telos*, for example, grounded in Aristotelian biology.

A direct consequence is that Heidegger places enormous emphasis on flexibility, on a capacity to avoid imposing assumption that say more about the viewer than the phenomena viewed. In his own early work, he expresses this in terms of "reticence" [*Verschwiegenheit*]: "a potentiality-for-hearing" or as McManus nicely puts it, a "readiness to judge *rather than pre-judge* one's situation."[54] In his later work, this theme of receptivity interweaves with that of submission to being: as Davis observes, thinking itself becomes "receptive listening . . . obedient [*gehorsam*] to the voice of being."[55]

Now consider the orthodox reading of Aristotelian virtue from this perspective. Virtue is, to borrow a phrase from Williams, *a moral incapacity*, a carefully acquired inability to see things other than in a certain way. As Aristotle famously put it, habit produces a new nature. In McDowell's modern idiom, the virtuous person is simply deaf to certain considerations: "Reasons to act contrary to what virtue demands are silenced . . . [T]he dictates of virtue, if properly appreciated, are not weighed with other reasons at all, not even on a scale which always tips on their side. reasons for acting otherwise [than virtuously] are silenced."[56] This makes ethical and epistemological sense if there is a substantive notion of the good: the virtuous person blinds themselves to factors that might distract from it. But once the good and the mean have been replaced by the particular circumstances of "each moment" or the "full presence of the situation encountered," such blindness starts to look like prejudice. Why is an inflexibility, an inability to tailor our stance to the matter in hand, desirable? It is this thought which underlies so much of Heidegger's work on Aristotle ethics.

The basic point is similar to one Heideggerians often made against narrative visions of authenticity. Agents who seek to maintain narrative consistency will often do so only by forcing the world around them into a set mould—rather than genuinely responding to it on its own terms. As Fisher suggests in an acute discussion of Malick's *The Thin Red Line*, for Heidegger the truly authentic person: "[D]oes not appropriate the situation to his life by projecting a life-gestalt in order to make sense of it. On the contrary, he allows his life to be appropriated for the sake of the situation."[57] What makes Heidegger's Aristotle so *unique* is the combination of this move with his supposed commitment to utter textual fidelity, to "philology" rather than philosophy.[58] The result is that Aristotle's text is subjected to almost continuous pressure, line by line, as it is gradually forced in a direction quite alien to it. *Hexis* lies at the epicenter of this process. On the one hand, Heidegger seeks to separate it from any stable, i.e., cross-situational, commitments: this is what we saw in §3. On the other hand, now equated with a notion of the mean severed from any substantive good, it plays a key role in articulating Heidegger's hermeneutic vision of normativity, of "genuine being that corresponds to the circumstances." This is what we saw in §4.

Here is another way to put the point. Textbook readings of Aristotelian virtue often stress its situation sensitivity: its rejection of general rules, for example. This even gives them a loose affinity to hermeneutics, as within the Gadamerian tradition. Heidegger's reading takes a radically different tack: he assumes that a standard Aristotelian framework cannot be situation sensitive enough. There are, as noted with respect to McDowell, some things that the virtuous have trained themselves not to see or imagine. This is blindness once our standard is not the Aristotelian good life but the "full presence of the situation encountered."

Suppose what I have said is right: what are the broader philosophical and exegetical consequences?

First, note the distinctive nature of Heidegger's position. He is not denying, as Sartre or contemporary situationists like Doris do, the existence of character traits in the Aristotelian sense. Instead, he is rejecting them as *undesirable* in his reconfigured epistemology. Withy, in a hugely insightful discussion of Heidegger on Aristotelian affects, sees the key point: "Heidegger's driving intuition is that habits, tendencies and settled dispositions are opposed to human excellence."[59] But I disagree when she explains this in terms of "Heidegger's Kierkegaardian aversion to conformity" or worries about "averageness."[60] The root is the hermeneutic model sketched above. What Heidegger tacitly rejects is not a model of average agency but rather one of exemplary agency, the Aristotelian virtuous man.

Second, we can now understand the central relevance of anxiety in Heidegger's account of individual development. Anxiety serves to distance an agent from even their deepest commitments: all are rendered "utterly insignificant" as the agent sees that they cannot be "at home" in them.[61] The original Aristotelian aspiration to *hexis* is precisely an aspiration to the kind of stability, the kind of being at home, that anxiety undermines. We can also see why *Being and Time* itself presents the justification for taking anxiety seriously as circular, i.e., as interwoven so closely with his other Heidegger's commitments.[62] There is no way to defend it, no way to explain why the man who suddenly experiences all meaning slipping away is not simply akratic or worse, without introducing large parts of the apparatus above, as well, ultimately as a much broader story about anxiety's capacity to expose the structure of Dasein.[63]

Third, what of the philosophical plausibility of Heidegger's account? One immediate way to boost that is to read Aristotle 'thickly.' Heideggerian anxiety distances agents from the concrete web of the world, of identities, tools, social structures, which define them. It can thus serve as a useful corrective in cases where agents over-identify with contingent aspects of their society: if Aristotelian virtue is taken to include the full complacent package of Athenian social arrangements, from natural slaves to feminine virtues, a dose of anxiety starts to seem attractive. But, of course, no contemporary Aristotelians defend this. So, the problem for Heidegger is to explain the preference for his model over one that recognises a substantive but more general Aristotelian vision of our telos.

A full confrontation on this issue is evidently beyond the current paper: it would require, among other things, a close treatment of authenticity and Heidegger's understanding of finitude. But the key to the *Basic Concepts of Aristotelian Philosophy* is the unanalysed hermeneutic notion of "doing justice to the particular situation." In some ways the driving intuition is a simple one: once we accept the basic hermeneutic premise that our commitments and interest determine what is visible to us and how we interpret it, it becomes plausible that any cross-situational commitments, beyond a meta-level commitment to reticent openness, will blind us in at least some cases. One can invert a McDowellian theme here: there are dimensions of a situation—angles, vulnerabilities—where a willingness to look with an evil eye opens up a fineness of grain that the virtuous miss. As Nietzsche put it, only he who is himself decadent, for example, who can fathom a decadent society.[64] At this juncture, the Aristotelian will naturally want to press on the notions of perception or "full grasp": in what sense does an agent genuinely perceive or fully grasp another's weakness if their motivational response is to exploit it? Such questions remain unaddressed by Heidegger in 1924.

I want to close by returning to the word "perversion" in my title. Heidegger's reading amounts to a rejection of the role of stable, cross-situational character traits in virtue ethics—with the exception again of a meta-level commitment to reticent openness, to flexibility. Yet he presents this as a piece of pure "philology," a simple reclamation of Aristotle's views. The result is a continuous process of distortion, passage by passage.

Yet what is striking is the crudeness of the exegetical framework Heidegger employs. Compare his reading of Kant a few years later. That is avowedly "violent," rejecting Kantianism to align Kant with Heidegger's own agenda.[65] But crucially Heidegger then draws a distinction precisely between what *he* is doing and '*mere*' philology: the laws of a true "dialogue," he states, are quite different from those of "historical philology."[66] This allows him to separate out two voices: the supposed "concealed, inner passion" of Kant's work, which is essentially Heideggerian, and an official Kant who "shrunk back" from his insights, burying them in a conventional rationalism.[67] The problem is that in 1924 Heidegger lacks this distinction. Hence, the treatment of Aristotle, while no less "violent," is presented throughout as an exercise in scrupulous "philology." The result is a perversion of Aristotelianism, as its language is forced, line by line, against its own purpose: an analysis of *hexis* becomes a rejection of *hexis*. Perhaps the most extraordinary thing about the *Basic Concepts* is that there is no sign Heidegger himself realized what he was doing.[68]

Notes

1. Franco Volpi, "Being and Time: A "translation" of the Nicomachean Ethics?," in Theodore Kisiel and John Van Buren (eds.), *Reading Heidegger from the start* (Albany: State University of New York Press, 1994), 195–211.

2. For example, Béatrice Han-Pile, "Early Heidegger's Appropriation of Kant," in Hubert L. Dreyfus & Mark A. Wrathall, eds., *A Companion to Heidegger* (Oxford: Blackwell, 2005); William Blattner, "Laying the Ground for Metaphysics: Heidegger's Appropriation of Kant," in *The Cambridge Companion to Heidegger*, ed. Charles B. Guignon (Cambridge: Cambridge University Press, 2006).

3. For a particularly sophisticated assessment see Denis McManus "Heidegger and Aristotle on Reason, Choice and Self-Expression," in *Transcending Reason, ed.* Matthew Burch and Irene McMullin (London: Routledge, 2020), 125–50; and Denis McManus, "Authenticity, Deliberation and Perception: On Heidegger's Reading and Appropriation of Aristotle's Concept of 'Phronêsis,'" *Journal of the History of Philosophy* (forthcoming), 173–98. For my own views see Sacha Golob, "Heidegger on Kant, Time, and the 'Form' of Intentionality," *British Journal for the History of Philosophy* 21: 345–67.

4. Daniel C. Russell, "Aristotle on Cultivating Virtue," in *Cultivating Virtue*, ed. Nancy E. Snow (Oxford: Oxford University Press, 2015), 17–48, here 18.

5. *Nicomachean Ethics*, trans. Roger Crisp (Cambridge: Cambridge University Press, 2000); *Nicomachean Ethics*, trans. Joe Sachs (London: Hackett, 2002); *Nicomachean Ethics*, trans. Terence H. Irwin (Indianapolis: Hackett, 1985).

6. Julia Annas, *The Morality of Happiness* (Oxford: Oxford University Press, 1993), 50.

7. Sarah Broadie, *Ethics With Aristotle* (Oxford: Oxford University Press, 1991), 104. There is also a widely discussed 'external' problem: how does one specify the set of just acts to be performed prior to acquiring the corresponding virtue?

8. Annas 1993, 57.

9. Julia Annas, *Intelligent Virtue* (Oxford: Oxford University Press, 2011), 12.

10. I use Sachs's translation here.

11. Annas 1993, 55.

12. GA 18: 169–71; BT: 140, 188.
13. Katherin Withy, "Owned Emotions: Affective Excellence in Heidegger on Aristotle," in *Heidegger, Authenticity and the Self*, ed. Denis McManus (London: Routledge, 2015), 21–36. I return to Withy's text below.
14. BT: 182, 7. I remain neutral here on whether imagining an experience anxiety would suffice for Heidegger: for helpful discussion, see R. Matthew Shockey, "Heidegger's Anxiety: On the Role of Mood in Phenomenological Method," *Bulletin d'Analyse Phénoménologique* XII (2016): 1–27.
15. BT: 186–87.
16. Hubert L. Dreyfus and Jane Rubin, "Kierkegaard, Division II, and Later Heidegger" in *Being-in-the-W: A Commentary on Heidegger's* Being and Time, ed. Hubert L. Dreyfus (Cambridge, MA: MIT Press, 1991), 332; Katherine Withy, *Heidegger on Being Uncanny* (London: Harvard University Press, 2015), 90; William Blattner, *Heidegger's Temporal Idealism* (Cambridge: Cambridge University Press, 1999), 80.
17. Robert Pippin, "Necessary Conditions for the Possibility of What Isn't: Heidegger on Failed Meaning," in *Transcendental Heidegger*, ed. Jeff Malpas and Steven Crowell (Stanford: Stanford University Press, 2007), 210.
18. BT: 186. I say "full blown form" to differentiate from the background awareness of anxiety that Heidegger believes is constantly present and almost always suppressed: I discuss the distinction further in Sacha Golob, "Methodological Anxiety: Heidegger on Moods and Emotions" in *Thinking about the Emotions*, ed. Alix Cohen and Robert Stern (Oxford: Oxford University Press, 2017), 253–69.
19. BT: 300.
20. Russell 2015.
21. BT: 287.
22. GA 29/30: 118.
23. BT: 211.
24. GA 18: 294.
25. BT: 327.
26. GA 18: 44–45.
27. GA 18: 41.
28. GA 18: 5.
29. GA 18: 188.
30. GA 18: 189; original emphases; translation modified.
31. GA 18: 189–90; original emphases; translation modified.
32. BT: 339.
33. One could push matters further, exploiting the links between "*fertig*" and "ready" to yield "stable readiness," a phrase that would also function as a very Heideggerian reading of "*hexis*." I am indebted to Joachim Aufderheide here for very helpful discussion.
34. GA 18: 191.

35. Nancy Sherman, *The Fabric of Character: Aristotle's Theory of Virtue* (Oxford: Clarendon Press, 1989), 157–59; Broadie 1991, 109.

36. Immanuel Kant, *The Metaphysics of Morals*, trans. Mary Gregor (Cambridge: Cambridge University Press, 1996), Ak.409.

37. GA 18: 247.

38. GA 34: 286; original emphasis.

39. GA 24: 99. For full discussion see Sacha Golob, "Was Heidegger a Relativist?," in *The Emergence of Modern Relativism: The German Debates from the 1770s to the 1930s*, ed. Katherina Kinzel, et al. (London: Routledge, 2020).

40. BT: 36.

41. BT: 143–44.

42. GA 18: 210.

43. GA 18: 228.

44. GA 18: 160.

45. GA 18: 170.

46. GA 18: 171.

47. GA 18: 180–181; original emphases.

48. GA 18: 186; original emphasis.

49. GA 18: 262.

50. GA 18: 119.

51. GA 18: 189; original emphases.

52. I am indebted to an anonymous referee for discussion here.

53. GA 18: 180–181.

54. BT: 165. McManus, forthcoming, 14.

55. Bret Davis, *Heidegger and the Will* (Evanston: Northwestern University Press, 2007), 226.

56. John McDowell, "Virtue and Reason," *Monist* 62 (1979), 331–50, here 332.

57. Tony Fisher, "Heidegger and the Narrativity Debate," *Continental Philosophy Review* 43 (2010): 241–65, here 262.

58. GA 18: 5.

59. Withy 2015a, 27.

60. Withy 2015a, 27.

61. BT: 187, 189.

62. BT: 194, 315.

63. For detailed discussion see Golob 2017.

64. Friedrich Nietzsche, *The Anti-Christ, Ecce Homo, Twilight of the Idols, and Other Writings*, trans. Judith Norman (Cambridge: Cambridge University Press, 2010): EH, 'Wise,' 1.

65. For detailed discussion see Sacha Golob, "Heidegger on Kant, Time, and the 'Form' of Intentionality," *British Journal for the History of Philosophy* 21 (2013): 345–67.

66. GA 3, xxvii.

67. GA 3, 201; BT: 23.

68. I am indebted to an anonymous referee for their extremely helpful comments: sadly, restrictions on space mean I am unable to take all of them up here.

9

The Temporality of Life

Reading Aristotle with and against Heidegger in
Two Unpublished Seminars 1923–1925

Francisco J. Gonzalez

A central and persistent commitment in Heidegger's reading of Aristotle was that the *Physics*, not the *Metaphysics*, is the central work of Aristotelian ontology. This commitment, which made the *Physics* a central and recurrent focus of Heidegger's many seminars and courses on Aristotle during the 1920s, remains when he returns to teaching Aristotle after the Second World War. In a seminar on the *Physics* from the Winter semester 1950–51 he characterizes *this text* as "the watershed in the fluvial land of Western thinking"[1] and even as "the fundamental text of Western metaphysics."[2] Of course, as is well known, the texts that have come down to us as Aristotle's *Physics* and *Metaphysics* are at least partly the products of editorial decisions made long after Aristotle's death and the term "metaphysics" itself was unknown to Aristotle. Nevertheless, Aristotle himself clearly distinguished what he called "first philosophy" from physics, the central distinction being that the former is concerned both with all beings *as beings* and with a primary being that is immaterial and unmoved, while the latter is concerned with *nature* as what possesses its source of motion within itself and thus with *beings in motion*. The central focus of the physics is therefore the nature of motion as such, its conditions (such as place and time), its different kinds, and its ultimate cause. The effect, then, of making the *Physics* the central and foundational text of Aristotelian ontology is to turn the latter into an *ontology of motion*, that is, an ontology for which being-in-motion and the being of motion are the central focus.³ In doing so Heidegger can be said to have a double purpose: to appropriate Aristotle's ontology of motion for his own project of an ontology of Dasein and simultaneously to critique Aristotle's ontology of motion as ultimately committed to a conception of being as presence.

What can be critiqued in such a reading is its failure to do justice not only to Aristotle's own distinction between physics and first philosophy (with the attendant distinction between nature and being as being)⁴ but also to his distinction between motion (*kinêsis*) and *energeia*: a term that has been given the disastrous English translation "actuality" (disastrous for reasons evident in what follows), but that is better approximated (though only approximated) with the translation "activity." Not only does Aristotle explicitly defend this distinction in Book Theta of the *Metaphysics* (1048b18–35), but it is indispensable to his characterization of the ultimate object of first philosophy as an *unmoved* mover whose being (*ousia*) *is energeia*. Furthermore, if this unmoved mover can be described by Aristotle as "alive," indeed as life itself, this is only because life itself is for him an *energeia and not motion*. Finally, if motion is inseparable from the "world-time" of past-present-future of which Aristotle gives an account in the *Physics*, the *energeia* that defines the being of not only the life of the unmoved mover but of life itself is said by him not to be *in* time and is therefore arguably characterized by a totally different temporality.

Heidegger of course does not neglect Aristotle's metaphysics, and he himself insists on the central importance of the notion of *energeia* in this metaphysics. In one of the unpublished seminars to be examined in what follows,⁵ he is even reported to have said: "ἐνέργεια is the fundamental ontological concept in Aristotle, his genuine discovery."⁶ The problem instead, as I aim to show, is that as Heidegger tends to read the *Metaphysics* from the perspective of the *Physics,* reading it more as a pre- rather than as a meta-physics, so he tends to interpret the notion of *energeia* from the perspective of motion, as a type of motion rather than as distinct from motion. This interpretative move, and the problems it raises, are most evident in seminars from the 1920s in which Heidegger reads and interprets the central Aristotelian texts on the notions of *energeia* and *dunamis*. Two of these seminars of particular importance are currently unpublished in any form and thus not even mentioned in the literature: a

1923–24 seminar on Book 2 of the *Physics* and a 1924–25 seminar entitled (somewhat misleadingly as we will see) *On the Ontology of the Middle Ages: the Small Summa [of Thomas]*.[7] It is on these seminars, as I have reconstructed them on the basis of student transcripts preserved among the papers of Helene Weiss, that I will focus here. The payoff will be a better understanding of the resistance Aristotle's texts offer to Heidegger's reading and thus, most importantly, of the alternative conception of the being and temporality of life they might offer. As we will see, Heidegger's overarching thesis is that Aristotle and the tradition that follows him fail to give an account of the being and temporality of life in being guided by the being and temporality of the world. The question is if this supposed failure is not instead an alternative conception that Heidegger's reading suppresses.

Heidegger on Aristotle in Two Unpublished Seminars

THE 1924–25 SEMINAR ON THE ONTOLOGY OF THE MIDDLE AGES

We begin with the 1924–25 seminar, as it is of the greatest importance for the present topic, as well as being one of the most extraordinary seminars Heidegger ever gave. Its title *On the Ontology of the Middle Ages: The Small Summa*[8] is misleading because most of the seminar is devoted to a breathtakingly wide-ranging and incisive reading of Aristotle and provides, in particular, Heidegger's most detailed and extensive interpretation of *Metaphysics Theta*, the goal of which is understanding the ontological significance of the notions of *dunamis* and *energeia*. At one point in this seminar (p. 21) Heidegger notes how Aristotle himself recognized time as a determination of the motion of *nous*.[9] Heidegger is referring to *Physics* IV.11 where Aristotle makes the argument that time and motion go together by pointing out that even when we are not affected through the body, the movement that takes place in the mind suffices for us to suppose that time has elapsed (219aff.) Heidegger comments: "Here Aristotle let matters stand; he did not press forward any further. This is a valuable reference to the inner sense: that I find within myself something that is an event and with this as a μεταβολή also time. One has chosen to understand this as Aristotle placing time in consciousness, as if time were something subjective. That is a misunderstanding" (21). But in what sense does Aristotle let matters stand without pressing forward?

Here we need to consider the general argument of the seminar, which is, in brief, as follows: in both medieval ontology and Aristotle, the being and temporality of the divine (eternal presence) is understood against, and therefore from the perspective of, the being and temporality of the world, rather than from the perspective of the being and temporality of Dasein. When Heidegger repeats this charge in the 1924 lecture *Wahrsein und Dasein nach Aristoteles*, which he delivered concurrently with the seminar, he also indicates its importance in defining his own project: "We are faced with the immense task of creating an ontology of Dasein in contrast to the ontology of the world."[10] This task is, of course, the one that will be carried out in *Being and Time* where Heidegger, in seeking to interpret the being of Dasein, must constantly work *against* Dasein's own tendency, as well as that of the philosophical tradition, to interpret its being according to the understanding of being derived from the beings encountered within the world. Thus in the introductory chapter of *Being and Time* in which Heidegger describes the task of a "destruction" of the history of ontology, we read the following: "Greek ontology and its history—which, in their numerous filiations and distortions, determine the conceptual character of philosophy even today—prove that when Dasein understands either itself or Being in general, it does so in terms of the 'world,' and that the ontology which has thus arisen has deteriorated [verfällt] to a tradition in which it gets reduced to something self-evident. . . . In the Middle Ages this uprooted ontology became a fixed body of doctrine."[11] What we do not get in *Being and Time* is any attempt to explain or justify this thesis concerning Greek ontology and its determination of medieval ontology that motivates Heidegger's own project. This is where the seminar of 1924–25 is of crucial importance.

To see why and how Heidegger maintains his thesis, let us consider briefly some of the major steps of the seminar's argument. Starting with medieval ontology, Heidegger maintains that the conception of time in Aquinas is the same as that in Aristotle: time as the measurement or number of motion. Yet Heidegger acknowledges that the eternity of God for Aquinas *cannot* be measured and therefore is not in time. This eternity does not involve any succession, being characterized as the "all at once" (totum simul); nor can one even say "now" in relation to this eternity. Furthermore, Heidegger notes that the motivation behind this characterization of eternity as completely outside of time is to *avoid* ascribing to God what can be ascribed to the being of the world. How, then, can Heidegger claim that in medieval ontology the being and temporality of

God is interpreted in terms of the being and temporality of the world? The answer is his claim that the concept of eternity here is *completely negative* and therefore still determined precisely by what it negates. What is lacking is a positive conception of being and time distinct from that which characterizes the world and things within the world, one that Heidegger believes can be found in *our own being*. Heidegger concludes as follows: "Most immediately, however, the concept of eternity is objectively won in line with worldly being, not Dasein, life—ζωή. In order to open up the possibility of determining, against the time in which the world is, the time in which Dasein is, where this determination as Dasein would indeed be the genuine ground, here too we are still in need of a remotio" (13).

The irony is that, while God is conceived of as a living being, the being and temporality of God is *not* interpreted on the basis of the being and temporality of life. The conclusion of this class of November 17, 1924, is worth citing in full as making this point perfectly clear: "The ground for the via remotionis is provided by the being of the world and the time in which the world is, and this despite the fact that the being of human Dasein provides the genuine ground for the being of God insofar as God is a *vivens*. The reason is that the being of life itself is explicated with the means of an ontology of the world, so that time, in the sense of the time that Dasein itself is, cannot at all provide the basis for the discussion of eternity" (14). The question I wish to address here is whether this is true of *Aristotle*, that is, whether we do not find in Aristotle an account of the being and temporality of life, and of the unmoved mover as alive, *not* grounded in an ontology of the world.

Before turning back to Aristotle, it should be noted that for Heidegger in this seminar it is the *Reformation* that represents a serious break with medieval ontology and its interpretation of the being of God from the perspective of the being of the world. This is because with the Reformation our being is given, in purely methodological terms, a certain ontological priority in relation to the being of God. "Purely methodologically: humans, with regard to their specific existence, are the only place from which one can say something about God. Precisely when one understands the existence of humans, and to the extent to which one understands it, will the possibility grow (I emphasize again: purely methodologically) of winning a genuine understanding of the being of God" (29). Thus at the very end of the seminar, when it is claimed that the Scholastics failed to inquire in an original way into the being of God and of man, the methodological alternative is identified with Luther (62).[12]

What then of Aristotle? A central focus in the seminar is on what Heidegger sees as Aristotle's impasse in attempting to explain the *unity* of thought (*phronêsis*) and desire (*orexis*). This is clearly for Heidegger a failure to explain the motion that we ourselves are. Commenting at one point on this problem, he observes:

> Φρόνησις is what it is through ὄρεξις, and ὄρεξις through φρόνησις. The difficulty that lies in this circle can be resolved only from the being of humans. More precisely: Aristotle himself knew no way out because *he did not examine praxis further with regard to the structure of its being*, in another respect because he saw the highest form of πρᾶξις in θεωρεῖν, because he thus wins the determination of the highest form of πρᾶξις from the being of the ἀεί. He therefore lacks the ontological basis for making the being of humans itself into a problem. (47–48)

As we see here, for Heidegger the failure of medieval ontology has its source in Aristotle, which is why the seminar turns from the one to the other. Heidegger furthermore claims that this orientation toward eternal-being is itself grounded on a way of being of Dasein, though one the Greeks fail to make an explicit object of inquiry. Citing *Metaphysics* 1050b22–24 and Aristotle's claim there that "therefore the sun, the stars and the whole heavens are eternally active, so that there is no fear that they will at one point not stand, which is what is feared by the natural philosophers" (διὸ ἀεὶ ἐνεργεῖ ἥλιος καὶ ἄστρα καὶ ὅλος ὁ οὐρανός, καὶ οὐ φοβερὸν μη ποτε στῇ, ὃ φοβοῦνται οἱ περὶ φύσεως), Heidegger observes that this anxiety is "nothing momentary, but is constitutive for Dasein itself, i.e., for the way in which Dasein is in the world and for how it sees the world" (55).[13] This is what explains that for the Greek interpretation of being "the eternal-being of the world is a completely immediate, indeed not explicit ontological presupposition" (55).

In the conclusion of the seminar Heidegger will explain the adoption of Greek ontology by medieval ontology as motivated by the desire on the part of the latter to find a way out of the difficulty of finding a common basis for the understanding of the being of God (ens infinitum) and of the being of creatures (ens finitum). This difficulty of course did not exist for the Greeks and the consequence of the adoption for medieval ontology was that it failed both to grasp the being of humans in an ontologically original way and to formulate the question of the determination of God

(60). The roughly parallel difficulty that did exist for the Greeks was that of determining the relation between being as such and the genuine being. Yet Heidegger suggests that Aristotle in a certain sense overcame this difficulty in interpreting the concept of being from the perspective of *energeia* (61).

This concept indeed retains a certain ambiguity on Heidegger's reading. On the one hand, he sees being-in-*energeia* as identified eventually in *Metaphysics* Theta (chapter 8) with eternal-being and believes that this identification is what Scholasticism will inherit (60). On the other hand, he insists in the seminar's conclusion that *nothing remains of the Greek concept of energeia in the medieval notion of actus purus* (62). This is presumably because *energeia* is for Aristotle *activity* and thus, at least from Heidegger's perspective, a kind of motion and indeed a motion that characterizes our being.[14] As Heidegger is well aware, the examples given of *energeia* in *Metaphysics* Theta 6 when it is contrasted to *kinêsis* are all human activities such as seeing, contemplating, indeed living and being happy. This is presumably behind his otherwise puzzling claim that interpreting the *actus purus* as *energeia* would mean that the being of God is present there in the activity of knowing itself (given that the latter is *energeia*). Heidegger's explanation of the ambiguity is that Aristotle himself eventually neglects the concrete grounding of *energeia* in motion or, in other words, its ontic ground in the "thing in motion" of the *Physics* and turns it into a purely ontological notion encompassing what is eternal and motionless as well as what moves (61). The question, of course, is whether this is how we are to interpret Aristotle's explicit distinction between *energeia* and *kinêsis* in *Metaphysics* Theta 6.

The 1923–24 Seminar on Aristotle's Physics

Before addressing that question, let us briefly turn to the unpublished seminar on Book 2 of the *Physics* from 1923–24[15] in which we find a similar argument with further details. Indeed, this seminar leads right into the seminar on medieval ontology we have been considering, introducing the thesis that will be defended in the later seminar and concluding the discussion of Aristotle with a reference to some of the central texts of medieval ontology. Thus at one point in the 1923–24 seminar Heidegger observes that Aristotle's four causes are seen in relation to nature (and specifically in the context of production, *Herstellen*) and then transferred later to proofs for *God's* existence. "The being of God is assumed to have the same meaning as the being of nature. Already in Aristotle οὐσία and φύσις alternate. The whole of ontology is uprooted from this its origin (incompatibility of theological categories with religious experience—taken up again by Melanchthon)" (7). With the reference to Melanchthon we have here too the suggestion that it is the Reformation that breaks with these theological categories originating in an ontology of the world by seeking to ground religious experience in our own being. While in these ways introducing the subsequent seminar, the 1923–24 seminar also has its specific focus: the notion of *archê* as that from which something is brought into being through either nature or *technê* (the structure, Heidegger insists, is the same in both cases). What Heidegger sets out to show is that explanation in terms of an *archê* goes hand in hand with a conception of being as *hypokeimenon*, as what always already lies before for a *logos*, and therefore as *Immer-Sein*, always-being. *What is always there* is what most fully *is*. Here we see again the ontology the Middle Ages will inherit from Aristotle and be guided by in its interpretation of the eternity of God.

But perhaps the most important moment of the 1923–24 seminar comes with Heidegger's discovery there of a different kind of temporality in Aristotle with the discussion of *tuchê* in *Physics* Book II, chapters 4–5: the temporality of the "sometimes, once in a while" as distinct from the "always" and the "for the most part."[16] Most importantly, he finds Aristotle locating *tuchê* in the sphere of *proairesis*, that is, in the sphere of those actions for the sake of something that involve choice (197a5–6). It is easy to guess what importance Heidegger must give this passage, and we are not left guessing when he comments:

> Never again such an original and fundamental discussion of temporality (Zeitlichkeit)—Not until Bergson was it attempted again. Temps est durée. But he did not arrive at the genuine ground since it was not seen historically but only biologically. With Aristotle time is oriented towards motion and number [He does not yet distinguish between the motion of φύσις and that of a προαίρεσις.][17] Through the orientation towards ἀριθμός he covers up again. Concerning a particular being of life, there where an always-being and a for-the-most-part-being are found (in the world). The ἀεὶ and the ἐπὶ τὸ πολύ does not come into consideration for the being of προαίρεσις. Sometimes I go to the market, sometimes I choose this and that, and sometimes something else. (Historical Being). (VI, p. 12)

This praise of Aristotle thus also reveals a double critique: (1) Aristotle fails to distinguish between the motion of nature and the motion of *proairesis*;[18] (2) Aristotle covers up the phenomenon of motion with that of number. The first criticism is crucial here since Heidegger wishes to privilege the motion of *proairesis* as the motion of being human from whose perspective all motion must be understood and he wishes to privilege the finite temporality that characterizes this motion against the temporality of the eternal that orients Aristotle's account of natural motion. The second criticism is not explained in the seminar, and it cannot be pursued in detail here. But evidently the reference is to Aristotle's definition of time as the number of motion and the point is that the phenomenon of motion is effaced as motion in being interpreted through something that is not itself motion: if counting is a motion, in the number counted all the units are simply *present* and *at the same time*.[19]

But what do we make of Aristotle's notion of energeia *in the context of such a critique?* This is a crucial question for the following reasons: First, *energeia* is the way of being Aristotle attributes to the soul in denying it is *kinêsis* in the first Book of *De Anima*: he indeed claims there that it is *impossible* for the soul to be motion because, all movement being an *ecstasis*, a departure from a thing's current state, if the soul in its essence moved, "the soul would depart from [its own] being [*existait' an ek tês ousias*]" (406b15–16).[20] Secondly, Aristotle explicitly distinguishes *energeiai* such as seeing, understanding, and living from *kinêseis* like building, most explicitly in the text from *Metaphysics* Theta 6 already mentioned and to be examined below; Aristotle will also be seen to argue in the same text that *energeia* is defined by a temporality distinct from that of *kinêsis*. Finally, even in the *Physics* Aristotle grants *energeia* priority over *kinêsis* in characterizing the latter as only an "incomplete" (ἀτελής) *energeia* (*Phys.* 201b32, 257b8). Aristotle's definition of motion indeed defines it as an *energeia, but only of what is dunaton,* "potential," *insofar as it remains dunaton* (201a10–12). The motion of building a house, for example, is the activation of the potential the bricks have of being a house, but only in so far as this potential remains potential; once the bricks are no longer potentially a house but have become a house, there is no longer any motion of building.

Heidegger in commenting on precisely this definition of motion in the 1924–25 seminar clarifies how he understands the relation between *energeia* and *kinêsis*: "In this moment of the There (τέλος) in ἐνέργεια there is something that does not exist solely in relation to motion. However, this concept of ἐνέργεια is *derived* from motion. Only *then* is it transferred as a fundamental concept to every being" (50). We see stated here the crucial thesis: whatever its difference from *kinêsis*, the concept of *energeia* is nevertheless derived from motion.[21] But how is this thesis sustainable if *energeia* is not itself a motion, even if motion is itself a type of *energeia*?

Heidegger's Interpretation of Metaphysics Theta

Here we need to consider Heidegger's detailed reading of *Metaphysics* Theta, which (as already noted) is a focus of the 1924–25 seminar. The initial five chapters of this book are a discussion of what Aristotle describes as *dunamis* and *energeia* spoken of in relation to motion (*kinêsis*). *Dunamis* in this context is a principle of change in something else or in itself as other, with a secondary sense being the power of being changed or affected. *Energeia* is accordingly in this context the change or the motion itself. In his later 1931 course *Vom Wesen und Wirklichkeit der Kraft*, Heidegger will focus entirely on these senses of *dunamis* and *energeia* in relation to motion, indeed not reading beyond the third chapter of *Metaphysics* Theta.[22] In the 1924–25 seminar, by contrast, he recognizes in chapter 6 a break (another basis of consideration and a different context, 44) and a transition toward what Aristotle characterizes as a sense of *dunamis* and *energeia* that goes beyond motion. Thus we read: "In chapter 6 in contrast *dunamis* as a character of being, as a way in which beings are present at hand. Methodologically a complete break, something completely new begins here" (45). *Energeia* too, Heidegger continues, is here a way of being present, but other than the way of being present of those things whose presence is characterized by *dunamis*. Heidegger recognizes in this context the importance of the second half of chapter 6 with its distinction between *energeia* as possessing its own *telos* and therefore complete, on the one hand, and *kinêsis*, as always only on the way to the *telos* and therefore incomplete. Heidegger even suggests that the chapter should be interpreted backward from this second half (46). But then do we not have in chapter 6 a transition to an interpretation of *energeia* that *opposes* it to the motion that characterizes objects in nature? Given that, as already noted, all the examples Aristotle gives of this *energeia* opposed to motion are activities that define *human being*, do we not have here an understanding of human being that does not conflate it with the being of things within the world? And given that it is precisely this *energeia* opposed to motion that will define the being of the unmoved mover, is it not the case that, for Aristotle at least, it is precisely in terms of our being that the being of the divine is understood?

Heidegger's response to the crucial passage from Theta 6 is complex. Immediately after noting that every motion is as such incomplete (ἀτελές), Heidegger continues: "With the determination of κίνησις through ἐνέργεια Aristotle wishes to grasp precisely *being-underway* itself. The essential thing to be seen is this: ἐνέργεια of a δυνάμει. To grasp precisely the Underway in its There. The τέλος that lies in the determinate ἐνέργεια signifies the having-come-to-a-stand, the There, the presence [Anwesenheit] of something, and indeed the presence of a δυνάμει ὄν" (50). We see here that *energeia* is itself for Heidegger motion in the sense of being-underway and thus is the *energeia* of *dunamis*; at the same time *energeia* contains that toward which it is on the way: the *telos* or end that is presence. The temporality that characterizes *energeia* is therefore that which characterizes motion: the number of motion with respect to before and after; a conception of time oriented toward the present, the "now," as that by which time is counted.

We need to understand here that Heidegger's own project is to radicalize Aristotle's conception of motion by destroying its "telic" structure and thus its orientation toward presence and production.[23] Or, in other words, Heidegger will identify the *telos* with death. As he says in the lecture *The Concept of Time* delivered in 1924: "But I am with my Dasein always still underway. It is always still something that is not yet at an end. Reaching the end, when it comes to that, it precisely no longer is. Before arriving at this end it is never actually what it can be; and when it is, then is it no more" (*Der Begriff der Zeit*, 15–16; my trans.). Note how this description of Dasein exactly parallels Aristotle's description of motion. But Heidegger goes on to observe that death as my "end" should not be understood as some point at which a course of events breaks off; instead, it is "the outermost possibility of itself that it can grasp and make its own as standing before it" (16). This appears to parallel Aristotle's description of *energeia*. However, the key point is that the *telos* here is, if a "certainty," a radically indeterminate one that renders Dasein in its very being a being-underway, not indeed as a course of events but as a being-possible: "*Dasein* as human life is *primarily being-possible*, the being of possibility as a certain and also undetermined 'gone' [Vorbei]" (17).

If we return to the 1924–25 seminar we see Heidegger interpreting *energeia* in Theta 6 as follows: "ὁρᾶν [to see] is the presence [Anwesenheit] of that which is complete [fertig] and in its being-complete *still becomes [wird]*" (47).²⁴ It is because *energeia* is treated here as still or precisely a motion in its being-completed that Heidegger, while acknowledging that in Theta 6 "ἐνέργεια as a way of being is opposed to motions, κινήσεις," adds: "not to κίνησις!"(47). Proceeding to address the apparent contradiction between the distinction in Theta 6 and the definition of *kinêsis* in the *Physics* as a type of *energeia*, that is, an "incomplete" one (ἀτελές), Heidegger explains: "In relation to κίνησις, ἐνέργεια serves to bring out the *presence of what is not yet complete*." If *energeia* is not *a* motion, this is because it is the *being* of motion as the *presence* of what is *not yet* complete. We can surmise that *energeia*, as itself the being-complete of motion, is for Heidegger an interpretation of "the motion of Dasein itself," but one that covers over the finite temporality of the "sometimes" through an interpretation of being and time as constant presence. For Heidegger the temporality of *energeia* is presence. Briefly and crudely put, *energeia* is motion interpreted as presence, motion seen as coming into its own only as presence.

It is in this context that we must understand Heidegger's insistence on distinguishing between *energeia* and another term Aristotle tends to use interchangeably with it: *entelecheia*.²⁵ In the 1923–24 course, for example, we see that for Heidegger it is in *entelecheia* that the conception of being as always-being-there, which *energeia* already implies as a movement toward such being, attains full expression. It is *entelecheia* that gives *energeia* its perfect tense, and the perfect tense is here interpreted as the tense of what is completed, finished, perfected: "Being-completed [Fertig-sein]. Perfectum. (finis and perfectio)" (III). Following an 1873 study by Teichmüller,²⁶ the importance of which for understanding his reading cannot be overestimated, Heidegger takes the Aristotelian *entelecheia* to be derived from the earlier word *endeleches* that means "persisting" ("fortdauernd" in Heidegger's translation). The suggestion is that Aristotle transformed the *d* into *t* in order to make it fit "his conceptional structure" (seine Begriffsstruktur), that is, in order to bring it into relation with *telos*. The philosophical significance of this thesis is that *endelecheia* has the sense of continuity in time, of uninterrupted persistence (Fortdauern) in time (Teichmüller 1873, 106–7), so that to derive the sense of *entelecheia* from it is to interpret *entelecheia* as "a motion that persists without stopping" (Teichmüller 1873, 120). On this basis Teichmüller explicitly defends the thesis so crucial to Heidegger's own position: that *entelecheia* and *energeia* (with the latter term being interpreted in terms of the former, which Teichmüller takes to be the suggestion of Met. 1050a22 and 1047a30: 114–15) are both derived from the phenomenon of motion. Heidegger himself thus concludes: "ἐντελέχεια is abidingness [die Ständigkeit]. The always-being-there [Immer-Da-Sein]. Genuine being [Eigentliches Sein]. What has come to a stand [zustande gekommen ist], what is there as produced [als hergestellter da ist]. What is not in need of being-produced. From there δύναμις; from it first ἐνέργεια and ἐντελέχεια" (page III). The distinction of *entelecheia* from *energeia* and its identification with eternal presence makes it possible to interpret *energeia* itself as a *coming-to-presence* dependent as such on a conception of being as presence.

What should be evident by now is that the distinction between *energeia* and *kinêsis* in Theta 6 is weakened by Heidegger's reading to the point of disappearing. Even if it is in its being-at-an-end and being-finished that *energeia* becomes what it is, as a *becoming*-finished and *coming to* an end that continues *becoming* after having reached its end, it still has the structure and the temporality of *kinêsis*. This reading was already evident, if not yet explicitly defended, in a translation Heidegger gave of 1048b18–35 in a SS1922 course on Aristotle: already here the *kinêsis* opposed to *energeia* is only motion "in a special sense," while *energeia* itself is a being-in-motion (Bewegtheit) that has reached its end *and continues to move itself* in possession of its end.[27] But is such a reading defensible?[28]

In turning to this question, it is first worth noting that the study by Teichmüller that so influenced Heidegger's reading depends precisely on the interpretative moves that will be challenged in what follows. First, Teichmüller must misinterpret the distinction in Theta 6 as maintaining only that with an *energeia* "the time-distinction falls away and past and present change nothing with regard to the thing itself" (105). Thus for him an *energeia* is simply a movement that persists as the same throughout time. But Aristotle's point will be seen to have nothing to do with "persistence" or "duration" or "remaining the same": an *energeia* is complete in the moment because it does not exist *in time at all*. Secondly, Teichmüller gives as his example of a perfect *energeia the movement of the sun, the stars and the heavens* (117–19) since he takes perfect *energeia* to be "eternal and ceaselessly continuing movement" (119); of the *energeia* of the *unmoved mover* there is, incredibly, no mention whatsoever! Finally, his interpretation of *energeia* requires him to interpret the soul, and therefore all life, as "the movement or reality of the body that continues without pause" (122), in clear contradiction, as we will see, to Aristotle's own account.

Aristotle on the Temporality of *Kinêsis* and *Energeia*

The Temporality of *Energeia* in Metaphysics Theta 6

Aristotle himself insists in the passage of Theta 6 that the temporality of *energeia* is *not* that of *kinêsis*. According to Aristotle, *energeia* differs from *kinêsis* not only because the perfect tense can apply to it and not to *kinêsis*: such a distinction by itself would be compatible with interpreting *energeia* as a completed *kinêsis*, as Heidegger does. The difference is, instead, that in the case of *energeia* the perfect tense is "simultaneous" with the present tense, while in the case of *kinêsis* they exclude each other. "For one cannot simultaneously [ἅμα] be walking and have walked, be building and have built . . . But the same [τὸ αὐτό] can have seen and be seeing simultaneously, and be thinking and have thought. This I call ἐνέργεια, the other I call κίνησις" (1048b30–35). What does this mean? It cannot mean that an *energeia* has simultaneously reached its end and is still moving towards its end. It cannot mean that, as Heidegger puts it, an *energeia or praxis* simultaneously has been completed and still continues to *become*.[29] It is the evident incoherence of such a thesis that leads Aristotle to deny the simultaneity of the present and perfect tenses in the case of motion. In order for "having-seen" to be compatible with "still seeing," the perfect *cannot* have the sense of "being-finished, being-completed, being-at-an-end." In order for "still seeing" to be compatible with "having-seen," the active present tense *cannot* have the sense of "becoming" or "being-underway": cannot indeed be the *aorist* present.[30] But this means: *the simultaneity of the perfect and present active tenses* that ontologically distinguishes *energeia* shows its being and temporality to be radically other than the being and temporality of motion. An *energeia* is never simply *present* or *at-hand* for it is always still active, still φ-ing. An *energeia* is never moving toward full presence or completion in some end, can never even be said to *have come to be at an end* since it is always, at every moment, its own end; in other words, it is in itself indistinguishable from *entelecheia*.[31] An *energeia* cannot be not-yet, no-longer, present-at-last, present-for-now, or everlastingly present. All of these are attributes of the time that numbers motion. But if that is what we mean by time, then an *energeia* does not exist in time. Thus Aristotle in the *Nicomachean Ethics* can distinguish pleasure from *kinêsis* by asserting that while something can be moved only *in time* (μὴ ἐνδέχεσθαι κινεῖσθαι μὴ ἐν χρόνῳ), this is not the case with the *energeia* of *being-pleased* (ἥδεσθαι) since it exists "as a whole in the now" (τὸ γὰρ ἐν τῷ νῦν ὅλον τι, 1174b8–9). The consequence should be clear: Aristotle's account of the distinction between *energeia and kinêsis*[32] by itself shows that the being of *energeia cannot* be understood from the perspective of the being of motion. Indeed, I would suggest that for Aristotle all motion, in both its positive and privative forms, can be understood only from that *energeia* that we ourselves are.[33] For life and its activities for Aristotle, as Theta 6 again shows, is neither static presence nor radically finite and open-ended motion, neither always-being nor *tuchê*, but an *energeia* whose being and temporality is neither that of motion nor that of motionlessness.[34] This is only an assertion that cannot be fully demonstrated within the confines of the present paper. My goal in what follows is simply to make the assertion appear plausible.

THE TEMPORALITY OF THE "NOW" IN THE *PHYSICS*

Let us first note that even in the account of time in the *Physics* as the number of motion with respect to before and after, the "now" is not a "part" of such time as distinct from the past and the future, nor a mere dimensionless point separating past from future which, if it were actually to divide time as a point divides a line, would bring time to a standstill (220a11–13). Instead, the "now" is, as Aristotle says, the "continuity of time," that which holds all of its dimensions together, that which runs through time and is therefore more strictly comparable to the line as a whole than to a point on the line (222a10–17).[35] This character of the "now" also allows Aristotle to compare it to a body that moves through different places in remaining the same body, but with this crucial difference: the "now" is not some substance that persists as self-same beneath changes that thereby remain outside of it, as if it made sense to say that "now at 9:35" is *the same thing* as "now at 9:36" with just different accidents; rather, the "now" has the peculiar character of remaining the same *precisely in being continually different* (219b12–30).[36] Aristotle can therefore say quite consistently, in a text that unfortunately appears to have been corrupted in the manuscript tradition, that the "now," if not in time as a part of time, *is time* (220a21–22).[37] It must indeed be time in a much stricter sense than that numbering of motion that depends upon it. To claim that Aristotle's interpretation of time in terms of the "now" reduces time to a timeless present and thus suppresses temporality as such is not to understand at all what the "now" means and how it functions in Aristotle.[38] It holds time together not as some self-repeating self-same present but as continual self-differentiation. This is significantly a point that the student Gadamer rightly insisted on against Heidegger's reading in an unpublished seminar from 1925–26 I discuss elsewhere.[39] The "now" has a "span,"[40] but not one that can be measured. It is only for this reason that *energeia*, in both its having-been and continuing to be, can exist as a whole in the "now." I can be both still seeing and having seen *now* because the "now" is in itself that continuity in self-differentiation that *holds time together*. In brief, even the account of time in the *Physics* shows the "now" neither to be a part of time as "the present" opposed to the past and the future nor to have the ontological character of presence but rather to be time itself as the self-differentiating holding-together of past, present, and future. This is why *energeia*, for which these temporal tenses are not mutually excluding, can exist as a whole in the "now."

The Temporality of Common Sense in *De Anima*

This conception of the "now" also seems to be assumed by the account of the temporality of common sense in *De Anima* Bk. 3, chapter 2. As we have seen, Heidegger himself recognizes the need to ground the conception of time in Aristotle in an account of the temporality of the soul. However, he appears to miss what is perhaps the most important text in this regard. Aristotle is maintaining that there exists a common perception (αἴσθησις κοινή) of the common sensibles (425a27). But this raises a significant problem. This common sense, as discriminating the difference between sweet and white, must be both one, single, and undivided while divided between the two objects it is comparing (426b). This problem is immediately seen by Aristotle as a temporal problem: how, he asks, can one thing be affected by two forms at one and the same moment (427a5–10)? How can we see whiteness, taste sweetness, and perceive the difference between them *in an undivided time*? As in the *Physics*, Aristotle appeals to an analogy with the "point": as the point can be treated as both one and two (i.e., as the beginning of one segment of the line and as the end of another segment), so the soul can use the same sign (τῷ αὐτῷ σημείῳ) twice (δίς) simultaneously (ἅμα), for example, in applying the concept of difference to both what is seen and what is tasted (427a12–13). But this analogy obviously can go only so far. If the point can be treated as two, this is only at different times: we take it first as the end of one line and then as the beginning of another. As Aristotle remarks at 430b12, if you think each half of the line separately, "then by the same act you divide the time also." What is required in the case of common sense, by contrast, is that the soul discriminate two different forms *at the same time*. The "twice simultaneously" is the problem.[41] How can we not conclude that the moment itself in which the discriminating occurs is both undivided *and divided*? In discriminating between sweet and white, I am thinking each separately, and therefore in a divided time, while also thinking them "at once" and therefore in an undivided time. This is possible not in a "now" understood as self-identical presence, but only in a "now" understood in the way already suggested: as the same only in continual self-differentiation. Here the analogy with the point holds only if we mean not the actual point that has divided the line but the potential point that is the line itself. What is grasped both in the case of such a point and in the case of the "now" is a whole both undivided and divided.

The Temporality of the Divine in Met. Λ and De Caelo

But none of this yet provides a positive understanding of the *energeia* that would as such exist only in the "now" rather than being counted and thus held together by the now as is *kinêsis*. For such a positive understanding I turn finally to that being characterized by Aristotle as nothing but *energeia* and therefore as in no way *moved*: the unmoved mover or god.[42] We must never cease to be amazed (or have we even begun to be amazed?) by the fact that what is for Aristotle the first *ousia*, both ontically and ontologically, should be identified in *Metaphysics* 12 with pleasure (1072b13), living (1072b26–27) and thinking.[43] What explains this identification is that the *energeia* argued in chapter 8 of Book Theta to be prior to *dunamis* in being is, if excluding δύναμις and therefore motion, nevertheless not some static presence, but *activity*. It is what Aristotle calls in the *Nicomachean Ethics*, in a phrase whose sense defies both Heidegger and practically all Aristotle interpretation, an ἐνέργεια ἀκινησίας, an "activity of immobility" (1154b26–28).[44] What, then, is the temporality of this divine immobile activity?

Aristotle indeed argues that the unmoved mover must be imperishable (ἀΐδιος, 1072b28). But we need to be extremely careful in interpreting what this means. If the unmoved mover is pure *energeia*, then it cannot strictly speaking exist *in time*. If it is eternal, therefore, this cannot be in the sense that it is "everlasting," that it exists throughout or takes up an infinite time. If it will never cease to be, that is not because it is present throughout all time but rather because it fully and as a whole does not exist in time at all: in contrast to ourselves who *tire of* our activities because we *do* exist in time on account of our *dunamis*.

But then do we have here simply that conception of "eternity" that Heidegger finds in medieval ontology and that he argues to be nothing but the negation of being-in-time? Here we first need to note something of great importance: Aristotle's concept of *energeia* contradicts rather than confirms that identification of true-being with everlasting-being that Heidegger has been seen to identify as the Greek inheritance in medieval ontology. This is because an *energeia* that lasts one second is on Aristotle's account no less complete or perfect than an *energeia* that lasts forever. This is precisely what it means for an *energeia* not to be in time: the extent of its duration makes absolutely no difference to the quality of its being.[45] We might have very good reason to conclude that the divine *ousia* can never perish (namely, because as pure *energeia* it excludes any limiting *dunamis*[46]); but if the divine *ousia* were to go out of existence today, it would have been no less perfect. This is because what makes it perfect is not lasting forever nor being unaffected by time, but rather being a complete activity. Thus Aristotle can object to Plato that the Idea of the Good is not any more good on account of being eternal, just as a white thing that lasts a long time (πολυχρόνιον) is no whiter than one that is "ephemeral" (ἐφημέριος, 1096b3–5). For Aristotle, the ephemeral can be as good and as perfect as the everlasting.[47]

Once we conclude that the divine *ousia* does not take up time and therefore should, strictly speaking, not be described as "lasting forever," it is easy to fall into the opposite error: concluding that Aristotle denies the highest type of *ousia* any temporality whatsoever and thereby identifies being with some time-effacing absolute self-presence. I hope that what has already been argued here will at least cause us to pause before reaching such a conclusion and for the following reasons: the divine *ousia* is identified here not with some static actuality but with the activity of thought, life, and pleasure; this god has little to do with the God which the Scholastics understood as pure *intuitus*. Furthermore, the activities that characterize Aristotle's god have been shown not to lack temporality altogether but rather to be characterized by their own distinctive temporality that allows for the "simultaneity" of the perfect and present active tenses. Finally, the "now" in which such activities exist, if not a part of time understood as the number of motion, has the function of unifying the different dimensions of time in their very difference and is to that extent *not* analogous to the dimensionless point. Considering briefly Aristotle's description of god's temporality will now confirm these points as well as further develop them.

The word Aristotle uses to refer to god's temporality is *aiôn* (1072b29).[48] This *aiôn* is here qualified as "eternal" (ἀΐδιος) and thus provides an answer to the question of what kind of eternity characterizes god if not simple "everlastingness." What, then, does *aiôn* itself mean? For clarification of this term, we must turn to *On the Heavens* I.9, where Aristotle addresses the being and temporality of what exists outside the heavens.[49] We are told that this type of being cannot exist in time and therefore cannot be aged by time: time clearly being understood here as defined in the *Physics*, that is, as the counting of motion with respect to before and after.[50] But Aristotle proceeds to provide a positive characterization of the temporality of such a being when he observes that it lives the best life throughout a whole *aiôn*. Aristotle then comments that our forefathers were inspired when they coined this word to refer to *a living being's entire period of life*, a period that encompasses all the natural stages of such a life and leaves nothing out: "τὸ γὰρ τέλος τὸ περιέχον τὸν τῆς ἑκάστου ζωῆς χρόνον, οὗ μηθὲν ἔξω κατὰ φύσιν" (279a23–25).[51] The *aiôn* is identified here with an *end*, a *telos*, but not in the sense of a completion of motion at a particular time, as in the house that has been built, nor in the sense of constant presence, but rather in a sense unsuspected by Heidegger: that of *encompassing a whole time*.[52]

Time here is not *succession*, not a counting of motion by means of discrete "nows," but *an encompassing whole*: a 'duration' that holds together past, present, and future in their unity. In the *Metaphysics* Aristotle therefore qualifies the *aiôn* as *synechês*, "holding-together, continuous" (1072b29). In *On the Heavens* he elaborates when, proceeding to apply the ancient notion of the *aiôn* to the divine, he describes it as an end *encompassing all time, even limitless time* (τὸ τὸν πάντα χρόνον καὶ τὴν ἀπειρίαν περιέχον τέλος, I 9, 279a26).[53] If the *aiôn* can encompass limitless time—a seeming impossibility—this is because it signifies not a measure of time but a unity of time that can be lived *now*.[54] "Lifespan" signifies here not a quantity of life but a quality of life: living a whole life where this "whole" is not countable in terms of the number of years but is rather a whole in the sense of encompassing all of the different temporal phases (birth, youth, adulthood, old age, death) that naturally belong to life.[55] The crucial point here is that the *aiôn* expresses the temporality of life itself as not reducible to, but rather encompassing, time as the number of motion.

Aristotle proceeds to tell us that the term *aiôn* is derived from *aei einai*: *to be always*. But such a derivation only tells us that being-always cannot here mean being-always-at-hand.[56] If the word *aiôn* can describe even a finite human life, this is because even such a life is characterized by temporal wholeness such that at each moment I can have lived in still living. If not eternal in quantity on account of our *dunamis*, our lives are still eternal in quality. Thus in *Metaphysics* Theta 6 Aristotle can contrast living with *kinêsis* by claiming that it never stops (ποτε παύεσθαι,1048b26). This does not mean, of course, that what lives can never die; the point instead is that living, unlike building a house or becoming healthy, can never *come to an end* because in having lived one is still living and in living one already has lived; in other words, it cannot come to an end in time because it *is an end* that encompasses a whole time. As Aristotle says, the life of the unmoved mover is like our own life, though never worn out by a potentiality in tension with it. If the temporality of the *aiôn* can be applied to the divine unmoved mover at all, this is only because this first *ousia is life*. Contrary, therefore, to Heidegger's central thesis in the 1923–24 and 1924–25 seminars, it is not the being and temporality of the world, but rather the being and temporality of *life* that, at least in the case of Aristotle, provides the guideline for the interpretation of divine being. In the critique of medieval ontology, therefore, we can side with Aristotle instead of Luther.[57]

Life after Aristotle: The Aiôn in Medieval Ontology

One may wonder if this heritage of Aristotle did not also work its way into medieval ontology. Boethius's definition of eternity, cited by Heidegger in the 1924–25 seminar (11), is after all the following: "Eternity is the completed, simultaneous and perfect possession of unending *life* [Aeternitas est interminabilis vitae tota simul et perfecta possessio]" (*De Consolatione Philosophiae* V.6). Heidegger asks: "Why vita?" Why indeed! Perhaps because it is an ontology of life, and not an ontology of the world, that proves decisive here.

Heidegger, after citing Boethius and claiming that Aquinas is indebted to Boethius's conception of *aeternitas*, nevertheless proceeds to argue that, while the distinction between aeternitas and sempiternitas and the ascription of the former to God is an attempt to distinguish the being and temporality of god from that of the world, the notion of aeternitas itself is determined from the perspective of world time, instead of from the perspective of the time that characterizes Dasein and life. Evidence of this for Heidegger is the association of aeternitas with immobilitas. But as noted above, "immobility" for Aristotle characterizes *life itself*. Furthermore, the important intermediary here between Aristotle and Boethius is Plotinus.[58] There can be no doubt that Plotinus not only understands time in terms of the temporality of life, but sees time as inseparable from life. First, for Plotinus time (χρόνος) is "the life of the soul in its changing motion from one way of living to another" (ψυχῆς ἐν κινήσει μεταβατικῇ ἐξ ἄλλου εἰς ἄλλον βίον ζωὴν, 3.7.11.44) and the world moves in time *only because it moves in soul* (3.7.11.33–35). In short, world-time is derived from, indeed is nothing other than, soul-time.[59] But even more significantly in the present context, the *aiôn*, of which time is only an image for Plotinus, though characterizing the being of the intellect and the intelligibles beyond soul, *is itself life*, though life that is unextended and that does not move from one thing to another—always remaining in the same, all at once (ζωὴν μένουσαν ἐν τῷ αὐτῷ . . . ἅμα τὰ πάντα, καὶ οὐ νῦν μὲν ἕτερα, αὖθις δ'ἕτερα, 3.7.3.16–19). Furthermore, this unmoving life in which the *aiôn* is found cannot help but recall Aristotle's distinction between *energeia* and *kinêsis*; this echo is brought out especially by Beierwaltes when he writes of Plotinus's *aiôn*: "In eternity the unchangeable-moved constancy (die unwandelbar-bewegte Ständigkeit) of the spirit comes to appearance. Eternity is therefore the timeless 'occurrence' (Ereignis') of self-thinking being" (42); and Beierwaltes himself draws attention to the reflection here of Aristotle's *energeia akinêsias* (161). The point to stress is that both time (chronos) and eternity (aiôn) *are life* for Plotinus, as Beierwaltes rightly concludes (67).

As for differences between Aristotle and Plotinus, Plotinus in his account of the *aiôn* does not explicitly address Aristotle's account of this notion, but he critiques Aristotle's definition of time as "the number of motion with respect to before and after," importantly insisting, among other things, that even as a measure of motion time would need to have *its own nature* (3.7.9.12–15), which for Plotinus is the nature of the soul. Significantly, however, after insisting that, having its own nature apart from motion, time is more what is measured than what measures, Plotinus allows that he may have misunderstood his predecessors since "they didn't make clear in their writings whether time is measuring or being measured, since they were writing for people who knew and were present in their lectures" (3.7.13.15–18; Gerson trans.) Of course, Aristotle is clear on the fact that time is "number" in the sense of *what is numbered* rather than what numbers; and what does the numbering is the soul. So Plotinus's position may indeed not be as distinct from Aristotle's as he thinks. Worth citing in this context is the revealing remark of Simplicius in his commentary on the *Categories*: "How I admire Aristotle's perspicacity! How is it that he too made the soul the immediate cause of time? For searching for what does the numbering, he claimed it to be the soul. For if the soul is the principle and cause of all movement, whether as self-moving according to Plato or as unmoved according to Aristotle, then it would plausibly be the cause also of temporal movement" (351.8–13; my translation; for discussion of this passage, see Hoffmann, 513–14). Beierwaltes is of course right to insist (289) on the important distinction here between Aristotle and Plotinus: in the former the connection between the soul and time is mediated by number (time as a number counted requires a counting soul), whereas there is no such mediation in Plotinus, time instead being found immediately in the activity of the world-soul itself; time is not an accident of motion that presupposes the existence of the soul, but an essential characteristic of the soul itself in its activity. But if we recognize that for Aristotle the soul in its activity of living has its own temporality that is prior to, and the condition for, the time that numbers motion, then the two positions become closer. The major difference between Aristotle and Plotinus, I suggest, is instead the latter's distinction between two forms of life, one unmoved (the life of the intellect) and one moving (the life of the soul), with the correspondingly sharp opposition between the temporality of the one (*aiôn*) and the temporality of the other (*chronos*). But what is to be stressed here is what they have in common: it is the phenomenon of *life* that for Aristotle and Plotinus, and arguably also for Plato,[60] shapes and informs their conceptions of being and time. Furthermore, it is this Greek ontology of life that comes at least partly to guide medieval ontology through, among what are likely to be other chains of transmission, Boethius's enormously influential definition of eternity.[61]

Conclusion

In conclusion, the temporality of Aristotle's god is not that of some timeless present, but that which characterizes a *whole life*.[62] The temporality of *energeia* is neither presence nor radical openness to the future as pure potentiality and negativity but rather that perfect in which something can *have been* while continuing *to be*. [63]And it is this "sunective"[64] temporality that explains the possibility of that numbering of motion that defines the temporality of natural objects since such a numbering requires a "now" that remains the same while constantly changing, that divides time while "simultaneously" holding it together (συνέχεια χρόνου). Indeed, the passage cited from *On the Heavens* can be taken to suggest that the time that goes together with motion is derived from the temporality of *energeia*: there can be no counting of motion, and therefore no time in *that sense*, without a time that holds the past, present, and future together without effacing their difference. It is only because activity exists as a whole in the "now," and because the "now" therefore has its own *span*, that the "now" can count motion with respect to before and after, thus giving rise to time as the number of motion. Furthermore, this activity in the "now" that constitutes its temporality and enables the "now" to count time as the number of motion is *the activity of the soul or, less misleadingly, the activity of life*. While Heidegger is right to insist that Aristotle does not make time "subjective," what he does do is ground the temporality of the world in the temporality of life. If the unmoved mover is ultimately that on which all motion, and therefore time, depends, that is only possible because the unmoved mover is *alive*. It is only because the first *ousia* is not *in time* but rather encompasses time *in one lifespan* that there can be time as the number of motion. When Heidegger asserts in a 1922 lecture course what is a presupposition of his entire reading of Aristotle, namely, that "the concept of the θεῖον first becomes fully understandable from the phenomenon of κίνησις,"[65] we must maintain *the exact opposite*. The being and temporality of motion can be understood only from the perspective of the radically different being and temporality of *energeia* as it characterizes *both* human *praxis* and divine *praxis*.[66] It is not that Aristotle fails to understand "the motion of Dasein itself": it is rather that he conceives of life as something distinct from and ontologically prior to motion: *energeia*. The temporality of such *energeia* is neither the temporality of absolute differentiation and radical finitude nor the temporality of the self-effacing repetition of a self-same present.[67] In this case Aristotle's "perfect" is not a denial, motivated by anxiety, of the being of Dasein as "care," but *an alternative interpretation* of our being. What Aristotle's texts therefore demand is not "destruction" but dialogue.

Notes

1. GA 83: 206; see also 209 and 506.
2. GA 83, 477.
3. The book on Aristotle by Walter Bröcker, openly inspired by Heidegger's Aristotle seminars of the 1920s, is thus motivated by "the conviction that the

question of movement is the fundamental question of philosophy" (*Aristoteles*, fifth ed. [Frankfurt am Main: Vittorio Klostermann, 1987], 5; see also 6). Bröcker even writes that "the riddle of movement is the life's breath of Aristotelian philosophy" (44). See also p. 62: "Movement is the fundamental problem of Aristotelian philosophy."

4. On the objection that could be made here, see Dimitrios Yfantis, *Die Auseinandersetzung des frühen Heidegger mit Aristoteles* (Berlin: Duncker & Humboldt, 2009), 352.

5. For this and other unpublished seminars referred to in this paper I am basing my discussions on the transcripts produced by Heidegger's student, Helene Weiss, currently held in the Department of Special Collections at the University of Stanford. When the transcript pages are numbered, these numbers will be provided; otherwise, references will be to the dates of the sessions as provided by Weiss herself. The 1924–25 seminar is found in MO631, Box 3, Folder 5, Helene Weiss Papers, Courtesy of the Department of Special Collections, Stanford University Libraries; the claim cited is on p. 44.

6. In the 1924 lecture *Wahrsein und Dasein nach Aristoteles*, Heidegger observes of the term Aristotle tends to use interchangeably with *energeia* (more on this below): "ἐντελέχεια is not some hackneyed notion for Aristotle but the concept in which his entire philosophy dwells" (translated by Brian Hansford Bowles based on an auditor's transcript, in *Becoming Heidegger: On the Trail of his Early Occasional Writings, 1910–1927*, eds. Theodore Kisiel and Thomas Sheehan [Evanston, Illinois: Northwestern University Press, 2007], 226; this statement is not found in Heidegger's draft of the lecture published in *Vorträge 1915–1932*, *Gesamtausgabe* 80.1 [Frankfurt am Main: Vittorio Klostermann, 2016]; see corresponding context on p. 70). The assessment persists: see "Vom Wesen und Begriff der Φύσις: Aristoteles, Physik B, 1 (1939)," in *Wegmarken* (Frankfurt am Main: Vittorio Klostermann, 1978 [2nd ed.], 1967 [1st ed.]), 280–81/352–53.

7. Theodore Kisiel, though listing the two seminars in an appendix, apparently is unaware of their contents since he says nothing of them in his account of Heidegger's reading of Aristotle during this period (*The Genesis of Being and Time* [Berkeley: University of California Press, 1993], 464, 472). Basing my work on the Weiss transcripts, I reconstruct both seminars in full, class by class, in my book, *Human Life in Motion: Martin Heidegger's Unpublished Seminars on Aristotle as Preserved by Helene Weiss* (Indiana University Press, 2024).

8. MO631, Box 3, Folder 5, Helene Weiss Papers, Courtesy of the Department of Special Collections, Stanford University Libraries.

9. In a SS1921 course on *De Anima* Heidegger suggests that the δύναμις—ἐντελέχεια distinction is to be understood from the "Ich kann" of *nous* (MO631, Box 3, Folder 5, Helene Weiss Papers, Courtesy of the Department of Special Collections, Stanford University Libraries, 13). See my "The Birth of *Being and*

Time: Heidegger's Pivotal 1921 Reading of Aristotle's *On the Soul*," *Southern Journal of Philosophy* 56, no. 2 (2018): 216–39.

10. *Becoming Heidegger*, 231. There is interestingly no hint of this thesis in Heidegger's draft for the lecture published in GA80.1, just as there is, as noted below, no reference there to *Metaphysics* Theta 6. The talk Heidegger actually delivered in December of 1924 in Cologne was clearly informed by the seminar on medieval ontology that he began teaching on November 10 of that year (as dated in the Weiss transcript).

11. BT: 21–22.

12. On the role of Luther in Heidegger's reading of Aristotle, see Christian Sommer, *Heidegger, Aristote, Luther: les sources aristotéliciennes et néotestamentaires d'Être et Temps* (Paris: Presses universitaires de France, 2006), especially 60 and 62; and Yfantis 2009, 72–75, 87, who also shows the role the courses on religion in WS1920-21-SS1921 play in Heidegger's turn to Aristotle (70). Neither Sommer nor Yfantis mention, or even seem aware of, the unpublished seminars considered here. That Luther represents for Heidegger a return to early Christian experience before its suppression by Aristotelian scholasticism is shown by the notes of Oskar Becker for the SS1921 course "Augustine and Neo-Platonism": "In his earliest works, Luther opened up a new understanding of primordial Christianity. Later on, he himself fell victim to the burden of tradition: then, the beginning of *Protestant scholasticism* sets in" (Martin Heidegger, *The Phenomenology of Religious Life*, trans. Matthias Fritsch and Jennifer Anna Gosetti-Ferencei [Indiana University Press, 2004], 213). In the WS 1920–21 course, "Introduction to the Phenomenology of Religion," Heidegger, in speaking of the lived temporality of Christian religiosity which one cannot find "in some sort of objective concept of time," asserts: "The meaning of this temporality is also fundamental for factical life experience, as well as for problems such as that of the eternity of God. In the medieval period these problems were no longer grasped originally, following the penetration of Platonic-Aristotelian philosophy into Christianity . . ." (73). Even earlier, in notes from 1918–19 for a course on medieval mysticism that Heidegger never delivered, we read that "in the strongly natural-scientific, naturalistic theoretical metaphysics of being of Aristotle . . . , which is renewed in medieval Scholasticism, the predominance of the theoretical is already potentially present, so that Scholasticism, within the totality of the Medieval Christian world of experience, severely endangered precisely the immediacy of religious life, and forgot religion in favour of theology and dogma" (*Phenomenology of Religious Life*, 238). Though here mysticism is identified as a countermovement, elsewhere in the notes we read: "In Luther an *original* form of religiosity—one that is also not found in the mystics—breaks out" (236).

13. Heidegger cites this text to the same purpose in the course *Grundbegriffe der aristotelischen* Philosophie, GA 18: 289–90.

14. But in a way that shows particularly clearly the distance between them and Aristotle, the medieval theologians did not hesitate to ascribe *dunamis* to god. Arguing, for example, that whatever acts has the power to act, Thomas continues: "Deus autem est agens et movens. Igitur potens est agere, et potentia ei convenienter adscribitur activa, sed non passiva" (*Summa contra Gentiles*, II.7). What we see emerging here is a conception of *dunamis* as 'power' or 'force': precisely the conception that will prove so important to Heidegger. In this respect, and perhaps in many others, Heidegger is much closer to the medieval philosophers than he is to Aristotle, despite his constant critique of the "Scholastic" interpretation of Aristotle.

15. MO631, Box 3, Folder 6, Helene Weiss Papers, Courtesy of the Department of Special Collections, Stanford University Libraries.

16. The reading Heidegger is pursuing in this seminar is the one he announces in the 1922 introduction to the proposed book on Aristotle: "Es wird gezeigt, wie Aristoteles unter den Titeln τύχη, αυτόματον (die bezüglich ihrer eigentlichen Bedeutung schlechthin unübersetzbar sind) die 'historische' Bewegtheit des faktischen Lebens, die Bewegtheit dessen, 'was einem täglich so passiert und passieren kann,' ontologisch expliziert. Diese ontologischen Analysen sind bis heute nicht nur unübertroffen, sondern nicht einmal als solche verstanden und ausgewertet" (*Phänomenologische Interpretationen zu Aristoteles [Anzeige der Hermeneutischen Situation]*, (GA 62: 395). D. Yfantis, ignoring the unpublished seminars, believes that Heidegger's interpretation of *tuchē* and *automaton*, along with most of the interpretation of the *Physics* projected in the 1922 introduction, has not come down to us (194, 280). The "more or less" that characterizes the temporality of the world as revealed in *proairesis* is also thought by Heidegger through the Aristotelian concept of the *kairos*: see GA 18: 170.

17. Square brackets in the transcript itself.

18. On this critique as presented elsewhere by Heidegger, see Yfantis 2009, especially 163 and 181.

19. This is why Heidegger can at one point in the Cassel lectures say of using a clock to count time: "Die Uhr gebrauchen besagt, alle Zeit zur Gegenwart machen" (*Les conférences de Cassel* [1925] [Paris: J. Vrin, 2003], 194). Likewise in the 1924 lecture *Der Begriff der Zeit* Heidegger observes: "Die Zahlen sind nicht früher oder später, weil sie überhaupt nicht in der Zeit sind. Früher und Später sind ein ganz bestimmtes Vorher und Nachher. Ist einmal die Zeit als Uhrzeit definiert, so ist es hoffnungslos, je zu ihrem ursprünglichen Sinn zu gelangen" (*Der Begriff der Zeit*. [Tübingen: Max Niemeyer, 1995], 24). Heidegger speaks here of the *Homogenisierung* of time.

20. I analyze Aristotle's argument in another article in which I also examine critically an important part of the story of Heidegger's *Auseinandersetzung* with Aristotle that cannot be addressed here: his interpretation of *De Anima*. See my "Movement versus Activity: Heidegger's 1922–23 Seminar on Aristotle's Ontology of Life," *British Journal for the History of Philosophy* 27, no. 3 (2019): 615–34.

21. Here Bröcker follows very closely what he learned from Heidegger's seminars: "Wirklichkeit und Möglichkeit im weiteren Sinne werden zwar ausdrücklich den auf Bewegung bezogenen entsprechenden Begriffen gegenübergestellt, sie haben aber ihren Ursprung nichstdestoweniger ebenfalls in der Analyse des Seienden als bewegten. Nur von da aus hat dies Begriffspaar überhaupt einen Sinn" (77; see also 81).

22. See my "Whose Metaphysics of Presence? Heidegger's Interpretation of Energeia and Dunamis in Aristotle," *Southern Journal of Philosophy* 44, no. 4 (2006): 533–68. D'Angelo in discussing the 1931 course must acknowledge that Heidegger is neglecting the distinction between *energeia* and *kinêsis* in his exclusive focus on the latter: see *Heidegger e Aristotele: La Potenza e l'Atto* (Napoli, 2000), 414, 427.

23. S. Jollivet expresses well Heidegger's transformation of Aristotle in writing of Dasein: "Sein Unvollendentsein verweist weniger auf seine eigene Vollendung als vielmehr auf sein mögliches Ende, also auf sein unabwendbares Verschwinden, das nicht so sehr als ein immanenter Zweck oder 'äußerstes Ende' gedacht werden muß, sondern als eine existentiale Struktur die Heidegger schon 1924 als 'Sein zum Ende' bezeichnet" ("Das Phänomen der Bewegtheit im Licht der Dekonstruktion der aristotelischen Physik," in *Heidegger und Aristoteles, Heidegger Jahrbuch 3* [Freiburg: Karl Alber, 2007], 147–48). That Heidegger first called "Sein zum Ende" what he came to call "Sein zum Tode" shows the origins of the latter concept in Aristotle's teleology. For an account of being-towards-death in *Being and Time* that shows it to be a unity of *dunamis* and *energeia*, see D'Angelo, 301–15. See also Yfantis who argues that "being-towards-death" in *Being and Time* is a transformation of the concept of *entelecheia* (476–77).

24. "ἐνέργεια is the way of being of this being [the one which sees]. Such a comportment that when this being has arrived at an end, it *then first is*" (46). What Heidegger appears to be getting at here is perhaps expressed more clearly in the 1924 lecture *Wahrsein und Dasein nach Aristoteles* where he takes Aristotle's point to be that it is only when one "has seen" that one is "really and truly seeing" (*Becoming Heidegger*, 230). But, as will be seen below, this is clearly *not* Aristotle's point. Interestingly, in Heidegger's own draft for the 1924 lecture published in GA 80.1 there is no reference whatsoever to the characterization of *energeia* in contrast to *kinêsis* in chapter 6 of *Metaphysics* Theta.

25. As Heidegger himself had to acknowledge in a 1928 seminar according to the published protocols: "Beide Termini gebraucht Aristoteles häufig promiscue" (GA 83, 234).

26. *Aristotelische Forschungen, Band 3: Geschichte des Begriffs der Parusie* (Halle, 1873; reprint Scientia Verlag Aalen, 1964), 111, 113.

27. See GA 62: 105–8. Heidegger's translation here includes a revealing mistranslation. At 1048b30-33 we read: οὐ γὰρ ἅμα . . . κινεῖται καὶ κεκίνειται, ἀλλ᾽ἕτερον [καὶ κινεῖ καὶ κεκίνηκεν]. If the phrase in brackets belongs in the text (itself highly doubtful), the translation needs to be something like: "but different, and moving and being moved too [i.e., are different]." Yet Heidegger translates:

"but it is another mode of being in which 'he moves' and 'he *has* moved' " (sondern es ist ein anderes Wie des Seins in dem 'er bewegt' und 'er *hat* bewegt,' 108). What Heidegger is clearly trying to do is turn *energeia* itself into a simultaneous κινεῖ καὶ κεκίνηκεν, whereas Aristotle's point is that *kinêsis* cannot be *energeia* *because there is no such thing as a simultaneous* κινεῖ καὶ κεκίνηκεν. Something peculiar to the SS1922 course, however, is Heidegger's translation of *energeia* as 'Zeitigung': a translation he unfortunately never explains, much less justifies. Does this represent a recognition of the distinct temporality of *energeia*? If so, it still seems to be assimilated to some sort of presence. See his translation of 'τὴν μὲν τοιαύτην ἐνέργειαν λέγω': "Eine solche Bewegtheit spreche ich an als Wiesein in der verwahrenden Zeitigung als zeitigender Verwahrung [ἅμα τὸ αὐτό]" (108).

28. A related problem here is that *energeia* is being treated as the product of a motion. As Mylène Dufour rightly objects against a similar reading in analytical interpretations, an *energeia* cannot be the product of a *kinêsis* for the same reason it cannot be a *kinêsis*: the product of a *kinêsis*, like the *kinêsis* itself, must be composite and divisible ("La distinction ἐνέργεια-κινήσις en *Métaph.* Θ, 6: deux manières d'être dans le temps," *Revue de philosophie ancienne* 19 [2001]: 22).

29. This is how D'Angelo appears to interpret the text in simply assuming that the continuity of *energeia* requires it to include *dunamis* (274; see also 297). He recognizes the apparent contradiction here (276) and, as far as I can see, does not adequately address it. Instead he simply asserts later that the "dynamism" of *energeia* requires its *identity* with *dunamis* (279) and our attribution to it of 'becoming' (divenire) if not time (278–79).

30. Dufour correctly identifies the problem in claiming that an interpretation of the temporality of *energeia* must explain how it can be *both* instantaneous (complete at every moment) *and* continuous (present tense), while "La conciliation des deux determinations n'a jamais été envisagée par les commentateurs" (12). Dufour proceeds to show how commentators have either favored the perfect tense over the continuous present tense, thus tending to treat *energeia* as a "state" and as the "outcome" of a motion, or, more rarely, have favored the continuous present tense over the perfect tense, thereby running afoul of Aristotle's distinction between *kinêsis* and *energeia* (16–25). Dufour's own solution is that *energeia* is instantaneous in its production but continuous in its existence (30) and that this is possible because, as produced in the moment, it links past and future as their limit in the way the moment does (42). But the sense in which Dufour situates *energeia in time*, even if only indirectly by way of the existence of the "now" in time, still seems at odds with Aristotle's insistence that *energeia* exists as a whole in the "now"; on Dufour's view, for example, the future of the activity does not yet exist and its past exists no longer (42). See note 45 below.

31. Yfantis rightly notes that Heidegger's distinction between ἐνέργεια and ἐντελέχεια is contradicted by Met. Θ 6 (284, n. 563). He also rightly notes

against Heidegger that the term in the definition of motion is ἐντελέχεια whereas Heidegger's reading would lead us to expect ἐνέργεια (p. 291, n. 580).

32. A distinction that is neither ontic in the sense of simply distinguishing between two types of beings nor even ontological in the sense of simply distinguishing between two regions of being, but fundamental-ontological in the sense of seeking to determine what it means *to be* in the strictest and most radical sense.

33. In considering possible objections to Heidegger's thesis that Aristotle interpreted being on the basis of an explication of the being of motion and in particular according to the model of production, Yfantis expresses succinctly the crucial claim defended in the present paper: "Bezüglich der Begriffe ,Potentialität (δύναμις), ,Aktualität' (ἐνέργεια) und ,Vollendung' (ἐντελέχεια) ist wohl die Annahme plausibler, daß diese Begriffe primär aus der Erforschung der Lebensphänomene gewonnen werden" (2009, 355).

34. Like Heidegger, Sommer assumes that Aristotle conceives of the telos of human life in the same way in which he conceives of the telos of something like a house: human life is a movement to be completed when what is presently absent to it becomes present. To this Sommer and Heidegger oppose a conception of human life as a movement whose end is nothing but this movement (2006, 174) and which is therefore always in movement, inherently imperfect, always characterized by negation and deprivation: the *Christian* conception of human life (175). But what this opposition ignores is precisely the way in which human life is its own end according to Aristotle: *not* as something finished and statically present *nor* as a radically incomplete and imperfect movement (*semper in motu*, 185), *but as activity, as energeia*.

35. Serge Marcel rightly notes the *disanalogy between the now and the point*: « De la sorte, le maintenant n'est pas identique au point. Il ne saurait se confondre avec le point, dans la mesure où ce dernier se définit comme une limite fixe, qui permet à la fois d'arrêter et de commencer la longueur d'une ligne. Ainsi conçue, par conséquent, la représentation graphique deviendra profondément inadéquate » (*Le Concept de Temps : Étude sur la détermination temporelle de l'être chez Aristote* [Bruxelles: OUSIA, 1999], 167). If the analogy is to be maintained, it is not with the actual point but with the potential point (168; see also 170 and 177).

36. According to Marcel, what makes the moving body correspond to the now is not its being a subject or substance (since the now is neither), but rather its function of at the same time dividing motion and rendering it continuous (159).

37. The text that has come down to us in the manuscripts, although with some variants, reads: "In so far, then, as the now is a limit, it is not time but is something merely involved in the nature of time, but in so far as it numbers, it is number (ἀριθμός)." Ross in his commentary notes that this reading does not supply the antithesis we would expect and that the text Philoponus read apparently did: "in so far as it numbers, it is *time* [χρόνος]" (*Aristotle: Physics* [Oxford:

Clarendon Press, 1936], 603). In his French translation, Pellegrin adopts this reading: rightly, in my view (*Aristote: Physique* [Paris: Flammarion, 2000], 256).

38. The thesis of Marcel's book on Aristotle's concept of time, namely, that time is understood by Aristotle in terms of a presence that is not temporal and is thereby effaced as such (180), must and can be challenged by appeal to what the book completely neglects: reflection on the temporality of *energeia*.

39. "Gadamer and Heidegger on Hegel's Greek Conception of Being and Time in an Unpublished Seminar of 1925/26" (*Archiv für Geschichte der Philosophie* 104, no. 4 [2022]: 735–58).

40. This is a point on which Heidegger himself insists in his reading of Aristotle's account of time in GA 24: 351–52. Yfantis critiques this reading (439n884), but only by insisting that the now can have no measurable or divisible span. He does, however, rightly critique Heidegger's interpretation of Aristotle's account of time on other points: see 448n900.

41. H. G. Apostle comments: "Can that faculty [i.e., the common] sense its objects simultaneously or must it sense them at different times? It may sense a white object, then sense a black object, and later judge that blackness differs from white. But it appears that it can also sense at one time an object which is partly black and partly white and then make the judgement. Would this be Aristotle's position?" (*Aristotle's On the Soul* [Grinnell, IA: Peripatetic Press, 1981], 143). It is hard to see how either could be Aristotle's position. The former is ruled out by Aristotle's insistence that the time is undivided. The second position does not really offer an alternative: even if the whiteness and the blackness can be judged to belong to the same object, they are themselves different objects of sensation as is the difference sensed between them. Here too we have the seeming impossibility of the common sense sensing different objects and relating them to one another in one undivided time.

42. It is probably no accident that D'Angelo, in a book of 437 pages, never once discusses the pure *energeia* of the unmoved mover. Not only is he to some extent following Heidegger in this omission, but a central thesis defended throughout the book is clearly incompatible with Aristotle's characterization of the unmoved mover: the thesis, namely, that *energeia* is always *energeia* of a *dunamis* that preserves this *dunamis* as such (see, e.g., 373–74). Christopher Long, in a book inspired, like D'Angelo's, by Heidegger's reading (*Aristotle on the nature of truth* [Cambridge; New York: Cambridge University Press, 2011]), has the merit of confronting the problem of the unmoved mover head on, but finds himself compelled to attribute *dunamis* to the unmoved mover. On p. 236 he suggests that while the *ousia* of the unmoved mover cannot be *dunamis*, this does not require that the unmoved mover be without *dunamis*. Not only, however, is no explanation given of what it would mean to have a *dunamis* when one's very being excludes *dunamis*, but Aristotle's own argument infers that the unmoved mover's being is not *dunamis* from the fact that as the unmoved mover it cannot possess

the *dunamis* to move the universe (since a *dunamis* need not be exercised and the eternality of motion would thus be undermined, 1071b17-20). For a different sense in which Aristotle might attribute *dunamis* to the unmoved mover, however, see note 46 below.

43. As Franco Volpi observes in a rare article devoted to the topic, "Il faut dire d'abord que la détermination de Dieu comme vie (ζωή) et comme être vivant ou 'animal' (ζῷον) paraît, d'emblée, curieuse et bizarre » (« La Détermination Aristotélicienne du Principe Divin comme ζωή [*Mét.*, Λ, 7, 1072 b 26-30]," *Les Études philosophiques* 3 [1991]: 370).

44. Volpi asks, "L'idée d'une ἐνέργεια ἀκινησίας, qu'Aristote nous suggère, n'est-elle pas une *contradictio in adiecto*?" (371). The task of any adequate interpretation is to show why this is *not* the case.

45. Dufour takes a similar claim I make in 1991 ("Aristotle on Pleasure and Perfection," *Phronesis* 36, no. 2: 147) to mean that "temporal continuity" is completely accidental to the nature of *energeia* (16). Here we need to be careful. My point is that the *extent* of an *energeia*'s duration is completely accidental to what it is: it is what it is just as completely whether it lasts one second or lasts an eternity. This is *not* to say that having some sort of temporal duration is accidental to the nature of an *energeia* and that an activity can be some timeless dimensionless point (something hardly conceivable). The task is precisely to understand what kind of temporal duration this is that can exist as a whole in the "now" and that is therefore not subject to the measure of motion. See also note 50 below.

46. But if the unmoved mover excludes *dunamis* in the sense of matter and thus *dunamis* in the sense of passive, unrealized potential, there is a passage that suggests that it could be characterized by *dunamis* in another sense. At 1073a8 we have the argument that the unmoved mover cannot have magnitude because an infinite magnitude cannot exist, and a finite magnitude is incompatible with "infinite power" (δύναμις ἄπειρον). This argument appears to imply that the unmoved mover has infinite *dunamis*; and in *Physics* VIII.10 we have a much more developed version of this argument in which the implication is quite clear. But if god's *ousia* is *energeia*, how can god be characterized by infinite *dunamis*? Both texts make clear that god has infinite *dunamis* only in the sense of moving the universe through infinite time. But as the preceding argument has made clear, this *dunamis* can be the *dunamis* to move through infinite time only if it has no *dunamis* to stop moving. In other words, this *dunamis* can be infinite only if it is always and necessarily fully realized, that is, only if it is always *energeia*. So the point here could be to suggest that while excluding *dunamis* in the sense of unrealized potential, the unmoved mover as a cause of motion through infinite time is nothing static, but rather something whose *energeia* is an infinite power. It might therefore be that case that Aristotle's position is not so far as it might seem from that of Plotinus as succinctly stated by Werner Beierwaltes: "δύναμις ist im Bereich des Intelligiblen mit ἐνέργεια identisch. Sie ist *aktuale Mächtigkeit*"

(*Plotin:* Über Ewigkeit und Zeit, 5th ed. (Frankfurt am Main: Vittorio Klostermann [2010], 203).

47. One might object that in this case the *energeiai* we engage in would be no less perfect than god's. It suffices, I think, to say that it is sufficiently comparable for Aristotle to be able to maintain at Met. 1072b14-15 that god's activity is like our best activity, except that in our case it lasts only a short time. The point is clearly expressed by Dufour: "La valeur ontologique de l'ἐνέργεια est certainement comparable chez le dieu et chez l'homme. La différence se trouve bien plutôt entre ceux-ci qui l'exercent" (43). But Aristotle goes on to claim that god's activity is not only without interruption but also is *better* than ours (1072b24-26). This is presumably because it is its own end and its own object to such an extent that our own noetic activity could never be. If all *energeia* is by definition "complete," Aristotle does appear to recognize different levels of completeness.

48. Against the tendency to equate the *aiôn* with 'timelessness,' and the argument that it instead expresses the temporality of life, see the excellent comments of G. Böhme, *Idee und Zahl: Studien zur Zeittheorie bei Platon, Aristoteles, Leibniz und Kant* (Frankfurt am Main: Vittorio Klostermann, 1974), 73-74. Rémi Brague focuses on another term used for the temporality of the unmoved mover: the term διαγωγή with which the state of the unmoved mover is first described at line 1072b14 (*Aristote et la question du monde* [Paris: 1988], 437).

49. When Aristotle speaks of the things τἀκεῖ as not existing in place or affected by time, the reference is clearly back to the ἔξω δὲ τοῦ οὐρανοῦ where neither place nor time are to be found (279a16-18). As has been often noted, what Aristotle in *De Caelo* envisages as existing outside the heavens is not necessarily the unmoved mover of the *Metaphysics*. Indeed, it is clear that in *De Caelo* Aristotle does not yet make the distinction between *energeia* and *kinêsis* indispensable to his conception of the unmoved mover. This is particularly evident in the following passage: "Θεοῦ δ'ἐνέργεια ἀθανασία. τοῦτο δ'ἐστὶ ζωὴ ἀΐδιος. ὥστ'ἀνάγκη τῷ θεῷ κίνησιν ἀΐδιον ὑπάρχειν" (285b9-10).

50. See the claim in the *Physics* that what is eternal (τὰ ἀεὶ ὄντα) does not as such exist in time because not having its being measured by time (221b3-7). By contrast, *rest* does exist in time because measured by time (221b7-14). As Aristotle notes, not everything that is unmoved is at rest since to be at rest a thing must by nature be capable of being moved and thus capable of being deprived of motion. It is important to note that Aristotle in this whole passage (see 221a5) distinguishes between (1) being measurable by time and (2) and having one's being measurable by time. The distinction is unimportant in the case of motion since it is both but appears important in the case of *energeia*. There is certainly a sense in which an *energeia* can be measured by time: I can think for half an hour or feel pleasure for twenty minutes. This does not mean, however, that the *being* of these activities is measurable by time. Likewise, we might measure the divine activity as lasting through all time, but this does not mean that the being

of this activity is measurable by time. And where Aristotle explicitly makes the distinction between *x* being measurable by time and the *being* of *x* being measurable by time, it appears to be only the latter that makes *x* exist in time (221a7). The fact that my feeling-pleasure can be measured as taking up a certain length of time does not by itself make my feeling-pleasure exist in time.

51. As Helen M. Keizer has noted, and as Aristotle's own reference to the inspiration of the forefathers suggests, Aristotle here remains true to the prephilosophical meaning of the word *aiôn* which Keizer summarizes as follows: "My investigation of *aiôn* in Greek literature from Homer to Hellenism has shown a coherent complex of meaning of the word, which turned out to be built up from the following three notions: 'life,' 'time,' and what I call 'completeness,' 'wholeness,' or 'entirety.' *Aiôn* refers to 'life' as a 'whole' of 'time.' . . ." (" 'Eternity' Revisited: A Study of the Greek Word αἰών," *Philosophia Reformata* 63, no. 1 [2000]: 55); on Aristotle's own definition as "fitting in perfectly" with this earlier conception, see 65. Aristotle's definition is also clearly indebted to the conception Keizer finds in Plato's *Timaeus*: "The *aiôn* of the (ideal) cosmos is lifetime as a completeness and this is what gives the time of our (material) world its form" (64).

52. Heidegger cites and discusses briefly the *De Caelo* passage in the *Sophist* course of 1924–25 (GA 19: 33–34), recognizing there that αἰών refers to the determinate time of a living being. But he immediately adds that it expresses more broadly the duration of the world and the heavens, "und ewig im Sinne der sempiternitas, nicht der aeternitas" (34). He defends the last point with the claim that the αἰών is not in time only in the sense that its "nows" (Jetzte) are without limit and uncountable. I have not been able to find any place where Heidegger discusses the term αἰών in reference to the temporality of the unmoved mover, a temporality that clearly cannot be identified with the sempiternitas of eternal motion. The discussion of Boethius's "totum simul" and Aquinas's aeternitas referenced below is one place where one would expect this discussion, but in vain. If Heidegger had seen that for Aristotle this notion expresses more *life*-time than *world*-time, his conclusion that the Greeks interpreted the temporality of life from the perspective of the temporality of the world would have been much harder to reach.

53. See also II 1 283b28–29 where, given the *aiôn*'s character of encompassing all time, the whole heavens can be described as having no beginning or end of its *aiôn*: "Ὅτι μὲν οὖν οὔτε γέγονεν ὁ πᾶς οὐρανὸς οὔτ' ἐνδέχεται φθαρῆναι . . . ἀλλ' ἔστιν εἷς καὶ ἀΐδιος, ἀρχὴν μὲν καὶ τελευτὴν οὐκ ἔχων τοῦ παντὸς αἰῶνος, ἔχων δὲ καὶ περιέχων ἐν αὑτῷ τὸν ἄπειρον χρόνον."

54. This suggests, therefore, that the unifying temporality of the αἰών grounds time in the sense of succession. If instead, then, of speaking of an absence of time we speak of a different sense of time, we can affirm the insightful suggestion of D'Angelo: "Nel caso dell'ἐνέργεια sembra pertanto che vi sia una assenza di tempo che fonda il tempo, mentre nel caso della κίνησις sembra que vi sia un

trascorrere del tempo che elimina la possibilità stessa del tempo" (279). D'Angelo indeed a little later speaks of a "tempo originario" that characterizes ἐνέργεια and according to which it never ceases (284). See also 383.

55. Böhme has well explained that the "lifetime" that is the *aiôn* must not be understood as a quantity of time that measures the duration of life: it is the time that characterizes life itself. "Für Aristoteles wie für Plato es ist das Leben, das sich seine Zeit schafft" (81). That the telos that is the *aiôn* is not any arbitrary measure of time is made clear by the consideration that a life that ends in youth would not be a complete life (81–82). The whole here must encompass all the phases that naturally belong to life.

56. Plotinus, while repeating Aristotle's suggestion that *aiôn* is derived from *aei on* (3.7.4.42–43), notes later that the "*aei*" is not employed here in its usual or dominant meaning (ἐπεὶ τὸ γε ἀεὶ τάχ᾿ ἂν οὐ κυρίως λέγοιτο, 3.7.6.23–24). "Being always" means simply "being truly" (ἀληθῶς ὄν) when applied to the *unextended* power (ἀδιάστατον δύναμιν) that is the *aiôn* (3.7.6.34–35). See Beierwaltes 2010, 46. The difference Beierwaltes sees between Aristotle and Plotinus here (190) depends on identifying Aristotle's *aiôn* with "endless time" rather than noting that for Aristotle the *aiôn* is a *telos* that *encompasses* endless time. It is fundamentally wrong to claim, whether one is speaking of Aristotle or Plotinus, that the Greeks identified being with presence, or that, as Helene Weiss claims in defense of her teacher's thesis, "eternity *is nothing other than* lasting, present existence, or lasting presence. The quality of lasting *does not add any new or foreign character* to the idea of being present" ("The Greek Conceptions of Time and Being in the Light of Heidegger's Philosophy," *Philosophy and Phenomenological Research* 2, no. 2 [1941]: 180; my emphases). Weiss herself cites on the very next page (181) the passage in which Plotinus asserts that the word "always" is not properly said of the eternal. In another paper Weiss rightly argues that the meaning of the passage is that the word "aei" is not properly applied to true being and explains this in terms of a distinction between the "successive everlastingness" (the Latin *sempiternitas*) suggested by the "aei" and not applicable to true being and the "presence all at once and in one" that characterizes true eternity (the Latin *aeternitas*). But here she insists that *sempiternitas* and *aeternitas* have in common "that either means *infinite and never failing presence* or ever present being" ("An Interpretative Note on a Passage in Plotinus' *On Eternity and Time* (III.7.6)," *Classical Philology* 36, no. 3 [1941]: 232). Helpful resistance to such an insistence is provided by Keizer who maintains: "*Aiôn* is the 'entirety' of time; 'eternity' is too much an 'anachronistic,' misleading or unclear rendering" (70). Drawing attention to an asymmetry between the notion of *aiôn* and the development of the Latin *aeternitas*, Keizer concludes: "Thus we should recognize all the more that *aiôn* cannot be explained as 'eternity' without qualification" (70). See also R. Brague who notes how translating *aiôn* in Plato's *Timaeus* as "eternity" is an *interpretation* and not simply a rendering of the

meaning the word would have had when Plato chose to use it (*Du temps chez Platon et Aristote* [Paris: PUF, 1982], 29–30). As Böhme notes, even if the translation of *aiôn* as "eternity" has some justification, it suggests itself for the first time in the passage of Plato's *Timaeus* (69) and is in danger of eclipsing entirely the original and ordinary meaning of the word in abstracting the notion of eternity from the paradigm's nature in the *Timaeus* as a living thing, so that it is understood as being "eternal" in the same way the number 2 is "eternal" (70). The crucial point, as Böhme sees, is this: if the word *aiôn* can come to mean "eternity," this must be understood as a kind of "eternity" that uniquely and exclusively characterizes a *living* thing and not as some generic "everlastingness" that can apply indifferently to anything, living or not. Therefore, the *aiôn* means neither 'everlastingness' (lacking beginning or end in time) nor "timelessness," contrary to what we read in a recent book: "Remarquons d'emblée que, par 'éternité' (αἰών), Aristote entend ici ce qu'on appellera plus tard la 'sempiternité,' à savoir l'absence de commencement et fin dans le temps, et non pas l'atemporalité . . ." (S. Delcomminette, *Aristote et la nécessité* [Paris: J. Vrin, 2018], 245; see also 520–21).

57. Referring to the "immobile activity" of Aristotle's god, Sommer describes the opposition between Heidegger and Aristotle as follows: "Or Heidegger entend inscrire ce néant [δύναμις] au Cœur du mouvement et spécialement dans la πρᾶξις humaine sublunaire. Ce qui présuppose la destruction de la doctrine aristotélicienne du premier moteur immobile posé comme étant suprême situé hors de tout changement" (108). But this position is both a philosophical and hermeneutical error. Like Heidegger, Sommer sees in the unmoved mover the symptom of a desire for constant presence (114–15). One can agree that Aristotle's god is opposed to the incarnate god of Christianity (113) without reaching this conclusion. And here is the major error: "Le mouvement que l'être-là *est* en lui-même l'arrache (*ek-statikon*) à la prédominance du paradigme grec de l'οὐσία comme présence constante. Le sens de l'être de l'être-là n'est pas ἐνέργεια pure mais ἐνέργεια *atelès* comme temporalité ekstatique originaire: puissance (*Mächtigkeit*) pure" (300). Here the alternative is between constant presence and pure potentiality and therefore between atemporality and an ecstatic temporality characterized by pure negativity. But the temporality of *energeia*, and therefore the temporality of that pure *energeia* that is god cannot be understood according to either alternative.

58. For proof of Boethius's dependence on Plotinus, see Beierwaltes 2010, 198–99.

59. As Phillipe Hoffmann has helpfully expressed the point, "Le temps du Monde et de la Nature n'est que dérivé par rapport à un temps 'premier' qui n'est autre que le procès d'autotemporalisation de l'Âme déchue, curieuse, inquiète, lasse de la tranquille contemplation des intelligibles" ("La Définition Stoïcienne du Temps dans le Miroir du Néoplatonisme (Plotin, Jamblique)," in *Les Stoïciens*, ed. G. R. Dherbey and G.-B. Gourinat [Paris: J. Vrin, 2005], 491–92).

60. Böhme's study concludes: "So viel aber ist unzweifelhaft: daß es die Idee des Lebens ist, von der her Ewigkeit und Zeit bei Platon ihren Inhalt erhalten" (77).

61. Beierwaltes, after showing the dependence of Boethius' definition on Plotinus, concludes: "Dadurch, daß die boethianische Ewigkeits-Definition für die gesamte Philosophie des Mittelalters geradezu zu einer Modell-Definition wurde, ist ein zentraler Gedanke der Philosophie Plotins in der Gotteslehre des Mittelalters indirekt wirksam geworden" (200).

62. Gwenaëlle Aubry makes the important suggestion that it is precisely through the notion of *life* that the distinction between *energeia* as act and *energeia* as activity is overcome: "La notion de vie, zôê, intervient précisément à la jonction du sens ontologique et du sens pratique de l'ἐνέργεια . . . , venant ainsi nommer l'activité de ce qui est acte par soi » (*Dieu sans la Puissance:* Δύναμις *et* Ἐνέργεια *chez Aristote et chez Plotin* [J. Vrin, 2006], 172). It is in contrast consistent with Pierre Aubenque's reduction of *energeia* to pure presence and actuality that he dismisses talk of life here as a mere biological metaphor (*Problèmes Aristotéliciens: Philosophie Théorique* [Paris: J. Vrin, 2009], 90–91).

63. Aubenque in rejecting Hegel's interpretation of *energeia* as "activity" absurdly objects to Hegel's substitution "au parfait de l'Acte pur l'aoriste d'une activité" (91), apparently forgetting that Aristotle attributes to *energeia* not only the perfect tense but also the active present tense (*Soph. El.* 178a9, *De Sensu* 446b3–5, *Met.* 1048b18–36).

64. This barbaric neologism is intended as a contrast to Heidegger's ecstatic temporality as described, for example, in *Grundprobleme der Phänomenologie* (GA 24: 377–78).

65. GA 62: 100.

66. It is not enough to object to Heidegger, as does Beierwaltes (175–76), that the Greeks were able to conceive of being as beyond and outside of time. As Heidegger repeatedly asserts, to conceive of being as not in time is still to interpret it from the perspective of time. The important response to Heidegger is that Aristotle in his conceptions of *energeia* and the *aiôn*, as well as Plotinus in his conceptions of the *nous* and the *aiôn*, are thinking being in relation to a temporality radically distinct from the temporality of "present, no-longer-present, not-yet-present."

67. Aubry constitutes a rare exception in arguing, in agreement with what I am maintaining here, for an interpretation that makes Aristotle's ontology "une ontologie qui ne réduit l'être ni à la puissance, ni à la présence" (15). And her disagreement with Aubenque parallels my own: where the latter sees "une métaphysique de l'inachèvement et une sagesse des limites," she sees "une ontologie de la perfection, qui porte, aussi, une éthique du dépassement" (143 n.1). See also pp. 186 and 204.

10

The Sky, from Below

Heidegger, Aristotle, and the Orientation of the Gaze

CLAUDIA BARACCHI

... any meditation on that which now *is*, can only rise and thrive if, through dialogue with the Greek thinkers and their language, it thrusts its roots into the ground of our historical being-there. This dialogue is still waiting to begin. It is hardly prepared at first and still remains for us the precondition for the inevitable dialogue with the East-Asian world. . . .

That which was thought and poetized at the dawn of Greek antiquity is still present today, so present that its essence, still closed off to its very self, above all awaits us and comes towards us from any direction. . . . In order to experience this present of history, we must free ourselves from the still dominating historiographic representation of history [*aus der . . . historischen Vorstellung der Geschichte*].

—M. Heidegger, "Wissenschaft und Besinnung"[1]

In what follows I offer a reflection on Heidegger's approach to Greek thought, particularly Aristotle, toward the mid-1920s.[2] As far as his teaching activity is concerned, Heidegger turns to Aristotle already in Summer Semester 1921, offering a seminar on *De Anima*[3] that will be followed by lecture courses in Winter 1921–22 (*Phenomenological Interpretations relating to Aristotle: Introduction to Phenomenological Research*, GA 61), Summer 1922 (*Phenomenological Interpretations Relating to Aristotle: Ontology and Logic*, GA 62),[4] and Summer 1924 (*Basic Concepts of Aristotelian Philosophy*, GA 18, on *Rhetoric* II, with particular focus on the question of *pathos*),[5] as well as further seminars in Winter 1922–23 (on *Nicomachean Ethics* VI, *De anima*, *Metaphysics* VII), Summer 1923 (on *Nicomachean Ethics*), Winter 1923–24 (on *Physics* II), and Summer 1924 ("High Scholasticism and Aristotle").

However, around 1924–25 Heidegger's *Auseinandersetzung* with Aristotle seems to display novel developments, or perhaps to draw original elements into sharper focus. To be sure, in the early 1920s Heidegger turns to Aristotle, in particular *De Anima*, in order to address the phenomenon of life and ultimately cast the ontological question in terms of the being of life. But very soon it becomes evident that the concern with life (with life in the broadest sense, that is, the phenomenon of animation and animality, bare life, one would say) gradually closes in on human life, on the specific phenomenon of the being of the human as Dasein—the being on which alone the question of being (of being as being-there, i.e., as existence) imposes itself. Or, to put it in the later language of *Sein und Zeit*—the being for which its own being is a question. Hence, in Heidegger's analyses the *Nicomachean Ethics*, and notably the discussion of *psuche* in Book VI, becomes increasingly prominent, while *De Anima* loses its centrality. This is precisely what becomes apparent in the 1924–25 lectures on Plato's *Sophist*, containing a conspicuous preparatory meditation on Aristotle.

This shift already foreshadows difficulties to come, albeit for the moment only dimly noticeable. First of all, we seize here the prodromes of Heidegger's later declarations on the poverty, indeed the insignificance, of the condition of the animal vis-à-vis the question of being and the overall existential framework. The 1929–30 lecture course *The Basic Concepts of Metaphysics* (GA 29/30) is the *locus classicus* (but by no means the sole document) of the formulation of anthropocentric privilege, which in recent years has come under massive critical scrutiny. But another problematic implication of this move is Heidegger's gradual dissociation of the ontology of human life from the ontology of the cosmos, which amounts to severing human Dasein from *phusis* as *enveloppement*, thus reducing the natural situatedness of humans to the most proximate surroundings and eventually leading to the fracture between earth and world.

As we shall see, in the context of his lectures from the years 1924–25 this dissociative scheme signals a peculiar ambivalence, a conflict internal to Heidegger's thinking, which oscillates between contradictory positions and remains both at odds with itself and unresolved in its hermeneutical approach to Greek philosophy. As far as the latter is concerned, the sharp distinction between ontology of Dasein and ontology of the physical world (*phusis*, *kosmos*) grounds the divarication of practical and theoretical thinking. Such a dichotomy forces ancient Greek thinking, yet again, into the systematizations, both conventional and utterly questionable, consolidated through a millenary tradition. Above all, it counters (or even undoes) other strands of Heidegger's reading that would resist such reductive restorations and, rather, open unprecedented vistas of antiquity.

The task here is twofold. It is a matter (1) of tracing Heidegger's tense and ultimately ambiguous approach to Greek beginnings, showing its both disclosive and obscuring operations. Simultaneously, we should (2) draw out of Heidegger's interpretation those insights contributing to an emergence of the past in its unheard-of, profoundly enigmatic, and ultimately irretrievable character. For this is what Heidegger's stance encourages and promises—a coming to pass of the past (for the past has yet to come to pass), an undergoing of the past in its disruptiveness and unforeseen character. So that the past may take place for the first time, that is, as future. Perhaps.

Before delving into the 1924–25 course, let us briefly consider a lecture dating from the same period, announced by the title "Dasein und Wahrsein nach Aristoteles (Interpretation von Buch VI der Nikomachischen Ethik)."[6] Replicated a few times in the Ruhr region in early December 1924, the talk was given in Cologne on December 3, 1924, at the *Kantgesellschaft*, according to Max Scheler's report. In its conciseness, it highlights themes and preoccupations underlying the lecture course from that winter.

In the title of the address the question of truth is reformulated in terms of being-true and joined to being-there, that is, situated within the compass of existence. It is clear from the outset that the discussion will exceed the bounds of merely scientific inquiry. The opening moves are worth considering:

> Today I will try to explain the concept of truth as it is found in Greek philosophy or, if you will, in the Greeks' natural everyday awareness of life [*im natürlichen alltäglichen Lebensbewusstsein*

> *der Griechen*]. Such a clarification of the sense of truth—or of "being-true"—in Greek philosophy is not merely of antiquarian interest. Its aim is, rather, to bring us to a radical fundamental reflection [*zu einer radikalen Grundgesinnung*] in the context of a fundamental question of science and, more generally, of human existence. I shall present my treatment of the concept of truth by way of an interpretation of *Nicomachean Ethics*, Book VI.[7]

Far from being reified as subject matter, object of investigation, archival material simply available for inspection, the ancient experience is intuitively cast as the primordial ground of modern and contemporary inquiries—as the mostly unacknowledged conditions of "us" (whatever this pronoun may mean, and this is precisely the issue).[8] It is already a matter of attempting a *Wiederholung*, in which the movement of interpretation (with its choral character, translations, and transitions) is hardly separable from the movement of thinking. At issue in it is not the acquisition of a determined grounding principle, but an approach to a source that, though inappropriable, allows for regenerating, reenergizing otherwise drained words:

> The foundations of contemporary science as well as of philosophy are rooted in the investigations carried out by Greek philosophers—ultimately and especially in those of Aristotle. This is true to such an extent that in many areas of thinking we no longer know about these origins and simply make our way among clichéd, worn-out meanings, or with words that have been torn from their roots. It is entirely up to us whether we get a clearer sense of the historical foundations of how we see, think and interpret, or whether we instead treat history as a mere collection of antiquities.[9]

Heidegger could not be more peremptory in warning against an objectification that would divest his own hermeneutical analysis of all radicality and, indeed, bring it back to the routine of conceptual operations that, in the academy as well as everyday life, fail to interrogate what is basic, fundamental, original—that is, fail to confront the arduous, most consequential questions:

> We must first understand that history does not lie behind us like some object, but rather that *we ourselves are history*, and

consequently that we bear the responsibility for how we deal with it—only then will our engagement with the historical past, *that is, with ourselves*, become a truly burning issue. The aim of the present interpretation is to enable Aristotle to speak again, not in order to bring about a renewal of Aristotelianism, but rather in order to prepare the battleground for a radical engagement with Greek philosophy [*um den Kampfplatz zu schaffen für eine radikale Auseinandersetzung mit der griechischen Philosophie*], in which we ourselves still stand.[10]

In its radical character, this inquiry is at once a hermeneutical exercise, a methodological revolution, and an attempt at reassessing the meaning of logic, metaphysics, scientific research. It involves above all a contestation of common sense—which, in its stolid procedure, is literal without actually adhering to the letter, without acknowledging the silences and enigmas harbored there, the mysterious roots of the text. Rather than opening itself to such questions, common sense experiences words as binding in the most myopic sense and proceeds to reduce them to conceptual/categorial schemata abstractly available through an unconscious historical sedimentation. In these opening remarks, Heidegger declares in no uncertain terms that ultimately the aim will be heeding the exchanges between silence and utterance, seizing *logos* in its very emergence out of the unspoken and inarticulate, and locating in such an abysmal conversion the ground and origin of word: "An interpretation is a genuine interpretation only when, in going through the whole text, it comes upon that which common sense never finds there, but which, although unspoken, nonetheless makes up the ground [*Boden*] and the genuine foundations of the kind of vision from out of which the text itself came to be."[11]

Having thus introduced the inquiry, Heidegger turns to Aristotle, more precisely *Rhetoric* and *Nicomachean Ethics* VI, through which the question of the proper *locus* of truth is addressed, leading to the shift, by now well known to Heidegger scholars, away from the traditional posture locating truth in the distant, disembodied, purely logical space of judgment. Of course, moving away from truth understood as a merely propositional affair involves relinquishing the will to protect truth from the ebb and flow of being-there: the dream (or hallucination) at the heart of the philosophical discourse of modernity.

The turn away from truth in judgment does not lead away from the phenomenon of language, but rather allows for a decisive amplification and deepening of it, taking *logos* well beyond logic and propositions. In the first place, Heidegger restores Aristotle's *Rhetoric* in its philosophical dignity, for, he says, this treatise addresses language as the "basic phenomenon of everyday living, of the speaking-with-one-another as a being-with-one-another."¹² Here Aristotle casts light on the fundamental structures of the human in its essentially communal traits. And this would be the site of truth, wherein being-there, precisely as being-with, that is, speaking-with, is receptive to the self-showing of phenomena. Yet, language in its ordinary exercise may be disclosive (let beings appear as they are) as well as concealing (obscure beings in their self-manifestation and cover them over), and this motivates Heidegger's shift to *Nicomachean Ethics* VI, in which *logos* is examined in its excellent manifestations (*aretai*). *Logos* thus understood may be most apt to let beings come forth in their self-showing, to let them be seen as such. By reference to this text, Heidegger may more incisively draw out of ancient Greek thought the situation of truth, namely, in existence, in being-there, open to the self-disclosure of that which comes to be.

At stake is an understanding of truth as more primordial than the truth opposed to falsity—truth coinciding with emergence into being out of latency, that is, with the coming to be of that which is, in its self-disclosure and manifest outline. It turns out that truth is a matter of ontology rather than of judgment. It is situated in dynamics of disclosure—in that which discloses itself and in the disclosing receptivity to it; in the things themselves and in the unveiling work of *psuche*; in *phainomena* and in *logos apophantikos*, the *logos* that lets appear and is a fundamental determination of Dasein. Situated *in* such dynamics, truth emerges out of them *as* their unitary expression.

It should be underlined that already at this stage Dasein may be understood neither in terms of subjectivity nor in terms of humankind in a determined and circumscribed sense. Dasein rather names an openness, the there, the "in which" of phenomena. Hence, it indicates the human, individually and collectively, as a disclosing disclosedness. As Heidegger will point out much later on, "The there in *Being and Time* does not mean a specification of place for a being, but rather must name the openness [*Offenheit*] in which a being can be present for the human being, even he himself for himself. *Being the there* [*Das da zu sein*] is distinctive of being human [*das Menschsein*]" (emphasis added).¹³ And again, in a letter to Beaufret (November 23, 1945) making explicit the connection with truth: "'Dasein' is a keyword of my thought and therefore also the occasion for gross misinterpretations. For me 'Da-sein' means not so much 'here I am!' ['*me voilà!*'] but rather, if I may say it in a perhaps impossible French: being-the-there [*être-le-là*]. And the-there is the same as *aletheia*: unconcealment—openness [*Unverborgenheit—Offenheit*]."[14]

The human being, then, is indicated as an infinitely, indeterminately open field, which at once is the site of truth and is-truth, that is to say: the human being, being-there, at once harbors truth and belongs in truth, receives truth, and is the variegated region within which truth receives its lineaments. This strand of Heidegger's thinking blurs the distinction between being-true and being-in-truth, between being-there and being-in-the-world. (It does so even in an anticipatory fashion, preemptively unsettling the language of later works, from *Being and Time* to "On the Essence of truth"—always already keeping this language in oscillation, announcing its constitutive instability, preventing its ideological crystallization.)

If, however, being-there should be taken as being-the-there, as the openness within which worldly interactions are configured, then the conclusion of the 1924 address must sound rather surprising. For, indeed, in bringing the lecture to a close Heidegger launches the task of sharply distinguishing between an ontology of Dasein and an ontology of world (cosmos, sky, sun, stars). To be sure, he observes, ancient thought unfolds the fundamental insight of human situatedness in-the-world. And yet, the acknowledgment of such a situation eventually led to an assimilation of the human phenomenon to the comprehensive articulation of the world, so that the inquiry concerning the being of the human being ended up reflecting the categories, criteria, and overall conceptuality of the investigation of the world—an investigation already scientific or metaphysical in tenor. But of course pursuing an understanding of the phenomenon of life, specifically of human life, by reference to that which always is (and can be examined with precision, determined in its objectivity, exteriority, immutability) cannot but involve a fundamental misunderstanding and dramatic inadequacy. Life, in its constant variation and infinitesimal detail can only be missed by a mode of inquiry secured to the ideality of presence.

This interpretive twist appears ideologically laden, if not capriciously arbitrary, above all as it is compelled by a preoccupation with the outcome of Christian-Scholastic Aristotelianism. In the impossibility of discussing this in depth and by reference to the ancient texts, here I limit myself to recalling Heidegger's closing statement:

> Dasein means being-in-the-world—this is our fundamental finding [*Befund*]. There is not first of all a subject, which is

enclosed in and for itself as in a box, with an object outside. Rather the fundamental finding and first level of reference is: being-in-a-world. From that there comes the task of ontologically determining this Dasein qua being-in-the-world in as precise a way as the Greeks determined the being of the world. That is, one can show that all the basic concepts of Greek ontology are concepts taken from the being of the world. When this stock of concepts enters into Christian theology and is used to define the being of God, one can see (and a radical critique can show this clearly) that one is now speaking about one reality in categories and ways that are all taken from another reality and transferred to an entity that presumably has quite a different mode of existence than, say, the sun and the eternal cycles of the heavens. We are faced with the immense task of creating an ontology of Dasein in contrast to the ontology of the world; and we shouldn't think because we stand within an entirely different tradition that the task will be any easier for us than it was for the Greeks. That is why a radical critique is needed and why, in the first place, we have to learn again what real philosophical research looks like, and in fact we have to learn this from the Greeks.[15]

This concern is well attested in Heidegger's very early career and grounds the establishment of the practical-theoretical dichotomy consistently (if surprisingly) surfacing in his hermeneutical as well as speculative discussions.[16] Certainly Heidegger's pressing concern is to inaugurate a novel discipline of attention and of attending to things as they are, above all, to Dasein and its situation—temporal, worldly, historical. Again, in his reply to Scheler, who responded to the talk, Heidegger stresses: "Beginning from the basic phenomenon of time as a characteristic of Dasein itself, we have to press forward to a radical ontology of history and of the human world."[17]

Yet, one attempting to alleviate the hold of hermeneutic automatisms and undertake a radical reading of antiquity might find there, most evidently in Aristotle, an abundance of resources for an understanding of the theoretical in its continuity with the practical, indeed, as imbued with the latter and itself a matter of *praxis*. This does not mean erasing differences but rather realizing that there is a difference between difference and separation. But one may well guess that Heidegger would not have been unaware of this.

In the 1924–25 lecture course on Plato's *Sophist*,[18] conspicuously devoted to a preparatory reading of Aristotle's *Nicomachean Ethics* VI, Heidegger again presses the question of history, of historical inquiry, as another way of posing the question concerning us. In the final analysis, philosophical research will have had to do with us[19]—with us wondering about ourselves, abiding unfathomed, and belonging in that which is irreducible to us: "This past, to which our lectures are seeking access, is nothing detached from us, lying far away. On the contrary, *we are this past itself.* And we are it not insofar as we explicitly cultivate the tradition and become friends of classical antiquity, but, instead, our philosophy and science *live* on these foundations, i.e., those of Greek philosophy, and do so to such an extent that we are no longer conscious of it: the foundations have become obvious."[20] Accessing "this past" means accessing ourselves. The inquiry concerns our being, how we understand ourselves—and, more broadly, how we are, how we live. The proximity, even the immediacy, of the past in and as us comes to the fore.

Realizing this coincidence, the immediacy of the past in and as us, in no way involves an experience of the past in terms of familiarity or obviousness. On the contrary, precisely in regarding ourselves as well as our provenance as obvious, we miss the enigmatic depth of this question and fail to undergo the anguish (*Not*) of being obscure to ourselves. Experiencing such a coincidence casts a shadow across us. It opens us up to that which we cannot appropriate, far from allowing us to bring the past to presence in the mode of naïve historicism and rest secure on that ground. We are revealed to ourselves as dispersed, stretched out, traversed, constituted in such an openness. Here lies the possibility of reawakening to our uncanny conditions and becoming aware of its obscuring strangeness, beginning to recapture a primordial insight, however fleeting, of the remembrance of forgetfulness. Experiencing mystery at the heart of ourselves means beginning to become aware of oblivion as such. Distress accompanies this incipient awareness that stares into the opacity of the withdrawing, that is, into the impenetrable. Heidegger underlines: "To understand history cannot mean anything else than to understand ourselves—not in the sense that we might establish various things about ourselves, but that we experience what we *ought* to be. . . . The authentic possibility to *be* history itself resides in this, that philosophy discover it is guilty of an omission, a neglect, if it believes it can begin anew, make things easy for itself. . . ."[21] The paradigmatically antimodern comment on the "new beginning" sounds like an admonishment—an ethical demand, or even an injunction, experienced in the interruption of any self-positing and self-establishing. The cultivation of intimacy with the open that we are results in an ethical directive—in an orientation of action, of becoming.

⁓

In the later stages of the lecture course, and surely in his later work, Heidegger will distance himself from this kind of language. It is telling that, even in the middle of his analysis of Aristotle's ethical discourse, he should avoid discussing the question of *eudaimonia* and *agathon* in terms of that which moves life and orients becoming. He instead maintains that, taken "as a properly *philosophical* term,"[22] "the *agathon* is nothing else than the ontological character of beings."[23] Consequently, since "the *agathon* is not primarily related to *praxis* but instead is understood as a basic constitution of beings in themselves, the possibility is predelineated that the *agathon* as *arche* is precisely the object of a *theorein*."[24] The *agathon*, the fugitive[25] first principle and final cause, is thus assimilated to the order of the theoretical. In turn, *theorein* is understood here less (or not at all) as a contemplative endeavor, but rather as the proper approach to that which abides immutable, over against becoming, phenomenality, being-there. For "exactly with regard to a being as *aei on*, as everlasting being—in relation to which I can take no action—the correct comportment is *theoria*."[26]

This assessment is problematic, if not altogether absurd, with regard to Plato as well as Aristotle. Plato, most notably in the *Republic* and the later dialogues, consistently points to the good as that which exceeds being and ontology—as the nonontological *arche* of ontology. So much so that the good remains utterly impervious, inaccessible to rigorous investigation or definition. Or maybe, more accurately, the rigorous investigation is that which stands in the face of such a difficulty and acknowledges the good as that which marks the limits of investigation, as the fugitive always beyond investigation. Maybe rigorous investigation is indeed that which withstands the good as a symptom of its own finitude and maintains an awareness of itself in its always coming to an end (after all, *theorein* is an altogether human pursuit) but also in its always continuing, in its indeterminate openness—investigation ceasing and incessant. This can certainly be said in the context of Plato, suffice it to mention the discussion of the divided line in Rep. VI, where the good signals the utmost comprehensiveness and, at once, ineffability, and brings to the fore the overcoming of the distinction between subject and object. It can be said, *a fortiori*, in the context of Aristotle, constantly focusing on the many ways of signification and especially on the good as that which fosters life, grants its thriving, ultimately pointing to an accomplishment named *eudaimonia*. In this light, Heidegger's treatment of the *agathon* as the archic ontological structure,[27] having nothing to do with action, would deserve close scrutiny, particularly in relation to Heidegger's distinctive reluctance to broach the ethico-political question.

But here Heidegger is most probably motivated by a concern with what happens when the "stock of concepts" of Greek thought "enters into Christian theology and is used to define the being of God."[28] As a consequence, he does exactly what, in the talk on "being-true," he is striving to avoid, namely, speaking "about one reality in categories and ways that are all taken from another reality."[29] In the *agathon* at the center of ancient thought, he already foresees the *summum bonum*, not even in the original Ciceronian conception, still linked to action and the realization of life, but within the compass of Christian theology, viewing the highest good as coterminous with being and ultimately with God.[30]

This dissociation, or even opposition, of *praxis* and *theoria* (the good would be that "being" "in relation to which I can take no action") projected onto the Greeks lends itself to a few observations. First, as suggested above, it seems prompted by the project of an ontology more attuned to Dasein, its unique traits, time, and circumstances, instead of claiming to measure its ventures by reference to the firm standard of that which always is. It is such a preoccupation that urges not only a separation but a shift from the theoretical to the practical, hence an inversion of priorities. But this turn from the theoretical to the practical misses both, especially as it insists on their opposition. And, above all, it completely misses the reach of ethics in the ancient discourse, the way in which ethics (the question of life, of the how of life) grounds theoretical inquiry in its possibility and grants the continuity, the unitary articulation of practical and theoretical considerations.[31]

Exhibiting an analogous aversion to certain crucial categories in ancient thought (thus failing to think them anew), in later years Heidegger will consistently avoid the language of life and aliveness, claiming that it is within "the history of metaphysics" that the human has been thought in terms of animality, of life (*zôe*).³² In this lecture course, however, and particularly in its opening considerations, Heidegger, after Aristotle, undertakes to think through the question of Dasein in light of life primordially understood. *Logos* itself, as *phanai* and *deloun*, the speaking that makes clear, perspicuous, and lets appear, is inscribed within the flow of life, within the motility of *zoe*, whose being is *psuche* ("*psuche* is the *ousia zoes*"). *Legein* is, then, recognized as "a mode of the being of life."³³ It belongs to life, in the sense that the living (*zoon*) embraces and holds (*echei*) it. Hence *aletheuein*, the unveiling and letting shine forth that is the work of *logos*, inheres in the living. Indeed, the metabolic operation that life is encompasses practical as well as noetic endeavors: "We are used," Heidegger remarks, "to attributing movement to the phenomenon of life. But movement is not understood here merely as motion from a place, local motion, but as any sort of movement, i.e., as *metabole*, as the coming to presence of some alteration. Thus, every *praxis*, every *noein* is a movement."³⁴

Again, the phenomenon of *logos* is fundamentally situated in life, belongs in the being of the living beings and speaks through them. More to the point, *logos* belongs in that mode of animality whose *phone*, voice and vocalization, possesses particular powers of articulation. In fact, so crucial is the phenomenon of speaking, of language, that the human being is comprehended as the *zoon logon echon*. But what does it mean to be such a being? What does it mean to live, to be alive, to be a living being in the midst of all that comes to pass in the luminosity of phenomena? And, being there under such circumstances, what is involved in living as that being that *has logos*? How is one to understand such a having, the having of something like *logos*? How is one to understand the possession, property, or endowment of that which cannot be owned in any straightforward, subjective sense of owning? How does *logos*, the *aletheuein* that *logos* effects, inhere in the living?

Heidegger turns to Aristotle in order to shed light on the modes of *legein*, that is, *aletheuein*. Around the beginning of *Nicomachean Ethics* VI, Aristotle states: *aletheuei he psuche* (1139b15). The *psuche* enacts truth, truth becomes an action. The *psuche* "truths," as it were. Following the privative construction of *a-letheia*, we could say: *psuche* dis-closes. As a matter of fact, such is the work of life: disclosing. As the living (most notably that living being that holds the *logos*) moves through the world and opens itself to the world in utter fragility (existence is, after all, standing out, being exposed), it discloses, uncovers, discovers—the world. The living, *he psuche*, does not quite bring forth, let alone bring forth from out of nothing. Yet it touches and is touched, stretches out beyond itself and takes the beyond into itself. The living, *he psuche*, draws out of withdrawal (such is the movement of *aletheia, aletheuein*). And, in the interaction of the living with the world, of the living with itself, in its multitude of modes, truth emerges, is drawn, brought into focus—if transiently, never once and for all.

Aristotle goes on to discern modes of disclosure occurring in the involvement in action (in the peril and uncertainty of existence) from others pre-eminently characterized by the suspension of such an involvement or, at least, by the receding of practical preoccupations into the background (1139a–b). The distinction between practical and theoretical, then, is determined by the comportment toward worldly endeavors broadly understood—comportment whose possibilities range from absorption to detachment vis-à-vis the challenges of existence. At stake, however, is not so much the contrast between ensnarement in and emancipation from the pressing demands of life (the age-old contrast between interested and disinterested posture), but rather the varying gradation of their urgency and peremptoriness. The variation in the intensity of these concerns suggests that, however inescapable, they may not simply exhaust the range of human possibility and rule unmitigated. Human life, in which *logos* belongs, unfolds through moments of sheer engagement in quotidian affairs and moments of release, in which one looks around oneself with no pressing project, no instrumental urge. The human being oscillates between these moments. It participates in worldly affairs with full adherence *and* steps back, if intermittently. *Aletheuein* occurs in the deliberative evaluation of ever-changing circumstances as well as in the perception of encompassing constancy. And the intertwinements of these different modes are diverse and indissoluble, so much so that Aristotle discerns *theorein* at the heart of *phronesis*,[35] acknowledges *techne* as a manner of exploration and not the mere application of eidetic knowledge,[36] and on this ground recognizes an essential bond between *techne* and *sophia*.[37] *Logos* manifests itself in many ways.

Life is disclosive (*he psuche aletheuei*) in many ways. From this perspective, it is quite peculiar that Aristotle's text should have become the ground of subsequent systematizations of the practical/theoretical distinction—systematizations turning the distinction into an opposition and the modes of disclosure into practical and theoretical *rationality*. Which amounts to reducing both to the same logic and neglecting the obscure ground from which rationality itself stems, a ground more ancient than anything in the order of *logos* as *ratio* or *scientia*—neglecting the irreducibility of *nous* (intellect or intuition) to *logos*. Heidegger himself, as noted above, intermittently plays into this schematization of the ancient discourse. It is an impoverished tradition, if well established, that would not need further reinforcement.

Nevertheless this lecture course remains relevant precisely because of a few dazzling moments interrupting millenary interpretive automatisms and insightfully delving into the basic experience of being there. This may let transpire how *logos* (*aletheuein*) is deflected and inflected through the living of life: through the ways in which life takes place, the ways in which human beings experience different degrees of involvement and distance, engagement and disengagement, necessity and possibility.

One such moment is couched in a preliminary reflection on *episteme* and *sophia* as concerning "that which always already was, that which man does not first produce."[38] On the emergence of *sophia* and *episteme*, on the one hand, and *phronesis* and *techne*, on the other, Heidegger notes:

> This initial and most primitive ontological distinction does not arise primarily in a philosophical consideration but is a distinction of natural Dasein itself; it is not invented but lies in the horizon in which the *aletheuein* of natural Dasein moves. In its natural mode of being, Dasein busies itself with the things that are the objects of its own production and of its immediate everyday concerns. This entire surrounding world is not walled off but is only a determinate portion of the world itself. Home and courtyard have their being under heaven, under the sun, which traverses its course daily, which regularly appears and disappears. This world of nature, which is always as it is, is in a certain sense the background from which what can be other and different stands out. This distinction is an entirely original one. Therefore it is wrong to say that there are two regions of being, two fields, as it were, which are set beside one another

in theoretical knowledge. Rather, this distinction articulates the *world*; it is its first general ontological articulation.³⁹

The reach of *sophia*, here still associated with *episteme*, is said to exceed that of *phronesis*, for *sophia* opens onto the world beyond this "portion" here, takes the world in as such, in a momentary suspension of existential concerns, preoccupations, and challenges. In the movement of *sophia* Dasein understands itself in relation to the elemental manifold (on earth, "under heaven, under the sun"), that is to say, within the compass of the "world of nature," which is always as it is—or thereabouts.⁴⁰

The sight of *sophia* perceives the *aei on*, always-being, in terms of nature—that which abides, to be sure, but in motility and recurrence. The *aei on*, that which *always is*, is disclosed as that which *always returns* to itself, unfolding cyclically—as do day and night, the seasons, planetary motions in their rhythm. Always being means always coming back, recurring. The analysis discloses sameness not without any qualification, but in the paradoxical terms of moving sameness, *becoming other* while *staying by* itself. That which always is (i.e., always returns) remains in the vicinity of itself: by itself, but not without motion, not without time. Indeed, always-being unfolds (itself as) archaic time.

Sophia discloses that which cannot be reduced to the domain of human affairs—that which envelops, the environment. The nascent distinction between the practical and the theoretical rests on this basic experience of irreducibility. The excess of *sophia* with regard to *phronesis* entails no division of their domains, let alone their mutual exclusion, or even the resolution and dissolution of the practical, of sensibility, into the intelligible. Rather, what distinguishes *sophia* is the spaciousness and orientation of the gaze.

Again, we take note of Heidegger's determination to establish different ontological registers. But difference here does not involve the demarcation of "two regions of Being," separated and juxtaposed "in theoretical knowledge." As a matter of fact, the ontological difference is said to arise out of a pre-philosophical layer of experience. Ontology originates in the pre-ontological—in the language of *Beings and Time* (§ 39), it rests on a "pre-ontological confirmation." For it is from its worldly situation that Dasein looks upwards—if and when it does. And from this gazing Dasein may understand itself as having "quite a different mode of existence than, say, the sun and the eternal cycles of the heavens."⁴¹ The remoteness of the sky, the uncanniness of the natural world, its being radically otherwise—the experience of such a discontinuity did not originally result in a severance of heaven from what is below. Rather, the constancy and stability of the distant environment proved a kind of "background" against which what constantly changes, what is always becoming other may be set into relief and "stand out." Ontological difference issues from the gathering of the different modes of being and their dynamic interplay. It therefore operates inside the system of home, courtyard, environing nature, sun, and stars, and is not established by an aloof "theoretical knowledge."

The ontological distinction is an articulation. And it depends on a redirection of the gaze, a lifting of the gaze from the courtyard, that is, from the manifold involvements in action and concern with the necessities and hardships of life. In lifting the gaze Dasein, still caught within its world, comes to embrace that within which such involvements take place, that which surrounds the ventures in which the human is entangled. Catching a glimpse of the difference between that which admits of being otherwise and that which does not (that which, if not always and fixedly self-same, still abides close to itself, in returning) entails an amplification of one's vision—one's vision becoming more comprehensive. It implies situating oneself in the cosmos as well, in that which is irreducible to one, that which is indeed inhuman, in the sense of nonhuman, beyond-human.

Heidegger's reflection here quite literally follows a decisive passage in *Nicomachean Ethics* VI, in which the meditation on *sophia* develops into a genuine critique of anthropocentrism. Indeed, leaving aside the question whether or not *sophia* might enjoy a privileged status with respect to the other excellences of *logos*, the central issue is—how is *sophia* to be understood? What would be distinctive about it? Is it simply a matter of acknowledging the broadest reach of this mode of disclosing? Is the dignity of *sophia* resting on its access to an all-encompassing vision, as if this were in and of itself worthwhile? Does worth coincide with hegemony? In order to flesh out *sophia* in its basic character, Aristotle first contrasts it to *phronesis*. But before long it becomes evident that the peculiar outcome of disclosing in the mode of *sophia* is the awareness that the human being may *not* be the most remarkable or excellent being in the cosmos. Let us follow Aristotle's line of thinking:

> [I]t would be absurd to regard politics or *phronesis* as the most serious [disposition], if the human being is not the best [*ariston*] of beings in the cosmos. If indeed the healthy and

the good differ for humans and for fish, while the white or the straight is always the same, everyone would say that the wise [*sophon*] is always the same while the prudent [*phronimos*] may be different; for they would say that a prudent being is one which perceives well [*eu theoroun*] matters which are for its own good and they would entrust those matters to that being. It is in view of this that they say that some beasts too are prudent, namely, those which appear to have the power of foresight with regard to their own life [*bion*]. It is also evident that wisdom [*sophia*] and politics are not the same (1141a20–30).[42]

This passage would demand extensive analysis, but let us highlight only a few themes in passing. In the first place, the good of humans is said not to coincide with the good of other living beings. Nor is it the good in an unqualified sense. In relation to this, secondly, Aristotle leaves open the possibility of acknowledging *phronesis* in animals other than the human. This, however obliquely, would signal the possibility of recognizing *logos* itself, at least in its deliberative/estimative mode of disclosure, at work in diverse manners of aliveness.[43] Thirdly, as anticipated above Aristotle resorts to the language of *theoria* in discussing the insightfulness of *phronesis*. Far from being a matter of "theoretical" assessment, *theorein* seems first and foremost to designate contemplation as circumspective outlook.

But what should above all be underlined is the intimation that the cosmos is neither in function of the human nor hinging upon the human. Precisely in thrusting the human beyond the human, in opening the human to that which indefinitely exceeds it, *sophia* obtains the highest dignity. Thanks to this particular mode of uncovering or discovery, the human is defined in its *constitutive* openness to the inhuman. It is constituted in the receptivity to the excessive, the irreducible, the radically other. At its best, thanks to the insight of *sophia*, the human being catches a glimpse of this. In Aristotle's words:

> And if one were to say that the human is the best [*beltiston*] of the animals [*ton allon zoion*], this too would make no difference; for there are also others much more divine in their nature than the human, like the most shining ones [*phanerotata*] of which the cosmos is composed. From what has been said, then, it is clear that wisdom [*sophia*] is scientific knowledge [*episteme*] and intuition [*nous*] of the objects which are most

> honorable by their nature. It is in view of this that Anaxagoras and Thales and others like them, who are seen to ignore what is expedient to themselves, are called 'wise' but not 'prudent'; and they are said to have understanding of things which are extraordinary and wondrous and difficult and daimonic but which are not instrumental for other things, for they do not seek human goods. (1141a35–1141b8)

The prominent character of *sophia* does not presuppose the domination of the theoretical based on a simple practical/theoretical opposition: the contemplation at stake in *sophia* still belongs in the phenomenal, indeed, it is of the *phanerotata*, those which most shine. The bifurcation between the practical and the theoretical does not presuppose the split between sensibility and intelligibility but instead is thoroughly internal to phenomenality. The gaze, the *theoria* of *sophia* is a gaze turned to the sky enveloping us, to the radiance of the sun and stars, to their appearance and all that appears within their enfoldment. It is in looking at the sky in its vibrant aliveness that the intuition of the abiding may at all arise, along with the awareness that the sky is one and each living being shares in common this situation—on earth, under this one sky. That which abides is also that which binds, that which gathers. Thus, this movement beyond itself, leaving Dasein open to that which it is not, does not exhaust itself in a solitary relatedness to what is far and above. It is, on the contrary, utterly consequential in matters here below and in the horizontal plays of forces and relations in which Dasein is caught. In other words: it has everything to do with how one lives—always along with others.

That what is abiding may be understood as source, orienting principle, and, ultimately, the good, is in itself worth considering. However, what should be underlined in this context is that, thus understood, *sophia* does not and cannot mean the quest for objectivity and objectifying mastery—all-encompassing knowledge for its own sake. Rather, *sophia* indicates the human recognition of the finitude, situatedness, and peripheral position that mark the human condition.

∽

The interpretive approach outlined above has not been pursued, let alone legitimized, in the tradition of Aristotelian exegesis and its systematizations—at least in the Western/scholastic context. Heidegger's reading renews the ancient words, releases the energy they harbor, and receives and is summoned by them. Nevertheless, Heidegger will not always pursue the possibilities inherent in his opening gestures. On the contrary, in a way he will betray his own problematization of the dichotomic structures of the metaphysical tradition by reverting in his turn to all too familiar splits: between an ontology of involvement in action and an ontology of scientific detachment, worldly involvement and theoretical contemplation (understood in its purely rational sense, as unqualified disengagement from the phenomenal), or even sensibility and intelligibility, the practical and the geometrical.

The possibility of hearing the unheard-of in Aristotle is brushed against, provocatively offered, but not fully taken up. This problem in Heidegger's reception of Aristotle is not merely a matter of "interpretation." Or, more precisely, the work of interpretation itself does not simply dissolve into historiography and its methodology, the procedures of the history of ideas—as if ideas were inert, transhistorical entities merely to be documented, compiled, and reported. Of course, this adds nothing to what young Heidegger already knew with unique lucidity. From the very start, the hermeneutic engagement, the movement and comportment of interpretation, has for him everything to do with the task of thinking. It lets transpire the intimate structures, the way of thinking, thinking at work, drawing its course.

As Heidegger insists in his exchange with Max Scheler in Köln, following the talk "Being-There and Being-True," the clarification of a basic problem such as truth, carried out through hermeneutical engagement with the past, takes us to the root of thinking. It does not so much, or not at all, take us to a foundation established through historiographic documentation, but rather it may allow us to reach out to those roots of thinking presently (if obscurely) operative in our own thinking, to the origin that keeps originating, always differently, through epochal transformations. In his response to the paper, Scheler had asked for historical-interpretive clarifications on truth as *adaequatio*, feeling that, unlike his "colleague Heidegger," he had not delved as deeply into "these purely historical matters" (BH: 230), "since this question is too far removed from my own philosophical perspectives, which are systematically and not historically oriented."[44] After reiterating the essentially philosophical stakes of his confrontation with the past, thus rejecting the distinction between systematic thinking and historical research, Heidegger could not hold back one last slightly abrasive comment: "These are the positive tendencies that actually guide this research, which has not the slightest interest in serving antiquarian concerns."[45]

Yet Heidegger's reading of Aristotle, often regarded with suspicion by classicists for its apparent license and arbitrariness, seems in this respect not to be radical enough, not to reach sufficiently far, even according to its own premises. It could be said that, with regard to its beginnings, Heidegger's approach lacks rigor, or perhaps watchfulness. It lacks that which would allow it to unfold *in* the wake, *in* the aliveness of its own inceptual insight. As though drawn by an irresistible tropism, whose nature and power it would be important to investigate further, Heidegger would turn away from his own work (from himself), toward a dogmatic reading of Aristotle. It is as though his insight, in its intermittence, were the prelude to a disclosure still unsustainable to him at the time.

Thus, as far as the reading of *Nicomachean Ethics* VI is concerned, the lecture course proceeds by reaffirming and enforcing an increasingly dichotomic structure, despite the caution and discrepancies in Aristotle's discourse. Heidegger's strategy relies on a few moves.

(1) First, it involves the exclusion of *aisthesis* from the formation of universals. Yet, the function of *aisthesis* in such a formation is consistently affirmed by Aristotle, especially in the overall elaboration of *epagoge* (*Posterior Analytics*), but also in an explicit statement that Heidegger's line-by-line reading of the *Nicomachean Ethics* skips altogether.[46] Indeed, at 1143b3–5 Aristotle speaks of "the singular," "ultimate and variable beings" as "origins" or "principles of final cause," since, he adds, "universals proceed from singular beings." Those that are according to the all proceed from those that are according to the singular: Heidegger does not even report this latter clause. He goes on to cite the next sentence: "Hence, it is necessary to have sensation [*aisthesin*] of these, and this is *nous*."

Aristotle's reference to singularity as "principle of final cause" gets interpreted in narrowly practical terms, so that the finality (the *hou eneka*) at stake here would be the merely contingent pursuit envisioned through *phronesis*. But the remark ignored by Heidegger, stating that what is according to the whole (the universal) is "from" singularity, would inevitably cast a problematic shadow on such a reading. However, as noted, Heidegger skips this statement and goes straight to the following one, which admittedly affirms the necessity of *aisthesis*. But if *aisthesis* as structurally bound to the formation of universals goes unnoticed (if, forgotten, it sinks into latency), then the necessity of *aisthesis* can easily be circumscribed to practical matters and demoted to a quite secondary role. The excision of singularity as the provenance of universals is, then, highly strategic. By virtue of this, *aisthesis* can be relegated to the domain of action (as if the domain of action were marginal in ancient thought, particularly in Aristotle). Indeed, the practical and theoretical domains are constitutively conceived in their demarcation thanks to this operation—thanks to the denial of the implication of sensation in the perception of that which is according to the whole.[47]

In the lecture on "being-true" Heidegger asserted: "If an examination of Aristotle's text should show that much of what we say here is not to be found there in the text, that would not be an argument against our interpretation."[48] When quoting this passage above I did not comment on its peculiar, questionable character. But much more troubling than this is the posture whereby certain parts of the text are *deliberately* omitted, which would disallow the proposed interpretation.

(2) Second, referring to *De Anima* III Heidegger separates "practical" from "theoretical" *nous*, but this distinction is not enunciated by Aristotle in the text under consideration. In Aristotle's discussion at 1143a33–b14, the difference between *nous* "according to demonstrations" and *nous* "according to practical matters" appears to be aspectual. *Nous* is of the "immovable, first terms or delimitations" (in which demonstration finds its beginnings) as well as of the ultimate particulars (which are the subject matter of practical assessment). And if, as pointed out above, "it is from singular beings that universals proceed," the singular seems to be involved in the intuition of that which is primary, or first, in the apodictic procedure—of that which even precedes and is presupposed by the apodictic procedure as such. Hence, the intellection or intuition providing the principles of demonstration could hardly be severed from the intuition at work in the apprehension of the sensible (variable, fluctuating).

And yet, in Heidegger's analysis the undeniable convergence of *nous* and *aisthesis* is limited to "practical" *nous*. In its "theoretical" function, *nous* is crucially associated with *logos*, a *logos* now apparently emancipated from life and its muteness. Indeed, Heidegger goes as far as to say that "*noein* concerns the last outcomes of *apodeixis*, the theoretical demonstration of the *akineta*, of beings which are not in motion."[49] As if the principles (*archai*) yielded by *nous* resulted from a discursive process, from the syllogistic/demonstrative articulation of *episteme*, coming at the end of the *logos* of *episteme* and not constituting its indemonstrable beginning. As if the noetic beginnings were secondary, dependent upon the tactics of reason, and not vice versa.

In contrast to the *nous* of *sophia* and *episteme* in its essentially *logical* character, the *nous* pertaining to practical involvements is said to be "no longer a matter of discourse" but instead a "simple," silent grasping. But the Aristotelian text, in the very lines Heidegger is examining (PS: 108–9), most clearly disallows this turn. Indeed, it states that *nous* is of the "ultimate," in the sense of both theoretical beginnings and practical singularities and that "of *both* the primary terms and the ultimate [beings] there is *nous* and not *logos*" (*kai gar ton proton horon kai ton eschaton nous esti kai ou logos*) (1143a35–b; emphasis added). The same position is even more forcefully exposed in another passage from the same context, again neglected by Heidegger, where it is said that "*nous* is of the terms or definitions (*ton horon*), for which there is no *logos* (*hon ouk esti logos*) (1142a26). Aristotle's view of the *nous* of *sophia* as also non-discursive, unmediated, a matter of immediate apprehension, is covered over—with immense consequences.

(3) Then there is a third set of strategic implications. On the ground of the above considerations, the priority and strictly rational character of *sophia* is put forth and demonstrated. It is demonstrated, to be sure, in a provocative way: namely, so that a poietic dimension, a moment of *techne*, is shown to be in play in *sophia* (PS: § 24). Potentially this could decide upon the nature of disclosure in the mode of *sophia* and acknowledge its roots in a practical and creative involvement in the world.

However, even despite the retrieval of technicity at the heart of *sophia*, the troubling and paradoxical outcome of Heidegger's interpretive trajectory is the reinstatement of the theoretical/practical opposition. *Sophia* as contemplation of *phusis* becomes ontology, physics, metaphysics. Its relation to *phusis* and to the aisthetic is still recalled, but now only a pale, formal reflection of the initial insight—formal because sensibly deprived, void of sensuousness. But rigorously heeding Aristotle's thought and language would show that the contemplation of *phronesis* (pertaining to that which may or may not be, to that which is in the mode of nonabiding or change) is no less "theoretical" than the contemplation of *sophia* is "aisthetic." Granted, these words cease to signify in the accustomed fashion and would have to be understood, thought, heard anew.

Heidegger's remarks on *eudaimonia*[50] and the *agathon*[51] as "purely ontological" expressions should be situated in the wake of this strategic reassertion of the ontological or theoretical in its rational purity. Yet, in Aristotle the *agathon* contemplated by *sophia* is prior not qua principle of being as a whole, but qua human thrust beyond the human, at once the environment of and excess to human self-involvement, and even human knowing (e.g., *Nicomachean Ethics* X).

～

To conclude, let it be mentioned that the *theoria/praxis* dichotomy appears all the more unlikely when extrapolated from an author who, quite pervasively and occasionally with remarkable limpidity, strives to indicate thinking *as* deed—to think the energy of thinking, its being en-acted and in action, operative and at work. This is the case in a notable (if not especially perspicuous) statement in the *Politics*, disclosing thinking, precisely in its highest mode, as inherently practical:

> But the practical [human being] is not necessarily in relation to others, as some suppose; and practical thoughts [*dianoias . . . praktikas*], too, are not only those occurring for the sake of what comes to be from acting [*prattein*], but much more those which are complete in themselves [*autoteleis*] and are speculations [*theorias*] and [acts of] thinking [*dianoeseis*] for their own sake; for a good deed [*eupraxia*] is an end, and so it is a certain action [*praxis tis*]. Outward actions [*exoterikon praxeon*] in the highest sense, too, we say to be mainly those which master artists [*architektonas*] [carry out] by thoughts [*dianoiais*] (1325b17–23).

Thinking as *theoria* gives itself as *praxis*. It *is* a kind of *praxis*—*praxis* in its highest actualization. As Heidegger will have noted in the "Letter on Humanism": "Thinking does not become action only because some effect issues from it or because it is applied. Thinking acts insofar as it thinks. Such action is presumably the simplest and at the same time the highest, because it concerns the relation of Being to man."[52]

～

The originality of Heidegger's interpretation of Aristotle stands out particularly in the intuition of the continuity of *phronesis* and *sophia*, both considered in terms of gazing, only differing in their respective comprehensiveness and orientation. In fact, both practical and contemplative wisdom are shown in their essential belonging in the order of the phenomenal, remaining within the compass of the sensuous. This does not at all mean to reduce them to the same but rather that their irreducible differing takes place as a bifurcation internal to the phenomenal domain, not as a movement instituting two separate worlds.

Yet, despite its groundbreaking novelty, despite its promise to release resources yet to be thought through, Heidegger's treatment of fundamental categories of ancient discourse, at least in those winter months between 1924 and 1925, ends up reasserting some of the most entrenched conventions in the history of Aristotelian commentary, at least in this corner of the world. Albeit construed in innovative terms (in relation to *techne* and thus seized in its commitment to the world), *sophia* comes to be opposed to and detached from what concerns action. The most radical Aristotelian gestures, intimating the constitutively sensible character of formal-intelligible constructs and the arising of universals out of experience, lie ahead of us, still waiting to unfold their radical implications. "Dialogue is still waiting to begin."

Notes

1. In GA 7: 41–42. My translation.

2. The present remarks follow in the wake of earlier encounters of mine with Heidegger vis-à-vis the Greeks, in particular (1) "Contributions to the Coming to Be of Greek Beginnings: Heidegger's Inceptive Thinking," in *Heidegger and the Greeks*, ed. Drew Hyland and John Manoussakis (Bloomington: Indiana University Press, 2006), 23–42 (focusing on the *Beiträge zur Philosophie*, especially the reception of ancient Greek thought in the movement from the first to the other beginning) and (2) "On Heidegger, the Greeks, and Us: Once More on the Relation of *Praxis* and *Theoria*," *Philosophy Today* 50 (Supplement 2006), 162–69 (on Heidegger's lectures on Plato's *Sophist*).

3. The notes from this seminar taken by Oskar Becker were published in A. Denker, G. Figal, F. Volpi, H. Zaborowski, eds., *Heidegger und Aristoteles. Heidegger-Jahrbuch 3* (Freiburg: Karl Alber, 2007). See Francisco J. Gonzales, "The Birth of *Being and Time*: Heidegger's Pivotal 1921 Reading of Aristotle's *On the Soul*," *The Southern Journal of Philosophy* 56, no. 2 (2018). Also, again by Gonzales, "Movement versus Activity: Heidegger's 1922/23 Seminar on Aristotle's Ontology of Life," *British Journal for the History of Philosophy* 27, no. 3 (2019): 1–20.

4. A text related to this teaching program is the 1922 outline of a projected book on Aristotle, entitled "Phänomenologische Interpretationen zu Aristoteles (Anzeige der hermeneutischen Situation)," *Dilthey Jahrbuch für Philosophie und Geschichte der Geisteswissenschaften* 6 (1989) (GA 62).

5. But one should note also the lecture course offered in 1923–24 (*Introduction in Phenomenological Research*, GA 17), reading Husserl through Aristotle, including *De Anima* II.

6. "Being-There and Being-True According to Aristotle," in *Becoming Heidegger: On the Trail of his Early Occasional Writings, 1910–1927*, ed. T. Kisiel and T. Sheehan, 2nd rev. ed. (Seattle: Noesis Press, 2009), 211–34 (GA 80). Hereafter indicated parenthetically as BH.

7. BH: 216; translation modified.

8. ". . . for they trained the habit for us [*ten gar hexin proeskesan hemon*] . . . but there were others before who caused them to become [what they were]" (*Metaphysics* alpha elatton 993b14–19). My translation.

9. BH: 216.

10. BH: 216; emphases added, translation modified.

11. BH: 216.

12. BH: 219.

13. *Zollikoner Seminare*, ed. Medard Boss (Frankfurt am Main: Klostermann, 1987), 156–57. My translation.

14. The letter to Beaufret is included in Martin Heidegger, *Lettre sur l'humanisme*, ed. and trans. Roger Munier (Paris: Aubier, 1964), 182–83. My translation.

15. BH: 228.

16. Let this be clear: Heidegger's insistence on the two contrasting ontologies is not meant naively to contrapose near and far, human world and physics, time and timelessness, but rather to introduce a mode of ontological inquiry that, regardless of its subject matter (whether earth or celestial bodies), may disclose beings in their intermittence and vibratory field, but above all seize the fleeting, manifold dimensions of finite, situated life: Dasein. See John van Buren, *The Young Heidegger: Rumor of the Hidden King* (Bloomington: Indiana University Press, 1994) for Heidegger's attention to the diverse modes of intentionality in relation to the sun, sunrise, and such phenomena, for instance in the Black Forest, or in Sophocles's *Antigone*, or in astronomy (115, 270, 272–74, 277, 286, 289, 292, 298, 304, 343, 344, 374, 381). He also reports the many early signs of Heidegger's call for a doubling, or even a multiplication, of the ontological gaze (81–84, 207, 258, 290).

17. BH: 231.

18. GA 19. In the present discussion I refer to the English translation, PS.

19. I am deliberately using the future perfect on occasion, to intimate the anteriority of what is to come, of what will have come to pass, as if under a dictation only retrospectively discernible.

20. PS: 7; emphases added.

21. PS: 7.

22. PS: 85.

23. PS: 84.

24. PS: 85.

25. Plato (*Philebus* 64e) attributes to the good a flight for refuge, away from further inspection.

26. PS: 85.

27. Many years later, and in apparently modified circumstances, Heidegger will recognize the good, qua *epekeina tes ousias*, as the failure to think the ontological in a more primordial fashion, as a retreat before the task of fundamental ontology (*Beiträge* § 110).

28. BH: 228.

29. BH: 228.

30. See the paradigmatic statement by Thomas Aquinas, *Summa Theologiae* I, q. 6, a. 2. But the identification of the *summum bonum* and God can be ascribed already to Augustine (*De Moribus Ecclesia Catholicae et de Moribus Manichaeorum* 1. 15. 8).

31. Showing in some detail the textual evidence available in ancient sources that lends support to the present interpretive hypothesis, and furthermore laying out the main features of a radically reconfigured interpretation of antiquity, are endeavors clearly exceeding the scope of the present essay. While a portion of my work has been devoted exactly to this task, here I limit myself to mentioning a couple of contributions of mine originally in English: *Aristotle's Ethics as First Philosophy* (Cambridge: Cambridge University Press, 2008) and "Measure, Excess, and the All: *To Agathon* in Plato," in *Companion to Ancient Philosophy*, ed. S. Kirkland and E. Sanday (Evanston: Northwestern University Press, 2018).

32. The question of life developed in this context will be vital to the development of the existential analytic. After *Sein und Zeit*, this question is progressively lost. Against these early meditations, in the "Letter on Humanism" and, for example, the Parmenides lectures, Heidegger will assert the metaphysical character of the concept of life and bypass it on this ground. Remarkably enough, in the "Letter," despite the explicit reservations about humanism, in a quintessentially humanistic gesture Heidegger employs the language of *Ek-sistenz* and *Dasein* in order to reinstate the classical human/animal distinction, the claim being that it is metaphysics that has thought the human by reference to the animal (*Basic Writings*, ed. D. F. Krell [New York: Harper Collins, 1993], 226–254. Hereafter indicated parenthetically as BW. Of course, it could be pointed out that metaphysics/humanism has not thought the human in terms of animality at all—that, rather, in thinking the human as rational animal, metaphysics has precisely forgotten *both* the human and the animal, reducing the human to reason and subjugating the animal to it. What is avoided in the avoidance of the problem of life would require careful consideration, especially vis-à-vis the ethico-political implications of a turn away from the mystery of embodiment, of bare life, of *phusis* itself understood (with the Greeks) as living. In this regard, Heidegger's essay "*Aletheia* (Heraclitus, Fragment B 16)" is especially relevant (*Early Greek Thinking*, trans. D. F. Krell and F. A. Capuzzi [New York: Harper Collins, 1984]).

For an illuminating reflection on this theme, see Giorgio Agamben, *The Open: Man and Animal* (trans. K. Attell [Stanford: Stanford University Press, 2004]).

33. PS: 12.

34. PS: 12–13.

35. *Phronesis* is endowed with vision, it develops through the "eye of the soul" (1144a28–30). On the explicit connection with *theorein*, see 1140b8–10 and 1141a26–27.

36. *Techne* discloses not simply by bringing forth that which is not a being of nature (*phusei on*) but also by experimentally acquiring new knowledge, unearthing previously unknown aspects of the world, occasionally stumbling upon unpredicted discoveries. Decisive in this regard is the emphasis Aristotle places on chance, *tuche*, in the creative process ("*techne* is fond of *tuche*, and *tuche* of *techne*," 1140a20). See also 1140b23. This should warn one against attributing to Aristotle an understanding of *techne* as simply harboring a purely technical, proto-technological vision, the anticipation of techno-scientific rationality.

37. See 1141a9–12. The rapprochement of *techne* and *sophia* should, however, retain an understanding of *techne* in its broadest sense, as just mentioned. Indeed, it should not be forgotten that, if *sophia* surpasses *episteme* in excellence and dignity, it is not by virtue of a superior apodicticity or enhanced rationality, but quite the contrary—by virtue of its comprehending the apodictic-syllogistic procedures and, at the same time, transcending them, showing them in their finitude, remaining aware of the fact that the ground of scientific procedure is not itself scientific, let alone demonstrable. *Sophia* marks the limits of rationality because it is consciously rooted in *nous*.

38. PS: 20.

39. PS: 20.

40. The situation of Dasein in the pulsating and circulatory movement of the surrounding natural environment, here developed in terms of archaic temporality, is analyzed towards the end of BT (especially §§ 80–81).

41. BH: 228.

42. Here and in the next citations, the rendition of Aristotle's texts is mine, although I have consulted Hippocrates G. Apostle's translation of the *Ethics* (*Aristotle's Nicomachean Ethics* [Grinnell, Iowa: Peripatetic Press, 1984]) as well as Hippocrates G. Apostle and Lloyd P. Gerson's translation of the *Politics* (*Aristotle's Politics* [Grinnell, Iowa: Peripatetic Press, 1986]).

43. At 1153b25–34 Aristotle goes as far as to intimate that "all animals," whether human or beast, may perhaps, even unbeknownst to them, have access to a perception of the good (here in the guise of pleasure) "that is the same for all, for all have by nature something divine in them." But this amounts to attributing to all animals a perception beyond that of *phronesis*!

44. BH: 229.

45. BH: 232.

46. PS: § 23, 109.

47. Analogous problems mark Heidegger's discussion of the "universal," *katholou*, earlier in PS: § 12. To recall all too schematically, there Heidegger distinguishes the *katholou*, which can be accessed by *logos*, from the singular (*kath'hekaston*), which is immediately known to us through *aisthesis*. In so doing, he nearly obliterates the fact that, for Aristotle, the language of the *katholou* is equivocal and the perception of the whole may be associated with *aisthesis* as well (*Phys.* 184a23–25). Heidegger resists the fact that the *katholou* can be understood on the basis of sensibility, as originating from the aesthetic, as the togetherness of what is mingled together, perceptively gathered even in its as yet unanalyzed compositeness (the whole "at a glance"). Yet, just as *logos* both gathers (is constitutive of the *holon*) and takes apart (analyzes), so *aisthesis* both gives ultimate particulars (ultimate determinacy, the "this") and the synthesis to be analytically or dialectically dissected.

48. BH: 216.
49. PS: 109.
50. PS: 118.
51. PS: 85.
52. BW: 217.

11

Pity, Fear, and *Catharsis* from a Heideggerian Perspective

ROBERT EAGLESTONE

Introduction

Discussions of pity, fear, and *catharsis* are the Sargasso Sea of Aristotelian interpretation: currently filled with an astonishing amount of floating plastic waste—a region where mariners get lost and uncertainties abound. Stephen Halliwell, for example, notes how the "catharsis controversy of the past century and a half has been marked by a display of confidence on the part of many interpreters that stands virtually in inverse ratio to the quality of evidence available on the subject."[1] My only excuse for sailing these waters is that these terms orient the analysis of tragedy. Tragedy is existentially significant in navigating our own lives. Moreover, like Paul Gilroy's vision of the "Black Atlantic" and following the currents of this volume, tragedy is a place of connection between disciplines: as Miriam Leonard writes, tragedy "has repeatedly provided a common lexicon for arguments between philosophers, political theorists and literary critics."[2] While Angela Curran's excellent handbook for the *Poetics* rightly reminds readers that the concept of *catharsis* (and, I'll add, the concepts of pity and fear) are "not the key to unlocking" the "true meaning" of tragedy, Aristotle's definition of tragedy is the chart that many, if not all, travelers refer to at the start of their voyage.[3] The aim of this chapter, then, is to revisit fear, pity, and *catharsis* from a point of view formed by Heidegger: or, at least, by the Heidegger of the 1920s.

For Aristotle, tragedy, through "pity and fear" (*Poetics* 1449b27) leads to "the purification of the emotions" (1149b28), *catharsis*. In the introduction to his beautiful translation of the *Poetics* (these days, Aristotle's best-selling work), Anthony Kenny makes a thought-provoking point when he suggests that while pity and fear are the emotions that arise from tragedy, *catharsis* might also arise from other emotions in relation to other forms of literature or drama: perhaps the lost volume on comedy explored "the relation of the emotions of amusement to the virtue of wittiness or conviviality" and he notes how Vàclav Havel's plays "circulated in samizdat served to purify the emotion of anger against communist tyranny, and a reading of *Anna Karenina* may teach us to love wisely rather than too well."[4] However, a Heideggerian account suggests something very different: pity and fear are not just some emotions among others, contingently chosen by Aristotle. Rather they are fundamental and revealing forms of our attunement to the world, other people, and ourselves—they uncover the deepest structures of being. That is, an ontological account puts these terms into a different perspective.

For Halliwell, many scholars who study Aristotle's philosophy regard the *Poetics* as "marginal to the system" while "literary scholars . . . often show little interest" in Aristotle's "wider thought." And while there have been recent attempts to bring the main body of his ideas and the *Poetics* together, these parts remain sundered.[5] At first sight, Halliwell's judgment seems to fit Heidegger. The crucial significance of Aristotle for his thought is very widely recognized, yet in his work there are scant references to, and no extended discussions of, the *Poetics* (as far as I am aware) and the two mentions I note below are tangential to the main argument in which they appear.[6] However, part of Heidegger's power as a reader of Aristotle in the 1920s lay precisely in his reevaluation of the relationships between different areas of Aristotle's work. This was one of the ways in which, according to Gadamer, Heidegger "freed the original Aristotelian text" from "the overlay of scholastic tradition and from the miserable, distorted perspective of the critical philosophy of the period."[7] One central aspect of this was Heidegger's reading of the *Rhetoric*, and it is with his revaluation that I will begin my account of fear, pity, and catharsis.

Everyday Conversation and Fear

Aristotle's *Rhetoric* is an odd work. Assumed for centuries to be a textbook for teaching rhetoric, Aristotle says explicitly that the point of the book is *not* to teach persuasion (*Rhetoric* 1355b10): he is not a sophist selling lessons in hustling. And sure enough, the book is full of examples, topics, fragments of poetry, analyses of people's character, views, and opinions (*endoxa*) that seem to have nothing to do with a well-crafted lawyer's or politician's speech. Even sympathetic accounts find it problematic.[8]

In his lectures on Aristotle from 1924, Heidegger declared that the "current way of considering rhetoric" was "a hindrance to the understanding of Aristotelian rhetoric."[9] He scoffs that no one really understands the point of the book and in the famous Berlin Academy edition of Aristotle, "they did not know what to do with it so they put it at the end! It is a sign of complete helplessness." He went on: "The tradition lost any understanding of rhetoric long ago, since it had become simply a school discipline even in the time of Hellenism and in the early Middle Ages. The original sense of rhetoric has long ago disappeared."[10] Heidegger offers another, more profound interpretation of the book and of Aristotle's interest in rhetoric: "Rhetoric is nothing other than the discipline in which the self-interpretation of being-there is explicitly fulfilled. *Rhetoric is nothing other than the interpretation of concrete being-there, the hermeneutic of being-there itself.*"[11]

Formal occasions "in public meetings, before the court, at celebratory occasions" are examples of "customary speaking" of how "being-there speaks itself."[12] He repeats this claim in *Being and Time*: that *Rhetoric* was the "first systematic hermeneutic of the everydayness of being-with-one-another."[13] This is much more than a "unique spin on the rhetorical tradition."[14] It is a total reevaluation.

Heidegger's argument is this. Aristotle notes that many technical forms of language have been (or are being) developed: *dialectic* as a form of philosophy, technical languages for specific skills, carpentry-talk for carpenters, medic-talk for doctors, and so on. But in contrast to these specialized forms of languages, there is a nonspecialized language that we use every day. While this everyday talk may lack precision and certainty, it is absolutely central to all our shared activities, whether to do with governing the state or other public activities (weddings, funerals, any shared events). It's crucial, too, in our more run-of-the-mill daily lives: talking with our friends, asking advice, working out what to do, deliberation. The *Rhetoric*, while taking public speeches as its central examples, is for Heidegger the first study of this everyday nontechnical, shared kind of talking that we do with each other: a philosophical response to the increasing specialization of expertise (including the specialization of philosophy itself). It's a book about how we speak to each other not as philosophers or logicians (or carpenters or doctors) but as everyday people in everyday language. This is why, for Heidegger, Aristotle says rhetoric does not have a special *techne* or subject area. It deals with "speaking as a basic mode of the being of the being-with-one-another of human beings themselves": how we talk to each other, what we talk about and what this means.[15] Speaking is communication, "deliberative . . . speaking-with-one-another" and "*logos* is the mode of being of human beings in their world such that this being is, in itself, being-with-one-another."[16] As Theodore Kisiel puts it, rhetoric is not "immediately the power of persuasion, as the sophist would have it, but rather the cultivated power of a situational insight, *phronesis*, of being able to see, hear and feel, in a temporally particular situation of action."[17]

This is why, for Heidegger, the *Rhetoric* is full of sayings, thoughts, opinions, *views*: as Heidegger says, our "being-with-one-another moves in a definite, always modifiable views regarding things: it is not an insight, but a 'view,' *doxa*."[18] A *doxa* here contrasts with something that has been investigated and worked out. To be in the world means we have, and are constantly offered, opinions and ideas. Some things can be investigated as certainties (triangles have three sides), but other matters can only be deliberated (what should I do about . . . ?). Or, as Heidegger puts it, what we deliberate "cannot be 'scientifically proven'" and is not worked out by "theoretical axioms": instead it "consists of basic opinions . . . that life has cultivated in everydayness."[19] Rhetoric does not offer specific knowledge but "treats what one debates in life in a customary way, and the manner and mode of talking it through."[20] He's talking about deliberation and about *phronesis*: indeed, as Michael Hyde argues, for Heidegger's Aristotle, "rhetoric, *phronesis* and collaborative deliberation go hand in hand" and "collaborative deliberation is a 'knowing together.'"[21] In all, the account of language in the *Rhetoric* is an account of who we are and how that is disclosed: as Daniel Gross writes, "We are human in so far as we can generate shared contexts, articulate our fears and desires, deliberate and judge in the appropriate terms of our day and act meaningfully in a world of common concern. Moreover in all such activities we are simultaneous agent and patient, mover and moved (to use Aristotle's terminology)."[22]

A famous and beautiful metaphor from Wittgenstein illuminates part of this idea about the different sorts of language we speak. He writes: "Our language can be seen as an ancient city: a maze of little streets and squares, of old and new houses, and of houses with additions from various periods; and this surrounded by a multitude of new boroughs with straight regular streets and uniform houses."[23] The specialized and technical languages make up some areas of the city: over here, mathematics; the sciences are close by; and over there the argot of a certain business sector.

These languages can be very different (scientific notation refers to reality in a very different way from our hopes and expectations, for example, and both differ from language about dreams). Following Heidegger's line of argument, "everyday language" is how we talk in the *agora*, our communal meeting place. Having a sense of the general views and opinions is "knowing-the-way-around in everyday being-there for those who wish to be occupied within the circle of the *polis*."[24] You need to know how to talk about everyday things in an everyday way to be a person in the city. The *Rhetoric* is not about a skill, it's an understanding and orientation to our daily life: in a sense it is more like a "conduct book" than a "text book." (The influence of this idea is clear, for example in both Arendt and in Gadamer, and in other philosophical accounts that turn to or rely on ideas of shared public spaces or languages. It is open as well to many of the same critiques: does everyone have equal access to this metaphorical central square? Is everyone welcome and able to speak? These are more challenging questions than this gentle metaphor of the agora suggests, and they open up to both to ontological problems of, say, the relationship between dasien and mitsein, as well as, more obviously, to questions of ethics and politics).

I want to note three consequences of this view. First, this fundamental everydayness is why *all* (!) topics of conversation seem to be covered in the *Rhetoric*: everything we talk about when we are not delving into some technical, scientific, or specialist matter. Aristotle made detailed observations of animals and sea life: here, his observations in an analogous mode focus instead on what we are like in our shared human life, paying attention to our everyday talking with examples collected by him from his own experience and from extensive evidence, drawn in large part from poems and drama.

Second, poems and plays (what we would simply call "literature" today), are in common, in the "public square": not a technical language but a version—intensified and patterned, perhaps—of everyday talk and so open (in principle at least) to all. This is how and why they can play a role in our personal and shared deliberations.

However, it is the third consequence that reveals the importance of fear. Everydayness is also why the *Rhetoric* is interested in *pathos*, roughly in emotions. There is not space here to unfold Heidegger's full thoughts on emotion and on mood. In his Aristotle lectures, he argues that *pathos* has a "fundamental significance" for Aristotle in three ways: in an immediate way it describes our "variable condition," our changing feelings; the ontological significance is that it describes the movement of external forces on us that lead (most often) to suffering; and finally, stemming from that, it designates a "variable condition in relation to definite concrete context, variable condition with a definite being-region of life: 'passion.' "[25] It is this last sense, *pathos* as our passions, our emotions—that is the "topic of the *Rhetoric* and the *Poetics*."[26] What he means is explained at its clearest, and most relevant to my topic, in *Being and Time*.

In that book, Heidegger shows how emotions and mood play a key role in what he calls attunement. Attunement is made up of thrown-ness, disclosure of "the whole of being-in-the-world"[27] and heedful encounters with things that matter in the world. Mood, which we have all the time (we are always "in a mood": even calm contemplation is a mood) plays a role in disclosing being-in-the-world and in making how what we "encounter in the world . . . matter" to us.[28] Indeed, the "moodedness of attunement constitutes existentially the openness of the world to Dasein."[29] Feeling-hungry or loving-cuisine attunes us to food; feeling-humiliated attunes us to our bodily responses and to the social strata in which we are enmeshed. A speaker "speaks to" mood "and from out of it" and so "needs an understanding of the possibilities of mood in order to arouse and direct it in the right way."[30] Lawyers and politicians can use this because at a deeper level, mood concerns what the speaker wants or is oriented toward, that is, how the world is disclosed in attunement.[31]

Heidegger's (much more carefully chosen) example of a mood is fear, which demonstrates both how mood works to disclose the world and, in this case, the profound ontological significance of fear. Fear is about something (a virus may infect me on my commute), is a physical feeling (we often say feel fear "in the pit of our stomachs"), and is *for* something: we are afraid *for* our lives; we are afraid in case we die. The significance of this is that fear is the specific mood that reveals our care for ourselves, makes us pay attention to our own life. Fear attunes us to what he calls "care" (*sorge*) and is how we come to individuate ourselves and pay attention to what concerns us.

Heidegger discusses Aristotle's account of fear in the second book of the *Rhetoric*. Fear is not just "any emotion": rather, as I have suggested, it has a profound ontological significance. Aristotle says that fear makes men deliberative: "Fear sets us thinking what can be done" (1383a6): when "it is advisable that the audience should be frightened, the orator must make them feel that they really are in danger of something, pointing out that it has happened to others who were stronger than they are, and is happening, or has happened to people like themselves, at the hands of unexpected people, in an unexpected form and at an unexpected time" (1383a8–12). For Heidegger, then, "fear" attunes us to care, to ourselves. This is the profounder ontological significance of fear in the *Poetics*. For Heidegger, Aristotle has not simply chosen one mood, as it were, contingently inspired by tragedy: instead, tragedy turns us to our most profound awareness of ourselves.

Obviously, in literature, the tiger is not real, nor does the "pit of the stomach" feeling last long, but the paying attention to our life lasts (a little while, at least) because (as I discuss below) we can "leap in" to a literary work. Normally, we don't pay much explicit attention to our life: we are just thinking about what to make for lunch, or what we have to do at work tomorrow, or what he said about what she said (all this *is* a kind of *inexplicit* attention to our life, of course). But our focus on and the intensity of a literary work throws us out of our normal run-of-the-mill daily life and can make us feel "not at home," a stranger to ourselves, filled with anxiety or concern. This anxiety *does* make us pay explicit attention to ourselves and reveals what Heidegger calls "care." Tragedy, through fear, reveals this care to ourselves and leads us to think attentively and clearly about our lives.

Pity and Being-with

Like fear, *pity*, the other mood that Aristotle notes, is for Heidegger not simply one mood among others. Like the analysis of fear, pity will turn out to reveal our fundamental concern with (but not necessarily for) others. And like fear, it has an everyday sense and a profounder ontological significance. Chapter 4 of *Being and Time* makes this clearest in turning to the question of "*Who* is it that Dasein is in everydayness?"[32] Answering this question leads to two structures of Dasein that are "equiprimordial"[33] with being-in-the-world: being-with (*Mitsein*) and Dasein-with (*Mitdasein*).

This exploration of who begins with Heidegger's refusal to take the "I" as a given: indeed, the "I" it is only a "noncommittal formal indication of something which perhaps reveals itself in the actual phenomenal context of being as that 'beings' opposite."[34] "I" am no I, and "we" are often deceived as to who "we" are: indeed, as "Dasein is always only itself in existing, the constancy of the self as well as its possible 'inconstancy' requite an existential-ontological kind of questioning."[35] Dasein encounters others like itself in the world, others "from whom one mostly does not distinguish oneself, those among whom one also is."[36] These others are not "encountered by first looking at oneself"[37] and then turning to look at them: instead, they are always already encountered in Dasein's dealings with the world. Indeed, we are entangled with the world and so "even one's own Dasein initially becomes 'discoverable' by looking away from its 'experiences' and the 'centre of its actions,' or by not yet 'seeing' them at all. Dasein initially finds 'itself' in what it does, needs, expects, has charge of, in the things at hand which it initially takes care of in the surrounding world."[38] We meet people doing things, at work, at play, not as "present thing-persons."[39] This is Dasein-with. But this Dasein-with itself relies on a more primordial structure of Dasein itself, which is being-with. This doesn't mean actually being with a person, real or fictional. Rather, he means that what makes you who you are is, simply, the capability of being with others: it is integral to our own being.

The beings that being-with encounters are, for Heidegger, matters of concern. This does not mean for him that we have ethical responsibilities for them (Heidegger claims he is simply describing—and while we may not be completely convinced by this claim, the ramifications of this doubt open up questions too broad to be broached here). "We are concerned with" not "concerned for." We might feel compassion or indifference (indeed, we don't feel compassion if people are comic, or wicked or too powerful or too good for Aristotle). Pity names one emotional state, but it also designates the very possibility for feeling compassionate or indifferent because its more profound ontological significance names this very fact of our being-with others. Usually, we are deficient in our concern for others: Heidegger writes that "being-for, against-, and without-one-another, passing-one-another-by, not-mattering-to-one-another, are possible ways of concern" and indeed, these illustrate very well our "every day and average being-with-one-another."[40] Heidegger adds, we can "leap in"[41] for the other, taking their place: this takes the other's care from them, as a servant might, or as a parent might help a child do a task that is beyond them (we might morally judge this as helpful or unhelpful: aid can also infantilize). We can also "leap ahead" of the other, which in turn enables them to "become transparent" to themselves,[42] as when a parent enabled a child to undertake a task on their own. The phenomenon "none too happily designated as" empathy is not the source of being-with but a consequence of it: without being-with, empathy would not be possible.[43]

This allows us to see pity, too, from an ontological viewpoint. Again, pity is not simply one emotion among others but has a profound ontological significance. Pity, or empathy, arises from the very fact that we exist with other people in the world, sharing our world and our lives. Pity is a term to express this fundamental concern with others, being-with that is "existentially constitutive."[44]

This discussion of pity also sheds light on the importance of the idea of unity in the *Poetics*. Following on from his account of being-with, Heidegger (famously, even infamously) develops his analysis of the "they-self" in section 27. He argues that knowing oneself "is grounded in being-with"[45]: we come to know our own Dasein through our mindful dealings with others. However, because our mode of being-with is usually deficient, our knowledge of ourselves is usually deficient. In its everyday being, Dasein finds itself lagging behind, and so subservient to, others—not particular others, but what Heidegger calls a "neuter" they. This "dissolves one's own Dasein completely into the kind of being of "the they."[46] Everything is averaged, leveled-down, obscured: "everyone is the other and no one is himself."[47] This is not (he claims) a type of moral judgment: the "they" is "a primordial phenomenon in the positive constitution of Dasein."[48] In contrast to the "they-self" is the "authentic self . . . which has explicitly grasped itself."[49] However (and unlike, for example, Sartre) this "they-self" is not understood as inauthentic but as "dissolved" or "dispersed": "As the they-self, Dasein is dispersed in the they and must first find itself."[50] Heidegger sums up:

> Initially "I" "am" not in the sense of my own my own self, but I am the others in the mode of the they. In terms of the they and as the they, I am initially "given" to "myself." . . . If Dasein explicitly discovers the world and brings it near, if it discloses its authentic being to itself, this discovering of "world" and disclosing of Dasein always comes about by clearing away coverings and obscurities, by breaking up the disguises with which Dasein cuts itself off from itself.[51]

This account of dispersal contrasts with a point that Aristotle makes repeatedly in the *Poetics*: that a plot has a unity, that it focuses on an action "single and entire" (*Poetics* 1051a34). An action is, if you like, the product of the tragedy. This unity is precisely working against dispersal, like Eliot's "objective correlative": something we engage with that offers back an image that is correlative to ourselves. In addition to attuning us to care and concern, the tragic also attunes us to the authentic, undissolved self. It does this through our attention paid to a character, their disclosed world, and their unified authentic self. (Of course, in watching a tragedy, we may instead pay attention to other things: the acting style of our favorite thespian; the key quotations we can use for an exam; how long until the interval in this uncomfy seat? None of these are essential to the experience of the tragic, however).

Catharsis (again)

These understandings of fear, as revealing care, and pity, as revealing concern, and unity, as disclosing the authentic and undispersed self, allow us to say something about *catharsis*, one of the most famous and widely discussed ideas from *Poetics*.[52] The word "catharsis" had a range of linked meanings in classical Greek: clarification, medical purgation, religious and ritual purification (that is, purgation of the soul).[53] A key issue for commentators on Aristotle is which of these nuances Aristotle is seeking to draw out.

To oversimplify, there are roughly three "standard" interpretations of *catharsis*. The first, and most influential, stems from Jacob Bernays who argued in 1857 that *catharsis* was best understood by comparting it to a "pathological bodily phenomena."[54] "Let no one primly wrinkle his nose and allege that this reduces aesthetics to medicine" he wrote, as he suggested that the effect of a tragedy was the same as a medical purgative.[55] A bodily purgative makes you excrete: an emotional purgative allows you to vent your feelings. Bernays was influenced by Aristotle's many medical metaphors and by an account from *Politics* in which Aristotle suggests that music can work as a "relief of the passions" (*Politics*. 1341a22–3). This idea implies that "pity and fear" are harmful emotions that need to be evacuated and that the audiences of tragedy need emotional healing. Jonathan Barnes is even more blunt: "Philosophical readers have found it strange of Aristotle to suggest that tragedy is, by definition and essentially, a form of rhubarb."[56] However, as ever, there is more to this idea. Angela Curran, in her very clear introductory account, offers a modified version: experiencing pity and fear in art works to "diminish" these feelings in our real life and so does not vent excess emotion but helps us cope with it.[57]

Similarly Kenny argues that *catharsis* helps us "calibrate the emotions of pity and fear when felt in real life . . . helps us put our own sorrows and worries into proportion."[58]

A second view responds to the repeated insistence on the idea of unity and on the importance of plot construction in the *Poetics*. G. R. F. Ferrari's reading, akin to that of Gerald Else, argues that fear and pity are "the emotions engaged by tragic suspense" and not "an audience being braced with a sense of its own tragic vulnerability."[59] This means that the "pleasure of *catharsis* is the pleasure that the audience feels when the suspense that has been tightening throughout the play is suddenly released. It is the pleasure of relief."[60] Jonathan Lear makes a similar argument and notes too that the audiences were not children who needed educating in the virtues but adults.[61] This pleasure in closure, in finding out "whodunnit" or what happens at the end, is very gripping and relies on well-made plots; however, it doesn't really explain why we go to see a play, say, whose ending we already *know*. Nor does it explain why we find ourselves so involved with literary texts afterward (apart from the satisfaction of admiring the cogs of the plot). Further, Aristotle often reminds his audience that they (and we) have constantly and practically to work at being virtuous (it's not a kind of finished state). (Who, after all, is not a person "in between," "not outstanding in virtue or justice") (*Poetics* 1453a8). Narrative is gripping and closure is pleasurable, but perhaps *catharsis* is more profound than this.

A third view is offered by Martha Nussbaum, among others. She argues for the nontechnical meaning of catharsis as "roughly . . . 'clearing up' or 'clarification,' i.e., of the removal of some obstacle (dirt or blot or obscurity)": the word is used of "water that is clear and open, free of mud or weeds; of a space cleared of objects; of grain that is winnowed, and so clear of chaff."[62] She argues that the medical and moral senses stem from this. For her, then, *catharsis* is "the clearing up of the vision of the soul by the removal of these obstacles" (389). For Aristotle "the viewing of pitiable and fearful things, and our responses of pity and fear themselves, can serve to show us something of importance about the human good" (388) and the experience of *catharsis* leads to a form of knowledge, a kind of understanding crucial for *phronesis*.

The discussion above would support the argument made by Nussbaum but for even more profound ontological reasons. The action of catharsis is precisely one of "'clearing up' or 'clarification.'" What is revealed in this "clearing away coverings and obscurities" and "breaking up . . . disguises"

(BTS: 125) is Dasein itself, its structures of care and concern, as unified and authentic, and its world. This kind of insight is not, as it were, a scientific depiction of the psyche or a list of facts but rather a "vision of the soul"[63] achieved through *phronesis*, learning by reflection and experience. Catharsis offers Dasein a clear vision of authentic Dasein, bringing one back to oneself. (Interestingly, Arendt, who studied the courses with Heidegger from which much of this material is taken, explicitly and repeatedly writes of that "'reconciliation with reality,' the catharsis, which, according to Aristotle, was the essence of tragedy."[64] The intellectual consequences of this for understanding Aristotle, Heidegger and Arendt and their differences are too significant to discuss here, and I mention this only further to suggest this Heideggerian reading of catharsis). Something like "leaping in" occurs when you pay attention to a tragedy: you cannot disburden the fictional Oedipus of his cares, of course, but emotions are stirred for "one who does not deserve" their suffering and who is like us in vulnerability to suffering "which we might expect to befall ourselves" (1385b13–15). This need not happen of course. One can simply ignore the action on stage and agree with whatever the "they" says: a tragedy is a work of art not a magic spell. More, as both Aristotle and Heidegger agree, this vision does not last. One cannot live by aesthetics or philosophical contemplation alone. Aristotle writes that "all human things are incapable of continuous activity" (1175a4) and "one will also need external prosperity; for our nature is not self-sufficient for contemplation but our body also must be healthy and have food and other attention" (1178b33–34): one's everyday affairs need management. For Heidegger, we "fall" back to the "they-self," we go back to reading the newspaper or scrolling through Twitter.

Conclusion

This chapter has offered a provisional Heideggerian reading of fear, pity, and catharsis in the *Poetics*. Fear and pity are not simply contingent feelings but also have a more profound ontological significance. Fear discloses care, our care for our own Dasein; pity discloses being-with and our concern with (not necessarily for) others and so with ourselves not as dispersed but as unified authentic selves: both these disclose the world. Both, too, lead to catharsis, here understood as a form of clarification, of understanding (rather than venting or a pleasure in closure). Catharsis is a vision of one's authentic self and of the structures of one's being. This is why tragedy is existentially significant. Finally, as a coda, this also allows us to see why it is that tragedy is a common lexicon for critics, classicists, philosophers, and political scientists. It is because it has disclosive power not only for our lives but also, in care and concern, for what Heidegger identifies as part of the fundamental structure of our being-in-the-world.

Notes

1. Stephen Halliwell, *Between Ecstasy and Truth: Interpretations of Greek Poetics from Homer to Longinus* (Oxford: Oxford University Press, 2011), 237.

2. Miriam Leonard, *Tragic Modernities* (Cambridge, MA: Harvard University Press, 2015), 13.

3. Angela Curran, *The Routledge Philosophy Guidebook to Aristotle and the Poetics* (London: Routledge, 2016), 216. Tragedy has the most demanding bibliography of any literary genre. Even within only relatively recent literary criticism, there are too many significant books to list, and all engage with Aristotle. These include *Rethinking Tragedy*, ed. Rita Felski (Baltimore: Johns Hopkins University Press, 2008); Terry Eagleton, *Sweet Violence* (Oxford: Wiley-Blackwell, 2002); George Steiner, *The Death of Tragedy* (London: Faber and Faber, 1974); Ato Quayson, *Tragedy and Postcolonial Literature* (Cambridge: Cambridge University Press, 2021); Raymond Williams, *Modern Tragedy* (London: Chatto & Windus, 1992).

4. Kenny, *Aristotle's Poetics*, xxvii.

5. Stephen Halliwell, *Aristotle's Poetics*, 2nd ed. (London: Duckworth, 1998), 2–3. By contrast, see, for a recent exploration of the links between the *Poetics* and the rest of Aristotle's work, *The Poetics in its Aristotelian Context*, ed. Pierre Destrée, Malcolm Heath, Dana L. Munteanu (London: Routledge, 2020); Robert Eaglestone, *Truth and Wonder: A Literary Introduction to Plato and Aristotle* (London: Routledge, 2022).

6. On Heidegger and Aristotle, see, *intra alia*, Theodore Kisiel and John van Buren, eds., *Reading Heidegger from the start* (Albany: State University of New York Press, 1994); Walter Brogan, *Heidegger and Aristotle* (Albany: State University of New York Press, 2005); Drew Hyland and Johan Panteleimon Manoussakis, eds., *Heidegger and the Greeks* (Bloomington: Indiana University Press, 2006); Franco Volpi, "In Whose Name? Heidegger and "Practical Philosophy," *European Journal of Political Theory* 6, no. 1: 31–51 (2007); Thomas Sheehan, *Making Sense of Heidegger* (London: Rowman & Littlefield International, 2014).

7. Hans-Georg Gadamer, *Heidegger's Ways*, trans. John W. Stanley (Albany: State University of New York Press, 2004), 32.

8. For example, the "unity of the whole has often been questioned. Each of the three books hardly displays any continuity with the two others" Michael Meyer, *What is Rhetoric?* (Oxford: Oxford University Press, 2017), 20.

9. BCArP 75.
10. BCArP: 79.
11. BCArP: 75.
12. BCArP: 75/6.
13. BTS: 139.
14. Daniel Gross, "Introduction" in *Heidegger and Rhetoric*, ed. Daniel Gross and Ansgar Kemmann (Albany: State University of New York Press, 2005), 5, 11.
15. BCArP: 80.
16. BCArP: 43.
17. Theodore Kisiel, "Rhetorical Protopolitics in Heidegger and Arendt" in *Heidegger and Rhetoric*, ed. Daniel Gross and Ansgar Kemmann (Albany: State University Press of New York, 2005), 131–60,146.
18. BCArP: 80.
19. BCArP: 90.
20. BCArP: 84.
21. Michael J. Hyde, "A Matter of the Heart: Epideictic Rhetoric and Heidegger's Call of Conscience," in Gross and Kemmann, 81–104, 91.
22. Daniel Gross, "Introduction" in *Heidegger and Rhetoric*, ed. Daniel Gross and Ansgar Kemmann (Albany: State University Press of New York, 2005), 4.
23. Ludwig Wittgenstein, *Philosophical Investigations*, trans. G. E. M. Anscombe (Oxford: Blackwell, 1963), 8e paragraph 18. See also: Robert John Ackerman, *Wittgenstein's City* (Amherst: University of Massachusetts Press, 1988).
24. BCArP: 92.
25. The second of these is what Bernard Williams, in *Shame and Necessity*, analyzes as the belief that a "supernatural necessity" "is, so to speak, playing against you," or, once that belief has died, the "psychological, social and political" obstacles and "constraint exercised by the power of others." Bernard Williams, *Shame and Necessity* (Princeton, NJ: Princeton University Press, 2008), 14, 52.
26. BCArP: 113. This is the first mention of the *Poetics*. The second is in passing on the next page, where he is discussing various ramifications of *pathos*: *ethos* in the *Poetics* is what "makes manifest, at the moment, the being-resolved of the speaker" (BCArP: 114) (*Poetics* 1450 b8). Kenny's translation is "moral character is what reveals the nature of people's fundamental options: that is why there is no such thing as speeches in which the speaker reveals no choice or rejection" (p. 25)
27. BCArP: 133.
28. BTS: 133, H. 137.
29. BTS: 134, H. 137.
30. BTS: 135, H. 139.
31. BCArP: 114.
32. BT: 111.

33. BT: 111.
34. BT: 113.
35. BT: 114.
36. BT: 115.
37. BT: 116.
38. BT: 116.
39. BT: 117.
40. BT: 118.
41. BT: 118.
42. BT: 119.
43. BT: 121.
44. BTS: 118.
45. BT: 120.
46. BT: 123.
47. BT: 124.
48. BT: 125.
49. BT: 125.
50. BT: 125.
51. BT: 125.

52. The term is so contentious that some scholars even suggest it is a later interpolation to Aristotle: a clear discussion and opinion can be found in Stephen Halliwell, *Between Ecstasy and Truth* (Oxford: Oxford University Press, 2011), 260–65.

53. Halliwell, *Aristotle's Poetics*, 185–90, 197.

54. Jacob Bernays, "Aristotle on the Effect of Tragedy," trans. Jennifer Barnes, intro. Jonathan Barnes, in *Ancient Literary Criticism*, ed. Andrew Laird (Oxford: Oxford University Press, 2006), 158–77, here 166.

55. Bernays, 'Aristotle . . .' 166.

56. Bernays, 'Aristotle . . .' 159.

57. Angela Curran, *The Routledge Philosophy Guidebook to Aristotle and the Poetics* (London: Routledge, 2016), 231, 232. See also her (really useful) ch. 11 "The Distinct Pleasure of Tragedy."

58. Kenny, *Poetics*, xxvi.

59. G. R. F. Ferrari, "Aristotle's Literary Aesthetics," *Phronesis* 44, no. 3 (1999): 181–98, here 194.

60. Ferrari, "Aristotle's Literary Aesthetics," 196.

61. Jonathan Lear "Katharsis" in *Essays on Aristotle's Poetics* (Princeton, NJ: Princeton University Press, 1992), 315–40.

62. Martha Nussbaum, *The Fragility of Goodness* (Cambridge: Cambridge University Press, 1986), 389; further references in the text.

63. Nussbaum, *Fragility of Goodness*, 388.

64. Hannah Arendt, *Between Past and Future* (London: Penguin, 2008), 45.

12

Rationalizing the Animal in Humanity
On Speaking with Neither Cause nor Purpose

LAURENCE HEMMING

Philosophy seeks definitions. Philosophers very often ask us to "define our terms," and many arguments, especially in the Anglophone, or Analytic, tradition begin by asserting "for the purposes of this argument I will define *x* to mean *y*," where *y* is a very precise and narrow explanation of the range of possible meanings of *x*. In relation to this approach, philosophers will often refer to "natural language," those species of language whose range of meanings is not fixable in advance. Words escape us, which means in the face of our attempts to pin them down, words, language itself, leaks, and exceeds our capacity to discipline what is said, or to secure in advance what and how words are (and language is) to speak. Even the most linguistically schooled among us fails to impose limits on what words will say.

An old definition of philosophy in the West is one that speaks of man as the *animal rationale*. This definition appears by the time of the first century CE, seemingly with Epictetus, and is frequently attributed (earlier still) to Aristotle, to the *Nicomachean Ethics*, or *Metaphysics*, or *De Anima*. Aristotle was writing long before Latin overtook Greek as a language of thinking. Martin Heidegger frequently draws our attention to how the phrase *animal rationale* is a translation, a rendering of a definition of the human being that he traces to "the Greeks," and to Aristotle in particular. Greek thought, Martin Heidegger claims, speaks of the ἄνθρωπος, the human being, as ζῷον λόγον ἔχον,[1] living being that is possessed of language and speaking.[2] This essay seeks to explore that claim by following the contours of Heidegger's inquiry into the phrase itself, into the history of metaphysics, and the history of being. In a discussion of this length it will not be possible to present the full range of Heidegger's thought: indeed, that is not the aim. Rather I want to show the breadth of the discussion and how it relates to both classical and contemporary sources. In one case I will consider a text that (to my knowledge) Heidegger does not ever mention, let alone consider systematically. I will conclude by asking where, or rather in whom, might Heidegger locate the origin, we might say, the ἀρχή, of language?

Heidegger's use of the phrase ζῷον λόγον ἔχον is not without a certain difficulty: Aristotle did not ever directly employ or coin the precise phrase ζῷον λόγον ἔχον (nor did Plato) in any text we currently have. In the *Politics* Aristotle does say something very close, however, when he says that "the human being alone of [all] living beings possesses speaking,"[3] but this has more the feeling of an observation than a formal definition. In the *Nicomachean Ethics* Aristotle speaks of two parts of the soul: τό τε λόγον ἔχον καὶ τὸ ἄλογον, "one possessing speaking and equally one without speaking," and further, he adds, the part (μέρα) possessing speaking does so in two ways.[4] The talk here is all of the soul (ψυχή) not "living being" (ζῷον), let alone the human being (ἄνθρωπος), and in both places the soul and, again, the forms of life in question are being described and explicated, not defined. The phrase ζῷον λόγον ἔχον is therefore an interpretation, an abstraction, from what Aristotle says. The exact phrase, strictly speaking, was never his.[5]

Heidegger is frequently criticized, especially among classical philologists, for his often-daring etymologies and interpretations, especially of classical texts. However, the problem is not as simple as it seems. Many of Heidegger's philosophical neologisms are, in fact, nothing of the sort: the phrase "being toward death" (*Sein zum Tode*), found throughout *Being and Time* (but, in the works published in his lifetime, almost nowhere else) is a straightforward rendering of θνητός. The entry for θνητός in Liddell and Scott is itself instructive on this since it first says "liable to death" (a good rendering of *zum Tode*) and only then mentions the abbreviation of that careful thought in the word "mortal." Despite the debate over the α-privative of ἀλήθεια, Heidegger's definition of "dis-closure" and the relation to λήθη, λανθάνομαι, is referenced not only in Liddell and Scott but also the pages of the Byzantine *Etymologicum Magnum* dating from the twelfth century CE. If the definition is controversial for Heidegger, it is not less controversial in the pages of those works too. *Mitsein*, "being-with," "being-with-one-another," is a straight rendering of σύνειμι, συνεῖναι, although I have never seen it documented by anyone except Heidegger himself.[6] It would be possible to provide numerous examples of how Heidegger renders important Greek terms into German constructions of his own, but what is essential to understand is that in every translation from Greek into German or English a decisive interpretation has been made somewhere: even when one is oneself employing those decisive interpretations with the authority of the dictionary or of historical convention. In the question of the passage from which the phrase ζῷον λόγον ἔχον appears to have been taken, Ömer Aygün has pointed out (without reference to Heidegger, although it's possible he had Heidegger in mind) that one is never free from the demands that interpretation make, even if those demands are to a certain extent taken as givens (from the dictionary). He shows how, even if we can try by an inductive and statistical method to establish the meaning of the words λόγον ἔχειν because we know "that *logos* means this here . . . and so on"—and "even if in an ideal situation *logos* turns out to be always followed by *ekhein*" (in fact, the two do occur together with remarkably high frequency)—we are left with two difficult questions: first, "how does this give us any insight into the meaning of *that* particular occurrence?" and second, "to answer this, we are rather led to the question of what *ekhein* means and thus we fall into infinite regress."[7] To think and understand what a word means, means being able to take over and make one's own the decisions that interpretations in their *decisiveness* demand.

Heidegger invites us to understand that the Greek word ζῷον can mean "animal," but only because it first means "thing that has life," "living being": that which is akin to, the likeness of, everything ζωός, alive, living, animal. Only as living being is an animal "animal." In what he says from the *Politics* Aristotle appears to secure the being of the ἄνθρωπος, the human being, on the basis of λόγος, "speaking," "discourse," "language." *How* Aristotle does this, and on what basis, is not yet clear. The phrase ζῷον λόγον ἔχον could rather be understood to be a reconstruction of the Greek origin of the phrase *animal rationale*. It shows the extent to which the Latin phrase *animal rationale* is a Latin "summing-up" of Aristotle, perhaps for the school room or lecture hall. As a definition, it is a most decisive interpretation. It could well be that the phrase *animal rationale* is the direct interpretation of the original line of Aristotle's *Politics*, from which Heidegger, or another, inferred the phrase ζῷον λόγον ἔχον. Certainly no text of Greek antiquity that I can identify, from the earliest fragments up to, and contemporaneous with, Epictetus or later, appears to have written or deployed the exact phrase ζῷον λόγον ἔχον—and so the formal definition came later.

What is the difference between the two definitions, one Latin, one Greek? A definition seeks out two things: first, it seeks out what is most basic, its "ground." A definition lays out the most basic trait of what it defines. Second, it lays this basic trait out over against the other things that are similar but different to what is to be defined: it identifies and specifies the unique ground—the only ground the thing in question could have. A definition therefore both defines (and settles) what something is, and it excludes alternative possibilities. In doing this, it singles the thing out. In the Middle Ages, this came to be known as the technique of defining by specific difference. By seeking out what is at one and the same time "what it is" that is the most basic trait of something, and "what it is with respect to what it is not" (i.e., that specifies it over against everything else it could otherwise be), the "essence" of a thing is brought, through a clear and rigorous intellectual procedure of differentiation, to a formal definition. Like a process of distillation, the "essence" of a thing is therefore and simultaneously twofold: what it *is* and what it *could not be other than*. Both elements are required for a formal definition to be binding. Both: that the definition sums something up in its most basic trait; and that it excludes every other possibility of what the thing could be.

In the Latin language *ratio* means "reason," as in (Latin) *reor*, "I think," but in the sense that "I count," and so "I reckon." Very decisively, therefore, *animal rationale* equates speaking and discourse with thinking, thinking as "ratiocination": this would appear to be an essentially correct rendering of the phrase ζῷον λόγον ἔχον into Latin. In one way, there is no difficulty with that. Every thought *can* be spoken aloud. But precisely because thought and speaking are equated, and in a very specific way, the definition of the human being is secured *only on the basis of* the spoken, the said, the uttered. Now a very specific kind of speaking has been selected as the ground of the definition: rational speech. The consequences of this we will return to later. What, then, is meant by reason? In what way is speaking (as thinking) reason? To think by means of reason is to assemble into an order, where one thing follows from (and is in consequence of) another. The human being, as the rational animal, is the animal that understands by arranging what is to be understood and spoken about in thoughtful order. What is the most basic trait of this assembling of what is thought into an order? For Kant, what fundamentally distinguishes humanity from every other possible animal is the thought that says *reor*, "I think": I think (by means of *ratio*, reason).[8] *This* is the unique characteristic of man as that one who has self-reflexivity, who can think *himself*, herself, thinking alongside whatever and everything he or she thinks.

This most basic of all thoughts: the "I think," is at the same time the thought that *each* thinking animal thinks and that *every* thinking animal thinks "as" the "thinking animal." The "I think" lies at the beginning of every ordered thinking, and is first in the series of what is to be thought. It is co-given in every subsequent thought. In this, the question of whether non-human animals can think or not (which has troubled some philosophers) seemingly becomes irrelevant: *I think* is only thinkable by one who *knows himself or herself in thinking* and so can *think* himself or herself *thinking*.

In Aristotle's original phrase, λόγον ἔχον, λόγος ἔχειν, "having λόγος" is ambiguous: it does not decide how and in what way living being holds to λόγος. On the contrary, the translation with its division of human being into "animal" and "rational" brings with it an ambiguity of a quite different order. Often, in the history of thinking, of philosophy, of literature, the two halves of human being are held as contraries: opposites that must be reconciled—the "animal" and the "rational." The "rational" is said to tame the primordial, the animality, of humanity. The animality is said to situate, to give body and place—actuality—to the rational, the spiritual, to *Geist*. Quite early on, Martin Heidegger draws attention to what emerges from this definition of the *animal rationale*: beginning with Descartes, and spurred on by British empiricism, philosophy is transformed into a "science of consciousness," of the analysis of the "inner experience" of the mental states of the rational animal. Heidegger points out that neither Greek philosophy, nor even the philosophy of the Middle Ages thinks in this way, where inner psychic life is set off from an "exterior" world and understood through what comes to be called "consciousness." This consciousness comes to be conceived through a science, the science of consciousness itself. This development then divides the understanding of experience (as inner mental states) from what it is experience of (an "external world"), while being able only with great difficulty to reconnect these two now separated spheres. The result is "*not knowledge of the soul as of a substance, but of the psychic manifestations of whatever is given in inner experience.*" With this development, Heidegger argues, scientific psychology came to be "the *basic science of philosophy itself*."[9]

What has become the most basic trait of thinking, the activity of the human being as "animal," is "I think," *reor*, "I assemble into an order (a structure)." Even when this is reversed, when, as Heidegger argues, Nietzsche and nihilism inverts the priority of the rational over the animal and privileges animality over reason, this merely puts reason in the service of embodiment and its drives, urges, and passions. This is the "'willing' of life itself," which deploys reason as the ground for the positing of values, so that "reason is just 'living' as embodied reason."[10]

This basic trait, the "I think," seeks out what is *first* in every order of thinking (what stands at the beginning of the sequence). What stands prior in every case is "I think," the thought which (for Kant) thinks the most individual, individuated, thought, and thinks the *same* thought that every thinking being, every rational animal, thinks whenever it thinks: "I think." It is in this sense that *ratio* can also mean "ground," for Kant as much for Nietzsche and beyond: the "I think" that assembles into an order at the same time provides the ground, *ratio*, for that order. "I think" as the ground for everything thought, everything that has been placed into an order, according to its *ratio*, its "reason." [11] The most individual thought turns out at one and the same time to be the most universal thought. This most universal thought at the same time turns out to be the thought that is the *same* thought at every point in time as well as in space. '–I– think.' What does this thought think? Even with its body, it need think nothing other than the "*I think me thinking*." In this sense the most universal thought is at the same time the emptiest of thoughts. It must think: "I think": everything else it thinks subsequently is superadded to the "I think." This definition goes beyond, therefore, the merely individual, and it is wider than the universal. It accounts for both: the individual in his or her individuality, and the universality of the *species* or "genus" of humanity as a whole. Individual and species are (as Marx, following Feuerbach, asserted) understood to be "the same."

Have we, therefore, pinned down what makes *me* the same as you, and every *you*, and even all of *them*? Surely not, because I am differentiated from every other person. Have we specified our sameness, our universality among ourselves? Surely not, for I do in fact differ from you and them. What have we achieved in what we have said so far?

The most empty, the most universal, thought—"I think me thinking"—prepares the way for every other thought and grounds and secures all other subsequent thinking. It also conceals within itself an ambiguity. For it is the most individuating of thoughts. Only I can think the "grounding" or "rational" thought of "I think me thinking." At the same time, *every thinking I* is said to think this thought.

How then can we secure the origin of thinking as speaking? Who, then, or what, "thinks" and "speaks"? Is "to speak" the same as "to denote," "to inform," "to tell" or "to say," or are these ways of speaking consequent on something prior? What is this "prior," and how do we find it out? Or are we so familiar with what it is that through its very closeness it hides itself?

One of the possible answers to the question "from where does speaking and thinking spring?" is not to look for its most "universal" origination but to look for its origin historically. The answer given here is that speaking and thinking originally sprung from use and need. Thus we are accustomed to hearing it said that language is a "tool" the human being "uses." This takes for granted that this animal, "man," *is* and was before ever language spoke: that language "evolved" for humanity out of, in the words of one evolutionary theorist, "a form of pre-linguistic representation," based on a development of animal communication, which, he goes on to say, "starts with [animals] doing things to each other dyadically."[12] This understands language to be fundamentally a purposive "projecting" of a "constructive" humanity, a humanity emerging from animality. Speaking is in each case, therefore, "willed" and "intended," the animal learns to direct its will and so "intend." Here we have a "scientific psychology" of the rational animal at work. We should note that a decision has already been made in this interpretation of the "evolution" of language: that it is through a certain kind of already present intending and willing that comes to be expressed as language, in which humanity moves from an originary individuality into other kinds of relation, specifically the "dyadic" or twofold. The whole of "anthropology" is grounded in this thought. Humanity, in evolving, attains to sociality and to a higher life *through* the perfecting of the tools to do so, as an effect of a not-yet-even-named willing. Language, thought in this way, is a tool for the accomplishing and perfecting of (social) human life. Language is one of man's perfecting social techniques. Language is a "technology," it is an element of man's making: what we "make" our most basic life with: his and her life as an individual "within" society. Hegel constructs the *I think*, the relationship between thinking and activity and production, the "ascent" of the individual subject into absolute subjectivity, in exactly this way.

We construe the "before" to humanity with recourse to the basic outlook of "progress" that grounds the sciences of anthropology and evolution. Since the nineteenth century, and certainly since Hegel, Marx, Weber, and others, philosophy has presupposed an essentially constructive understanding of humanity, taking the individual first, then his or her being in the family, which then is the basis for "civil society," "society in general," and even the state. This understanding conditioned the basic outlook of Hegel, of Marx, indeed of the "science" of "social anthropology" in general. In this "historical" understanding, we are still thinking sequentially: rationally. Indeed the sequential is still an essential part of the thinking. Indeed it is *only* because we are still seeking an adequate and incontestable (rational) ground for the most universal thought: "I think me thinking," that we *also* require a historical origin for the reason (ground) of this thought. The historical origin supplied here is not another or different account of the origin of thinking, it is the necessary counterpart to the "working out" (rationality) of its universality as a definitive thought. As part of the definition, we trace back from what we know and have now to what "must have been" before.

In this way humanity understands language, the word itself, to arise on the basis of the *needs* of the species that it is, as it develops. What evolves through these needs is a passage from the lower to the higher: the emergence of language accounts for the drive to "the cooperative" (as what masters and perfects the most immediately proximate, producing the neighboring, the familial, the tribal),[13] which gives rise to social relations and then society itself. The evolution of language, to quote the evolutionist, occurs because of "humans' great willingness to give each other useful information in language, altruistically and/or cooperatively."[14] Altruism and co-operation are then fortunate outcomes favored by evolutionary history: "the good" itself, is an effect of humanity's historical progress. Humanity is originarily disposed both to produce, and to privilege as it proceeds, "the (ethically) good" (Hegel would have not put it better). We understand the "before and after" to be explicable by a theory that governs the purposiveness of the coming-about of the animal, of the species, of that region of understanding we deem to be "the biological" as such, and through one of its dependent sciences, "evolutionary biology": that entire region covered by what the Greeks denoted with their word ζῷον.

What is it that the translation *animal rationale* overlooks in its securing of the human being as the being that itself *speaks* and *thinks*. What is it, therefore, that is occluded by the decisive interpretation of λόγος through *ratio*? If we return to Aristotle's politics, from where the definition ζῷον λόγον ἔχον appeared to have come, but in fact turned out be to an interpretation of a phrase to be found there, we make a most surprising discovery early on in the text. We discover that what is prior for Aristotle is not the effects of the drive from animality to something higher, a progress from individuality through household and tribe to "society" through the emergence of the utility of language (as philosophy, certainly since Hegel, has taken for granted), but the exact opposite. Aristotle is explicit about this: the polity is first. This is because, Aristotle tells us, "the whole necessarily is prior in being to the part."[15]

If the definition of the ἄνθρωπος, the human "living being," as ζῷον λόγον ἔχον, is formally absent from the text of the *Politics*, is there any other definition of the "living being" to be found there? What kind of living being does Aristotle think the human being to be? Aristotle replies, several times, that the ἄνθρωπος, the human being, is *first* ζῷον πολιτικόν, "political animal" (there is no article),[16] *that* living being (animal?) whose proper being and place is the πόλις. This is the actual definition Aristotle himself supplies for the human being (rather than ζῷον λόγον ἔχον). Are they one and the same, as Martin Heidegger has suggested they were? [17] Perhaps. How are we to translate this word πόλις? This word is most often translated as both "city" and "country," and means both the physicality of the citadel, and its land (the land that supports it and on which it relies), and the community or body of citizens, and at the same time is akin to what we would now call "the state," and even "the nation." We can translate it (as I already did) with the old English word "polity." Aristotle says "and so the polity is first among things which are present in and of themselves, prior to the household [i.e., the family] and each of us individually."[18] Household, family, tribe, and individuality are only possible because the polity first "is," and was, and goes on being. The polity lets the other forms of human being "be." Thought like this, something else comes into view. For the definition "rational animal" is itself a rational ground, a claim of pure reason. But every polity is itself historical; there is no "politicality," no "essence" of the political as such. Each πόλις has a place and a time, even if it has great duration. Indeed, for the Greeks, every (free) person belonged to a specific πόλις, and no two were quite alike, even if one was founded out of another that had laid down for it its customs, its laws, and its existence.

Thought like this, the purposive character of language falls into the background and ceases to be the driving ground for the emergence of "communication." Humanity first "is" at all because he and she is among others: and among others with a wherefrom and a whereto, which these others also have. And at the same time, the first and prior *being* of language itself need not be (and in fact is not) "information." Humanity does not come to speak *merely* to satisfy his and her immediate "needs." Rather, the opposite pertains: speaking has need of humanity. Language *is* what lets us *be*—lets us be who we are. Language informs us, informs me (and in that order).

When we say humanity is "possessed of" speaking (λόγον ἔχον) we need to ask: Does humanity possess language, as one thing among (many) possessions (tools)? Or does language possess humanity, as what uniquely lets us, jointly and individually, be human? How is this relation of possession to be understood? Aristotle distinguishes very firmly (as Hurford does not: in fact Hurford conflates precisely where Aristotle distinguishes) between speaking, possessing language, and the semantic possibility of φωνή, by which is meant vocalization (the voice), the calling-out that has a capacity for σημεῖον, "indication": for instance, of pain or pleasure. Animals call out and use "indications," signs, calls, and so forth by which they inform each other of what is happening in the surrounding world. These calls, however elaborate and structured or nuanced, are not, and indeed are quite other than, words and speech—certainly for Aristotle. In this sense speaking is, for Aristotle, already quite other, and much more than mere indication or "information": "semiosis." Even humanity has calls and signs (of pain perhaps, or when smiling, for just two examples). Language is quite other than the σημεῖον that Aristotle says characterizes much animal life.

If we take together Aristotle's understanding of the ζῷον πολιτικόν with the ζῷον λόγον ἔχον, we would say, and taken at the widest, πόλις and λόγος (language as a whole, discourse in itself, speaking as such) name the same. They name, for Aristotle as much as for Heidegger, the πρότερον, that which is prior and first, the ground, and the *through which* "humanity" appears. This would mean that humanity appears because λόγος is, rather than because man thinks the "I think," so that world appears *for him* and *her*, each of us, respectively. This word λόγος is, after all, another word for thinking, as much as it is a word for discourse, speaking, or language. This means that nothing like "biology," nothing like "evolution" is first, or prior, in explaining the being of humanity. It also means that it is not in her taking possession of language (the *I* that thinks "I think," such that each time it is the *first* person singularly) that *I* think, by grasping and taking over and taking up what is to be thought or said. Rather it is because language already is, thinking already is and is already thinking, that humanity can appear. It is in language that "humanity" is first explained. Language has possession of, "has," humanity.

To the most ancient authors, thinking is a "speaking to ourselves" that is the activity of the soul: Plato and Aristotle both speak of this, and more than once. Thinking and speaking belong together. We can now see how this is. For if man is first and foremost the political living being, the being whose abode is the polity, the one who *first* lives by being among others in the widest sense, then thinking and speaking is therefore, and even when I am alone, and always in some sense, with respect to those others, and so with respect to the whole. This is a quite different orientation on the universal to that which we uncovered earlier of the universal as "the same," such that every *I* thinks "the same thought," "*I think me thinking.*" Now, with this changed (or rather older) understanding, *I think*, or *I* speak, but with respect to, and from my being from out of, among, others: thus in-among-the-whole. I speak, as already belonging to the (historical) πόλις, that *wherein* where speaking is already both a possibility for speaking (λεγεῖν) and a being-spoken (λεγόμενον), wherein thinking thinks.

Speaking already had to be, before my specified *I* could think or speak. Does this mean that speaking is antecedent to human being? What does it mean even to ask this question? Does this question not seek how it would transform into "scientific fact" every myth of creation? If language has need of humanity as much as the human being is nothing other than living being possessed of λόγος, at what point can it even be said that either preceded the other? Is not their appearance one and the same, a simultaneity? Who could *say* otherwise, or how? Speaking summoned others with speech before ever I spoke. Or is there pre-linguistic thought, as many philosophers are fond of claiming? What could thinking think, that it could not speak—even to itself—*of*? Which is to say, in which order do they stand? The thinking before the speaking or the speaking before the thinking? Is philosophy really a psychology, of interior states that gain exterior expression, or is psychology only that which can come about because I uncover myself through learning to correspond with, and make my own, what others have already been able to say, and so have said (before, before *me*)? Even if there is anything like "pre-linguistic thought," it can only be accounted for by speaking of it. This is why animals might indeed do something akin to thinking, but Kant is not wrong in identifying something very specific and necessary in the self-reflexivity of thinking. "I think" is never enough to explain how thinking speaks of itself, when it speaks of what thinking thinks. The definition *animal rationale* therefore already says much more than when we simply let it be concerned with the *ratio* alone. It now speaks not only of the whole of humanity taken as a general and basic "trait" within a definition (each one thinks "the same"), but, and for each of us, it speaks of our (your, her, their, my) belonging to the whole (each one thinks within the *same* whole that speaking always speaks *from out of*, whenever there is speech). How are we to understand the kind of whole is it that is meant here? Surely, the whole in question is that to which we are accustomed and to (as much as with) which we correspond? Accustomed does not just mean "familiar," but rather our "from whence," our place of belonging. Our abode. The Greeks thought of this "whole" as the ἦθος (from which we get the word "ethics," although nothing "ethical" in the modern sense is indicated by this word ἦθος). Thinking thinks, speaking speaks, from out of the abode of humanity, our *ēthos*.

What else does Aristotle say of the ζῷον λόγον ἔχον, the ζῷον πολιτικόν? There are, as we have seen, passages in the *Nicomachean Ethics* that come very close to the phrase ζῷον λόγον ἔχον, but they also say something altogether more important, a more again that the phrase *animal rationale* otherwise overlooks and excludes. We should remember first of all that Aristotle's *Politics* and his *Nicomachean Ethics* belong together, and have even (at times) been considered as a single text. They treat of the same: of the being of the human being in the polity. We should recall that the only definition that Aristotle has given us of the human being is "political living being" and *not* "living being possessing speaking." In that part of the *Nicomachean Ethics* where the phrase "possessing speaking" (λόγον ἔχον) appears, the matter under discussion is not the "living being" (ζωόν) of humanity, but the word we translate for soul, ψυχή. This word is perhaps among the most misunderstood in philosophical thought.

What does Aristotle mean by "soul," and in what relation does it stand to the "living being" of humanity? The word ψυχή originally meant something more like "life," but life taken in a very specific way. Whereas life, as ζωή, is the force of life, the activity and zest of living itself, ψυχή indicated the whole of life in its unity. It is for this reason that the so-called Latin Averroists of the thirteenth and fourteenth centuries debated hotly the issue of a single "world-soul"—whether there was only a single soul in which all participated. What they intuited as an unresolved question in Western thinking was to return again and again in the Idealism of the eighteenth and nineteenth centuries and what followed from them. In Homer, the soul, ψυχή, was that which the body gave up when it died: not in the sense of a spirit, or in the final gasp for breath (*Geist*, πνεῦμα), but in the sense of the totality of the life lived by the one deceased, and this life having been finished, by, and *through*, its coming to its, her, his, end. In Homer we find the word *soul* fundamentally connected with another word, αἰών, in two places: one in the Iliad, the other in the Odyssey. In these two places the words appear conjoined: ψυχή, αἰών.[19]

In both places where the conjunction appears, the Epic texts employ the same construction in Greek to connect them: τε καὶ (these two words together say: "and, and," but in a manner akin to the logical "if and only if"), a construction that stresses very vigorously the identity of meaning of each word with the other: ψυχή τε καὶ αἰών. The two words say the same: each can be used in place of the other. And again, in his work on the heavens, *De Cælo*, Aristotle remarks that the immortality and divinity of the whole heaven is disclosed through the word αἰών. This word therefore says, in a very particular way, "the all," not only of all things, but at the same time, the "all" of time. The origin of this word, Aristotle argues, is ἀεὶ εἶναι, ever-being (the span allotted to the deathless gods), and he adds that it was a "divinely inspired" name given by "our predecessors" because originally it meant the surrounding time (περιέχον χρόνον), literally the encapsulation or containment a being has within its time as a whole, which is each living thing's portion or allotted time.[20] Thus, Aristotle concludes, "according to the same thought the 'all' of the heavens and all time and the unlimited final containment (περιέχον) is αἰών, taking the name ἀεὶ εἶναι (being ever) without death, and as if divine."[21] Aristotle calls the whole of the span of a living being, the duration of its life-force, ζωή, the αἰών, the entire allotted span, of the life it has. He says this is because it is in this manner that its surrounding time is analogous to the eternal being of the heavens. *This* "whole," within the "all" or time and the "whole" of place, is the finality and totality of the soul.

How does this connect to speaking and thinking, which has been our concern so far? In the *Nicomachean Ethics*, Aristotle speaks not of the ζῷον λόγον ἔχον, the living being that is possessed of language and speaking, but, using the verb ἔχειν, to possess, to have, rather of how it is a commonly held doctrine that the soul is possessed of speaking. The soul, and nothing else, is that which is possessed of language. This means that the soul, the inner unity of the human being, is brought to light and *is*, through speaking, through what it can say, and how it says it (and in all the manners it has of speaking).

How are we to understand what it means to "be possessed of language"? The verb ἔχειν in Greek says more than mere "having" in our modern English sense. It names possession in both the objective and subjective senses: language pertains to humanity, humanity has speaking. So we ask again, in what way does language possess humanity or is language in humanity's possession? The "purposive" explanation of the origin of language says: "Language is for saying. Language is at our disposal and for our use. With language we say some*thing*." This seems to be in accord with a statement that Plato puts in the mouth of Socrates in the dialogue the *Ion*, when Plato has Socrates say: "I, indeed, pronounce from nothing other than that which truly lies before me."[22] To pronounce, for Socrates, is to speak from out of what is most clearly present. Taken in a philosophical sense, this kind of speech "tells it as it is," and plainly, speaking of what is most present. This is consonant with the claim Plato makes in Socrates's name in the *Phaedrus*, when Socrates says that, contrary to all (poetic) myth, a word "always indicates one and the same thing."[23] Socrates is in command of his language (he "has" it at his disposal) for the sake of the truth of what is present. This is speech as science, the specific, singular, knowledge of what *is*. This is the word in its univocal sense that the philosophers intend when they say "for the purposes of this argument, I will take the word *x* to mean *y*" (irrespective of whether the word can also, and has at times, been said to mean *z*, and *a*, *b*, *c* . . .).

Aristotle several times discusses what it means to be "possessed of" speaking in preeminent places in his writing. In the place in the *Nicomachean Ethics* where Aristotle speaks of the commonly held doctrine that soul pertains to language, he explains this in a very particular sense. He reports that the doctrine that the soul is possessed of speaking (λόγον ἔχον) is to be understood because the soul is first possessed of ἄλογον.[24] What does this word ἄλογον mean? The word begins with what we call an alpha-privative: the letter α- indicates that what we are trying to name is deprived of, removed from, without, what follows. In English we express this with the prepositions "un-," "dis-." Something that is discontinuous is the breaking, or privation, of the continuous: it is not-continuous. But "the discontinuous" at the same time reminds us that we were looking for something continuous when we found out that what we were looking at turned out, in fact, to be *dis*continuous. The α-privative puts something in front of us to show that it is really missing.

Thus what is ἄλογον is therefore outside-λόγος, that is to say it is a privation that is nevertheless oriented on what it is the privation of. Even the ἄλογον brings the presence of λόγος to the fore, by indicating that, and in what way, it is absent, and draws our attention to it by at the same time noting where and in what manner it is absent. To take up our earlier example, we use the word "discontinuous" where we want at the same time to indicate that continuity might otherwise have been expected or found. Otherwise we might have spoken of the "periodic," or "intermittent."

Very often, especially in English translations of Aristotle, this Greek word ἄλογον is translated as "irrational." Is this a good translation? Since the movement of Romanticism in the nineteenth century, since the place accorded "feelings" and the subconscious in the life of the personal self, since the scientific analysis of the "body" as the inquiry into the animality of the *animal rationale*, since Nietzsche, since the entire nineteenth-century taking in hand of the human being as a bundle of drives, passions, of biologically- and evolution-derived functions, of psychic states and presenting the self as an essentially electro-chemical machine (whose own history and emergence is attributed to wild conjectures about availability of food-types, mates, and the drive to preserve, or moderate, the growth of the species through reproduction), the irrational has functioned as the name of the animality of humanity that the rational seeks to bring under the dominion of its cool and ordered system, or (in the reversal that we named earlier), the χάος, the primordial state of being (that which is always present as the surrounding and abyssal) that reason wills to master.[25] The irrational stands in for a *rational* deference to our animal-being. Is this what Aristotle, indeed what Plato, mean by the irrational as ἄλογον?

The word ἄλογον does have a range of meanings, including "the irrational."[26] How are we to understand this word as it occurs as Aristotle uses it here, "without-λόγος"? What is said at this point in the *Nicomachean Ethics* is largely unable to help us, except that, whatever else these two are, ἄλογον and λόγος, they are not to be understood to be parts or aspects of the (workings of the) body. They are not, in other words, themselves faculties, like hearing, smelling, or touching. Rather they tell us how some faculty or faculties of the body function. Those functions that are concerned with ἄλογον and λόγος. We assume in each case these are concerned above all with the ear and the tongue: whatever acquires and utters λόγος.

There is another text that some attribute to Aristotle (others not)[27] but whom for the sake of what I want to say I am going to assume is in fact Aristotle himself. for even if it is not Aristotle who speaks, or it is some text of Aristotle's heavily altered by another hand, nevertheless, this text speaks from out of the same province of understanding, the same understanding of being, from which Aristotle speaks. The author of this text connects being possessed of language, λόγον ἔχον, to the parts of the soul, a division he traces back to Plato (as having been ὀρθός, "correct" in the matter in question).[28] The text reports that Plato divided the soul into two parts: τε τὸ λόγον ἔχον καὶ εἰς τὸ ἄλογον.[29] This is ordinarily translated as "a rational and an irrational part," [30] translating ἄλογον conventionally. We should also not overlook the reappearance of the τε καὶ construction here: the two parts belong together; fundamentally, they share something, and their connection and belonging together is stressed.

The question is that of the scope of possession of language: *How is speaking possessing?* As speaking itself, λόγος, or in its counter, ἄλογον, the word that Aristotle had put first in his discussion of these two terms in the *Nicomachean Ethics*, thus suggesting that it is the governing word, the word that stretches over and yields the *subsequent* meaning of what follows it, λόγος (even as here the τε καὶ suggests they are commensurate, or of equal and interchangeable value). In what way are these two contraries—as, perhaps, we might say in modern parlance, that the irrational is the proper contrary of the rational? Plato's Socrates seems already to have decided how, in speaking as denoting: speaking plainly, which is always a reasonable way to speak. In this, Socrates stands entirely with the "purposive" function of language as a "technology" for "information": language "denotes" through one who says. Socrates's statement in the *Ion* comes after a long discussion between Socrates and Ion in which Socrates taunts Ion that whereas he (Socrates) speaks merely from what is true and present, these poets and rhapsodes who claim to be speaking wisely (σοφός) are in doing so in obfuscations.

In the text I have referred to, Aristotle gives examples of what falls within the province of the two parts of the soul, the part which is λόγος and that part which is ἄλογον.[31] To the first, he says, belong judgment, acuity, wisdom, capacity for learning, recall. All of these "spring forth" naturally, they themselves arise spontaneously (ἐγγίνεται), in the soul.

These are compared with the "excellences" (the ἀρεταί, we sometimes say "virtues") of temperance, uprightness, and literally "manliness," but we could more inclusively say "poise" or "courage." All of these are concerned with ἦθος, what I earlier called the abode of humanity.[32] Aristotle says of this second list two things: first, they are things "having been said" (λεγόμεναι, λεγόμεθα), which means things already understood and established elsewhere—and so not spontaneously "here," in the moment and not arising spontaneously in the particular soul. Second, and, in order to come to fruition, these things require and deserve praise (the verb is ἐπαινέω) in order to be accomplished. The things that need and deserve praise are those that are brought to appearance and maintained through a particular kind of speaking: speaking-up, the highest speaking. All of these "excellences," virtues, are acquired through encouragement, cajoling, a bringing of the one addressed up to a higher life.

This encouragement and exhortation occur through an actual life in the polity, a being-together of one another.[33] We could not achieve these things for ourselves, on our own, except with the greatest difficulty (if at all). We need to be helped in these excellences of character, from being among others, if we are to attain them. Perhaps others must see in us possibilities that we do not easily or quickly perceive for ourselves. Rarely, for instance, can we speak in fulsome praise of our own quiet modesty, or proudly tell how humble we really are. We may be possessed of modesty and humility, but in possessing them, we may not claim them with our own tongue.

The word ἄλογον in connection with the having and possession of speaking, that part of the soul which Plato had noted is most disposed to waywardness, most at risk of "going off the rails," is surely not that part which is to be described as irrational (in what possible sense are these highest virtues "irrational"?). Rather, we should say, these things are concerned not with the speaking that comes spontaneously from us, but with the contrary to which speaking is most akin, namely with our being spoken-to: addressed. And so we can see, at last, they are concerned not with speaking but with hearing. This is hearing as attentive *listening*, "attending to": an active, careful, listening—"listening out for," "being attuned to."[34] Any fool can have the innate capacity of being quick-witted (one of the virtues Aristotle assigns to λόγος): by contrast, temperance and courage, the virtues that are ἄλογον, are not mere aptitudes or innate capacities, but have to be formed and shaped with assistance from others and through long experience. They come about from our knocking-around a bit and having the corners knocked off ourselves. They are difficult to accomplish in any particular soul, and so their meaning cannot simply be taught or told, but must be listened out for, attended to, and discovered; proved through experience and nurtured as much from rebuke and cajoling as through praise and encouragement. They are acquired as much from our peers as from our mentors. If we are humble we gain them as much from those over whom we stand as from those in charge of us.

Is this part of the soul, the part without-λόγος, at the same time the part that longs and desires and needs, the part most apt, therefore, to go astray, the part that is "appetitive"?[35] Are we, once again, addressing the animal nature of the human being? Is not the appetitive merely that aspect of human life that experiences drives, thirsts that it must slake, impulsions it must either give in to or bring under control? None of these things are what the rational soul tames in the animal nature, nor—nihilistically—what we make reasons of by giving purpose to the chaos of our drives and feelings. To be alive is to unify the soul that is the life we are, *in* its being. Λόγος is how the being *of* our present being is brought to accomplish itself as the presence that it is.

What does this say? It says that no-one rises higher by making language a tool for themselves but, on the contrary, that language has the possibility and capacity, in its unfolding through the polity, that is through certain kinds of being with others to bring about the higher and more excellent appearing and being of a man, a woman.

What kind of language is capable for this? Is it (mere) exhortation, cajoling, praise, and approbation, as I suggested earlier? Why does Socrates taunt Ion with his ironic reference to the "wisdom" of the poets and rhapsodes? To understand Socrates's complaint, we must look, not to the *Ion*, but to another of Plato's dialogues, the *Protagoras*. Here Socrates's complaint about the poets is that they "may not be interrogated concerning what it is they speak of." [36] For it is not that the poets are absent, or dead, that means that at *symposia*—educated, formal gatherings—the meanings of poets' words become a cause of dispute (because they do not speak plainly and do not speak of what is immediately present), but rather that the poets do not themselves own or originate the words they speak. The poet claims to speak words given by the gods.[37]

The words of the poet are a cause for dispute because the polity—in one of its more leisurely (but still quite structured, strongly conventional) forms, the symposium—is comprised of some who are ready to hear and others who are not. But the symposium is not the primary place where the poet's speaking should be attended to, but rather the polity as a whole, and in the most decisive moments of its life (its greatest triumphs, its most disastrous tragedies and losses): or rather, the πόλις is constituted, not by the most general, informative, disputatious, word that it hears, that word that can be bandied about and whose meaning can be picked over in relaxation and at leisure. The πόλις is constituted, *made* (brought to *be*), by the highest word it can ever hear and be attentive to, for which it requires one who can himself or herself *hear* and *attend to* with the greatest capacity, and speak *of*, what he or she hears with the noblest acuity: the "maker" of the word who has been heard: the poet. For this, the πόλις assembles at some more solemn moment: solemnity commemorated in a festival, but solemnity experienced at first hand at some dread moment—when facing war, or famine, plague or threat, or even at times of triumph, or after victories hard-won.

The poet is the ποιητής, the very maker and bringer-about of the highest word that makes the πόλις what it is. For this the poet must attend to the before and after, the origin and destiny, of the life of the πόλις, not just what is most immediately present, or plain for all to see (not from the mere presence from out of which Socrates pretends to speak). The poet speaks not merely of, and from, the excellences or "virtues," the *ēthica*, of man, but from humanity's ἦθος, abode, *entire*. The poet names, and is alone (as one who has come to be possessed of the highest kind of speaking) qualified to name, the whereof and the whereto of the polity. The whereof and the whereto is the whole of its life, the destiny of the polity, the way its beginning and its end are brought out before it *now*, at the moment when the poet must speak. The poet speaks in sight of the life, ψυχή, and the history and allotted span and destiny, αἰων, of the πόλις. The poet upholds this destiny, and so, by speaking, even when he or she must speak of tragedy to unloose the polity's fate, he, she, the worthy poet, preserves the polity in life. In Greek, to uphold and preserve in life is named by the verb σῳζεῖν, σώεσθαι: it is the proper activity and life of gods—above all, of Apollo and of Zeus.

The poet, as the one who knows and understands what has already been said and named (who, ἀλόγος, attended to, and was shaped by, the λόγος of the πόλις itself) is the one who hears and makes through speech the ἦθος, the abode, of humanity. The ἦθος here is not only the abode but the "before and the after," above all the "wherein." The wherein for humanity is that place where man properly stands out. Properly thought, and before this word became the name for something else, it was called δαίμων. The poet lets that which lets man himself stand out and take possession of his or her abode, also be seen. The word δαίμων is at the same time another name for a god. The poet attends to the words of a θεός or θεά: he or she speaks the holy, brings out into the open the word of a god or goddess. In this "bringing out," the god also comes to be seen and known for who he and she is. The poet is the bringing to presence of the divinity, as what or who is σωτήρ, one preserving, for the polity, the people, the nation, the tongue (language) as a whole.

Is, then, the birth of thinking better thought by understanding that one who prepares the ἦθος, the abode, for humanity? This is not humanity's own instrumental need, but that *one* and those *ones* who unfold what is needful to be said in χάρις, in the radiance of the holy, *for* men and women, and call forth an abode for humanity? Is this not the lifting up of the poet to speak and the uplifting of those attuned to hear what the poet has to say? Does the birth of thinking originate in the poet's capacity to be ready, actively, ἄλογον, to listen, listen out for, and hear, and attend to what appear as the words of a god, of a goddess? Is it in attending to this that I attain to my particularity, discover who I am, alone—yet as one among others, as a woman, a man, of the πόλις entire: Are we then ζῷον λόγον ἔχον because we are not, and cannot *be*, other than ζῷον πολιτικόν?

Notes

1. The first published place where he says this is in GA 2:34, but he repeats this claim multiple times and almost from the beginning of his writing (near ten years before *Sein und Zeit*), right across the volumes of his *Collected Works* or *Gesamtausgabe*.

2. All translations of works cited are my own, unless otherwise expressly noted to the contrary. I provide below details of English translations where they exist, but these are quoted or cited in the text only when expressly indicated.

3. *Pol.*, 1253 a 10. λόγον δὲ μόνον ἄνθρωπος ἔχει τῶν ζῴων.

4. Arist.*EN.*, 1193 a 1-6. τὰς μὲν εἶναι τοῦ ἤθους ἔφαμεν τὰς δὲ τῆς διανοίας. περὶ μὲν οὖν τῶν ἠθικῶν διεληλύθαμεν, περὶ δὲ τῶν λοιπῶν, περὶ ψυχῆς πρῶτον εἰπόντες, λέγωμεν οὕτως. πρότερον μὲν οὖν ἐλέχθη δύ' εἶναι μέρη τῆς ψυχῆς, τό τε λόγον ἔχον καὶ τὸ ἄλογον: νῦν δὲ περὶ τοῦ λόγον ἔχοντος τὸν αὐτὸν τρόπον διαιρετέον. καὶ ὑποκείσθω δύο τὰ λόγον ἔχοντα.

5. In fact I have never been able to find it existing antecedent to Heidegger himself, and I am not alone in trying. The phrase is unknown in the *Thesaurus*

Linguae Graecae, the vast electronic compendium of ancient texts hosted at the University of California, or to the *Digital Loeb* at Harvard University Press.

6. Compare GA 19: 343, "mit solchen zusammenzusein [ ], συνεῖναι" and GA2 "im 'nächsten' Miteinandersein können mehrere 'zusammen' 'jetzt' sagen." There are similar references to συνουσία in a number of works. None of the references to σύνειμι and συνεῖναι are in the recently published *Heidegger Concordance*, and only about half the references to συνουσία are there.

7. Ömer Aygün, *The Middle Included: Logos in Aristotle* (Evanston IL: Northwestern University Press, 2017), 15.

8. Kant says (in entire conformity with Descartes's argument *cogito, ergo sum*), "the: 'I think' must be able to accompany all my representations" ("Das: Ich Denke, muß alle meine Vorstellungen begleiten können") (AA3: B131). We could almost say that the relationship Kant envisages between *reor* and *ratio* is that the assembling of things into an order (*ratio*) is carried out by the only one capable of being so-assembling and does so through the I-think-by-assembling-into-an-order (*reor*).

9. GA 20: 15–16. "Nicht Wissenschaft von der Seele als einer Substanz, sondern von den seelischen Erscheinungen, von dem, was sich in der inneren Erfahrung gibt . . . [das] zur *Grundwissenschaft der Philosophie selbst* zu werden." (Heidegger's emphases)

10. GA 50: 42 f (=GA 6.2: 264–265). "Die ausgezeichnete Einheit des Herrschaftsgebildes aller Triebe, Dränge, Leidenschaften, die das Leben selbst 'wollen' [. . .] Die Vernunft ist nur eine »lebendige« als die leibende Vernunft."

11. We cannot avoid the connection here with Leibniz's "principle of sufficient reason," which says "nihil est sine ratione," "nothing is without a reason." See for an extended consideration of this, GA 10: 139–51, esp. 148–51. Much earlier Heidegger had indicated the formal connection made by Leibniz between "the principle of non-contradiction," a form of which we have just considered, and "the principle of sufficient reason" See GA 26: 135. Here Heidegger also notes the difficulties with the ambiguous and completely unclarified connection that is nevertheless asserted between the two "principles," although he says merely that a more radical formulation of metaphysics would be required than we find in Leibniz.

12. James R. Hurford, *The Origins of Grammar: Language in the Light of Evolution* (Oxford: Oxford University Press, 2012), x.

13. Cf. James R. Hurford, *The Origins of Meaning Language in the Light of Evolution* (Oxford: Oxford University Press, 2007), 252. For Hurford, language answers a need for cooperation in the history of evolution, or, as he argues (p. 241) "a crucial precursor to the appearance of [. . .] proto-linguistic abilities was not in itself a specifically linguistic change, but rather a shift in the normal social relationships between individuals in a group."

14. Hurford 2007: 255.
15. *Pol.*, 1253 a 20. τὸ γὰρ ὅλον πρότερον ἀναγκαῖον εἶναι τοῦ μέρους.
16. *EE.*, 1242 a 23; *Pol.*, 1253 a 3–8, 1278 b 19. The phrase was taken up by, among others, Galen (*De usu partium*, vol. 3, p. 5 and *passim*), Aspasius (*In Ethica Nicomachea commentaria*), and Plotinus (*Enneads*, 3, 4.2).
17. See GA 18: 50. The argument is further clarified in GA36/37: 158. Heidegger is explicit that what is not meant by ζῷον πολιτικόν is that the human being is a social being, but that the human being is the *rhetorical* being.
18. *Pol.*, 1253 a 19 f. καὶ πρότερον δὴ τῇ φύσει πόλις ἢ οἰκία καὶ ἕκαστος ἡμῶν ἐστίν.
19. Il: 16.453; Od: 9.523.
20. Cf. Cael: 279 a 5–279 b 5.
21. Cael: 279 a 25 f. κατὰ τὸν αὐτὸν δὲ λόγον καὶ τὸ τοῦ παντὸς οὐρανοῦ τέλος καὶ τὸ τὸν πάντα χρόνον καὶ τὴν ἀπειρίαν περιέχον τέλος αἰών ἐστιν, ἀπὸ τοῦ ἀεὶ εἶναι αἰληφὼς τὴν ἐπωνυμίαν, ἀθάνατος καὶ θεῖος.
22. Io: 532 d. ἐγὼ δὲ οὐδὲν ἄλλο ἢ τἀληθῆ λέγω.
23. Phdr: 275 c. ἕν τι σημαίνει μόνον ταὐτὸν ἀεί.
24. EE: 1102 a 29. οἷον τὸ μὲν ἄλογον αὐτῆς εἶναι, τὸ δὲ λόγον ἔχον.
25. The editors of Nietzsche's *Nachlaß* placed his discussion of chaos from a note of early 1888 at §842—"to become master over the chaos that one is, to compel one's chaos to take shape ("Über das Chaos, Herr werden, das man ist; sein Chaos zwingen, Form zu werden." Friedrich Nietzsche, *Nachlaß 1887–1889* (KSA13), 14[165]. See 'Der Wille zur Macht' (GOA.XVb, §842).
26. Heidegger has a discussion of ἄλογον in relation to λόγος in GA 18: 103–13.
27. The author of the *Magna Moralia* is often either thought to have been a pupil of Aristotle's, writing perhaps as late as around the second century BC, or perhaps related to the school and thought of Theophrastus, or possibly reproducing an account of what he had heard himself from Aristotle. Schleiermacher on the other hand, emphatically thought the text authentic: see Friedrich Schleiermacher, *Über die ethischen Werke des Aristoteles*, pp. 306–333. Two important summaries of the arguments for and against Aristotle's authorship exist: A. Mansion, *Autour des Éthiques attribuées à Aristote*; and E. J. Schacher, *Studien zu den Ethiken des Corpus Aristotelicum* in *Studien zur Geschichte und Kultur des Altertums* 22 (1940). More recently Franz Dirlmeier published a major defense of Aristotle's authorship of the *Magna Moralia* in *Aristoteles: Magna Moralia übersetzt und kommentiert*. Dirlmeier certainly thinks the text as we have it now has been redacted. See also John M. Cooper, 'The "Magna Moralia" and Aristotle,' but see also the reply to him by Christopher Rowe in the same journal two years later. The passage to which I make appeal in this paper without doubt reflects arguments and constructions that parallel others in Aristotle's texts. Compare EE: 1219 b 26–1220 a 13 and NE: 1103 a 6 f. Importantly, however, while the list of "irrational" virtues we will discuss

(σωφροσύνη; δικαιοσύνη; ἀνδρεία) can be found in several places in Aristotle, the list of those connected with λόγος: φρονήσις; ἀγχίνοια; σοφία; νήμη, can be found nowhere else in Aristotle's writing in this form. Indeed, in the *Nicomachean Ethics* the argument at the end of Book I and beginning of Book II seems to make a considerable alteration of the character of the parts of the soul—here *both* (NE: 1103 a 1-2) are said to be τὸ λόγον ἔχον, one (otherwise thought of as ἀλόγον) subordinated to the other. In this sense, however, the *Nicomachean Ethics* could be said to be contradicting an earlier argument that accepted Plato's division of the parts of the soul into τε τὸ λόγον ἔχον καὶ εἰς τὸ ἄλογον, which substantially strengthens the argument that the *Magna Moralia* is an earlier work whose basic outlook Aristotle later modifies. This might also account for how it is that Aristotle appears to become less interested in the place of hearing in thinking.

28. The other places Aristotle discusses this division are in the *Nicomachean Ethics* Book 1, (NE: 1102 a 5–1103 a 10), the *De Anima* (cf. De An: 432 a 25-30) and the *Rhetoric* (Rh: 1369 a 2). Plato discusses the parts of the soul—whether there are two or three, and how they are, in the *Republic*, Book 4, Chs. 15 and 16. He divides the soul into the λογιστικόν, the ἐπιθυμιστικόν, and the possibility of a third.

29. MM: 1182 a 8. Μετὰ ταῦτα δὲ Πλάτων διείλετο τὴν ψυχὴν εἴς τε τὸ λόγον ἔχον καὶ εἰς τὸ ἄλογον ὀρθῶς. The reference in Plato is to Book IV, Ch. XVI.

30. See G. Cyril Armstrong, "Magna Moralia" (Cambridge MA: Harvard University Press, 1989 [1933]), 451.

31. MM: 1185 b 1-12.

32. MM: 1185 b 8. ἄλλαι τοῦ ἤθους . . . εἶναι. In the *Nicomachean Ethics* and the *Eudemian Ethics* the various names of the 'irrational' powers of the soul at issue here are at times referred to as τάς ἠθικάς (cf. NE: 1103 a 7).

33. In the *Magna Moralia* the suggestion is that they are not taught but are gained through actual living: this is in contrast to the *Nicomachean Ethics* where the *ethica* are learned through instruction.

34. See for a parallel argument from Heidegger, but based on Aristotle's *Rhetoric*, GA 18: 111. "Sofern der Mensch sich etwas sagen läßt, ist er in einer neuer Hinsicht λόγον ἔχον: Er läßt sich etwas sagen, sofern er *hört*; er hört nicht in der Sinne, etwas zu lernen, sondern eine Direktive für das konkrete praktische Besorgen zu haben." This remark speaks directly *with* the argument of the *Magna Moralia*, which is concerned with what is ἀλόγον as praiseworthy in the course of actual life itself, what must be attained to in places and situations that are decisive, rather than in the *Nicomachean Ethics*, where the issue is directly (in the opening of Book II) what can be taught and instructed (NE: 1103 a 15, ἐκ διδασκαλίας ἔχει καὶ τὴν γένεσιν καὶ τὴν αὔξεσιν). Heidegger has a lengthy and important discussion of the term ἀλόγον (103–13).

35. Aristotle, arguing for a different dividing-up of the soul, connects it with ὄρεξις, which we find in Spinoza's and Descartes's *conatus*, what becomes the "thrustingly-appetitive." Cf. Rh: 1369 a 2.

36. Prot: 347e. οὓς οὔτε ἀνερέσθαι οἷον τ'ἐστὶν περὶ ὧν λέγοθσιν.

37. E. N. Tigerstedt calls attention to the extent to which this claim is a modification—even a caricature—of what the poets claimed for themselves. If, on occasion, the poet speaks *only* what the god requires, "far more frequent are expressions of a belief in a collaboration between the poet and his divine inspirator." The clear implication is that the poet brings about and lets unfold what the god has brought before the poet. E. N. Tigerstedt, "Furor Poeticus: Poetic Inspiration in Greek Literature before Democritus and Plato," *Journal of the History of Ideas* 31 (1970): 163–78, here 167.

13

Hiding in Plain Sight

Κίνησις at the Core of Heidegger's Work

Thomas Sheehan

On May 12, 1971, at his home in Freiburg/Zähringen, Heidegger told a young visitor that if he wanted to understand Heidegger, he first had to understand the two interrelated issues that had guided him to the heart of his thinking:

- Husserl's categorial intuition of being in *Logical Investigations*, vol. 2, VI/6 and

- Aristotle's doctrine of κίνησις in *Physics* III 1–3.

The first text, he indicated, led him to revise his earlier understanding of the second. That is to say, once he correctly understood it, phenomenology reshaped his reading of κίνησις in Aristotle.[1]

The basic presupposition informing all of Heidegger's work, both early and late, is his retrieval of the unsaid in Aristotle's κίνησις. Like any fundamental presupposition, this one operates in the background of everything he wrote; and yet if κίνησις is the hidden presupposition of Heidegger's work, it is a presupposition hiding in plain sight. It massively informs his early courses on Aristotle as well as the famous 1922 "Natorp Bericht," his first major text on Aristotle, where the term *Bewegung* is mentioned 52 times in a 51-page manuscript.² In a 1928 seminar he declared that we human beings are the *Urbewegung*, and that as such, we can understand the being of things only as a form of movement.³ Or in the language of SZ: insofar as we are existential κίνησις (*Zeitlichkeit*), we necessarily understand being as ontological κίνησις (*Zeit*). Indeed, the bond between *Dasein* as κίνησις and *Sein* as κίνησις is itself kinetic.⁴ That fundamental fact is the source of Heidegger's discussions of *Ereignis* throughout the last forty years of his career.

And yet this crucial issue is hardly mentioned in the scholarship. The result: The less the centrality of κίνησις in Heidegger's work is thematized, the harder his work is to understand, whether that be the formative pre-SZ courses or the volumes published in his own lifetime, or the thousands of notes that populate the later volumes of his *Gesamtausgabe*.

What follows is the prologue to a longer work-in-progress on Heidegger's retrieval of the unsaid in Aristotle's κίνησις. The complete text will analyze (1) Heidegger's phenomenological reinterpretation of κίνησις and (2) some consequences that has for rereading Heidegger's corpus. The work draws on the whole of the *Gesamtausgabe*, as well as on the student protocols from his seminars on Aristotle as found in GA 83 and GA 76, supplemented by the contemporary handwritten and typed notes of Helene Weiss, which are archived at Stanford University's Green Library.⁵ The present text introduces the work-in-progress. It focuses more narrowly on how Heidegger's approach to phenomenology laid the groundwork for his rereading of κίνησις.

What Heidegger said in 1951 about reading Nietzsche—"first study Aristotle for ten or fifteen years"⁶—applies as well to studying his own works Aristotle famously declared that if you do not understand κίνησις, you cannot understand φύσις (*Physics* III 1, 200b14f.), and Heidegger might gloss that with: And if you don't understand κίνησις, you'll never understand *Dasein*, much less *Sein* as φύσις.

As Heidegger intimated in 1971, his interpretation of κίνησις was radically reshaped by a *phenomenological* reading of Aristotle. But what does this mean? In the interests of answering that question this prologue unfolds as follows:

1. Phenomenological experience

2. Intentionality and the self

3. The phenomenological reduction

Hiding in Plain Sight | 363

4. *Sein* reinterpreted as *Anwesen* and κίνησις

- re *Sein* as presence
- re *Sein* as stability

5. Ἀλήθεια as κίνησις: three moments

- ἀλήθεια-1: The dynamic sphere of intelligibility that *Existenz* itself is
- ἀλήθεια-2: The understoodness of something
- ἀλήθεια-3: The *correct* understoodness of something

Phenomenology is often described in terms of the structure of intentionality and the method of description, and that is helpful as far as it goes. But those two elements need to be unpacked in order to sort out and highlight the fundamental features of phenomenological method that are specific to Heidegger.

Phenomenological Experience

Description, for Heidegger, is always the description of phenomenological experience. Such experiences are not detached, theoretical observations of the world; they are direct, first-person lived engagements with what is given in experience (*das Was*). More importantly, they are lived engagements with what is given *in terms of the way it is given* (*das Wie*). In the often misleading ontological terminology that Heidegger uses, phenomenological experiences are of beings (*das Seiende*) in their being (*das Sein*). Such an ontological formulation can be misleading if, as Heideggerians often do, one were to take "being/*Sein*" as referring to the intrinsic essence and/or existence of a thing apart from the person or persons relating to that thing. This would be "in-itself-ness" in the classical metaphysical form of Aristotle, for whom the thing one encounters is considered ἔξω ὂν καὶ χωριστόν, independent of and apart from thinking.[7]

Like any philosophical investigation, Aristotle's position on in-itself-ness is laden with presuppositions, both positive and negative, that are mostly tacit but need to be made explicit. The same goes for Heidegger's very different approach to the topic of in-itself-ness.

The most fundamental presupposition that Heidegger brings to any investigation (most fundamental because the denial of it only instantiates it)[8] is a phenomenological one: a human being is essentially τὸ ζῷον λόγον ἔχον, where λόγος primarily refers to "gathering into meaning" rather than to the consequences of that, namely the ability to interpret, speak, and reason.[9] As a necessary consequence, all human experience is a priori embedded in meaningfulness (*Bedeutsamkeit*). In phenomenology, this entails that the in-itself-ness of a thing—its being/*Sein*—is always understood in terms of direct, personal, first-order experience as

- the meaningful presence (ἡ παρουσία, *das Anwesen*)
- of the thing (τὸ παρόν, *das Anwesende*)
- to the person or persons relating to that thing (παρὰ τῷ ἀνθρώπῳ)
- within a meaning-giving context or "world of meaning"
- shaped by the purpose for which (the reason why) the person or persons is relating to the thing (τὸ τέλος, τὸ οὗ ἕνεκα).

For Heidegger, the "what" and the "how," i.e., the thing and its meaningful presence aka "being," are experienced *together* within a "phenomenological correlation" between what is experienced and the full experiencing of it. As Heidegger puts it, "The philosophizing person . . . belongs together with the matters being treated."[10] Unlike the metaphysics of Aristotle, phenomenology is concerned exclusively with intelligibility and meaning (*Sinn, Bedeutung*), which occur only with a person's *relation* to what is experienced. Thus the full structure of the phenomenological correlation consists of

- the *Gehaltsinn*, the sense/meaning of the *thing experienced* in the relation
- the *Vollzugsinn*, the sense/meaning of a *person's enactment* of the relation
- the *Bezugsinn*, the sense/meaning of the *relation itself*, i.e., the *Anwesen* itself aka "being."[11]

Thus Heidegger will argue that the "in-self-ness" of a hammer—what and how the hammer *is*, its "being"—is not baked into the tool as its metaphysical essence-and-existence. Instead, it consists in how and as what that tool is experienced by

- the person using it (e.g., a carpenter)
- for a purpose (to build a bookcase)
- within a meaning-giving framework that orders things to that purpose.

If the carpenter were to use that same hammer to hold down her blueprints so that they don't blow away in the wind, the in-itself-ness of the tool would thereby change from "hammer" to "ersatz paperweight."[12]

For Heidegger, the object of lived experience is not raw sense data (e.g., a range of decibels) as a first stage in then construing something as intelligible ("Oh, that must be a motorcycle"). Quite the contrary, even in its perceptual moments, experience is entirely suffused with λόγος, right down to one's senses: we hear those sounds *as a motorcycle*. The object of experience, *as* experienced, is meaningful from the start.

What is more, we experience objects not as separate, individual things but rather as related to yet other things

- within a meaningful context (*Welt*)
- that is unified by a certain regard (*Woraufhin*)
- based on a provisional "reason why" (*Worumwillen*).

In turn, that "reason why" is traceable back to the enactment (*Vollzug*) of the experience in its relation (*Bezug*) to what is experienced (*Gehalt*). Hence, as above, phenomenological experience is structured in terms of *Vollzugsinn, Bezugsinn,* and *Gehaltsinn*. And finally, phenomenological experience is neither presuppositionless nor blind to its presuppositions. For Heidegger, those presuppositions are always subject to deconstruction (*Abbau*), so that, once they are analyzed and seen for what they are, one can accept, reject, or revise them.

As contrasted with Husserl's *reflective* phenomenology, Heidegger calls his own approach *hermeneutic* phenomenology.[13] What is the difference?

And more specifically, what does Heidegger mean by "*Hermeneutik*"? (The word "interpretation," without qualification, is wholly inadequate for translating what Heidegger means by that term.)

To begin with, Heidegger and Husserl both agree that phenomenology

- is a fresh and radical new start in philosophy, free from any inherited content-related starting points or directions;[14]
- is strictly focused on lived experience as immediately given and as intentional;[15]
- reads its information directly off "the things themselves";[16]
- requires a decisive modification of one's absorption in the *intentum* of intentional acts, generally speaking via a "phenomenological reduction";[17]
- examines the structure of intentionality rather than some supposed "inner self";[18] and thus
- is always a matter of correlation research.[19]

Heidegger's first and decisive step away from Husserl's reflective approach was to insist that freedom from inherited directions and standpoints entails avoiding a theoretical-objectifying approach to lived experience and beginning instead with everyday practical lived experience. This has major consequences for how Heidegger carries out a phenomenological reduction. Husserl's reduction steps back from lived experience and takes a stance "outside" of (distinct from) the experience in order to objectify and theoretically reflect on it, thereby, as Heidegger argues, sucking the life out of lived experience.[20] By contrast, Heidegger's approach (1) begins with and remains within the practical experience *not* of observing things but of *dealing* with them; (2) follows out the intrinsic directionality that an act of purpose-oriented intentionality takes, (3) while *spelling out* the experience from within, as the experience unfolds its movement.

In both Husserl and Heidegger, the phenomenological reduction is a distinct, second-order act; but for Heidegger it is not a theoretical-observational act that denatures lived experience. Rather, it is one that remains engaged with first-order intentional experience as the moments of that experience begin to unfold

- from the ever-operative field of intelligibility that is *Existenz* itself
- through the projection of a practical purpose
- with its attendant goal-oriented context that "discloses" something *as for* that purpose
- to the emergence of declarative sentences that might make correct sense of the thing in question.

For Heidegger, the most basic meaning of "hermeneutic" is not merely "interpreting" in the sense of explaining something. It is a matter of *auslegen*, that is, *spelling out the meaning of something from within.*[21] That entails not reading a meaning into the thing from an external, observational-theoretical position but, on the contrary, following its intrinsic movement as it unfolds of itself before one's eyes (*ex-plicare, ex-foliare*) so that the thing itself provides an insight into what it is (cf. *kundgeben*).[22] Whatever we encounter is never presuppositionless but always already meaningful simply by our having encountered it.[23] In any such encounter we already *have* the thing within a world of meaning, already *see* it as directed to a purpose, and thus already *have a sense* of what it means (= *Vorhabe, Vorsicht,* and *Vorgriff*).

In short, phenomenological description is focused on one's direct first-person meaning-fraught relation to persons and things that, as experienced, are encountered *as meaningful* in terms of a "how" (the *Vollzug* and its *Bezug zu*) and a "what" (the *Gehalt* to which the experiencing is directed). The term "first-person" applies first of all to the singular "I" *in propria persona*. But in order to be confirmed as adequate, such experiences have to be submitted to the give-and-take of a συμφιλοσοφεῖν with others, the plural "we."[24]

INTENTIONALITY

Intentionality is often described in terms of "consciousness is consciousness *of* something." That, too, is true as far as it goes, but it can lend itself to the mistaken notion of an inside-versus-outside, the self as an interior subject reaching out to exterior objects, which it then drags back into the closet of consciousness. But for Heidegger there is no self "inside" as over against the world "outside." Rather, the self is always already "outside," and whatever interiority it possesses lies wholly within its exteriority.[25] This is because of what we saw above: everything in human experience, including the very act of experiencing, is already *in-der-Welt*, embedded in meaningfulness: we always already live in a world of meaningful persons and things.[26] There is no *hors texte*, no "outside of meaning," except in death.

Modern philosophy begins with the insight that we cannot know a *thing* without *knowing* that thing. This led to the *Wende zum Subjekt*, the "turn to the subject" that, already implicitly operative in elements of late Scholasticism, eventually charted an explicit path through Descartes to Kant and beyond.[27] Reflecting on the achievements of seventeenth- and eighteenth-century science, Kant saw that knowledge is active as well as passive, not just receptive but also spontaneous and projective, so much so that "we know a priori of things only what we have [already] put into them."[28] But for Heidegger, the a priori constitution of known objects is not the work of an "interior subject," whether psychological or transcendental.[29] All efforts to discover that subject through introspection come up empty—precisely because there's nobody at home. As the early Husserl put it, "I must frankly admit that I am entirely unable to find this 'I,' this primitive, necessary center of relations."[30]

Looking for the self "inside" always comes too late, insofar as the self has long since escaped such Plotinian-Augustinian-Cartesian interiority and can be found only "outside" in the world of meaning.[31] Heidegger speaks of such ontic-existentiel intentionality as "*Aussein auf etwas*" (as *ratio cognoscendi*), whereas he locates its ontological-existential foundation in *Existenz* as transcendence (as *ratio essendi*).[32] Moreover, he claims that long before Brentano and Husserl had rediscovered the intentionality of consciousness, Aristotle had expressed his inchoate awareness of it in terms of the ψυχή as πὼς πάντα, as did Aquinas with the *anima* read as *ens quod natum est convenire cum omni ente*.[33] Neither of them, however, saw *Existenz*-qua-transcendence as undergirding intentionality.

The Phenomenological Reduction

Phenomenology is not primarily a "turn to the subject." In describing intentionality as "consciousness of something," the emphasis falls on neither "consciousness" (the subject) nor the "something" (the object), but squarely on the "of." Intentionality has to do primarily with the correlation or togetherness (*das Zusammengehören*, τὸ αὐτό) between the *Wie* and the *Was*, between the enactment of experience and its content. Rather than a turn to the subject, phenomenology is a *return* to where we always already stand without noticing it, namely in and as the ever-operative correlation. For Heidegger as much as for Husserl, phenomenology is always correlation research, where the correlation is like a transparent medium, a μεταξύ that operates in intellection analogous to the way Aristotle's τὸ διαφανές operates in sensation.[34] In the natural attitude, we look *through* the medium—i.e., ignore it—as we focus entirely on objects.

The phenomenological reduction leads our gaze back (cf. *re-ducere, zurück-führen*) *from* our absorption in objects *to* that transparent medium, the "in-between" (*das Inzwischen*), where experiencing is ineluctably bound to the experienced. Although Husserl had failed to find the pure ego when writing *Logical Investigations*, he eventually discovered it by working "backwards" from the phenomenological correlation to the transcendental subject as constituting the object as known. Heidegger, however, moved in the opposite direction, that is, *ahead* not backward, insofar as his hermeneutical approach remained with the forward directionality of practical meaningfulness. He agreed with Husserl that the reduction refocuses our attention on where we always already stand without noticing it. But that meant leading the gaze not backward to an observing-theorizing self as sub-ject but *forward* to the living-practical self as e-ject, thrown ahead (*geworfen-entworfen*), as possibility into possibilities (see fig. 13.1).[35]

Heidegger wrote to Husserl in 1927, "Transcendental constitution is a central possibility [not of the transcendental ego but] of the *Existenz* of the factical self,"[36] where *Existenz* refers to the ontological condition of "being made to stand out ahead" (cf. ἐξίστημι: to be projected). Hereinafter I will translate *Existenz*—the being of *Dasein*—as "ex-sistence," hyphenated and misspelled in order to bring out this etymology.[37]

Figure 13.1.

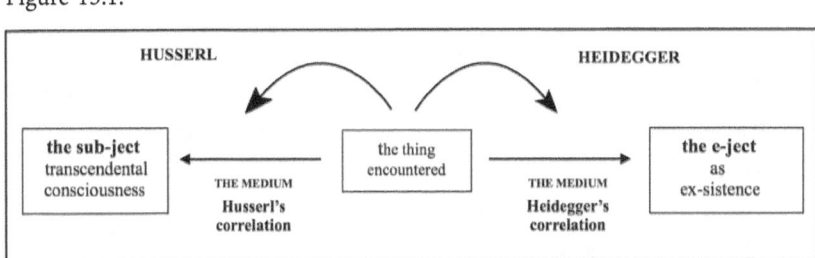

As Aron Gurwitsch famously declared, after the phenomenological reduction "there are no other philosophical problems except those of sense, meaning, and signification."[38] Through the reduction we come to see things explicitly as meaningful (*bedeutsam*) where "meaningful" means *mich-bezogen*, intelligibly related to me.[39] And for Heidegger, that meaningfulness comes from one's aheadness in purposes, one's kinetic stretching *forward*. The medium to which the phenomenological reduction directs our gaze is the fundamental issue of all Heidegger's work: *das Urphänomen, die Ur-Sache, die Sache selbst*.[40] Throughout his career he gave it various titles, each of them with a distinct nuance but all of them ultimately ex aequo (see Table 13.1).

But to speak of *die Sache selbst* as a "transparent medium" runs the twofold risk of considering it (1) as *separate* from us, and (2) as *static*, an inert something that we peer through in order to see things as meaningful. Even Heidegger's description of it as an open space that we traverse[41] can contribute to that misunderstanding by bringing together in one metaphor those two misleading tropes.[42] Far from being static (as terms like "the clearing" and "the open" might suggest), this medium is utterly dynamic and kinetic—precisely because it is *our own ex-sistence* as the Ur-κίνησις, the existential movement that issues in the meaningful presence of things. Ex-sistence is intrinsically in movement, always becoming, ever *unterwegs*. Never static, we are always "stretching out ahead" as the ability to make sense of things in terms of the possibilities we are thrown into.[43] The dynamic medium of sense is ourselves, living "In the middle, not only in the middle of the way / But all the way. . . ."[44]

Table 13.1.

die Mitte	die Lichtung	das Offene
das Seyn	die Welt	das Inzwischen
das Da	die Gegend	die Gegnet
das Ereignis	der Zeit-Raum	der Entwurfbereich
der Ort	der Wesensort	das Freie
die Wahrheit	das Sein der Wahrheit	die Wahrheit des Seins
das Wesen der Wahrheit	die Wahrheit des Wesens	das Wesen des Seins
das Geheimnis	das Heilige	der letzte Gott
Ἀλήθεια	Φύσις	τόπος (etc.)

Sein as Anwesen and κίνησις

Heidegger argues that in classical Greek ontology a fundamental characteristic of "being" is constant presence, *Beständigkeit in Anwesenheit*.[45] However, Heidegger's phenomenological reduction institutes a revolution in that notion and therefore in the foundations of Greek metaphysics. When he declared that "only as phenomenology is ontology possible,"[46] he was implicitly announcing the deconstruction of the ontology of constant presence.

First, "presence." After the reduction, what the tradition had previously spoken of as οὐσία, εἶναι, *esse*, *Sein*, etc. radically shifts location, it is no longer found "within" a thing, as its in-itself-ness in the sense of what and how that thing is apart from human experience (see note 3 below). How could we know such in-itself-ness? We have no experience of things without *experiencing* them; and things are given to us as intelligible only in correlation with experience. Thus the phenomenological revolution begins by reorienting our attention to the *givenness* of things, to *how*-they-are-given-to-us as our only access to *what*-is-given-to-us. The shift is from the in-se-ity of traditional metaphysics to the pro-me-ity of first-person experience, from οὐσία as "is-in-itself" to παρ-ουσία as "is-as-given-to-me": παρὰ τῷ ἀνθρώπῳ (see note 6 below).

"Being" as a thing's *inseitas* disappears from Heidegger's later work. He uses the word *Sein*, as he says, "only as a provisional term. Consider that [in Greek thought] *Sein* was originally called 'presence' in the sense of a thing's staying-here-before-us-in-disclosedness."[47] That last phrase—*her-vor-währen in die Unverborgenheit*—is Heidegger's phenomenological reconstruction of the tradition's "being" in terms of the meaningful presence of something to someone. The German phrase expresses three things:

1. *the locus* of meaningful presence: the lived world of human concerns (*-vor-*);

2. *the relative stability* of that meaningfulness (*währen*); and

3. *the phenomeno-ontological movement* of a thing from not-understoodness to now-understoodness (*her-* . . . *in die Unverborgenheit*).

One of Heidegger's early insights was that Aristotle employs an implicit, proto-phenomenological approach to the question of being insofar as he tacitly understands οὐσία as παρουσία, the presence of things in correlation with λόγος. Heidegger highlights a phrase that Aristotle uses time and again: τὸ ὂν λεγόμενον, a thing insofar as it is taken up into meaning. We can take a look at *things* but not directly at being. The being of something does not come into view unless and until the thing is subsumed into intelligibility (λεγόμενον) and understood *as* this or that, that is, as *being* this or that.[48]

Before Plato and Aristotle took up the word οὐσία as a technical philosophical term, it already had the common, everyday sense of "that which is one's own, that which one possesses" (*die Habe*).[49] Heidegger writes:

> In Greek οὐσία means things—not just any things but things that in a certain way are *exemplary in their realness*,[50] namely the things that *belong* to you, your goods and possessions, house and home (what you own, your wealth), what is at your disposal. These things—goods and possessions—are able to stand at your disposal because they are *fixed, steadfastly within your reach*, at hand, present in your immediate environment. What makes them exemplary? Our goods and possessions are invariantly within our reach. Ever at our disposal, they are what lies close to us, they are right here, presented on a platter; they are *constantly present*.[51]

Basing themselves on that everyday sense of the word, Plato and Aristotle adopted οὐσία as a philosophical term, where it has the double sense of both a *thing* and its *thingness*—that is, a being and its beingness—which in fact are inseparable. Thus οὐσία can refer equally to either things *in* their being or the being *of* things (*das Seiende in die Seiendheit* or *die Seiendheit des Seienden*). But Heidegger goes a step further and reads οὐσία phenomenologically in terms of *intelligibility*/παρ-ουσία: things as intelligible, or the intelligibility of things. Presence/παρουσία/*Anwesen* is not a matter of mere possession (as in the text above) and least of all spatial presence. For Heidegger, it is first of all the *understandability* of things, which is the foundation of every other relation we may have with the thing, such as possessing it or being aware that it is spatially near or far. The first step in Heidegger's phenomenological revolution was to reread the ontology of Plato and Aristotle within the parameters of the phenomenological reduction.

Second, "constancy." In Heidegger's world, everything is a matter of movement: *Alles ist Weg*.[52] His *Gesamtausgabe* bears the motto "*Wege— nicht Werke*" in order to indicate that those 102 volumes are examples not of thoughts set in stone but of the *movement* of his thinking. The phenomenological reduction brackets the traditional notion of "being" as the out-there-now-real-ness of things in order to focus on the dynamic correlation in which the meaningful presence of things gets opened up to understanding. And for Heidegger that correlation is our own ex-sistence as movement, the Ur-κίνησις that is ever stretched ahead and constrained to understand the meaningful presence of things as itself kinetic. When reread as meaningfulness, presence is no longer a *constant, unchanging* presence. But it is a *stable* presence, that is, stable-for-a-while. It can be understood and understood correctly, even if that understanding holds only for now (*jeweilig*, currently) before being surpassed or proven wrong or forgotten. Meaningful presence as the intelligibility of a thing is both stable and kinetic.[53]

In brief, Heidegger's first step in the phenomenological revolution was to deconstruct the traditional notion of being as presence in order to reconstruct it as intelligibility. But the second step consisted in deconstructing being as static constancy and reconstructing it as ontological becoming, that is, κίνησις as the movement of ἀλήθεια. That movement is not a pure, unchanging presence but a pres-abs-ence, the ever-on-going movement of *Anwesung*: *becoming* intelligible. In a way that is analogous (but only analogous) to Nietzsche, Heidegger took the characteristics that Greek philosophy had reserved for *being* and stamped them on *becoming*.[54]

Heidegger deconstructs constant presence in order to reconstruct it in terms of ἀλήθεια as κίνησις. But what kind of movement is that?

Ἀλήθεια AS κίνησις: THREE MOMENTS

Heidegger distinguishes between ontic things-in-motion (*das Bewegte*) and the ontological movement (*Bewegtheit*) that accounts for their being in motion. Both I and my dog Fido notice that things move: we see them change their place, size, properties, and so on. But Fido cannot envision movement as the *being* of those things because, even though he is a very smart ζῷον, he lacks the prerequisite for noticing being: τὸ λόγον ἔχειν.

The first step in the phenomenological revolution, as we saw, consists in regarding everything—and above all the *being* of everything—exclusively within the phenomenological correlation, where things and the way they are present are opened up to understanding. The Greek term for "opened up to understanding" takes the form of a double negative: ἀ-λήθ-εια, "not-hidden-ness." As Heidegger understands it, ἀλήθεια names a thing's ontological movement into intelligibility at three distinct but interrelated levels, the first two of which are not at all a matter of "truth."

ἀλήθεια-1: **The dynamic sphere of intelligibility that *Existenz* itself is.** In the presence of ex-sistence as the kinetic sphere of intelligibility, everything becomes *able to be known*. That kinetic sphere whereby anything we encounter is moved from unknownness into intelligibility (i.e., into the ability to be known) is the first and most fundamental form of ontological κίνησις. It is ex-sistence itself, the sphere of what Heidegger calls *Anwesen für das Verstehen*, what Aquinas calls *convenientia ad intellectum* or *praesentia intelligibile*, and what I will call "presence to mind."[55] Anything that enters this sphere that we ourselves are—anything we encounter—is rendered knowable but is not yet actually known. Ἀλήθεια-1 is always and only the movement of ex-sistence that *allows things to become* intelligible.

For Aristotle, the degree of a thing's intelligibility is measured by the degree of that thing's reality.[56] The most real entity, God, is completely intelligible: it knows itself and is known *by* itself in the perfect self-coincidence of a divine νόησις νοήσεως.[57] In God there can be no kinetic sphere that renders the unknown knowable, because in God there is no κίνησις at all. For Heidegger, such perfect intelligibility is nowhere to be found in first-person phenomenological experience: ex-sistence is ineluctably kinetic, in fact it is the Ur-κίνησις.

ἀλήθεια-2: **The understoodness of something.** That which *can* be known becomes *actually* known only when a specific person encounters that thing intelligently in theoretical or practical activity. If ἀλήθεια-1 is the movement from unknownness to know*ability*, ἀλήθεια-2 is the movement from knowability to knownness. As Aristotle puts it, the thing moves from being know*able* but "hidden from understanding" to being "no longer hidden" (λανθάνειν → μὴ λανθάνειν), from not-being-actually-known to being-actually-known (ἀγνοουμένον → γιγνωσκόμενον).[58]

Note, however, that ἀλήθεια-2 as κίνησις is not of itself a movement into "truth" as *adaequatio rei et intellectus*, the correct understanding of something.[59] Instead, it is only a thing's movement into *understoodness*, into being taken *as* something or other (τὶ κατὰ τινὸς σημαίνειν)[60] even if the understanding is incorrect.

For example, say I tell a first-year philosophy student that Socrates was born in Thebes. If she is familiar with the references of "Socrates," "born in," and "Thebes," and if she believes what I have said, then in her case Socrates's birthplace has moved from "hiddenness" to "un-hiddenness," from not-previously-known to now-known. Insofar as her mind has come to rest in that understanding, she has performed an act of ἀληθεύειν,[61] and Socrates's birthplace, for its part, has moved into a state of ἀλήθεια-2—even though what the student understands is incorrect. Her understanding will become correct when she finds out that Socrates was born about a mile outside the walls of Athens.

In other words, ἀλήθεια-2 is the status of something that has moved from possible to actual understanding, even if the understanding is wrong. In any case, the unhiddenness of ἀλήθεια-2 is at best a chiaroscuro presence-to-mind that can always slip back into λήθη, perhaps to be brought back and made present to mind again, perhaps to be lost forever.

ἀλήθεια-3: The *correct* understoodness of something. The word "truth" in the sense of "what is actually the case"[62] applies only at this third moment, which presumes and builds on the other two. Given that I am ex-sistence (ἀλήθεια-1) and that I take something as having this or that meaning (ἀλήθεια-2), I may occasionally get it right (ἀλήθεια-3). For example, say I am walking through a forest at twilight and notice a deer up ahead. As I get a bit closer and see more clearly, I realize that, no, it's not a deer: it's actually a bush that only looked like a deer. And when I walk right up to the bush, I finds out that, no, it's not really a bush at all: it's actually a moss-covered boulder. There in the darkening forest, I have worked my way through two instances of ἀλήθεια-2 and ultimately have arrived at an ἀλήθεια-3.[63] And in fact, as with ἀλήθεια-2, the "unhiddenness" of ἀλήθεια-3 can likewise fall back into λήθη. In a few days' time, I may well forget the whole experience.

Unfortunately Heidegger was not always crystal clear on these distinctions. At the beginning of his career, and again in the middle, and yet again in a *retractatio* toward the end,[64] Heidegger made it quite clear that ἀλήθεια should never be translated as "truth" except when it refers to *adaequatio rei et intellectus* (ἀλήθεια-3). Nonetheless, Heidegger violated his own prescription throughout much of his career. Only in 1967 he did acknowledge, *en passant*, that "*Wahrheit*" had occasionally and unfortunately "slipped in" to his texts.[65]

Ultimately, ἀλήθεια-as-κίνησις is the only kind of movement that interests Heidegger the phenomenologist. To be sure, when he reads the *Physics* on κίνησις and φύσις, he interprets both of them ontologically, as forms of being—but so had Thomas Aquinas seven hundred years earlier, and brilliantly so, in his commentary on the *Physics*.[66] But what

Heidegger offers over and above that ontological reading of κίνησις is a *phenomenological retrieval* of what Aristotle had left unthematized, namely that κίνησις and φύσις, when read in correlation with λόγος, are forms of ἀλήθεια and therefore have to do first of all with intelligibility rather than just "nature."

⁓

In the seven years leading up to the writing of SZ, Heidegger worked out the fundamentals of his phenomenological approach and, from within that, his retrieval of the unsaid in Aristotle's κίνησις. He did it all in the name of clarifying the central topic of his thinking, which he boldly delineated in the 1922 Natorp Bericht: "The object of philosophical research is *human beings* investigated with regard to the character of their being"[67]—a focus that continued to orient all his work over the next fifty years.

Whatever twists and turns his philosophical trajectory took, and regardless of the reorientation (*Wendung*) that he carried out in the 1930s, Heidegger never took his eye off *Dasein* as the central topic of his thinking, including when he focused on *Ereignis* in the last four decades of his career. And operating at the very core of *Dasein* there was always the alethic-existential movement that Heidegger had retrieved from the Stagirite. Using the term *unterwegs* to name that existential movement, he wrote: "In one way or another we are forever propelled on-our-way. Standing still and waiting are merely limited phases in the trajectory of our being always on-our-way."[68] *Alles ist Weg*: For us, there is nothing prior to this ontological movement of our ex-sistence and nothing after.

The topics in the next installment of this work-in-progress deal with Heidegger's reading of Aristotelian κίνησις and the question of how that phenomenon bears on the issues of *Dasein* and *Ereignis*. Here we will merely allude to three elements of that discussion.

The first issue will be to sort out how Heidegger retrieved his own notion of phenomenological κίνησις from *Physics* III 1–3 and *Metaphysics* IX 1–5. Movement, as Aristotle himself remarks, is a difficult topic in philosophy, and Heidegger echoes the sentiment.[69] In any case, if Heidegger's fundamental presupposition has always been hiding in plain sight, the same goes for Aristotle's analysis of κίνησις. Consistent with the Greek cathexis on τὸ τέλειον (the complete or per-fect: *per-factum*), Aristotle's tacit, if counterintuitive, presupposition is that rest / standing-still (ἠρεμία, στάσις) lie at the very core of movement and thus are the key to understanding his central terms, ἐνέργεια and ἐντελέχεια.[70]

The second issue will be to show that Heidegger's retrieved sense of movement shaped his early reading of *Dasein* and especially the nodal topics of SZ: embeddedness in meaning (*In-der-Welt-sein*), concern for meaning (*Sorge*), temporality (*Zeitlichkeit*), and historicity (*Geschichtlichkeit*). To sort all that out, we will have to redefine and retranslate some of Heidegger's technical terms (mistranslations of which has thrown off the scholarship for decades) including *Gewesen, Zeitigung, Sein-zum-Tode,* and *Zurückkommen* in SZ § 65 (as contrasted with §18). We will also have to work out how Heidegger understands τὸ τί ἦν εἶναι and the difficult issue of "existential aspect" in *Metaphysics* IX 6 (e.g., ἑώρακε, πεφρόνηκε, νενόηκε, etc.).

The third issue will be to show how Heidegger's understanding of κίνησις shaped his later work on *Ereignis*. This will entail analyzing his 1928 seminar on *Physics* III 3 in light of his insight in 1930 that what we have called the transparent medium is intrinsically "hidden," that is, unknowable in the sense of Aristotle's τὴν αἰτίαν γιγνώσκειν (*Posterior Analytics* I 2, 71b10f.), even as it remains the ever-operative force in the Ur-movement that is *Dasein*.

Those three tasks make up the "what" of Heidegger's retrieval of κίνησις, whereas the present prolegomenon has been devoted only to the "how" of his phenomenological approach—a necessary prologue, however, insofar as "Only as phenomenology is ontology possible" (SZ 35.39 = 60.2).[71]

Notes

1. At the meeting, Heidegger expressed his hope for an English translation of his "Vom Wesen und Begriff der Φύσις. Aristoteles *Physik* β 1," GA 9: 239–301. The English translation appeared five years later: Heidegger, "On the Essence and Conception of Φύσις in Aristotle's *Physics* B, 1," trans. T. Sheehan, in *Continental Philosophy Review* [then *Man and World*] 9:3, 219–70, and with slight revisions a dozen years after that: Heidegger (1998). The German text is now found in GA 9: 239–301 = 183–230.

2. GA 62: 346 et seq. = 149 et seq.

3. GA 83: 256.23.

4. GA 83: 20.3.

5. I am grateful to Professor Tugendhat for inviting me to photocopy Helene Weiss's handwritten Nachschriften at Heidelberg University (January 1974), along with his own typewritten notes from Heidegger's later courses. Particularly helpful for this present project has been Weiss' Mitschrift of Heidegger's 1928 seminar on *Physics* III found in the Green Library Archive, "Weiss, Helene," Box 2, Folder 7.

6. GA 8: 78.9 = 73.32.

7. *Met.* XI 8: 1065a24. Cf. ἔξω [τῆς διανοίας]: "outside" [i.e., independent] of thinking: *Met.* VI 4: 1028a 2, taken with 1027b34–1028a1: See GA 6, 2: 380.2–13 = 16.17–26.

8. That is, via argument by retorsion (περιτροπὴ τοῦ λόγου). See Sextus Empiricus (1958–), II, 128.

9. On λόγος as gathering into meaning: GA 9: 279.1–7 = 213.10–15, Re τὸ λόγον ἔχον: *De An* III 9: 432a31, *NE* I 13: 1102b15 and 1103a2; V 15, 1138b9; VI 1, 1139a4; etc.

10. GA 9: 42.25f. = 36.25f.

11. GA 61: 53.

12. On "in-itself-ness" after the reduction see SZ 71.37f. = 101.27f: "Zuhandenheit ist die ontologisch-kategoriale Bestimmung von Seiendem, wie es 'an sich' ist" (italicized in the original) and ibid., 74.31–34 = 105.1–6: "Die Struktur des Seins von Zuhandenem als Zeug ist durch die Verweisungen bestimmt. Das eigentümliche und selbstverstandliche 'An-sich' der nächsten 'Dinge' begegnet in dem sie gebrauchenden ... Besorgen." also ibid., 75.23 et seq. = 106.5; 87.22–26 = 120.25–28; 106.34ff. = 141.15ff.; 118.3 = 154.2; etc.

13. For an extended treatment of the contrast, see Friedrich-Wilhelm von Herrmann, *Hermeneutik und Reflexion* (Frankfurt am Main: Klostermann, 2000) on which I rely for the following paragraphs.

14. SZ 27.26f = 50.2f. Husserl, *Ideen I* (Husserliana III), 46.11f.= 38.32.

15. Husserl, *Logische Untersuchungen* (Husserliana V, 352 et seq. = 533 et seq); cf. GA 24: 90.9 et seq.= 64.20 et seq.

16. SZ 27.21= 49.38 ("aus den 'Sachen selbst' "). Husserl, *Logische Untersuchungen. Zeiter Band* (Husserliana XIX/1), 10.13f. = 252.11or ppbk. ed., 168.17 ("Wir wollen auf die 'Sachen selbst' zurückgehen").

17. Husserl, *Phänomenologische Psychologie* (Husserliana IX), 243f. = 90ff. and 260f. = 113f.

18. GA 17: 318.2f. = 240.39f.: "Das Dasein spricht sich gewissermaßen *aus sich heraus—von sich weg*."

19. See Husserl, *Cartesianische Meditationen und Pariser Vorträge* (Husserliana I), 38.1 and 121.2 = *Paris Lectures*, 38.3 (mistranslated) and *Cartesian Meditations*, 88.21. Also *Krisis der europäischen Wissenschaften* (Husserliana VI) §§ 41 and 46 = *Crisis of European Sciences*, 151ff. and 159ff. Heidegger's reading of a phenomenon as "das Sichzeigende" ("what shows itself," SZ 28.30 = 51.6) implies a correlative dative to which the phenomenon appears.

20. For Heidegger's polemic on this cf. GA 56/57: § 17: ent-lebt, ent-deutet, ent-geschichtlicht, Infizierung, etc.

21. SZ 37.34 = 62.6.

22. Re "following out the movement": GA 56/57: 117.4–8 (gehen mit, leben in, mitgehen) = 99.3–6; cf. 66.19f. (gehen wir seinem Sinne nach und sehen darauf hin) = 56.2 (mistranslated). Re kundgeben: SZ 37.32 = 62.3.

23. SZ 151.23ff. = 192.35ff.; re "presuppositionless," op. cit. 150.31f. = 191.30.
24. Re "I": see GA 2: 56, n. "a": "je 'ich.'" Re συμφιλοσοφεῖν: *NE* IX 12, 1172a5.
25. On "draußen" and "Draußensein" see SZ pp. 62.13 = 89.17f.: immer schon "draußen"; 62.16f. = 89.21: Draußen-sein; also 162.22. = 89.27: "bleibt das erkennende Dasein *als Dasein draußen*." Cf. Aquinas, *Summa theologiae* I, 14, 1c: "cognoscens natum est habere formam etiam rei alterius"—and yet he adds an easily misunderstood "in": "nam species cogniti est in cognoscente."
26. SZ p. 87.19f. = 120.25: In-der-Welt-sein = Vertrautheit mit der Bedeutsamkeit.
27. Re the turn to the subject in late scholasticism see Johannes Metz, *Christliche Anthropozentrik. Über die Denkform des Thomas von Aquin* (Munich: Kösel, 1962).
28. *Critique of Pure Reason*, B xviii: ". . . daß wir nämlich von den Dingen nur das a priori erkennen, was wir selbst in sie legen."
29. Re constitution in Heidegger see GA 9: 244.25–28 = 187.22ff.: Ausmachen; in her Blick heben; das Gesichtete feststellen; and ibid., 264.2–22 = 202.11–27.
30. Husserl (1984), *Logische Untersuchungen*, II, V § 8, p. 374.1–3 = 549.35f: "Nun muß ich freilich gestehen, das ich dieses primative Ich als notwendiges Beziehungszentrum schlechterdings nicht zu finden vermag"—only later to find it: see ibid., p. 364 n. = 542n.: "Die sich in diesem Paragraphen [= § 4] schon aussprechende Opposition gegen die Lehre vom 'reinen' Ich billigt der Verf. wie aus den oben zitierten *Ideen* [I, § 57, § 80] ersichtlich ist, nicht mehr." Before Husserl replaced "the stream of consciousness" with his newly discovered transcendental subject, he held that the phenomenological correlation conjugated the enactment of an intentional act with its object.
31. Re Plotinus see *Enneads* V 1, 12.13–14: εἰς τὸ εἴσω ἐπιστρέφειν (= Henry/Schwyzer [H/S], II, 288). Ibid., VI 7, 34.12: ἰδοῦσα δὲ ἐν αὐτῇ (= H/S III, 256). Ibid., VI 8, 18.1: μηδὲν ἔξω ζήτει αὐτοῦ ἀλλ' εἴσω (= H/S III, 299). Ibid., VI 8, 18.3: εἴσω ἐν βάθει (= H/S III, 299: cf. Augustine, *Enarratio in Psalmum 41*, vers. 8, in *Patrologia Latina* 34: 473.13–47). Augustine, "Noli foras ire, in teipsum redi," *De vera religione* 39, 72, *Patrologia Latina* 34: 154.23.
32. Aussein: GA 62: 352.18 = 153.33. Ratio cognoscendi, ratio essendi: GA 24: 91.20ff. = 65.15f.; cf. Aquinas, *Scriptum super sententiis*, d. 14, q. 1, a. 1, s. 4. At GA 83: 21.24 Heidegger calls transcendence "das ursprünglichste Entgegenkommen gegenüber. . . ."
33. Respectively *De anima* III 8, 431b21 and *Quaestiones de veritate* I, 1, c, cited respectively at SZ 14.6 and 14.20–21 (= 34.23 and 34.37). At SZ 14.6 = 34.23 Heidegger mistakenly omitted the word πάντα. In his course *Übungen im Lesen*, on February 13, 1952, Heidegger noted: "Das πάντα ist in S.u.Z. aus Versehen herausgeblieben": cited from the Tugendhat Nachschrift, p. 45.8–9 (see note 2 above). This remark is omitted at GA 83: 654.8.
34. On τὸ διαφανές see *De anima* II 7, with μεταξύ at 418a20.

35. Cf. ἐπαγωγή: GA 9: 244.12-35 = 187.12-30 and 264.2-22 = 202.11 = 202.11-27.

36. "Die transzendentale Konstitution ist eine zentrale Möglichkeit der Existenz des faktischen Selbst." Heidegger (1962). p. 601f.

37. Like ἵστημι, ἐξίστημι is a *causative* verb with the meaning: *to be made to stand out ahead*, which Heidegger will interpret with his term Geworfenheit.

38. Aron Gurwitsch, "Gaston Berger's Le Cogito dans la Philosophie de Husserl," in *Philosophy and Phenomenological Research*, 7/4 (1947), 649-654, here 652.8-9, italicized in the original.

39. GA 62: 105.12f. = 84.3.

40. GA 14: 81.13f. = 65.30f.

41. GA 15: 380.6 = 68.43.

42. ". . . eine offene Weite zu durchgehen." Cf. GA 14: 81.35 = 66.19 and 84.3f. = 68.9; also GA 7: 19.12 = 18.32.

43. Re Erstreckung, see SZ: 371.32 = 423.15 and 375.2 = 427.9.

44. T. S. Eliot, "East Coker," in *The Complete Poems and Plays of T.S. Eliot*, ed. Valerie Eliot (London: Faber and Faber, 1969), 177-83 here 179. with a clear nod to Dante's "Nel mezzo del cammin di nostra vita."

45. GA 3: 240.19f. = 168.35f.

46. SZ 35.36f. = 60.2f.

47. GA 7: 234.13-17 = 78.21-24; cf. GA 83: 213.24f.; re "before us": ibid., 214.8: "Unverborgenheit wo, wie? D.h. wofür an? Für den Menschen."

48. Cf. τὶ κατὰ τινὸς λέγειν: *De interpretatione* 5, 17a21 and 10, 19b5.

49. GA 62: 374.1= 169.9; GA 3: 240.18 = 168.34. Cf. GA 40: 65.17-24 = 66.18-25.

50. I here translate "Sein" as "realness" in the sense of an entity's existence in what one takes to be "the nature of things." See GA 84, 1: 396.9-10 and Suarez *Disputationes metaphysicae* XXXI, I, 2: "esse aliquid in rerum natura" and "aliquid reale."

51. GA 31: 51.11-15 and 51.31-52.3 (= 36.8-11 and 36.21-25) See also GA 3: = 168.35f. and GA: 9, 260.7-18 = 199.19-29. Cf. John Locke, *Two Treatises of Government and a Letter Concerning Toleration* (ed. Ian Shapiro) (New Haven: Yale University Press, 2003, 111: "to have a property in something": chapter V § 25). According to *Theaetetus*, 144c7 Theaetetus's father, Euphronius, left behind "an exceedingly large fortune" (οὐσίαν μάλα πολλήν). At *Republic* VIII, 551b2-3, Plato has it that no one shall hold office whose property or possessions (οὐσία) do not reach the required amount. (Heidegger comments on this last text at GA 34: 326.1-4. = 231.6f.) Heidegger translates οὐσία at *Phaedrus* 240a2 as "das vorhandene Verfügbare": GA 83: 118.8. See "zur Verfügung anwesend" at GA 33: 179.25f. = 154.6.

52. GA 12: 187.23 = 92.22.

53. Plato has Socrates gloss Heraclitus frag. 91 as: δὶς ἐς τὸν αὐτὸν ποταμὸν οὐκ ἂν ἐμβαίης (*Cratylus* 402a9–10), whereas Aristotle says Cratylus went Heraclitus one better by holding that no one could step into the same river *once* (ᾤετο οὐδ' ἅπαξ: *Metaphysics* II 5, 1010a15). When it comes to the stable fluidity of intelligibility, it seems Heidegger would side with Heraclitus. Regarding "fluidity": see GA 9: 270.7 = 206.28, nunc fluens, read in terms of intelligibility.

54. Cf. "Dem Werden den Charakter des Seins *aufzuprägen*," Nietzsche (1980), VIII, 1, n. 617, p. 320.15. Cf. Heidegger on ἐνέργεια at GA 83: 13.8: "'*Werden*' ('Sein' 'ist' 'Werden')—Hegel!"

55. Heidegger: GA 83: 80.8; Aquinas, respectively *Quaestiones de veritate*, 1, 1, responsio, and *Scriptum super* sententiis, I, d. 3, q. 4, a, 5, c (id quod est praesens intelligibile). "Convenientia ad intellectum" refers to the transcendental status of verum in the medieval sense of "transcendental."

56. *Metaphysics* II 1, 993b30–31, ὥσθ' ἕκαστον ὡς ἔχει τοῦ εἶναι, οὕτω καὶ τῆς ἀληθείας. (See also GA 45: 122.4f. = 106.27f.: "Die Wahrheit und das Seiende in seiner Seiendheit sind dasselbe.") On the convertibility of being and knowability see further Aquinas, *Summa contra gentiles* I, 71, 16: "quantum habet de esse, tantum habet de cognoscibilitate" and *Summa theologiae* I–II, 3, 7 c.: "Eadem est dispositio rerum in esse sicut in veritate," On the use of "reality" see n. 50 above.

57. *Metaphysics* XII 9, 1074 b 34f.

58. *Physics* III, 1 200b13f. Cf. Aquinas, *Summa theologiae* I, 84, 3c.: "homo est quandoque cognoscens in potentia tantum . . . [et] de tali potentia in actum reductitur."

59. Thomas Aquinas, *Summa theologiae* I, 16, 1, c.

60. *Metaphysics* VIII 3, 1043b 30f.

61. Respectively: ὁ ἀκούσας ἠρέμησεν: *De interpretatione* 2, 16b21 and ἀληθεύει ἡ ψυχή: *NE* VI 3, 1139b15.

62. *Metaphysics* IV 7, 1011b26ff.

63. See GA 21: 187.15–23 = 158.13–20.

64. Beginning: SZ 219.33–37 = 262.26–29; middle: GA 45: 98.8–12 = 87.20–24; toward the end: GA 14: 86.16–20 = 70.2–5.

65. GA 15: 262.10 = 161.34: schob sich dazwischen.

66. Aquinas, *In octo libros Physicorum Aristotelis Expositio*, ed. F. M. Maggiòlo, Turin, Marietti, 1954.

67. GA 62: 348.29f. = 151.17ff.: "Der Gegenstand der philosophischen Forschung ist das menschliche Dasein als von ihr befragt aus seinen Seinscharakter." Emphasis added.

68. SZ 79.18f. = 110.12ff.

69. *Physics* III 2, 201b33–202a3 and GA 9: 283.23–27 = 216.25–28.

70. GA 9: 283f. = 216f.

71. SZ 35.39 = 60.2f.

Additional Bibliography

Heidegger, M. (1962), [Heidegger's letter to Husserl, October 22, 1927], in Husserl (1962; 1968²), (*Husserliana IX*), *Phänomenologische Psychologie, Vorlesungen Sommersemester 1925*. Nijhoff, Den Haag, pp. 600-602.

> E.T. by Thomas Sheehan in Edmund Husserl, *Psychological and Transcendental Phenomenology, and the Confrontation with Heidegger*, edited and translated by Thomas Sheehan and Richard E. Palmer, in the series "Edmund Husserl: Collected Works," Dordrecht, Boston, London: Kluwer Academic Publishers, 1997, 136f.

14

Animal and World in Heidegger and Aristotle

SARA BRILL

Near the end of his life, Jacques Derrida concluded a career-long engagement with Heidegger's thought with an unsettling observation: for all of his efforts to ground the difference between human and animal on something other than one of the traditional philosophical bases—consciousness, self-awareness, reason, language—on the question of the animal, Heidegger remains staunchly Cartesian.[1] Derrida's critique is devastating precisely because of its generosity. The care with which he traces Heidegger's development of the theme of animality renders especially sharp his conclusion that Heidegger never really puts the relationship between animal and human into radical question—never really takes up whether there is any abyss between animal and human, only where it lies—and that, in the end, the question of the animal eludes his grasp.[2] This is disquieting, not only because of Heidegger's own critique of Cartesianism but also because, as Matthew Calarco has demonstrated, Heidegger's notion of animality plays a fundamental role in his development of some of the most essential aspects of his thought; the animal's poverty in world is inextricably bound up with Heidegger's understanding of being-in-the-world, being-with-others, and the *Da-* of *Dasein*, concepts that would receive further development in Hannah Arendt's work on human action and political life, and, through his engagement with Arendt, have shaped Giorgio Agamben's construction of a *zōē* /*bios* distinction in Aristotle's thought and thus also the many streams of contemporary critical theory that employ Agamben's construction.³ To detect a subterranean Cartesianism here would be to strike at the heart of some of Heidegger's most foundational philosophical projects, a fact of which Derrida is quite aware; the challenge the animal supplies to ontological difference and the question of being is a challenge to, "the whole framework of Heideggerian discourse."⁴ To address this challenge properly would require a reorientation to life itself, or, as Derrida puts it, "a radical reinterpretation of what is living."⁵

I would like to suggest that we find a radical alternate interpretation of what is living in the very ancient Greek texts from which Heidegger drew inspiration. Heidegger's infamous claim that the animal is poor in world presents a concise formulation of an approach to animality developed, in part, through Heidegger's critical engagement with ancient Greek conceptions of life and living beings, particularly those of Aristotle.⁶ Scrutiny of this engagement, however, has yielded significant concern regarding the comprehensiveness and accuracy of Heidegger's approach to the Greek texts. Wolfgang Kullman and Guenter Bien both register their discontent with Heidegger's treatment of the concepts of *zōē* and *zōion*, particularly his alignment of 'living being' [*zōion*] with 'beast' [*thērion*].⁷ The overarching aims and motivation of Heidegger's development of what he describes in the 1929–1930 seminar (published in English translation as *The Fundamental Concepts of Metaphysics: World, Finitude Solitude*) as a comparative approach to animality—expressed in the three-part claim the stone is word-less, the animal is poor in world, the human is world-building—are not easily generalizable outside of the particular historical and intellectual context in which they arise. This is particularly so for Heidegger's concern to avoid the reductive materialism of biologism and what he sees as the reactive response of vitalism.

It is not as though these concerns are entirely unrecognizable in ancient Greek philosophy—both the staunch materialist and the new materialist find ancient Greek sources from which to draw—but neither are they identical, and we do ourselves no service if we ground conclusions on a comparison too hastily drawn.⁸ Heidegger's explicitly preliminary use of the formulation that animal is poor in world in order to arrive at a clearer understanding of world and to assert the primacy of metaphysics operates at some remove from the aims and motivations of a thinker like Aristotle, whose philosophic investigations require a zoology, that is, whose "first philosophy" would be unthinkable without the contribution to an understanding of substance that is provided by attention to living beings. And while Aristotle himself will feel compelled to defend his study of even the smallest of animals by affirming a Heraclitean sentiment that "here too there are gods" (PA 645a23), affirm it he does, in both letter and spirit.

And yet, in contemporary Aristotle studies, sustained exploration of the significance of Aristotle's zoological research on his larger philosophical projects is a relatively recent scholarly endeavor.[9] Heidegger's conservatism on the question of the animal is quite consistent with a dominant trend in nineteenth- and early twentieth-century Aristotle scholarship and translation practices that also tended to marginalize Aristotle's zoological works, insist on a radical division between human and animal, and elide *zōion* and *thērion*.[10] His influence on Arendt and Agamben further enshrines this nonquestioning of the animal in contemporary engagement with Aristotle's thought and in recent efforts at genealogical study of the conceptual apparatus of critical theory, for example, biopolitics, bare life, etc.[11]

As I will argue here, if we locate Aristotle's investigations of living beings within the intellectual context in which it arises, we encounter a quite different approach to animality; in marking a divergence between Heidegger's understanding of animality and that of Aristotle, then, we have the opportunity to revisit contemporary reception of Aristotle's political theory and reorient the central questions of these genealogical projects. To do so, I will focus on the conceptual framework Heidegger builds in the 1929–30 seminar around the claim that the animal is "taken" (*nehmen*) by its surroundings.[12] Because, for Heidegger, the animal is "held" in its environment, it can neither leave its sphere of life nor see itself as situated therein; it is thus neither without world nor able to attune itself to its "world." Its "impoverishment" lies with this deprivation. This model of animality is far removed from the alignment of vitality and vividness evident in a variety of strands of Greek literature and the association between embodiment, signification, and sociality that accompanies them; this sensibility proves decisive for Aristotle's zoological investigations. And while Aristotle will indeed mark the exceptional character of the human animal, the qualities and capacities that make it so are not treated as outside of human animality but rather as the most distinctive feature of it. In exercising the capacity for thought and contemplation, humans are not more than animals; rather, they are most vividly expressing the kind of animal they are. But in order to see this, we have to put aside the conception not only of animality but of life itself, which Heidegger develops. Consequently, I will begin by drawing in greater detail the conception of animality that emerges from the 1929–30 seminar and sketching some points of con- and divergence with Aristotle's thought (part 1). I will then locate Aristotle's research into living beings within a broader cultural and intellectual context that places the body of the animal at the center of theorizing *kosmos* and the human place within (part 2), before turning to dig deeper into Aristotle's contribution to these efforts (part 3).

Heidegger's Cartesianism?

Heidegger characterizes his comparative study of the animal's poverty in world as methodologically distinct from the historiographical exercise he offered in "On the Essence of Ground" and the phenomenological investigation of our everyday engagement with the world attempted in *Being and Time*. Heidegger is equally clear that the study he undertakes in the seminar is aimed at an understanding of world and not of the animal; animality may provide essential insight into world, but it is epiphenomenal to the ultimate object of inquiry here. We could not read this seminar, then, as Heidegger's final word on the animal. Nevertheless, the consistency between this exploration of animal poverty in world and comments Heidegger makes throughout his work is striking, as is, more importantly, the sidelining of the question of animality to a peripheral or instrumental place in his engagement with being as such.[13] Here, as elsewhere, Heidegger is relatively clear that human being-in-the-world, that is, *Dasein*, is the higher object of investigation. Not only is this being-in-the-world the aim of the inquiry, but also some nascent disclosure of world is what makes the venture to, as Heidegger puts it, "transpose" oneself into the animal possible: "The question as to whether we can transpose ourselves into the animal assumes without question that in relation to the animal something like a going-along-with, a going along with in its access to and in its dealings with its world is possible in the first place and does not represent an intrinsically nonsensical undertaking."[14]

And yet, while the assumption of the possibility of this going-along-with would seem to extend naturally to other humans as well, Heidegger takes the opportunity to mark an essential difference.[15] We cannot assume the possibility of going along with other humans because we are essentially and already so transposed: "For the being-there of Da-sein means being with others, precisely in the manner of Dasein, i.e., existing with others. The question concerning whether we human beings can transpose ourselves into other human beings does not ask anything, because it is not a possible question in the first place. It is a meaningless, indeed a nonsensical question because it is fundamentally redundant."[16] It is against this essential givenness to others that we can see the full import of the human capacity for detachment in the form of extreme boredom. In turn, it is against the disclosure of world made possible by the fundamental attunement of radical boredom, the possibility of the world appearing as such and the stance toward mortality that is necessary to this possibility, that the animal's living is measured. Against this vision of human being-in-the-world, the animal emerges not as a being for whom the world appears as such, but as taken by its location, driven by its instincts, captivated by the intimacy of its enmeshment in its environment. This dimension of animal life has bearing on the very character of its living, a point made especially clearly, Heidegger argues, in the case of the domestic animal: for while we do live with our pets in some sense, "this being-with is not an existing-with, because a dog does not exist, but merely lives [*nur lebt*]."[17]

Thus, for Heidegger, contemporary biological theories of the intimacy of animal and environment do not go far enough; it is not enough to say, as does the Dutch biologist Buytendijk (whom Heidegger cites directly), that that animal's intimacy with its environment is nearly as intense as the unity of its body itself: "Against this we must say that the way in which the animal is bound to its environment is not merely almost as intimate, or even as intimate, as the unity of the body but rather that the unity of the animal's body is grounded as a unified body precisely in the unity of captivation." This is because, Heidegger continues, "Captivation is the fundamental essence of the organism."[18]

Heidegger goes on to summarize "the characteristic structural moment of captivation" in six points that draw out the various senses of *nehmen* at work in this concept. First, captivation indicates an essential withholding of the possibility of beings appearing as beings. Lacking this possibility, the animal is bound within its environment in a manner that is not accessible to it, that is, "an animal can only behave [*sich . . . benehemen*] but can never apprehend [*vernehmen*] something as something."[19] Second, the being-taken of the animal extends not only to its relation to its environment but also to the motivating mode of engagement with the "things" in its environment that the animal encounters, that is, its instinctual engagement: "The captivation of such behaviour is at the same time a being taken of the instinctual activity in which the animal is open relation to other things."[20] Third, the animal is completely absorbed by the collection of its instinctual drives; it is driven. This drivenness does not foreclose the animal to its surroundings but rather charts the horizon within which the animal conducts its life: "Absorbed as it is into this driveness, the animal nevertheless always pursues its instinctual activity in being open to that for which it is open."[21] It is this "that for which it is open" that distinguishes what openness Heidegger allows to the animal to the open allowed Da-sein.[22]

Indeed, fourth, this openness is open to a distinct realm that defines what the animal affects and by which it is affected. It is that within which the animal conducts its life, that is, "With this openness for something else, which is involved in captivation, the animal has an intrinsic encircling ring within which it can be affected by whatever it is that in each case disinhibits its capability for . . . and occasions the redirecting of its instinctual drives."[23] Heidegger next specifies the character of this ring, emphasizing its flexibility—"It is not like a rigid armour plate fitted around the animal"—but also its permanence: "It is something with which the animal encircles itself as long as it lives."[24] While Heidegger explicitly rejects one martial image, his subsequent description of this encirclement conveys the sense of an arena, a bounded field of play; the vital activities performed within would then have the sense of a contest or, as Heidegger puts it, a struggle that is endemic to life: "This struggling [*Ringen*] with the encircling ring which circumscribes the totality of its instinctual activity is an essential character of life itself."[25] Finally, Heidegger draws a sixth point that spells out clearly what, in his mind, are the stakes of these claims about animal captivation: animal behavior is made possible by merit of captivation; no biological study of such behavior is possible without first taking this character of captivation into account, "for this fundamental conception of captivation is the prior basis upon which any concrete biological question can first come to rest."[26] Metaphysics thus takes precedence over biology, handing down to biological study its necessary and essential concepts and conceptual tools as well as the demarcation of what can and cannot fall under its purview.[27]

Here, this supremacy of metaphysics is bound up with the priority of the human. For even when Heidegger observes the preliminary, contingent, and limited character of the thesis that animal is poor in world, he does so in order to mark its service in distinguishing animal from human. Thus, while he will observe that, "Our thesis that the animal is poor in world is accordingly far from being a, let alone the, fundamental metaphysical principle of the essence of animality. At best it is a proposition that follows from the essential determination of animality, and moreover one which follows only if the animal is regarded in comparison with humanity,"[28] this comparison is precisely the point: "Through the apparently purely negative characterization of world in our examination of animal's not-having of world, our own proper essence has constantly emerged in contrast, even if not in an explicit interpretation."[29] Thus, even if Heidegger will assert the possibility that the contingency of the investigation may require him to "repudiate it altogether,"[30] he ends this section by concluding that because the real aim here, the understanding of world, has not yet been attained, then "we have no right now, or at least as yet no right to alter our thesis that the animal is poor in world or to level it down to the indifferent statement that the animal has no world, whereby not having is taken as a mere not-having rather than as a deprivation."[31] Heidegger continues, in a passage that also returns him to a deeper motivation of the larger inquiry, that is, to assert the priority of metaphysics over biology: "Rather, we must leave open the possibility that the proper and explicit metaphysical understanding of the essence of world compels us to understand the animal's not-having of world as a deprivation after all, and to discover poverty in the animal's specific manner of being as such. The fact that biology recognizes nothing of the sort is not counter-argument against metaphysics. That perhaps only poets occasionally speak in this way is an argument that dare not be allowed to cast metaphysics to the winds."[32]

A properly metaphysical orientation toward the animal, like that expressed in the animal's poverty in world, would locate that poverty in the animal's absorption in its environment, in the totalizing effect of its servitude to its capacities and their servitude to its survival. This servitude characterizes the very unity of the animal's body, its character as an organism; or, to put it in terms on which Heidegger insists emphatically, its organs are determined by its capacities and not the other way around. An animal cannot detach from its drives and absorption any more than it can detach from its head or heart; it *is* as driven, and so while it lives it does not exist and, moreover, its life is its being-driven and its end a cessation of drive.

Following Heidegger's terms, the animal cannot generate sufficient distance from its place in order to have an attunement toward that place. It may win cessation of one drive but this is always replaced by another, and it never leaves the totality of its drives so long as it lives. In a word, the animal cannot be bored. And because it cannot be bored, detached, it cannot have the experience of the world as such; world is withheld from the animal: actively, permanently, and essentially withheld. This is the crux of the difference between the animal's poverty in world and the stone's worldlessness for Heidegger. But it is also the crux of what Derrida would describe as his Cartesianism, his proximity to consciousness and self-awareness, even if it is discussed in terms of a being-toward-death. Heidegger's conclusions about the animal's inability to distance itself from its surroundings sufficiently to experience the world *as such* place his claims about the originality of his thinking perilously close to sitting on a distinction without a difference.

If we turn now to Aristotle, and to the divergence between the two thinkers, it is worth observing their continuity first: Aristotle too will assert that nonhuman animals do not have a reflective sense of themselves, other animals, or their environment, although for Aristotle their lack of self-awareness is a function of their lack of self-regard, that is, because they do not appear to themselves as good, they do not appear to themselves at all; they do not exercise forethought or deliberation; they cannot form a *polis* or be happy. Aristotle too will assert that humans are exceptional for their ability to contemplate and think, for their proximity to the divine, and exceptionally political for the depth of their depravity if they are without law and political community. But the contemplative distance that would allow them to behold, allow them *theoria*, allow things to appear to them as such—that makes them especially godlike—is treated by Aristotle not as an exception to their animality but rather as the most distinctive feature of it. This is possible because Aristotle's conception of animality includes among the field of living beings not only plants and animals but also the divine, in a clear attestation to life as deeply and profoundly choiceworthy, as an object of desire. This sense of *zōē* stands at far remove from the struggle for animal survival enacted within an animal's encircled place and from the 'mere' living of the domesticated animal.

And so we encounter, even granting the points of intersection we observed above, moments where Heidegger will also assert something that seems radically un-Aristotelian; that, for instance, "in a fundamental sense the animal does not have perception,"[33] or, I would add, that the human exceeds the category of living being. This is an assertion Derrida draws out with particular clarity in charting the fissures that arise from Heidegger's failure to pose the question of the animal in its own right.[34] As Derrida points out, an insistence that one cannot approach the essence of animality without getting a clearer sense for the character of living being is an insistence on the very character that human and animal would have in common. And so it is as an indication of Heidegger's commitment to the abyss between human and animal that we should read Heidegger's equally emphatic insistence that on a fundamental level the being that is Dasein is not essentially living, or at least, as Derrida puts it, that "the determination regarding life, reference to it, is not essential in order to determine Dasein."[35] He will have to insist on this even though, as Derrida so effectively shows, the apophantic "as," the ability to see the world and beings as such that marks the divide between human and animal for Heidegger, is tied to an apprehending of death, mortality, and finitude: "This is why death is also such an important demarcation line; it is starting from mortality and from the possibility of being dead that one can let things be such as they are, in my absence, in a way, and my presence is there only to reveal what the thing would be in my absence."[36] Derrida follows this line with the question that will mark for him the challenge to Heidegger's thinking about the animal, not a giving back to the animal what was taken, for example, logos or world, but rather whether this engagement with death and thus with being as such really does belong to the human: "So can the human do that, purely?"[37]

In the next two sections, I will engage this question by focusing on what we miss about ancient Greek thinking if we adopt Heidegger's approach to animality. For one, as we will see, Aristotle will indeed emphasize the degree of intimacy between *zōion* and *topos*, and in particular the deep relationship between animal embodiment and place, down to the level of morphology. But for Aristotle, animal intimacy with environment is not an impoverishment but a successful expression of nature; the animal is not trapped or limited by its integration in its place, but freed and given the potential to succeed in its living (*eubiotos*). Human striving, choice, action, and contemplation are also embedded in a place that nourishes them and without which they would founder. In short, successful integration with one's *topos* is a crowning achievement, not an impediment to thought. For Aristotle, human exceptionalism is not conceived on the basis of human isolation, but rather, quite the opposite, on its exceptionally political character. Such isolation would be necessary only if we accepted a broadly Cartesian understanding of self-awareness, of the cogito. But this is not an understanding we can attribute to Aristotle, for whom a sense of self requires the presence of others and is formulated within a very different sense of the relationship between *zōion* and *topos*, especially the *topos* that is the *polis*.

Similarly, animal impulse, *hormē*, is treated by Aristotle as a gift of nature to assure survival; in the human context it is aligned with the human capacity for deliberate choice, not against it.[38] Both are considered a natural response to necessity, not an aspect of it. If impulse and capacity are bound up with a kind of servitude, this is a function of a principle of mastery in nature by means of which human well-being is aligned with the *kosmos*. We could not say of *hormē* and *dunamis*, then, what Heidegger says of *trieb* and capacity, nor can we recognize a clear correlate to the sense that stimulus is an irritant to be dispensed with. For Aristotle, to have one's perceptual organs "stimulated" is to have their mode of being most fully expressed; if this counts as an excitation it is one by way of which we know ourselves to be alive and is deeply, profoundly choiceworthy.[39]

Ultimately, these points of divergence stem from a fundamental difference between *zōē* as Aristotle conceives it and a concept of *Leben* that Heidegger inherits from the very position he is working against, a reductive conception of life as mere life (recall the dog who *nur lebt*, merely lives).[40] Ironically, for all of his efforts to avoid a reductive materialism in approaching the purposiveness of animal action and unity of animal organism, Heidegger imports a reductive approach to the very concept central to the living of the living being—life itself. By contrast, only very rarely do we encounter reference to something like "mere" life in Aristotle and rarer still in the larger context of Greek philosophy and literature, where, as we shall see, the tendency to align the animal body with vividness, vibrance, and meaning (reflected at even the linguistic level) is so strong that it carries over even to the animal corpse.

The Animal Body as World-ordering

If we follow Plato, the living body is philosophically useful as, simultaneously, an object of interpretation and a model for critique. Socrates's famous observation in the *Phaedrus* that logos should be structured like a *zōion*, "with a body all its own," provides the terms not only for how to construct an argument but also for how to criticize one. For the "body" of the *logos*, like that of an animal, must have that necessary organization that establishes both unity and hierarchy of which the living body is taken to be a paradigm: a speech, like a body, "must be neither without head nor without legs; and it must have a middle and extremities that are fitting both to one another and to the whole work" (264c2–5).

So constructed, this body's order would be illuminated by its opening, and it is the image of cutting into the body that proves useful for demonstrating one essential aspect of Lysias's failure to properly praise love. For his speech neither gathers together its material properly, nor performs the second essential task well, which Socrates describes as being able "to cut up each kind according to its species along its natural joints, and to try not to splinter any part, as a bad butcher might do" (265e1–3). Taken together, Socrates's encomium and palinode follow this process of collection and division, gathering the various phenomena described as "love" and dividing them into two "just as each single body has parts that naturally come in pairs of the same name" (266a1–2), so too Socrates discerned a left- and right-handed love and "justly denounced" (266a5) the former while praising the latter. Following along the natural joints includes, then, not only a standard of analysis but also a standard judgment and imparts discernment not only of what *is* but also of whether it is *good*, determining the proper stance or position (comportment) one should take toward them.

Plato returns to this image of cutting into the animal body along natural lines of cleavage in the *Statesman*, where again it serves as a model for the method of division, one that would receive significant critical treatment in the dialogue (259d). Here the terms of animal embodiment also serve to give shape and style to a form of rule: the divine shepherd who tends flocks of the living, humans included, in an earlier, idyllic age, the Age of Chronos. The extent to which Plato accepts or rejects a pastoral model for political rule is a matter of debate, but it remained a powerful image of the duties of the ruler in what is largely considered Plato's latest extant dialogue, the *Laws*.[41] If we move to the *Timaeus*, this signifying aspect of the living body extends beyond the human political world to the *kosmos* itself, which Plato will find useful to depict as alive, and filled with the necessary animal kinds in order to be complete, kinds that are also expressions of human moral failings.

These observations are embedded in a larger linguistic and religious context that treated the animal body as foundational for establishing a coherent, liveable world and draw upon a deep reservoir of images and concepts connecting the terms of embodiment with those of signification. To follow the line of the sacrificial body for a moment, the butchering of the sacrificial animal's corpse illuminates the ritual use of the animal body to simultaneously demarcate essential boundaries and honor them, to indicate the difference between human and divine and between different kinds of humans.[42] The traditional animal sacrifice, *thysia*, would have involved the removal of select body parts to be offered to the gods via burning, with variations including also the offering of uncooked choice morsels on altar or at a table setting.[43] Of the parts left for human consumption, these too were divided into two components: choice parts to be consumed by honored attendees given closest access to the altar, designated by their shared consumption of the *splanchna* (*sysplanchneuontes*); and the remaining meat and bones, apportioned by weight and handed out equally among the remainder of the attendees. In this, the sacrificial body is community-creating and serves to underscore order and hierarchy; its organs are not viewed as "mere" parts or reduced matter but gifts and offerings arrayed to bestow honor. Even the packaged remains, weighted out in equal parts, are meant to convey a dignified equality.

Similarly, animal divination, and especially the "reading" of animal entrails occurs within a grammar already established by the terms of living embodiment.[44] The natural joints, *arthra*, that prove so vital to Socrates' illustration of dialectic are composed of elements (*stoicheiai*) that would also serve to indicate letters, and are connected to the numbering (*arithmos*) by means of which they could be measured and the standard of harmony (*harmonia*) by which they would be evaluated. The movements of the living body provide the terms for conceptual understanding itself, from the "down-step" in dance (*thesis*) to the grasping, seeing, and beholding of contemplative understanding. The very demarcation between what is to be done and what is to not be done provided by *nomos* evokes the principle of distribution embraced in the verb *nemein*, "to deal out, distribute, dispense," "to apportion," which is itself also connected to the terms of animal embodiment, "to pasture" (as providing the basis for the noun *nemos*, "a wooded pasture, glade"), "to graze," "to devour." The root from which it stems, *nem-*, which provides a common root to *nehmen* as well, connects what is right or just (and the indignation over its abrogation, both of which are indicated by *nemesis*) with the needs of living embodiment; in fact, it suggests a reciprocity: the needs of the living body dictate a certain order to things.[45]

The animal body thus serves as a privileged site for encountering a kind of natural order. This is so even when, as with a running trope in tragedy, its innards convey passions and desires that evade scrutiny.[46] Even the insistence on bodily incursion in thinking and disruption of good order that we encounter in several Platonic dialogues is offered in language filled with bodily metaphors and references, in images that participate in their own critique. For Plato and Euripides alike, the body, with its shining exterior and hidden interior, provides the horizon of meaning, the measure by which what is meaningful and what is meaningless can be determined. Or, as the author of the medical treatise "On Techne" puts it, what cannot be read on the surface of the body can be made, through the physician's art, to elicit a sign.[47]

And so even as Plato's Socrates takes precious time before his imminent demise to point out the inadequacy of an account of bones and sinews alone to arrive at cause, he will do so having already observed the account of form nascent in our sense of the striving of two sticks for the equal (*Phaedo* 74a–75e); that is, he will do so having already gestured toward a capacious account of causality that could include not only the strivings of sticks but also, to draw from a few other sources, the axe that remembers the death of which it was the instrument, the statue that crushes its namesake's detractor, the wall of granite that Ajax becomes to hold the battle line, evocative of the stone that marks a boundary, *horos*, for instance, or the line of stones that mark a sacred precinct (*temenos*).[48] Thus, while we can observe a Platonic concern to avoid a reductive materialism that robs the human of purpose, we should keep in mind also the vibrant materialism that grants a world-building function to things, and a sense for their "responsibility" as carriers of miasma, a legal agency, if not a philosophical one.[49] By these terms, Heidegger was off the mark from his very first thesis that the stone is poor in world.

To be clear, there is no room for romanticization here. The terms of the body included categories and distinctions that were enlisted in efforts, often violent, to instantiate who and what was or was not worthy of care, defense, love, grief. Stone or animal legal 'agency' tended to result in their expulsion from political order. And to be sure, this efficacy does not belong to the things as something they have won, nor is it treated as something of which they are aware, save in the case of Clytamnestra's axe; rather, it is written into the nature of the *kosmos* itself, and this brings us to the larger question of Heidegger's "Welt" and ancient Greek conceptions of *kosmos* and the means by which they come to be known, a question we will enter by way of Aristotle's zoological research. When Aristotle turns to discern the terms of animal embodiment, to observe the signs of character in physical features, to anticipate the course of life that would follow from the possession of natural "virtues," to locate human political animality within this context, he does so from within this broad alignment of animal embodiment and signification.

Aristotle's Vitalism?

Zoology

In the second book of *De Anima*, Aristotle makes an observation about living that should sound familiar to readers of his *Metaphysics* and Heidegger's alike: "living is meant in more than one way" (413a22). Whether the polyvocity of *zēn*, like that of being, is best understood as an instance of core-dependent homonymy, or whether it is such to admit at best a modal unifying common account, Aristotle's attempts at disambiguation proceed by way of hierarchizing.[50] But at this point we should mark a difference between Aristotle's science of being and his science of life. The central concept that fixes the meaning of being, "substance" is not treated by Aristotle as admitting of the incrementalism he famously attributes to the difference between inanimate and animate: "Nature proceeds from the inanimate to the animal by such small steps that, because of the continuity, we fail to see to which side the boundary and the middle between them belongs" (HA 7.588b4–6). As an effort to sharpen our eyes to discern "the boundary and middle," Aristotle's psychology follows a different path than his metaphysics. For while he begins with the starting point that "what is ensouled is distinguished from what is soulless by living" the immediate consequence of his observation that living is meant in many ways is the demarcation of four aspects or "capacities" of life—nutritive, perceptive, desiderative, intellective—all of which offer a sign of life. In his subsequent discussion of these capacities, Aristotle will turn not only to distinguish the capacity that serves as the most basic sign of life, possessed by all living creatures (nutrition/reproduction) but also to identify those capacities that distinguish between animal kinds and treat these as the most vivid indicator of a living being's living. That is, he marks *both* a threshold and a pinnacle.[51]

In his zoological work, we encounter both the differentiating impulse and the hierarchizing impulse on display in *De Anima* carried into the very terms of animal embodiment. The forms of character indicated by the nick of the eye, or the shape of the ear, or the size of the body, for instance, resonate with the interlacing of embodiment and signification we traced in the previous section, and give substance to Aristotle's affirmation of the wonder-provoking character of the animal body. More specifically, the division into four capacities of soul gives structure to Aristotle's investigation of animal morphology, physiology, and anatomy as he seeks to discern their most vivid differentia, of which he again counts four: parts (*moria*), manner of life (*bios*), character (*ēthos*) and action (*praxis*) (*HA* 487a10).

Throughout this body of work, much of Aristotle's attention falls to parts, to the homogenous substances that stabilize morphology and support the complex (heterogenous) instruments of nutrition and perception as they navigate the in-comings and out-goings of the animal body necessary to manage vital heat.[52] But the difference between differentia, that is between parts, manner of life, actions, and character, is not nearly as clear, and if Aristotle's focus is often on parts, this is because they afford a path to indicating the relationship between animal *organa*, the actions they support, the manner of life and character that arises from them, and the environmental context in which they arise and to which they respond.

Animal *bios* proves especially useful to Aristotle in this regard, as it indicates the integration of parts and place, and helps explain why certain parts (long neck and long beak, for instance), arise in certain places and why certain places invite particular organizations not only of animal *organa* but also of animal sociality or the lack thereof (e.g., the gregariousness of cranes or the solitude of eagles). When, in the *History of Animals*, Aristotle turns to focus in particular on animal character and action, the two are treated as deeply intertwined (as any reader of Aristotle's ethics would recognize) and oriented toward maintaining the intimacy between body and place that forms the animal's life from the start, such that, as he observes in *On Respiration*, the material of the animal's body "is of the same nature as the region in which they exist" (477b30). This intimacy between *zōion* and *topos* is especially vivid in Aristotle's explanation for why plants do not emit a waste product: the warmth of the earth itself concocts the plant's food for it, serving as its "external stomach." Most animals approximate this relationship by having within them a bag (the stomach) that is, "an earth inside them, as it were" (*PA* 650a20–5).

Success at this integration is often described by Aristotle as *eubiotos*, which indicates less a kind of basic survival than a spectacular example of a vitality, a success at living, that would be most on display in the case of the divine. Any assessment of Aristotle's approach to life and animality must accommodate his description in the *Metaphysics* of the divine as living (1072b26–30). At the same time, we should resist the temptation to over-interpret this claim. Given the larger context in which the assertion is made, the description of the divine as alive would seem to follow from the fact that here, as elsewhere, being alive is treated as choiceworthy and good, and the divine has what is choiceworthy and best in the highest degree. Hence, the divine is not only alive but best and eternally so.

This sense of hierarchy infuses Aristotle's discussions of the broader field of living beings. All living beings live, but for Aristotle, some have more life—they live better—than others. Or, as he puts it in *De Caelo*, some adhere to life more or less articulately, others feebly (279a17–279b3). And so while it is indeed important to observe that when Aristotle wanted to investigate life he had two words at this disposal, it is equally important to note that what seems to have particularly spurred his thinking is that one word, *zēn*, would have been used to describe the nutritive capacity of the plant, the perceptual capacity of the animal, and the contemplative action of the divine. *Bios*, manner of life, offered the possibility of drawing some distinctions between these capacities and activities, and qualifying the living of the living being in the context of both time and space, thereby marking the superlative character of the living of the divine, whose *zēn* requires no such qualification.

As an integrative concept, *bios* helps Aristotle discern how an animal responds to the demands of living in a particular time and a particular space, as well as discern the relationship between organ, impulse, capacity, life, and the broader context in which life occurs, whether the scale be *topos* (most often for Aristotle) or *kosmos*. In this, Aristotle treats the living body as a paradigm of the unity of part and whole, and thus as a paradigm of just or meet apportionment, as a model of right distribution, or distribution according to what is due. The capacities that shape the organs and the impulses that animate them are indeed in service to an end—living—but this end is thematized as among the best and most choiceworthy, as an object of desire. Thus, capacity and impulse are not an encroachment on animal agency but in the service of pursuing this object of desire, that is, in the service of meeting the demands of living.

It is in this context that we should read Aristotle's observation that a wooden hand is a hand in name only (*PA* 640b36–641a6). That one can indeed have a hand that is made of something other than flesh does not vitiate Aristotle's point here. The prosthetic limb functions as such only to the extent that it can be taken up within the vital needs and capacities of the living being, that it can answer to the demands of life. That these demands admit of prosthetic supplement and enhancement is accommodated by a claim Aristotle makes about life: *zōē* requires many instruments (*Pol.* 1328b6–7). These instruments include both the inanimate and the animate, indeed the demands of *zōē* serve as a basis for a hierarchy of living beings, as will become particularly clear as we turn to Aristotle's discussions of the properly human *zōē*, with its several forms of *bios*, and its need to choose the best.

ANTHROPOLOGY

In his zoological works, the human fluctuates between serving as one example among many and as a heuristic paradigm, depending on the state of knowledge concerning the organ or action under question. In the *History of Animals*, for instance, the first reference to *anthrōpos* is one example among many of a land-animal (487a30), the second as dualizing between the *bioi* of gregarious and solitary animals (488a7–8), and the third as one example among several (bees, wasps, ants, and crane) of *politika* animals, that is, animals "which have some one common activity" (488a81–1).[53] In Aristotle's subsequent discussion of the common action of political animals we encounter a shared awareness of both space and time, that, for some at least, requires some form of signification: for example, the cranes' shared task of migration includes the leader giving a sign (614b18–27), and bees mark the close of day with collective buzzing until a single bee flies around buzzing, "as though signaling for sleep" (627a24–8).[54]

In the *Politics*, Aristotle treats human *bios* as simultaneously an extension and intensification of animal *bios*: extension because it too is shaped by the need for food and desire for pleasure and intensification because, for Aristotle, the human is the most political animal (1253a7–8). This intensification is most immediately asserted in the array of human *bioi* from which the human must choose with greater or lesser degrees of freedom/flexibility, an array that reflects the diversity of *bioi* found in the field of animal life (1256a28–30). The lists of human *bioi* Aristotle provides include accommodation of both human nutritive needs—the *bios* of the farmer or nomad, or the pirate, for instance (1256b1–2)—and the human capacity for choice: the lives of pleasure, politics, and contemplation. Both need and choice are treated as oriented toward living, toward *zōē*, and both indicate a certain potential for failure on the part of the human with respect to *zōē*, a failure in the collective enterprise of living and thus centered in the success or failure to produce the proper conditions for collective life. Because the human may fail at *zōē*, *eu zēn* is useful in marking its success. And while it is true that Aristotle does not attribute *eu zēn* to nonhuman animals, and thus that it stands in some form of difference from the *eubiotos* that indicates successful accomplishment of manner of life (of integration between *zōion* and *topos*), I take this difference not as asserting an ontological divide between human and animal, but rather as specifying a risk particular to the intensified politicality that is characteristic of the human animal: humans are more dependent on one another not only for the manner of their life, but for the successful accomplishment of their living in any environment, and thus are more vulnerable to a failure to meet the conditions of collective living.

The human dependence on one another for living, its intensified politicality, is made especially clear in Aristotle's development and use of the concept of *suzēn*, shared life or living together, which serves in Aristotle's ethical and political works to indicate the forms of intimacy (*sunētheia*) that arise from the possession of *logos* and the capacity for choice.[55] Aristotle often uses the term to help mark the active state of human *philia* (friendship), which he will describe in the *Politics* as "the intentional choice of living together" (1280b35). In his ethical texts, shared life indicates a heightened awareness of one's being made possible by sharing one's most cherished activities with one's friends (see e.g., NE 1171b32–1172a8), and that proves essential for describing the most complete form of *philia*, virtue friendship. At its most vivid, it includes three aspects that prove useful in describing more specific features of *philia* as well: first, sharing in joy and sadness, and more broadly feeling-with, (*sugchairein, sunalgein, sunēdesthai, sunachthesthai, sunōdos, sullupeisthai*); second, the shared perception (*sunaisthēsis*) that forms the basis of political community (*Pol.* 1253a15): a democracy or an oligarchy, for instance, are by way of a particular vision of justice, they endure to the extent that this vision of justice is shared by citizens and they collapse when it is not shared, indeed, they are inclined to collapse precisely because of the error in their model of justice; and third, a shared understanding (*suggnōrizein*) and contemplating (*suntheōrein*) that would accompany philosophizing together (*sumphilosophein*).[56] And while Aristotle is clear that *suzēn* is not the end toward which the *polis* aims, he is equally clear that a failure to live together successfully precludes the possibility of living well. There is no *eu zēn* without some form of *suzēn*, and this is a direct function of the intensified politicality of the human animal.

Human Animality

If we accept human animality as Aristotle constructs it, then, the need to accomplish *eu zēn* is a function of the intensified political character of human life, the intensified need humans have for one another, the possibility of failure at living allotted to the animal whose flourishing requires not only the distribution of labor assured by sexual difference and the division into natural slave and master, but also a shared perception of justice and injustice, in the absence of which the human becomes the most depraved animal (1253a31–7). This negative exceptionalism does not remove the human from the realm of the animal, so far as Aristotle is concerned; rather, it marks the possibility of the human serving as the lowest threshold of animality as well as approximating the highest, that is, the human can be the worst animal as well as aspiring to the best. The very exercise of intellectual capacities that marks humans as especially godlike animals requires the presence of others, not only with whom to think but also to supply the conditions for a contemplative life, which, like life itself, requires many instruments. And while the successful exercise of these capacities brings humans closer to a divine whose living is the highest and most vivid expression of what it means to be alive, failure to properly exercise these capacities brings humans below the beasts. What we need to acknowledge is that neither in this assertion of human negative exceptionalism, nor in his observations about human excellence, does Aristotle treat *anthrōpos* as something other than a *zōion*. In neither its godlike nor beastly character is the human removed from the animal.

But we need to be equally clear in acknowledging that *zōē*'s role in this model of the human does not exempt it from being used to bolster an oppressive and patriarchal ideology, quite the opposite in fact. Here too, there is no room for romanticization. The shared living of citizens is also bound up with the unequal and oppressive apportionment of work, with the use of some bodies as tools for living, as external body parts, with the farming out of vital functions to those perceived as "naturally" suited to such a task, and with the creation of political institutions designed to "assist" nature where it may fail in supplying such bodies.

Any investigation into Aristotle's approach to human animality needs to consider the fact that, for Aristotle, the shared life of friends, and the enactment of citizenship more broadly, also requires the relation between master and slave, which Aristotle treats in starkly organicist terms: the slave is a living instrument (1253b32), a separable organ (1255b12), a partner in the master's life [*koinōnos zōēs*] (1260a40). Master and slave stand to one another as soul to body, as two parts of the single living being. In this, the living they produce, what Pierre Pellegrin will call their fused life, is an expression of a principle of mastery Aristotle sees in nature itself—the *zōion* lives by merit of the soul's ruling over the body and for the vast majority of living beings, this rule takes the form of mastery (1254b3–5)—and has echoes in the relation between, for instance, the plant and its external stomach, that is, the earth in which it is rooted.[57] This is all underwritten by a model of ownership noteworthy for the degree of intimacy it imagines between owner and what is one's own: according to Aristotle, the first possession is the nourishment provided to the newborn, the yolk of the egg or the milk of the breast, and the natural generosity to which this "gift" is attributed is extended to the rule and use of all nonhuman animals (1256b7–22) and enlisted in the argument that certain people are also made, by nature, to be owned by others, and whose life is for the sake of another life.

For Aristotle, the purpose of the use of slaves, a work that Aristotle views as in itself ignoble and performed by overseers for those citizens who can afford them (1255b35–37), is to free up the master's time for cultivating virtue and performing the noble deeds for which the city has its purpose, for things like politics and philosophy, both of which require a community of some sort (even if, as in the case of the contemplative life, the community serves to create the conditions of its own transcendence Aristotle still insists that such a life is indeed a life of action). The political bond emerges as a form of intimacy, and the closest friendships, in which one shares one's most cherished activities with another, is best realized in those who have been most successful in the use of their leisure for responding to the rigors of character development.

In short, the shared life of friends is made possible by the fused life of master and slave. What this fusion buys the master is the leisure to develop the relationship with himself and others that serves as the core of the city. He will share joy and pain with his fellow citizens, he will share their perception of what is just and unjust, a sharing that provides the heart of political community, and, for those who opt for the contemplative life, he will share even his philosophizing and theorizing. And upon his death he returns his body to the city, to which it had belonged all along, formed by reproductive legislation and kept alive by a variety of other forms of legislation, including the prohibition on suicide which, Aristotle argues, is not an injustice against oneself (as this is impossible so far as he is concerned) but against the city.

For Aristotle, the life that has been assured in the relationship between master and slave belongs to the citizen. Or, perhaps even more accurately, it belongs to that of which the citizen is himself a possession, the city itself. And here we can mark a certain instrumentalization of citizen life in Aristotle's thought worth tracking closely for its relevance to Heidegger's concerns about animality: citizens are the "wool" (1258a20–7), the "material" (1325b40–1326a4), the "equipment" (1326a5, see also 1325b37), the "possessions" (1337a27–9) of the city. Their bodies have been shaped by eugenics legislation designed to render them amenable to the will of the legislator (1335a5), their early childhood education has been designed to calibrate their senses in order to assure a shared perception of justice and injustice, and their civic duties allocated according to significant stages in their life cycle. On the other hand, the living (*zēn*) this model is designed to support, that is, living well (*eu zēn*), is treated as a differentially distributed cosmic "force" exemplified by the highest cosmic bodies, the *polis* that does the supporting is there to assure the strongest degree of imitation of these bodies possible, and the paradigm to which all aspire, the highest object of desire, is a remote and distant divine whose life is best and eternal.

By these terms, we could read Aristotle as a proponent of a reductive instrumentalization of human life that is at home with an expansive vitalism. But I take this to simply mark the need for care in attributing these terms to Aristotle.[58] When Aristotle treats citizens as the wool, or the matter, or the equipment, or the possessions of the *polis*, he takes himself to be performing an ennobling gesture, as speaking to the value of role of the citizen. To be a citizen is to be worthy of legislating; this is why citizens will be legislated far more than their slaves. To be worthy of receiving and enacting the law: this is the aspiration, and the legislative project Aristotle sketches at the end of the *Politics* is designed to do precisely this. What worries Aristotle is the failure to meet this "challenge," the refusal, both individually and collectively to meet the demands and rigors of character development, the danger of softness, slackness, etc. And these too are accommodated within Aristotle's understanding of human political animality.

Thus, most constructions of human exceptionalism, whether the traditional emphases on consciousness or self-awareness, rationality, language or the Heideggerean development of the human formation of world, and the attunement of radical boredom, the apophantic as, and the comportment toward death that allow for the world to appear as such, fit within Aristotle's understanding of human political animality. For Aristotle, self-awareness, knowing oneself as such, is a collective effort, down to the level of perception and affect. The sharing of perception on which the political bond is based includes also the perception of oneself as good that is won from friendship both with oneself and others; it is because they have a shared orientation toward and perception of the good that one can say of one's friend that they are another self, and see oneself in them.[59] (We should be careful to mark the profound difference between the model of self-awareness that arises from *sunaisthēsis*, which could not come to be without a community of co-perceivers, and that arising from Cartesian consciousness, which assumes a kind of isolation that would have been inimical to Aristotle).[60]

Moreover, the intimate connection between human rational and perceptual capacities involved in human shared life, that renders it exceptionally political, insists upon the location of the human within the context of the animal, and not outside of it. The ability to share a perception of justice and injustice is granted on the basis of the possession of logos, a possession Aristotle does indeed not grant (in its fullest form) to other animals, but treats as an expression of the particular animal humans are and, even more specifically, as a particular intensification of human politicality, a category that is not exclusively human. For Aristotle, we do not need to leave the "realm" of *zōē* in order to fully understand logos, that is, we miss nothing of logos by conceiving of it as an expression of the particular living of a particular living being, because of the capacious field of what constitutes the living.[61] By this understanding, we are no more given license to ask how we would be transposed toward the animal than we are to ask how we would be transposed to other humans. In both cases we are, to follow a Heideggerean locution, always already so transposed. Aristotelian *suzēn*, then, is not identical to Heideggerean *mit-sein*.

The detachment of radical boredom is accounted for in Aristotle's thinking by the status of the human as a dualizer, which indicates that standing outside of human community, that resisting the *hormē* toward human community, is within the horizon of human possibility, and further that this standing outside is not a standing outside of human animality but a further affirmation of it. That is, through the category of the dualizer, Aristotle can accommodate human antisocial tendencies, human alienation, human detachment, human distance, human angst without needing to assert an ontological difference between the human and the animal.[62] Even the event that is taken by Heidegger to be ineradicably singular, the event of one's death, is treated as a collective event. For Aristotle, not even my death is my own. This is true for my birth as well, and more obviously so. By these terms, the city should be the guarantor of citizen birth and death, the legislation concerning natality and mortality forms its matrix.

And all of this is to serve the demands of life, to live well, which includes integrating into one's environment, even (especially) if that environment includes the *polis*. What distinguishes human life as especially political is the degree to which human living is a collective effort and serves the intergenerational project of human intimacy that is the city, by means of which humans attempt to approximate the eternal life of the divine.

Conclusion

In the summer semester of 1943, fourteen years after the lecture course in which Heidegger develops his thesis that animal is poor in world, Heidegger returns to the question of the animal and this time explicitly in an ancient Greek context, in a lecture course on Heraclitus fragment B16.[63] Here Heidegger asks how *leben* is to be understood, "if we accept it as a faithful translation for the Greek word *zēn*."[64] Heidegger's 'if' is significant here. For while he will assert again the distance between the Greek *zōion* and 'any biologically conceived animality,' and will even do so by means of a gesture toward the Greek construction of the gods as *zōia*, a construction at which he himself marvels, he concludes that "because the animal does not speak, self-revealing and self-concealing, together with their unity, possess a wholly different life-essence [*Lebe-Wesen*] with animals."[65]

Heidegger does not here go on to answer whether *leben* is a 'faithful translation' of *zēn*, nor does he develop his own sense of *leben*, choosing instead to align *zōē* with *phusis*.[66] In the years between the 1929–30 lecture course and this study of Heraclitus, Heidegger's approach to life and metaphysics alike was profoundly altered, in part by a long-running engagement with Nietzsche's work, beginning with four lecture courses in the mid- to late 1930s, and culminating in the publication of a two-volume set in 1961.[67] When he addresses the question of life in his *Beitraege*, for instance, he does so with a sense of the relation between a metaphysical conception of life and nihilism, and thus for the complicity between a concept of life and what he took to be the pathologies of his time.

If we want to answer whether, in Heidegger's opinion, *leben* translates *zōē*, then, we are left to fall back on the comments about life Heidegger makes in his development of the thesis that animal is poor in world. And we have charted here the distance between Aristotelian *zōē* and *leben* in both Heideggerian and "biologically conceived" senses. Far from serving as the struggle to maintain one's capacities within a sphere of living, from a conception of living as a reduced or "mere" exercise of "vital capacities" or "biological processes," life itself, *zōē*, serves as a form- and meaning-granting force. If humans too are subjugated, especially to the need of life for many instruments, this is far less important to Aristotle than the deeds to which their subjugation gives rise, deeds that constitute for Aristotle not a source of dismay but of happiness itself.

And here we run up against the limited nature of Heidegger's engagement with Aristotle's zoological works. A more comprehensive survey of Aristotle's research into living beings would include acknowledgment that not only do we encounter an alternate vision of life in Aristotle's *zōē*, but also an alternate vision of the human, whose political nature does not vitiate its dualizing between gregarious and solitary, whose living is a collective effort, whose bios depends upon the labor of others to create a horizon of choices, whose contemplation requires a community not only of others with whom to think but of others whose labor is for the sake of another's thinking.

We have thus seen as well that Aristotle's vision of *zōē* in general and human *zōē* in particular is not without its inconsistencies and pathologies, many of which arise as a function of Aristotle's attempt to diagnose his own time and place. The human weakness/slackness in the face of the rigors of character development, the attracting power of pleasure and the repulsing power of pain, the possibility that even the noble deed will be made mercenary to the aim of the limitless acquisition of money and the misunderstanding of human life on which it rests, are not fully allayed by the measures in his ethico-politics to address them. Quite the opposite, in some cases. Aristotle's efforts to draw distinctions that thwart these human errors fail, and they do so in spectacularly revealing fashion: the alienated natality behind his insistence on private ownership and understanding of the first possession serves as the basis for a model of ownership that includes the ownership of other humans; this model is underwritten by an understanding of life's instruments as including the animate kind and by life itself as an object of desire and a cosmic force distributed so differentially as to include lives that are only for the sake of others. This understanding of life, in turn, supports the very commodification of life that Aristotle attacks in his critique of the limitless acquisition of money, and threatens the coherence of his account of animal embodiment as such. What all of this tells us is that a theory of "the animal" gets the image of life it deserves.

Notes

1. This critique is most concisely offered in the concluding essay of the collection *The Animal that Therefore I Am* (see especially Jacques Derrida, *The Animal that Therefore I Am*, trans. David Wills [New York: Fordham University Press, 2008, 160]), but as Derrida points out there, the critique is developed in various points throughout his work, see, for example, *Of Spirit, Geschlecht, Aporias*, etc. Derrida is not alone in pointing to the flaws in Heidegger's approach to animality. See, for instance, David Krell, *Daimon Life. Heidegger and Life-philosophy* (Bloomington: Indiana University Press, 1992); Susanna Lindberg, "Heidegger's Animal," *Phänomenologische Forschungen* (2004): 57–81, Stuart Elden, "Heidegger's Animals," *Continental Philosophy Review* 39 (2006): 273–91; and Gerard Kuperus, "Heidegger and Animality," in *Phenomenology and the Non-Human Animal*, ed. Christian Lotz and Corinne Painter ([Dordrecht] Kluwer/Springer, 2007).

2. Heidegger will insist on an abyss separating humans and animals throughout his published work; see, for example, his comments on the gulf separating the speaking human from the speechless animal in the 1934–35 lecture course on Hölderlin (39/75), and the abyss separating humans and animals in the "Letter on Humanism" (BW 206), even when (as is the case in this second reference) that abyss is treated ambiguously as also a form of connection, or, as David Krell puts it, even when the chasm is also a chiasm, see Krell, *Daimon Life*.

3. Matthew Calarco, *Zoographies: The Question of the Animal from Heidegger to Derrida* (New York: Columbia University Press, 2008). For Arendt on animality, and Heidegger's influence therein, see in particular her development of the conception of *animal laborans* (and her critique of Marx based thereon) in Hannah Arendt, *The Human Condition* (Chicago: University of Chicago Press, 1958). The influence of Arendt's and Heidegger's conception of animality on Agamben's engagement with Aristotle can be seen throughout the homo sacer series (see, e.g., Giorgio Agamben, *Homo Sacer: Sovereign Power and Bare Life*, trans. D. Heller-Roazen (Stanford, CA: Stanford University Press, 1998); *The Highest Poverty: Monastic Rules and Form-of-Life*, trans. Adam Kotsko (Stanford, CA: Stanford University Press, 2013); *The Use of Bodies*, trans. Adam Kostko (Stanford, CA: Stanford University Press, 2016), as well as Agamben's study of Heidegger on animality, see Agamben (2003). On Heidegger's influence on the contemporary reception of Aristotle's political theory more generally, see Walter Brogan, *Heidegger and Aristotle: The Twofoldness of Being* (Albany: State University of New York Press, 2005), and Sara Brill, *Aristotle on the Concept of Shared Life* (Oxford: Oxford University Press, 2020), introduction.

4. Derrida, *Animal*, 160.

5. Ibid.

6. Heidegger's relatively recently published early lecture courses in Aristotle have proven to be especially useful in explicating the influence of his reading of

Aristotle on the course of his thinking leading up to and just after *Being and Time*; see, for example, the 1922 introduction to a never-completed book on Aristotle available in English translation as "Phenomenological Interpretations with Respect to Aristotle: Indication of the Hermeneutical Situation" (Martin Heidegger, "Phenomenological Interpretations with Respect to Aristotle: Indication of the Herrneneutical Situation," trans. Michael Bauer, *Man and World* 25 [1992]: 355–93), and the lecture courses of 1921–22 (Martin Heidegger, *Phenomenological Interpretations of Aristotle: Initiation into Phenomenological Research*," trans. Richard Rojcewicz [Bloomington: Indiana University Press, 2001]), 1924 (Martin Heidegger, *Basic Concepts of Aristotelian Philosophy*, trans. Robert Metcalf and Mark Tanzer [Bloomington: Indiana University Press, 2009]), 1924–25 (Martin Heidegger, *Plato's Sophist*, trans. Richard Rojcewicz and Andre Schuwer [Bloomington: Indiana University Press, 2003]), 1926 (Rojcewicz [2007]), 1927 (Martin Heidegger, *The Basic Problems of Phenomenology*, trans. Albert Hofstadter [Bloomington: Indiana University Press, 1998, rev. ed.]), and 1931 (Martin Heidegger, *Aristotle's Metaphysics [theta] 1–3: On the Essence and Actuality of Force*, trans. Walter Brogan and Peter Warnek [Bloomington: Indiana University Press, 1995]). The lecture course that is the focus of the present study, that of 1929–30 (Martin Heidegger, *The Fundamental Concepts of Metaphysics: World, Finitude, Solitude*, trans. William McNeill and Nicholas Walker [Bloomington: Indiana University Press, 1996], is not directly a study of Aristotle, but resonates with the ongoing study of Aristotle in these other lecture courses. Heidegger himself observes the importance of his work on Aristotle for the development of his thinking on several occasions; see, for instance, History of the Concept of Time (136) and My Way to Phenomenology (86 German text). But we should be careful not to move too quickly when assessing the influence of Aristotle, and ancient Greek thought more broadly, on Heidegger's thinking about life and animality, a focus I will parse presently. For general studies of Heidegger's engagement with Aristotle, see Brogan, *Twofoldness*; William McNeil, *The Glance of the Eye: Heidegger, Aristotle, and the Ends of Theory* (Albany: State University of New York Press, 1999); and William McNeil, *The Time of Life: Heidegger and Ethos* (Albany: State University of New York Press, 2006); Ted Sadler, *Heidegger and Aristotle: The Question of Being* (London: Athlone Press, 2001); and Michael Bowler, *Heidegger and Aristotle: Philosophy as Praxis* (New York: Continuum Press, 2008). For assessment of the degree of influence of Heidegger's engagement with Aristotle on his thought, often with a focus on the early lecture courses, see Theodore Kisiel, *The Genesis of Heidegger's Being and Time* (Berkeley: University of California Press, 1993); William Richardson, "Heidegger and Aristotle," *The Heythrop Journal* 5, no. 1 (1964): 58–72, Thomas Sheehan, ed., *Heidegger: The Man and the Thinker* (New York: Routledge, 1981); and John Van Buren, *The Young Heidegger* (Bloomington: Indiana University Press, 1994). See also Josh Hayes, "Heidegger, Aristotle, and Animal Life." *Philosophy Today* 51 (2007): 82–88.

7. Guenther Bien, *Grundlagen der Politische Philosophie bei Aristotle* (Munich, 1973), 123, n. 27; and Walter Kullmann, "Man as a Political Animal in Aristotle," in *A Companion to Aristotle's Politics*, ed. D. Keyt and F. Miller (Oxford, 1991), 94–117 and Walter Kullman, "Der Mensch als politisches Lebewesen bei Aristoteles," *Hermes* 108: 419–43, 1980), 107, commenting in particular on a passage from Heidegger's "Letter on Humanism" (p. 66 of the second German edition).

8. Most famously in Marx's engagement with Democritus's atomism and the connection between the new materialism of Jane Bennet, *Vibrant Matter: A Political Ecology of Things* (Durham: Duke University Press, 2010); and Diana Coole and Samantha Frost, eds., *New Materialisms: Ontology, Agency, and Politics* (Durham: Duke University Press, 2010) and ancient Greek texts, for example, Homeric epic, see Alex Purves, "Ajax and Other Objects: Homer's Vibrant Materialism" *Ramus* 44, no. 1–2 (December 2015): 75–94.

9. See, for instance, the work collected in D. Devereaux and P. Pellegrin, eds., *Biologie, logique et letaphysique chez Aristoteles* (Paris, 1990); A. Gotthelf, and J. Lennox, eds., *Philosophical Issues in Aristotle's Biology* (Cambridge, 1987); M. Leunissen, *From Natural Character to Moral Virtue in Aristotle* (Oxford: Oxford University Press, 2017). Beyond his reference to Aristotle's report of the Heraclitus story in *Parts of Animals* in the *Letter on Humanism*, Heidegger's own engagement with Aristotle's zoological works appears limited as well, especially when compared to his work on Aristotle's *Nichomachean Ethics*, *Metaphysics*, *Physics*, and *De Anima*.

10. See, for example, D. Keyt. "The Meaning of BIOS in Aristotle's Ethics and Politics." *Ancient Philosophy 9: 15–21.* (1989) and throughout Joe Sachs' translation of the *Nicomachean Ethics*.

11. See Mike Ojakangas, *On the Greek Origins of Biopolitics* (New York: Routledge, 2016); Jussi Backman and Antonio Cimino, *Biopolitics and Ancient Thought* (Oxford: Oxford University Press, 2022); and the possibilities for alternate genealogies suggested in Emanuela Bianchi, Sara Brill, and Brooke Holmes, eds., *Antiquities Beyond Humanism* (Oxford: Oxford University Press, 2019).

12. In the difference between Heidegger's use of *nehmen* and the Greek verb *nemein*, words that share an Indo-European root, we see especially clearly the divergence between Heidegger's construction of "the animal" and Aristotle's.

13. I will trace this consistency throughout the chapter, and note here just a few signposts along the way: worldlessness and poverty in world return in Heidegger's *Beitraege*, a text that signals his turn away from an aspiration to return metaphysics to "first philosophy" and toward replacing it with what he took to be a more authentic engagement with the question of being on the basis of the complicity between metaphysics, and especially a metaphysics of life, with nihilism, themes he would deepen in the course of his extensive engagement with Nietzsche's work and his focii on technology, art, and language.

14. FCM: 204.

15. On the apparent (and misleading) obviousness of this extension to human beings: "Indeed it appears much less questionable to us, indeed as not questionable at all, that in certain contexts and situations other human beings on average comport themselves to things exactly as we do ourselves; and furthermore, that a number of human beings not only have the same comportment with one another, without this shared experience being fragmented in the process; it appears that it is possible, accordingly, to go along [*Mitgang*] with others in their access [*Zugang*] to things and in their dealings [*Umgang*] with those things. This is a fundamental feature of man's own immediate experience of existence" (FCM: 205).

16. FCM: 205.
17. FCM: 210.
18. FCM: 258.
19. FCM: 259.
20. FCM: 259.
21. FCM: 259.

22. On the openness of human and animal, see Giorgio Agamben, *The Open: Man and Animal*. Trans. Kevin Attell (Stanford, CA: Stanford University Press, 2003).

23. FCM: 259.
24. FCM: 259.
25. FCM: 259.
26. FCM: 260.

27. Or, as Heidegger will put it in his later lectures on Nietzsche "Biological thinking [. . .] can only be grounded and decided in the metaphysical realm and can never justify itself scientifically" although what Heidegger means by the metaphysical realm has undergone quite a bit of transformation (N2: 45) (cited in Bernasconi [2012] at p. 170).

28. FCM: 271.
29. FCM: 271.
30. FCM: 271.
31. FCM: 272.
32. FCM: 272.
33. FCM: 259.

34. For instance, Heidegger will have to say that the animal doesn't die and that it does (see e.g., discussion in Derrida 150–1 and 154; D. also references a citation of Heidegger D. makes in Aporias in which H. says the animal doesn't die).

35. FCM: 155. See also the early critical discussion of the concept of "life" and life-philosophy in *Being and Time* (Stamb, 42–47); see also an alignment of animals and plants with the realm of the biological, against and outside of which stands the free human being in his lectures on N2: 121–22 (cited in Bernasconi [2012], 174).

36. Derrida (2008) 160.

37. Ibid.

38. See, for instance, *EE* 1224a 18 and 22 in which *hormē* is aligned with nature against force and violence, and *Metaph.* 1015a27 where necessity is treated as contrary to both impulse and choice.

39. Heidegger's approach to drive and capacity is much closer to Freud's, for all of this insistence to the contrary, than Aristotle's. See, for example, Freud's "Instincts and their Vicissitudes."

40. See 209–10, cited in D at 158. See also the reference to *nur-nach-leben* (which Krell renders as "just-plain-life" [1992], and Stambaugh as just-being-alive, p. 46) in *Being and Time*. While Dasein cannot be so understood, Heidegger insists, "the animal" or at least the dog, can. Heidegger's own engagement with the concept *zōē* is complex, and a comprehensive treatment would have to unravel the tensions and complications at work in the differences between this engagement and Heidegger's ambivalences about the term '*Leben*' (see, e.g., the stated aspiration to avoid attributing terms like "life" and "human being" to those whom we are in *Being and Time* Stam 42–47, compared with the call for "a metaphysical interpretation of life" in his 1929–30 lecture course [FCM: 188–89]), the *lebens-philosophie* of his predecessors and contemporaries (ibid., and also the marginal note refuting his own concession in *Being and Time* that something of Dasein is heard in the *lebens-philosophie* of thinkers like Dilthey and Bergson; cited in R. Bernasconi. "Heidegger, Rickert, Nietzsche, and the Critique of Biologism." In *Heidegger and Nietzsche*, Ed. B. Babich, A. Denker, and H. Zabarowski (New York: Brill, 2012), 159–80, 169), and his engagement with Nietzsche, particularly his "defence" of Nietzsche against charges of biologism (on this last aspect, see especially Bernasconi [*Biologism*]). Bernasconi traces the relation Heidegger comes to see between a metaphysical conception of life and nihilism, anticipating Foucauldian "biopower" (see 176–77), but Bernasconi also observes that Heidegger's keen diagnosis of the complicity between concept of life and nihilism does not offer any forms of resistance: "Heidegger offered a powerful diagnosis of the ills of his time, but it left little or no room for a political response that was capable of combatting it" (180).

41. See discussion in M. Naas. *Plato and the Invention of Life* (New York: Fordham University of Press, 2018).

42. The scholarship on Greek sacrificial practices is vast. Helpful recent bibliographic review can be found in V. Mehl and P. Brulé, eds., *Le sacrifice antique: Vestiges, procédures et strategies* (Rennes, Presses Universitaires de Rennes, 2008), 111–38; Gunnel Ekroth, "Animal Sacrifice in Antiquity," in *The Oxford Handbook of Ancient Animals* (Oxford Handbooks in Classics and Ancient History), ed. G. L. Campbell (Oxford: Oxford University Press, 2014), 324–54, and "Why Does Zeus Care about Burnt Thighbones from Sheep? Defining the Divine and Structuring the World through Animal Sacrifice in Ancient Greece," *History of Religions* 58, no. 3 (2019); and Sarah Hitch and Jan Rutherford, *Animal Sacrifice in the Ancient*

Greek World (Cambridge: Cambridge University Press, 2017). Signposts of major movements that serve to mark shifting attitudes toward specific ritual acts and the proper human comportment toward the animal body include Walter Burkert's agenda-setting work on the role of blood guilt in explaining particular aspects of ritual: for example, W. Burkert. "Greek Tragedy and Sacrificial Ritual" *Greek, Roman and Byzantine Studies* 7, no. 2 (1966); and *Homo Necans: The Anthropology of Ancient Greek Sacrificial Ritual and Myth*, trans. P. Bing (Berkeley: University of California Press, 1983), the structuralist approach to ritual as attempting to instantiate, as Claude Levi-Strauss puts it, "good distance": see C. Lévi-Strauss *Mythologiques I. Le Cru et le cuit* (Paris: Plon., 1964), see also J-P Vernant. *Myth and Society in Ancient Greece*, trans. J. Lloyd (London: Methuen, 1974) and M Detienne and J-P Vernant. *Cunning Intelligence in Greek Culture and Society* (Brighton: Harvester Press, 1978). Giulia Sissa's "neo-structuralist" revision of this requires a broader context of interpretation; see G. Sissa "Nonhuman Animals: A Shared Life and a Licence to Kill," in *The Animal Inside: Essays at the Intersection of Philosophical Anthropology and Animal Studies* (New York: Rowman and Littlefield, 2016); the reassessment of the question of blood guilt in F. S. Naiden. "The Fallacy of the Willing Victim." *Journal of Hellenic Studies* 127 (2007): 61–73; S. Georgoudi, "Le consentement de la victime sacriicielle: une question ouverte," in Le sacrifice antique: Vestiges, procédures et stratégies, ed. V. Mehl and P. Brulé (Rennes: Presses Universitaires de Rennes, 2008), 139–53; and Ekroth, as well as Ekroth's argument for ritual practices as having grown out of practices designed to honor heroes (e.g., G. Ekroth, *The Sacrificial Rituals of Greek Hero-cults in the Archaic to the Early Hellenistic Period* [Liège: Presses universitaires de Liège, 2002] and *Why does Zeus*, 2019). My point here is relatively simple: in ritual sacrifice, the animal body is treated as a meaning-granting and world-ordering force.

43. Cf. Ekroth (*Sacrificial Rituals*).

44. On animal divination broadly, see the sources collected in Struck (2014).

45. See Emanuel Laroche, *Histoire de la racine nem- en grec ancien (nemō, nemesis, nomos, nomizō)* (Paris: Librairie C. Klincksieck, 1949). Its embrace of a sense of embodied order heard in the *nomos* evokes both song and custom, and here we can mark a divergence between *nemein* and *nehmen*; to get at this sense of harmony Heidegger must leave the verbal territory of *nehmen* for the sense of voice in *Stimme* that would prove so decisive for his formulation of the fundamental attunement [*Stimmung*], of radical boredom.

46. See, for example, Ruth Padel, *In and Out of the Mind: Greek Images of the Tragic Self* (Princeton, NJ: Princeton University Press, 1994).

47. For example, 1.1–161 and 13.5–34.

48. Axe: (Sophocles, *Electra* 484–86 (Jebb), Hyde ii 294; statue: Pausanias 6.2.9, Hyde ii 290, see also Aristotle's reference to the statue of Mitys of Argos (*Poetics*, 9. 12. 1452 a,7), Theocritus's to a statue of Eros (*Idylls*, XXIII, 59–60)

and a similar story in Callimachus, Epigr. VIII (Sch.); Ajax as wall of stone: Schol. D. Il. 6.5 (on Ajax), see discussion in Purves (2015).

49. Attested to in the (albeit rare) practice of legal prosecution of nonhuman animals and inanimate things; see sources and discussion in Walter Hyde, "The Prosecution of Lifeless Things and Animals in Greek Law: Part I," *The American Journal of Philology* 8, no. 2 (1917): 152–75; and Walter Hyde, "The Prosecution of Lifeless Things and Animals in Greek Law: Part II," *The American Journal of Philology* 38, no. 3 (1917): 285–303.

50. On *zēn* as core dependent homonym, see C. Shields. *Order in Multiplicity: Homonymy in the Philosophy of Aristotle.* Oxford. (1999) and (2008); as modal unifying common account, see C. Coates, *Aristotle on the Concept of Life* (PhD diss., DePaul University, 2021). For broader relevant discussion see R. King. *Aristotle on Life and Death* (London: Duckworth, 2001); C. Cohoe, "Living without a Soul: Why God and the Heavenly Movers Fall Outside of Aristotle's Psychology," *Phronesis* 65, no. 3: (2020): 281–323; C. Coates and J. Lennox, "Aristotle on the Unity of the Nutritive and Reproductive Functions," *Phronesis* 65, no. 4: (2021): 414–66.

51. Agamben's focus solely on the threshold in his development of what he takes to be a fundamental feature of Aristotle's method in studying life, what he describes as "the strategic device par excellence of Aristotle's thought," overlooks this dual strategy and risks attributing an overly reductive methodology to Aristotle; see Agamben 2003, 13.

52. At HA 491a15–16 he describes parts as the most vivid differentiators.

53. The primary differentia of bios for animals is that of *topos*; animals are either land dwelling or water dwelling (7.589a10–11). But there are other significant differentia as well. Some animals, for instance, are gregarious (*agelaia*), others solitary (*monadika*), and others dualize [*ta de epamphoterizei*]; of those that are gregarious, some are *politika* and some are *sporadika* (scattered). And here, Aristotle could not be clearer: humans are dualizers: ὁ δ' ἄνθρωπος ἐπαμφοτερίζει (HA 488a7). When Aristotle goes on, just a few lines later, to identify the human as one among several examples of political animals—political because they all pursue a common deed—there is no contradiction here provided we keep in mind his general approach to dualizing animals: namely, that while they or some of their kind exhibit behaviors outside of a kind, they are by and large identifiable as tending toward that kind. See the discussion of dualizers in Balme's notes to his translation of *HA* 7 (note on 66–69) and also J. Cooper, *"Political Animals and Civic Friendship,"* in *Aristotle's Politik: Akten des XI. Symposium Aristotelicum.* Ed. G. Patzig. Goettingen, 221–41 (1990). Whether this approach is true of all animals Aristotle describes as dualizing has been the source of some debate; for the basic terms of the discussion, see N. Carraro, "Dualizers in Aristotle's Biology," *Apeiron* 52, no. 2 (2019): 137–65. Carraro distinguishes between two senses of

dualizing: (a) ambiguity regarding essential properties, and (b) possessing either of two opposites as an accidental property; Carraro himself locates human dualizing within the latter.

54. Perhaps it is true to say that in neither case does the animal in question experience time as such, but we would have to add here that even in Heidegger, the resources for humans' ability to do so is found in the intergenerational collective of human community, in what Aristotle would have called oikos and polis.

55. For a more extensive discussion of *suzēn* in Aristotle's ethical and political thought, see Brill 2020.

56. *Suggnōrizein*, *Eudemian Ethics* 1244b26; *suntheōrein*, *Eudemian Ethics* 1245b4; *sumphilosophein*, *Nichomachean Ethics* 1172a5, see also *Eudemian Ethics* 1245a22. This construction of "shared philosophizing" is striking, appears in the Aristotelian corpus in only these two passages, and anticipates both the move toward living contemplation Agamben identifies in Plotinus and Agamben's own conception of philosophical exile and intimacy, developed near the end of *Use of Bodies*.

57. Cf. Pierre Pellegrin, *Aristotle's Classification of Animals: Biology and the Conceptual Unity of the Aristotelian Corpus* (Berkeley: University of California Press, 1986).

58. The stakes here are similar to the tension Katherine Nielsen observes between Aristotle's insistence on the private ownership of property and his equally committed insistence on the need for public, common education (see K. M. Nielsen. "Economy and Private Property," in *The Cambridge Companion to Aristotle's Politics*, ed. M. Deslauriers and P. Destrée. Cambridge: Cambridge, 2013), 67–91. This tension comes about in part because Aristotle does not want to deny his citizens the pleasure of dispensing with their property as they choose and specifically of the free or liberal use of their property for others. The resolution Aristotle attempts is a common teaching tool designed to train the citizen in the proper use of his property, a liberal education in "freedom" made possible by leisure purchased through the exercise of mastery.

59. The height of this intimacy is the forgoing of a noble deed so that one's friend can perform it (an indifference as to whether it is oneself or one's friend who performs the noble deed, and echo of the love Aristotle sees as emblematic in maternal sacrifice: the mother's sense of her child as her own is so strong she will give up the child and give up its recognition of her as mother, if it is in the child's best interest).

60. See discussion in D. Heller-Roazen. *The Inner Touch: Archaeology of a Sensation* (Princeton, NJ: Princeton University Press, 2009).

61. Whether we could say the same of nous is worth exploring but would take us too far afield here.

62. See, for instance, HA 487b33–488b4 (a passage that includes the observation that any kind of animal that is tame exists in a wild state as well, e.g., horses, oxen, swine, humans, sheep, goats, and dogs). See also PA 643b5-9.

63. Followed in the summer of 1944 with a second lecture course entitled "Logic" that dealt with Heraclitus fragment B 50.

64. Translated by Krell and Capuzzi (1975), 116.

65. Ibid., 116–17.

66. "But *zōē* and *phusis* say the same" albeit with his own sense of *phusis*, as that which grows or springs forth into the light, and its relation to a Heraclitean sense of *Welt*, as "the event of lighting," and logos, as "*to pur* [fire]" (118).

67. On the development of this relationship in Heidegger's thought, see Bernasconi (*Biologism*). See also the hints of this shift in the 1943 lecture "Nietzsches Wort 'Gott ist tot.'" published in Germany in 1950 and in English translation (Young and Haynes 2002).

Abbreviations

Heidegger

AS	"Art and space." Translated by Charles H. Seibert. *Man & World*, vol. 1 (1973): 3–8.
BC	*Basic Concepts*. Translated by Gary E. Aylesworth. Bloomington: Indiana University Press, 1993.
BCAP	*Basic Concepts of Ancient Philosophy*. Translated by Richard Rojcewicz. Bloomington: Indiana University Press, 2008.
BCArP	*Basic Concepts of Aristotelian Philosophy*. Translated by Robert Metcalf and Mark Tanzer. Bloomington: Indiana University Press, 2009.
BH	*Becoming Heidegger: On the Trail of his Early Occasional Writings, 1910–1927*. Edited by Theodore Kisiel and Thomas Sheehan. Evanston: Northwestern University Press, 2007.
BNII	*Ponderings VII–XI: Black Notebooks 1938–1939*. Translated by Richard Rojcewicz. Bloomington: Indiana University Press, 2017.
BN III	*Ponderings XII–XV: Black Notebooks 1939–1941*. Translated by Richard Rojcewicz. Bloomington: Indiana University Press, 2017.
BPP	*The Basic Problems of Phenomenology*. Translated by Albert Hofstadter. Bloomington: Indiana University Press, 1982.
BQP	*Basic Questions of Philosophy: Selected "Problems" of "Logic."* Translated by Richard Rojcewicz and André Schuwer. Bloomington: Indiana University Press, 1984.
BT	*Being and Time*. Translated by John Macquarrie and Edward Robinson. New York: Harper & Row, 1962.

BTS	*Being and Time*. Translated by Joan Stambaugh. Albany: State University of New York Press, 1996.
BW	*Basic Writings*. 2nd ed. Edited by David Farrell Krell. New York: Harper & Row, 1993.
BWP	*The Beginning of Western Philosophy: Interpretation of Anaximander and Parmenides*. Translated by Richard Rojcewicz. Bloomington: Indiana University Press, 2015.
CP	*Contributions to Philosophy (From Enowning)*. Translated by Parvis Emad and Kenneth Maley. Bloomington: Indiana University Press, 1999.
CPC	*Country Path Conversations*. Translated by Bret W. Davis. Bloomington: Indiana University Press, 2010, 2016.
CT	"The Concept of Time." In *Becoming Heidegger: On the Trail of His Early Occasional Writings, 1910–1927*. Edited by Theodore Kisiel and Thomas Sheehan. Evanston: Northwestern University Press, 2007.
DT	*Discourse on Thinking*. Translated by John M. Anderson and E. Hans Freund. New York: Harper & Row, 1966.
EHF	*The Essence of Human Freedom: An Introduction to Philosophy*. Translated by Ted Sadler. London/New York: Continuum, 2002.
EGT	*Early Greek Thinking*. Translated by David Farrell Krell and Frank Capuzzi. New York: Harper & Row, 1975.
EHD	*Erläuterungen zu Hölderlins Dichtung*. 6th ed. Frankfurt am Main: Vittorio Klostermann, 1996.
EHP	*Elucidations of Hölderlin's Poetry*. Translated by Keith Hoeller. New York: Humanity Books, 2000.
EM	*Einführung in die Metaphysik*. 5th ed. Tübingen: Max Niemeyer, 1987.
EP	*The End of Philosophy*. Translated by Joan Stambaugh. New York: Harper & Row, 1973.
ETP	*The Essence of Truth: On Plato's Cave Allegory and Theaetetus*. Translated by Ted Sadler. New York/London: Continuum, 2002.
FCM	*The Fundamental Concepts of Metaphysics: World, Finitude, Solitude*. Translated by William McNeill and Nicholas Walker. Bloomington: Indiana University Press, 1995.
FS	*Four Seminars*. Translated by Andrew Mitchell and François Raffoul. Bloomington: Indiana University Press, 2003.
G	*Gelassenheit*. 10th ed. Pfullingen: Neske, 1992.

GA Gesamtausgabe. Frankfurt am Main: Vittorio Klostermann, 1975–. Cited by the volume numbers listed below.
- 4 Erläuterungen zu Hölderlins Dichtung.
- 5 Holzwege.
- 7 Vorträge und Aufsätze.
- 9 Wegmarken.
- 10 Der Satz vom Grund.
- 11 Identität und Differenz.
- 12 Unterwegs zur Sprache.
- 13 Aus der Erfahrung des Denkens.
- 15 Seminare.
- 16 Reden und andere Zeugnisse eines Lebensweges.
- 18 Grundbegriffe der aristotelischen Philosophie.
- 22 Die Grundbegriffe der antiken Philosophie.
- 24 Die Grundprobleme der Phänomenologie.
- 26 Metaphysische Anfangsgründe der Logik im Ausgang von Leibniz.
- 29/30 Die Grundbegriffe der Metaphysik: Welt, Endlichkeit, Einsamkeit.
- 31 Vom Wesen der menschlichen Freiheit. Einleitung in die Philosophie.
- 34 Vom Wesen der Wahrheit. Zu Platons Höhlengleichnis und Theätet.
- 36/37 Sein und Wahrheit.
- 38 Logik als die Frage nach dem Wesen der Sprache.
- 39 Hölderlins Hymnen "Germanien" und "Der Rhein."
- 40 Einführung in die Metaphysik.
- 41 Die Frage nach dem Ding. Zu Kants Lehre von den transzendentalen Grundsätzen.
- 45 Grundfragen der Philosophie. Ausgewählte "Probleme" der "Logik."
- 49 Die Metaphysik des deutschen Idealismus. Zur erneuten auslegung von Schelling: Philosophische untersuchungen ueber das Wesen der menschlichen Freiheit und die damit zusammenhaengenden Gegenstaende (1809).
- 50 'Nietzsches Metaphysik,' in Nietzsche. 1. Nietzsches Metaphysik; 2. Einleitung in die philosophische Denken und Dichten, edited by Petra Jaeger (1990), 11–87.

51	*Grundbegriffe.*
52	*Hölderlins Hymne "Andenken."*
53	*Hölderlins Hymne "Der Ister."*
54	*Parmenides.*
55	*Heraklit.*
56/57	*Zur Bestimmung der Philosophie.*
60	*Phänomenologie des religiösen Lebens.*
61	*Phänomenologische Interpretationen zu Aristoteles: Einführung in die phänomenologische Forschung.*
62	*Phänomenologische Interpretationen ausgewählter Abhandlungen des Aristoteles zur Ontologie und Logik.*
63	*Ontologie: Hermeneutik der Faktizität.*
64	*Der Begriff der Zeit.*
65	*Beiträge zur Philosophie (Vom Ereignis).*
66	*Besinnung.*
67	*Metaphysik und Nihilismus.*
69	*Die Geschichte des Seyns.*
70	*Über den Anfang.*
75	*Zu Hölderlin / Griechenlandreisen.*
77	*Feldweg-Gespräche.*
78	*Der Spruch des Anaximander.*
79	*Bremer und Freiburger Vorträge.*
80	*Vorträge*
82	*Zu eigenen Veröffentlichungen.*
83	*Seminare: Platon-Aristoteles-Augustinus, Gesamtausgabe.*
90	*Zu Ernst Jünger "Der Arbeiter."*
95	*Überlegungen VII–XI.*
96	*Überlegungen XII–XV.*
98	*Anmerkungen VI–IX.*
HAS	*Heidegger und der Antisemitismus.* Freiburg: Verlag Herder, 2016.
HBB	*Martin Heidegger/Elisabeth Blochmann Briefwechsel.* Edited by Joachim Storck. Marbach: Deutsche Schillergesellschaft, 1990.
HC	*The Heidegger Controversy: A Critical Reader.* Edited by Richard Wolin. Cambridge, MA: MIT Press, 1993.
HGR	*Hölderlin's Hymn "Germania" and "The Rhine."* Translated by William McNeil and Julia Ireland. Bloomington: Indiana University Press, 2014.

HHI	*Hölderlin's Hymn "The Ister."* Translated by William McNeil and Julia Davis. Bloomington: Indiana University Press, 1996.
HHR	*Hölderlin's Hymn "Remembrance."* Translated by William McNeil and Julia Ireland. Bloomington: Indiana University Press, 2018.
HJB	*Martin Heidegger/Karl Jaspers: Briefwechsel 1920–1963.* Edited by Walter Biemel and Hans Saner. Frankfurt am Main: Vittorio Klostermann, 1990.
HK	"Die Herkunft der Kunst und die Bestimmung des Denkens." In *Distanz und Nähe: Reflexionen und Analysen zur Kunst der Gegenwart,* Jaeger, Petra, und Lüthe, Rudolf (eds.), 11–22. Würzburg: Königshausen und Neumann, 1983.
HKB	*Martin Heidegger, Kurt Bauch. Correspondence 1932–1975.* Freiburg: Alber, 2010.
IDS	*Identity and Difference.* Translated by Joan Stambaugh. New York: Harper & Row, 1969.
IHS	"Phenomenological Interpretations with Respect to Aristotle: Indication of the Hermeneutical Situation." In Theodore Kisiel and Thomas Sheehan, eds., *Becoming Heidegger: On the Trail of His Early Occasional Writings, 1910–1927.* Evanston: Northwestern University Press, 2007, 155–184, 477–480.
IM	*Introduction to Metaphysics.* Translated by Gregory Fried and Richard Polt. New Haven, CT: Yale University Press, 2000.
KPM	*Kant and the Problem of Metaphysics,* 4th ed. Translated by Richard Taft. Bloomington: Indiana University Press, 1990.
M	*Mindfulness.* Translated by Parvis Emad and Thomas Kalary. London and New York: Continuum, 2006.
MFL	*The Metaphysical Foundations of Logic.* Translated by Michael Heim. Bloomington: Indiana University Press, 1984.
MHNS	*Martin Heidegger and National Socialism: Questions and Answers.* Edited by Gunther Neske and Emil Kettering. Translated by Lisa Harries. New York: Paragon House, 1990.
MLS	*Mein liebes Seelchen.* Edited by Gertrud Heidegger. Munich: Deutsche Verlags-Anstalt, 2006.
Ni	*Nietzsche. Erster Band.* 5th ed. Pfullingen: Neske, 1989.
Nii	*Nietzsche. Zweiter Band.* 5th ed. Pfullingen: Neske, 1989.
N1	*Nietzsche,* Vol. I, *The Will to Power as Art.* Translated by David Farrell Krell. New York: Harper & Row, 1979.

N2	*Nietzsche*, Vol. II, *The Eternal Recurrence of the Same*. Translated by David Farrell Krell. New York: Harper & Row, 1984.
N3	*Nietzsche*, Vol. III, *The Will to Power as Knowledge and as Metaphysics*. Translated by Joan Stambaugh, David Farrell Krell, and Frank A. Capuzzi. New York: Harper & Row, 1987.
N4	*Nietzsche*, Vol. IV, *Nihilism*. Translated by Frank A. Capuzzi. Edited by David Farrell Krell. New York: Harper & Row, 1982.
OBT	*Off the Beaten Track*. Edited and Translated by Julian Young and Kenneth Haynes. Cambridge: Cambridge University Press, 2002.
OG	"'Only a God Can Save Us': *Der Spiegel*'s Interview with Martin Heidegger." Translated by Maria P. Alter and John D. Caputo. In *The Heidegger Controversy*.
OHF	*Ontology—The Hermeneutics of Facticity*. Translated by John van Buren. Bloomington: Indiana University Press, 1999.
OTB	*On Time and Being*. Translated by Joan Staumbaugh. New York: Harper & Row, 1972.
OWAF	"Of the Origin of the Work of Art (first elaboration)." Translated by Markus Zisselsberger. *Epoché* 12, no. 2 (Spring 2008): 329–47.
OWL	*On the Way to Language*. Translated by Peter D. Hertz. New York: Harper & Row, 1971.
PA	*Parmenides*. Translated by André Schuwer and Richard Rojcewicz. Bloomington: Indiana University Press, 1992.
PM	*Pathmarks*. Edited by William McNeill. Cambridge: Cambridge University Press, 1998.
PIA	*Phenomenological Interpretations of Aristotle: Initiation into Phenomenological Research*. Translated by Richard Rojcewicz. Bloomington: Indiana University Press, 2001.
PLT	*Poetry, Language, Thought*. Translated by Albert Hofstadter. New York: Harper & Row, Perennial Classics, 2001.
PMH	"Preface by Martin Heidegger." In William J. Richardson. *Heidegger: Through Phenomenology to Thought*. 3rd ed. The Hague: Nijhoff, 1974.
PR	*The Principle of Reason*. Translated by Reginald Lilly. Bloomington: Indiana University Press, 1991.
PRL	*The Phenomenology of Religious Life*. Translated by Matthias Fritsch and Jennifer Anna Gosetti-Ferencei. Bloomington: Indiana University Press, 2004.

PS	*Plato's Sophist*. Translated by Richard Rojcewicz and André Schuwer. Bloomington: Indiana University Press. 1997.
QCT	*The Question Concerning Technology*. Translated by William Lovitt. New York: Harper & Row, 1977.
R	*Die Selbstbehauptung der deutschen Universität. Das Rektorat 1933/34*. Frankfurt am Main: Vittorio Klostermann, 1990.
RFT	"The Rectorate 1933/34: Facts and Thoughts." In *MHNS*.
SA	*Schellings Abhandlung Über das Wesen der menschlichen Freiheit (1809)*. 2nd ed. Tübingen: Max Niemeyer, 1995.
SG	*Der Satz vom Grund*. 7th ed. Pfullingen: Neske, 1992.
SP	"Nur noch ein Gott kann uns retten." Interview which took place in 1966, and published posthumously in *Der Spiegel* in 1976. Reprinted in *Antwort: Martin Heidegger im Gespräch*. Edited by Günther Neske and Emil Kettering. Pfullingen: Neske, 1988.
ST	*Schelling's Treatise on the Essence of Human Freedom*. Translated by Joan Stambaugh. Athens: Ohio University Press, 1985.
SU	"The Self-Assertion of the German University." Translated by William S. Lewis. In *HC*.
SZ	*Sein und Zeit*. 17th ed. Tübingen: Max Niemeyer, 1993. Both *BT* and *BTS* contain marginal references to the pagination of *SZ*.
TB	*On Time and Being*. Translated by Joan Stambaugh. New York: Harper & Row, 1972.
TDP	*Towards the Definition of Philosophy*. Translated by Ted Sadler. London: Athlone Press, 2000; paperback edition of 2003 under the Continuum imprint.
UKE	"*Vom Ursprung des Kunstwerks: Erste Ausarbeitung*." Edited by Hermann Heidegger. *Heidegger Studies* 5 (1989): 5–22.
UV	"Unbenutzte Vorarbeiten zur Vorlesung vom Wintersemester 1929/1930: *Die Grundbegriffe der Metaphysik: Welt, Endlichkeit, Einsamkeit*." *Heidegger Studies* 7 (1991): 5–12.
VA	*Vorträge und Aufsätze*. 7th ed. Pfullingen: Neske, 1994.
WCT	*What is Called Thinking?* Translated by J. Glenn Gray. New York: Harper & Row, 1968.
WhD	*Was heißt Denken?* 4th ed. Tübingen: Max Niemeyer, 1984.
WP	*What is Philosophy?* (bilingual edition). Translated by William Kluback and Jean T. Wilde. New Haven, CT: College and University Press, 1958.

WT	*What is a Thing?* Translated by W. B. Barton Jr. and Vera Deutsch. Chicago: Henry Regency Co., 1967.
Z	*Zollikoner Seminare. Protokolle—Zwiegespräche—Briefe.* Edited by Menard Boss. Frankfurt am Main: Vittorio Klostermann, 1987.
ZS	*Zollikon Seminars: Protocols—Conversations—Letters.* Edited by Menard Boss. Translated by Franz Mayr and Richard Askay. Evanston: Northwestern University Press, 2001.
ZSD	*Zur Sache des Denkens.* 3rd ed. Tübingen: Max Niemeyer, 1988.

Kant

AA3	**Kritik der reinen Vernunft 1787 (B-edition)**, edited by Benno Erdmann (1911). Cf. *Critique of Pure Reason,* translated and edited by Paul Guyer and Allen W. Wood. Cambridge: Cambridge University Press, 2019.

Ancient Sources

De An.	Aristotle, *De Anima*
Cael.	Aristotle, *De caelo*
EE.	Aristotle, *Eudemian Ethics*
HA	Aristotle, *Historia Animalium*
MM.	Aristotle, *Magna Moralia*
Met.	Aristotle, *Metaphysics*
NE.	Aristotle, *Nicomachean Ethics*
PA	Aristotle, *Parts of Animals*
Pol.	Aristotle, *Politics*
Rhe.	Aristotle, *Rhetoric*
DL.	Diogenes Laertius, *Lives of the Eminent Philosophers*
Il.	Homer, *The Iliad*
Od.	Homer, *The Odyssey*
Io	Plato, *Io*
Phdr	Plato, *Phaedrus*
Prot.	Plato, *Protagoras*
Theat.	Plato, *Theaetetus*
Thuc.	Thucydides, *History of the Peloponnesian War*

Contributors

Babette Babich is Professor of Philosophy at Fordham University, New York. She is the author of *Günther Anders' Philosophy of Technology* (2022), *Nietzsches Antike: Beiträge zur Altphilologie und Musik* and editor of *Reading David Hume's 'Of the Standard of Taste'* (2020).

Charles Bambach is Professor of Philosophy at the University of Texas at Dallas. He is the author of *Of an Alien Homecoming. Reading Heidegger's "Hölderlin"* (2022), *Thinking the Poetic Measure of Justice: Heidegger, Hölderlin, Celan* (2013), *Heidegger's Roots: Nietzsche, National Socialism, and the Greeks* (2003) and *Heidegger, Dilthey, and the Crisis of Historicism* (1995).

Claudia Baracchi is Associate Professor of Moral Philosophy at the Università di Milano-Bicocca. She is the author of *Friendship: The Future of an Ancient Gift* (2023), *Of Myth, Life, and War in Plato's Republic* (2002), and *Aristotle's Ethics as First Philosophy* (2007). She is also the editor of *The Bloomsbury Companion to Aristotle* (2015).

Sara Brill is Associate Professor of Philosophy at Fairfield University. She is the author of *Plato on the Limits of Human Life* (2013) and *Aristotle on the Concept of Shared Lives* (2020) and has published articles on several Platonic dialogues, the Hippocratic corpus and Greek tragedy.

Bret W. Davis is Professor and Higgins Chair in Philosophy at Loyola University Maryland. He is the author of *Zen Pathways: An Introduction to the Philosophy and Practice of Zen Buddhism* (2022), *Heidegger and the Will: On the Way to Gelassenheit* (2007), and the editor of *The Oxford Handbook of Japanese Philosophy* (2020).

Robert Eaglestone is Professor of Contemporary Literature and Thought at Royal Holloway, University of London and Deputy Director of the Holocaust Research Centre. He is the author of *The Holocaust and the Postmodern* (2004), *The Broken Voice: Reading Post-Holocaust Literature* (2017), and *Truth and Wonder: A Literary Introduction to Plato and Aristotle* (2022).

Sacha Golob is Professor of Philosophy and Co-Director of the Centre for Philosophy and Art at King's College London. He is the author of *Heidegger on Concepts, Freedom, and Normativity* (2014), and the co-editor (with Jens Timmerman) of *The Cambridge History of Moral Philosophy* (2017).

Francisco J. Gonzalez is Professor of Philosophy at the University of Ottawa. He is the author of *Plato and Heidegger: A Question of Dialogue* (2009), *Dialectic and Dialogue: Plato's Practice of Philosophical Inquiry* (1998), and editor of *The Third Way: New Directions in Platonic Studies* (1995) and the editor of *Human Life in Motion Heidegger's Unpublished Seminars on Aristotle as Preserved by Helene Weiss* (2024).

Laurence Hemming is Honorary Professor at the University of Lancaster and Director of the Knapp Foundation. He is the author of *Heidegger and Marx: Over the Language of Humanism* (2012), *Heidegger's Atheism* (2002) and coeditor (with Aaron Turner) of *Heidegger and Parmenides* (2024).

David Farrell Krell is Professor Emeritus of Philosophy at DePaul University. He is the author of *Three Encounters: Heidegger, Arendt, Derrida* (2023), *Cudgel and the Caress, The: Reflections on Cruelty and Tenderness* (2019), *Ecstasy, Catastrophe: Heidegger from* Being and Time *to the* Black Notebooks (2015).

Mark Payne is Chester D. Tripp Professor of Classics and Comparative Literature at the University of Chicago. He is the author of *Flowers of Time: On Postapocalyptic Fiction* (2020), *Hontology: Depressive Anthropology and the Shame of Life* (2018), and *The Animal Part: Human and Other Animals in the Poetic Imagination* (2010).

Dennis J. Schmidt is Research Professor and Chair at Western Sydney University. He is the author of *Idiome der Wahrheit* (2014), *Between Word and Image: Heidegger, Klee, and Gadamer on Gesture and Genesis* (2012), and *On Germans & Other Greeks: Tragedy and Ethical Life* (2001).

Thomas Sheehan is Professor Emeritus of Religious Studies and, by courtesy, German Studies and Philosophy at Stanford University. He is the author of *Making Sense of Heidegger: A Paradigm Shift* (2015), *Heidegger, the Man and the Thinker* (1981), and coeditor (with Theodore Kisiel) of *Becoming Heidegger: On the Trail of His Early Occasional Writings, 1910–1927* (2007).

Aaron Turner is a Research Associate at Royal Holloway, University of London, and a Knapp Fellow at the Knapp Foundation. He is the editor of *Reconciling Ancient and Modern Philosophies of History* (2020); *Parmenides, Plato, and the Crisis of Sophistry* (2025); and *The Essence of History* (2025). He is currently working on his monograph, *Thucydides and the Ground of History*.

Index

Aeschylus, 221, 232n
Agamben, Giorgio, 234n, 385, 414n
Anaxagoras, 43, 83n, 141–143, 158n, 185, 310
Anaximander, 2–5, 10n, 18, 40, 42–48, 51–53, 56–59, 61–63, 65–70, 72–78, 83n–90n, 94n–96n, 114–115, 139–140
Anaximenes, 140
Aquinas, Thomas, 260, 276, 289n, 318n, 368, 374–375
Arendt, Hannah, 211n, 325, 332, 383, 385, 407n
Aristotle, 2, 5, 7–9, 16–18, 39–42, 48, 50–51, 53, 59–60, 63–65, 68, 73, 74, 76, 79n–82n, 91n, 93n, 103, 107, 115, 128, 143, 159n, 175, 180–181, 184, 191, 208n–209n, 239–253, 257–279, 280n–292n, 293–294, 296–298, 300–305, 308–309, 311–315, 319n–320n, 321–332, 335n, 337–339, 341, 345–353, 358n–359n, 361–364, 368–369, 371–372, 374, 376–77, 381n, 383–386, 390–392, 395–404, 406, 407n–409n, 411n–414n
Aristotelianism, 4, 7, 48, 60, 70, 73–74, 80n, 114, 138, 182, 239–240, 242–246, 249–252, 257–258, 268, 280n–282n, 310, 314, 316, 321–323, 376, 390, 404–405, 414n

Cassirer, Ernst, 3, 41, 80n, 84n
Carnap, Rudolf, 41, 80n
Classical Philology, 2–3, 10n, 19, 39–41, 44–47, 50–51, 54, 56, 65, 67, 239, 244, 250, 252–253

Democritus, 87n, 101, 142
Descartes, René, 5, 341, 368
Cartesianism, 121, 368, 383–384, 386, 390–391, 404
Diels, Hermann, 46, 50, 53–54, 58–59, 63, 66, 71–72, 76, 89n, 94n–95n
Diogenes Laertius, 45–46, 53–55, 57–58, 69, 73–74, 121, 142

Empedocles, 5, 20, 42, 78, 82n, 113–130, 132, 133n, 141–144, 158n
Euripides, 114, 395

Friedländer, Paul, 10n, 137–138, 214n–215n

Gadamer, Hans-Georg, 39–40, 53, 58, 60, 63, 79n–81n, 83n, 233n, 272, 322, 325
Goethe, Johann Wolfgang von, 51, 53, 88n, 116
Gorgias, 143–144, 158n–159n, 172

Hegel, Georg Wilhelm Friedrich, 5, 57, 63–64, 70, 173, 207n, 236n, 343–345
  Hegelianism, 104
Heraclitus, 2, 4–5, 10n, 18, 36n, 43, 48, 53–54, 56, 58, 60, 76, 78, 83n, 114, 116–117, 139, 141–142, 152, 167, 176–178, 181, 200, 207n, 318n, 381n, 405, 409n
Heraclitean 153, 385, 415n
Hesiod, 45, 130
Hippocrates, 149–150, 160n, 319
  Hippocratics, 147–150, 156, 159n
Hitler, Adolf, 182
Hölderlin, Friedrich, 5, 14–20, 23–27, 31, 33–35, 36n, 42, 47, 60–62, 114–127, 130, 132, 133n, 164–165, 171–172, 182, 203, 407
Homer, 45, 51, 67, 70, 74, 149, 349

Jaspers, Karl, 3

Kant, Immanuel, 5, 8, 43, 46, 79n, 207n, 215n, 239, 244, 246, 249, 252, 295, 341–342, 348, 357n, 368
  Kantianism, 8, 249, 252

Leucippus, 87n, 142

Marx, Karl, 342, 344, 407n, 409n

Nazism, 1, 48, 50, 55, 60, 63, 233n
Nietzsche, 5–7, 17, 40–64, 66–68, 71–78, 80n, 82n–94n, 96n, 104, 113, 115–121, 126–127, 131–132, 165, 169–170, 192–193, 206n, 211n, 222, 233, 252, 342, 351, 362, 373, 410n–411n

Parmenides, 2–6, 10, 18, 41, 43, 48, 54, 56, 58, 60–61, 76, 114, 127–128, 137–144, 151, 155–158, 199, 202, 204, 224, 226, 228, 318
Pindar, 18, 25, 42, 45
Plato, 2, 4–7, 16–18, 40, 42–45, 48–54, 58, 63–64, 68, 78, 79n–80n, 82n, 84n, 87n, 90n–91n, 93n, 115, 137–139, 143–144, 156, 157n, 163–175, 180–190, 192–195, 197–204, 205n–215n, 217–224, 226–230, 230n–234n, 236n, 274, 278, 289–292, 294, 301–303, 318n, 338, 347, 350–354, 359n, 372, 380n–381n, 392–395
  Platonic/Platonism, 4, 6–7, 42, 48, 54, 59, 138, 163–166, 168–169, 171–173, 175, 179, 182–188, 190, 192, 195, 198–202, 206n, 208n–209n, 211–212, 214, 219, 222–223, 230n–234n, 281, 394–395
  Pre-Platonic, 4, 40, 44, 49–50, 56–58, 129, 190
Plotinus, 209n, 277–278, 287n, 290n–292n, 358n, 379n, 414n
Protagoras, 143
Pythagoras, 44, 51, 53, 87n
  Pythagoreanism, 87n, 192

Rilke, Rainer Maria, 47, 115

Socrates, 51, 53–54, 64, 82n, 172, 174, 184–185, 188–196, 209n, 213n, 217, 222, 224–225, 227, 235n, 350, 352, 354–355, 374–375, 381n, 393–395

Solon, 45
Sophocles, 4, 13–23, 25–27, 29–35, 92n, 114, 119, 123, 125, 203, 317n

Thales, 42, 45, 53, 62, 64, 140, 310
Theophrastus, 42, 47, 50–52, 64–65, 69, 74, 76, 358
Thucydides, 6, 139, 144–157, 159–160

Wagner, Richard, 43, 46, 50–51, 56, 60, 88n
Wilamowitz-Moellendorff, Ulrich von, 60, 91n

Xenophon, 68

Zeno, 142

www.ingramcontent.com/pod-product-compliance
Lightning Source LLC
Chambersburg PA
CBHW020118240426
43673CB00038B/524